EISENHOWER

and the American Crusades

EISENHOWER

and the American Crusades

Herbert S. Parmet

THE MACMILLAN COMPANY, NEW YORK, NEW YORK

COLLIER-MACMILLAN LIMITED, LONDON

The Macmillan Company
866 Third Avenue, New York, N.Y. 10022
Collier-Macmillan Canada Ltd., Toronto, Ontario

All photographs appear through the courtesy of
Wide World Photos, Inc.

Library of Congress Catalog Card Number: 73-189680

FIRST PRINTING

PRINTED IN THE UNITED STATES OF AMERICA

TO JOAN

for so many reasons . . .

Contents

Part Three "MODERN REPUBLICANISM"

Illustrations following page 308

Preface

"What can you possibly write about him?" an acquaintance asked at the start of my work on the Eisenhower Presidency. "So little happened when he was in office." Later, during the process of conducting interviews, a prominent civil rights leader had little to offer beyond recollecting that Ike had demonstrated that the country does not "need" a President. Others recalled the contemporary joke about the "Eisenhower doll": just wind it up and it does nothing for eight years. Yet, however widespread such reactions, they represented a minority of the American public. Much more common was the response of a small businessman from Lubbock, Texas. Learning that Eisenhower was my subject, he turned to his wife and said, with obvious admiration, "Now, *there* was a President!"

Neither a period of tranquillity nor extraordinary turmoil, considered in retrospect as perhaps our most successful postwar years, the Eisenhower era nevertheless contained not only the residue of the preceding decade but the germs that became endemic to the 1960s. For a historian who had twice voted for Stevenson, a foray into the period carried the almost automatic assumption that somehow the victory of the GOP led by a general—or leading a general—had resulted in negativism and waste, denying to the American people either the hope of what John F. Kennedy later branded the "New Frontier" or the more radical solution of a complete overhaul of society, capitalism and liberal democracy. Only a closer view of the situation as it existed can restore balance to that judgment. And no such consideration can possibly ignore the multitude of deeply felt currents, or crusades, that emanated from a democracy more genuine than most of its critics realized. No understanding of Eisenhower and his problems can, similarly, be complete without an appreciation of what he faced, both within the country and his party. Once recognized, both his own role and the problem of realistic alternatives become more formidable. The more one probes, the more complex the questions; the closer one looks at the General who occupied the White House during those years, the less possible to be glib about an "Eisenhower doll."

Much more will be written about his Presidency, both as over-all generalized evaluations and as accounts of different aspects and personalities. Much remains to be said that is far beyond the scope of the present book. Carloads of material are already available for many conceivable purposes, and much more will be unveiled in the future, particularly with the release of classified documents. Therefore, in making the present broad overview, I have had to be selective. There was no intent to write an encyclopedia of everything that happened during the Eisenhower years. Nor should the reader expect a careful chronology. One, therefore, has to settle for the hope of being able to glean some useful glimpses and ideas. Perhaps some rethinking about the 1950s and its major figures may result, all of which may be as ephemeral as any of our cultural and intellectual trends. There is, one should also remember, no such thing as a permanent and definitive history of any subject.

Many individuals helped to make the present work possible. Foremost were the archivists and librarians who extended their vital patience, labor and information. At the Dwight D. Eisenhower Library in Abilene, Kansas, in particular, many weeks of labor spanning two summers were greatly facilitated by Dr. John Wickman and his staff, especially Mr. Roland Doty and Miss Joan Howard. Access to the John Foster Dulles papers at Princeton University was obtained through the cooperation of Mr. John Hanes, Jr., and the Dulles committee. Mrs. Wanda Randall helped me find my way through the vast collection of Dulles oral history memoirs as well as the papers of the former Secretary of State. At Lancaster, New Hampshire, Mr. Sinclair Weeks interrupted his retirement to talk to me extensively about his Washington years and then gave me unrestricted access to twenty-nine cartons of papers comprising his personal collection. His "neighbor" at Lincoln, New Hampshire, Governor Sherman Adams, extended the courtesy of two interviews and enabled me to examine his private collection deposited at Dartmouth College's Baker Library. Professor Robert K. Merton of Columbia University's Department of Sociology kindly furnished a summary of his group's analysis of the Eisenhower-for-President mail sent by the public long before the General became a candidate. Mrs. M. Lucile Tudor supplied me with a copy of her late husband's useful and revealing

Washington diary. Others who went out of their way to provide exceptional courtesies and assistance were Mr. Maxwell Rabb, Mrs. Eleanor Lansing Dulles, and Dr. Gabriel Hauge. The staff at Columbia University's Special Collections department also made possible my extensive use of the Dwight D. Eisenhower Oral History Project. Most helpful, too, for completion of the project was the library of my own institution, the Queensborough Community College of The City University of New York, where Mr. Charles Pappalardo and his staff gave me unrestricted access to microfilm copies of the New York *Times* and other material. My own departmental secretaries, Mrs. Roslyn Arnow and Mrs. Marie Buonomo, provided indispensable services. Mrs. Marie B. Hecht, with whom I twice collaborated on earlier books, read the entire manuscript and offered much that was useful and encouraging, as did my brother, Dr. Robert D. Parmet, whose careful scrutiny of the work in progress was invaluable. My daughter, Wendy Ellen Parmet, contributed her share by tolerating with mature understanding having Dad "lost" for the duration of "the book."

Still, nothing would have been possible without the dedication and sacrifices of my wife, Joan Parmet, who, despite an unusual and extended illness that debilitated her energies, provided the encouragement and understanding so necessary to sustain a huge project. With Spartan determination, she forced herself to overcome physical limitations to type every word of the massive manuscript. Without her courage, there would have been no book.

Herbert S. Parmet
Bayside, New York
1972

PART ONE

"A New Kind of Candidate"

CHAPTER I

Abilene, June 4, 1952

Once west of Topeka the trees gradually disappear, and motorists along Interstate 70 can see rolling plains as far as the horizon on all sides. Even the distant farmhouses become fewer, the fields drier and somewhat flatter, and the great road across Kansas simulates an orbital track carrying speeding cars through space. About one-third of the way across the state, some forty-five miles past the university town of Manhattan, white grain elevators and the towering old Sunflower Hotel, visible for many miles around, mark the village of Abilene; and, seconds later, large and very modern neon motel signs appear alongside the road. Abilene, the oasis on the plains that was once the Chisholm Trail's northern terminus, now gets a steady flow of visitors seeking nostalgia about its most famous name, Dwight D. Eisenhower. On their way across the empty stretches of the Midwest, between the Mississippi and the Rockies, the boyhood home, gravesite, museum and library become to them more than a convenient pause from monotony. The hour or two spent with the memory of Eisenhower provides the regeneration to sustain their image of America.

After the White House years, Ike and Mamie Eisenhower had also crossed the nation many times. Usually, because of Mamie's adverse reaction to heights, they traveled by train. Viewing the countryside, they could see evidence that the General's optimism and ideas of progress were not shared by many Americans. Great billboards, particularly numerous in the South and Midwest, carried a simple slogan: "Impeach Earl Warren!" Such symbols of protest recalled the domestic part of his containment policies; and by the time he died on March 28, 1969, millions who had had complete faith in his patriotism and honor were

3

displaying the stars and stripes, in almost any form, as though the flag were a hex sign to frighten off mysterious evils. Had he been presented to them as a candidate, once again, there would have been less insecurity. Only three months before his death and shortly after Richard Nixon was elected to the Presidency, Americans asked to list the ten men they admired most still placed Eisenhower first.[1]

Less than two months after the end of the European war he had been honored by Abilene as tumultuously as a village of less than six thousand can muster. Americans had spent the preceding years with countless photographs of the General that revealed the smiles and the expressions that had become inseparable from the man. Repeatedly they had read about his boyhood nickname of Ike; and Ike was Ike Eisenhower and nobody else. General Douglas MacArthur, that brilliant soldier with aristocratic ways, had inspired many nasty stories, jibes, allegations, rumors of pernicious self-interest. But Ike was what an American general should be: a humane battler for virtue and freedom, a leader desiring above all the restoration and maintenance of peace, a man who truly was a "soldier of democracy." That all those things applied to Eisenhower few Americans doubted. And, standing on the speaker's platform in little Eisenhower Park, which was a short distance northwest of his boyhood home on Southeast Fourth Street, he addressed the admiring crowd.

Among those hearing his words of appreciation for Abilene and America, few were aware of what he had told another audience, in London's Guild Hall, only two weeks earlier. "I am not a native of this land," he had said. "I come from the very heart of America." And then he had gone on to say: "To preserve his freedom of worship, his equality before law, his liberty to speak and act as he sees fit, subject only to provisions that he trespass not upon similar rights of others—a Londoner will fight. So will a citizen of Abilene. When we consider these things, then the valley of the Thames draws closer to the farms of Kansas and the plains of Texas. . . . No petty differences in the world of trade, traditions or national pride should ever blind us to our identities in priceless values."[2] Whether he spoke such words in Abilene, London, Paris, New York or Washington, few doubted the sincerity of the most unwarriorlike man in uniform.

The wonder was that, seven years later, on June 4, 1952, when once again he returned to Eisenhower Park a hero, the reverence was still there. That day's festivities had followed a long and astonishingly persistent effort to make him a Presidential candidate, a movement that had begun while the Nazis were still fighting. Even during his first visit to Abilene he had had to deny any political ambitions. But on that June 4, 1952, while millions watched on television, the planning, the desperate dreams of political salvation, the expected restoration of confidence, all threatened to collapse.

The General was no longer in his famous uniform. In fact, he had left the military payroll, having forfeited over $19,000 a year in salary and allowances to become a political candidate. Standing in heavy rain, he did not resemble the legendary Ike. His raincoat and gray suit were pedestrian substitutes for his famous khaki jacket. He looked his sixty-one years, even to people who never thought about his age before. He carried a straw hat and had rolled both trouser legs up several inches above the mudline. Not until five o'clock airtime did he mount the speaker's platform. Just then, providentially, the rain stopped, and the umbrella that had been installed was no longer necessary. The General wiped his glasses and began to read the prepared speech before the weather-limited crowd in the 2,800 seat stadium.

It was then that the TV viewers, perhaps more so than those present that day in Abilene, could see, instead of the much-loved radiant image that had given credence to the inevitability of virtue triumphing over evil, the picture of a grayish-looking, somewhat bewildered and troubled, rather ordinary man speaking with difficulty in a very uninspiring setting. As he wrote a decade later, "Probably no televised speech up to that moment was ever delivered under greater difficulties and more uncomfortable circumstances."[3]

The speech equaled the drabness of the image that reached the TV screens. All the familiar orthodoxies were repeated: communism was bad, of course, but, even worse, foreign Red dictatorships were ready to exploit the first sign of American weakness; contributing to the destruction of supremacy and thus endangering national security were the free-spending bureaucrats who did not seem to care or understand that "a bankrupt America would mean the loss of all we hold dear and would leave much of the world almost naked before the Kremlin menace." He stressed that we must "hold fast to our faith and ideals, which are fundamental to the free system. We must work together in an atmosphere of good will and confidence."[4] At best, millions were hearing confirmation of their fears spoken by one of undisputed integrity. But, to others, his remonstrations about the preservation of the "American way of life" and the lethargic delivery recalled the shallow heroism of Hawthorne's general, also returning to address his old neighbors, in the shadow of the Great Stone Face.

Political scientists will, of course, always debate the importance of a candidate's ideology and charisma to his voter appeal. However they may assess that relationship, Eisenhower's words were incapable of salvaging the event. For the message to be prosaic was one thing, but for the famous soldier to look so unlike a sure winner was much more important.

For the Old Guard in the GOP, that performance almost induced complacency and dissipated fears that the General's return would launch an irresistible crusade. One prominent Taft supporter, Representative Carroll Reece of Tennessee, was quick to call the speech "pretty much for home, mother and heaven."[5] Marquis Childs has noted that, on the TV screens, Ike "looked like an old man who read from his manuscript in a halting and uncertain fashion."[6] James Reston of the New York *Times*, after acknowledging that Eisenhower had done better during an earlier, untelevised talk that day, explained that the soldier had "staked out a compromise position between those who are urging him to attack Mr. Truman openly and those who are urging him to attack Mr. Taft openly."[7]

CHAPTER 2

The General's Constituency

No PARTICULAR EVENT, no specific political consideration (except winning elections), no cause was necessary to get the American public excited about a possible Eisenhower candidacy. Sufficiently vague was the notion that, somehow, he had those qualities that were desirable for the White House, or, at least, that such assets would make him a deserving and trustworthy occupant of 1600 Pennsylvania Avenue. Consequently, the years before 1952 had been marked by the longest continuous non-partisan Presidential boom in American history.

It was made possible by the phenomena of what appeared to be the General's simultaneous appeal to a great array of interests, all of whom were convinced that he was their man. Their desire to have Eisehhower as President was the clearest solution for the plague of corruption, limited wars, twenty years of Democratic rule, communism and greedy labor unions.[1] His victory in 1952 was the direct result of circumstances favorable to the man whose ascent had been anticipated by millions.

On that day in Abilene in 1945 when reporters had inquired about the Presidency, the General heard a suggestion that was no longer new. Eisenhower himself reported that, in 1943, Virgil Pinkley, a West Coast journalist, had been the first to discuss the idea with him seriously. The General's comment, according to his own account, was "Virgil, you've been standing out in the sun too long."[2] Also in 1943 the World War Tank Corps Association, headed by a former corporal in Eisenhower's command at Camp Gettysburg adopted a resolution that, although lacking any knowledge of his political convictions, declared that Ike was fit for the Presidency because of his "leadership qualities." Eisenhower, concerned that suspicions that he sought a political career "will promote disunity at a time when our whole future as a nation demands complete unity among us all," felt that a public denial would appear ridiculous or might give credence to thoughts that he was guilty of disloyalty to his civilian chiefs in Washington.[3] But to a friend he wrote: "And I furiously object to the word 'candidate'—I ain't and I won't."[4] When Republican Senator Arthur Capper of Kansas wanted his party to nominate the General for the 1944 campaign, Eisenhower dismissed the suggestion privately with the thought that ending the war must remain his only ambition.[5] Informed that same autumn that professional sensationalist Walter Winchell had said that FDR was ready to have Eisenhower as his running mate if the Republicans ran MacArthur, Ike called the gossip "badly misinformed." Furthermore, he added, "I can scarcely imagine anyone in the United States less qualified than I for any type of political work."[6] All denials were consistent with his comments in personal letters, such as one to "Swede" Hazlett. Ike had told his boyhood friend that he hoped to "never again hear the word 'politics' " once the war had ended, and then he commented: "But I do have the feeling of a crusader in this war and every time I write a letter or open my mouth, I preach the doctrine that I have so inadequately expressed above."[7] Nevertheless, in their first meeting after the end of hostilities in the European Theater of Operations, in Potsdam during July 1945, President Harry S Truman turned to the General in the back of a car in which they were riding and said, "General, there is nothing that you may want that I won't try to help you get. That definitely and specifically includes the Presidency in 1948."[8]

All overtures, from ordinary veterans to the President of the United States, came without any evidence of the General's party preference. More than rhetoric, however, events had created a political category, so the suggestion that he was backed without regard to ideology has been greatly exaggerated.

There can be no doubt that the absence of direct political verbiage did little to dissuade those who liked Ike that they might not like Ike politically. What fostered the appearance that his appeal was entirely apolitical was the General's ready acceptance by the majority of Americans who generally remain within an ideological range that spans little more than moderate liberal to moderate conservative—in short, the great field that Arthur Schlesinger, Jr., has called the "vital center." There was, then, much less mystery about his basic attitudes than his opponents later charged, and that intelligence was communicated to the American people in a number of ways.

Victory and a friendly press had played significant roles. Probably no commander was more cognizant of the press and its fickleness. "Almost without exception," he wrote to his brother Edgar, "the 500 newspaper and radio men accredited to this organization are my friends."[9] Of the visible high-ranking war heroes—MacArthur, General Jonathan Wainwright, General George S. Patton, etc.—Eisenhower received the most consistently favorable press, which presented him as the antithesis of stuffed shirts or martinets.

Eisenhower also had two distinct advantages that enhanced his attractions. The most obvious one, to the general public, was his direct leadership in the European theater of war as the Commander of Supreme Headquarters, Allied Expeditionary Forces. Such dramatic events as operations TORCH, the invasion of North Africa, and OVERLORD, the June 6, 1944, opening of a so-called Second Front in France, shattered the forces responsible for the mass slaughters.

Those with a more sophisticated knowledge of the war could also appreciate the diplomatic skills and political perceptions that had gone into what was the most astonishingly successful joint command of combined military forces in history. Any man who could hold together such disparate personalities as Roosevelt, Churchill and De Gaulle and, at the same time, deal with matters involving such controversial and even sordid individuals as Admiral Darlan and General Giraud, while never veering from the requirements of the joint Anglo-American, French and Russian mission, must, inevitably, they reasoned, have the talents necessary for the Presidency. The superficial alliance of the major powers, the attempted fulfillment of military roles while keeping watch on nationalistic political ends had required leadership at the very top command that was more political than military. It was Eisenhower to whom most of the credit must be given for making it work. His personality had been generally recognized as having lubricated the sources of friction. Thus, both the political and the sophisticated could find that Ike was indeed the sort of man to occupy the White House.

Nor were there many hints about his probable political position if he did seek public office. Liberals were romanced by the General's obvious humanity and his "Crusade in Europe" into assuming he was one of their own. Conservatives, normally more congenial to the military, immediately identified the General of Denison, Texas, birth and Abilene, Kansas, boyhood as a characteristically American type who could be trusted to preserve the traditional virtues. Nevertheless, it was not that simple.

Even at the outset, reasonably accurate political identifications were made. Left-wingers had been distressed by Eisenhower's expedient deal with Admiral Jean Darlan in North Africa. The arrangement to confirm as the chief French power in Algeria an ex-Nazi collaborator to save the fleet at Toulon and help make Tunisia more vulnerable before the invading Allies brought sharp criticism at home. Treasury Secretary Henry

Morgenthau, Jr., was a strong opponent within the Roosevelt Cabinet of the deal with the pro-Fascist French militarist.[10] The 1940 Presidential candidate of the Republican party, Wendell Willkie, complained that the "moral losses of expediency always far outweigh the temporary gains."[11] The major focus of criticism, in fact, hit directly at Eisenhower.[12] Weathering the reaction, the General wrote to his son John: "Apparently the people who have been creating the storm do not like Darlan. The answer to that one is 'Who does?' The only thing that a soldier can use for a guide is to try to do what appears right and just at the moment of crisis. If it turns out wrong—or if it appears to turn out wrong—the reaction may be serious. But there is no other course to follow. That is one reason we train people all their lives to be soldiers, so that in a moment of emergency they can get down to the essentials of situations and not be too much disturbed about popularity or newspaper acclaim."[13]

After the German defeat, with the start of the cold war, Eisenhower was criticized from the political right. They charged him with the responsibility for having enabled the Russians to capture Berlin by halting his armies at the Elbe River and pursuing the remnants of Hitler's troops to the last redoubt in the south. Eisenhower's reasoning was unconvincing to those eager to attribute Russian gains to American laxity or even treachery.[14] That Eisenhower's move achieved a swift military end to the war and that West Berlin was nonetheless kept within Western control without the loss of a single American life did not occur to the more hysterical postwar critics who, instead of realizing that both the Americans and the British were working to thwart Communist domination of regions where they hoped to establish their own influence—such as Italy and Turkey—preferred the delusion that the Soviets were so weak that only American duplicity could have made their expansion possible.[15]

Conservatives, or the more extreme rightists, were, additionally, not as charmed by the zeal to defeat Hitler first, which had been a basic motivation behind Eisenhower's military strategy. To them, it seemed more appropriate for Americans to pursue the main war against Japan, the aggressors at Pearl Harbor. American interest in the Far East had, after all, been of long standing. Merchants had traded with China even during colonial times. Expressions of Manifest Destiny that justified expansion into Oregon and California had paralleled rising interest in the trans-Pacific trade.[16] Moreover, the whole chain of events, from the purchase of Alaska by Secretary of State William Seward, the conflict with Great Britain and Germany over the Samoan Islands, the annexation of the Philippines, the Open Door Policy, to the eventual Japanese bombing of Pearl Harbor resulted from continuing and increasing American aims of hegemony in that area of the world. It was more difficult, then, for the advocates of an Asia-first military strategy to be enamored by the man who was leading the crusade in Europe.

Therefore, a long series of events, refined by the personalities and conflicts of World War II, gave General Eisenhower a natural political constituency even before any hints emerged about his partisan feelings.

CHAPTER 3

From Europe to Columbia

REMINISCENT OF NAPOLEON BONAPARTE before his return to Paris, prior to the *coup d'état* of 18 Brumaire, Eisenhower's political emergence was achieved by those who appreciated his value, appraised his positions, then wooed and seduced him. While he was in Washington during those early postwar years, the Presidential talk was quiescent. All of that changed, however, in June of 1947 with his announcement that he would soon resign from the Army to succeed Nicholas Murray Butler as president of Columbia University.

The prospect of Ike's leaving the military to assume a prestigious civilian post rekindled the White House fervor of Ike admirers. In Connecticut, the co-founder of the advertising agency of Young and Rubicam, John Orr Young, who had worked for Wendell Willkie's candidacy in 1940, began a one-man advertising campaign to stimulate interest in Eisenhower. Young placed an advertisement for the General in the *Westporter-Herald* during December of 1947 and then had the satisfaction of seeing his idea spread to the formation of Eisenhower clubs in thirty-five cities and towns, creating a milder version of what Oren Root, Jr., had done for Willkie.[1] In New York City, the Headquarters Restaurant, owned in part by Ike's former wartime mess sergeant, Marty Snyder, had a large sign over the entrance that urged DRAFT IKE FOR PRESIDENT. That these instances were merely indicators of what was happening nationally was confirmed by a Presidential "trial heat" conducted by Dr. George Gallup's Institute of Public Opinion, which reported in September that with Eisenhower as the Republican candidate opposed to President Truman, the GOP would have a nine percentage-point advantage. Three months later, at the end of 1947, the Gallup poll showed Eisenhower as the leading candidate among political independents.[2]

Some have gauged the Columbia appointment as a deliberate attempt to prepare the General for the 1948 nomination.[3] An academic post would avoid either business ties or political controversy. Dedication to useful public service would be consistent with his image, and a civilian career would overcome the obstacles created by his military connection. While such speculation does make the proper attribution of Thomas J. Watson of IBM as the prime mover in luring the five-star general to the university on Manhattan's Morningside Heights, some inconvenient facts are thereby overlooked. First, there is no reason to doubt the legitimacy of the General's own denials of interest in the Presidency. "I am neither a Republican nor a Democrat," he had said in September, in response to persistent questioning during the months following the announcement about Columbia. Such rejection of interest in either party, as well as denial of any political interest, could not have been designed to endear him to the politicos who would be needed to realize such a nomination. Finally, what was regarded as a finish to the boom was supplied by Eisenhower himself when he released on January 22, 1948, a letter to Leonard V. Finder, the publisher of the Manchester (New Hampshire) *Evening Leader*. Going beyond a flat rejection of any Presidential offers that might be made, he cited the importance of subordinating the nation's military power to civilian rule. And that "necessary policy," he wrote, "will be best sustained, and our people will have greater confidence that it is so sustained, when life-long professional soldiers, in the absence of some obvious and over-riding reasons, abstain from seeking higher political office."[4]

More likely Columbia simply needed Ike; and the General, his gross income recently $625,000 higher from the outright sale of *Crusade In Europe* to Doubleday and Company, was ready for the life style that had been in his mind for a long time. When he had graduated from Abilene High, the school yearbook had predicted his future as a professor of history at Yale.[5] His propensity for historical facts, particularly dates, and his zest for reading about history was regarded as sure signs of an incipient historian. Eisenhower himself had visions of a collegiate life, but not for an urban complex of colleges such as Columbia. A smaller, more congenial school, the kind of place boys read about in the prep-school fiction of Ralph Henry Barbour, a rural college with, as Eisenhower later wrote with a touch of regret, a "campus character whose lack of scholarly achievements would be offset by an ability to talk freely and fully about the world."[6] Amherst would clearly have been his ideal.

He was, therefore, only partly ready for the offer. But the trustees of Columbia University, particularly Thomas Watson, Sr., of IBM, and Doubleday president Douglas Black, had their own problems. The university needed money badly. Its financial condition had been aggravated by the personal style of fund-raising used by Butler. Within the academic community at Morningside Heights, in fact, there was some feeling that Butler had remained at the head too long. His methods had prepared only a void upon his departure.[7] Eisenhower had, by then, become very friendly with a substantial array of businessmen and financiers. One cannot fail to observe that the non-military portion of his correspondence was dominated by such figures as Bernard Baruch, George Whitney, Clifford Roberts, Young and Rubicam president Sigurd Larmon, Denver multimillionaire Aksel Nielsen, Kansas City *Star* publisher Roy Howard, Clarence Dillon, Walter Robinson, Paul Hoffman and Robert Woodruff. And they gave him an entree to others. When the Dillons, for example, invited him to dinner it was to introduce him to Wall Street bankers and lawyers.[8] When on the golf links, playing bridge, hunting or drinking cocktails, it was usually in their company. After he came to New York as Columbia's president, he was immediately persuaded by friends to join the prestigious Blind Brook Golf Club. Just as most of Eisenhower's other associates, his golfing companions there were also businessmen, and the General found them delightful.[9]

They were men who knew their fields, as well as national and international politics and finance. Their wealth was to Eisenhower, as well as to most Americans, evidence of industry, wisdom, prudence and sobriety. Eisenhower's proximity to this coterie was almost as complete as if he himself were a member of the United States Chamber of Commerce or the National Association of Manufacturers. Columbia's Board of Trustees was merely a subsidiary of that complex. Whether any members of that board had the Presidency of the United States in mind when they sought Ike for Columbia is hard to prove. Hindsight may offer temptations to take credit for having been a king-maker. Scruples, morality, on the other hand, may prompt denial of such plotting. Both possibilities have been raised and also denied. But one thing is certain: There was no arrangement for a Presidential attempt in 1948, and any effort to deal with 1952 was, at that time, too clouded with imponderables, not the least of which was the real possibility—and even probability—that Dewey—or perhaps Stassen—would then be President and ready for a second election in 1952. If the affluent circle around Eisenhower and the Board of Trustees would have been happy to make the General President of United States as well as of Columbia, they were, in 1947 and 1948, undoubtedly more concerned with placing a Republican in Washington and the General on Morningside Heights. Only clairvoyance could have predicted Truman's subsequent victory in 1948.

Eisenhower, thinking that he would prefer a small school, where personal relations with students and faculty were possible, nevertheless succumbed to the offer. Having brought him to the Watson place up the Hudson River for that purpose, a committee pounced on the General with a series of hard-sell pitches to get acceptance. He would, they assured him, have plenty of opportunity to see students. Knowing the Eisenhower attitude, they minimized the task they thought his prestige would help accomplish—fund-raising. Once ensconced in his office at Columbia's Low Library, however, he found that there was a vast distance between the president and the students, that a "wall of deans" separated him from the faculty and that money-raising was indeed a major function.

Nor did he proceed to help matters much. Colonel Robert Schulz, who had been his military aide since 1945, was brought in to perform a similar function at Columbia. Dr. Kevin McCann was placed in charge of Eisenhower's public relations and correspondence and also to aid in speech writing. Together they served as a quasi-military staff, trying to protect the General from the faculty and having him direct his attention to the appropriate deans of the various faculties, which was one of the biggest problems Eisenhower had at Columbia. His non-academic background, lack of sophistication suitable for a major Ivy League school and reputation as a non-intellectual reader of Westerns were not appreciated by those who preferred to equate a university president with scholarship. Eisenhower and the super-intellectual climate of Columbia were not compatible.

CHAPTER 4

Why They Liked Ike

ALTHOUGH MANY WERE certain that the General had prudently given himself latitude by using the words "in the absence of some obvious and overriding reasons" in his "I do not choose to run" letter to Leonard Finder, the statement was widely regarded as a fine argument for not having a military man as President and as a firm, if un-Sherman-like, no. The letter, a response to Finder's newspaper editorial call for Eisenhower's participation, via delegates pledged in his behalf, in the New Hampshire primary elections of March 1948, was necessary to halt the pro-Ike activity in the Granite State.

But, coinciding with his arrival at Columbia, the national boom continued. Politicians, most of them Democrats bent on dumping Truman, went to Morningside Heights in persistent droves. One estimate states that at least eight Senators and a half dozen Governors reached the campus.[1] Publicly, endorsements of support came from a wide range of sources: Jersey City's strong-arm Mayor Frank Hague; "Boss" Jacob Arvey of Chicago; Mayor Hubert Humphrey of Minneapolis; Governor William Tuck of Virginia; other Southern politicians, both liberal and conservative, such as Senators John C. Stennis of Mississippi, John Sparkman of Alabama, Richard Russell of Georgia and Claude Pepper of Florida, the latter an outspoken New Dealer.[2] Furthermore, they were all Democrats. But a relatively early call for Ike came from Alf Landon of Kansas, the GOP's loser to FDR in 1936. In March, Franklin D. Roosevelt, Jr., a vice-chairman of the Americans for Democratic Action, and the policy committee of New York's Liberal party both announced for Ike, thereby abandoning Truman.[3] Organized labor also offered support—CIO secretary-treasurer James B. Carey, in a speech before the strongly liberal Americans for Democratic Action, and Emil Rieve, the general president of the Textile Workers Union.[4] The June 6, 1948, report of the Roper public-opinion poll confirmed the politicians' estimate of prevailing sentiment by showing that, if only they could saddle him, Eisenhower would ride into the White House as either a donkey or an elephant.

The Morningside Heights post office was probably in the best position to substantiate Roper. That spring alone almost twenty thousand letters, telegrams and postcards arrived for Columbia's president. On June 21, the opening date of the Republican convention in Philadelphia, more than 4,425 items were received. In fact, 56 percent of the total arrived during the period immediately before, during and after the convention, while the corresponding period of the Democratic convention, which took place two weeks later, brought 19 percent of the total.[5]

Columbia sociologist Dr. Robert K. Merton, who headed the university's Bureau of Applied Social Research, had been conducting an analysis, with staff members Joan Doris, Marie Jahoda and Leila Sussman, of letters to presidents from the public. The massive mail pile-up led Professor Merton to suggest, on June 19, 1949, that the bureau could make good use of the material by analyzing the contents. Eisenhower agreed.[6] The complete Merton report, issued two months later, consisted of 160 pages. To Eisenhower, however, Merton carefully submitted a twenty-nine page summary and digest. Faculty members who had had the privilege of sitting in on meetings with the university president had circulated reports that Eisenhower was an unsophisticated "hayseed" and his well-known preference for concise papers led Merton to simplify the summary.[7] From the analysis, the bureau and Eisenhower received a profile of the General's supporters and an examination of the sources of his political strength. Fifty-six percent of the mail centered around the period of the Republican convention and only 19 percent around the time when the Democrats met—probably a reflection of Eisenhower's additional public statement of July 5 that he would not consider becoming a candidate. The items received during the later period were less involved with an actual Eisenhower candidacy and more concerned with how the letter-writer himelf viewed the world. Moreover, 80 percent of the total mail that came in showed indifference about which party should nominate him, with about one in five voicing explicitly their lack of concern with that technicality. This also indicated the essential nonpartisanship of the correspondents, or, just as accurately, the apolitical qualities of the appeals.[8]

Most interesting were the reasons for wanting Ike. Of the 9 percent who said he should not run, 74 percent explained that doing so would, as the report explained, "mar his otherwise unimpeachable position in the eyes of the American people."[9] Those hostile to his becoming a candidate usually complained that he was being supported by the "New Deal Communists." A careful examination of the contents of the mail showed that the writers were mainly "independents" who cared more for the man than for the party, only 11 percent identifying themselves in any way with a partisan interest.[10] In fact, those who associated him with a policy position or seemed to care how he stood on such questions of national policy as civil rights also comprised 11 percent.[11] Very few, then, expressed a desire to have his candidacy offer some partisan purpose, such as ending the long Democratic hold on the Presidency or preventing the Republicans from replacing Truman. Overwhelmingly, by 85 percent, they were behind the General because of his personal qualities rather than his achievements. His appeal was attributed mostly to sincerity and human warmth and to competence. "Because of his sincerity and warmth," the summary explained, "they expressed *affection and loyalty*, and because of his competence, they expressed a sense of *newfound security*, were he to become President." Impressions of sincerity had come because the General had never shown himself to be self-seeking and because he had no association with any political interest. Truman, they felt, had lacked competence, and Dewey, the Republican loser in 1944, was insincere, whereas Eisenhower was rated positively for both qualities. The General, they were convinced, said in public what he believed in private and acted through conviction, not for effect—a relief from the self-interested scheming of most politicians.[12]

Perhaps even more significantly they saw Ike as a healer or a symbol of national unity. While he was a military man, he was not *militaristic*, and his accomplishment had been the coordination of the Allied armies. That was viewed as a major qualification for a President, who would have increasing relations with foreign powers. Since he was a "born leader," there would be no problem moving from military to political leadership. About one-third of the writers expressed a strong desire for internal national unity, showing strong distaste for conflict and disagreement or a "bickering atmosphere," and wanted to improve the political climate. Dewey had sensed with accuracy the desire for national unity, but his use of the appeal in the subsequent election of 1948 had been ineffectual because he was viewed as a "party man" or a machine politician. In short, he was the wrong man with the right slogan. When, as with Roosevelt, the report noted, "mass support *and* a political machine are behind the same man, the political machinery does not stand out in bold relief—its workings are not regarded as 'undemocratic.' But when, as with Eisenhower, a man with mass support does not have the backing of a political machine . . . *his supporters feel that the political machinery frustrates the popular will."* Fully half expressed the need for peace and security and the "establishment of national unity and preservation of American ideals." A farm wife's letter was quoted as saying that to achieve a feeling of security "will mean a lot of hard work on our part, but it will also mean that we must have a competent, progressive, capable leader handling our country and giving us leadership that will enable us to help ourselves."[13]

Letters from rural regions were by no means dominant, however. Figured on the basis of the 1948 population distribution, mail from farms and towns under 10,000 showed a deficit of 34 percent, while the volume from metropolitan areas reached a surplus of 29 percent. Again in relation to population distribution, the Pacific Coast region was most highly represented, with the Middle Atlantic area second and the South last. When analyzed for educational levels, the conclusion was that all degrees of literacy and economic groups were represented, with the majority giving clear evidence of belonging "to the more literate strain." Also noted was the marked departure from the usual political mail, where men generally outnumber women by two to one. The Eisenhower correspondents were almost equally represented by sex.[14]

Most emphatically, the report shows the political independents' role in the Eisenhower boom of 1948. The independent or least partisan segment of the population is also well known to political scientists as the group normally most uninvolved in politics.[15] It consists, almost by definition, of middle-of-the-roaders, political moderates, occupying the vast center of American politics and susceptible neither to the passions of the left nor the right. Their political commitment is to the traditional concepts of patriotism and the cultural definitions of virtue and morality.

The study by Herbert H. Hyman and Paul B. Sheatsley of Eisenhower's supporters offers substantiation. "The voters who fanned Eisenhower's candidacy at the time reflected majority sentiment on every issue," they noted. "They were somewhat more conservative than the Democrats, more liberal than the Republicans."[16] Although the General's views on important questions were unknown, he was able to attract more support from Democrats than could MacArthur. Both generals had, at the time, said little about national politics, and MacArthur was off administering the Japanese occupation. Nevertheless, political lines were adequately delineated so that admirers of Henry A. Wallace, on the left, and of Douglas MacArthur or Robert A. Taft, on the right, were far less likely to call for Eisenhower's nomination than were mildly liberal Democrats or mildly conservative Republicans.

CHAPTER 5

The Despair of the GOP

Ｉｆ Dwight D. Eisenhower's installation at Columbia had not been with the Presidency of the United States in mind, 1948 was nevertheless a good time for the retired soldier to be there. Tom Dewey's perplexing loss to Harry Truman had created a mood of desperation among Republicans. The certain return of the GOP to Washington after four White House terms had been, incredibly, thwarted by a President who, it was assumed, few were taking seriously. Perhaps it was the GOP that was dead, some were saying. With almost gloating despair, Colonel Robert McCormick's super-nationalistic Chicago *Tribune* promptly editorialized that, "For the third time, a Republican convention fell under vicious influences and nominated a 'me-too' candidate who conducted a 'me-too' campaign. For the third time the strategy failed. That is why Mr. Truman was elected and with him a Democratic House and Senate." And then the paper warned: "After this experience, we may hope the Republicans have learned their lesson. If the same forces control the next Republican convention the party is finished and the millions of patriotic men and women who have looked to it for leadership will have to look elsewhere."[1] Whether the GOP followed the Colonel's admonition or approached 1952 with similar candidates was evolving as the great political question. Continuing a crusade that had begun even before the New Deal had had a chance to prove what it could not do, conservatives of both parties were becoming far more desperate than Al Smith's old American Liberty Leaguers.

The election of 1948 was, in some ways, the greatest shock of all to the Republican party. With the sole exception of analyst Louis Bean, the experts had virtually written Truman off; but what the election had demonstrated was even more significant. The losses in 1932 and 1936 could be explained as the party's penalty for the Great Depression, while in 1940 and 1944 everybody knew that the war and the enormous personal popularity of FDR had kept Democrats in control. When the GOP acquired a majority in Congress in 1946, the inevitable return of Republican domination seemed at hand. The upset victory, however, was not only for Truman but for his party, too. Republicans reverted to their minority status as the Democrats regained the House by winning an additional seventy-five seats and getting nine more in the Senate. Moreover, candidates supported by the two major houses of organized labor, the CIO and the AFofL, did very well. Of the 215 candidates backed in House races by the CIO's Political Action Committee, 144 were successful, and similar union triumphs were made in the Senate.[2]

That election also brought to power several Democrats who were destined to play prominent roles during the next decade. In Illinois, Paul Douglas, a professional economist, defeated Old Guard Republican Senator C. Wayland Brooks, and Adlai E. Stevenson, whose grandfather had been Vice President under Grover Cleveland, won the governorship with a margin of over half a million votes. Texans elected Lyndon B. Johnson to the Senate for the first time by a scant eighty-seven-vote plurality. The mayor of Minneapolis, Hubert H. Humphrey, went to the Senate via an easy victory, and an ex-chairman of the Republican National Committee, Carroll Reece, was defeated in a senatorial election by Estes Kefauver of Tennessee.

A Republican casualty in his first attempt at political office, even before November, had been General Douglas MacArthur. Although still in Japan with American occupation forces, MacArthur had consented to let backers test his political appeal in Wisconsin's Presidential primary, the same one that had eliminated Wendell Willkie from contention in 1944. The military hero of the Pacific, however, won only eight of the twenty-seven convention delegates, with Harold C. Stassen, the ex-"Boy Governor" of Minnesota, taking the rest. MacArthur, having made a clear association with conservative forces in that state, was thus stigmatized both by losing and by his followers. Only in 1951, after Truman had relieved the general from his Far Eastern Command, would his political prospects evoke further excitement.

The president of Columbia University was, however, untouched by the political debris. Very few Democrats who had tried to draft him in lieu of Truman could be certain of his party affiliation. As has already been shown, that was far more elusive than the nature of his appeal. In reality, Eisenhower's instinctive convictions were proportionately as far to the right of dead center as Kansas is west of the Mississippi.

CHAPTER 6

The Centrist from Mid-America

EVEN IKE'S BIRTH placed him in the middle. Born on August 14, 1890, he was the third of seven sons of David and Ida Stover Eisenhower. Only six survived into childhood, as the fifth boy, Paul, died shortly after birth. Arthur and Edgar were older than David Dwight*; Roy, Earl and Milton were the youngest children.

The Eisenhowers were descendants of a German Palatinate family that had taken its religion from the teachings of Menno Simons, a contemporary of Martin Luther and John Calvin. Menno Simons carried the rebellious creed to a greater extreme, denying not only the justification of a special spiritual estate that sanctified sacerdotalism, as did Luther, but also the concept of the Trinity and infant baptism. A more moderate branch of the Anabaptists, Menno Simons's disciples, known as Mennonites, believed that the Word of God was available through the Bible to all who had faith. Their belief in regeneration was thus also incompatible with Calvin's concepts of predestination.

When the Eisenhowers reached Pennsylvania in the middle of the eighteenth century, they settled just above Harrisburg and east of the Susquehanna River, at a place called Elizabethville. Their local Mennonite congregation accordingly took the name River Brethren, which was later also used in Dickinson County, Kansas, after the westward migration of Jacob Eisenhower. When they met, David and Ida Stover were students at Lane University in Lecompton, which was run by the

---

* He was christened David Dwight but called Dwight and used the name Dwight David upon his enrollment at West Point.

United Brethren churches. The pacifism and strong faith in the Bible that characterized their religion would always be a cohesive force in the Eisenhower home, contrasting with the rather diverse political views of the boys. General Eisenhower would one day cite their varied opinions to Russian Army Marshal Zhukov as an example of the freedom of thought that was possible in America.[1]

In their company, Eisenhower was the moderate, middle-of-the-roader, to the right of the more liberal views of brothers Milton and Earl and certainly less conservative than Edgar and Arthur. Roy, the Junction City druggist who died in 1942, was a Republican stalwart in the GOP stronghold near Fort Riley.[2] There is no record of Dwight Eisenhower's ever having taken an extreme position on any political issue, except, possibly, for the sake of a family discussion. The one instance offered by his biographer described his helping Edgar attack Earl and Milton's defense of the New Deal.[3] Even when young Ike represented his high-school speech class at a Democratic club banquet in Abilene to speak on the subject of students in politics, two other boys represented each of the major parties while he spoke as a non-partisan.[4]

The usual image of the Kansas Eisenhowers is that of a hard-working, Bible-centered family that could have been created by Willa Cather or O. E. Rölvaag. David Eisenhower, who had been trained as an engineer at Lane University, ran a general-merchandise store in the Dickinson County hamlet of Hope with a man named Milton Good until, apparently swindled by his partner, the business collapsed and he was forced to move to Denison, Texas, and a menial job with the Missouri-Texas-Kansas Railroad. It was there that David Dwight was born. Later, returning to Abilene, David Eisenhower managed to support his family by working as a mechanic in the Belle Springs Creamery. While trying to earn money for his own education and also raise enough money for his brother Edgar's college expenses, young Dwight later also worked at the creamery, laboring twelve hours every night in the week.

Their home soon thereafter was the little house on Southeast Fourth Street, which still stands just west of the museum and library. The collective portrait of a family on the poor side of town, south of the railroad tracks, after the hard times of David Eisenhower, hardly suggests that the children were accustomed to middle-class comforts. And Dwight, reared in pious and impecunious circumstances, worked as a youth at various odd jobs in Abilene, in addition to his period of time at the creamery, and had every reason to trust the Horatio Alger success stories that were a fulfillment of, as Herbert Croly called his 1909 book, "the promise of American life."

For Dwight D. Eisenhower, reared in the rural Midwest during the first decade of the twentieth century, the American ideals portrayed in his textbooks were as sacred as the truths of the Bible. Fear of God was synonymous with virtue. Thrift, honesty and the avoidance of debt were the basic characteristics of morality. "Because of my father's reputation and his insistence on paying cash for all he bought," Dwight Eisenhower later recalled, he gained a reputation for "unimpeachable honesty."[5]

"Abilene thought that most everyone could succeed in the American environment," he wrote, if they were willing to work hard, had "native" intelligence and could "cipher" accurately.[6] He pointed out, in appropriate frontier concepts, that his parents "profited more from their association with people than with books or with expensive laboratory equipment."[7]

Although the Mennonites had been unable to avoid fighting battles on the frontier, the faith was highly pacifistic. Of his mother, whose gentle tolerance he admired, he wrote that she had always been a woman of peace. He never forgot the stories that were told about her early years in Virginia's Shenandoah Valley, when Yankee troops seared the lush countryside with all the destruction they could deliver. Having been caught as a baby in the Civil War, Ida Stover Eisenhower had experienced the ravages of war "in a devastated land and in broken bodies. If her hatred of war arose out of childhood memories, she had justification. War's tragedy, inescapable in its waging and in its aftermath," Eisenhower wrote, "was no tale she had read or heard."[8]

The Eisenhower boys had never been able to take security for granted. They also learned to be careful about judging others. Although no one could prove that Milton Good had been dishonest, the disaster to David Eisenhower and his family had resulted from the other man's ways. Later, recalling the experience of baseball's Black Sox scandal of 1919 but also alluding to his own past, Eisenhower noted that he had learned to "grow increasingly cautious about making judgments solely on reports." He also observed that "Behind every human action, the truth may be hidden. But the truth may also lie behind some other action or arrangement, far off in time and place. Unless circumstances and responsibility demand an instant judgment I learned to reserve mine until the last proper moment," even, he conceded, if such caution was not always proper.[9]

Going off to West Point and leaving his mother in tears was Ike's boldest move. He had known, of course, that Ida Stover Eisenhower, with her feelings toward anything connected with war, would be dismayed; but it was his choice and she felt it improper to thwart him. Eisenhower, as he realized later, had underestimated how deeply she felt.[10] Both Eisenhower and his biographers have repeated his friend "Swede" Hazlett's role in enticing him to apply for Annapolis. However, he was ultimately disqualified as too old for the Naval Academy, and so he went to West Point instead. Bold as that move may have been, the military academy did hold several attractions for the young man from Kansas: the patriotic call of service to his country, for one, and, aside from a government career with financial security, an opportunity to get a higher education despite his limited funds and without making financial problems for his family. "With Ed already in college and receiving some help from Father and with Earl and Milton coming on in the future," he has since explained, "I could see that if I could make it, I would take a burden off my family."[11]

When he married Mamie Geneva Doud just before his twenty-sixth birthday in 1916, he became a part of a more than routinely comfortable middle-class Denver family. They had a large home, a maid, a telephone, a car. The Douds, in fact, had had money since the financial successes of Royal Houghton Doud, Mamie's paternal grandfather, in the grocery and meat-packing fields. The lieutenant had no trouble becoming part of his new family. The smooth start of his early military career and marriage was marred in early 1921 by the death of their first child, Doud Dwight Eisenhower, called Ikey, at the age of three years, three months. A second son, John Sheldon Doud Eisenhower, was born during the summer of the following year.

By the time Japanese bombs fell on Pearl Harbor, Ike was Brigadier General Dwight D. Eisenhower, having been promoted only recently as a direct result of his superlative direction of Army maneuvers in Louisiana. His career had already included service in the Panama Canal Zone and five years under General MacArthur in the Philippines. Assigned, at the age of fifty-one, as Chief of Operations under General George Catlett Marshall in Washington, he could hardly have predicted what the next two decades would bring. Less than one year earlier he had been promoted to colonel, which would have been, as he noted, a respectable and normal level for the completion of his career.

CHAPTER 7

Ike

Eisenhower's personality and style of operation were particularly well suited to the responsibilities given to him during the war. Broad optimism and genuine modesty made him particularly easy to take. Although brief exposure to his papers may cause cynics to conclude that such humility was contrived, thorough acquaintance with both the man and his writings dispels any skepticism. When, for example, he was informed early in the war that magazines were carrying articles about him back in the States, he wrote to an old friend: "When I have time to think about the matter at all, I merely wonder what kind of fanciful picture of my very ordinary characteristics all this publicity is building up in the popular mind."[1] At the same time it would be misleading to conclude that such nonchalance connoted insufficient appreciation of his own talents and intelligence. He simply had too much appreciation of the abilities of others to regard himself as extraordinary, which may be why he was uncomfortable with "yes" men.[2]

The lack of conceit precluded a proclivity to make rapid judgments on insufficient evidence. If he had learned the need for caution, it was best illustrated by his daily style. Problems were, to him, challenges that, like hands in a card game, had to be examined for every possibility. Little, he insisted, could be judged without weighing all facts and circumstances thoroughly before coming to any conclusions. Not only were all the possible alternatives studied, but he had learned to consider the options open to the other fellow and to anticipate the most effective way of meeting the probable moves taken as a result of those possibilities.[3] Once his own course had been decided, Eisenhower expected each subordinate to follow through within his own area of responsibility.

Thus, he promptly relieved an American officer during the war for referring to an ally as a "British son of a bitch" instead of merely a son of a bitch. Those who observed Eisenhower at close range claimed they never saw anyone move as quickly once his mind was made up.[4]

To each problem he brought total dedication. He prepared himself carefully, preferring oral briefings so he could probe further by asking questions and raising arguments to test for fallacies. So he could best get at the "meat of the coconut," he preferred that whatever written reports were necessary be summarized on one page.[5] He often liked to test advocates of a position by challenging whatever was being proposed. Those unwilling to go all the way in countering his arguments, or who simply conceded the weakness of the points, often turned away in defeat without being aware of having failed the General's effort to test the validity of what they were saying.[6] Many were amazed at how quickly he familiarized himself with totally new subjects.[7]

That Eisenhower was dedicated to his country, above every other consideration, is, of course, taken for granted and is hardly surprising. For one, he had received the conventional patriotic indoctrination at West Point. But, more importantly, for an American of his time and place, greater sophistication in his unquestioning loyalty would have been unusual. He was more than merely a product of small-town Kansas; his impulses were those of a representative American. He was optimistic, proud and never doubting that his country's democracy was superior to anything the world had ever seen and as good as its people desired. To his brother Arthur, for example, he pointed out the importance of adhering to Stephen Decatur's much-quoted "our country, right or wrong" toast of 1816.[8] When another brother, Milton, became president of Kansas State College, the General used the occasion to wish that his youngest brother's inaugural speech had referred to "the necessity of teaching and inculcating good, old-fashioned patriotism—just that sense of loyalty and obligation to the community that is necessary to the preservation of all the privileges and rights that the community guarantees."[9] Still bothered about the problem, two days later he wrote to "Swede" Hazlett that those "influencing the teaching of the younger generation" have perhaps the most responsible task of all, teaching the "obligations as well as the privileges of American citizenship," which would involve the "virtue of old-fashioned patriotism." Characteristically, he also added, "the need for a clean, honest approach to intricate problems and the necessity for earnest devotion to duty. . . ."[10] But another aspect of this devotion to country must have conceivably been influenced by his extensive international military and diplomatic experiences, particularly during his unique World War II role and the almost total lack of chauvinism in his patriotism, a quality more easily desired than found.

That the authorship of *Crusade in Europe*, Eisenhower's personal ac-

count of his World War II experience, was essentially his was no surprise to those who had witnessed him as a writer, editor or had heard
him speak informally. His prose was characteristically clear, even if some
did find the tiny script hard to decipher. He searched for accurate
phrases, not the pompous or fancy. When others prepared drafts for his
signature, he was adept at tightening and clarifying the prose, sometimes
with astonishing attention to details. Later, when he was President, Sir
Howard Beale, the Australian ambassador to the United States, prepared
with an Assistant Secretary of State a document for Eisenhower to send
to the Prime Minister in Canberra. When the State Department man
showed it to Eisenhower, the President read it carefully and promptly
asked, "Did that Australian write this?" "We wrote it together," said the
Assistant Secretary. "He must have," replied Eisenhower, who then explained that the word "chances" had not been used as an American
expression and promptly replaced it with "happens."[11]

Others noted that General Eisenhower had the unusual talent for delivering every spoken word as part of a perfectly formed sentence.
Stenographers were often pressed to race in order to keep up with his
rapid dictation of smooth-flowing prose. Carter L. Burgess, who served
as an assistant to General Eisenhower's aide, General Walter Bedell
Smith, recalled hearing Ike dictate a long situation message to General
Marshall that, when it emerged from the typewriter, required only limited changes. His facts, too, were neatly arranged in his head and reeled
off his tongue effortlessly even without notes.[12] Later, at Columbia, he
was again witnessed as speaking best when not burdened with notes.[13]

Eisenhower's rapid rise to the top during the war and his ability to
gain and hold the confidence of all elements in the tenuous wartime
alliance also proved his political skill. He learned politics as the art of
compromise and that a statesman is a politician who always compromises
in the right direction. Shrewdly, however, he avoided compromises that
would reverse his objectives.[14] When clarifying the controversial deal
with Darlan in North Africa, the General pointed out to his brother
Milton, who had been concerned about the unsavory aspects of the
affair, that "it was obviously necessary to recognize the manifest interdependence of maximum military requirements and pressing political
needs. . . . Such success as we have accomplished over the whole front
has come about, I firmly believe, because we did not attempt to put the
cart before the horse."[15] To an American journalist he explained the
politics of the African affair by saying that "You can't drastically reform
everything at once, though the extremists always want you to. If you
strive to gain everything at once, without compromise, you end up with
nothing."[16]

His cautious approach to problems had, in a way, been the antithesis of the popular notion of the rash military man. Political acumen and personal qualities had, at the same time, made an enormous contribution toward the success of the wartime alliance. His entire career and reputation, it seemed, had provided him with qualities tailor-made for conciliation.

CHAPTER 8

Truman's Troubles

Eisenhower RECALLS THAT the drive to persuade him to run for the
Presidency began "almost within hours of Truman's defeat of Dewey."[1]
While that was not unique in American history, more distinctive was the
desperation that agitated Republicans after that horrendous disappointment in 1948. For the party stalwarts there was frustration over failure
to recapture the federal bureaucracy with all its rewards. For business
interests, troubled by the growth of Big Labor, it was a lost chance to
oust the Administration that had vetoed the National Labor Relations
Act of 1947 (Taft-Hartley) and excoriated the Republican-controlled
Eightieth Congress for having enacted it into law. For conservatives in
general, the unbalanced budgets, "fiscal irresponsibility," taxation, enlargement of the federal bureaucracy—all associated with New Deal–
Fair Deal Democrats—had to be halted before, as Senator Taft and his
followers warned, there would be no return from a steady march toward
"socialism." For those perplexed and frightened by the advances of European and Asian communism, it was time to get rid of those inheritors
of the party responsible for having negotiated secret and "immoral"
deals with Stalin at Yalta. In New York a former New Dealer, Alger
Hiss, had been named by Whittaker Chambers as the transmitter to the
Reds of classified State Department documents; and within six weeks of
Truman's upset victory, Hiss was indicted by a federal grand jury on
two counts of perjury. For the followers of South Carolina Democratic
Senator J. Strom Thurmond there still remained the task of getting rid
of the Administration that had rent the Philadelphia convention by writing a bold civil-rights plank into the platform. Even on the left there was

consternation because over one million—half of them in New York alone—had voted for Henry A. Wallace, who had turned against the Administration by accusing it of provoking the Cold War.

Yet, although the pro-Eisenhower people were serious after Dewey's defeat, the forces that were to assure his return from Europe as a candidate had not developed in full by 1949. During those four years, the ones that were Truman's "reward" for his triumph, Americans experienced the apotheosis of their postwar despair. If Eisenhower, therefore, had not been ready for the nation in 1949, the nation was his for the asking in 1952.

Internal communism, hinted at when Truman had instituted the federal Loyalty-Security Program in 1947, had created national paranoia. Alger Hiss, in his second trial, had been found guilty and sentenced to five years in prison, an achievement widely credited to the determination of Representative Richard M. Nixon, a young Republican from Southern California. Eleven top U.S. Communist party leaders were accused of violating the Smith Act of 1940 and given prison terms. Moreover, Judith Coplon, Valentin Gubichev, Harry Gold, Klaus Fuchs, Morton Sobell and Julius and Ethel Rosenberg were all names everyone associated with internal Communist treachery in the United States, Canada and Great Britain. When the Russians then revealed, in the fall of 1949, that they had solved the mystery of how to make atomic bombs, it was easier to credit their spies than their scientists. As though such jolts to the national well-being were insufficient, Senator Joseph R. McCarthy of Wisconsin had adopted a crusade peddled by anti-Communists in Washington.[2] At Wheeling, West Virginia, he shocked the nation with the allegation that there were 205 Communists working in the State Department. The millions of Americans who considered the suddenly famous Senator a savior of the free world also welcomed the passage of the Internal Security Act of 1951 that provided for the registration, internment and exclusion from war plants of American Communists in case of a national emergency. Senator Nixon, accepting McCarthy's theme, told the 180th dinner meeting of the Economics Club of New York that not only was a growing distrust of politicians increasing the popularity of Eisenhower and MacArthur but that the Administration "has consistently failed to recognize that the United States can be destroyed just as effectively and completely by forces within as by enemies abroad."[3]

Taft, too, so typical of the Republican party that his nickname as "Mr. Republican" was taken for granted, adopted the McCarthy line with even more enthusiasm than did Nixon. While not engaging in the irresponsible personal accusations that was the style of the Wisconsin demagogue, he sought to capitalize on the anti-Communist hysteria and mania that had surfaced again. Campaigning in McCarthy's home state, he told a Beloit crowd that McCarthy's demands for an investigation of the State Department were "fully justified" by its "pro-Communst policies."[4] In Wyoming, Taft charged that years of information-gathering by the FBI on Communists in government had been neglected by the soft attitude of the Executive Department toward Communists, who were merely viewed as "just another form of Democrats."[5]

Overseas there had been even more bad news. On top of the Soviet atomic debut, Chiang Kai-shek's forces had finally abandoned the main-land and had decided to make the island of Taiwan Chinese. An airlift lasting nearly one year, directed by General Lucius Clay, had been needed to defy the Soviet blockade of West Berlin. The Korean war was still being fought. General MacArthur had miscalculated Chinese Com-munist reactions toward American troops driving to the Yalu River, and a whole "new war" had developed. Less than half a year later, the President fired the determined general.

Even worse, perhaps, the man in the White House had little prestige left. There had been scandal after scandal, involving so-called "five-per-centers," and everybody was concerned about deep freezers and mink coats being used as payoffs. Senator Estes Kefauver's subcommittee to investigate interstate crime had given television its first big show. All over the country, Internal Revenue officials were judged more culpable than the tax-dodgers, and removed. There had even been a brazen at-tempt by Puerto Rican nationalists to assassinate the President. The man whose popularity had soared after his much-admired personal achieve-ment in 1948 was still regarded as a good President by only one quarter of those responding to Dr. Gallup's poll.[6]

Only their dismal experience of four years earlier checked Republican confidence. For Eisenhower, having resisted the calls in 1948, the timing could not have been better.

CHAPTER 9

The Forces for Ike

THE MOVEMENT TO get Eisenhower to run and the campaign to win the GOP's nomination resembled, in many ways, the Willkie drive of 1940. Both drives were for political amateurs and, not surprisingly, both were suspected of having been engineered by Democrats. Unquestionably also they were strong personalities who were regarded by the public as "above politics." A popular following among the apolitical centrists, therefore, became a vital constituency in 1952 as it had been a dozen years earlier. That neither had ever stood for elective office was more of an asset than a liability. Their cadre and so-called grass-roots support were mobilized largely by businessmen concerned about international as well as domestic commercial interests; and, although such devotees to the crusades behind Willkie and Eisenhower were often small-town bankers and investors, the most influential and powerful sources were in the country's major financial quarters, particularly New York and Boston. Furthermore, the 1952 campaign aimed against a continuation of the New Deal that Mr. Willkie had failed to stop. Both campaigns brought convention victories for the so-called Eastern Establishment of the Republican party.

Such comparisons become important only when trying to understand the persistent dilemma of the moderate and liberal wings of the GOP, largely in the East. A closer view, however, suggests some contrasts. The same businessmen who had helped Willkie against Arthur Vandenberg, Robert A. Taft and Thomas E. Dewey had aligned themselves, by the early 1950s, with Dewey to elect Eisenhower. And their advantages were significant. Unlike Willkie, Eisenhower had never been a Democrat but

33

had descended from a traditionally Republican family with an equally firm tradition of ideological indifference. His own affiliation had never been publicized. Where Willkie, through his battle against TVA when he tried to defend the interests of Commonwealth and Southern, was a creature of domestic political controversy, Eisenhower's career had created few significant enemies. Different, too, was the fervor behind the return-to-power momentum that had mounted by 1952. The professionals had become even more desperate. But the businessmen, amateurs only in a technical political sense but highly professional in responding to their self-interest, were convinced that corporate and patriotic goals were identical. Perhaps their only real disadvantage over the early period was their need to persuade the candidate even more than the voters.

The businessmen behind the Eisenhower movement had another reason for consternation. For them, continued absence from power by the GOP threatened to create a Republican party ever more resentful of "me-tooism." The conservative reaction against such outbidding of the Democrats had led to a shift of control away from the Eastern Establishment back to the small-town, Midwestern-based sentiments that minimized desires to commit American money and soldiers to rehabilitate postwar Western Europe. When the results of the mid-term elections of 1950 became known, the impact of the Chicago *Tribune*'s anti-"me-too" attitude seemed close to realization. Not only did the swing to the Republicans cut the Democratic majority (by about three-fourths in the Senate and two-thirds in the House), but the shift was unmistakably away from liberal or moderate Republicanism. Of the eight new GOP Senators, six were conservatives, and only Jim Duff of Pennsylvania could be called liberal. Of the five members of the party's Congressional hierarchy, only Senate Whip Leverett Saltonstall of Massachusetts was not an Old Guard-type reactionary. When the party's state chairmen were polled, immediately after Election Day, to determine their man for the 1952 Presidential nomination, their clear-cut choice was Taft.[1] Once again a certain victory seemed ahead, but this time few dared to express unguarded optimism.

With General Eisenhower at their center as president of Columbia and with his ear easily available, it was only natural that he became the liberals' chief hope. Among those close to the General during this period was the Reid family, owners of the New York *Herald Tribune*, the virtual organ of the Republican party's Eastern Establishment. Having met Eisenhower during their postwar efforts to reopen the Paris edition of the *Herald Tribune*, they maintained a close social relationship that became even easier after the General came to Columbia. The General's association with William Robinson, the paper's publisher, also intensified during this time, and the Reids saw to it that Eisenhower was feted at their home along with many distinguished visitors. As their paper represented the opposite end of Colonel McCormick's notion of Republicanism, the Reids wielded significant influence among those advocating continued bipartisanship in foreign affairs. Aid through such programs as the Mutual Security Act, which provided funds for economic and military assistance, was typical of the kind of support given to the Truman Administration by *Herald Tribune* Republicans. Quite naturally, Eisenhower emerged from this circle as the logical favorite, especially after Dewey's defeat.

However biting the New York Governor was in criticizing the Democrats' domestic ineptitude and corruption in Washington, he had been a steady supporter of obligations to Europe by advocating strengthening of the structure begun by the North Atlantic Treaty Organization, which had, in 1949, united eleven nations in a collective-security program. With the death of Senator Arthur Vandenberg, Dewey was left as one of the GOP's outstanding advocates of internationalism. On February 12, 1951, just two months before the Michigan Senator died, Dewey told a Lincoln Day dinner of the National Republican Club that NATO should be extended along the Mediterranean and even beyond its eastern shores to minimize what was available for Russian aggression. He also urged that Greece and Turkey be brought into the pact.[2]

Eisenhower, the next day, ended his Army status of "on active duty without assignment" and went to Europe as the Supreme Commander of the Allied Powers in Europe (SACEUR). Reactivated by President Truman, who assured him that all NATO countries had sought him as the man for the job, Eisenhower, certainly sympathetic to the project, responded to the new assignment as another call to duty. During the little more than two weeks between his return from a brief preliminary trip overseas to determine what kind of structure would be feasible and his departure to take command of NATO forces, General Eisenhower had two conferences of future significance. The first, on the night of his return to Washington, January 31, 1951, marked his initial meeting with Texas banker Robert B. Anderson, whose advice Eisenhower had sought on Federal Reserve Bank policy applicable to Europe. From that moment on, a steady correspondence between both men increased their mutual respect. The second meeting, far less congenial, was a clandestine arrangement in the privacy of the massive Pentagon. Acknowledging that Senator Taft was the Republican party's chief opponent of full American economic and military guarantees to the NATO countries, Eisenhower had hoped to win assurances from the Senator that would enable him to leave for Europe with sufficient bipartisan support. With his usual optimism, Eisenhower drafted in advance a statement announcing Taft's cooperation for collective security. But, to Eisenhower's dismay, which was a shock he never forgot, the Senator's main concern was over whether he should vote for two, four or six divisions. The mission was completely fruitless. "This aroused my fears that isolationism was stronger in the Congress than I had previously suspected," the General later wrote.[3] Of even greater importance, it was a confrontation with the realities of Republican leadership that would ultimately make Eisenhower vastly more receptive to political pleas.

Eisenhower's differences with Taft largely over foreign policy had become clear. During his presidency of Columbia, he referred to domestic matters and gave ample evidence that neither the New York financial establishment boosting his candidacy nor the Ohio Senator could brand him as any kind of a New Dealer. When, for example, he spoke before the American Bar Association in St. Louis in praise of mutual contributions of labor and management to the nation's economy, he also eulogized the "middle of the road between the unfettered power of concentrated wealth . . . and the unbridled power of statism." At Galveston, Texas, that same year, 1949, he said, "If all Americans want is security they can go to prison."[4] He later gave more evidence of traditional conservatism by denouncing the desire to "wear fine shirts and have caviar and champagne when we should be eating hot dogs and beer," stating that those who died for freedom "believed in something more than trying to be sure they would not be hungry when they were sixty-seven."[5] At Columbia in early 1950 he complained that too often "we incline to describe the ultimate in human welfare as a mule's sort of heaven—a tight roof overhead, plenty of food, a minimum of work and no worries or responsibilities." He called for a rekindling of our understanding to "make Marxist devotees see that things of the spirit—justice, freedom, equality—are the elements" really important to satisfy man's creative needs.[6] Most speeches dwelled on overcentralization of the federal government and cheapening of the currency.[7] Liberal complaints that a professional soldier was ungracious to complain about welfare-state security were more often than not regarded as poor manners.

At least one sympathetic student of Eisenhower's fiscal ideas, Charles J. V. Murphy, believes that his European stay at the NATO headquarters (SHAPE) actually deepened those conservative convictions. Murphy, citing the General's constant correspondence with business and banking figures—Robert B. Anderson now among them—points out that much of that mail was concerned with "high economic theory, not excluding such mysteries as the gold standard."[8] More explicitly they dealt with the soundness of the dollar; their fear was the continuation of inflationary spending policies threatening to go even higher because of increased defense costs. Distressed by the situation, George Whitney judged that the upward spiral is "a fearful picture of what might happen when necessary expenditures for defense actually do flow into the economic bloodstream."[9] Another financier, Lewis Douglas, cited his past Washington experiences to recall that Executive Department expense estimates are always padded and added that "I have known enough about the terrific power that the Pentagon exercises over the Executive Branch and the Legislative to realize that it can be restrained only by the most courageous and objective controls." And the kind of control that was needed, Douglas made clear, was "dedicated and strong political control" over the pressures for increased defense spending.[10] Whitney, despite his concern over the evils of mounting "socialistic" controls since 1933, advised Eisenhower in Keynesian terms that government action might be needed, after all, "through the use of credit and taxes when there is an inflationary tendency." A depression, he added, would even justify deficit financing.[11] The brand of conservatism thus conveyed to Eisenhower showed that financial interests were no more ready than labor leaders, small businessmen and academicians to trust the operation of the "free market." Some, apparently, were not even quite willing to trust Ike's brand of conservatism. Cyrus Sulzberger recorded hearing that "Winthrop Aldrich is going around telling people that if Eisenhower wins, he thinks he will have to accept a job in Washington to 'keep Ike on the beam.' "[12]

There is also the possibility that the General's natural conservatism may have been furthered by what he actually saw in Europe. He concluded that countering inflation and financial chaos with productivity was essential for any hopes of self-defense for the NATO countries. Also vital for that end was a strong American domestic economy. Murphy has observed that Eisenhower thereby became even more convinced that the way to preserve and intensify American productivity "was to turn the U.S. Government back to the traditional paths of fiscal morality and free enterprise."[13]

Those views were largely ignored by the rising demand for his candidacy, except that they served to increase the confidence of Republican promoters that the General was at least an intellectual, if not an actual, member of their clan. However, a local radio broadcaster in North Carolina proposed a plan to make possible the selection of Eisenhower electors by that traditionally Southern Democratic state "without a third party and without the state going Republican."[14] A recipient of the plan, "Swede" Hazlett, promptly forwarded the proposal to his good friend Ike. And while Governor Dewey had already told a "Meet the Press" TV interview panel, as early as October 1951, that he would prefer Eisenhower for 1952, Senator Henry Cabot Lodge of Massachusetts seconded that endorsement on the same program the following August. It was notable, however, that Lodge had taken care to warn that involvement in partisan politics would be harmful to what the General was trying to achieve in Europe.[15]

Both statements were, of course, significant. Dewey, the party's titular leader, was signaling his forces to get behind the man he had determined was most likely to reinstall the party in the White House. The New Yorker, who had seen a lot of the General since Ike had arrived at Columbia—including at the Governor's Pawling estate—was attempting to exploit the popular notion that, in Eisenhower, the GOP had a sure winner. It is also certain that, knowing the General as well as he did, Dewey did not attempt to launch a "trial balloon" with Eisenhower's approval. Instead, he made his move first and then told the General that he could not refuse.[16] Eisenhower, however, reacted by issuing a prompt public rejection that included such words as "I don't know why people are always nagging me to run for President. I think I've gotten too old."[17] Dewey, however, continued to press his pro-Eisenhower preference and tried to dispel any notions that he was merely attempting to create machinery for his own third nomination. When the Governors held their annual conference at Gatlinburg, Tennessee, in 1951, Dewey pressed the Eisenhower drive among the Governors. Progress was achieved through announcements of support from Gatlinburg by Governors Sherman Adams of New Hampshire, Val Peterson of Nebraska, Edward Arn of Kansas and Walter Kohler of Wisconsin.[18]

The way was thus opened for Dewey's people to move into the campaign in Eisenhower's behalf. They included a number of well-placed, highly competent individuals: General Lucius Clay, retired from the Army and now chairman of the board of the Continental Can Company; Wall Street attorney Herbert Brownell, Jr.; J. Russel Sprague, Republican leader of Long Island's Nassau County; James C. Hagerty, Dewey's press secretary; National Committeeman Barak T. Mattingly of Missouri. During the coming months they were more likely than Dewey to become visibly identified with the Eisenhower cause, as the New York Governor realized, quite accurately, that Old Guard hostility toward him had become so bitter that his presence at the General's side would be no blessing.[19]

Lodge, the grandson of the Republican leader whose concepts of internationalism and domestic politics had blocked American participation in the League of Nations on Woodrow Wilson's terms, was as concerned as Dewey with the attitude of the GOP toward European affairs. Simultaneously, he also wanted the party to present a strong Presidential candidate to Massachusetts voters in 1952. As he was up for re-election that year, and with a young, well-financed and attractive Democratic Congressman, John F. Kennedy, looming as his probable opponent, Lodge feared that the combination of Taft's anti-labor reputation and isolationism would repel Massachusetts voters. They had not given a majority to a Republican Presidential candidate since Calvin Coolidge in 1924. Lodge's most ardent efforts, therefore, were devoted to convincing the General that he was needed by both the country and the party.

The Lodge arguments were persuasive. As inadequate as was his attitude toward Europe, Taft's view of the Korean war had seemed inconsistent and confusing. Having originally supported Truman's response to the invasion across the Thirty-eighth Parallel, by early 1951 he was calling for outright American withdrawal. "It is far better to fall back to a defensible position in Japan and Formosa than to maintain a Korean position which would surely be indefensible in any third world war," he told the Senate.[20] Yet, when Truman fired MacArthur for public advocacy of a more hawkish policy than the Administration would undertake, Taft became one of the general's staunchest defenders. By the middle of the year, the Senator was adding his voice to calls for bombing the Chinese mainland, blockading their coast and using Chiang Kai-shek's troops. Holding that it was American policy that was inconsistent, he pointed out that the nation was risking war with Russia in Europe by implementing NATO plans, so why not take the same risk in Korea?[21] The major element in the Senator's thinking about the "police action" was his denial of the feasibility of limited war; Taft's more traditional view called for either a traditional military victory or complete withdrawal.

Obviously campaigning hard for the nomination, by early fall, Taft made it official on October 16 by declaring himself a candidate. His immediate and undeniable strength was, from that moment on, with the party professionals. A poll of 455 of the 1,094 Republican delegates to the forthcoming convention that was taken by NBC radio commentator Ned Brooks revealed the obvious fact that the Senator was their favorite by a vote of 244 to 114 for Eisenhower and that Harold Stassen was a poor third with thirty-four.[22] Taft hoped that impressive early strength would discourage Republican delegates from gambling on the uncertainties of a hazy Eisenhower candidacy. The major mysteries were Eisenhower's party preference, if he had one, and his willingness to abandon SHAPE to return home as an active contender. That both uncertainties could prove negative posed a dilemma for wavering delegates, who would consequently find themselves without a place in the winner's circle. Enough delegates going to Governor Earl Warren of California, who announced his candidacy on November 14, or to the still to be heard from Harold E. Stassen, could create a sufficient holding action to block Taft; but a strong, convincing drive could build a "bandwagon" that few could spurn.

By the time the pre-convention competition for delegates began, the

Eisenhower people were optimistic enough to believe some progress had been made. A front-page New York *Herald Tribune* editorial on October 25, with format and sentiments similar to their call for Wendell Willkie during the Philadelphia convention of 1940, declared that "At rare intervals in the life of a free people the man and the occasion meet. . . . We believe that for the Republican party the occasion has now come. We believe that Dwight D. Eisenhower is the man." It continued by claiming that his past responsibilities had "required the vision of the statesman, the skill of the diplomat, the supreme organizing talents of the administrator, and the human sympathies of the representative of the people. All these gifts General Eisenhower has shown in abundance. . . . He is a Republican by temper and disposition. He is a Republican by every avowal of faith and solemn declaration of America . . ."[23] One week later the same paper was quick to report that, when interviewed by the United Press, Eisenhower said he did not aspire to the Presidency but was ready to put duty before all other considerations in 1952. Most important, observed the reporter, was that the General did not say no.[24]

Meanwhile, recruitment of other professional politicians added to the opponents of the Taft candidacy. Lodge brought together Senator Frank Carlson and Republican National Committeeman and former Senator Harry Darby. Both Kansans had already been working to develop the Eisenhower boom. To their group also came Senators James Duff of Pennsylvania and Irving Ives of New York.[25] Public statements of support were also made by New York Representative Jacob Javits, who said that it was Eisenhower's "duty" to accept the Republican nomination, and Representative Hugh Scott of Pennsylvania, who told the Young Republican convention that Ike "will react on a patriotic basis" and that he would accept the GOP nomination if enough people demonstrate that they want him for their President. Scott then pressed the theme being pushed more and more by the party's "left wing"—that Eisenhower would be the "one candidate who would be certain to become President on the Republican ticket."[26]

Dewey, working to unify the various factions, called a meeting in his suite at the Roosevelt Hotel in New York. Taft's progress had made essential a rapid, well-organized and sustained drive that would attract enough politicians and, at the same time, convince friendly businessmen that it was an organization worth supporting. The Dewey caucus, calling itself the Initial Advisory Group, thus undertook the task of selecting a campaign manager.

All of the participants agreed that naming a prominent figure from west of the Mississippi would be desirable to counter suspicions that the Eisenhower forces were merely representative of the Eastern Establishment. As each possibility was mentioned, however, personal objections were made, usually by rival Republicans from the same part of the country. Finally, Dewey and Barak Mattingly turned to Lodge. But Lodge protested. He cited impolitic personal liabilities. An obvious product of Harvard, he was from the Eastern Establishment. Nevertheless, the essential fact was the dearth of high-ranking politicians willing, at that point, to join their cause and, among the professionals, Lodge had an important asset. Unlike most of the others in the room, he could not be resented as having been a Dewey supporter. The Massachusetts Senator had, in fact, worked to deadlock the 1948 convention between Dewey and Taft to secure the nomination for Arthur Vandenberg. Lodge, who had been assured by General Lucius Clay that Eisenhower was a Republican, therefore became the campaign manager.

Increasingly, businessmen joined the crusade. Roy Howard, the publisher of the Kansas City *Star* and a good friend of the Eisenhower family, announced that the General "is a Kansas Republican like his forbears" and would accept a genuine draft for the Presidency if he felt that his European job could be left in good hands.[27] Raymond Pitcairn, the principal stockholder and director of the Pittsburgh Plate Glass Company, circulated an appeal in Pennsylvania to raise money for Eisenhower's candidacy because "we need a candidate free from the handicap of previous defeats, a candidate who does not carry the scars of party strife, a candidate unfettered by prejudice engendered by previous political commitments, a statesman who is not identified with partisan political issues, a man who can lead in establishing an era of peace, security, and well-being at home and abroad."[28] The same concern with peace was very much on the mind of Harry A. Bullis, chairman of the board of General Mills Corporation and frequent correspondent of Eisenhower's. Bullis was disturbed that foreign business associates of General Mills feared that, if Taft were chosen, they "might as well give up because we would have World War Three immediately."[29] Bullis subsequently rearranged his business affairs to devote himself as financial representative in Minnesota for the Eisenhower National Committee. Other business figures, such as Cliff Roberts, Aksel Nielsen, W. Alton Jones, Sigurd Larmon, Douglas Black and William Robinson, supported the Initial Advisory Group. Their major concern was that, as Washington *Post and Times-Herald* publisher Eugene Meyer wrote to Bullis, "The Republican Party cannot afford to take another licking. . . . Ike is the sure thing, and I do not think Truman would run against him."[30] On the other hand, Sinclair Weeks, chairman of the Republican National Finance Committee and a prominent New England businessman, decided for Eisenhower because he feared that Taft, an advocate of public housing, would be more liberal than the General.[31]

Others stressed not so much the two-party system, private enterprise or preventing the nation from lapsing back into isolationism but, rather, their concept of Eisenhower as a man of high moral purpose who would somehow rectify the mounting improprieties. Not unlike the progressives of half a century earlier who feared that democracy, free markets and morality were the lost virtues of industrialized America, the Eisenhower crusaders also worried that the "real America" had been lost. The combined evils of the labor behemoth, commercial monopolies, government regulations and controls, urban political bosses (usually Democrats) and a denial of individualism would ultimately destroy the society if the Democrats were not checked. Truman himself they viewed as a small, undignified President who had unsavory associates he hated to lose. A New Jersey lady, concerned about the quality of American society, informed *Herald Tribune* readers that she wanted Eisenhower because of the deteriorating moral fiber of a nation where even the children were beginning to say, "So what, why not get what I can while the going is good?"[32] "Certainly an overwhelming majority of Constitutional or honest Jeffersonian Democrats and Independents will not vote for an old-line party candidate," Pitcairn had written in his letter to fellow businessmen. He also called for "preconvention work to organize a demand for a candidate whose integrity and statesmanship will inspire nation-wide support."[33] "The people want another George Washington," wrote Harry A. Bullis to Eisenhower. "They really think of you as a modern George Washington. To them you are the man who can best help them keep their liberty and their freedom."[34] To Senator Ralph Flanders of Vermont, Paul Hoffman, the former head of the Studebaker Corporation, the first administrator of the Marshall Plan and a long-time Eisenhower-for-President man, wrote that "we have a new kind of candidate. I think we have. I think he is going to put 'new heart' in the Republican Party and recast it in the image of Abraham Lincoln. We can use a party which takes its orders neither from the N.A.M. nor the C.I.O."[35]

Having tried to persuade Eisenhower since 1949, Hoffman had no doubt that the General could lead a moral crusade. Vital to this new morality was the trust that an Eisenhower Presidency would bring the best possibility of achieving the realization of a cause Hoffman had long advocated—disarmament. Allied with the director of the Ford Foundation was Senator Flanders. Realistic in their view that John Foster Dulles, the party's most prominent foreign-policy expert, would be Secretary of State in an Eisenhower Administration, both men undertook the task of lobbying for disarmament as an integral part of the morality that could be achieved in a new era.

In the matter of disarmament, Eisenhower himself had contributed the substance of what was to become the Big Three proposal to the Sixth

General Assembly of the United Nations. The SHAPE commander, on October 17, 1951, told reporters that a successful military build-up for the eleven NATO countries would induce the Soviet Union to consider the whole question of general disarmament. A minimum demand for the West, he added, would be the right to inspect the USSR's atomic industry.[36] Joining with England and France, the United States successfully dominated the headlines by announcing to the packed chamber in the Palais de Chaillet in Paris a proposal to limit arms, including atomic weapons, that could be verified by international inspection. When Russia's Andrei Vishinsky responded by telling the delegates that he could "not sleep because I kept laughing" after having read President Truman's "fireside chat" description of the plan, the State Department felt it had succeeded in scoring a major propaganda triumph.[37] New York *Times* correspondent James Reston, however, pointed out that there were many people in Washington who "believe there is some justification for the charge" made by Vishinsky. He also noted that the disarmament proposal contained nothing new and was, in fact, a less specific version of a position that had been defined by Acheson in a University of California speech in March of 1950.[38] Just hours after Secretary of State Dean Acheson elaborated on the plan at the Palais de Chaillet, Paul Hoffman warned that mere proposals were not enough to counter Soviet propaganda that the United States was bent on war and called for the nation to dedicate itself to help "achieve the aspirations of men everywhere."[39]

The predictable Russian rejection of the Western propaganda initiative demonstrated to the Flanders–Hoffman disarmament lobby the difficulties placed before their goal by both East and West. Flanders, hopeful that the State Department–White House conflict over making such initiatives was resolved, noted that a recent Truman speech at Winston-Salem, North Carolina, had contained "less of the donner and blitzen" and might, therefore, be indicative of future hospitality to such ideas. After consultations with newspaper and magazine publisher John Cowles, General Clay and Clark Eichelberger of the American Association for the United Nations, Flanders asked Hoffman to lead a group into the White House to persuade the President to follow through on his own disarmament proposals.[40]

The table-of-organization route, however, was through Ambassador-at-Large John Foster Dulles, the Republican corporation lawyer serving as a foreign-affairs expert in the Democratic Administration. After repeated attempts to interest a rather indifferent Dulles, Flanders finally succeeded in getting a hearing for Hoffman and Milton Katz, an associate director of the Ford Foundation and a former special representative in Europe with the Economic Cooperation Administration. They found

Dulles cordial but decidedly cool. He pointed to the intricacies of the problem and warned, as Hoffman reported, that there were "great dangers in discussions of disarmament, which might lead only to endless haggling on technicalities" that could produce even deeper misunderstandings between East and West. He left Hoffman with a promise to give the problem closer attention after ratification of the Japanese Peace Treaty, of which Dulles was the principal author.[41]

Flanders, informed of Dulles's reaction, lectured to the Ambassador-at-Large that the moral approach to problems has one advantage over the strictly intellectual route. "The moral approach," the Senator wrote, "brings positive results whether the proposals in which it is incorporated are accepted or rejected. Rejection is not failure. Rejection can contribute to what Paul [Hoffman] calls a 'proper climate of opinion in both the free world and Russia.' "[42] Flanders then toured the country delivering speeches on the need to counter Soviet military and economic power by using a moral approach that could result in "moral solutions or moral containment." Referring to Truman's possible successors in the White House, Flanders decided that the "only one of the candidates in the position to propose such solutions is General Eisenhower. If he can do it simply, forcibly, and honestly he will sweep the country. He cannot do it where he is now because the people of the country have to be reached by him." With that, he urged Hoffman to leave for Paris by the earliest plane to speak to the General.

The director of the Ford Foundation was the same Hoffman who, in April, told a group of leading Chicago businessmen and industrialists that Eisenhower was "a reluctant candidate," but he "can do more to give us a win than anyone else," and he also warned against "a small group of men in the Republican party who would rather wreck the party than lose control."[43]

CHAPTER 10

The Decision to Return

GENERAL EISENHOWER HAD every reason to believe that his NATO job would be very temporary. His Pentagon meeting with Senator Taft and the visit to France of Henry Cabot Lodge in September had left little doubt in the General's mind that, under the proper conditions and with appropriate assurances, he would enter the contest for the Republican party's Presidential nomination. From late 1951 until the following spring, the SHAPE commander was a cautious non-politician in full command of his strategy.

There were, of course, the usual visits to his headquarters from politicians looking for personal gain from an Eisenhower campaign and possible Presidency. Such solicitations could be warded off by pleading that he was too preoccupied with his important duties even to consider any other responsibility, or by conveniently citing from paragraph 18 of Army Regulations No. 600-10, which forbade active solicitation for elective office by members of the Regular Army. Then, too, there was a steady flow of mail either asking for him to run or even congratulating him for allegedly having agreed to become a candidate. One American magazine even offered him $40,000 simply to reveal whether he was a Republican.[1]

If Eisenhower's ambivalence seemed to reflect the disposition of a highly cautious and troubled man who had difficulty making a decision, those closest to the General were at least aware of the considerations being weighed in his mind. Together they portray a man whose concept of duty and patriotism were inseparable from the best interests of his own career. His caution, he never doubted, was for the protection of the

45

future of the United States rather than Dwight D. Eisenhower. He could make no serious distinctions between the two. The elements he weighed may be isolated into three different categories.

The first was the importance to the nation of a strong system of collective security under NATO. Whether he could best fulfill this objective from his headquarters at Rocquencourt, near Paris, or from Washington was a leading question. Yet, as he viewed his position, suddenly to declare himself an active candidate for the White House would risk the stability of the incipient project. To General Lucius Clay, who was serving as Eisenhower's liaison with those campaigning in the States, he explained his resistance to such political pressure. "Time and time again," he wrote, "I have tried to make clear that the American Military Commander of the Allied Forces in Europe cannot possibly allow his own actions or words to inspire partisan argument in America concerning the merits or demerits of this whole project. To my mind, this would be close to disloyalty."[2] A week later he informed Clay that there would be a "bleak future for our country" with failure to complete the effort to produce collective security.[3] Not only could such partisanship undermine support of NATO among detractors back home; it could also cause European friends to become resentful of his becoming "just another candidate."[4] He viewed European unity as a prerequisite to the Western alliance's economic, military and political strength. If that could be achieved and a protective shell could be woven above it, he believed, his real mission would have been accomplished.

After praising Paul Hoffman as one of a "tiny group" that recognized the importance of his work in Europe, Eisenhower added: "The fact is that our economy and our way of life depend upon great quantities of imports—some of them coming from remote corners of the earth." Abandonment of our overseas interests would be myopic isolationism. Furthermore, the situation in such places as France and Italy, with their precarious postwar economies, only emphasized the importance of the mission. He made clear to Hoffman that while America would design, mold and support such recovery, he was, at the same time, telling all foreign governments "that there is no possibility of America undertaking the completely hopeless and futile task of 'buying' collective security for NATO."[5] He also wondered whether many Americans were aware of the significance behind the inducement to non-Communist nations to produce collective security through cooperation. "The success of the whole effort," he wrote to Harry A. Bullis, "is so important to our country that nothing must be allowed to interfere with its progress."[6]

But the argument that Eisenhower himself reveals in his memoirs to have been most compelling was the one advanced by Lodge on September 4, 1951. On that visit to the General's NATO headquarters the Senator reviewed the deterioration of the Republican party's moderate faction. Their long absence from power had increased the stridency of the rhetoric. A growing right-wing faction actively sought to exploit and enhance existing doubts and fears troubling the American people, whether of communism or internationalism, to recapture their lost partisan advantage. Their prolonged absence from power, the Senator told the General, had compounded such passions and had enhanced their irresponsibility. One ominous result, and a departure from the American political tradition, was the growing polarization of the historically broad-based parties. The two-party system itself was in jeopardy. Lodge cited the prominence of the Old Guarders and their indifference or even hostility to programs that had been created to fortify Western Europe against Communist expansion. Shortsightedness and political opportunism from such quarters threatened the viability of democratic, private-enterprise economies outside the Soviet sphere. "You," Lodge told the General, "are the only one who can be elected by the Republicans to the Presidency. You *must* permit the use of your name in the upcoming primaries."[7]

Eisenhower's memoirs later recalled that of all the visits to his headquarters—which constituted an endless succession that included such people as the newly elected Senator from California, Richard M. Nixon—the Lodge trip "turned out to be, for me, significant." Thereafter, he also noted, "I began to look anew—perhaps subconsciously—at myself and politics."[8]

Having a fine sense of political perception and fully cognizant of how the American public had always regarded him, as his reading of the Merton report had made clear, the General was convinced that his strength as an opponent of Republican reaction must not be diluted by hasty actions that would cast him as just another self-seeking politician. If becoming a candidate should prove to be the most vital thing he could do to protect the objectives, he must start such a campaign as he would enter any battle—with strength—and, at the moment, his most powerful weapon was his image. For that reason, he confided to Bullis that his participation, directly or by implication, "would do much to destroy such reputation I have had for a disinterested and loyal public servant."[9] He was also fully aware that public knowledge of his communication with the professional politicos "could obviously be embarrassing."[10] To minimize such risks, Eisenhower had General Clay work as his intermediary with the "pros." To several of his close supporters he pointed out in March that "as long as I am performing a national duty and doing it as well as I know how, I am possibly providing as much ammunition for your guns as I could in any other way."[11] His Boston banker friend, General Robert Cutler, while conceding that the press speculation about his possible return could possibly do more harm than good, substantiated Eisenhower's own convictions by pointing out that the "enormous belief the American people have in your integrity and sincerity is the greatest asset for victory. Nothing must be permitted to derogate from it."[12] Only increasing pressures for him to declare his candidacy forced him to retreat to the protective wording of Army Regulation No. 600-10, with an interpretation that General MacArthur had not considered valid when entering the Wisconsin primary or, later, campaigning for Taft.[13]

The General's decisions for a political campaign also had to be based on ample evidence of probable success. Although Herbert Brownell was quietly at work, on behalf of the Dewey group, persuading delegates to avoid premature commitments to Taft, Eisenhower knew there had to be not only public praise for his patriotism and wartime accomplishments but overwhelming popular support for his Presidency. A Gallup poll released in November that showed him the favorite in a sampling of all voters with 28 percent of the total and MacArthur and Truman tied for second, each with 13 percent, was undoubtedly helpful. But the Eisenhower people, too, were constantly telling him that he could not fail. Winthrop Aldrich, chairman of the board of the Chase National Bank, returned from a trip to Texas and fed the General reports of a poll of the Lone Star State newspapers showing that 77 percent of the editors believed he would carry the state. Aldrich also informed Eisenhower that Governor Allan Shivers, a Texas Democrat, had confided to him that the General's nomination would provide "a very good chance of bringing the Southern Democrats and the Northern Republicans together in some permanent manner."[14] Underlining such reports from the South was the endorsement of Eisenhower by the Montgomery *Advertiser*, the newspaper's first Republican preference in its 124-year history. It had even backed Al Smith in 1928.[15] Bullis, while also urging his friend to enter the competition, filled him with similar optimism from the Midwest.[16] Additionally, a national survey revealed that, of the newspapers that had endorsed one of the leading candidates, Eisenhower was ahead of Taft by fifty-four to twenty-eight.[17] An Elmo Roper poll even showed him leading Taft in Cincinnati, the Senator's home city.[18] More dramatic and personally exhilarating was the bringing to Rocquencourt, via a solo flight by the noted aviatrix Jacqueline Cochran, of the cinematic description of fifteen thousand cheering for Ike in a midnight rally in New York's Madison Square Garden. Held after the close of the regular Friday-night boxing matches on the night of February 8, the event was a direct effort to demonstrate that the people were behind Ike.[19] Most of the politicians working to persuade the General also implied that he needed only to return home and declare his candidacy to be nominated.[20]

He did return, but only briefly, in early November, and the visit was advertised as a "non-political" trip to Washington for a discussion of NATO matters with the President. The trip, made at Truman's request, heightened speculation that the President wanted to find out whether his general expected to relinquish his command. Senator Duff's public announcement that he planned to consult with Eisenhower during the two-day stay in Washington provided some confirmation of the obvious, that the General's personal interest in his stay would not exclude politics.[21] But, more important than Duff, was a visit that Eisenhower received while in the capital from Lucius Clay.

Clay's purpose was to convince Eisenhower that, unless something unforeseen should occur, it was not fair to his many friends and supporters not to be ready to accept at the proper time. The General's reply was that he would run but would not work in his own behalf or give it any publicity until after he had left the Army. To what he told Clay he also added an intentionally ambiguous public statement that "If I have friends that have been my friends for so long they believe they know how I would react that is their business and I never interfere in their business."[22]

To the dismay of those who had taken the General's statement as an "all-clear" signal, Eisenhower later informed a member of the Dewey group that he had not yet made up his mind. He even implied he might still decide against running at all. That brought from Clay a strong letter that acknowledged his problems about making a public commitment but also pointed out that it was not necessary to add to their difficulties by going overboard in the opposite direction.[23] Eisenhower's reply showed his state of mind. "I hasten to admit of the possibility that I may have given some impression in our Washington conversation that I have now forgotten," he explained; "these days, I sometimes wonder at myself when I find I am still outside a mental ward. However, in the absence of information as to the specific point in which I have apparently diverged from the understanding of our conversation, I can address myself only to generality. . . . Frankly," he continued, "my current decision not to come home until the transfer could be on a permanent basis was partially formed as a result of my experiences in Washington the last time I was there. My life was almost unendurable." Then he reiterated the importance of his preoccupation with providing for collective security.[24]

Nevertheless, only two days after Eisenhower had left Washington, Arthur Krock's New York *Times* column revealed that, despite a vehement denial by Truman and a rejection by Eisenhower as being wholly "fictional," he had learned from an individual whose "public position can be correctly described as 'eminent' that during the General's visit to Washington Truman had offered to support him for the Democratic nomination in 1952. Krock, noting that such leverage would be tantamount to his nomination, pointed out that "evidence is growing that the President's proposal was the culminating point in a major enterprise by important Democrats that seems to have failed."[25]

Eisenhower and Truman had been unable to agree, Krock wrote, because the General could not accept the Democratic President's pro-labor attitude and, in particular, his opposition to the Taft-Hartley Law. Their conversation had ended at that point.

Later that same day, November 5, Truman received the members of the Supreme Court at Blair House. With Justices William O. Douglas, Fred M. Vinson and Sherman Minton alone in a corner with the President, Truman observed that he had "had a big day; that he had an interesting talk with Eisenhower; that he told Eisenhower his offer of 1948 held good for 1952; that Eisenhower said that would present a great problem to him, his differences with the Democratic (Truman) Party over the Wagner Act and labor policy alone being typical." Only years later did Krock, after many denials by others that the incident had ever occurred, reveal his private memorandum made at the time with the fact that his information had been supplied to him in the office of a Washington dentist by Supreme Court Justice William O. Douglas.[26]

The Krock piece, however, was sufficient to provoke the controversy Eisenhower was trying to avoid. Taft's followers were quick to cite the information as proof that the General was not a Republican, after all; and, even if he were, his credentials were doubtful enough for so partisan a Democrat as Mr. Truman even to consider naming him as his successor. Conservative columnist David Lawrence, who had, only a few days before Eisenhower's arrival in Washington, written that Truman could be paving the way for a Democratic endorsement of Ike if the Republicans failed to nominate him, accepted the Krock account without any reservations. Other conservatives had no trouble lauding Krock's impeccable reputation. Meanwhile, the *Herald Tribune* was highly critical of the story's legitimacy and even ran a report that interviews with "close" but unnamed friends of the General disclosed that such an overture had almost certainly not been made. In Paris, Eisenhower himself confided to New York *Times* correspondent Cyrus L. Sulzberger that the story was not true; in fact, by mutual agreement, both men had avoided any discussion about politics.[27]

Nevertheless, the story fed the continuing assault on the General's Republicanism being made by the party's right wing. The Chicago *Tribune* resurrected the account of Eisenhower's boyhood talk before the Democratic club in Abilene and also condemned the General's drive as "ballyhoo" coming from "New Dealers, New Deal propagandists, Europe-firsters and other brands of world savers," including the "un-American press in New York."[28] In much the same vein, ultra-conservative George Sokolsky said Republicans could not take Eisenhower because MacArthur had "linked him with Dean Acheson in his address to the American Legion."[29]

Shortly after Christmas, Senator Lodge began the draft of a letter to Governor Sherman Adams of New Hampshire to agree with the placing of Eisenhower's name on the ballot of the New Hampshire primary scheduled for March 11. He assured Adams, who had previously stated that the General's name would be entered in the primary, that Eisenhower was a Republican. The entry into the first popularity contest held a valuable psychological reward for the winner, which was more important than merely winning the state's fourteen convention delegates. Lodge's letter, in addition to being the first concrete move to enter the General as a candidate, also nipped an effort by the vice-chairman of the Grafton (N.H.) Democratic Committee, who said he intended to "smoke out" Eisenhower by entering his name on the ticket as a Democrat.[30] Meanwhile, a Washington Eisenhower-for-President office had been opened.[31]

Lodge, concerned that further delay would benefit the Taftites, and spurred by the attempt to get Eisenhower on the New Hampshire ballot as a Democrat, moved rapidly. He mailed his letter to Adams on January 4 and, two days later, presided over a press conference at the Eisenhower headquarters in room 600-G of the Shoreham Hotel in Washington. Referring to New Hampshire's January 11 deadline for entering the primary, he announced that Eisenhower's name would be included and that he was in the contest to the finish. Additional headlines were made by his statement that "General Eisenhower has personally assured me that he is a Republican. His name therefore cannot be entered as a Democratic candidate in the New Hampshire primary or elsewhere." Then, going still further, he assured them that Eisenhower would accept a nomination and even invited the reporters to check with Ike at his headquarters in Rocquencourt. "I know I will not be repudiated," he declared.[32]

Lodge's tactics represented a gamble, designed to force the issue. His statement about Eisenhower's readiness to accept a nomination made the General so furious that he came close to responding by issuing a statement of withdrawal.[33] While aware of the New Hampshire announcement that Lodge was going to make, Ike had not expected him to go that far.

Eisenhower's concern about disassociating himself from blatant political moves reflected his sensitivity to petty political chicanery. For example, he wrote to Harry A. Bullis with more than mild contempt that "someone came in the other day to tell me of a trick that some of the politicians learned out of the experience in Minnesota. They passed a rule in the Nebraska primaries that no write-in names would be counted unless the spelling was correct. Now I am told that Illinois has gone even further and stated that the name must be spelled correctly, the first name likewise, and the middle initial given. They think of everything!"[34]

When the United Press attempted to get a response from the head-quarters at Rocquencourt, they could only come up with a comment from another general on the staff, presumably General Alfred Gruen-ther, that "Silence is more eloquent than any statement."[35]

The next day, however, Eisenhower issued a statement that Lodge's announcement "gives an accurate account of the general tenor of my political convictions and of my Republican voting record" and added that he was also correct in stating that "I would seek no nomination to political office" and then reiterated his intention of remaining at his "vital task" in the absence of a "clearcut call to political duty."[36]

Taft, meanwhile, had sent to Eisenhower via a visitor a letter designed to dissuade the General from becoming a candidate because of the urgent need to prevent the election of an opponent of NATO. The Sena-tor's message supported the completion of the European army project and said he would do nothing to wreck foreign military and economic-assistance programs. Reports had also circulated that Taft had told sev-eral colleagues in the Senate that he did not fully agree with ex-President Hoover's proposal for eventual withdrawal of all American ground forces in Europe except those that may be needed to protect American air bases outside NATO nations. But there was very little that Taft could do by then to rehabilitate himself with Eisenhower, who had long since concluded that the Senator was a very stupid man with no intellectual ability, who had shown himself unable, in their talks, to grasp basic problems. His inconsistencies had demonstrated weakness and confusion, and Eisenhower felt he could no longer trust whatever he might have to say.[37]

For the NATO commander, then, the most prudent course was to make his own preparations for what had clearly become more inevitable. Kevin McCann, on leave from the presidency of Defiance College in Ohio, returned to Eisenhower's side, where he had not been since the General was at Columbia. This time, at Rocquencourt, his mission was handling political correspondence. Cliff Roberts, the New York invest-ment banker charged with the General's personal finances and occasional political adviser, was also at the headquarters with greater frequency.[38] Robert B. Anderson, whom Eisenhower had first met in Washington when he had sought information about Federal Reserve Board matters, was in steady communication with him on problems related to interna-tional finances. From Chester Davis, of the Ford Foundation and an authority on agriculture, Eisenhower solicited an outline of his general ideas on the "farm problem."[39] His brother Milton, who had been a director of information in the Department of Agriculture, was also helpful in that area, as in many others. Aksel Nielson, the president of the Title Guaranty Company in Denver, gathered information about housing and the question of government housing subsidies.[40]

Careful plans had already been made with Harold Stassen by the Eisenhower group. The former governor of Minnesota was regarded as the perfect man to declare his own candidacy in an effort to attract delegate support and consequently reduce Taft's chances of establishing a solid majority even before the convention. Bernard Shanley, a Newark lawyer and national chairman of the Stassen-for-President Volunteer Committee, met with Herbert Brownell and Stassen to plan the running of a delayed action for Eisenhower before the General returned from Europe. Without Stassen as their "stalking horse," they decided efforts to stop Taft would be hopeless.

This plan was discussed in full when Stassen made a much-publicized trip to visit Eisenhower in early December. Stassen told the General that he would engage in an "all-out campaign" for himself that would be prepared for three possible conclusions: 1) insufficient strength to subtract from Taft's delegate total and subsequent victory for the Ohioan; 2) a decisive victory over Taft that would enable Stassen to go on to his own nomination; or 3) he could develop, along with Earl Warren, sufficient preconvention support to achieve a stalemate that, when added to the Eisenhower support being accumulated in a number of states, would result in an overwhelming draft for the General.

Other points were also covered. He assured Eisenhower that any statement made to the press after leaving Rocquencourt and returning to America would express his conviction that the NATO commander would not become a "seeker" for the Republican nomination, nor would he participate in any prolonged battle with Taft. Eisenhower would avoid anything that would spoil his image of selfless patriotism. Only an unmistakable summons to greater responsibility or the fulfillment of the basic tasks involving the establishment of European unity and strength, Stassen recalled, could alter the General's plans. Stassen also agreed to point out that Taft, unless countered, would emerge as the Republican nominee and that, thereby, the party would have selected the one candidate with the poorest chance of beating Truman.[41]

There were, it is apparent, several levels of understanding. With their assumption that Stassen could not, in any case, win, the Eisenhower people were convinced that Stassen was a "stalking horse." Stassen himself, brilliant, personable, highly competent but unrealistic when tantalized by the prospects of his own Presidency, had thus prepared for his own possible failure by being able to retreat into an Eisenhower Administration.

When Stassen returned from Europe abroad the *Queen Mary*, he refused all questions about his own political intentions but praised Eisenhower's NATO accomplishments for having bolstered Western European defenses.[42] In Philadelphia on December 27, the ex-"Boy Governor" announced his own candidacy. He would cope, he said, with the four major threats to America's future—"corruption, inflation, the strife of group against group, and Communism." If elected, he promised to consult with MacArthur on Far Eastern matters and with Eisenhower about Europe.[43]

Stassen, by his evasiveness with reporters about what he and Eisenhower had talked about in Europe and the fact that, only a month earlier, he had proposed that Taft abandon the race to Eisenhower, plus his new announcement that he would use Ike as his consultant on European matters, had created suspicions that his private conferences with the General had given him the information that Ike did not intend to run. That was particularly heightened by his statement that the Paris conferences had a "direct bearing" upon his decision. The possibilities were causing consternation among those followers of the General who were not privy to the Eisenhower-Stassen talks.[44] Two days after New Year's, Stassen announced his entry in the coming primary elections of Ohio, Pennsylvania and Minnesota. In Milwaukee, a few days later, he denied that he was acting as a shadow for Ike.[45]

The first primary, in New Hampshire on March 11, provided a dramatic display of Eisenhower's appeal to the voters. Delegates pledged in his name received 50 percent of the total Republican vote and won all fourteen of the state's delegates. Taft came in second with 38 percent and Stassen third with 7 percent. Other votes were in the form of some two thousand write-ins for MacArthur and less than one thousand pledged to a local political figure. The victory had been achieved despite the pro-Taft position of publisher William Loeb's highly conservative Manchester *Union-Leader*, the most important paper in New Hampshire. Eisenhower had even run well in many areas that had been regarded as Taft strongholds.[46]

In France, Eisenhower told reporters that he was "very moved" and "deeply touched." The results must have been more than a relief to the General, however, for in a February meeting in London he had told a delegation of General Clay, George E. Allen and Texas oil magnate Sid Richardson that he would run if nominated. The primary victory in New Hampshire thus fortified his belief that he could be chosen without fighting for the honor. Just one day before the people of New Hampshire had shown their preference, Eisenhower, responding to a letter dated February 22 and signed by nineteen Republican Congressmen—thirteen of them from the Northeast—ruled out for the "immediate future" his return to campaign actively. Once again he stressed his NATO commitment, although the Republican legislators had argued that returning home would be the "surest way to preserve your efforts in Europe and to promote peace in the world."[47]

Where New Hampshire had failed to bring him home, however, Minnesota succeeded. Stassen's former state voted one week after the New England election. Since only Stassen's name was on the ballot, Eisenhower supporters secured a court order withdrawing the General's slate, which avoided a meaningless contest that could only "divide if not destroy the liberal element of the party in Minnesota."[48] The inconvenience of having Eisenhower's name absent from the ballot, however, did not prevent 108,692 voters, many of whom had only a phonetic concept of how the name Eisenhower was spelled, from writing it in one way or another. Stassen, with his name on the ballot, received 129,076 votes.[49]

At Rocquencourt, France, on March 20, just ten days after Eisenhower had informed nineteen Congressmen that he would remain at his post and only two days after the Minnesota turn-out, it became known that the General was prepared to return to America at the end of May or June to present himself for the Republican party's nomination. The Minnesota vote, he left no doubt, had convinced him.[50] At about that time Eisenhower had another significant visitor. Herbert Brownell, Jr., spent two days giving the General his analysis of the situation. Its conclusion was that the nomination was within Eisenhower's reach but not without a fight. When Brownell left Rocquencourt he was convinced that Ike was ready to do whatever might be necessary.[51]

Eisenhower then wrote letters to Secretary of Defense Robert A. Lovett, Lieutenant General Paul Ely of the French Army, chairman of the Standing Group of NATO, and a personal note to President Truman. Then the President, in a surprise announcement, tacked on to the end of a Jackson Day dinner speech on March 29, revealed his decision not to be a candidate for re-election. His mind, Truman wrote in his *Memoirs*, had actually been made up as early as April 16, 1950, and revealed to his White House staff in Key West in March of 1951.[52] On April 11 the White House released the news about Eisenhower, and the same day Paul Hoffman, chairman of the Advisory Committee of Citizens for Eisenhower, revealed that the active candidate would probably make his first major address at Abilene on June 4.

Once the decision had been made, Eisenhower seemed more ill at ease than ever. He had not convinced himself that he was making a legitimate response to a "clear call to duty." Robert B. Anderson has remembered that he was "working himself into physical exhaustion" during that period and had to have a medical conference.[53] Sulzberger, also at Rocquencourt, noted that Ike was often crotchety, tired and pale. In the locker room after a round of golf the General said, "Anybody is a damn fool if he actually seeks to be President. You give up four of the very best years of your life."[54] With plans finally made for his departure from Paris at the end of May, he was noticeably disturbed and tired.

During his last days at SHAPE, while undergoing his personal ordeal, he received a bit of advice from Kansas City *Star* publisher Roy Roberts, an old friend. Recalling Wendell Willkie, "who was quite a fellow, but not a politician," as one who had "listened to so much advice that he laid an egg at Elmwood in his opening speech," Roberts counseled Eisenhower about the handling of all those who would be volunteering advice during the coming days. "Don't pay a damn bit of attention to any of them," wrote Roberts. "That goes for Lodge, Duff, Carlson, Darby and, above all, Roberts. Be yourself. The American people want a leader—a sincere and genuine one. They would rather have you speak out and make a mistake than to give them a political document that doesn't represent Ike Eisenhower."[55]

CHAPTER 11

Abilene, June 5, 1952

Eisenhower's return to the familiar Kansas soil marked the debut of the General as a contender for public office, a role very different from the kind of politics he had perfected while in uniform. At SHAPE, for example, he was strictly General Eisenhower to all callers; nobody dared to call him Ike in any kind of an official situation. Even his closest aide, General Alfred Gruenther, reserved that nickname for private, off-duty moments. Eisenhower's own sense of dignity was immediately understood and accepted by his associates. He was never one for off-color humor or ribaldry. His baptism into a different kind of political world was noted by correspondent David Schoenbrun, who stood alongside the General under the floodlights of Kansas City's Fairfax Airport on the night of June 3, 1952. Governor Dan Thornton of Colorado, a big, outgoing man who customarily wore cowboy boots and a ten-gallon hat, greeted the General with an enthusiastic "Howya, pardner!" and a hearty slap across the back. As Schoenbrun has noted, "there was a tense moment as the General's eyes blazed and his back stiffened. Then, with great control, he gradually unfroze into a smile and reached out his hand to say, 'Howya, Dan.' "[1]

The next day Eisenhower went on to his disappointing political performance at Abilene. If his image on that day showed him as something less than a military hero and worried his followers that, without his military uniform, he was a dull, gray figure very much out of his field, the following day brought the first real indication that Taft's rival was not merely a patriotic apparition. Within the confines of Abilene's little Plaza Theater he conducted a press conference that salvaged his image.

Again before television cameras, he left little room for listeners to mistake his political position or wistfully to believe, as so many had been doing for some half dozen years, that his creed would inevitably be compatible with their own. More relaxed than during the outdoor speech, and smiling and scowling with natural ease, he thrust considerably to the right of the men who had promoted his candidacy.

Although, in 1950, Senator Lodge and Governor Dewey had both criticized the party's "Declaration of Principles" for its rigid conservatism, Eisenhower volunteered the statement that it best described his own political philosophy. Drafted for the 1950 Congressional elections by a writer of popular fiction and a national committeeman from Arizona, Clarence Budington Kelland, the paper had defined the issues as "Liberty versus Socialism." It took a dim view of the social and economic legislation that had been contributed during the years of Democratic rule. Eisenhower, resurrecting the document, said that as a good Republican he would support any candidate who subscribed to its views. Although he did say that he could not agree with the entire statement, he never specified just where and how he differed. And it was easy to avoid being more precise, since few in the room could recall the "Declaration of Principles" and were in a poor position to ask any embarrassing questions.

The candidate then continued with an adroit mixture of charm and conservatism. No, he did not care if people called him Mister. He did not have the faintest idea of whether he would beat Taft for the nomination. He had no secret formula for ending the Korean war and pointed out that there were serious military risks involved in bombing beyond the Yalu River but held that we should work for a "decent armistice." Civil rights demanded fairness and equality for all citizens; but since that was a responsibility best left to the states, he specifically opposed establishing a Fair Employment Practices Commission (FEPC). He would rid the economy of "artificial direct legislative controls" and would rely on the operations of a free market. While conceding that "every American has the right to decent medical care," he attacked nationalization of medicine and bureaucratic controls. Government itself, he explained, needs a thorough overhauling with the elimination of unnecessary agencies. For education, his policy would include a program of limited federal aid to the poorer states that lacked the resources to meet minimal needs, but even such assistance should be accompanied by safeguards to preserve local control. Labor should be permitted to retain its present gains, he said, and he opposed punitive legislation to cope with industrial strife. The farmer must be protected from such economic disasters that result from flood and drought and the soil must be conserved; but he could not say whether parity payments should be set at 75, 80 or 85 percent. When a reporter asked whether he would support the reelection of Senator McCarthy, he cited an earlier statement that he did not intend to indulge in personalities. Cautiously, however, he added that no one was more determined than he that "any kind of Communistic, subversive or pinkish influence be uprooted from responsible places in our government" but added that the job could be done under competent leadership and through existing agencies.

About his own political record he was candid. Desire to avoid partisan politics, he explained, had kept him from registering as a Republican when leaving the Army in 1948; nevertheless, he had voted for Dewey's Presidential candidacy that year. He had also been for Senator John Foster Dulles during the special New York State election of 1949 and had supported Dewey's re-election as Governor in 1950. A segment of the audience, which was supposedly restricted to members of the working press, applauded when he declared, "I have never voted any Democratic ticket."[2]

Whatever loss had followed the previous day's performance was recovered by the conference.[3] James Reston noted that every reporter he met thought that Eisenhower had shown himself as the greatest master of the press conference since FDR; if anything, he was even more effective, since he lacked Roosevelt's weakness for petulance and sarcasm. "He is direct," wrote Reston, "and what is equally important, he seems to be more direct in his answer to some questions than he actually is. He speaks in sentences and avoids intellectual detours, a political rarity not practiced since the days of Woodrow Wilson."[4]

Nevertheless, Brownell had been correct about the need to fight. The hard, right-wing core of the party refused to yield easily; to them, the destroyer of Nazism was an alien interloper, an emissary from an "unAmerican" Paris–London–New York-dominated axis. Richard Nixon had already notified the General, as early as January, that people calling themselves Partisan Republicans of California had been circulating defamatory anti-Eisenhower literature; and the Senator's purpose had been to assure their victim that its sources were anathema to the party in his state.[5] But, quite openly, at a meeting of the Republican National Committee in San Francisco in mid-January, Taft's manager, David S. Ingalls, had warned the party not to nominate a candidate because of "hero worship," glamour or "sex appeal" and stressed that, if they did, they would be merely choosing a "good-looking mortician."[6] Another highranking Taftite, Clarence Brown, had told the Women's National Press Club that there was "no breath of scandal" associated with Taft's name, thus leaving his listeners free to judge the validity of the Eisenhower stories being peddled around the country. In New Hampshire, for example, during the primary campaign, a cropped picture altered from an official British photograph showed the General in close conversation with Marshal Zhukov. Its caption read: "Zhukov, Communist general, decorates drinking partner Eisenhower, at Frankfurt, Germany." Also in circulation was gossip about Eisenhower's continuing "affair" with Kay Summersby, his wartime Irish ambulance driver; stories about Mamie Eisenhower's alleged alcoholism; that Ike was a Jew; or that he had been baptized by the Pope; or that some mysterious disease had made his election too risky. Some even accepted the story that he was a Soviet agent.[7] Much of the hate literature floating around the heart of the country had originated from Wichita, Kansas, with the authorship of Joseph P. Kamp, a veteran American pamphleteer who had penned similar political smut against Wendell Willkie. One of Kamp's charges was that Eisenhower was an originator of the Morganthau Plan to pastoralize and demilitarize postwar Germany. Not only did Kamp charge that the idea had been hatched under Ike's aegis but that the plan, which was never implemented, had somehow "cost countless American lives." In South Dakota newspaper ads sponsored by the Taft campaign people in that state repeated Kamp's charges.[8] At the same time, battles, many of them particularly acrimonious—especially in Texas—erupted at all but a handful of state conventions over the seating of delegates for the party's national convention. The major conflicts were between the heavily pro-Taft party regulars and the younger insurgents trying to carry their states for Eisenhower.[9] By the end of the first week of June, the Associated Press claimed a Taft delegate lead of 462–389 over the General.[10]

All Ike's circumspection had been insufficient to spare him from the realities of political life.

PART TWO

Launching the Crusade

CHAPTER 12

The Road to Chicago

At 8:56 p.m., Eisenhower's big DC-6 flagship, the *Abilene*, came down in the deepening darkness of the runway. The throng of between five hundred to a thousand watched the General guide his wife down the steps and then, almost spontaneously, erupted with the already familiar "We want Ike" chant. Present also was just about every prominent Republican leader in the region. After a brief exchange of greetings to the excited crowd, Eisenhower and Mamie stepped into Governor Dewey's car, which then led a motorcade of twenty limousines and five busses along the Grand Central Parkway, over the Triborough Bridge and up to Columbia. A few minutes later, as the Eisenhowers watched from a second-floor porch above Morningside Drive and waved to the crowd, a torchlight parade moved along the street. The men, women and children carried signs saying, "We Want Ike" and "Vote for Integrity, Knowledge, Efficiency," with the letters of the last three words arranged to spell IKE. A bagpipe band from Stamford, Connecticut, contributed to the celebration on Morningside Heights that Friday night.

The cheers and adulation, however, were merely a prelude to the real function of the coming weeks that remained before the opening of the GOP's national convention at Chicago on July 7: the battle for delegates. Having already confided to reporters that he planned to woo the uncommitted by seducing them with frankness, he prepared for a long flow of Republicans from all over the Union.

Most important was the delegation from Pennsylvania. The Keystone State group, led by Governor John Fine, was still unpledged. Fine, enjoying the power of his hand, had been coyly saying wonderful things about Taft, MacArthur and Eisenhower. Nevertheless, the most recent Associated Press poll of his delegation showed twenty for Ike, eighteen inclined toward Taft and the largest single bloc, thirty-two, either uncommitted or unwilling to announce a preference.[1]

On Eisenhower's first Sunday back at Morningside Heights, Fine visited for a three-hour conference. There the Governor, still circumspect and clutching his king-making powers, agreed to a meeting with the General and the Pennsylvania delegation at the recently purchased Eisenhower farm near Gettysburg on Friday, June 13. Fine, who held more gubernatorial patronage power than any of the other state chief executives, also discussed job-distribution problems pertaining to rivalries within his state. After the session he met with reporters in front of the mansion and disclaimed any personal preference. Conceding that there was a split within the Pennsylvania delegation, he was nevertheless optimistic that a united front would be achieved by roll-call time in Chicago. At the same time, however, he warned reporters not to expect any clues of his state's probable course to come out of the Gettysburg meeting and pointed out that the seventy delegates would, within the next two weeks, hold a similar session with Mr. Taft.[2]

During the days after that meeting, Eisenhower continued his preoccupation with the ritual of meetings. Most of them were with large groups of delegates and usually on a regional basis, a process he had started while still in Abilene, where he had met with ninety-one Midwestern Republicans. Returning to New York had meant, besides holding a large-scale press conference at the Commodore Hotel on June 7, the continuation of similar sessions. Monday, for example, was reserved for three New England states and Delaware, while Tuesday gave the same opportunity to Alabama, Georgia and North Carolina. Wednesday was reserved for the massive but overwhelmingly sympathetic New York delegation and the uncommitted Marylanders; on Thursday he hosted visitors from the three remaining New England states plus New Jersey, South Carolina and Virginia. By Friday he was at the farm for the appointment with the Pennsylvanians.

Entertaining nearly 120 delegates and alternates at a midday picnic, Eisenhower offered nothing he had not stated over and over again since his return to the States. His comments about labor, finance, foreign responsibility, civil rights and the general area of governmental powers were not newsworthy to any follower. Furthermore, the differences between his position and Taft's in many of these areas was inconsequential. But what was advanced at the session, as at all face-to-face meetings, was the warmth of the Eisenhower personality. He joked and bantered with them as though he were enjoying a good outing with "the boys," answered their questions in a simple, forthright manner that lacked the usual political jargon susceptible of free interpretation, repeatedly drew their applause and, several times, their laughter. After the affair, Fine reaffirmed his prediction that no important indications would result from the picnic but acknowledged the possibility that "two or three delegates at most" may have been won to the General's cause. One thing was certain, the Governor was willing to admit: Eisenhower had not harmed himself. Pressed further for his own preference, Fine said he doubted he would make a decision before reaching Chicago. When a reporter inquired whether he was now closer to the General, the Governor answered, "Oh, I wouldn't say that."[3]

Fine's position clearly stemmed from his own political dilemma in Pennsylvania. Eisenhower had received about 75 percent of the total party vote during the state's primaries on April 22, and, although it was achieved with only Stassen in opposition, that figure was nevertheless more than 800,000 greater than the total Republican primary vote of 1940.[4] The statewide situation, therefore, resembled a pattern that was becoming familiar elsewhere. Despite the undoubted grass-roots popularity of the General, the leading Pennsylvania politicos, all tied to Fine, were sharply divided. National Committeeman G. Mason Owlett, Joe Grundy's successor as president of the Pennsylvania Manufacturers Association and one of the state's leading conservative powers, was for Taft. Senator Duff had, of course, overlooked his own hostility toward Dewey and had declared himself for Eisenhower early. The state's other Senator, Ed Martin, was with the Owlett camp. Fine himself had been reported as basically leaning toward MacArthur.[5]

The purpose of Eisenhower's confrontation with the delegates, then, was not for them to take a position as in a popularity contest but to meet the man they might support in July and November and, if possible, to be reassured about control of the campaign and patronage and his position on the issues. Since he was a political amateur, the professionals were skeptical that his nomination would be followed by a vigorous campaign. Further doubts were unquestionably induced by the prominence of the novices in the Eisenhower movement.

When the General was asked whether he was prepared to wage an enthusiastic campaign, he replied that it was a "funny kind of question to put to a man who has spent forty years of his life fighting." Then, adroitly removing the possibility that such words might be interpreted too broadly, he added that "I shall not and will not engage in character assassination, vilification and personalities." That response was an early distinction from those ready to profit from a McCarthy-type position.[6]

The Pennsylvanians and others were concerned about the validity of the thesis that an Eisenhower candidacy would have great "coat-tail" strength. This argument, of personal concern to Lodge in his own Massachusetts campaign, was already being pressed throughout the country. As early as March 29, *Business Week* had appeared with an article by Dr. Gabriel Hauge, an economist and one of the Dewey workers for Eisenhower, that emphasized the General's popularity as capable of salvaging the fortunes of many others on Republican tickets. In the New York *Times*, Arthur Krock had speculated that, when the professionals really got down to business, that consideration would be especially persuasive.[7] For most politicians, the desire to win, even with an unpredictable novice rather than with "Mr. Republican," was the most compelling. It was also true for those with only a secondary interest in control of the White House. Their inspection of the man, therefore, at such personal meetings, also served to confirm his flesh-and-blood appeal to their own constituents.

The evidence of his popularity was, of course, quite clear. In early May the Gallup organization released the results of a double breakdown of the Eisenhower appeal. When pitted against fellow Republicans, he was first with 44 percent. Only Taft, with 33 percent, was even in the running. But providing greater ammunition for those advancing Ike as the best man for November was his standing with independents. There he was preferred by 52 percent, while Taft had 14 percent, Warren 12 percent and MacArthur 9 percent. Stassen, who still hoped for a convention deadlock to give him an opportunity, could command just 5 percent of the non-partisan group and a mere 3 percent among Republicans.[8] Such primary results as in New Hampshire, Pennsylvania, New Jersey, and Minnesota, provided further evidence.[9]

Still, with just one month remaining before the Chicago convention and with Truman retiring and the Democrats forced to select a candidate who inevitably would have to defend the unpopular President's record, there was room to argue Taft's case. In state after state, as in Pennsylvania, he was the choice of the old-line Old Guard, politicians who wanted to convince themselves and others that Taft could win. They cited his 431,000 re-election margin of 1950, although that required ignoring the perfunctory nature of his opposition. But they could also total the popular votes cast in all the primaries and show that there was little difference between their performances. Moreover, Taft had won in South Dakota, although by a tiny margin, but he had trampled even a sizable Eisenhower write-in vote in Illinois by 935,867 to 147,518. In Nebraska, where there were write-ins for both men, Taft had taken over 54 percent.[10] Behind the Taft advocacy was also the hope of avoiding a "me-too" candidate, a position which assumed that untold numbers of voters, having been too discouraged to vote through the lack of a "real choice," would suddenly dash to the polls in gratitude for the opportunity to elect a true conservative.

Professionals preferring Eisenhower had concluded that choosing the Senator was too risky; they and often the younger, more moderate or liberal political neophytes constituted the stop-Taft forces. Their mission was, in many cases, to counter the impression that Ike was a good-hearted but naïve fellow. One of the Maryland delegates, for example, admitted that he had been impressed with the General's frankness but observed that that very quality "makes me feel Taft is the man we ought to have."[11] Others were more ready to lose with Taft than win with a fake Republican.

The Eisenhower forces, denying the existence of a "hidden" conservative vote, had to present their man not only as a winner but as one who would thereby salvage the GOP by rescuing it from the feverish excesses of frustrating impotence. Their patriotic goal would be achieved by preserving the virtually sacred two-party system. Once again, rivalries would yield to the inspired, prestigious leadership of a new George Washington.

Thus, Henry Cabot Lodge, even while the General was still in Europe preparing his return, sounded the theme of anti-Taft Republicans. Writing in the May 1952 issue of *Harper's* magazine, the campaign manager summoned his readers to join a crusade to save America. Keeping the Democrats in the White House, he wrote, "could introduce a really dangerous period of one-party government."[12] Using an argument that had appealed to Eisenhower himself as early as September 1951, he suggested that defeating the incumbents would also repair the extremist excesses that were already dividing the Republicans, since lack of "leadership at the top" had created an absence of discipline that was causing "it to break down into factions and give to extremists a disproportionate influence."[13] More important than trying to engage "in a game to test the popularity of abstract political doctrines," he reminded believers in a "hidden-vote" conservatism, was a "general rebirth of a national unity and enlightened resolve."[14]

The promotional portrait of the General that followed was of a man not only peculiarly qualified by his background record of military diplomacy but of a leader whose political creed was virtually a euphemism for "Americanism." Just as he would reject the idea that there were no social responsibilities, so would he not bring a mere continuation of New and Fair Deal programs. While it would be "inconceivable" that he might ever respond to needs with a "sterile grant of authority to the states or a corrupting handout of public funds," it would be equally unthinkable that "he would stand back hopeless or inactive where a plain need for housing or flood control or some other measure existed."[15] One familiar with his past record knows he will bring harmony by convening diverse elements "around practical endeavors." "He is," assured Lodge, "neither like the Democrats of the past two decades who have been resigned to destroying piece by piece the free enterprise system, nor like those who have opposed with unconstructive bitterness every measure of reform."[16] He would be a healer, not a political ideologue. Eisenhower also, he stressed, does have an "intuitive sense of political ways."[17]

The assumption, of course, was that winning votes would somehow accomplish the restoration of a severely fractured party. The Republican Senate representation in the Eighty-second Congress, for example, contained a determined corps of crusaders against internal communism: McCarthy of Wisconsin, Jenner of Indiana, Nixon of California, Cain of Washington, Malone of Nevada and Mundt of South Dakota, plus many part-time zealots. Jenner, Malone, Kem of Missouri and Langer of North Dakota had voted against both the Marshall Plan and the North Atlantic Treaty Organization, a fairly reliable index of isolationism. Negative votes toward the inception of NATO were also cast by Langer, Young of North Dakota, Cordon of Oregon, Watkins of Utah and Flanders of Vermont and Taft, while Williams of Delaware, Dworshak of Idaho and Capehart of Indiana had opposed the Marshall Plan that provided assistance for the economic recovery of Western Europe. Most Republicans tended toward a greater emphasis regarding Asian affairs, as Dewey had stressed. Senator William Knowland of California, in fact, led the Congressional concern about the communization of the Far East. Some pessimists, considering all this, were already comparing the mission of a possible Eisenhower Presidency with the problem that had confronted another soldier, William Henry Harrison, who had been elected in 1840 by a Whig party united only in opposition to Andrew Jackson. Would Taft, it was asked, become the Clay of the Eisenhower Administration and would Ike be as unable to command leadership as John Tyler, the unfortunate successor of an even more uncomfortable Harrison?[18]

From the outset, the Eisenhower candidacy, with its vast appeal to the so-called "middle of the road" of American politics, was anomalous with the Republican Congressional delegation. Even leaving aside, for convenience, the disproportionately heavy rural representation in the House, with its strong conservative bias, the Senate Republicans were sharply to the right of the independents being wooed by the Eisenhower campaign. Of the forty-six Republicans in the Eighty-second Congress, only a dozen or so could be called liberal to moderate as measured by their votes on key issues. For example, on an issue closest to the General's own interest, the recovery of Western Europe, Everett Dirksen's amendment to the Mutual Security Act of 1951 reducing economic aid to Europe by $250 million was opposed by only five Republicans—Irving Ives of New York, Jim Duff of Pennsylvania, Wayne Morse of Oregon, Ed Thye of

Minnesota and Nixon. Six others, including Henry Cabot Lodge and Ralph Flanders, were paired against the cut. At the same time, twenty-six Republicans upheld the Dirksen amendment, while the Democrats opposed it by twenty-nine to ten.[19] Two other votes on key issues while Eisenhower was conducting his pre-convention campaign substantiated the image of a highly conservative GOP. After President Truman's seizure of the strike-bound steel mills was ruled unconstitutional by the Supreme Court, Virginia's patriarchal conservative Democrat, Harry Byrd, introduced an amendment requesting the President to invoke the eighty-day Taft-Hartley "cooling-off" anti-strike injunction. Falling in line with a position anathema to pro-labor liberals, the Byrd measure was passed forty-nine to thirty. But the opposition represented only three Republican Senators—Ives of New York, Morse of Oregon and Charles Tobey of New Hampshire.[20] A little more than two weeks later, on June 27, the GOP liberals could produce just eight votes to uphold Truman's veto of the quota-plagued and restrictive McCarran-Walter Immigration Act of 1952, although Lodge and Tobey were both paired in favor of the President's position.[21]

As conservative as Eisenhower's views were on domestic issues—and that was mostly related to what he regarded as sound fiscal principles—it was plain that choosing the General would give the GOP a candidate much less representative of Republican thinking than was Senator Taft. On the issue of American aid to Europe, Eisenhower was far more advanced than the heart of his party. He had decided to leave SHAPE, in fact, largely with the assumption that he could be more useful in the White House. Discussing immigration while campaigning for the Presidency, he hit out unmistakably at the McCarran-Walter Immigration Law in an Alfred E. Smith memorial foundation speech by saying, "we must strike from our own statute books any legislation concerning immigration that implies the blasphemy against democracy that only certain of Europeans are welcome on American shores."[22] He was, however, closer to his party on using the anti-strike injunction provided by the Taft-Hartley Act. In fact, CIO President Phillip Murray reacted to the General's statement of June 12 that he favored the weapon to end the national steel strike by calling Eisenhower a "me-tooer" for Taft. On the other hand, he believed that Taft-Hartley inequities, mostly to the disadvantage of labor, should be corrected.[23]

Failure of the Lodge assumptions that an Eisenhower Presidency would salvage the GOP from the far right could conceivably produce an even greater conservative thrust from frustrated romanticizers about a bygone American *laissez-faire*. An Eisenhower-led GOP would have to straddle the dangerous center line by selling respectable restraint upon an enlarging federal government while, at the same time, convincing perplexed conservatives that there was no choice but to accept obnoxious regulations and taxes. Even more, as President and leader of his party he would need to continue working toward European unification by assuaging Taft's fears about growing American international involvement and by satisfying those whose interests were more with economy than with overseas commerce.

Lodge's own concern about having Eisenhower at the head of the ticket to attract independent votes appealed to such Senate liberals as Irving Ives of New York, also a candidate for re-election. While Minnesota's Edward Thye obviously supported Governor Stassen, he would also find Ike safer then Taft. But among Senate incumbents up for re-election, they were outweighed by the fourteen clearly conservative-to-reactionary Senators. Dependent upon conservative constituencies, such people as Joe McCarthy of Wisconsin, John Bricker of Ohio, Jim Kem of Missouri, Zales Ecton of Montana, George "Molly" Malone of Nevada, William Jenner of Indiana and Owen Brewster of Maine were scarcely free to take public positions in opposition to Taft or MacArthur.

Moving westward to Mamie's hometown of Denver and the Brown Palace Hotel for the last three weeks of the pre-convention campaign, Eisenhower staged a shrewd, unadvertised public debate with Taft. In Detroit he announced to a throng of 40,000 in Cadillac Square that he was abandoning his prepared speech and declared that he had no panaceas. "If I make blunders," he told the crowd, "I know my friends will excuse it. I hope the others will realize at least that I'm sincere." Without saying anything about conservatives or right-wingers, he told the fiercely anti-Communist workers that he had no personal responsibility for diplomatic blunders at Yalta and Potsdam. He had, in fact, recommended—but in vain—that we should not divide Germany into two parts or invite Russia to get into the Japanese war; regarding the decision to leave Berlin to the Russians, that had been political and beyond his control, he claimed. Then he reminded his audience that "None of these brave men of 1952 have yet offered to go out and pick the 10,000 American mothers whose sons should have made the sacrifice to capture a worthless objective." Ending his speech, he asked the crowd in the square to recite the Pledge of Allegiance with him.[24] In Denver he told members of the American Agricultural Editors Association that he would appreciate being educated by them on the farm problem because, although brother Milton had "done his best to give me a little real education" in the field of agriculture, the instruction had been definitely hit or miss, although Milton had "inherited all the brains in the Eisenhower family."[25] There was a lot of "scarey talk about Russia," he conceded to a local meeting of the Sigma Delta Chi journalistic fraternity, but he did not believe "every Russian is fourteen feet high." And, besides, there is no more reason to fear the Russians "than there is to fear polywogs swimming down a muddy creek." The American people, he assured them, could conquer all the nation's problems by working together.[26] At a luncheon with correspondents he denied the possibility of a convention foreign-policy plank that would be acceptable both to himself and to Taft, and then complained that his earlier remarks about a $40 billion cut in the budget had been "taken from context" and misinterpreted by Taft people.[27] Before Oregon and Arizona delegates he went directly counter to Taft's position on the Korean war. He warned that seeking a military victory would risk a general war and denied there was any justification for Korean deployment of Chinese Nationalist troops from Formosa. Japan, he reminded his listeners, is "the real outpost of our civilization" in the Far East and must not be jeopardized by ill-advised ventures in Korea and Formosa."[28]

The General was doing his utmost to counter the Senator by presenting himself as a political amateur devoid of glib theories but, in contrast to his opponent, a sincere, plain-talking American always ready to learn whatever may be necessary for his country's benefit. Matters pertaining to the bloodshed in Korea, he was insinuating, could hardly be left to a man who was an amateur in that field. For Eisenhower to have agreed with Taft on conducting the Korean war would have been to surrender his strongest claim to expertise.

On the night of June 19 Taft had his turn. Speaking at the CBS-TV theater in New York City, the Senator played right into Eisenhower's hands by calling attention to his amateurishness regarding several matters. Taft's theme was that the General was either ill-informed or did not understand the issues. He pointed to what he regarded as Eisenhower's imprecision on the Taft-Hartley Act, saying that Ike had not understood the law because he had said "you can't make men work," when everybody knows, Taft pointed out, that the act was not for that purpose but to provide for collective-bargaining rights for both employers and employees. He even noted that Eisenhower had asked a group of farm editors to help him come up with an agricultural program. And although Eisenhower had talked in terms of reducing the budget by some $30 or $40 billion, Taft was quick to seize an erroneous newspaper report as a pretext for claiming that the Presidential hopeful had been talking about a $40 billion tax cut, which, he pointed out, would leave nothing for foreign aid. Despite the General's sharp dissent from Taft's international views, particularly his statement about Korea made just one day earlier, Taft, recognizing his own Achilles heel, denied that their chief difference was on foreign policy. Eisenhower had, after all, told a news conference in Abilene that he subscribed to the Declaration of Party Principles, which Taft said, "I largely wrote in 1950."[29]

In Denver on June 26 Eisenhower achieved the tone of orthodox

Republicanism in an "Eisenhower Day" radio-TV address that served as the chief feature of fund-raising dinners being held throughout the country by the various Ike clubs. The Coliseum crowd of 11,000 that had been entertained by a succession of motion-picture stars that included Humphrey Bogart and Susan Hayward was then aroused when the General rode into the stadium on top of the back seat of an open convertible with two giant spotlights pinpointing him as the car circled the blacked-out arena. His nationally broadcast speech then invoked the standard rhetoric of his party, Lincoln and God and attacked the Truman administration for having been too easy on corruption at home and on communism abroad. The Democrats were blamed for the "loss" of China, the dangerous situation in Europe and the war in Korea. "If we had been less trusting," he said, "if we had been less soft and weak, there would probably have been no war in Korea!" With the end of corruption and the introduction of businesslike efficiency, much, much more could be accomplished and greater economy could still be achieved.[30]

In Paris, his old friend and aide General Gruenther was puzzled. Who was advising Eisenhower? he wanted to know. "I know damn well it isn't like Ike," he told Cyrus Sulzberger, "to come out and say he wants a $40 billion budget reduction."[31] Even Gruenther did not understand the depth of Eisenhower's commitment to the most pragmatic methods of achieving his ends. To Dulles, just one week before the Denver speech, the candidate for the Republican Presidential nomination had written: "There are innumerable instances of method, detail and procedure on which I am always ready to accept almost any revision of my own views."[32] Furthermore, the goal of "fiscal responsibility" was, next to the importance of a viable Atlantic Alliance, his most common theme as the best means of ensuring American strength.

Seeking the Republican nomination with all the accouterments of his party's jargon, the General and his people were ready to take on the challenge that would most likely decide the outcome; the bumping by Taft forces of pro-Eisenhower delegates.

CHAPTER 13

Deception at Houston

THE PRELIMINARIES OF the 1952 Republican National Convention centered on the ability of the son of President William Howard Taft to repeat the control of the nominating session that his father had commanded in 1912. At that time the party's national committee, dominated by the President, had decided most of the unusually large number of contested seats in his favor over the claims of Theodore Roosevelt's insurgents. Taft's subsequent first-ballot victory precipitated a second convention, that of TR's Progressives, and the Bull Moose campaign then divided the Republican vote and installed Woodrow Wilson, a Democrat, as a minority President.

This time the essential difference was that neither side presented an incumbent. However, the Taft–Eisenhower clash did have many of the characteristics of an insurgent trying to usurp the *status quo*. Rebellion was particularly evident in such areas as the South, where Eisenhower boosters were joined by large numbers of conservative Democrats. Only four years earlier Governor J. Strom Thurmond of South Carolina had led the Dixiecrats in open rebellion against the Democratic national leadership. Now, enticed by the prospects of an Eisenhower candidacy and still reluctant to return to their traditional party, there was the possibility of the greatest Southern interest in the GOP since 1928. For some of the heretofore tiny Republican organizations, often held as the virtual fiefdoms of national committeemen from the various states, such as Texas's R. B. Creager and his successor, Henry Zweifel, swollen numbers of party activists were as ominous for their leadership as was the population expansion of Puritan Massachusetts to the early Congregationalist

73

churches. State Republican organizations were small patronage vehicles virtually owned by such national committeemen as Creager and Zweifel. Newer groups, such as those headed by Jack Porter in Texas and John Minor Wisdom in Louisiana, were distinct threats to their power. Such proprietary state party organizations tended to be safe, conservative centers, ready to respond to patronage deals. Inadvertently, however, they furnished Lodge and the other Eisenhower managers with the issue that was needed so badly.

When Taft appeared on the "See It Now" TV program in early June and scoffed at the opposition by saying, "I think they'd rather have the issue than the delegates," he was also making an important point. More simply, and, of course, what he was trying to get across, was that they needed the issue because they did *not* have the delegates. Yet the two were inseparable. The issue arose because Eisenhower people were charging that their duly elected convention delegates were being "stolen," that local potentates were employing tactics that, later in Chicago, would be rewarded by the Taft-dominated Republican National Committee and its chairman, Guy Gabrielson. Inability to make any headway with this complaint would virtually seal Taft's nomination.

By every count of delegates, however inaccurate a specific number may have been, Taft was well ahead. With 604 votes needed for the nomination, the Senator's figures suggested that those in opposition were risking alienation from the winner. At the close of the first week in June, with Eisenhower in New York, the Taft people were claiming 588 delegates. Completing the first ballot with that total would be unlikely because of the haste from certain "favorite son" delegates to get credit for his nomination by changing their votes to clinch the victory. More realistically, however, the Associated Press calculated, at the same time, that Taft could count on 462, while Eisenhower had 389. But the efficacy of the General's conferences with the delegates was, nevertheless, showing signs of success. An Associated Press poll in late June reported that thirty-two Pennsylvania delegates were now inclined toward Ike, a gain of twelve, while Taft also penetrated the uncommitted to increase his number by six. Overall, by the eve of the Chicago convention, the press service box score showed that 427 delegates were for Eisenhower and 530 for the Senator.

Possibly more important than such arithmetic was the Taft control of the party machinery. Having a majority of the national committeemen as well as the Committee on Credentials meant that adoption of procedural rules would inevitably repeat the 1912 experience and enable the Senator to duplicate his father's achievement. The Committee on Arrangements, meeting in Chicago a month ahead of the convention, ignored the protests of the Eisenhower minority and chose General Douglas MacArthur to rouse the delegates by delivering the keynote address on the opening night. Having the prestigious general face a national television audience with a speech undoubtedly keyed to the Taft position, as MacArthur had already supported the Senator, could have a powerful influence on public opinion and, hence, on the delegates. Even more disturbing to the Eisenhower people, and particularly illustrative of the Taft monopolization of the GOP's national leadership, was their choice of Walter S. Hallanan of West Virginia as the temporary chairman. Hallanan was one of Taft's regional campaign managers.[1] His convention role could give him crucial decision-making powers over the seating of contested delegates, much as that exercised by Elihu Root in 1912.

Lodge reacted bitterly. He accused the Taft backers of using shyster methods to create a "kangeroo court" in Chicago. Moreover, he charged them with violating all the ethics of fair play and popular government. But Hallanan, reacting from his strong position, called the Eisenhower manager a "completely spoiled political child" who was "obviously having a political nightmare."[2] All that was fine for Lodge, who thereby succeeded in getting exposure for his efforts to portray the Taft candidacy as the product of a self-interested political clique trying to thwart the popular will by imposing the product of a "smoke-filled room." There was, however, an even more promising issue, one that held the only realistic chance of ultimate success, the controversy surrounding the choice of delegates from several Southern states.

In all, some seventy-five delegate seats were at issue. Half were from Texas, while seventeen Georgians and eleven from Louisiana were also involved. Additionally, there were disputes concerning delegates from Mississippi, Florida, Virginia, Missouri and Kansas. Overwhelmingly, the complaints were from pro-Eisenhower people who alleged that their right to represent the voters had been overturned by the controlling powers of their states. In Florida, however, the clash was between two factions both strongly for Taft, while elsewhere, such as in Kansas, a scattering of pro-Eisenhower seats were under fire.

The Texas situation, because thirty-eight delegates were involved, provided the greatest controversy. Moreover, it was the locale of the most dramatic confrontations between a tightly dominated and comfortably small fiefdomlike party and people the regulars like to call "enthusiasts"—largely newcomers to partisan political activity. In traditionally Democratic Texas, rebellious at the concentration of power in Washington and eager to overturn Truman-backed Supreme Court rulings that gave tidelands oil deposits to the federal government rather than to the state, there was little wonder that many of the new participants were not identifiable as Republicans.[3]

The battle had begun early in the year. In February, national committeeman Henry Zweifel, the virtual proprietor of the state's GOP, attempted to secure himself and his organization against so-called "one-day Republicans" by extracting a pledge to be signed by all voters at the May 3 precinct conventions. The statement was that "I am a Republican and desire to participate in Republican party activities in the year 1952."[4] In Dallas County, the Eisenhower people, led by Jack Porter and Alvin H. Lane, instructed their own followers to sign the pledge by pointing out that "The Supreme Court of Texas held that, in effect, you can vote Republican one day, Democratic the next, and vote in the general election the next day. You CAN vote in BOTH Democratic and Republican elections—DO NOT BE INTIMIDATED!" Bexar County voters, where San Antonio is located, were given a similar message via a postcard campaign.[5] Mrs. Oveta Culp Hobby, the former wartime leader of the WACs and the wife of an ex-Governor and publisher of the Houston Post, used her newspaper resources for great partisan effect. Having run a front-page endorsement of the General in the April 13 edition of the Post, Mrs. Hobby managed to distribute a "non-partisan" political primer to over 400,000 Texans informing them, in essence, that party ties did not prevent them from voting for Eisenhower delegates. Furthermore, a statewide telecast service provided by the paper's station KPRC-TV gave instructions on how to hold precinct conventions.[6]

In May, conventions were held throughout the state on three levels—the precinct, the county and, finally, on the 27th, statewide in the town of Mineral Wells. Although there were 185 precinct conventions held simultaneously on the third, the Post managed to have a reporter cover each one. Their observations testified to the wide occurence of a similar phenomenon. Whereas such gatherings were normally intimate affairs that could be confined within private homes, attendance numbering several hundreds was common. Often the crowds had to abandon living rooms and convene on lawns. Even Zweifel, captain of his precinct in Tarrant County, was bewildered. When a vote within his home yielded 110 for Eisenhower and only thirty-one for Taft, he and his astonished followers fled from his living room and reconvened on the front lawn, where they chose their own delegation. In meeting after meeting at other precinct conventions, pro-Eisenhower delegates were chosen; and Taftites, finding themselves badly outnumbered, usually walked out and held their own rump sessions and chose rival delegates to attend the county conventions. When, for example, the Harris County chairman, who was for Taft, appointed a group of three Taftites and two Eisenhower people to study the situation, they found that the meetings in the county, where Houston is located, had chosen 146 Eisenhower and nineteen Taft delegates. Rump meetings, however, had created sixty-nine disputed seats at the county convention.[7] When the county conventions met, just three days later, the Taft people, contending that the Eisenhower men were really Democrats who had signed the pledge in bad faith, staged similar walkouts in thirty-one counties and held additional rump conventions, thus negating the Eisenhower claims of 743 "duly elected" delegates to only 275 for Taft.[8]

Zweifel reacted by continuing the scurrilous campaign that had been going on for some time. A vehemently anti-Eisenhower, anti-Semitic periodical called *Headlines*, edited by Joseph P. Kamp and carrying such headlines as "REDS, NEW DEALERS USE IKE IN PLOT TO HOLD POWER" and "SIDNEY HILLMAN AND ANNA ROSENBERG FATHERED 'IKE-FOR-PRESIDENT'" and "IKE CODDLED COMMUNISTS WHILE PRESIDENT OF COLUMBIA UNIVERSITY" was distributed by Zweifel workers for Taft.[9] Zweifel himself got into the spirit of such tactics by issuing press releases that were almost on Kamp's level. He charged that the Texans behind the General consisted of "notorious New Deal–Fair Deal supporters of the past 20 years, Labor-Internationalists, CIO Political Action Committee members and left wingers so far left that the Texas Democrats don't want them."[10]

The state convention at Mineral Wells on May 27, however, was a much more carefully scrutinized affair and not left to a mere pledge. The state executive committee, serving as a credentials committee, had "scrutinized" the contested seats with such care that pro-Eisenhower decisions were made only after the Taft forces were assured majority control even though they spoke for mere minorities at both precinct and county levels. When the rejected Eisenhower delegates were then barred from the meeting hall, the Porter group held its own rival convention. The Zweifel people chose an uninstructed delegation (in accordance with the Taft instructions) that, nevertheless, consisted of thirty for Taft, four for MacArthur and four for Eisenhower. The Porter convention elected thirty-three delegates instructed for Eisenhower and five for Taft.[11]

With similar conflicts arising elsewhere, notably in Georgia and Louisiana, the best the pro-Eisenhower people could do was to exploit the situation by calling attention to the "steal." In Dallas on June 21, Eisenhower charged the Texans for Taft with corruption and denounced the disregard of majority will. By disenfranchising Eisenhower delegates, the General declared, the "rustlers stole the Texas birthright instead of Texas steers."[12] He also advocated barring all disputed delegates from voting on any convention contests. In New York, meanwhile, Henry Cabot Lodge called on ex-President Herbert Hoover at his Waldorf Towers suite and detailed what had happened at Mineral Wells. Hoover suggested that Eisenhower and Taft each choose an "eminent citizen" to discuss the matter and offered his assistance to work out an agreement between them. Lodge, however, held firm and maintained that there was nothing to mediate. Nationally, the situation was widely publicized by the news media.

An obstacle for the Eisenhower people was Rule Four of the convention, which, ironically, had been adopted at the 1948 session through Dewey's efforts. Basically, in trying to guide outcomes of contested delegations, it stipulated that the credentials committee could exclude all controversial choices that had been disposed of by state conventions or state committees, with the exception of delegates elected not from specific districts but at-large. Invoking that rule would now mean that only a small fraction of those challenged could be overturned. It would result in another 1912-type spectacle by enabling contested Taft delegates from certain states to pass on the validity of challenges raised by Eisenhower people elsewhere. But it was still possible for the credentials committee to decide, by a two-thirds vote, to accept new evidence concerning contests that had already been settled by the national committee.

When the national committee convened in Chicago on the first day of July to begin hearings on the seating disputes, it became more evident that the party's highest council would not do anything to jeopardize Taft's momentum. Taft's people hoped for a quiet, undramatic settlement that would minimize the popular loss both for the convention and with the electorate in November. Eisenhower managers, underdogs in need of an issue, were adamant about not compromising and getting more publicity for their claims. The night before the hearings began, Lodge made the point very simply. "There is nothing to compromise," he said. "In Texas, for instance, the Taft people laid down the rules, the Eisenhower people obeyed the rules, and then the Taft people changed these rules." Henry Zweifel, on the other hand, maintained that the Eisenhower forces had no basis for compromise.[13] Lodge, however, was also ready to show the committee a photostat of a letter written on January 1, 1949, by the late R. B. Creager officially designating Jack Porter as chairman of the "Campaign Committee for Two-Party Government in Texas." Lodge, talking as much for public consumption as for the committee, also pointed out that the designation of the man now being charged by the Taftites with packing the present conventions with Democrats had had the approval of Zweifel, Creager's successor, whom he called the "mastermind of the Texas steal."[14] Lodge's people had also opened the hearing room to radio and TV coverage, and the national committeemen found microphones, lights and cameras ready when they arrived. Promptly, by a vote of sixty to forty, they voted to prohibit such publicity for the hearings on the delegate contests. Representative Clarence Brown, one of Taft's campaign managers, led the fight against holding open hearings, explaining that the logical result of such practice would be for a Chicago newspaper to insist upon the right to install linotype machines and one of its presses in the hearing room to compete with radio and television.[15] Rather than waiting for the equipment to be removed, they simply went to another large room of the Conrad Hilton. On the hearings' second day, they gave Taft his first impressive victory at Chicago by seating the solidly pro-Taft delegation from Georgia and refusing credentials to the group that included thirteen Eisenhower people among its seventeen members.[16] The Georgia Taftites, led by Roy Foster, had not been recognized by the party's national convention in two earlier attempts to be seated, 1944 and 1948. Only with the state's recognition provided by the ruling of a Democratic judge not adverse to splitting Republicans had the largely rural group won its place.[17]

Possibly the most vigorous denunciation that came from outside the identifiable Eisenhower circle came from California's Senator Richard M. Nixon, who, along with the rest of his state's delegation, was ostensibly behind Governor Earl Warren. He warned about the importance of following up that decision by doing justice to the Eisenhower claims in Texas, which was scheduled to be considered on the fourth day of the hearings. If the party approves the "Texas grab," he said, "we will be announcing to the country that we believe ruthless machine politics is wrong only when the Democrats use it." Concerned, then, that the Republicans would lose the "corruption issue" if their hands were not clean, Nixon added that the party "can't hope to win this November if it limits its memberhip to the minority which has not been large enough to win for national elections."[18]

Eisenhower also reacted vigorously. Returning with his banker friend Aksel Nielsen after an all-day fishing trip, he declared, "I'm going to roar out across the country for a clean, decent convention. The American people deserve it."[19] Taft retorted by saying, "I only hope that he roars out against Truman, Acheson and Brannan in the farm district as well as against Republicans."[20]

But then, with Louisiana and Texas still unresolved, the most important break for the Eisenhower challengers came from an unexpected quarter.

Coincidentally meeting that year in Houston, Texas, the center of the battle between the Zweifel and Porter factions, the forty-fourth annual Governors' conference was still in session while the national committee meetings were continuing in Chicago. Both parties were almost evenly represented, with twenty-five of the forty-eight state houses controlled by the GOP, although attendance at Houston was not 100 percent. Some Governors feared exposing their families to the polio epidemic that had plagued Texas earlier.

Occurring as it did on the eve of the Republican convention, the

inevitable sparks came from that highly political setting. For the Democrats, Illinois's Adlai E. Stevenson said that he would consider a genuine
draft for the Presidency and appealed for North-South party harmony
by reiterating that the states should be able, at least for the near future,
to deal with racial discrimination in employment instead of being subjected to a Federal Fair Employment Practices Commission. But Republican concern centered on the delegate battle being waged in Chicago.
Governors Dewey, Douglas McKay of Oregon and Sherman Adams of
New Hampshire sent a telegram to the Republican National Committee
urging the seating of the pro-Eisenhower delegation from Texas. Utah's
arch-conservative J. Bracken Lee conceded that, "in fairness," Eisenhower could be considered a stronger candidate than Taft. But, Lee
stressed, that was only true for July. In November, Taft would be a
better bet. Dewey predicted an Eisenhower victory by the third ballot
and said his information showed forty Taft delegates preparing to shift
to the General.[21]

Fear that the Taft steamroller would seize the convention before July
7 preoccupied the Eisenhower Governors. Accordingly, in the Sham-
rock Hotel room of Sherman Adams a special caucus convened to see
what could be done to stop the Senator. Adams, who had called the
meeting, also served as its chairman. The nineteen Governors present
comprised the General's leading supporters among the state chief executives. Walter Kohler of Wisconsin, acting as secretary, jotted down
their suggestions on a handy telephone pad. Determined to send a manifesto to Guy Gabrielson with as many names as possible while, at the
same time, advancing the Eisenhower candidacy, they searched for ways
of getting approval from the three Taft supporters in Houston. Lee was
the most important figure, as it turned out, as the other two were ready
to follow his lead. After ending the meeting with agreement to avoid a
frontal attack on the Democrats, Lodge and Dewey afterward held a
brief session with Kohler. From that three-man conference, in all likelihood, came the idea for a manifesto proposing that contested delegates
be kept from voting on the right of others to be seated. The next day
Richard Pittenger, the press aide to Governor Dan Thornton of Colorado, suggested a way of getting an endorsement from all the Governors,
even the Taftites.[22]

Pittenger's idea was to send a two-page telegram to Gabrielson with
the signature of every Republican Governor present. That would certainly win publicity for their counterattack and might deter many pro-
Taft delegates. Their manifesto would be revealed at a special press
conference and read to the news media by such diverse men as Lee and
Thornton. That kind of an endorsement, with sponsorship from both
Taft and Eisenhower men, would be bound to influence the delegates, if

not the national committee. Getting it accomplished was another matter.

Lodge and Thornton helped Kohler compose the telegram. The opening page was harmless enough. Mostly it was a platitude about how the Republican party "aspires to the highest standards of honor, integrity, and fairness." Then, gradually getting to the real point, deep into the second page, it urged "your support of a ruling that no contested delegate may vote to determine the outcome of any contest." "We believe," it also stated, "that if contested delegations are permitted to vote on the seating of other contested state delegations, the Republican party, no matter who ultimately may become the Republican nominee, will enter a vital and difficult campaign under a serious moral cloud."[23]

Adding the other signatures was the trick. Sherman Adams took charge of getting the ones from New England and Kohler took care of the Midwesterners. Val Peterson of Nebraska accomplished the difficult but important task of getting the approval of Earl Warren, who, of course, was nursing his own ambitions. Lee was the important holdout. While the host Governor, Allan Shivers, held the attention of his audience during the farewell address to the conference on July 2, Val Peterson was under instructions to keep the session going until he received a signal from Dan Thornton. The Colorado Governor, complete with cowboy boots, was working on Lee. Lee's support was clinched by the appeal to his appetite for publicity when informed that he and Thornton would share the press conference to be held immediately after the meeting. Once Lee had consented, there was no trouble getting the other two Taftites, Len Jordan of Idaho and Norman Brunsdale of North Dakota. Kneeling in his boots, Thornton approached the two men as they listened to Shivers. Assured that Lee had been amenable and not bothering to be sufficiently distracted from the proceedings by reading beyond page one of the manifesto, they were easy conquests for Thornton.

His goal accomplished, the Colorado Governor signaled to Peterson, who then announced that there would be a special press conference in the basement as soon as the meeting adjourned. Peterson also said that Lee, who was scheduled to catch an early plane to return to Salt Lake City, would begin the reading of the telegram.

The press, having been furnished no advance copy, had to take it down in longhand. Not until Thornton had introduced Lee to read page one did the reporters know anything about it. And Governor Lee, surprised as well as flattered by the invitation, overlooked the significance of the contents.[24] When he finished the first page, the part with the high-minded passages, he was excused so he could get to the airport. When Lee was safely out of sight, Thornton continued with the real substance. By the time Thornton completed the manifesto, newsmen could no longer get to Lee for an explanation of his apparent support of the pro-Eisenhower position. Only when Lee was surrounded by newsmen upon his arrival in Utah did he realize what he had signed and read to the press. But he, just as the other Governors involved, could not admit that, as the chief executive of a state, he had signed a document without knowing what it was about. Furthermore, Thornton pocketed the telegram for an hour before actually sending it to Gabrielson to make certain that it would go over the wires without being countered by anyone.

The manifesto with the signatures of twenty-three Republican Governors was the first real breakthrough for the Eisenhower forces. As Thornton and Pittenger had hoped, it was front-page news throughout the country and could not go unanswered. Both Governors Fine of Pennsylvania and Theodore McKeldin of Maryland, who had not attended the conference, quickly announced their support. Gabrielson, angry also because the telegram had been released to the press before he had seen it, stated that their request was contrary to custom and former rulings and could be used by ruthless individuals in the future to thwart conventions by rendering most delegates unable to vote; furthermore, said the national chairman, such a rule "would affront the American and the Republican tradition of fair play and sportsmanship." Taft used the same theme by pointing out that, under such a system, it was conceivable that a minority of delegates could gain control. That brought a rejoinder from Tom Dewey, who said, "If the delegates who were elected illegally are seated in the coming convention, the nomination for President will be no more valid than the nomination in 1912, which was achieved by the same tactics."[25]

The irony, then, was that while they were complaining that the Taftites were trying to steal the convention, the Eisenhower people had "stolen" the Governors' conference at Houston.[26] Their power as the heads of state delegations, plus the psychological impact of the issue upon the gathering at Chicago, reduced the prospects for a repetition of 1912.

CHAPTER 14

Chicago, July 1952

SPURRED BY THE GOVERNORS' manifesto, the Eisenhower camp moved to bring the issue to the convention floor and before the public. Unlike any previous political gathering in history, the Republican party's twenty-fifth Presidential nominating convention was geared to complete coverage by television cameras. Even the site, the International Amphitheater rather than the more accessible Chicago Stadium, was chosen because it was more suitable for TV. To the leading Eisenhower strategists, Cabot Lodge, New York attorney Herbert Brownell, Jr., and Governor Dewey, shouting "foul" in plain view of the national audience would be a lot more effective than complaining before a closed and stacked meeting of the party's national committee.

For the first time since his return to the country, Eisenhower, too, seemed infected with the spirit of a crusade. At the Coliseum in Denver, speaking on what had been proclaimed as "Eisenhower Day" by the Ike clubs throughout the country, he said, "You young people both in and out of these Eisenhower clubs are helping to get that train ready and on the right track. It is a Republican train on a Republican track." Then, ostensibly directing his attack upon Truman and the Democrats but actually keeping the delegate issue in the forefront, he acknowledged that while we have had corruption in the past, "never before has it reached such epidemic proportions. . . . In little more than twelve months of this year and last, 177 persons in the Bureau of Internal Revenue were fired for dishonesty or other improper activities."[1] Later, while traveling toward Chicago on his special train, he castigated the "chicanery" and "crookedness" used to deny the claimed seats. Passing through the Midwest on July 4, he chose the holiday theme to complain that the handling of the contests by the national committee had flouted the Founding Fathers' concept of a "decent respect to the opinion of mankind" as embodied in the Declaration of Independence. Barring radio and TV reporters, he charged, had given the country the spectacle of "star chamber" methods and "smoke-filled room." Those responsible for having deprived the people of vital information, the General said, are not "true Americans." In a nationally televised speech from Ames, Iowa, he defined the issue as whether "politicians are to be loyal servants or arrogant masters" and held that the battle was "a straight-out issue between right and wrong. It is a struggle against a little group of men whose purpose of controlling the Republican party overrides respect for majority decisions."[2]

At each whistle stop along the way the crowds cheered the increased tempo of his attacks. Reporters noted that the throngs must have equaled the total population of the communities on his itinerary. At every stop people had to fight their way to reach the platform of the General's train. Then, just before he spoke in Boone, Iowa, he received news of a Taft "compromise" offer.

Taft, analyzing the district delegates chosen in Texas, offered to split that state's delegation by giving the General sixteen seats and leaving himself twenty-two, eight less than he had had. "If General Eisenhower and his managers hold with me that the good of the party comes first," Taft wrote to Guy Gabrielson, "they will not hesitate to accept my proposal." Taft also wrote: "While I will suffer a delegate loss in making this proposal, I am doing so because I think it is so generous that its equity cannot be questioned, and I am willing to take that loss as a contribution to the strengthening of the Republican party."[3]

Eisenhower's immediate reaction to the Taft proposal was "Gee, that sounds good."[4] His advisers, however, convinced him to tell the press that any public reaction would have to come from Senator Lodge. Lodge promptly denounced the maneuver.

A quiet, "out of court" settlement was the last thing that the Eisenhower strategists wanted. Not only would such a move concede that there were two possible versions to the Texas story and would leave the aroma of a cynical division of the spoils, but it would deprive the General's people of their most persuasive issue. With the Senator claiming more than the 604 delegates needed to win, and with the wire services agreeing that he had a substantial lead, quiet diplomacy was clearly not in the Eisenhower interest. This was also the reason Lodge continued to reject former President Hoover's insistence that he be permitted to play the role of "honest broker" in resolving the disputes.

After Lodge's visit to the ex-President at the Waldorf Towers, Hoover continued to press the matter. By telegram he notified the Senator on June 26 that he had not discussed his proposal with Taft but would "do my best to secure his cooperation," if only Lodge would agree to let each side appoint one "eminent citizen," not one of their managers, to sit with Hoover for the purpose of finding some basis of agreement. "There would be no public announcement nor publicity if such a committee were agreed to," assured the last Republican occupant of the White House. "Do you still think such an approach is hopeless?" But Lodge, holding to his position despite the other man's prestige, continued to maintain that only by having the convention settle the issue could the "public have confidence in the integrity of the proceedings of the Republican National Convention." Hoover then responded by sending Lodge a copy of a newspaper column by right-wing journalist Fulton Lewis, Jr., "to indicate that the law and right can have different interpretations" and included the petulant observation that "I refuse to construe your remarks as an insult to my integrity." Lodge, still adamant, replied, "I am surprised that any such thought should ever occur to you."[5] Reminding Hoover that Eisenhower was clearly the popular favorite, he also pointed out that the total vote of the precinct conventions held in Texas was one-third of the Republican vote cast for Dewey in that state in 1948.

There was no choice for the Eisenhower people. The day before the Taft "compromise" offer on Texas, for example, the national committee gave the Senator sixteen more seats by deciding the Louisiana and Mississippi contests in his favor. After the committee voted by sixty-one to forty-one to seat two pro-Eisenhower people from Louisiana's third Congressional District, whose election had been voided by the state's party organization, Chairman Gabrielson ruled out of order a challenge to seven other contested pro-Taft Louisiana delegates.[6] When the national committee then voted on Independence Day night, they agreed by sixty to forty-one to split the Texas delegation precisely by the twenty-two to sixteen margin Taft had suggested. Turned back by a vote of fifty-eight to forty-three was an attempt to seat the pro-Eisenhower Porter delegation. As a result, the Associated Press tallied 527 safe for Taft and 427 for the General.[7]

The challengers announced they were ready to take the issue to the floor of the convention by appealing to the 1,206 delegates to comply with the spirit of the Houston manifesto. En route to Chicago, Governor Earl Warren of California, who stood with Stassen in hoping for an Eisenhower-Taft deadlock, gave his full support to the anti-Taft side of the seating issue. Consistently, California's national committee man and woman had opposed the Taft compromise on the Texas issue, indicating certain support from the state's seventy-member delegation in any floor fight. Also with the Eisenhower side in that vote were, in addition to most of the ninety-six-member New York delegation, such other major states as Pennsylvania, Michigan, New Jersey, Massachusetts and Indiana.[8] Tom Dewey, having reached Chicago on July 3, busily conferred with delegates. His objective was to reach those who had supported him in 1948.

Eisenhower, arriving two days before the convention's scheduled opening, read to the press a prepared statement that reminded the nation of the support given to his position on voting by contested delegates at Houston and declared: "There will be no Iron Curtain between the convention and the people—any more than there should ever be an Iron Curtain between our people and the Government."[9] To reporters on the train before they reached the city the General had remarked, "If they do give me this job, brother, it's going to be a slugging match from beginning to end."

The threat of a repetition of 1912 was very real that weekend. Just to make sure that that catastrophe was not forgotten, Ed Russell, the editor of the Harrisburg *Record*, had prepared reprints of a page from *Collier's* magazine of July 27, 1912. Entitled "The Stolen Delegates," it carried the following subhead: "Comment on the Illegality of Taft's Nomination from Newspapers of Every Shade of Political Belief." Superimposed in a facsimile of handwriting at the upper right-hand corner of the flyer was the admonition: "Don't let history repeat itself!"[10] Copies were distributed to all delegates and visitors to the Eisenhower headquarters at the Conrad Hilton Hotel. The New York *Times* editorialized that the decisions of the National Committee were "suicidal" and stated that the decision of the convention would be "whether the Republican party belongs to the people who want to vote Republican or to a small and highly organized group that happens to be in control of the party machinery."[11]

The plan proposed by the Eisenhower people was simple and reasonable. Offered by Representative Christian Herter of Massachusetts, it proposed the substance of the Houston Governors' manifesto, which held that contested delegates should not be able to vote on the seating of those who were challenged from other states. But it added one compromise stipulation that was designed to meet the Taft-Gabrielson objections to the Houston manifesto. Those who had been approved by more than 80 percent of the 106-member national committee could be seated; the others would be denied the right to vote in the convention or committees until their credentials had been certified by the Credentials Committee and the convention itself. In effect, that bypassed any fight over the disputed delegates from Florida, Mississippi, Kansas and Missouri but focused the fight on Georgia, Louisiana and Texas. Not permitting those delegates to be seated would, of course, also keep them off the Credentials Committee, which was one of the significant by-products of the move.

At the urging of Herbert Brownell, Eisenhower went over this proposal at a dinner on the eve of the convention's opening with National Committeeman Arthur Summerfield of Michigan and Governor Fine of Pennsylvania. Fine, who had already announced on TV that afternoon that he would support Ike on the convention floor, also agreed to the psychological move of announcing early in the week his outright support for the Eisenhower nomination. Later that evening the General met with Harold Stassen's Minnesota delegation and with Governor McKeldin of Maryland.[12] They also represented support for the amendment to the voting rules drawn up by Herter. Advanced under the politic description "Fair Play Amendment," it was scheduled to be introduced on the floor by Governor Arthur B. Langlie of Washington.

More simply, the issue was over control of the Republican party. Abandoning all pretexts of neutrality, national committee chairman Gabrielson had moved to open support for Taft. Talk of a possible walkout was heard if Gabrielson or Hallanan tried to prevent a direct test of strength on changing the rules. There was the distinct possibility that Gabrielson, as chairman, might ignore Governor Langlie's attempt to be recognized so he could introduce the "Fair Play Amendment." "If that happens," Dewey was reported to have told a strategy meeting in Lodge's Conrad Hilton suite, "I'll go to the platform and grab the microphone myself."[13] Taft, on the day prior to the opening of the floor fight, announced that he had written pledges to support him and "become working members of the Taft team" from 510 delegates. He was not, however, ready to predict a first-ballot nomination, preferring to announce the possibility that some delegate strength might be held in reserve on the first ballot so they might be released at an opportune time if needed later.[14]

The big Eisenhower fear was that a floor fight would not take place, that the Taft people would line up behind the "Fair Play Amendment" without a battle. That would deprive them of a big psychological boost. When Senator Knowland, representing Governor Warren, arranged conferences with Lodge and other Eisenhower people on the "Fair Play Amendment" on Sunday night, the advantage of a floor showdown remained the major goal. Knowland's purpose for the sessions, which lasted throughout that night, was to arrange a compromise on the voting issue. To Lodge and others, however, the Senator, ostensibly committed to Warren, was suspiciously upholding the Taft interest in his zeal for a back-room settlement. But the Eisenhower forces refused to give way. Their only concession was in agreeing to modify the amendment by reducing from 80 to 67 percent of the national-committee vote required to permit seating, a change that made no difference in the state-by-state results.[15]

The constant meetings even delayed the opening of the convention itself. Just some ten minutes before the scheduled 11:30 A.M. start, Guy

Gabrielson called for Lodge. In the national chairman's little office behind the speaker's platform, Lodge found Knowland with David Ingalls,
Tom Coleman and Representative Clarence Brown of Ohio, Taft's main
strategists. Knowland, revealing that the California delegation had just
caucused, said they had agreed to support the "Fair Play Amendment."
Nevertheless, he held to his position of the night before—the desire to
resolve the matter without a floor fight. Brown also expressed a willingness to approve a solution similar to what Langlie was about to offer but
not the precise amendment. To Lodge, fearful that the Taft people were
ready to accept the "Fair Play Amendment" itself, without a vote,
Knowland was actually trying to accomplish what Hoover had suggested. After conferring with Brownell on the telephone, Lodge refused
to compromise. He held to his position that the "way to avoid bitterness
is to vote this up or down on the floor of the Convention."[16]

The waiting delegates on the noisy, jammed floor milled among themselves or gave interviews to the members of the press. For the first time
at any convention TV men carried hand-held portable units, quickly
dubbed "peepie-creepies." An organist provided entertainment by playing songs of the various states and got the loudest cheers for a rendition
of "Dixie." At 12:33 P.M., one hour and three minutes late, Guy Gabrielson gaveled the opening of the party's national convention.

The General, in his Blackstone Hotel room, seemed curiously detached
about the coming clash. To visitors arriving that morning he repeated
Fox Connor's advice to "Take your job seriously; never yourself." What
happened to him, he told them, was not important. What mattered concerned the principles of any group fighting for what was right. That,
he emphasized, was "of paramount importance." His longest talk was
with Governor Earl Warren, the California "favorite son" who had his
hopes geared on a deadlock. After Warren had left, one hour later,
Eisenhower observed that both had similar views; both were middle-of-
the-roaders. "Neither Warren nor I is going to get involved with a lot of
pinkos," said the General, "but we're not going to get dragged back by a
lot of old reactionaries either."[17] Asked by Floridians whether he would
campaign in the South and what he would say if he did, Eisenhower
replied that there were no "sections" of this country so far as he was
concerned and that despite his hope that the Republican party could
create a two-party system in Dixie, he would say the same things in all
parts of the country.

In the convention building, a color guard of Chicago's American
Legion Post 985 took the flag down the center aisle. Representative
James E. Van Zandt of Pennsylvania, a former commander of the Veterans of Foreign Wars, then led the assemblage in the Pledge of Allegiance. After the preliminaries, which also included songs by baritone

William Warfield, came the first partisan notes. Illinois State Treasurer and candidate to succeed Adlai E. Stevenson as Governor, William G. Stratton, called for the removal from power of the "New Dealers, Fair Dealers and little dealers."

The big fight began when Senator John Bricker of Ohio, a loyal Taft man, moved that the rules of the 1948 convention be ruled in effect until a permanent organization was formed. That brought a signal to the chair from Governor Langlie, who was promptly recognized by Hallanan. Langlie then proposed the "Fair Play Amendment" as modified the previous night.

Anticipating the move, the Taftites had decided to raise a point of order. Seven of the Louisiana district delegates who had been seated by the state committee in accordance with Rule Four were among those affected by the Langlie move. For Chairman Gabrielson to uphold the point of order, which they could well expect him to do, would mean that Eisenhower efforts to seat their own seven from Louisiana would face the disadvantage of having to get the convention to overrule the chair. But their plans suddenly became confused because Bricker's motion, apparently engineered by Gabrielson, upset the timetable. Representative Clarence Brown of Ohio then took the floor. But Brown, having been told by Gabrielson that he feared subsequent criticism and would overrule his motion, offered instead an amendment to amend Langlie's "Fair Play" revision of the rules. That precipitated a fierce two-hour debate.[18] Bricker offered to acquiesce to Langlie's move if the Eisenhower people would agree to Brown's proposal.

No such easy out was forthcoming, however, and the first roll call of the convention, made on Brown's amendment involving the seven Louisiana seats, gave the Eisenhower forces an impressive 658–548 victory. The results offered convincing evidence that the Taftites did not control the convention. Then, acting by acclamation, they went on to approve Langlie's "Fair Play Amendment."[19]

The psychological momentum was obvious. But there was an important practical side as well. The vote cost Taft a net of thirty-two in seating contests since fifty of these delegates favored him and eighteen were for Eisenhower. It also left doubt that the convention would uphold the rulings of the national committee, since future tests on the floor would leave him with fifty less than he had on the Brown amendment. Furthermore, the uncommitted delegates had gone to Eisenhower by a big majority.

Later, the Credentials Committee met. Before its organization votes began, the temporary chairman, abiding by the results of the Langlie amendment, excluded committeemen from Georgia and Texas. Nevertheless, when voting for a chairman of the committee, Ross Rizley of

Oklahoma, a Taft man, defeated a Minnesota lawyer by twenty-five to twenty. The lawyer, Warren Burger, was pledged to Stassen but was supported by the Eisenhower people on the committee. The vital function of the Credentials Committee was to hear appeals from delegates who lost their seats to opponents following decisions by the national committee.

Eisenhower had watched the voting on a TV set while having his hair cut. One hour after the balloting, dressed in a gray suit, a red and blue tie and wearing old officers' brown buckled shoes, he called in reporters and read a statement declaring that the vote was "heartening to millions of Americans." Extemporaneously, he added, "I think this vote will really go a long way for gaining the trust of young people."[20]

Practically buried in that day's events was the virtual recision by three of the pro-Taft Governors of their role in the Houston manifesto. Trying to extricate himself from his awkward position, J. Bracken Lee prepared a statement for Taft to announce to the press. Hardly in a position to admit to having been duped through his own carelessness, Lee's statement said that the manifesto "was signed in good faith for the purpose of appealing to the National Committee to see that everything that was done was above reproach." However, the Governor now pointed out, "by the same token, in fairness to everyone concerned, it is impossible for me to see how you can change long-established rules in the middle of the game." Joining him but also careful not to repudiate what had been done at Houston were Governors Len Jordan of Idaho and Norman Brunsdale of North Dakota.[21]

Their modification was far too late and much too weak. Anybody standing outside the Eisenhower suite at the Blackstone the next morning could tell by the constant flow of delegates around rooms 508 and 510 that the momentum was his. Even some with Taft buttons arrived to greet the General, who was greeting fifteen to twenty delegates going in at a time in relays. Most emerged more convinced than before that the General would be their candidate. Some of the Taft people, too, noted James Reston of the New York *Times*, departed making "distinctly anti-Taft sounds."[22]

The Taft forces were still not ready to concede defeat. Whatever "compromises" were offered, such as their plan for the seating of the Texas delegation, had the distinct aroma of concessions designed to induce an atmosphere that would bring enough harmony to the convention to salvage their important seats from Georgia and Texas. Once more the same maneuver was attempted. After an adjournment that came at 3:45 A.M. on Wednesday morning, allowing just enough time for a nap and breakfast, the Taft forces capitulated on Louisiana as all fifty votes cast by the Credentials Committee favored seating John Minor Wisdom's pro-Eisenhower delegation.

But the acrimony was too intense for such gestures. The Credentials Committee reports on Georgia and Texas became the main business of the convention that Wednesday. For about two hours, late that night, debate over Georgia held the floor. With few exceptions it was clear that Georgia was only a technicality, that the delegates were really arguing over whether they wanted Eisenhower or Taft. Senator Everett M. Dirksen, a fifty-six-year-old Republican from Illinois, took the floor to argue that the Foster delegates from Georgia had been seated by the ruling of a Georgia Superior Court and that Judge Chester A. Byars's decision must now be accepted by the convention, as it had been by the Credentials Committee. With a mastery of dramatic flair, and admonishing the Republican gathering in mellifluous tones, Dirksen urged the convention to "search their hearts" before voting to seat the Eisenhower Georgians.

As his audience responded with appreciation to his warning, the Senator from Illinois turned toward Governor Tom Dewey, who was standing in the aisle, and raised aloft his right arm with a forefinger aimed directly at the New Yorker and said, "We followed you before and you took us down the road to defeat." Then, lowering his carefully modulated tone, he added, "And don't do this to us again."[23] Then, as though the Senator had switched them on, hundreds of Taftites in the International Amphitheater booed and hissed Dewey. The crisis of the 1952 Republicans had reached its most intense point. When order was restored, Dirksen said, "This is no place for Republicans to be booing any other Republicans."[24]

From that point, it was all Eisenhower's. Shortly after midnight Governor Fine announced that he was for the General. When the vote finally came, fifty-one Pennsylvanians voted for Eisenhower, and the Taftites were defeated on the Georgia issue as the convention accepted the minority report of the Credentials Committee 607 to 531. The Warren and Stassen people also helped to secure his victory. The final coup came when a member of the Iowa House of Representatives and a Taft man proposed unanimous approval of the contested pro-Eisenhower Texans led by oilman Jack Porter of Houston. They were then seated by acclamation.[25] The rejection of all compromise offers, including one to seat the Porter faction in exchange for the re-election of Henry Zweifel as Texas GOP national committeeman, had been vindicated.

For the first time the Associated Press reported that Eisenhower was ahead. He had 501 delegates to 485 for Taft, while 109 remained uncommitted and 111 were divided among the other candidates. But the real source of Eisenhower's strength, the item that had defied even the earlier estimates, was his popularity with most of the delegates committed to casting first ballots for Warren or Stassen.

At the same time, Henry Cabot Lodge was presented with a new problem. The Chicago *Daily News* appeared with a report that Richard Nixon, the youthful Senator from California who had won much fame as an anti-Communist as a result of his prominence in the Alger Hiss case and bitter political campaigns in California against Jerry Voorhis and Helen Gahagan Douglas, was Eisenhower's most "probable" running mate. Lodge, reacting as would any campaign manager at a rumor that such a matter had been settled in advance, refuted the report with a statement that there had been no discussion of Vice Presidential candidates in the Eisenhower headquarters.[26] Much more useful, while the battle for the top spot was still incomplete, was the continued speculation that included a variety of personalities, such as MacArthur, Knowland, Dirksen, Driscoll, Warren, along with Nixon. Even Allen B. Kline, president of the American Farm Bureau Federation, was mentioned.[27]

Lodge may have been accurate about the absence of discussion on Vice Presidential candidates in the campaign headquarters, but only on a technicality. He and the others behind the General had been too careful to waste any resource. Their concern with the California delegation inevitably had led to Senator Nixon. Knowland was clearly committed to Warren only through the first ballot; but encounters with the Senator had left little doubt about his preference for Taft, which had been strengthened by his efforts to avoid a showdown vote on the "Fair Play Amendment." Warren, of course, did not merely regard himself as a "favorite son" candidate but as a serious contender with a chance of triumphing in case the two leaders deadlocked. The Eisenhower strategy needed someone on the California delegation who would hold the line for the General, particularly on the crucial seating test. They never believed they could have been as successful had the first roll call involved a direct clash of Eisenhower-Taft strength. Failure to succeed with that assumption would have provided ample evidence that the Taft powers had tied up the convention as well as the national committee. Lodge's political sense then led him to the one man on the California delegation with both influence and tractability—Richard M. Nixon.

The arrangement had been made before the Republicans even reached Chicago. On the Senate floor, in May, the Massachusetts aristocrat suggested the idea to the young Californian. Nixon responded with natural warmth to the notion of being Vice President. Although many ambitious politicians still viewed that office as unrewarding because so few had, in recent American history, gone on to win the Presidential nomination on their own afterward, for Richard Nixon, a thirty-nine-year-old freshman Senator, there were few swifter paths to national prominence. To the others who discussed the subject with him, Nixon gave much the same impression of availability.

That Nixon was more committeed to Eisenhower than to Warren had become quite obvious. Despite his delegation's commitment to their

Governor, Nixon polled 23,000 Californians to learn their favorite man for the Presidency and did not keep secret the results that showed Eisenhower far ahead. After the national committee had voted to seat the Foster delegation from Georgia, it was Nixon who responded with a vigorous denunciation of what he termed the "Texas grab." Late Sunday night and again on Monday it had been Knowland and not Nixon who had urged a settlement without a vote on the convention floor. Nixon was also conspicuously absent from the front lines of the Warren effort in Chicago; from Knowland alone had come continuing predictions of a Warren victory, even after the Eisenhower triumph on the Georgia situation.[28] Those who watched him closely, therefore, understood the pattern even before the Chicago paper carried he story. When asked about the possibility, Nixon offered such comments as "who dreamed that one up" and maintained that he was out of the running. That an observer of the California delegation from the American Political Science Association found no evidence of a Nixon nomination drive inspired by the California delegation was not surprising since the Warren people were still hoping for their Governor's nomination in case of the increasingly likely deadlock with Taft. As the political scientists who scrutinized the delegation observed, "it seemed the better part of political wisdom for the delegation to avoid any commitments or promises to [the] rival groups."[29]

Lodge had informed Eisenhower about his offer to Nixon. The General's response was entirely favorable. Eisenhower was pleasantly surprised to learn that he was only thirty-nine because, even before yielding his NATO command, he had been expressing interest in appealing to American youth, and a Nixon candidacy might be useful as an attraction to young people.[30] So when Eisenhower paid a visit to the California delegation on July 9, during which he was received with considerable enthusiasm, it was with the clear knowledge that the junior Senator, who had been elected to the Senate only two years earlier, had been lined up as his running mate.

But there were other reasons for the arrangement with the man from Whittier, California. Eisenhower, by the time of his return from Europe, and particularly since his Columbia presidency, was regarded as an Eastern candidate. Certainly, during the course of the subsequent campaign, he was to make much of his Denison, Texas, birth and Abilene, Kansas, upbringing, but he very much belonged to the so-called "Eastern Establishment." More important than the geographic accident involved, of course, was his connection with the New York financial circles. And, after all, his chief sponsor, as Everett Dirksen had reminded the convention, was Tom Dewey, the man who had lost in 1948, they said, because he had "me-tooed" instead of slashing at the Democrats.

Perhaps equally essential was Nixon's standing with the party and, in particular, his reputation dating back to the Hiss case as an ardent fighter against communism. Eisenhower, figuring that he would have to deal with Joe McCarthy, gave Nixon a prominent place in his strategy. To him, Nixon had demonstrated the ability to conduct a Congressional investigation "in the American way." Furthermore, unlike the General, there was no question about the legitimacy of Nixon's Republican credentials. If the GOP was about to swallow Ike, it was through desperation because, as a Republican, his standing could not begin to compare with Robert A. Taft. So if the party were now to reject Taft once more, it would be strictly because of "Mr. Republican's" uncertain appeal to the so-called "independents" or casual voter, who, nevertheless, carried sufficient numerical "swing" vote strength to take an election away from the Democrats. And the Republican party, as their representation in the Eighty-second Congress left no doubt, was extremely conservative. *Time* magazine, complaining about Old Guard domination of the convention, was engaging in romanticism—or propaganda—by observing that "The national committee chose to present a face that was not the Republican Party as it is, but the Republican Party as the Democrats say it is."[31]

The fact is that the major speakers chosen for the convention *did* represent the party in 1952. General Douglas MacArthur's keynote speech and addresses by Herbert Hoover, Senator Joe McCarthy and Representative Joe Martin were, in fact, decidedly representative of the GOP. MacArthur, speaking on the opening night, said that a crusade to rechart a course toward peace, security and prosperity would find "an aroused countryside ready and eager to march." Yet, while talking about "peace," the man who little over a year before had been relieved of his Korean command by President Truman assailed what he called a "headlong retreat from victory" after World War II and accused the Administration of failing to pursue policies that would have resulted in "a victory which would not only have discharged our commitment to the Korean people, but which in the long run might well have saved continental Asia from Red domination." The ingredients of the "crusade" to which he called the GOP were purging the American educational system of subversive and immoral influence, restoring youth to its "rightful heritage," raising the dollar to its true value and practicing greater economy in government in order to reduce tax burdens. In fact, he charged that there were "oppressive and arbitrary" controls on business, taxation "which withers initiative, reduces energy and, in the end, destroys the spirit of enterprise." His speech was interrupted by applause scores of times, and the cheers were particularly vehement when he declared that a "party of noble heritage has become captive to the schemers and planners who have infiltrated its ranks of leadership to set the national course unerringly toward the socialistic regimentation of a totalitarian state."[32]

Hoover, in the convention's most effective speech, warned that American efforts at arming Western Europe might result in "the bankruptcy which is Stalin's greatest hope." Even Eisenhower delegates on the floor applauded a statement that was the antithesis of the General's view of American responsibility toward Europe. "The sure defense of London, New York and Paris," added the ex-President, "is the fear of counterattack on Moscow from the air." Furthermore, he charged that the Constitution's words and spirit "have been distorted and violated" during the twenty Democratic years and that what was really at stake in 1952 was the freedom of men, an issue "which transcends all transitory questions of national life." Applause, yells and cheers interrupted him seventy-one times.[33]

When introducing McCarthy, Walter Hallanan explained that "when they tell you Joe McCarthy has smeared names of innocent men, ask them to name just one. Each man exposed has been publicly fired or quietly allowed to leave the government. We will not turn our backs at any time on that fighting Marine, the Honorable Joe McCarthy." McCarthy's speech warned that "We cannot fight Communists or communism in the Acheson–Lattimore fashion of hitting them with a perfumed silk handkerchief at the front door while they batter our friends with brass knuckles and blackjacks at the back door." Then, in a zestful peroration that the crowd loved, McCarthy orated:

I say, one Communist in a defense plant is one Communist too many.
One Communist on the faculty of one university is one Communist too many.
One Communist among American advisers at Yalta was one Communist too many.
And even if there were only one Communist in the State Department that would be one Communist too many.[34]

Martin, the convention's permanent chairman, charged the Administration "with victory in its grasp" in Korea, "apparently decided the best way to win was to lose." He went on to blame the Democrats for "higher deficits, higher debt, higher spending, higher taxes and higher prices." The men who have ruled from Washington for twenty years, he said, have "told us America no longer had a future."[35]

New York *Times* political correspondent Anne O'Hare McCormick observed that the absence of anyone to express General Eisenhower's views was a "notable feature of the convention" and that the "set speeches were obviously keyed to proclaim a policy completely at odds with many of the ideas for which General Eisenhower stands."[36] At least the man now lined up for the Vice Presidency, with an "anti-

Communist" record that was compatible with McCarthy's, was above suspicion. In the anti-Communist climate of the era, exploited as a political weapon by such people as McCarthy, Nixon, Senator William Jenner of Indiana, Senator Styles Bridges of New Hampshire and countless others who regarded nonconformity with their views as heresy, such terms as "pinkos" and "commies" were the icons of respectability. Marty Snyder, for example, Eisenhower's old wartime mess sergeant and the part owner of New York's Headquarters Restaurant, was in Chicago with a sound-equipped car to boost the Eisenhower candidacy. Momentarily stalled by the congested convention-city traffic, Snyder began to exploit the situation by using his microphone to preach the Eisenhower gospel to the other motorists and pedestrians. That prompted a man to step out of a nearby taxi and shout at Snyder, "Why don't you get a red flag?" Snyder recognized him as John Wayne, the Hollywood movie star.[37]

Undoubtedly David S. Ingalls, Taft's cousin and campaign manager, assumed that he was speaking for the party's majority when he circulated a newspaper-size broadside that bore the heading SINK DEWEY!! It also included the following vituperative passages:

TOM DEWEY IS THE MOST COLD-BLOODED, RUTHLESS, SELFISH POLITICAL BOSS IN THE UNITED STATES TODAY. He stops at nothing to enforce his will. His promises are worthless. He is the greatest menace the Republican Party has. Twice he has led us down the road to defeat, and now he is trying the same trick again hidden behind the front of another man.
Behind Tom Dewey is the same old gang of Eastern Internationalists and Republican New Dealers who ganged up to sell the Republican Party down the river in 1940 and in 1944, and in 1948. They are trying it again this year. . . .
Tom Dewey, his machine, and his cold-blooded, self-seeking ruthlessness have meant only sorrow and defeat to the Republican Party. Until and unless Dewey and Deweyism are crushed our party can never win and America can never be made safe from the insidious efforts of the New Dealers, whatever their party label, to take us down the road to socialism and dictatorship.[38]

ISSUED BY
TAFT COMMITTEEE
DAVID S. INGALLS
NATIONAL CHAIRMAN

Doubt about the responsibility for the diatribe was raised later when the Taft people denied that it was their work. The explanation was that Ingalls, as well as Taft and Tom Coleman, had all rejected the broadside, but "it was put over by a conspiracy outside the Taft Committee in spite of the fact that Ingalls's name was signed to it."[39] Nevertheless, there is no evidence that strenuous efforts were made to prevent its distribution; its existence, of course, was another drop of poison in the already embittered clash.

Such serious divisions were submerged, however, when the convention heard Senator Millikin read the draft of the platform put together by his Resolutions Committee. Although Eisenhower later admitted that references to the Democratic twenty-year rule "were in some sections written in purple 'prosecuting-attorney' style,"[40] there was no serious dissent. Inevitably, it contained the usual fiery propaganda of such documents. For example, the preamble contained the extravagant charge that Democratic Administrations, "by a long succession of vicious acts, so undermined the foundations of our Republic as to threaten its existence." Even the charge that the opposition had "national socialism" as its goal may be written off as having become fairly traditional Republican campaign rhetoric. Nevertheless, when Eisenhower made his comment and hinted that the charges about the past were excessive, he concluded that the platform's pledges contained terms that would not place him in a "false position" and so felt free to accept the statement.[41]

With that he also endorsed much that recognized the importance of the party's rightists. Echoing Senator McCarthy, the platform charged that the Democrats "have shielded traitors to the Nation in high places." Later on, in the section on communism, it gave complete sanction to the Wisconsin Senator by saying that "When such infiltrations became notorious through the revelations of Republicans in Congress, the Executive Department stubbornly refused to deal with it openly and vigorously" by crying "red herring" and taking "other measures to block and discredit investigations." A Republican President, it then promised, "will appoint only persons of unquestioned loyalty," after having made the insinuating statement that "There are no Communists in the Republican Party." Its foreign-policy plank, drafted largely by John Foster Dulles, promised that Republican leadership "will repudiate all commitments contained in secret understandings such as those of Yalta which aid Communist enslavement" and, like Dulles's article published in *Life* in May, referred to the containment policy as "negative, futile and immoral," charging that it "abandons countless human beings to a despotism and godless terrorism." Then, pursuing the political objective Dulles thought vital to attracting a large segment of the normally Democratic ethnic vote, it said that a Republican Administration would look "happily forward to the genuine independence of those captive peoples," referring to Latvia, Lithuania, Estonia, Poland and Czechoslovakia, which it had already accused the Democrats of having "abandoned . . . to fend for themselves against Communist aggression which soon swallowed them." A Dulles concern, as well as Eisenhower's, was the en-

dorsement of "collective security forces" for Europe; but, to please a
much larger segment of the party, it renounced any intention of sacrificing the Far East to preserve the West.

The civil-rights plank was pure compromise, designed to be read either way. For conservatives, the states were recognized as having the
primary responsibility for controlling such "domestic institutions."
Then, after having left little room for meaningful action, there was a
declaration that "the Federal Government should take supplemental action
within its constitutional jurisdiction to oppose discrimination against
race, religion or national origin." Singled out for areas of possible correction, all of which were no longer seriously disputed by 1952, were
lynching, poll taxes and desegregating the District of Columbia. The
most gingerly handling was reserved for the controversial question of
federal action to outlaw discrimination in employment. It called for such
legislation by coupling the statement with the warning that such action
"should not duplicate state efforts to end such practices; should not set
up another huge bureaucracy."

Of most importance to General Eisenhower, however, was that the
platform had rejected isolationism. Dulles, who had drafted the foreign-policy plank so that it could be acceptable to either of the two most
likely candidates, had been careful to do just that. When he had met
with Eisenhower in Paris about three weeks before the General left his
European command, he had been disturbed by Eisenhower's preoccupation with NATO's needs.[42] In gaining acceptance for strong language
against abandoning the Far East to communism, Dulles appeased critics
of collective action in Europe. Those closest to the General were convinced that failure to write a platform devoid of isolationist rhetoric
would lead to his rejection of the nomination.

The Presidential nominating session, which was held on Friday, July
11, was anti-climactic. Yet, down to the final moments, there was talk of
coalition efforts to stop Ike. With Hoover having formally announced
for Taft, the Ohioan seemed more and more determined to do anything
to prevent an Eisenhower victory, even if he had to lose. Taft hastened
to separate meetings with Warren and Stassen; both said they were
remaining in the race. Rumors that the anti-Eisenhower forces might be
desperate enough to strengthen their opposition by combining forces
behind another general were inspired by a long-distance telephone call
Taft made to MacArthur in New York.[43]

Stassen and Warren also saw their opportunities. Both men were determined to remain as viable candidates pending the success of any efforts
to stop Eisenhower. Stassen, now seeing a chance for himself, resisted all
pressures within his Minnesota delegation to declare for Eisenhower.
Releasing his forces to the General would have been in fulfillment of his
verbal and written commitment that had been made in December. Only

if Eisenhower could not get the nomination, he had agreed, would he move for himself with the delegates he had denied the opposition. Now, however, unable to resist the mirage of success, he did whatever he could to thwart the other man's chances. Most of Thursday he spent in his hotel room before two tiers of a dozen telephones doing everything he could to head off the Eisenhower drive.

Stassen's own delegation was at the point of rebellion. Its chairman, Senator Edward Thye, had calculated that Eisenhower was just eight to twelve votes short of a first-ballot nomination. Minnesota could easily deliver that number. Failure to win for Eisenhower on that ballot could, Thye feared, bring unpredictable results during the subsequent rounds. Aware of considerable pressure by others from his state to have Stassen release them, Thye called a caucus of the Minnesota people early Thursday morning, and Stassen was invited to attend. Removing from his pocket the tabulation showing how the pro-Eisenhower vote could be expected to go, Thye warned Stassen that it would be dangerous to permit the voting to continue beyond the first ballot without a victory by the General. Should the balloting proceed according to such expectations, Thye said, he would ask for recognition from the floor of the convention for a switch to Ike. But Stassen objected. He had, he explained, greater strength than he was being credited with and maintained that Thye had overestimated Eisenhower's.

Meanwhile, Minnesota delegate Warren Burger attempted to coordinate his delegation's contemplated shift with the Warren-committed Californians. He approached the chairman of the big West Coast state's delegation, Senator Knowland, and suggested that the inevitability of the Eisenhower victory made the interest of party harmony a primary concern. Therefore, why not strengthen the candidate's prestige by having the Minnesota and California delegations both give him their votes and thus help to create a substantial margin of victory? But the Senator merely replied, "We don't want any credit or any responsibility for *that* nomination."[44]

Nevertheless, after Minnesota had given Stassen nineteen votes, the conclusion of the first ballot showed Eisenhower with 595 votes, only nine away from victory, while Taft had only 500. Shortly after noon, after a cry of "Minnesota" had arisen from the galleries, Harold Stassen, emotional and puzzled at having received just twenty votes, capitulated. Senator Thye then signaled to Joe Martin, who was the convention's permanent chairman. In the confusion that followed, Martin called the name of Warren Burger because the Minnesota lawyer was nearby trying to call his attention to Thye's request. The recognition of Thye then gave the Republican party's Presidential nomination to Dwight D. Eisenhower. When additional switches were counted, the nominee's total reached 841, and Senators Bricker and Knowland moved to make the choice unanimous but were thwarted by a scattering of "no's" from the floor.[45]

Within a half hour, the new nominee had reversed the usual order of protocol. The normal procedure was for the winners to receive visits from their less fortunate opponents; this time, however, those in the Eisenhower suite of the Blackstone Hotel, including Paul Hoffman, were startled to see the General emerge from his room with his brother Arthur. Arthur was apparently trying to dissuade Ike from going through with his plan to telephone Senator Taft; that precedent would be broken was the major argument. But the General persisted, using his private switchboard to reach the Senator. After a brief conversation, he walked out into the crowd, inched his way across the jammed street, aided by a police guard, and entered the Conrad Hilton.[46]

Facing Taft, who had his sons with him, Eisenhower expressed the desire for friendship and hoped they would be able to work together.

"My only problem for the moment," said Taft, in his usual business-like manner, "is that for the twenty minutes it took you to get over here I have been bombarded by requests from photographers for a picture. Would you be willing to have one taken?"

Before the TV cameras the defeated Senator, normally a reserved personality, stood with what Arthur Krock thought was "dignity and graciousness" and so "demeaned himself that one watcher at least thought that this was his finest hour."[47] Then the visit ended. When Senator Bricker then announced that Taft would be ready to give his "unlimited and active support" to the new candidate, Eisenhower replied that he could not carry out his program without Taft's cooperation.

Only the formality of choosing the Vice Presidential candidate remained. That was done in Herb Brownell's Conrad Hilton office, where some twenty-five men gathered to evaluate a short "eligible list" that Eisenhower had prepared. Nixon's name was first. Behind him were such possibilities as Charles Halleck, William Knowland, Walter Judd and Dan Thornton. Serious consideration was also given to Governor Alfred Driscoll of New Jersey. The possibility of selecting Taft never got very far because they agreed he would be much more valuable in the Senate. When Senator Carlson reported that Taft would like to see Dirksen on the ticket, the sharpest opposition came not from the "Eastern Internationalists," as the Chicago *Tribune* later charged, but from Iowa and Colorado. Iowa's Governor William S. Beardsley said, "All I have to say is that after what Dirksen said the other night, the people of Iowa wouldn't use him to wipe their feet on." Dan Thornton voiced a similar but milder sentiment. But the Nixon "suggestion" received "a tremendously favorable response" and every hand rose for him.[48]

The "selection" was remarkably rapid. In great contrast with the start of the convention, Senator Knowland's nominating speech for his colleague from California was followed by no controversy. What had actually been decided, in effect, long before the convention had begun was given the politically necessary appearance of a judicious choice of the "best man" for the second spot. Eisenhower's memoirs recount the usual reasons given for the selection; but the most compelling consideration of strategy that led to the choice of the thirty-nine-year-old Senator and thus to place him on a line that led to the White House sixteen years later was omitted from the General's account. However, Dr. Milton Eisenhower has conceded that, on the choice of Nixon, his brother "was pretty much guided by the advice of the people who had been in politics for a great many years."[49] Mrs. Nixon, formerly Thelma Ryan, then answered reporters' questions by saying how surprised she was by her husband's selection.[50]

Both candidates appeared before a hysterical convention that night, a moment when nobody in the International Amphitheater doubted that the Democrats were finally on their way out of Washington. If not, Republicans would lose more than just their candidate.

Mamie Eisenhower and Pat Nixon were with their husbands. The Field Artillery march, "The Caisson Song," filled the huge hall near the stockyards; then, as Mamie stood by her husband at the microphone, the music changed to "Dixie."

"We want Ike!" the crowd chanted. "We want Ike!"

"If you keep quiet," Joe Martin shouted, "I'll give him to you."

Gradually, the tumult stilled and the party's Presidential candidate delivered his acceptance speech.

"I know something of the solemn responsibility of leading a crusade," he told them. "I accept your summons. I will lead this crusade." He called for an end to the "wastefulness, the arrogance and corruption in high places, the heavy burdens and the anxieties which are the bitter fruit of a party too long in power." With the crowd roaring its approval, the General then vowed a "program of progressive policies, drawn from our finest Republican traditions; to unite us wherever we have been divided; to strengthen freedom wherever among any group it has been weakened; to build a sure foundation for sound prosperity for all here at home, and for a just and sure peace throughout our world." Then he was Ike Eisenhower, the Supreme Commander, as he told his fellow Republicans that "Since this morning I have had helpful and heartwarming talks with Senator Taft, Governor Warren and Governor Stassen. I want them to know, as I want you now to know, that in the hard fight ahead we will work intimately together." He concluded by asking for the "prayers of all our people and the blessing and guidance of Almighty God."[51]

Now that he had the party's nomination, he needed the party.

Party Realities

In RETROSPECT, THE certainty of the Eisenhower victory undoubtedly made the election a *pro forma* exercise. Some have even suggested that the results would have been virtually unchanged even if the two candidates had delivered each other's speeches, that the public saw the candidate as a heroic anti-war general and a football-coachlike political amateur with far more concern for honor, morality and dignity than personal ambition. Such thinking recognized that his party had chosen to gain an inevitable triumph rather than risk the candidacy of their real favorite, the safe conservative who was so representative of Republicans in the Eighty-second Congress. The common cliché was that "nobody could have beaten Ike."

Those realities became far more obvious once the returns were in that November night; but while the campaign was on, even the Eisenhower leadership was not regarded as invincible. After the spectacular Truman upset of 1948, few could dare be overconfident again. Furthermore, the country was still overwhelmingly Democratic. The Great Depression Generation constituted the majority vote. Notions that the General was merely a captive of big business might frighten them from placing a Republican in the White House. There was also the reality of Eisenhower's political inexperience. The tendency among those within the Eisenhower camp, therefore, was to underestimate his strength and worry that Stevenson's cultivated speeches would appeal to the mass of voters.[1]

In many ways they were right. While the General did have an instinctive sense of what was politic, he had never waged a political campaign. Expediency having forced him upon the party—which was still not

entirely certain he was one of them—it remained to be seen whether the
Old Guard would work for him or whether they would, as Senator
William Jenner of Indiana suggested to a colleague, forget about the
Presidency and concentrate on electing a Republican Congress. Another
Dewey-like campaign, the Eisenhower brass reasoned, would be fatal.
Dewey, for his part, adhered to his determination to avoid close associa-
tion with the campaign.[2] When the Republican National Committee
held a secret strategy session they decided that the "me-too" approach,
designed to lure the independent voters, had to be jettisoned for an all-
out effort to attract the "stay-at-homes," who were far more numerous.[3]

More than anything else, this consideration also determined Eisenhower's response to an offer from President Truman. Although it came
after he had already so accommodated the Democratic candidate, the
President's proposal was consistent with the finest patriotic interests. It
was, in fact, a unique effort to further the best interests of the country
by facilitating an orderly transition of government. The handling of the
Korean war and America's other international involvements, as well as
the domestic economy, warranted the kind of preparations that had not
always been quite so urgent in the past. That the Truman Administration may have been embarrassed into the move was only incidental. It
was far more important that the President's plan was eminently consistent with the non-partisan national needs Eisenhower had continually
espoused.

The Truman proposal invited Eisenhower to a luncheon with the
President and his cabinet. There Eisenhower would also receive a briefing of the foreign situation from his old aide and associate, CIA Director
General Walter Bedell Smith, and a report on the situation in the White
House from the entire Executive Department staff. The Truman offer
also included the sending of weekly CIA briefing reports to each major
party candidate.[4]

But Eisenhower's wired response of August 14 reflected the deep antagonism that was developing between the two men, marking a continuous
deterioration in their relations since Truman's most recent offer to the
General of the Democratic candidacy during their White House discussion in November of 1951. The reply left the President convinced that
the Republican candidate had surrendered his purity to the wiles of "the
politicians."[5] While agreeing to receive the periodic CIA reports, Eisenhower rejected the rest of the President's offer. His excuse stated that no
"grave emergency" required such a course, and he declared it his "duty
to remain free to analyze publicly the policies and acts of the present
administration whenever it appears to me to be proper and in the country's interests."[6] Seeing through this transparent position, since the arrangement would in no way have bound the candidates from freedom to

criticize policies, the petulant President responded that the General had evidently made a mistake by allowing a "bunch of screwballs to come between us."[7]

Truman, of course, was correct in ascribing the response to political motivations. His charge, however, anticipated a reaction to Eisenhower that would become even more characteristic of such criticism: that the General had been misled by advisers. It was a point that assumed the inability of the war's most political general to perceive the realistic dangers of risking further association with the most important Democrat. That he was not an apostate, in the first place—as Willkie had been—was already a defensive argument. The Old Guardsmen, the Taftites, after all, had been the firmest accepters of the Arthur Krock account of how Truman had again offered him the Presidency. Therefore, the Eisenhower rejection called attention to avoidance of hints that there could be any private understanding with the other party. "I believe our communications," Eisenhower said in his public response to Truman, "should be only those which are known to all the American people."[8] Early the following week, moreover, in a personal letter to the President, Eisenhower explained that such an arrangement would have required elaborate explanations to the public.[9] Significantly, the 1952 campaign gradually alienated the President from both Eisenhower and Governor Stevenson, who offended Mr. Truman's pride by ignoring him and dignifying the "mess in Washington" by an unfortunate response to a challenge on that issue and by moving his campaign headquarters out of the capital and to Springfield, Illinois.

There was a real danger of repeating Wendell Willkie's experiences of 1940. The Eisenhower pre-convention drive had also been propelled throughout the country by political amateurs working at the grass-roots level. The Citizens for Eisenhower groups, organized by two youthful businessmen, Charles F. Willis, Jr., and Stanley Rumbough, had provided a means for such popular participation. However, just as with Jack Porter's well-publicized Texans, the Citizens were also a "non-partisan" haven to Democrats. Nevertheless, intramural resentments and the inability to coordinate the amateurs with the "regulars" would drive new wounds into sensitive flesh.

Their start was encouraging. The nation's press, both Democratic and Republican papers, embraced the Eisenhower candidacy as the palliative for the postwar troubles of America. All worth preserving, the two-party system, integrity, the popular will, freedom and peace had become identified as Republican objectives.

The New York *Times*, which had started the month with a persuasive three-installment editorial called "Mr. Taft Can't Win,"[10] exulted that if the GOP's Old Guard is thrown out once and for all, the "Republican revolution will have been successfully accomplished."[11] The *Herald Tribune* agreed that the party had a great opportunity "for its mission of leading America in a period of growing strength, fresh purpose and dedication to the goal of peace. Rarely has so great an opportunity opened before Republicans." Concluding that the GOP had chosen its "ablest and most popular candidate," the Pittsburgh *Post Gazette* emphasized that it "decisively turned its back on Old Guard reaction." The Atlanta *Constitution* rejoiced that the GOP had "voted itself into the future" by rejecting the "extreme reactionary isolationist wing of the party," while the Chattanooga *Times* hoped that "the effort to turn back social welfare to the Nineteenth Century will lose its force." The New Orleans *Times-Picayune* saw the workings of justice in having Taft "overwhelmed by a man whom so many Americans had come to associate with the simple virtues of integrity, fair-dealing and the humility which would allow him to seek the nomination only if he believed the people wanted him."

Others, however, were more concerned with the ability of the party to govern if it did not consolidate all factions and remain representative of diversity. Inevitably, they were optimistic that Republicans had chosen the one man with the talent for such an assignment. The Philadelphia *Evening Bulletin* recalled the General's "outstanding success in harmonizing discordant views among influential people having the most serious reasons to disagree" during the war and saw no reason why he should fail to repeat that achievement at home. "Mr. Eisenhower's nomination," proclaimed the Newark *Evening News*, "bails the party out of an untenable position." Such highly conservative forces of journalism as the Hearst papers, for example, although they would have preferred Taft or even MacArthur, expressed the hope that "the men and women who were Taft adherents will . . . put aside rancor and bitterness of defeat." The New York *Daily News*, barely recovering from the shocking events in Chicago, acknowledged that its major interest was in avoiding "four more years of Fair Deal creeping fascism and socialism, warmongering, inflation and excessive taxation," and concluded that any "Republican President . . . would be better for the country in the next four years than virtually any Democratic Mr. Big."[12]

But Colonel McCormick's gloom resulted in the following words from the Tribune Tower in Chicago:

> Some doubts and misgivings are finding expression in the wake of the maneuver by which Eisenhower got the fifty-five delegates from Texas and Georgia, without whose votes the general would not have been nominated. Those who visited their calumnies upon Senator Taft, an honest man, are uneasy about it all. We note that the New York *Times*, a New Deal organ, finds it necessary to beg for fair play in behalf of Governor Dewey, who

was properly put on the spot by Senator Dirksen in front of the whole nation. Mr. Dewey is at best a contemptible person, animated chiefly by the desire to spoil things for Senator Taft, out of the evident fear that if Taft ever had his chance before the people he would make Dewey look as sick as Truman. The shame of the methods used in behalf of Eisenhower at this convention is not something that can be scrubbed off with a quick shower.[13]

The Chicago *Tribune*'s vindictiveness was precisely what the General aimed to overcome. To him, the right wing, the disappointed, the disfranchised represented elements without which no campaign could possibly succeed. Meeting with the newly reconstituted National Committee on the day after the nomination, the General (who also announced his formal resignation from the Army that day) said he would regard them as his "general staff" and volunteered his desire to avoid Willkie's errors. Arthur E. Summerfield, the national committeeman from Michigan, was chosen as the new national chairman of the party to replace the fallen Guy Gabrielson. Summerfield, it was learned, was attempting to enlist Taft's floor manager for the convention, Tom Coleman, as "campaign director." Eisenhower had also met with Coleman that day, as well as with seventy-one Republican Congressmen.[14]

Since Henry Cabot Lodge had to attend to his own campaign for reelection in Massachusetts, Summerfield was appointed as the director of the Eisenhower effort, although the candidate himself was tentatively listed as his own campaign manager. Arthur H. Vandenberg, Jr., the son of the well-known late Senator from Michigan, was named as the executive assistant in charge of personnel. Ex-Dewey aide Thomas E. Stephens was placed in charge of appointments, and James C. Hagerty, the Governor's press secretary, replaced Robert Mullen for the General. Senators Frank Carlson of Kansas and Fred Seaton of Nebraska were also appointed as special advisers.[15] Despite the complexion of the Eisenhower staff, the press was told that the campaign would not be run by those who had directed the Dewey bids of 1944 and 1948 and that it would be "managed in a considerably different manner."[16]

The composition of Eisenhower's staff was, in truth, his most overt concession to those responsible for his nomination. In other ways the candidate placated the opposition and chastised those whose partisanship ignored priorities. Speaking in language acceptable to everybody, he said he hoped to bring a "message of militant faith and hope to the American people" rather than announce the details of any specific program. Turning to the reporters gathered for his departure from the convention city, he spoke the language that would become familiar to the American people during the coming years. "I'm not eloquent," he said. "I wish I were eloquent—but I am sincere. I hope to bring a message of militant faith and hope to the American people in what they have got the capacity to do, gol darn it, rather than go into details of a specific program."[17]

Three days later, from the Brown Palace Hotel in Denver, Eisenhower showed annoyance with the partisan zeal that, according to an interview carried in the Pasadena *Star News*, had been displayed by his good friend Paul Hoffman. "I do want to point out," Ike wrote to Hoffman, "that in our struggle to keep the crusade moving along and to insure its success in November, we should avoid pouring salt in the wounds of the defeated. In every conversation and in public statements," he reminded the director of the Ford Foundation, "I am careful to see that the principles on which we fought out this campaign are all restated and re-emphasized." He also explained that, once those had been accepted, "I then do my best to enlist the support of those who have been on the other side of the fence—or sitting on the fence. Speaking generally, I believe this the clearly indicated course of action. I trust you agree." With only minor changes the letter could have been a reprimand from the SHAEF or SHAPE commander.[18]

Having gone to Mamie's home town and having established temporary campaign headquarters on the second floor of the old, ornate and plush Brown Palace Hotel, he continued the major task of organizing his soldiers for the crusade. The most dramatic overture yet made to the opposition within his own party came in the form of a telegram sent by Eisenhower on July 15 to Representative Edward H. Jenison. Jenison, a Republican candidate up for re-election from the heavily pro-Taft state of Illinois, was given the General's complete endorsement. Going beyond that, however, the Presidential candidate promised to give his "wholehearted support" to all other GOP contestants. He also pledged to "leave nothing undone that will rejuvenate, invigorate and strengthen the Republican party from Coast to Coast and from north to south." Appealing to all Republican campaign workers, he urged that they put their "shoulders to the wheel" and "pound the sidewalks" to "knock on doors" and work "endless hours" in an all-out campaign to elect the entire Republican ticket in all parts of the country. Such an effort, he wrote, was necessary in support of his "crusade" to "save the essentials of America." "In any contest," Eisenhower added, "it is real fighters who provide the difference between victory and defeat. In the present one they are the bulwark against every assault upon American ideals and principles."[19]

On July 17, the Presidential candidate drove seventy-two miles west of Denver for a week's stay at the ranch of Aksel Nielsen at Fraser, Colorado, an 8,700-foot-high settlement at the western slope of the Continental Divide. Nielsen was an old friend of the Eisenhower family. Added to that attraction was an excellent place for trout fishing on

Nielson's 1,900-acre cattle ranch. Joining the General were assistants on leave from the Denver headquarters to formulate the basic plans for the campaign.

From there the General exuded detached confidence across the front pages of America's newspapers. Almost daily stories appeared about his trout fishing, painting and outdoor cooking. As to the Democratic convention, which was about to open in Chicago, the press was told the General planned to give it little attention until his rival had been chosen.[20] The news that he had, in addition to his other outdoor activities, finished four oil paintings in less than a week substantiated his casual attitude. When Senator Paul Douglas of Illinois told the Democratic convention that Eisenhower, as Chief of Staff, had been one of those responsible for encouraging the North Koreans to drive south of the Thirty-eighth Parallel by recommending the withdrawal of American troops from South Korea, Eisenhower's press secretary, Jim Hagerty, replied that the vacationing General would make no statement. He had, said Hagerty, gone fishing and was totally out of touch with events in Chicago.[21]

At the same time, the Eisenhower campaign strategy began to take shape. Sherman Adams, who had managed the General's forces on the floor of the International Amphitheater, was called to Colorado and induced to become his "chief of staff." The job of "liaison officer" with the national committee was also added to his chores.[22] Rather than appoint a separate campaign manager or personal campaign director, tradition was followed by making Arthur Summerfield, the new chairman of the national committee, double as campaign manager. In addition to pursuing the independent and Taft vote, as well as getting the stay-at-homes, the candidate's office also reported that the General would reject the usual Republican custom of ignoring the Solid South. A swing through the whole area, especially Texas, was being planned.

There was ample reason for optimism about breaking the Democratic hold over the South. Before the end of July fifty-four newspapers in the traditionally Solid South had endorsed Eisenhower or had indicated they had such plans.[23] Not only had there been support within the states involved in the convention seating battle, but such key figures as Texas Governor Allan Shivers and Virginia's patriarchal Democratic power Senator Harry Byrd were known friends of his candidacy. After the Democrats had rejected Tennessee Senator Estes Kefauver and nominated President Truman's choice, Governor Adlai E. Stevenson of Illinois, more than one disappointed Southern supporter of the Senator announced for Eisenhower. In telegrams to Senator James Duff and Jack Porter, for example, the publisher of the Longview (Texas) *News and Journal* said, "As soon as I can get rid of the New Deal fleas I picked up over the country during the last six months I want to start doing what I can to elect Dwight D. Eisenhower."[24]

In contrast to the promises of action emanating from the various Eisenhower headquarters was the continued nonchalance in Fraser. Enjoying his trout fishing and painting, the General extended his holiday to ten days. A visit from his running mate on July 27 resulted in newspaper pictures of Eisenhower demonstrating to Nixon the proper way to catch trout. The portrait of conviviality was furthered by reports that the General, aided by Master Sergeant Leonard Dry, prepared the dinner by cooking a fourteen-pound joint of Colorado beef that had been contributed by Governor Thornton. More germane politically, however, was Eisenhower and Nixon's first opportunity to become acquainted.[25]

Eisenhower's caution had not infected his running mate. Nixon, even while telling reporters he would first have to steep himself in the General's philosophy, nevertheless assumed the offensive early. Three days after their nomination he promised they would work for "an effective and fair program for dealing with subversives in government." He added that he had found "as many Democrats as Republicans disgusted with the way the Administration kissed off and pooh-poohed the Communist threat at home."[26] Only four days after his Colorado meeting with Eisenhower, Nixon spoke in Columbus, Ohio, and denounced Stevenson as the candidate of Jack Kroll, the director of the CIO Political Action Committee, which was widely reputed as supporting left-wing candidates. But the greatest handicap of the Democrat, Nixon told the Ohio state convention, was that "he is Harry Truman's candidate."[27] At the Illinois State Fair, two weeks later, Nixon challenged Stevenson to repudiate "Trumanism." Jibing at his opponent's literate speeches, Nixon demanded that Stevenson "tell where he stands in simple, down-to-earth language we can understand."[28] Also appealing to his party's right wing, he called the Administration's record in the Far East an obvious major issue in the campaign and asked Stevenson to reject Dean Acheson's foreign policy.[29] Even before the campaign had become very serious Nixon's function was very clear.

Having Nixon on the ticket was, of course, important for Eisenhower's attraction to the dissident Taftites. Of greater concern, however, was the future course of the embittered followers of the Senator. Everett Dirksen, for one, regarded Taft's defeat as a political disaster, not only for the country but for himself personally. His outburst at Dewey, after he had placed Taft in nomination, had made him a controversial figure. When the Eisenhower people caucused immediately after the General's nomination to confirm the choice of Nixon as his running mate, Senator Taft called to say he preferred to see Dirksen as the Vice Presidential candidate; but by then that would have been an unthinkable maneuver for the nominee's strategists, even if there had been no prior agreement with Nixon.[30]

During the two weeks after the Chicago affair, the Senator from Illinois was uncharacteristically reticent. As a prominent Taftite and also as the chairman of the Republican Senatorial Campaign Committee, his support was of great concern to the Eisenhower camp. On July 21 he said he would work for Eisenhower; yet even that statement was vitiated by his expression of primary concern for the election of Republicans to the Senate.[31] As an aftermath, he addressed his state's American Legion convention on August 1 and failed even to mention the General's name and, instead, attacked the Truman Administration's European policies, a matter closely identified with Eisenhower.[32] By that time Senator Hugh Butler of Nebraska, responding to Eisenhower's invitation, had visited with the candidate in Denver and had gone away telling the press that the General had his complete support.[33] When a similar invitation was sent to Dirksen, to meet at Denver with the other party leaders in the formulation of campaign plans, the Illinois Senator's afirmative reply was delayed until just two days before the scheduled meeting. Upon his arrival he said he was "without animus or bile" and was appointed to Eisenhower's six-man board of strategy. But, as his biographer has noted, "there was something less than enthusiasm in Dirksen for the man who had defeated Taft and thus also deprived Dirksen of his fling at national office."[34]

Other attempts were made in the direction of conciliation. Eisenhower spent most of Monday, August 4, meeting with additional pro-Taft people. Senator Karl Mundt of South Dakota, for example, was made a co-director with Representative Charles Halleck of Indiana of the party's Speakers Bureau for the campaign. He also held a secret meeting with former Senator C. Wayland Brooks. Brooks, the newly elected Republican national committeeman for Illinois, was known as a close political associate of Colonel Robert McCormick.[35] A liberal fortnightly, *The Reporter*, which had been warm toward the Eisenhower candidacy, wondered, "How much of his energy will Eisenhower have to devote to preventing the Taft-MacArthur wing of the party from again trying to pull it down to oblivion."[36] Another need was to harmonize the Citizens for Eisenhower groups with the regulars. Early in August, while the Denver headquarters was still in operation, the General agreed to retain the separate identity of the Citizens organization.

Willis and Rumbough were obscure businessmen who were unhappy with the continuing Democratic Administrations. Hoping to organize public opinion so that its impact could be directed toward convincing the General to run, they had put up some four or five thousand dollars of their own capital and opened a rented loft at 1426 Willow Avenue in

Hoboken, New Jersey. That location was selected because Tom Stephens and other professionals had advised that New York "was a dirty word, as far as the rest of the country was concerned." The office was furnished largely with the assistance of Jack Straus, the president of R. H. Macy's, who made a loan of the necessary furniture. They worked at distributing all the available pro-Ike literature, including magazine reprints, and ultimately succeeded in organizing over eight hundred "I Like Ike" clubs in thirty-eight states. They also helped organize the Madison Square Garden rally of February 1952. Of greatest value was their identification as political amateurs not connected with either party, an arrangement that was congenial for Democrats and independents.

After the General had agreed to run, the structure that Willis and Rumbough had organized received its "Citizens for Eisenhower" title, and its over-all direction was placed under Henry Cabot Lodge. The purely volunteer organization gradually became staffed with a number of salaried workers. Lodge named Arthur Vandenberg, Jr., as the chairman and Jock Whitney as the financial head, with the two founders as assistants to the chairman. Vandenberg was later replaced by Paul Hoffman, and then Walter Williams joined the organization.[37]

The post-convention meeting at Denver included Willis and Rumbough as well as the campaign organization under Summerfield. Fearing a future division of authority and a loss of power, particularly of patronage—as had happened in the past—the national committee pressed for placing the Citizens under their control. The amateurs, contending that that would compromise their appeal to the Democrats and independents, threatened to remain autonomous without any coordination with the rest of the campaign.[38] They won their point, and, from that time, the Citizens, under the direction of Walter Williams and Mary Oswald Lord, had a relatively free hand. The decision had the complete approval of the candidate, whose brief exposure to partisan politics had already taught him to favor the idealistic amateurs over what he perceived were self-seeking Old Guardsmen.[39]

For the balance of the campaign, the Citizens managed to coordinate their efforts with the work being done by the regulars. Their greatest difficulties came during the early weeks when many of the professionals still suspected Eisenhower's credentials as a Republican. In several instances the hostility was open. Difficulty, for example, was encountered in Chicago. A parade staged by the Citizens was stopped by the police, and further investigation showed that the roadblock was ordered not by Mayor Ed Kelly's Democrats but by the regular Republican organization. Their subsequent defiance of such intimidation, however, succeeded largely because the police were sympathetic toward the Eisenhower cause. Other troubles traceable to the regulars were experienced in Kansas City and Cincinnati. Aside from such incidents, they were instrumental in providing a basic organizational stronghold in areas where the Republican party was either weak or nonexistent. Wherever independents and Democrats were more numerous, the Citizens were stronger than the professionals. To the Citizens also fell the task of organizing branches based on ethnic or special-interest lines. So the campaign had its "Jews for Eisenhower," "German-Americans for Eisenhower," "Doctors for Eisenhower," "Lawyers for Eisenhower," etc. Particularly active and present in each strategic city and town was the local "Youth for Eisenhower," one of the most important groups.[40]

The Citizens also became adept at preparing cities for visits by the candidate. Starting with an Eisenhower visit to Houston, an advance team that arrived in the city rented a fleet of fifteen or sixteen tractor-trailers. Each was a self-contained unit with loudspeakers that could play such campaign songs as "I Love the Sunshine of Your Smile," a crew of girls wearing special wired-for-sound Ike dresses, relief drivers and two big barrage balloons. The balloons, with the words "I Like Ike," were hoisted above the trucks at the site of an Eisenhower speech. As the campaign progressed, the General would look forward to their presence as an indication that the advance team had prepared for his reception. One balloon had even been hoisted outside Colonel McCormick's *Tribune* windows in Chicago, but it was soon downed with a twenty-two rifle. That night it was patched up and airborne the next morning when the Colonel arrived in his office.[41]

Yet, as the summer progressed, there seemed to be a strange malaise from the man who headed the ticket. His call for a "crusade" began to seem vague. Reminiscent of Willkie's isolation at the Broadmoor Hotel at Colorado Springs in 1940, Eisenhower remained out of the firing line by staying close to his eighth-floor suite at the Brown Palace Hotel. When Nixon appeared with Arthur Summerfield at Columbus on July 31, Ohio's national committee woman, Katherine Kennedy Brown, complained about Eisenhower's silence. Alluding to Dewey as the man in real control, she said that Eisenhower "must divest himself of his shackles."[42] In a day letter to Paul Hoffman, Senator Flanders noted that "it becomes increasingly clear that Eisenhower can win only if he reaches the hearts of the American people. This he can do but will he? I remain on the anxious seat and want to get off."[43]

The evidence shows the extent of Eisenhower's own discouragement. Writing from the Brown Palace Hotel to General J. Lawton ("Joe") Collins, he described his disposition by conceding the possibility that "some day I shall conclude that I made a mistake in allowing myself to be drawn into the political whirlpool. However, that is past history—and

Mamie and I both are determined to give our best to the task that lies before us," he wrote to his friend. "It is not easy; we simply never allow ourselves to think of the serene, peaceful life that could be ours if I had not allowed friends and others to persuade me as to my public duty back in 1949, '50 or '51. Or indeed, if the fates had decided differently in Chicago."[44]

Further discouragement came the very day he wrote that letter. Speaking before the annual encampment of the Veterans of Foreign Wars at Los Angeles, where he presented a ten-point program to "win a just and lasting peace" and provide the domestic front with "a prosperity not based on war," he faced a crowd that was estimated at no larger than sixteen thousand. The event was held in the Los Angeles Coliseum with a seating capacity of one hundred thousand. Thus he spoke to "acres of empty seats, and his voice echoed in the big concrete bowl" as he called for a reinvigoration of America's "spiritual, creative and material" strength.[45]

Those blaming Dewey for Eisenhower's failure to hit hard often spoke for local popular consumption, not unlike Dirksen's theatrics at the convention. For some, it seemed a confirmation of a suspicious New Deal-type liberalism that prevented him from "sounding like a Republican" and reciting the party's catechism. Very few remembered what the General had said in Galveston back in 1949. After having described prison as the best place for security, he had warned that "if an American wants to preserve his dignity and his equality as a human being, he must not bow his neck to any dictatorial government."[46] To the son of one of his former West Point instructors, Eisenhower wrote from Colorado: "Next to war perhaps the greatest threat to our security arises from statism and its attendant bureaucracy. To overthrow this tendency is one of the principal aims of my candidacy."[47] With all this Taft was in agreement; but the General would have been less likely to have gone along with the Senator's advocacy of a federal program to provide for low-cost public housing.

Eisenhower also knew the value of patience. That August he indicated several times that the real fight would begin with the traditional Labor Day speeches. He and his aides realized the danger of hitting a high point prematurely. More than any of those around him, he was also well aware of the risk to his popular image if he appeared too eager for the job, if his tone was too reminiscent of other politicians. He thus viewed himself as a purveyor of lofty moral principles, as a man dedicated to the "middle of the road" where most Americans stood, to conserving traditional values and safeguards but not undoing the social and economic changes of the past two decades. He could do nothing, he knew, without retaining and enlarging his mass following. So when he faced a crowd of nineteen thousand at Boise, Idaho, during one of his side trips away from Denver, he pointed out that what had already been achieved would continue to be supported by Americans of both parties. However, he added, they were not the final goals but rather the "solid floor" upon which a better life could be built by private incentives. "Now we have had for a long time a Government that applies the philosophy of the Left to government," he said. "The Government will build the power dams, the Government will tell you how to distribute your power, the Government will do this and that. The Government does everything but come in and wash dishes for the housewife." That would be as extreme as he would get; it would be the crux of his domestic attack. In Kansas City, the next day, he rejected the role of a politician who would campaign behind what he called "manufactured words" such as "Trumanism" or "Pendergastism." Nor would he stoop to labeling an asserted evil in government by linking it with any person's name.[48] Shrewdly, he was making a grand distinction between himself and his political-creature running mate, Senator Nixon, to whom such terms as "Trumanism" and the linking of prominent names with the weakening of American security were already daily expressions. The more visible the politicians, the sharper the contrast.

Nevertheless, his understanding of the realities of American political life, which he seemed to grasp almost instinctively, was not appreciated by some of his most ardent supporters. Having brought up to the front lines their biggest gun ever in the battle against the spendthrift heirs of the New Deal, they were eager for salvo after salvo to smash the enemy's citadels. On August 25 many of the papers of the Scripps-Howard chain, which had supported the General before the Chicago convention, ran an editorial called "Ike, When Do We Start?" Appearing on the front page of the New York *World Telegram and The Sun* was the following complaint:

> We trust Dwight Eisenhower doesn't think that what he has been doing and saying this last month can classify as campaigning for office. . . . We are continuing our support . . . but we must admit that Ike has not done anything lately to fortify our belief that he can win. We still cling to the hope that when he does start campaigning he will come out swinging. . . . If he doesn't, he might as well concede defeat and go back to the cloisters of Columbia University or the tranquility of his Pennsylvania farm. . . . An exchange of correspondence in the last couple of weeks with men who work on these papers tell a story which is nationwide and can be summed up in one sentence:
>
> Ike is running like a dry creek.

Meeting with Western Republican governors in Idaho, Ike came out with a statement of middle-road political philosophy which, considered in the abstract, was a noble pronouncement of principles to which most Americans can adhere. Yet, evaluated in the context of this campaign, it was such a statement that his adversary, Gov. Stevenson—a shrewd and seasoned politician—used it conveniently and happily to label Ike as just another 'me-too' candidate. . . .[49]

The Scripps-Howard papers had spoken for a wide segment of the party that feared the possibility of throwing away still another chance to defeat the Democrats. Stevenson's speeches, getting considerable press attention despite the overwhelming newspaper bias in favor of the Republican candidate, did little to calm the Eisenhower people.

Probably the least bothered by all the agitation was Eisenhower. Forever optimistic (he often called himself the "world's greatest optimist"), he gradually began to substantiate that confidence by his ability to carry the campaign to the people and exploit his genius for the "popular touch." His obvious liking for people was probably his most important asset, but it was made much more effective by his ability to communicate that warmth. As with most candidates, he drew powerful strength from the reaction of the crowds. More accurately, however, they inspired each other.

All candidates faced with the need to speak almost incessantly, often several times each day, fall into an inevitable pattern. Reporters assigned to the party soon learn to anticipate the exact words, the points of emphasis and the surefire applause getters. So it was with Eisenhower. What was perhaps most repetitious about his spiel was the constant invoking of earnest moral principles, spoken as simply as possible, and always stressing himself as virtually predestined to lead a crusade for righteousness, honesty and wholesomeness. Over and over again, at virtually every stop along the way, he would repeat what the reporters would soon refer to simply as "the pledge," the promise to give the people a government of "men and women with the will and determination for honesty." The journalists soon learned to regard those words as a signal to pack up their typewriters and head back toward the train.

The major themes of his addresses, the research work, the drafts outlining what to emphasize in each area, how to acknowledge local politicians and conditions were usually the work of a varying number of aides. Emmet John Hughes and publisher C. D. Jackson, with occasional assistance from Harold Stassen and Herbert Brownell, manned the New York end of the operation. Usually anticipating a speech need by some forty-eight hours, they comprised a council that formulated ideas and words. The resulting drafts would be taken to the General or, when he was far from New York, sent to the train by teletype.

Their efforts were usually unrecognizable by the final draft. Working at a distance from the scene, they were at a severe disadvantage. The difficulties of writing a speech for another man were compounded by their remoteness from the temper of the situation and the mood of the man. As a result, the material from New York, when used, supplied only the theme for a particular speech. Too often the phraseology was discarded because of failure to mesh with the General's characteristic style. Dr. Gabriel Hauge, although an economist by profession, emerged as somewhat of an expert at translating the thoughts into the simple, homey language the General preferred. Hauge, working on the campaign train, labored with assistance from Sherman Adams and, later, a Boston banker and former novelist whom Ike invited along as a traveling companion, Robert (Bobby) Cutler. Others, with expertise in certain areas, occasionally contributed to this group.[50] Yet, more than was generally realized, the final speech was undeniably Eisenhower's. All material submitted to him was carefully scrutinized; often he reconstructed the papers completely, dictating entirely new paragraphs that were usually very accurate expressions of his sentiments.

The same diligence molded the final products of his campaign speeches. His involvement with what the corps of speech writers put together was very intense. He was deeply concerned with every word. One of the younger aides, Stephen Benedict, often had to retrieve speech drafts out of the wastebasket to keep up with all the General's delineations and comments for revisions. Changes would continue to be made until the actual delivery time. The candidate's editing usually consisted of writing softer versions of harsher political assertions that were contrary to his style. Excessively heavy cold-war rhetoric furnished by some of the others was usually toned down.[51]

One of the tritest observations about the 1952 campaign involves the contrast between Stevenson's witty, urbane speeches and Eisenhower's style. Indeed, the Democrat would have been quite incapable of some of his rival's performances. His "egg" and "economist" speeches were particularly good examples of how he could reach an unsophisticated audience. In Jacksonville, Florida, on the first of a two-day swing into the deep South, he used the device to address his listeners in terms calculated to make them feel that he was simply one of their own. "The other day an economist came in to see me," he told them, and then added, "and like the rest of you, I am a little bit frightened when a man uses that word to describe himself, but he told me something that was very interesting." The General moved from there into the following lesson on taxation:

> He said, "General, here's a fact: you've put a boiled egg on your table for breakfast and on that egg you are paying 100 taxes that you don't know anything about. If you go back to where they started to raise the feed and they process that feed, they shipped it to where it was needed, the farmer bought it, he raised his eggs, he paid his taxes, he put it in the

hands of the wholesaler, who paid more transport taxes; by the time you eat the egg you are paying 100 taxes, 100 different taxes."

Now I hope I haven't spoiled your appetite for boiled eggs. But it tends in that direction, doesn't it, except that it makes us angry that we free-born Americans have to put up with that kind of thing; and the fact is that we don't.[52]

In Birmingham, the next day, he told how "my wife has been giving me the dickens about prices." Then he recalled that "we got to talking about prices, and she said something about the butcher shop, the man who owned it, the man who operated it. I said wait a minute. I've been having one of these economists around to see me, and they're pretty smart fellows, and I learned something." The butcher, Eisenhower revealed, had become "Uncle Sam's collector of taxes the people don't think they pay." Then he repeated the economist-and-the-egg story.[53] At another time the General expressed his belief that we could get "a sound money" by proper use of "the Federal Reserve Bank and all that stuff."[54] In October he apologized to an Oklahoma City audience for having used the phrase *status quo* and explained that he was "not supposed to be the educated candidate."[55]

The speaker was clearly not the same man who had won such wide respect with his Guild Hall speech in London back in 1945. His mission was different and so was his strategy. The scoffs from intellectuals, especially in comparison with Stevenson's style, bothered Eisenhower hardly at all. He had never had much use for what he considered pretense anyway and had enough confidence in his own ability to pursue his own course without apologies. Let the Democratic candidate win the admiration of journalists and professors; he would win the people by moving even closer to a more complete realization of his already firm popular image. Benedict, who worked along with Dr. Hauge and was one of the "house intellectuals," recalled with admiration many years later that Eisenhower knew how to make "sophisticated use of the unsophisticated side of himself."[56]

CHAPTER 16

The Ordeal of Politics

THE SCRIPPS-HOWARD "dry creek" complaint became the campaign's most memorable editorial. Its appearance that August had confirmed the trepidation surfacing in the Eisenhower ranks. More important than its accuracy was its threat to the unity the General was trying to achieve. Another fainthearted GOP candidacy, possibly even worse than an impotent "me-too" appeal, might jeopardize the success of the national ticket. Republican after Republican, particularly in the traditional Old Guard regions, where Taft was the hero, would be tempted to agree with Senator Jenner that the Eisenhower crusade should be ignored. Money and energy might be more profitably applied to enhancing local interests. From the start, Stevenson compounded such fears by using sharp wit and ridicule that dissected the undeniable weakness of the GOP. For the remainder of the campaign the General, prodded by continuing jabs from the Illinois Governor and plagued by his own inherent problems, was forced to suffer the controversies and endure the compromises that are the ordeal of politics. Such hazards of the middle of the road were something less than an automatic unification of the American public behind the General's "great crusade."

Starting with his welcoming address at Chicago, Eisenhower's opponent had launched a campaign that became notable for elegant prose. Ridiculing the Republican convention, Stevenson said, "For almost a week pompous phrases marched over this landscape in search of an idea. . . . After listening to this everlasting procession of epithets about our misdeeds I was even surprised the next morning when the mail was delivered on time!"[1] When he appeared before the delegates as their nominee, he told them that "the Republican Party looked brutally alive a couple of weeks ago, and I mean both Republican parties!"[2] At the state fair in his own capital city of Springfield, one day after Richard Nixon had campaigned from the same spot, Stevenson introduced Vice President Alben Barkley by saying that "The Republican Party is the party which makes even its young men seem old. The Democratic Party is the party which makes even its old men seem young."[3]

As he continued across the nation, he was clearly everything the General was not: urbane, intellectual, compulsively preoccupied with making every speech a polished performance, satirical and incisive. It would have been just as unlikely to have heard Stevenson deliver an "economist and egg" talk as for the General to tell a crowd, as did the Governor, "The season when Republican hearts regularly throb with such thoughts is, of course, the autumn of Presidential years."[4] While the General hated oratorical ornamentations, Stevenson delivered clever phrases with zest regardless of how many perturbed politicians complained that his rhetoric was too lofty for the common man. Thus, he seemed to take particular delight at the kind of observation that he made one day in Springfield, Massachusetts. Addressing a crowd from atop a high railroad embankment, he said, "I have often been accused of talking over the heads of the people. Thank goodness, at last you have given me an opportunity to do it."[5] Although private pollsters—an understandably subdued lot that year—seemed to indicate that his popularity was only about 35 percent near the start of the campaign, he was clearly an unusual candidate whose efficacy seemed hard to gauge. Fears that he was receiving more attention than the General prompted hysterical complaint by the Eisenhower–Nixon Research Service of Washington that the Governor's campaign had at least "brought out into the open the major Democratic weapon of the past twenty years: *control of the mass media through shrewd and aggressive publicity that generated news*" not by winning the editorial pages but by commanding the front pages.[6]

Such exaggeration of the newspaper coverage of the campaign can be attributed more to fear than to exhortations against complacency. The reality, of course, was that while the working press was overwhelmingly Democratic, the publishers were just as decidedly behind the Republicans and on balance, the press favored Eisenhower. The General's support came from 67.34 percent of the papers, which represented 80.24 percent of the circulation. Moreover, despite the claims of the Eisenhower–Nixon Research Bureau, the Republican backers favored their candidate on the front pages.[7] Clearly, it was Stevenson who was the underdog. At the time of his nomination, the Governor was far from the nation's most prominent Democrat. Estes Kefauver, Tennessee's progressive Senator, had fought hard and had swept the primaries. Stevenson, meanwhile, was known only to those with a close interest in politics. Few were aware of his fine record as Governor of Illinois after his landslide election in 1948.

Compared with the General, then, he was a minor figure. Even more of a handicap was his emergence as the chosen candidate of the outgoing and very unpopular President. Much to Mr. Truman's annoyance, it was an association that Stevenson tried to minimize throughout the campaign. The Governor's formidable job was to convince most Americans that he, not the General with the reputation for victorious crusades, was better qualified to lead the nation through the period of divisive frustration. Eisenhower had only to "be himself" as friends were forever advising him—a very different mission from Stevenson's.

Therefore, the most partisan foreign-policy position taken by Eisenhower during the campaign adopted the views of John Foster Dulles. The descendant of a diplomatic dynasty, which had supplied Secretaries of State for Presidents Benjamin Harrison and Woodrow Wilson, Dulles had already established his own reputation. As early as 1948, before becoming the chief author of the Japanese Peace Treaty of 1951, Dulles was clearly Dewey's choice to head the State Department. So firm was his esteem in that field among Republicans that there is ample reason to believe that an Arthur Vandenberg Presidency would have similarly installed Dulles. When, after the retirement of New York Senator Robert F. Wagner, Sr., Dewey had the opportunity to appoint a short-term successor, the Governor chose Dulles for the vacancy. Facing a special election soon afterward, however, Dulles's highly conservative campaign and charges that he had stooped to exploit upstate New York anti-Semitic sentiments gave the victory to a proven vote-getter, Herbert H. Lehman. Dulles, with his previous experience as a United States delegate to the United Nations General Assembly and identification as an internationalist, returned to Washington as a Deputy Secretary of State. In reality, he was Truman's chief Republican foreign-policy adviser. Even then the enormously successful Wall Street lawyer and Council of Churches activist with strongly Calvinist views was already articulating a diplomatic position that, while fully consistent with the Truman–Acheson appeals for American participation *vis-à-vis* Europe, contained significant rhetorical distinctions.

His first book, *War, Peace and Change*, which appeared in 1939, warned about treaties that lacked provisions for change. He pointed out that drafters of the League of Nations covenant had neglected machinery to alter such pacts.[8] The chief reason for the failure at Versailles was, therefore, the attempt to maintain the *status quo*. Identifying "stability with rigidity" misconceived the nature of peace.[9] Therefore, he had concluded in a succeeding volume, eleven years later, American acquiesence to Soviet expansionism, permitting the completion of their planned encirclement "to isolate us, to weaken us, and eventually to strangle us," would be the most certain prescription for defeat.[10] Mere containment, he warned readers of *Life*, would be a disaster. Victory can be assured, he emphasized with underscored words, only by developing the will and the means to *"retaliate instantly against open aggression by Red armies, so that if it occurred anywhere, we could and would strike back where it hurts, by means of our choosing."*[11]

His warning contained aggressive overtones toward not only Europe but Asia, too. Consistent with the increasing concerns of Congressional Republicans were such alarms that "policies that do not defend freedom in Asia are fatally defective."[12] At about the same time, speaking to the French National Political Science Institute at the Sorbonne, Dulles asked, "Is it not time that the Chinese Communists know that, if, for example, they sent their Red armies openly into Vietnam, we will not be content merely to try to meet their armed forces at the point they select for their aggression, but by retaliatory action of our own fashioning?"[13]

During the spring of 1952, while Ike was still at SHAPE, General Lucius Clay had forwarded to him a draft of the *Life* article and a paper on Formosa prepared by Dulles. Eisenhower, who was only superficially acquainted with its author at the time, responded in his characteristic manner of contesting another's position. Pondering the idea of retaliation, he asked how the policy could possibly apply "if Soviet *political* aggression, as in Czechoslovakia, successively chips away exposed portions of the free world? So far as our resulting economic situation is concerned," he pointed out, "such an eventuality would be just as bad for us if the area had been captured by force. To my mind, this is the case where the theory of 'retaliation' falls down."[14] Eisenhower, increasingly adhering to the Wilsonian concept of linking free European markets with the economic soundness vital for American interests, thereby challenged what he regarded as Dulles's simplistic solution. Dulles's reply anticipated the course of their future relationship by not debating the point but conceding flatteringly, "You put your finger on a weak point in my presentation."[15]

Whatever feelings of oversimplification existed were mutual. One week later, arriving in Paris for his lecture series, Dulles had two meetings with Eisenhower. He gave his views on the need for a stronger post-containment policy, on the necessity for counterattacking wherever Communist pressure was greatest, of how to get the American people to respond at the polls by suggesting the need to do something about the stagnating acceptance of captive peoples behind the Iron Curtain in Eastern Europe. Such areas were essential as market places for Germany, Dulles pointed out, but holding out hopes for their liberation would provide encouragement to the millions of Americans, preponderately Catholics and Democrats, whose homelands of Poland, Estonia, Hungary, Latvia, Czechoslovakia, Lithuania, Bulgaria and Rumania had been consigned to communism by sterile containment. To all this Eisenhower seemed cool. And Dulles left distressed that the General was still preoccupied with NATO and the Western Alliance, that he was under excessive British influence, that he did not understand that a political challenge to the Democrats would require the formulation of a vibrant anti-Communist foreign policy that recognized the possibility of reversing the Red postwar gains. In an interview with an American correspondent, fresh from his meeting, Dulles said that he was "terribly worried about Eisenhower's preoccupation with European unity."[16] Nevertheless, they had found themselves in substantial agreement on the need for mutual security and preventing the resurgence of American isolationism.[17]

Formulating foreign policy had, of course, always been Dulles's ultimate goal. Having been frustrated before, he was not about to see his party botch another "victory," nor was he ready to subordinate his own ambitions to the outcome of the Republican nominating convention. Whatever his reactions to Eisenhower or to Taft, he determined to remain acceptable to all wings of the GOP as well as to either candidate. Not surprisingly, as a Dewey internationalist, Dulles had inclined toward Eisenhower during the preconvention period. His respect for Taft's intellect may have been greater than his regard for Eisenhower's; but he and the Senator did not have quite the same slant on world affairs and Dulles felt that Taft's stubbornness would make working with him more difficult.[18] At the most practical level, of course, in view of what Dulles thought could be achieved, was his realization that Taft would make victory less likely.[19] Nevertheless, he moved in every possible way to preserve his acceptability to Taft as well. Taft himself had informed Dulles that there was "a large area of possible agreement" between them, and Dulles suspected that the Senator was trying to stall him from openly endorsing Eisenhower.[20] The anti-Dewey people around Taft would most certainly have found Dulles much more acceptable than Dewey himself. Many close to Taft, including one of his long-time law partners, were convinced that the Senator would have chosen Dulles as his Secretary of State.[21] There also seemed to be little doubt that few other Eisenhower candidates would have been as acceptable.

Whatever private agreements Dulles may have reached with the General after their meeting in Paris, the lawyer's public deportment suggested loyalty to the party rather than to any of its potential candidates. After a visit with Eisenhower in mid-June, he told reporters that his main objective was to draft a foreign-policy plank acceptable to both the General and Taft. As always, he avoided any expression of personal preference.[22] When he reached Chicago with the draft of his contribution to the platform, he stressed the harmony between Eisenhower and Taft in criticizing the Administration.[23]

For his part, Eisenhower continued to maintain his earlier resistance to some of Dulles's more dramatic views, particularly *vis-à-vis* retaliation. Before Dulles could do much with the platform, the General reminded him of his opposition to any statement lacking a clear commitment to collective security and a high level of international trade. "Peace is our objective," he wrote to Dulles; "we reject all talk and proposals of preventive war."[24] A few days later, at Chicago, Eisenhower demanded the deletion of any reference to "retaliation."[25] Nevertheless, Dulles guarded the Eisenhower interests by skillfully resisting efforts of others to write a plank that would have reflected the isolationist point of view. Since that would have been just as unacceptable to the General as references to retaliation and since the platform was written before the candidates were chosen, the wrong kind of platform might have been fatal to the plans of the Eisenhower forces. Moreover, Dulles was able to satisfy both the Taft and Eisenhower positions.

Once the nomination was his, however, the Eisenhower mission had to change, a factor that undoubtedly accounts for both the personal and political depression the General suffered that August. No longer was he confined to the great middle of the road. His need to unify the party meant accommodating himself with at least the spirit of the fiercely partisan line the Republicans had been pursuing with the deepening cold war. That meant greater acceptance of Dulles's counsel, whatever his private reservations and attempts to ameliorate its tone. Dulles, who remembered the advice of a former Polish ambassador to Washington that the GOP could never regain its power unless it outbid the Democrats for the immigrants, returned to his concern for the "captive peoples." Formulating his words carefully—with excruciating deliberation, Eisenhower noted, as perfect as a printed page once they were delivered —he told a luncheon meeting at the Brown Palace Hotel how the party should exploit its "captive peoples" platform statement to cut sharply into the Democratic vote. Few of his listeners that day could ever again underestimate Dulles's political consciousness.[26]

Whatever agonizing the candidate did that summer about his principles was undoubtedly resolved in favor of the thought that the American people might not crown him merely because he was Eisenhower. He carried the liabilities of a minority party that still reminded many of bitter times. On the very day of the publication of the "dry creek" editorial, Eisenhower rejuvenated his campaign by carrying the Dulles theme to an American Legion convention in New York.

It was his perfect audience. Bedecked in a blue and gold Legion overseas hat with the name of his Abilene post, the General repeated the platform's rhetoric about the need to liberate the "captive peoples" from godless Soviet communism. The veterans cheered without restraint as he declared, "The American conscience can never know peace until these people are restored again to being masters of their own fate."[27] Liberals winced and *Pravda* charged the Republicans with Hitleresque plans to conquer most of Europe and Asia; and the New York *Times*, noting that he had also called for a home-front fight against corruption in government, racial discrimination and domestic Communist infiltration, called the speech "more reminiscent of the real 'Ike' than any he had delivered in some time" and approved of its presentation of a "broad program behind which Americans can unite."[28]

Whatever influence Dulles had achieved over foreign-policy statements was substantiated the next day when the adviser faced reporters after an eighty-minute conference with the General. Speaking in his usual confident manner, he promised that the candidate would soon offer a new foreign policy, one better designed to deter Soviet aggression. "What we should do is try to split the satellite states away from the control of a few men in Moscow," Dulles told them. "The only way to stop a head-on collision with the Soviet Union is to break it up from within, and a head-on collision means World War III."[29]

His explanation could only exacerbate rather than relieve the fears provoked by Eisenhower's speech to the legionnaires. From overseas—and not only from Moscow—unfavorable reactions were continuing to arrive. Dispatches from the vicinity of Ike's former SHAPE headquarters reported fear among American allies of Yankee adventures unleashing an aggressive military force whenever fully armed. The Parisian newspaper *Le Monde* termed the liberation pronouncement "violent." W. Averell Harriman, Truman's Mutual Security Director, told a meeting of political scientists in Buffalo that the liberation policy had spread the fear of war in Europe and it could only lead to premature uprisings and even future replicas of the Warsaw massacres.[30]

Eisenhower had fully accepted the concept of liberation. He could not understand how any other reaction could be moral. America's conscience, he felt, "would never be at ease until those states had the right of self-determination," and the United States should be prepared to use "all peaceful means" to effect such a goal. Any such pronouncement, therefore, had to stress our reluctance to go to war simply to satisfy moral indignation; moral means had to be used for moral purposes.[31] Reading Dulles's version upset Eisenhower not only for its belligerent tone but also because the words had come from a man clearly associated with the General and already destined, the candidate realized, to head the State Department in the next Republican Administration. By the time he could be reached, Dulles had already flown to Buffalo to address the same audience Harriman had faced the day before. Via long-distance telephone the candidate told Dulles that he had sounded more belligerent than was justified because he had overlooked their agreement to qualify such talk about liberating captive nations with the addition of the words "all peaceful means." Dulles, rarely one to fight when reprimanded by his chief, agreed that he had erred and replied that it was just an over-sight.[32] Then, when his turn came to face the academicians, he con-tinued to denounce the failures of containment, which condemned such captives to permanent imprisonment, but took care to explain that the policy eschews violence and was dependent upon peaceful revolution that could employ such "quiet" methods as passive resistance, non-coop-eration, discontent, slowdowns and industrial sabotage. He then called a press conference to denounce Harriman's specter of massacred rebels and fears of war as "nonsense."[33]

The vigorous anti-Communist foreign-policy line placed the General in pursuit of more than just the potential Taft voters. That conservative group was merely one segment of the total following behind Senator Joseph R. McCarthy. The Catholics, with strong emotional or family ties to traditionally anti-Communist areas of Europe, or regions that had actually become Russian satellites, were among the most ardent devotees of the Senator from Wisconsin.[34] In his own home state, for example, McCarthy's impact was greatest among the Poles and Czechs.[35] Among eastern Catholics, including Irish and Italian Americans, he was equally strong. The most that Henry Cabot Lodge, Jr., and John F. Kennedy, both competing for the Senate seat from Massachusetts, could do about McCarthy, as repugnant as he was to them, was to dodge the issue and to avoid his path as though he were a leper. Taft himself, recognizing McCarthy's strength among Ohio's numerous German-Americans, had declared that "the pro-Communist policies of the State Department fully justified Joe McCarthy in his demand for an investigation."[36]

Subsequent studies of the McCarthy "phenomenon" have demon-strated that it was not a phenomenon at all. His appeal was very much in the American mainstream, really an exploitation of a long-standing fear of communism. As early as 1937, Dr. George Gallup had reported that 54 percent of the Americans favored laws permitting the police to "pad-lock places printing Communist literature," and in June 1938 53 percent opposed allowing Communists to hold meetings in their community. In June of 1942, while the United States was allied with the Soviets against the Axis and Russian stock among the American people was at its height, exactly half of the sample interviewed wanted to outlaw membership in the Communist party.[37] Despite evidence showing his earlier indiffer-ence—and even ignorance—about the whole question of communism, the Senator's need for political publicity had led to his crusade against internal subversion. Even before the famous discussion with his friends at the Colony Restaurant in Washington, where he was supposedly searching for a dramatic issue, a group of rightists had, after having failed to interest some others, "sold" McCarthy a program designed to expose the domestic "Red menace."[38] Not only the postwar gains of Communists, both Russian and Chinese, but the actual presence of Reds and fellow travelers in such agencies as the Government Printing Office, the National Labor Relations Board, the Board of Economic Warfare, the International Monetary Fund and the ready access of the editors of *Amerasia* to State Department classified papers lent some credence seemingly to justify, in the eyes of many, the Senator's reckless accusations against individuals.[39] The total McCarthy appeal had become a powerful Republican means of liquidating the long-entrenched Democrats. Economic conservatives, also enthusiastic supporters of the Senator, never lost sight of that goal.[40] As a Republican fighting Democrats, he won support from individuals such as Taft, who had doubts and even anxieties about his methods. Enough Old Guarders considered McCarthy an asset to equate any opposition to him with attempts to destroy the party.[41] For conservatives, it was easy to equate "anti-business" policies with communism. If only as a way of removing the New Dealers from Washington, the upwardly mobile, economically conservative small-business interests with sentiments akin to the Jacksonians and the Populists of the nineteenth century constituted some of McCarthy's strongest supporters.[42] McCarthy himself, in a much less publicized passage in his Wheeling, West Virginia, speech of February 9, 1950, in which he announced his "list" of "205 communists" in the State Department, made the following revealing diagnosis about the source of America's domestic troubles:

> The reason why we find ourselves in a position of impotency is not because our only potential enemy has sent men to invade our shores, but rather because of the traitorous actions of those who have been treated so well by this nation. It is not the less fortunate, or members of minority groups who have been selling this nation out, but rather those who have had all the benefits the wealthiest nation on earth has had to offer—the finest homes, the finest college education, and the finest jobs in the government that we can give. This is glaringly true in the State Department. There the bright young men who are born with silver spoons in their mouth are the ones who have been worse.[43]

If McCarthy and Eisenhower were, then, both viewed by partisans as instruments of their crusade to oust New Dealers, it is not surprising that they made gains with similar appeals to the American mood. Eisenhower, of course, had adopted righteousness as his credo. From his acceptance-speech promise of a "great crusade," with its religious implications, he had stressed a high level of morality as the surest way of cleansing the capital city of Truman Administration larceny, of manliness in meeting foreign responsibilities against a "godless enemy," and restoring dignity to the Presidency. McCarthy, addressing an audience that was also ready for Eisenhower, assumed the same kind of moral justification. "The great difference between our western Christian world and the atheistic Communist world is not political . . . it is moral," he had declared. To his home-town audience in Appleton, Wisconsin, he said that "There are two fundamental truths of religion: there is a God who is eternal, and each and every one of you has a soul which is immortal."[44]

It was Eisenhower and not McCarthy who aroused a Billings, Montana, crowd on the fifth of October by equating honesty in government with "honesty as a deeply felt religion" and went on from there to promise that "we will find the men and women who may fail to live up to these standards; we will find the pinks; we will find the Communists; we will find the disloyal."[45]

To an American public perplexed that things should be going astray for people who had always been favored by God and eager for replenishment of faith in their own virtues, both men, one the "fighting marine" and the other a humane General who sounded not at all like the effete Easterners who had created his candidacy, had emerged as Saint Patricks. When, for example, Adlai E. Stevenson spoke to the American Legion in New York two days after Eisenhower had proposed "liberation," he missed the essential point. Referring to the attack on the loyalty and motives of General of the Army George C. Marshall, the Democrat who had promised to "talk sense" to the American people, recalled Samuel Johnson's reminder that patriotism was the "last refuge of scoundrels."[46] However admirable such sentiments as apologetic Eisenhower voters wrote to Stevenson in the hours immediately after his subsequent defeat, he was battling the obvious fact that it was "time for a change" of the leadership in Washington.[47]

Eisenhower could even agree, but his political mission was in McCarthy's terrain, not Stevenson's. In three notable instances the General submerged his personal feelings for the ultimate needs of the crusade, just as had the Supreme Commander of Allied Forces in Europe; and, in each case, events moved him further toward the direction of Republican numerical strength, however unwillingly he may have gone or however much the embarrassment.

His first ordeal confronted Ike with the man who had denounced General Marshall as "a front man for traitors" and "a living lie" in a speech months before McCarthy's attack, Senator William E. Jenner. An

Old Guardsman even before the age of forty-five, Jenner had an established reputation as a fervent supporter of the Wisconsin Senator. Unlike McCarthy, Jenner followed a consistent right-wing line: implacable anti-internationalism toward the United Nations, NATO, the Marshall Plan, foreign aid and hostility toward all domestic social programs. In short, his record left little room to his right. Only after he had decided that Eisenhower was a "winner" did he back his party's 1952 candidate.[48] Eisenhower, visiting Indianapolis for a speech on September 9, could not avoid the Senator from Indiana.

An overflow crowd, much larger than the sixteen thousand able to get into the Butler University Field House, had arrived to see the candidate, who was introduced by Jenner. The speech, designed to please the region's Taftite majority, contained some choice crowd-pleasers. He told them he had decided to run because he could not sit by while his country was "the prey of fear-mongers, quack doctors and bare-faced looters." Speaking also to a national radio audience, he asked Indiana voters to support the Republican statewide slate from top to bottom; much to the annoyance of local political leaders, he did not mention Jenner by name.[49]

But the Senator made sure he was not ignored. With every burst of applause from the big crowd, he reached out and grabbed Eisenhower's arm with a display of vehement approval. When the crowd cheered the candidate's final words, the camaraderie became warmer. Jumping to his feet, Jenner embraced Eisenhower, putting his arm around Ike's shoulder as the photo-flash bulbs went off.[50] Suddenly turning away and toward Congressman Halleck, the General, his face red with anger, said, "Charlie, get me out of here!" and they left before either the police or the bodyguards knew what had happened.[51] Eisenhower later told Emmet Hughes that he "felt dirty from the touch of the man."[52] The national reaction was predictable, with the liberals and many moderates of both parties indignant that the General had associated with Jenner and had even, at least by implication, endorsed him for re-election. Steve Young, one of the vice-chairmen of the National Young Republican Clubs, immediately announced that he was switching to Stevenson. "It is too much for an honest man to swallow," he told the press.[53]

The second incident, only three days later, involved his inevitable meeting with Taft. Whatever their differences, Republicans could hardly imagine their candidate without the full endorsement of the Ohio Senator. With his oft-expressed belief in Herbert Hoover's "fortress America" concept and his vigorous desire to limit the economic and social role of the federal government, achieving harmony had appeared an impossibility. That Dulles had been able to do so when writing the platform had been particularly noteworthy; but the position taken by

Eisenhower, the candidate, was another matter. Nevertheless, only by getting Taft's support could the crusade appear to carry the full endorsement of the Republican party. Eisenhower, therefore, continued to work toward what had been an objective ever since they had left Chicago, the wooing of Taft. While in the Senator's own part of the country, after the two-day early-September Southern venture, the General spoke to Mid-America conservatives and praised Taft profusely and met with a stream of state leaders who had supported the Senator. Meanwhile Arthur Summerfield and Frank Carlson combined efforts in Washington by meeting with Taft and thus fulfilling the national committee's desires by offering him a major role in the campaign, which he resisted. In Taft's own state, at the same time, Eisenhower told regional Republicans gathered at Cleveland of his willingness to meet "anybody anywhere in the world anytime I believe there is a worthwhile result to be accomplished."[54] He had already, in fact, arranged to receive the Senator at Morningside Heights for a breakfast conference on September 12.

Present with the General at the official residence of Columbia University's president were Jim Hagerty, Milton Eisenhower and Senator Carlson. On Thursday night Carlson, meeting Taft at the airport, was given the draft of a statement that the Senator had prepared for distribution to the press after the conference. Taft wanted Eisenhower to study it before their meeting. Since the General had already gone to bed, however, Carlson decided not to disturb him and kept the paper.[55] When the Senator arrived just after seven-thirty the next morning, with a flock of news photographers recording every footstep from the taxicab to the mansion door, the General had not read the statement.

There is no reason to believe their breakfast meeting was not very cordial. Those who were within the mansion at the time could not, even in later years, contradict the public impression of harmony. At least privately, Taft, aware that his Hooverish international position was his greatest source of contention with Eisenhower, continued to show signs of modification. Domestically, both were conservative, with Taft occasionally showing even greater flexibility than Eisenhower in his willingness to grant social powers to the federal government. Perhaps the harshness of the Senator's rhetoric, designed for his constituency, was the most profound difference with the General in the handling of the national economy.[56] Taft showed his prepared statement, and Ike had no reaction beyond a few suggestions. They did not, therefore, have any substantial area of disagreement. When reporters and photographers were summoned after the two-hour session, the General and the Senator were discussing fishing. One newsman asked Eisenhower whether he saw eye to eye with McCarthy. The General responded by turning to Taft, shaking his hand and walking out of the room without comment.[57]

The real burden was on Taft. He had been the loser; he had gone to Morningside Heights; he had just conferred with the man of doubtful Republicanism, whose backing contained some discredited members of the Eastern Establishment. How could he, with his strong reputation as a man of principle, embrace what only so recently had been so repugnant? Leaving the mansion, he walked south across West 116th Street and entered the temporary press headquarters that had been set up in the King's Crown Hotel. There he read his prepared statement, which urged complete support for Ike. It went on to declare that the issue separating them from the Democrats was the one of "liberty against the creeping socialization in every domestic field" and warned about the constant growth of big government. Such sentiments, he read, reflected Eisenhower's own philosophy; but the words came after his espousal, in conventionally conservative terms, of his own economic concepts and, therefore, were clearly meant to imply that they expressed the General's views just as accurately, including agreement to hold the budget to $70 billion in fiscal 1954 and to reduce it to $60 billion in fiscal 1955. Only in the field of foreign policy did he agree that there had been any differences, and those he minimized to just a matter of "degree" since, he said, "We are both determined to battle communism throughout the world and in the United States."[58]

Taft's shrewdness could be digested only by Eisenhower. Their profound differences over the Atlantic Pact nations and spending for European economic and military strength, as well as conduct of the Korean war, over which Taft had been a vehement critic and Eisenhower a supporter, had been passed over as an insignificant, almost academic matter. Even its description of domestic horrors, with its implicit condemnation of all that had been done since 1932, had gone well beyond any Eisenhower public criticism of the New or Fair Deal. Eisenhower paid for Taft's support by remaining silent while others talked about how the Senator had at last converted the politically naïve general to his own way of thinking.

Others were free to react. Stevenson charged that the "great crusade" had become the "great surrender" and also declared that, "Taft lost the nomination but won the nominee."[59] Republican Senator Wayne Morse of Oregon, clearly a maverick, already annoyed by Eisenhower's endorsement of McCarthy and Jenner, announced that he would not campaign for his party's Presidential candidate but would merely vote for him.[60]

Such heated reactions were mild compared to the results of Eisenhower's October campaign swing into the upper Midwest. From New York had come a suggested speech for delivery in Milwaukee on the night of October 3 that included, as a way of indicating some difference between the General and the Senator, mild praise for General Marshall's "patriotism to the service of America." Unfortunately the earlier attacks on the character and even the loyalty of Ike's old colleague had made Marshall's name controversial. Did one subscribe to the view that his mission to China and his burial of the Wedemeyer Report of the conditions in China prior to the completion of the Communist takeover cast enough doubts about Marshall's credibility or real aims? Having had the matter raised by Messrs. Jenner and McCarthy seemed, to many, adequate reason to re-enforce esteem for Marshall. Any favorable mention of his name in Wisconsin by candidate Eisenhower would, of course, be interpreted as a criticism of the Senator; and the writers on the train, working with the material sent out by C. D. Jackson's New York staff, decided to include a tribute to Marshall for the purpose of indicating Ike's continued loyalty.[61]

When the train made an overnight stop at Peoria, Illinois, and Eisenhower quartered at the Pere Marquette Hotel, he received a surprise visitor: Senator Joe McCarthy. Accompanied by Arthur Summerfield, who sympathized with the purpose of the visit, the controversial Senator made a firm request. He wanted no references made by Eisenhower to Marshall while speaking in Wisconsin. Their discussion, over the dinner table, reached a point of high tension as two determined men faced each other with firm positions. In a cold and controlled manner, Eisenhower clearly told McCarthy what he thought about his anti-Communist crusade and how he felt about Marshall. Adamantly, he refused to omit the passage from the speech. Kevin McCann, who was also present, has recalled that it was the only time he ever heard Ike speak "in red hot anger."[62] Leaving the hotel, McCarthy told newsmen he had had a "very, very pleasant" talk and announced he would be on the General's train the next day for the ride into Wisconsin. Speeches were scheduled for Green Bay and Appleton as well as Milwaukee.

The controversy continued on the train. Wisconsin's Governor Walter Kohler, also a candidate for re-election, pleaded that the Marshall reference was unduly provocative, that Eisenhower could praise the General at any other time, that it could jeopardize the entire Republican statewide ticket. Of the Eisenhower advisers, Gabriel Hauge and Bobby Cutler were adamant that the speech be delivered as written. Their biggest supporter was Eisenhower himself. Adams, however, sided with Kohler and, by circumstances, with McCarthy. He felt that the Governor, who feared the speech unnecessarily designed to praise Marshall, should have his wish as the host in the state.[63] Eisenhower, having gone to a forward car of the train to continue the discussion with Adams and the local politicians, later returned to the back car looking "purple with anger." He then announced to Hauge and Cutler, in a peremptory tone, that the passage had to go. Hauge, protesting to the General, was told the matter was closed. When Hauge complained to Adams, the chief of staff replied that it was the judgment of the political advisers. Hauge, distraught, contemplated abandoning the train and the campaign at that point; but, after all, what could he do when the General himself had agreed to the deletion?[64]

At Appleton, McCarthy, in a last-minute move, rushed onto the platform and introduced Eisenhower. Rather conciliatory, Eisenhower told a Green Bay audience that both he and McCarthy differed only over "methods" of how to rid the government of the "subversive and the disloyal." Continuing in McCarthy's territory in his major speech at Milwaukee that night, he talked about the hazards of Communist penetration of government.[65]

Once again the reaction was predictable. The New York Times, lamenting with an editorial called "An Unhappy Day," reported erroneously that the deletion had been at McCarthy's request. Unhappily, Arthur Vandenberg, Jr., reported from New York that press accounts were emphasizing Eisenhower's support of McCarthy and his apparent capitulation "over and above his disagreement with McCarthy respecting methods."[66] Adlai E. Stevenson campaigned in Wisconsin just five days afterward and called for McCarthy's defeat. "My opponent has been worrying about my funnybone," he jibed. "I'm worrying about his backbone."[67]

But Eisenhower's caution had tempered his concept of morality and principles in rather mixed proportions. In a Pulaski Day message he called for the repudiation of the Yalta Agreements; but, on the same day, he praised Marshall in Salt Lake City. He contributed additional kind words for the World War II General of the Army at the Alfred E. Smith Memorial Foundation dinner in New York City and later in Newark, New Jersey.

On October 27 Senator McCarthy, speaking from Chicago at a "McCarthy Broadcast Dinner" that had been arranged by a committee headed by Sears, Roebuck and Company chairman General Robert E. Wood, supported Eisenhower by attacking Stevenson viciously. Pretending, theatrically, to confuse the names Adlai and Alger, he accused the Democrat of having aided the cause of communism by having associated with such "leftist" speech writers as Arthur Schlesinger, Jr. The telephone lines of the New York Times were jammed by more than two hundred callers protesting the speech and demanding that the paper rescind its recent editorial support for Eisenhower.[68] Industrialist and financier George A. Sloan reacted to the McCarthy appeal by informing Eisenhower, "Thank God it is over. My reaction and that of several other men who were with me at the Union League Club is that it probably did not do as much harm as we feared."[69]

The cautious campaign of Eisenhower and his followers had developed recognizable lines of support as his following became better defined. Oregon's Senator Wayne Morse, for example, was so upset by the "reactionaries running a captive general for President" that he finally resigned from the GOP.[70] But what had bothered Morse had, at last, brought the desired conservatives to Eisenhower's side. Colonel Robert McCormick, after his earlier contemplation of forming an "American Party," finally acknowledged that Eisenhower was preferable to Stevenson, a view reflected by the Chicago *Tribune*'s editorial page in late October. Eisenhower's complete support of the rights of Texas and Louisiana, as well as California, to the tidelands oil deposits, while Stevenson held that they belonged to the federal government, brought him endorsements from Governor Robert Kennon of Louisiana and Governor Allan Shivers of Texas, both Democrats. Elsewhere there were other indications that he could breach the Solid South. With Stevenson finally advocating an FEPC and with Eisenhower deploring discrimination but holding that such evils had to be dealt with by the states rather than by the imposition of federal laws, Democratic Governor Jimmy Byrnes of South Carolina became another Ike endorser. In Virginia, Senator Harry Byrd, that state's real political power, announced that Stevenson's adherence to "Trumanism" had made him ineligible and, although he could not endorse the Republicans, he had to abstain from the Democratic campaign. As if to wrap up the conservative coalition, ex-President Hoover delivered a TV and radio speech for Eisenhower on October 18.[71]

Encouragement also came from the Nixon entourage. Campaigning widely and speaking without hesitation even for those whom Eisenhower had endorsed with embarrassment, the Californian was creating unusual excitement for a number-two man. Large crowds, overwhelming in even such Democratic centers as Boston and Rhode Island and record-breaking in Pennsylvania, heard him fire repeated charges at Stevenson, Truman and Acheson. Exploiting his connection with the Alger Hiss case, he blasted the President as "soft" on communism and "spineless" and told a nationwide TV audience in mid-October that Stevenson had disqualified himself for the Presidency by having provided a good character deposition for Hiss at the first perjury trial in 1949.[72] Over and over again, thereafter, particularly through the Midwest, he repeated the association of Stevenson and Hiss to enthusiastic crowds. He told a Pittsburgh audience that the Communists, both American and Russian, were eager for a Democratic victory.

By linking the opposition with the nation's sorest frustrations, the Eisenhower people had sparked the campaign and brought their party to a reasonable degree of harmony. In this effort, Richard Nixon's contribution had become notable.[73]

CHAPTER 17

Holding the Center

Having Nixon woo the hard-shell Republicans and ardent anti-Communists and pleasing Taft and McCarthy, however useful for expunging "me-tooism" from the campaign, constantly threatened to jeopardize the greatest potential source of Eisenhower's political strength: that fickle, uncommitted, apolitical, independent vote. "The vital center" would, in this case, make the vital difference. And, feared the liberals around Ike, spicing the campaign with militant partisanship was obviously the best way to repel both independents and Democrats. Advisers Herbert Brownell, Tom Dewey, Lucius Clay and others helped keep the General alert to that reality. A possible key to the success of the campaign, then, was his emergence with renewed strength among middle-of-the-roaders in the aftermath of one of the two boldest strokes made that fall.

The entire effort had seemingly reached its lowest point on the night of September 23. Eisenhower, present for a speech in the Cleveland Public Auditorium, had gone upstairs to the manager's office instead of following the original schedule. In that small room some thirty members of the entourage had gathered. Several stood along the back wall to see the corner television set. In front of the small screen sat General and Mrs. Eisenhower. New York *Herald Tribune* publisher William Robinson was near them. Three floors below, in the auditorium, as uncertain of what to expect as those in the room, were fifteen thousand Republicans who had gathered to hear Eisenhower deliver a speech on inflation. But first they awaited the piping-in of a radio broadcast of what many others were about to see on television.

Throughout the nation, the greatest TV audience assembled for a political event until that time, estimated at sixty million, was waiting to hear whether Senator Nixon was about to resign as a candidate. The Vice Presidential candidate's advance public statements on his intentions were sufficiently vague to enhance interest in what he was about to say. He had also refused to issue an advance text. The General, as well as all those around him in that room, were as uncertain of its contents as the public.

As they waited for him to speak, however, they were sure of one thing: He had to resign. All the campaign talk about the "mess in Washington" and restoring honesty in government threatened to become a sham if their own number-two man on the ticket was guilty of questionable ethics for having been the recipient of an $18,235 special fund that had been raised to facilitate his political purposes by a group of seventy-six wealthy businessmen. Since the New York *Post*, a vehemently liberal anti-Republican example of tabloid sensationalism, had released the story on September 18 behind a front-page headline proclaiming SPECIAL NIXON FUND! the dump Nixon sentiment had mounted. Harold Stassen had even sent a long-winded telegram that, helpfully, contained a suggested resignation statement. The Washington *Post* had joined the callers for Nixon's scalp. Much more disturbing to the Senator was the agreement from the New York *Herald Tribune*. So influential in the party, so close were the Reids and William Robinson to Eisenhower, the paper was virtually a *Pravda* of the Eastern Establishment. Even Milton Eisenhower contemplated having the matter, at best, referred for study by an *ad hoc* Senate committee on ethics that would be chaired by a distinguished Democrat, Paul Douglas of Illinois.[1] National Chairman Arthur Summerfield was virtually alone as a vigorous defendant of Nixon.

The General, worried about a loss of credibility if the Senator remained on the ticket, had, at the same time, confided to Sherman Adams that "if Nixon has to go, we cannot win."[2] He recalled a parallel with the famous slapping incident that had led to outcries that he relieve General George S. Patton, Jr., during the war. Judiciously, after having analyzed all of the facts—not least of all being Patton's value—he had settled for a reprimand but kept his effective officer. Nevertheless, what had galled Nixon about Eisenhower's reaction in this case was the General's comment to reporters on the campaign train "Of what avail is it for us to carry on this crusade against this business of what has been going on in Washington if we ourselves aren't as clean as a hound's tooth?" Nixon himself later wrote that "it made me feel like a little boy caught with jam on his face."[3] Determined to fight back rather than leave the ticket, he had responded by telling crowds of his persecution by Communists seeking to destroy him for his anti-subversive activities.[4] At Eugene, Oregon, he had reacted to taunting signs that mocked the

GOP for having criticized Democratic wrongdoing by proclaiming, "No Mink Coats for Nixon, Just Cold Cash," with the statement that "There are no mink coats for the Nixons. I am proud to say my wife, Pat, wears a good Republican cloth coat."[5] Clearly, with Eisenhower unprepared to make a decision until he got "all the facts" and leaving his running mate without a statement of support, and with Nixon's determination to fight back, there was a painful impasse. Dewey, using the name "Mr. Chapman" to continue his campaign policy of remaining inconspicuous, phoned Nixon to suggest a national radio-TV talk that would include an appeal to the public. Only an overwhelmingly favorable response, the Governor stressed, would constitute vindication and justify not quitting, for there must be no question about any lack of propriety.[6]

But the most important call that day came shortly after 10 P.M. from Ike himself. "If I issue a statement now backing you up," the General explained, "in effect people will accuse me of condoning wrongdoing." He added his agreement about the wisdom of a television talk. At that point, Nixon wanted to know whether he could expect a decision from Eisenhower, one way or another, after the program. Replied the General: "I am hoping that no announcement would be necessary at all, but maybe after the program we could tell what ought to be done."[7] Nixon, agitated by the lofty indecision that was making him squirm, then replied into the telephone, "General, a time comes in politics when you have to shit or get off the pot!"[8]

The preparations followed. Arthur Summerfield rushed to round up the needed $75,000 for both radio and TV time and arranged for a Tuesday-night spot that would be suitable for a national audience. Legal and financial statements on the fund, which had already been initiated by Sherman Adams, were being completed by the law firm of Gibson, Dunn & Crutcher and the accountancy house of Price, Waterhouse and Company. Their investigations showed that the fund was not a secret affair; that it had been carefully supervised by Dana C. Smith, its trustee; that its function was to supplement the Senator's campaign and political expenses, which included $4,237.54 for two years of Christmas cards alone; that the collection and disbursement of funds had violated no law; and, very clearly, that every aspect agreed with the explanations that had been made by Nixon and Dana Smith.[9] Additionally, on the very day the Price, Waterhouse report was received, came the disclosure of a fund for Adlai Stevenson that was used to augment the state salaries of the Governor's staff in Springfield. Its main difference from Nixon's fund was that it was not used for the Governor's personal campaign activities. But such distinctions were not always easy to make, and its supervision was not nearly as complete as what Smith had done for

Nixon. It did, however, dramatize the lack of uniqueness about Nixon's fund. Nixon, meanwhile, in preparing to answer the charges and ask the American people for support in his own far more publicized predicament, recalled the political use of FDR's dog Fala in the 1944 campaign against Dewey and his own comment in Oregon about Pat's "Republican cloth coat." The program was set to be televised and broadcast from the El Capitan Theater in Hollywood.

Just before he left for the studio, Nixon's phone rang. It was "Mr. Chapman" again. Dewey's latest message reported the Eisenhower staff decision that Nixon should submit his resignation after the broadcast. When the distraught Senator asked what the General's personal view was, the Governor hedged. Then Dewey made it clear that he would not have been asked to call Nixon unless the decision was consistent with Eisenhower's view. Telling Dewey it was too late to change his speech, he advised them to "listen to the broadcast" if they wanted to know what he would say.[10]

The Senator, in the role of the defendant, entered the studio without having gone through the elaborate technical preparations. He had been so eager to use every possible minute preparing the speech itself that there had been no studio rehearsals; a stand-in had substituted for lighting and sound adjustments. The speech was the main thing. There could be no distractions. Even William P. Rogers, his lawyer friend from Hiss trial days, and political coach and manager Murray Chotiner were kept out of sight to prevent distractions. Only his wife, Pat, sat nearby within picture range, ready to appear on camera when her husband discussed her with the TV audience.

Nervously, about to gamble with what could determine several political careers, he faced the camera as the little red light indicated he was on the air. He began with "I come before you tonight as a candidate for the Vice Presidency and as a man whose honesty and integrity have been questioned."

Well over two thousand miles away, the thirty people in the manager's office sat without a word. The General held a large yellow pad and a pencil and followed every word of the intensely delivered, emotional plea.

Nixon began by taking the offensive with moral indignation against the corruption in Washington and readily acknowledged that, had any of the $18,235 been for his personal use, it would have been a moral crime. But that, he emphasized, had not been the case. "Not one cent of the eighteen thousand dollars or any other money of that type ever went to me for my personal use." And, unlike Senator John Sparkman, the Democratic Vice Presidential candidate, his wife had not been placed on the Senate payroll. He had to make ends meet on his own $15,000 Senate salary. After reading the legal opinion from Gibson, Dunn and Crutcher, he proceeded to give the audience his own "complete financial history," how he had started from "modest circumstances," had worked through college and law school and then, in 1940, had married Pat. His career then interrupted by the war, he had entered the armed forces and compiled a "record that was not a particularly unusual one." Then, running for Congress, they were forced to save their earnings to buy a home, had lived modestly and had thus compiled only moderate assets and debts. "It isn't very much," Nixon added, "but Pat and I have the satisfaction that every dime that we've got is honestly ours." Looking directly into the camera he said, "I should say this—that Pat doesn't have a mink coat. But she does have a respectable Republican cloth coat. And I always tell her that she looks good in anything."[11]

The Cleveland Public Auditorium audience, as in the rest of America that night, watched intensely. Many had tears. Mamie Eisenhower and some of the men, too, dabbed their eyes with handkerchiefs. The General watched, fascinated.

Nixon then continued with the story of a Texan who, having heard that their little daughters, Tricia and Julie, wanted a dog, sent them a package one day. "You know what it was?" he asked earnestly. "It was a little cocker spaniel dog in a crate that he sent all the way from Texas. Black and white spotted. And our little girl—Tricia, the six-year-old—named it Checkers. And you know the kids love the dog and I just want to say this right now, that regardless of what they say about it, we're gonna keep it."

Then he declared: "I would suggest that under the circumstances both Mr. Sparkman and Mr. Stevenson should come before the American people as I have and make a complete financial statement as to their financial history. And if they don't it will be an admission that they have something to hide. And I think that you will agree with me."

In Cleveland, while the others sat absorbed and tearful, a much more perceptive viewer, Dwight Eisenhower, jabbed his pencil into the yellow pad with anger. He alone realized what Nixon was doing, how his running mate was turning the fire on him. For Nixon did not have to mention the General by name, but how could Ike be the only one of the four candidates not to make a disclosure? Doing so would inevitably publicize his having been the recipient of a special Congressional act that permitted him to save thousands on the lavish earnings from *Crusade in Europe* by paying a capital-gains instead of income taxes for the publication rights that he sold to Doubleday.[12] When the figures were subsequently released they showed that the General had earned $888,303.99 since 1942, including $635,000 on his book, but his total income and capital-gains tax payment had been less than 25 percent. Stevenson, whose ten-year income was almost exactly an even half million dollars, had paid 42 percent in taxes.[13] Eisenhower's anger was not without reason.

But the General's real fury was yet to come. "I would do nothing that would harm the possibilities of Dwight Eisenhower to become President of the United States," said Nixon in Hollywood. "And for that reason I am submitting to the Republican National Committee tonight through this television broadcast the decision which it is theirs to make. Let them decide whether my position on the ticket will help or hurt."[14]

This time, according to someone in the room who watched Eisenhower instead of the TV set, the General broke the pencil point on the yellow pad. The observer, who was interviewed by Stewart Alsop, commented, "Before that, I'd always liked and admired Ike, of course, but I often wondered how smart he really was. After that, I knew—Ike got what Dick was getting at right away, while the others were weeping and carrying on."[15]

Nixon asked his listeners to write and wire the national committee. Then he added: "But just let me say this last word. Regardless of what happens I'm going to continue this fight. I'm going to campaign up and down America until we drive the crooks and the Communists and those that defend them out of Washington. And remember, folks, Eisenhower is a great man. Believe me. He's a great man. And a vote for Eisenhower is a vote for what's good for America."

He continued with the mailing address of the national committee; but the little red camera light had gone off. His air time had expired. Realizing what had happened, he was disturbed that the public would not know where to send their responses.

Eisenhower turned to Summerfield and said, "Well, Arthur, you surely got your seventy-five thousand dollars' worth."

In the auditorium below, the audience had begun to shout, "We want Dick!"[16]

Eisenhower, determined to maintain full control over the situation, reacted quickly to the younger man's challenge. With the newsmen clamoring for a statement, he dictated to Jim Hagerty a telegram for Nixon that was also designated for release to the press. "Your presentation was magnificent," it began. Then, ignoring Nixon's comments about the national committee, he explained that before he would "complete the formulation of a decision" he felt the "need of talking to you and would be most appreciative if you would fly to see me at once. Tomorrow night I shall be at Wheeling, West Virginia." When he later faced the auditorium crowd, he praised Nixon in more lavish terms, as a courageous and honest man who, in a showdown fight, would be more useful than "a whole boxcar of pussyfooters." But the crowd, shouting, "We like

Dick!" was not told that he had reached a final opinion, only that he would not be "swayed by any idea of what will get the most votes. . . . I am going to say: Do I myself believe this man is the kind of man America would like to have for its Vice President?"[17]

The response was an unmistakable national outpouring of approval. Uncertain about where to send their communications, the public directed telegrams, cards, letters and petitions to various Republican headquarters. The party's Washington office alone received some three hundred thousand items. The Nixon appeal had, undoubtedly, provoked the correct popular response; even Harold Stassen wired his congratulations to Dick and Pat.

Forever remembered as a maudlin performance or as a political "soap opera" that would be recalled as the "Checkers Speech," it was ridiculed by the more sophisticated and forever coupled with the Nixon image. But, even as Nixon waited in Los Angeles that night for Eisenhower's reaction, both men understood that the real decision would not be made by the national committee or by the General. The verdict was the public's, with its warmth and understanding for a modest, decent man who had worked hard toward the American dream, who had a devoted family that wanted mere simple pleasures, including dogs and cloth coats; for a man who, having fought against his country's nefarious enemies, had found himself maligned just as he had risen to accept greater responsibilities. All that became clear within the next few hours. Yet, as he waited for a telegram from Cleveland, the only word of the General's reaction came from a news report that stressed his determination to reach a decision only after they had conferred together in Wheeling, West Virginia.

Nixon would have none of that. More agitated than ever and linking Eisenhower's latest statement with Dewey's pre-speech telephoned advice, he dictated to Rose Mary Woods, his secretary, a telegram announcing his resignation from the ticket. As Miss Woods left the room with the message for Arthur Summerfield, Murray Chotiner pursued her and ripped it up.[18] Within the next hour, when the Eisenhower telegram arrived, Nixon remained adamant. He would not go crawling to Wheeling as a child to father asking forgiveness. The American people, he knew, were on his side. He, instead, shocked the Eisenhower entourage by wiring his intention to continue his campaign schedule by going on to his next stop, Missoula, Montana. He would attend such a conference only *after* the General had made a decision. Eisenhower knew, of course, that he wanted Nixon to remain on the ticket.[19] Nixon, however, wanted that made clear to the public first. The Senator's campaign then headed toward Missoula.

The "clearance" to go on to Wheeling came the next morning. Summerfield, whom the Nixon people trusted, called Chotiner at dawn to give the General's assurance that the Senator would be received in West Virginia without any doubt about his standing. He would only go that far. After a brief appearance in Montana, Nixon flew to Eisenhower.

At the Wheeling airport there were three thousand people. Suddenly, as Nixon stood at the airplane door helping Pat with her coat, he saw Eisenhower himself rush up the steps toward the plane. Astonished, Nixon said, "What are you doing here, General? You didn't have to come out here to meet us."

"Why not?" said Eisenhower, putting his arm around Nixon. "You're my boy."[20]

Nixon, having pressed with his strength, had enhanced his stature. He had kept Eisenhower from humiliating him further by presiding over his distress before rendering the inevitable positive judgment, which would have been billed as the result of the General's heart-to-heart conference with his running mate. As the reward of Eisenhower's sufferance, Nixon's debt would have seemed real. For the rest of the campaign, wherever the Californian went, his reception compared favorably with what was normal for a popular candidate. Whatever their reaction to the style of the speech, there was general agreement that the net result was highly favorable. Eisenhower's political craft had been matched.

The Republicans had also retained exclusive monopoly over the corruption issue. As Senator Karl Mundt had defined them, the GOP's issues conformed to the formula K_1C_2—Korea, Communism, Corruption. With all the Republican big guns also promising, at best, to end the years of Democratic softness toward Reds, the matter yet to be presented with a distinctive position was the continuation of the war in the Far East. As the endless "peace" talks at Panmunjom threatened to match the permanence of the war itself, public concern had continued to mount. By October, Elmo Roper found that more than half of all Americans thought it was the number-one issue.[21] And, as Samuel Lubell noted in his soundings of grass-roots attitudes during the campaign, Democratic evocations of economic prosperity implicit in sloganeering like "You never had it so good" were being canceled out by the frustrations of a limited war.[22] Wavering somewhere between military victory and outright defeat, the unorthodox concept of war kept defying traditional solutions.

From the start, Eisenhower's promoters had also been the Republican supporters of the Administration's conduct of the war. After the popular approval of Truman's original deployment of MacArthur and the Seventh Army in June 1950 to save President Syngman Rhee's South Korean government, much of the GOP, including Taft, had plied back and forth between demanding full-scale war and outright withdrawal. Truman's bold sacking of MacArthur in April 1951 had made the commander more heroic than ever to that group and, forming behind his arguments for bolder action, they had increasingly accused Truman of a "no-win" policy.[23] Eisenhower, however, whose photographed expressive reaction to the MacArthur firing had left little doubt that he considered Truman's move a stroke of spectacular courage that was perhaps overdue, seemed to have returned from Europe with little appetite for offering an alternative Korean policy. His press-conference statement at Abilene on June 5 had amounted to precise support of continuing the limited war while seeking a decent armistice.[24]

For him to have maintained that approach would have demonstrated remarkable independence, as well as failure to exploit what had become a more partisan issue. His solution to a personal dilemma was adopting a middle ground between the hawk and dove extremes and, at the same time, avoiding mere duplication of the Truman–Acheson policy. Already, in Kansas City on August 21, he had warned that the Taft–Mac-Arthur approach would involve the U. S. in a Chinese war that would be "far more difficult to stop than the one we are in now."[25] Shortly after that, however, he turned his fire, instead, on Democratic culpability for having made Korea vulnerable to Communist attack and soon found himself in a hot debate with Harry Truman on the responsibility for having made the war possible. But that was merely an extension of prevailing Republican criticism. On October 2, at Champaign, Illinois, the General declared that there was "no sense" in having the nation "bear the brunt of the thing." "If there must be a war there," he said, "let it be Asians against Asians, with our support on the side of freedom."[26] As he continued that line, it combined with the debate about the war's origins to distinguish Eisenhower's position from the Democrats. Truman, by that time, as involved in the campaign as though it were a repetition of 1948, appeared in Hartford on October 16 and challenged the General to offer a plan for settling the war as a means of saving American lives.[27]

That was precisely what most Democrats feared. There was nothing Stevenson could do or say to compete with Eisenhower as a military authority. The Democrat had, in fact, already decided that, after his election, he would travel to Korea, Japan and India to see what could be done about the realities of the Asian power alignments in order to promote a settlement. He had rejected any notion of publicizing the plan during the campaign because that would have been regarded as a political move that might have jeopardized negotiations and promoted false hopes of peace that might only result in harmful despair, thus prolonging the war.[28]

For the General to make that announcement would obviously be far more dramatic and effective. On October 24, at Detroit's Masonic Temple, Eisenhower warmed up to his punch line on national TV by stressing that his Administration would give top proprity to ending the war. Then he added: "That job requires a personal trip to Korea. I shall make that trip. Only in that way could I learn how best to serve the American people in the cause of peace. I shall go to Korea. . . ."[29]

The brainchild of speech writer Emmet J. Hughes, who wrote the original draft in New York, the proposal had won swift approval within the Eisenhower inner circle. Eisenhower, hearing it read to him by C. D. Jackson, also bought it without objection. As an Associated Press political writer reflected about that event in Detroit, "For all practical purposes, the contest ended that night."[30]

What had become the country's greatest anxiety was thus promised the personal attention of her greatest living hero—Ike. Truman wondered what he could do that the Joint Chiefs of Staff had not been able to accomplish during their visits there, and Stevenson said he was raising false hopes, that if he wanted to go anywhere to end the war he should go to Moscow. But the issues raised by the Republicans during the campaign's last days were those of appeal to the independents and the Democrats in the industrial North. Even McCarthy was attacked by Eisenhower, although indirectly, when he told a Chicago audience on the last day of October that there was rightful concern about the methods being used to combat communism in government.[31] In Boston, on the campaign's last day, he identified himself with Wendell Willkie and progressive Republicans. His handling of the Korean situation had also been consistent with moderation, for it conceded nothing to the extreme solutions being promoted by important groups within his own party.

Liberals, however, who had assumed many things about Ike, remained thoroughly disenchanted. *The Reporter*, switching to Stevenson from Eisenhower, complained that after all the talk about the steal at Mineral Wells, "Who could have imagined that the Eisenhower faction, after having triumphed at Chicago, could let its victory be stolen? Who could ever have conceived that Eisenhower, the man who could revamp and cleanse the Republican Party, would go along, probably believing that it was still his party and that he was its leader?"[32] Rumors circulated that the New York *Times*, perhaps also surprised by Eisenhower's willingness to subordinate himself to the Old Guard, would abandon the General for Stevenson. On the campaign's final weekend, the *Times* responded with a special editorial denying the imminence of such a change and promised that, despite the letters and telegrams being received, the Election Day would still find that "General Eisenhower's name will be at the head of the list."[33]

Then, after campaigning in Boston on that final day, Ike and Mamie, weary and thankful for the end of the ordeal, returned to New York. Arriving early Election Day morning, they first voted and then went to bed at 60 Morningside Drive, confident of success. Popular song writer Irving Berlin expressed the national attitude toward Eisenhower that day when he noted how the statue of Father Duffy in Times Square had managed to exude a kindly glowing smile although hundreds of pigeons had covered it with muck.[34]

Nearly thirteen million more Americans went to the polls that day than in 1948, and almost thirty-four million shared Berlin's faith. By the early evening of November 4, the trend was obvious. Eisenhower's popular vote was 55 percent of the record total ballots cast. Even such reliable Democratic states as Texas, Tennessee and Virginia had gone for him. Not since Herbert Hoover in 1928, running against anti-Prohibition Roman Catholic Al Smith, had the GOP upset the Solid South. Stevenson, whose 27,314,992 votes nearly equaled what FDR had received in 1936, had done no better than eighty-nine electoral votes. Just before 1 A.M., Central Standard Time, he conceded defeat. To the distressed followers who surrounded him in the room, he recalled that Lincoln, asked how he felt after an unsuccessful election, had compared himself to a little boy who had stubbed his toe in the dark. "He said that he was too old to cry but it hurt too much to laugh," the Governor remarked.[35]

The Republican party's gamble, essentially a product of inadequate confidence, had paid off. It was almost hard to believe, but the twenty-year Democratic reign in Washington had finally ended. Industrialist Charles Hook, chairman of the board of the Armco Corporation, wrote to the President-elect in language that was commonplace among fellow businessmen: "All through the campaign I expressed the opinion (and I was sincere in the belief)," he stated, "that this was our last chance to stop the drift to socialism and save the freedoms that had brought to us the highest standard of living in the world."[36]

CHAPTER 18

Time for a Change

ANALYSES OF THE 1952 results brought considerable agreement. Republicans could not be credited with having wrought a change reminiscent of the Jeffersonian success of 1800, the Jacksonian triumph of 1828, the initial Republican victory behind Lincoln in 1860, the 1920 GOP return behind Warren Harding or the FDR sweep of 1932. The statistics showed clearly that Republican Congressional gains had been extremely modest in comparison with the Eisenhower endorsement. Only twenty-two seats had been picked up in the House, eight fewer than in the 1950 mid-term elections. Further, 359,397 more people voted for Democratic Congressional candidates than for Republicans. In the Senate, Wayne Morse's rejection of his old party affiliation had limited their majority to a single vote. Even Senator Henry Cabot Lodge, Jr., whose re-election hopes had banked on help from the General's name at the head of the Massachusetts ballot, lost by nearly seventy-one thousand votes to thirty-five-year-old Congressman John F. Kennedy. In Dallas County, Texas, heavy campaigning by John Roosevelt had brought the best-known Democratic name in behalf of the General and helped gain for Ike an astonishing 62.7 percent of the vote in that part of the state. Yet there was little confidence by local Republicans that the electorate had really abandoned traditional party lines.[1] In only seventy of the 199 House seats that had been held by the GOP did the Republican candidate run ahead of the General.

It seemed certain that popular confidence in Eisenhower, as a man of integrity, patriotism, moderation and particularly his bipartisan "above politics" appeal characteristic of a George Washington, had clearly overcome wide resistance against entrusting the government to Republicans. One of those closest to the General, whose association predated his return from Europe, observed that the Democrats who rushed to his support did so not through ideological reasons but because of confidence in the man.

Most voters in 1952 were sufficiently aware of Hoover and the Great Depression to vote for the GOP only with trepidation. The University of Michigan Survey Research Center found that one out of three studied spoke favorably of the Democrats as the party of the "common people," while such descriptions of the Republicans were rare. While the Democratic party evoked more feelings of both approval and disapproval than the GOP, the researchers reported, their net popularity was still greater. Reacting at a time of high employment, with only 2.7 percent of the labor force out of work, and during a Korean war-induced inflation, which had sent the consumer price index up to 113.5 from 102.8 in two years, 26 percent of those interviewed praised the Democrats for "good times," "higher wages" and "more jobs." The mere 6 percent who spoke favorably of the Republican party for economic conditions were mostly hopeful that the GOP could correct the inflation. All major groups of Eisenhower voters gave significant fractions of their votes to Democratic House and Senate candidates. And although 15 percent liked Stevenson because of his party, only 5 percent cited Eisenhower's political affiliation as an asset.[2]

The results can be understood best by considering what the voters did not like. Truman's decision not to seek re-election had obviously resulted from what even a superficial view of the American mood indicated about his popularity. His firing of MacArthur had brought demands for his impeachment and praise for the relieved General. Charges of malfeasance by Administration officials and Truman laxity in ridding the government of subversives, despite his inauguration of a loyalty program in 1947 and a militant Cold War stand, had combined in the public mind with the era's sensational Communist spy revelations and incomprehensible Red nuclear bomb and territorial achievements. The Dulles-inspired appeals to those outraged about the containment policy's acquiescence in the face of Russian hegemony in Eastern Europe had aroused the expected anger. Even where the Administration was giving communism direct military opposition, as in Korea, few found much reason to applaud the effort. Samuel Lubell's survey of grass-roots sentiment found the war so irksome that most people were inclined to feel that it more than negated the economic gains.[3] Texans, almost unanimous in opposing Truman's support of federal control of the tidelands oil rights, were so vehement about the issue that the fall campaign in the Lone Star State was dominated by the question of the most feasible ballot arrangement to permit Democrats to vote for Eisenhower. "Texans for Ike," organized by Corpus Christi businessman Maston Nixon, a newcomer to politics, was envisioned as an outlet for Democrats who, although "well satisfied with our Texas delegation in Congress," were behind the Republican candidate in large part because "Eisenhower is for returning the Tidelands to the school children of Texas." His group, however, he informed Mrs. Oveta Culp Hobby of the Houston *Post*, was "not about to become Republicans."[4] In Louisiana, where the oil issue was also compelling, only bitter statewide political rivalries between Governor Robert Kennon and the Long forces enabled Stevenson to slip by with 53 percent of the vote in a traditional Democratic stronghold. The fervent civil-rights position taken by Truman, which had caused the rebellion of 1948, had not been duplicated by Stevenson, but the Democrats' position was nevertheless sufficiently sympathetic to win him praise from the NAACP and condemnation by Harry Byrd of Virginia and Governor James F. Byrnes of South Carolina. In both Southern states, where the oil issue was more ideological than tangible, those leaders became Eisenhower assets, although Stevenson did take South Carolina by a flimsy five-thousand-vote margin. When journalist George McMillan interviewed voters in South Carolina's McCormick County, which had not cast a single Republican vote in 1948, he found that the anti-Truman sentiment was the strongest characteristic. Such issues as corruption and oil, in addition to civil rights, were convincing most voters to overcome their traditional antipathy to Republicans by going for the General. Fred Buzhardt, the county attorney and chairman of the McCormick County Democratic Committee, explained, "Well, you might as well know that this is one of the harshest anti-Truman counties in South Carolina. We just don't like him, and I'll tell you why: because we here in McCormick County don't like to think there are a bunch of thieves in Washington." Another reaction, which was typical, came from a lady who said, "People around here just don't like Truman. But they've all been raised Democrats."[5]

Truman, the heir of the responsibility for what had happened at Yalta, which both the Republican platform and Eisenhower had repudiated, had fallen in public esteem to where only 32 percent of the voters approved of his Presidency.[6] Schoolchildren throughout the nation responded with derisive laughter when teachers mentioned the President's name. The Michigan Research Center found that the "largest number of disapproving comments directed at any public figure were about President Truman." They also found that Stevenson's connection with the incumbent was the most objectionable quality about the Democratic candidate.[7] All Stevenson efforts to shake Truman had failed. The fighting campaigner of 1948 fame entered the battle with, as Arthur Krock noted, "a protracted assault on the personal integrity of General Eisenhower that is without parallel for a man in Mr. Truman's position."[8]

Eisenhower's involvement in politics, therefore, had been well timed. For a combination of reasons, Americans were ready not necessarily for a new party but for an end to Executive control by those who had permitted events to get out of hand. When the Research Survey asked why people had voted for Eisenhower, the most frequent single response was that it was "time for a change." Immediately behind that was an expressed concern with domestic policies and issues. Foreign policy was third. Only 15 percent said they favored him because he was the "best man," and his party ties and experience were at the bottom, each with just 8 percent.[9] Stevenson himself, within ninety-six hours after the election, had received about twenty-five thousand letters and ten thousand telegrams from both Democrats and Republicans praising his campaign; many felt compelled to confess that they had voted for Eisenhower because it was "time for a change."[10] The vote was clearly less for Eisenhower than an expression of protest against what had already happened. As political scientist V. O. Key, Jr., has pointed out, "the odds are that Eisenhower won, not so much so because of his 'personality' as because certain of his qualities happened to dovetail nicely with the requirements of the situation in which the country and the Republican party found itself."[11]

Two weeks after Election Day, Milton S. Eisenhower was interested in a report of the Opinion Research Corporation of Princeton, New Jersey, that confirmed the conservatism of the public mood: general opposition to FEPC laws, belief in the possibility of a $10 billion budget cut to be largely at the expense of foreign aid, demands for more zeal in cleaning up communism and corruption, opposition to government health insurance, for less government regulation of business and for a reduction of government aid to unions. At the same time it showed recognition for continued government welfare programs; doing more in regard to social security, veterans' benefits, loans to homeowners and loans to small businessmen. Sending the information to Arthur Vandenberg, Jr., with the suggestion that it be shown to Ike, the President-elect's younger brother added, "Please note the 'new conservatism' really means that we should keep what we have, catch our breath for a while, and improve administration; it does not mean moving backward."[12] When Dwight Eisenhower lunched with Herbert Hoover at Dulles's New York townhouse in December, the ex-President had some advice for his first Republican successor: It isn't necessary to reverse everything. You will have done a good job if you have merely slowed down the process by the end of your term. You'll find many things you want to reverse, you'll not be able to reverse, and if you can just slow down this trend in government, give it some new directions in your term of office, you will have succeeded mightily.[13]

That Hoover would have preferred Taft in Eisenhower's place was clear. Whether that could have been possible, in view of the anxieties that led to the heavy anti-Truman vote, was less clear. Republican stalwarts would speculate endlessly, but they could never be sure.

CHAPTER 19

Redeeming the Pledge

THE ENTIRE OPERATION, George Humphrey later recalled, was done in the "most hush-hush, cloak and dagger manner you ever heard in your life." Special agents brought instructions for carefully worked-out, top-secret departure plans that called for leaving homes and hotels at pre-dawn hours, walking specified numbers of street blocks in carefully prescribed and varying directions, driving through the darkness with dimmed or totally blacked-out headlights, emplaning at obscure landing strips, obeying restrictions against stepping out of planes at fueling stops and cryptic radio messages while aloft. Humphrey, the Secretary of the Treasury designate, was visited at his home near Cleveland by an agent; he was to meet him on a designated city street in the middle of the night, and from there they would leave for the flight to New York. Then, making a nocturnal departure from his hotel, he would travel by car to a given street, walk eight blocks in the dark, meet a man on the corner, and then be picked up in a car for the ride out to Long Island.[1]

At five-thirty on the morning of November 29, two men stepped out of 60 Morningside Drive. Their coats turned up against the thirty-degree temperature, they stepped into a black Cadillac limousine. With the city still quiet, the car cruised unimpeded across the Triborough Bridge; after a drive along a back road that paralleled the Air Force base at Mitchel Field, they reached the installation. As the gate swung open, another car pulled ahead of the limousine and provided an escort to the runway. There, with two big Constellations waiting in the dark, the Cadillac stopped and both men emerged. The driver was a Secret Service agent; the other man, wearing a brown double-breasted suit and camel's-hair coat, was President-elect Dwight D. Eisenhower.[2]

"I'm sorry we don't have coffee," an Air Force general explained, "but security cuts down the number of people we can use at this hour."

The others who boarded the two big planes had left the city just as mysteriously. Distinguished-looking and gray-haired Charles E. Wilson, the sixty-two-year-old president of the General Motors Corporation and now the man designated to head the Defense Department, had walked out of the Waldorf-Astoria Hotel alone and without luggage. He told a cab driver to drop him off at the southeast corner of Fifth Avenue and Fifty-eighth Street. Precise planning minimized his wait on the dark, cold and deserted street when a sedan met him at the spot. Wilson then headed toward Mitchel Field. At the same time as the President-elect and others were following their routes, from a half dozen other points in the city, before the general public had begun to stir very much that cold Saturday morning, six reporters and photographers had also left their quarters and begun to converge on Pennsylvania Station. As other early travelers waited for trains, the six were insignificantly deployed along the platform. Suddenly, a black limousine descended the ramp; and there, one by one, as the automobile made its way alongside the train tracks, the group, joined by press secretary Jim Hagerty, strolled to the car being driven by a Secret Service agent.

Eisenhower and the rest of his party, which included his close friend and future White House assistant retired Major General Wilton (Jerry) B. Persons; the chairman of the Joint Chiefs of Staff, General Omar N. Bradley; and the Attorney General-designate Herbert Brownell left in his Constellation at 5:55. The second plane, with Hagerty and the newsmen, followed ten minutes later. The others, who were scheduled to join the President-elect in the Pacific, such as John Foster Dulles, were due to leave the United States several days later.

Equally vital for security purposes were the cover stories that had been concocted to hide the General's absence. After the meeting at the Commodore Hotel headquarters on November 20, when the departure date was chosen, the subterfuge was planned to delay knowledge about Eisenhower's presence in the Far East until he was safely out of the Korean war zone. His absence from the hotel's sixth-floor headquarters, where he had been working full days since his return from a visit with President Truman on the eighteenth, was bound to stimulate unwanted speculation. By leaving early on a Saturday morning he had the weekend to make a getaway without attracting attention; but even that had to be set up in advance. To cope with the problem of his expected work habits, it was decided that the Saturday and Sunday before the flight would be spent with aides and visitors at Morningside Heights and not at the hotel. That would establish a precedent. In addition, arrangements were made for prominent people to arrive at the house on those days and for them to participate in stories that, with the aid of a cooperative press, gave the clear implication that they had been conducting business with the President-elect in person.

On Saturday afternoon, while the Constellations were already over the Pacific Ocean, John Foster Dulles emerged from 60 Morningside Heights and announced that he had visited with Eisenhower and, implying that he was at home, that they had decided on the appointment of Henry Cabot Lodge as the representative to the United Nations. Another announcement that afternoon said that Eisenhower had decided to forgo attending the Army–Navy football game but was watching it on television. On Sunday, photographers took pictures (which the newspapers carried) of Nelson A. Rockefeller, Milton Eisenhower and Arthur Flemming leaving the mansion after a "three hour meeting" to survey the possibilities of streamlining the Executive Branch of the government. The press also reported that Eisenhower had just made public an exchange of letters with Dr. Robert L. Johnson, the president of Temple University, that pertained to such reorganization. A string of additional announcements followed right after that, with all further implications of the President-elect's active involvement: Winthrop Aldrich was appointed Ambassador to England; Martin Durkin, unknown to the public, would be the new Secretary of Labor; Sinclair Weeks, who had headed the 1952 campaign finance committee, was nominated as Secretary of Commerce; and Walter Williams was named as his Under Secretary.[3] At the same time, speculation about the projected start of the trip virtually disappeared from the press, almost as though the project had been abandoned.

The elaborate precautions had at least been partly in response to the public concern that the trip would not be worth the risk. Even some of Eisenhower's closest advisers suggested the abandonment of such plans.[4] But the President-elect remained firm. He had promised the American people a personal inspection of the frustrating war, and the pledge had not only been made in Detroit on October 24 but had been repeated constantly during the closing days of the campaign. To those who discounted what he could achieve, he responded that he did not have any "patent medicine" that could solve the situation but that his intention was merely to get information.[5] He had made his commitment and to break faith with the American public, he knew, would stigmatize him as just another politician.

Other objections were also raised. Soon after the election returns had been tabulated, a joint statement by the GOP's 1936 Presidential candidate, Alf Landon, and a former Secretary of War under Roosevelt, Harry M. Woodring, had pleaded that the trip was not worth the great risk it posed for the "welfare of the American people."[6] Opposition also came from Walter Winchell, as well as the staunchly Democratic New York *Post*, the paper that had first exposed the Nixon fund story.

Such traditionally anti-Republican quarters had evidently not permitted their campaign barbs at the General's accommodations with the political right to destroy their trust that, however unholy his alliance with Satan, the country's future would be more secure under him than in the hands of any possible replacement necessitated by an emergency. His death before December 15, when the electors were due to cast their two ballots for President and Vice President, would have left the selection of a substitute up to the Republican National Committee. Taft would undoubtedly have been placed at the head of the ticket. The creation of a vacancy after the electors had completed their mid-December ritual would have given the Presidency to Richard Nixon.

Not until the fifth of December, then, was word of the actual trip released in the United States. The President-elect, news broadcasts revealed, had completed his visit to Korea and was en route to the United States via air to Guam and then toward Honolulu aboard the cruiser *Helena*. Pentagon fears that Communist aircraft might strike at Seoul during Eisenhower's presence almost materialized, it was later found, when eleven light enemy pursuit planes stabbed at the Allied defenses around the city in an effort that began just one hour before Eisenhower's Constellation departed.

In the days before Eisenhower's arrival, Seoul itself was the center of massive popular demonstrations staged by the government of President Syngman Rhee to promote his fervent desire for an all-out drive toward the Yalu River border with Manchuria. American flags and "Welcome Ike" banners were displayed. The Rhee administration was clearly working to bolster the lagging morale of large numbers of people who, more than two years after the start of the war that had waged back and forth across the Thirty-eighth Parallel, were tired of the conflict and would have liked nothing better than the restoration of peace to the peninsula nation.[7] Rhee himself, looking forward toward enlisting the new American President in his long-standing ambition of uniting the country under his own flag, had hoped for much martial mileage from the visit. Many Koreans had wanted the President-elect to spend at least a week in the country and then visit the National Assembly and participate in a giant military review to be staged in the capital city, all designed to enhance the public prestige of the Rhee regime. Eisenhower's promise to the American people, they reasoned, could be fulfilled only by a careful and lengthy study of the entire situation.[8]

But the visit became a major disappointment for President Rhee. Eisenhower landed in Seoul on December 2 and left in his Constellation almost exactly seventy-two hours later. The three days were devoted to a hectic round of conferences on virtually every military level. He met with Admiral Radford, the commander of the American Pacific fleet, and was accompanied everywhere by General Mark Clark, the com-

mander-in-chief of the United Nations forces and General James A. Van
Fleet, who led the Eighth United States Army in Korea. Eisenhower
reviewed the troops of the fourteen nations fighting under the UN flag,
flew over the front lines, visited the frozen, snow-clad battlefield and
heard the sound of shells plunging into enemy-held hills, inspected an
Air Force base, visited an American Mobile Army Surgical Hospital and,
during the morning hours of the third day, spoke with fifty-one military
commanders he had been unable to meet during the two days spent
visiting troops on the field. He also managed two conferences with Rhee,
for a total of one hour.[9]

In addition to attempting to persuade Eisenhower of the wisdom of his
military objectives, the Korean leader was clearly anxious to convince
the American visitor to include in his schedule a large public military
review in Seoul. Eisenhower had already declined to visit the National
Assembly. But the military review was a much more precious project of
the Korean President, who envisioned the presence on the reviewing
stand of himself alongside such notables as Eisenhower, Charles E. Wilson, Herbert Brownell, Generals Clark and Van Fleet, Admiral Radford
and other members of the military commands. The crowds had been led
to expect the big show. Some ten thousand had already gathered at the
site. Such a prospect, however, was a nightmare for the Eisenhower
entourage. South Korean claims that local Communists had been
rounded up in advance were not reassuring. A couple of well-placed
grenades from a single source would have brought a major disaster. In
the diplomatic embarrassment about how to get around Rhee's pet
project, which was not popular with those responsible for security in
Seoul, a simple solution that involved no further offense was found. The
schedule was devised to include the review at the latest possible time
before Eisenhower's scheduled departure. Happily, then, time spent by
the President-elect observing a hilltop assault demonstration by the First
Republic of Korea (ROK) Division and at a news conference was too
great to accommodate the review.[10]

There was also little comfort for Rhee in Eisenhower's remarks to the
reporters. He observed how difficult it would be to end that kind of
struggle with a "positive and definite victory without possibly running
the grave risk of enlarging the war." He reasserted the American willingness to "see it through," but offered no panaceas. His words contained not a hint about the POW issue or any reference to his own
position regarding the American debates over resolving the war.[11] In
New York, on that same day, a man whose views were far more compatible with those of President Rhee, General Douglas MacArthur,
spoke to the National Association of Manufacturers and hinted that he
had a plan to end the war and that, if requested, he would make it

available to Eisenhower. Even his brief stay in the Far East had strengthened the President-elect's willingness to listen to any reasonable solution.
As he later wrote in his memoirs, the Korean visit had left him with
the conclusion that "we could not stand forever on a static front and
continue to accept casualties without any visible results. Small attacks on
small hills would not end wars."[12] Thus, on the seventh of December,
from the *Helena*, Eisenhower radioed MacArthur: "I am looking forward to informal meetings in which my associates and I may obtain full
benefit of your thinking and experience" on Korea and the Far East.
MacArthur replied with an expression of gratitude for Eisenhower's
interest and pointed out that the successful solution of the Korean problem "might well become the key to peace in the world."[13]

The exchange exacerbated the downward course of Eisenhower's relations with Truman. Angrier than ever at the General for having digni-
fied MacArthur's offer, the outgoing President challenged the man he
had relieved from his command or anybody else having a "reasonable
plan" to end the Korean war to submit it to him "at once." "If we can
cut this fighting in Korea short by one day, we should do so," the
statement said. While there was no specific mention of MacArthur's
name, it was clear that the Truman message was tantamount to an order
to submit any plan to him before revealing it to Eisenhower or anybody
else. He was, after all, still the President.[14]

Regardless of what MacArthur might have to say, Eisenhower's mind
was clear about his options. When thanking Eighth Army commander
General James Van Fleet for having facilitated the arrangements for the
visit, the President-elect observed, "While one cannot learn everything
in such a brief visit, I feel that I now have a far better understanding of
the situation in Korea and the problems which you and your forces are
facing."[15] And the return trip, three days of it by sea in convenient
isolation with several of his future Cabinet members and other aides and
advisers, afforded a perfect opportunity to discuss that and other problems.

After the Eisenhower party had transferred to the *Helena* at Guam,
the cruiser proceeded along its easterly course despite the rough seas of
an incipient storm. Off Wake Island, a helicopter descended on the ship
and brought the last contingent: Cabinet nominees George Humphrey,
John Foster Dulles and Douglas McKay; future Director of the Budget
Joseph Dodge and General Lucius Clay; as well as speech writers Charles
D. Jackson and Emmet Hughes. Charlie Wilson, however, had left them
and flown to Pearl Harbor for conferences with Admiral Radford and
General Bradley.

After devoting the first day of the voyage to getting acquainted with
the other members of what Eisenhower liked to call his "team," they

spent almost all of the remaining hours before reaching Hawaii in thorough discussions about objectives. Eisenhower immediately made known his position on the Korean situation. Continuation of the *status quo* was intolerable. The fighting, caught between the nationalistic aspirations of President Rhee and the dangers of provoking a wider Asian war, had to be ended, even, Eisenhower stressed, if it meant accepting the stalemate. Stopping there would be justified because the original American and United Nations objective of clearing Communists from South Korea would be fulfilled. The greatest difficulty, it was already clear to Eisenhower after his visit, would come from Rhee; but that was a matter that needed special handling.[16]

Except for some outlining by Dulles of a policy that would involve the capability of concentrating American military power so that it could employ what soon began to be known as massive retaliation, there was little further discussion of foreign policy. The future Cabinet was drawn from the upper echelons of the managerial ranks of leading American corporations, and Eisenhower, thus surrounding himself with the businessmen whose success and judgment he admired, was perfectly at home with those who thought, as did he, that there was no point to any other consideration if the economy was not sound. Devoted as they were to minimizing the role of the federal government, their greatest concern was with ending inflation and preserving the "soundness" of the dollar, formulating a policy about the Korean war bred price and wage controls and fostering government economy by lopping $10 billion from the Truman budget for fiscal year 1954 (which would start on July 1, 1953) and aiming toward the earliest possible balanced budget.

But banker Joseph Dodge, whom Eisenhower had appointed to ease the problems of transition by working with the outgoing Director of the Budget, had disturbing news for the gentlemen on the *Helena*. Dodge revealed that the Truman budget with its projected $80 billion outlay would be almost impossible to cut. National-security appropriations alone, which included the armed forces, atomic-energy programs, foreign aid and other allied areas, made up some 70 percent of the total. Even more inflexible was the earmarking of much defense money to pay for military paraphernalia that had been authorized by Congress in the past but not yet delivered. When other fixed items were added, such as veterans benefits, farm price supports, interest on the public debt and statutory grants to state and local governments, cutting would require major ingenuity. If, in addition, the scheduled tax cuts were to be allowed, there would be a cash deficit of about $10 billion. How could Eisenhower, then, possibly comply with his campaign promise to balance the budget at the end of four years or his agreement with Taft to lower federal expenditures to $70 billion?

Furthermore, it illustrated the major dilemma, which they soon called the "great equation." At what point would the maximum amount of fiscal pruning threaten national security? Eisenhower and the business-men around him were convinced that generating inflation would weaken the economy and thereby make excessive spending counterproductive. Could this be accomplished by more selective expenditures rather than by shirking responsibilities?[17] The continuing controls of prices and wages, which most Republicans felt were preventing further desired economic expansion that could produce more revenue, compounded the problems. Left alone, they would expire on April 30.

George Humphrey had no doubts about how to handle controls: drop them. He had preached that line to Eisenhower, reasoning that expansion of productivity would inhibit the possibility of further significant infla-tion; and he argued, as did many Democrats, that the system of controls was simply not working, that they were strangulating the operation of a free economy. Eisenhower, beginning to succumb to the radiant per-sonality of the lawyer-businessman who had headed the Mark Hanna Corporation with its coal and iron-ore interests, bought his reasoning. What was left to decide was the question of how and when they should be removed. From the *Helena*, in the midst of their discussions, Eisen-hower sent a letter to Sinclair Weeks, his Secretary of Commerce-desig-nate. After informing Weeks of his desire to discontinue direct price, wage and other controls, he asked the party's experienced fund-raiser "to head a small group to examine the situation relating to present con-trols of materials, wages, prices, rent, etc., and to recommend to me by January 10 a schedule for future action. . . . I would suggest that you have John Henry Williams as one of the representatives of Mr. Durkin and selected members of the Business Advisory Committee on your group. Brownell or Clay can give you any further details you may need as to purpose and scope of study."[18] Clay arranged several meetings, one at the Links Club in New York with Weeks and such others as financier Sidney Weinberg, Ralph Cordiner of General Electric and several indus-trialists and bank presidents. Their general recommendation was to re-move the controls as soon as possible.[19]

By the time the *Helena* reached Hawaii and Eisenhower returned to New York on December 14, most of the new team had not only been exposed to one another through long hours of discussions, but a general consensus had been reached about the economy and the Korean war. "On the whole," the President-elect wrote to David Lawrence, who edited the conservative *U.S. News & World Report*, "I am entirely satisfied with the results of this trip. As you well know, there is no easy or obvious solution to the situation in the Far East, but I feel that we can now proceed on the basis of first-hand information and impressions."[20]

Three days after they reached New York, Eisenhower and Dulles met with MacArthur. During their more than two hours with Eisenhower's former military superior, in Dulles's East Ninety-first Street townhouse, they found that MacArthur's ideas did not constitute a plan at all but were merely tactical methods for ending the war. MacArthur advocated threatening to bomb wherever necessary beyond the Yalu to hit military bases and the sources of supplies and to warn in clear terms about the nuclear consequences of not getting out of Korea. If the Chinese refused to leave, MacArthur urged, we should go in and "crack them" with nuclear bombs. Dulles and Eisenhower said little while MacArthur went on. Finally, Eisenhower said, "General, this is something of a new thing. I'll have to look at the understanding between ourselves and our allies, on the prosecution of this war because if we're going to bomb bases on the other side of the Yalu, if we're going to extend the war we have to make sure we're not offending the whole world, the free world, or breaking faith."[21]

Undoubtedly, Eisenhower would have been very surprised to have received a realistic, moderate solution from MacArthur. When Mac-Arthur's original statement about his "plan" had been received aboard the *Helena*, some of Eisenhower's advisers were skeptical and even wondered whether the President-elect should involve himself with a man whose attitude about American military obligations in Korea were well known.[22] Eisenhower's view of MacArthur was no mystery, especially to those who saw the widely circulated photograph showing his expressive reaction to the news that Truman had just fired the Far Eastern commander. As far back as October 5, 1942, Eisenhower, who was rarely caustic about individuals, had recorded in his office diary a conversation with Walter Bedell Smith. Having said, "I wouldn't trade one Marshall for fifty MacArthurs," Eisenhower reconsidered for a second and then added, "My God! That would be a lousy deal. What would I do with fifty MacArthurs?"[23] But Eisenhower also realized, more than many of those who tried to discourage him from wasting his time with MacArthur, that the old general was still a hero to a large segment of the public and, of even more import, possibly to a majority of those who called themselves Republicans.

All that had been garnered since Election Day, the information obtained by those who had been working with the cooperative outgoing Truman Administration, the political relationships within the party, the impressions gathered during those three days in Korea and by the long discussions aboard the *Helena* were subjected to a final, pre-Inaugural review at a Commodore Hotel conference on January 12 and 13. After an opening prayer by Ezra Taft Benson, suggested by Eisenhower, the conference considered its agenda of problems in what amounted to a dress rehearsal: a reading of the Inaugural address by Eisenhower, final arrangements for the Inauguration, the problem of getting the Cabinet confirmed, the operation of the National Security Council, the distribution of patronage, a presentation by C. D. Jackson on "Planning a Cold War Program," Nelson Rockefeller on reorganization of governmental administration and the coordination of the White House staff.[24] But the dominant discussion continued to be federal finances and controls. The Weeks commission made its report in favor of reverting to a free market.

Weeks and his group had already made their recommendations known before the January 10 deadline that Eisenhower had set. Pointing out that, historically, controls cope with but the symptoms rather than the causes of inflation and should be reserved only for dire emergencies and for the shortest possible period, Weeks reported that keeping such controls in the present circumstances "would distort and impede our productive effort." The interests of a "dynamic economy to meet our changing and growing needs," he said, demanded prompt lifting of restrictions on wages and prices. As far as the impact on prices, there was the recognition that "adjustment to demand will result in individual price changes— some up, some down." The long-term gain for the economy, however, would be salutary.[25]

At the Commodore, following Weeks's presentation of this conclusion, Henry Cabot Lodge and Harold Stassen voiced the concerns of those who feared inflationary consequences. Both men, taking the view that was closer to the Democratic economists, favored the more cautious approach of delaying such action until possibly midsummer. Ike listened and, as was his practice in open conferences, remained noncommittal. But Humphrey, who spoke with determination in colorful terms and had a radiant smile that was second only to Eisenhower's, supported the report more emphatically than Weeks himself. Eisenhower's thinking, however, was no mystery.[26]

He had thus completed his major pre-Inaugural functions. The trip to Korea had fulfilled an election promise; there may also be some merit to the claims that Eisenhower had contributed to the morale of American troops bogged down on the peninsula, not so much by his presence during those few hours but by the strong implication that he meant to rectify their miserable condition. At the same time, such an excursion by "brass" undoubtedly brings cynical reactions from the overwhelming majority of GIs not visited, particularly when their lives in subsequent days show no evidence of any benefits. For President Syngman Rhee, the aggressive hopes of nationalist plans to invade North Korea with American assistance were, by Eisenhower's conduct during the trip, given a severe setback. President Truman had already permitted the twin militancy of MacArthur's dreams of glory and American anti-Communist jingoism to expand his original reason for deploying troops in Korea when, in defiance of warnings from both Europe and Asia, he had authorized the general to invade across the Thirty-eighth Parallel. The result had been the intervention by massive numbers of Communist Chinese "volunteer" forces and the most crushing defeat on land in American military history. For Rhee, astute, dedicated, Harvard- and Princeton-educated, the political nature of the trip had become evident and had signaled that the new administration in Washington would bring not continued partnership but disengagement. At home, too, the Eisenhower preliminaries had signified a change. As perhaps best illustrated by the questions relating to wage and price controls, the real issue for the Republicans was the imminence of having to translate not merely campaign rhetoric but their own shibboleths and credos of the past twenty years into a program that would prove the advantages of encouraging capitalism while at the same time reversing the persistence of Democratic majorities.

CHAPTER 20

The Restoration

Dwight D. Eisenhower spent his final collegiate hours saying good-bye to the numerous callers—and accepting a bronze Columbia lion, a key and a plaque signed by each trustee. The General had never been an integral part of the university. His NATO tour had shortened his stay; and as a military man, scorned by some as a Kansas "hayseed" with a West Point education, a self-effacing rejector of intellectual pretensions, a traditional conservative, he had made no effort to become representative of one of America's urban liberal intellectual centers. Most of the students and faculty members had, in fact, supported Adlai Stevenson during the recent campaign. That Friday night on Morningside Heights, in his final speech as the university's president, his remarks to the thirteen hundred faculty and administrative personnel gathered in the McMillin Theater on upper Broadway contained the aura of innocence that the professors ridiculed and the public appreciated.

He recalled having taken the job amid rumors that "our universities were cut and honey-combed with subversion and there was communism lurking behind every brick on campus and every blade of grass." If that was indeed the case at Columbia, he told the trustees, "I am intolerant. I will not stay in any institution where I can discover a known Communist. If we cannot get rid of a known Communist, I shall not be there, and they agreed." Then his very next words to those in the theater were "I have found universities in general engaged in how to bring up, how to teach, how to develop fine citizens to serve in a free democracy. That I conceive to be their basic purpose. . . . This is not just a casual argument against slightly different philosophies. This is a war of light against darkness, freedom against slavery, Godliness against atheism."[1]

Some 230 miles to the south, however, Washington was rapidly filling with a more appreciative audience. The Restoration had finally come. Good Republican faces, loyal, honest businessmen, not a Red or pinko among them, were back after the twenty-year interregnum of the long New Deal. Businessmen, weaned on the efficiency of American private enterprise, would make every dollar count for each taxpayer. Five hundred early celebrants jammed Union Station as the Pennsylvania Railroad's special five-car train arrived from New York with President-elect Eisenhower in private car No. 90, the same one he had used on his return to the United States in 1945. At 9:06 P.M., the train reached the station and, ten minutes later, Ike and Mamie appeared on the rear platform. He gave his admirers his famous smile while Mrs. Eisenhower responded with gracious waves to the cheering crowd. On the eve of the Restoration appeared the hero charged with the responsibility for bringing back good old American values.

The America the GOP was reclaiming, however, so little resembled what Herbert Hoover had given up on that somber March day in 1933 that it might, in a sense, be said that the Republicans had no experience for their task. No other two-decade span had ever brought so many changes. What had been an insular nation with 243,845 men in uniform had become a rapidly expanding nuclear military colossus with armed forces totaling three and a half million men and women. The nation that had stood and watched the League's acquiescence of Japanese aggression into Manchuria and passively mourned the submission of Ethiopia and the Spanish republic under the weight of fascist troops had become the leader of the largest power bloc in the newest version of a world organization, the banker of the Western world and the sponsor of the Atlantic Alliance as well as the promoter of the tenuous idea of a European Defense Community. The federal debt had grown from what the prudent had regarded as an unhealthy $24.3 billion to $288 billion.

There were other remarkable contrasts. In 1933, the federal government had 603,587 employees, but the GOP was inheriting a bureaucracy with over two and a half million on its official payroll. In the District of Columbia there were three and a half times as many federal workers as the capital had housed in 1933. The 125,000,000 who lived in the country in 1933 had produced a Gross National Product of some $56 billion, but with forty million more people the 1953 GNP was valued at $365.4 billion. Nineteen and a quarter million families had radios, and television still seemed far away when Hoover left the White House; but the nation of Eisenhower had almost forty-five million families with radios and twenty and a half million with TV sets. Only 11.5 percent of the non-agricultural workers were unionized in those days, but now 34 percent were card-carrying members. Net national income had gone from $48.8 billion to $338.9 billion. Despite the population increase, the number living on farms had declined by almost ten million and the rural population had hardly increased at all. At the same time, urban areas had grown by over 50 percent.

Some of the internal population shifts were, in fact, the most dramatic indicators of changes that had potential political as well as economic consequences. American Negroes, hardly a subject of much discussion in 1933, had resumed their First World War exodus from the South toward the industrial centers. During the two Democratic decades, the continuing shift had brought a black population decline of 316,400 in Mississippi, 281,500 in Georgia and 229,200 in Alabama, with a corresponding increase of over 900,000 for the states of New York, California and Illinois. At the same time, the general westward movement of the overall population had accelerated as the three Pacific Coast states went from barely over eight million to nearly fifteen million; in most of the Midwest, the population remained virtually static and numerous rural counties showed significant losses. Americans were clearly burgeoning toward the great industrial areas, and Negroes, so long a staple of an exploitive agricultural system during the days of post-Reconstruction neo-slavery, were the newcomers pushing the children of immigrants up and out of the urban core districts.

Whatever adjustments a modern Republican Administration would require to cope with such changes were clearly not the concern of the massive crowds that lined Pennsylvania Avenue that January 20. Pennsylvania Avenue seemed festooned with endless flags and bunting, as though proclaiming that Americans had retaken the capital city. The bleachers that had been set up along the avenue were filled early; many spectators carried lap blankets for protection against the chill winds, although the sun seemed warm and the temperature was rising to unseasonably high levels. The crowds, the largest for any Inaugural in history, included some fifty thousand from other parts of the country. The largest TV hookup ever, with 118 stations in seventy-four cities, prepared to make the scenes equally available to as many as seventy-five million additional viewers. Planned for after the formal ceremonies was an endless procession of military power and floats depicting all phases of Ike's life: his Denison, Texas, birthplace, his boyhood, his first job as a dairyman, his West Point days, his marriage to Mamie, his "crusade in Europe," his NATO tour of duty, his position at Columbia, his family and, finally, the culmination of a purely American success story, the Presidency. Such elaborate celebrating, which Eisenhower and Mamie would view from a special stand near the White House facing Pennsylvania Avenue, clearly exceeded his publicly expressed desire to favor more subdued festivities in recognition of the solemn international tensions and the killing still going on in Korea.

For the evening, of course, a full round of the usual Inaugural balls had been planned. One Republican politician, Congressman Fred E. Busbey of Illinois, cognizant of a governing party's responsibility to cleanse Washington of any possible softness toward the Communist enemy, had been vigilant enough to protect the patriotism of the concert that was going to be played by the National Symphony Orchestra. Busbey objected to the inclusion of a selection by Aaron Copland because, he complained, the composer had courted disloyalty to the American way by permitting his name to be used by such questionable organizations as sculptor Jo Davidson's Artists for Roosevelt and other groups that seemed leftish to the passionate right. The Congressman's complaint led to the immediate withdrawal of the offensive piece. When Washington music critic Paul Hume reminded Busbey that Copland's works were commonly on the repertoire of the Air Force bands and other tax-supported orchestras, the Representative from Illinois replied, "We must look into that!"[2] Others, not as cautious as Busbey, merely celebrated the long-delayed change in Washington.

The President-elect and Mamie Eisenhower started the day at à morning service conducted by the Reverend Dr. Edward L. R. Elson at the National Presbyterian Church. Eisenhower, who had never before maintained a formal church affiliation, thus aligned himself with his wife's religious denomination. "Religion was one of the thoughts that I had been mulling over for several weeks," he later wrote, and he explained that "there was embedded in me from boyhood, just as it was in my brothers, a deep faith in the beneficence of the Almighty."[3] Indeed, he seemed to be making up for lost time, as the First Family-elect entered the church with about 140 members of the incoming Administration, as well as with thirty-six relatives. It was, said Dr. Elson, the first time he could recall that an incoming President had invited his entire official family to such pre-Inaugural services.[4]

Two hours later, tradition was only partly preserved when the Eisenhowers arrived at the north portico of the White House to pick up President and Mrs. Truman. Their animosity, which had matured by then into a bitter feud, kept Eisenhower from the ritual of going into the White House to meet the outgoing Chief Executive. Moreover, he had also affronted Truman by rejecting an invitation to join him for lunch in the Presidential mansion.[5] Then, as the two men rode with their wives to the other end of Pennsylvania Avenue, their silence was rarely interrupted. The only conversation Eisenhower later remembered was Truman's admission that he had been responsible for ordering John S. D. Eisenhower back from the Korean combat zone so he could witness his father's ceremony.[6] But Truman attributed another conversation to that encounter. His version held that Eisenhower made a caustic comment about having stayed away from the 1948 Inauguration to avoid drawing attention from the President, and Truman's reply was "You were not here in 1948 because I did not send for you. But if I *had* sent for you, you would have come."[7] Whatever their actual exchange, it was their last personal conversation until both men were ex-Presidents and they met in Kansas City's Muhlenbach Hotel.[8]

The ceremonies took place on a platform that had been erected on the central east front of the Capitol building. There, before the massive crowds, Chief Justice Fred M. Vinson administered the oath to Vice President Nixon at 12:23 P.M. Minutes later, with both the historic Bible that had been used by George Washington and Eisenhower's from West Point days, the new President, bareheaded and wearing a dark blue double-breasted overcoat with a white scarf around his neck, repeated the oath after Justice Vinson at 12:32.

Then, as he turned to deliver his address, President Eisenhower's grim expression gave way to a warm smile and his hands went over his head in the familiar old V-sign. His first words consisted of an opening prayer for divine guidance that he had decided to include after having attended church that morning.

Beyond a doubt, it was the most internationalist speech ever delivered as an Inaugural Address. Ignoring any concrete references to domestic affairs and employing inspirational terms to appeal to the faith of a free people after declaring that "The world and we have passed the midway point of a century of continuing challenge," it was reminiscent of the Guild Hall address he had delivered in London in 1945. His citation of the "basic law of interdependence repeated the theme that had won him so much attention eight years earlier. Now as the thirty-fourth President of the United States, he declared that the "faith we hold belongs not to us alone but to the free of all the world." Then he added: "We know . . . that we are linked to all free peoples not merely by a noble idea but by a simple need. No free people can for long cling to any privilege or enjoy any safety in economic solitude." Peace, he emphasized, is a responsibility of our statesmanship, and can be achieved by sufficient strength to deter aggression, which will enable us to "stand ready to engage with any and all others in joint effort to remove the causes of mutual fear and distrust among nations, so as to make possible drastic reduction of armaments." "A people that values its privileges above its principles," he warned, "soon loses both."[9]

Although the speech had been worked on for a week by Hughes and Jackson, its dictation and final draft was clearly the President's. One cannot, moreover, imagine a more faithful rendition of his views. In one inspirational opening salvo, fitting in tone for an Inaugural Address, he had informed Hoover and Taft Republicans that the world had indeed changed and that the party had to revise its traditional concepts.

The chief criticisms of the speech deplored the President's failure to contend with specific problems, particularly regarding domestic affairs, thus confusing its function with a State of the Union address. Democrats, carping about its generalities and clichés, quickly pointed out that he had said nothing to refute their past international programs. "It was a statement," said Senator Lyndon B. Johnson of Texas, the new Democratic Minority Leader, "and a very good statement, of Democratic programs of the last twenty years."[10] Agreeing that the speech could have come from Truman or Stevenson, "Bertie" McCormick's Washington outlet said there was no place for Eisenhower in the Republican party.[11] *The Reporter*, a liberal biweekly, replied, "For once, Colonel McCormick agreed wholeheartedly with the Democrats," while *The Nation* complained that Eisenhower's view of a world of "moral absolutes" left little encouragement for those willing to negotiate differences to avoid a general war.[12] But the new Senate Majority Leader of the Eighty-third Congress, Robert A. Taft, was more gracious about a speech that had criticized most of his own basic assumptions about America and the world. It was, said the conservative from Ohio, "a great and inspiring beginning, a great and inspiring speech."[13]

Max Ascoli, writing *The Reporter*'s editorial, provided the best description of the nation's hopes and fears: "All in all, we feel like a people on a plane high in the air with a stormy, bumpy flight ahead. We tighten our seat belts, cling in our minds to the best we can think about the pilot, and trust God."[14]

CHAPTER 2 1

"*Walking into Bright Sunshine*"

Eisenhower's personal mission should not have been mysterious. The few who followed his public comments since the end of the war were able to perceive his delicate blend of conservatism and internationalism that somehow denied jingoism and excluded passion. Indeed, by the time he arrived at the White House, the years of recrimination and charges had rendered restoration of confidence in the nation's leadership as the first priority. However future historians might view Truman, his ultimate failure to keep the people with him must be regarded as a major inadequacy. Eisenhower, the conservative moderate and the famous healer of Allied forces, had little doubt about the nature of the mandate for change.

One of the big shortcomings of the New Dealers, of course, at least according to Republican rhetoric, was the failure of government by brain-trusters and ward heelers to appreciate sound business principles. The new Administration, while restricted by rigid previous spending commitments, would nevertheless attempt some fiscal pruning toward the ultimate ideal of a balanced budget. Regardless of the inherent difficulties that Dodge cited, the years of complaining about the excesses of the New and Fair Dealers, with charges of "waste" and "reckless spending," had made a shift necessary, if not for economic, certainly for political reasons. Eisenhower, hopeful that his budgetary aims would be aided by ending the Korean war, was finally in a position to implement his faith in fiscal strength as the major goal for the maintenance, as he was certain, of a free society. Restoring an economic climate conducive to investors by clear assurances that the new Administration opposed further restrictions upon private enterprise would, in turn, promote American capitalism and reap benefits for the entire nation. The United States could then give credible support to a Western European alliance and its hopes for military, political and economic integration that had been encouraged with the May 1952 signing of the European Defense Community treaty. In that scheme, West Germany was an extremely important cog; and such allies of America as France had to realize the fallacies of economic and political nationalism. Success would bring the realization of a trade zone with markets for all nations west of the Iron Curtain and the fortification of Europe against further Communist expansionism, an appealing climate for businessmen. Even the hysteria over internal communism in America that often puzzled Europeans might be relieved once Red inundation was no longer feared.

For Eisenhower, such massive tasks might be accomplished by creating a harmonious, well-integrated team that kept its eyes on the goals without being distracted by the numerous inevitable pitfalls. Organizing his government to implement the policies was a process that had gone into full swing almost immediately after Election Day. With New York City's Commodore Hotel as the pre-White House headquarters, the main burden of filling the requirements was undertaken by General Lucius Clay and Herbert Brownell. And the resultant nominees to head the executive departments and agencies of the federal bureaucracy had aroused few public complaints. For the most part, they constituted an array of conservative businessmen whose names did much to placate the segments of the party that had most bitterly opposed Eisenhower's nomination.

Only Martin Durkin, who had supported Stevenson and was president of the AFofL-affiliated United Association of Plumbers and Steamfitters, provoked anger among party stalwarts when he was named as Secretary of Labor. Taft heard the news while at lunch in the dining room of the Republican Senators and nearly exploded. Outrage overwhelmed his normally placid disposition and his face reddened. "This is incomprehensible!" he exclaimed. "It's incredible that this appointment could have been made without consulting any of us."[1] The senior Republican member of the Senate Labor Committee and the author of the Taft-Hartley Labor Relations Act of 1947 as well as the leader of the Senate, whose support for nominations was the most valuable of all, had good reasons for his reaction. Acting on a suggestion from Harold Stassen, Brownell and Clay had chosen Durkin after having decided that the labor post, which had been held by Maurice J. Tobin, should be manned by another Catholic, particularly since all other Cabinet designees were Protestants. Furthermore, he was the head of an important union and had a reputation for having been a highly competent leader. But, as with the selection of the other appointees, Taft was not consulted.[2] The procedure had been simply to obtain from Taft, through Tom Coleman, listings of suggestions. Eisenhower himself, having lacked prior experience with labor, had been more inclined to leave that appointment to his aides.[3]

Taft's anger over the Durkin appointment was particularly bitter because it had followed the selection of Humphrey to head the Treasury Department. Taft, of course, did not have the same objections to the Cleveland businessman as he had to Durkin, but the choice of an Ohioan had been done without consultation with Taft, the State's senior Republican.[4] The subsequent party crisis led to a meeting at the Commodore on December 30, when, over luncheon, the President-elect discussed liaison between the Executive and the Legislature and resolved future patronage proceedings with Senators Taft, Styles Bridges, Milton Young and Leverett Saltonstall. Taft later told reporters that an adequate method of consultation on appointments had been reached and that he expected no difficulty in "working out a harmonious relationship and a Republican legislative program that will be progressive and will put the country back on the road we abandoned twenty years ago before the New Deal."[5] A further meeting on these policies was held on January 12.

Such internal squabbles, however, had not marred the hopes of the Administration's well-wishers. George Murphy, the movie star and future Senator, who had contributed substantially to the Eisenhower campaign in California, sent the President-elect a New Year's greeting claiming that "your Crusade has solidified the American people as never before and for the first time in many years the country feels clean again." Then Murphy added: "It is all just so wonderful, it's like walking into bright sunshine after being in darkness for a long time."[6] Arthur Krock, who welcomed the departure of Democrats from the White House, also saw a bright glow. He prophesied that Ike was expected to become a strong President and, despite the clear evidence that the Senate would be controlled by such Republicans as Taft and Eugene Millikin, he wrote, "An enduring state of harmony between the executive and the legislative generally occurs when the President lavishly interprets the provision in the Constitution that Congress is a 'coordinate' member of the Government trinity."[7]

The strongest reservations came from opponents of the big-business-dominated Cabinet. In mid-December, *The New Republic* provided the tart observation that "Ike has picked a cabinet of eight millionaires and one plumber."[8] *The Nation* complained that "in surrounding himself with Big Dealers," Eisenhower "has cut himself off from the millions of little people who elected him."[9] At no time did Eisenhower himself express any concern that his Cabinet was overloaded with businessmen.[10] The public remained generally sympathetic and hopeful even after staffing the Pentagon had provided much unsolicited publicity that highlighted the affluence of the new Administration.

When Chief Justice Vinson again conducted a swearing-in ceremony, on the afternoon of Eisenhower's first full day as President, he faced evidence that the campaign and the period of transition had been replaced by the realities of government. Eisenhower's hope to have the entire Cabinet take office with him had been dashed by Senate objections. Not only was there a delay in the confirmation of such nominees as Harold Stassen as Mutual Security Administrator and Pentagon designees Roger M. Kyes, Robert T. Stevens, Harold Talbott and Robert B. Anderson, but more dramatically, trouble confronted Charles E. Wilson. Sometimes called "Engine Charlie" to distinguish him from "Electric Charlie," who had served Truman as Director of Defense Mobilization, he had been named to head the Defense Department. But he soon found himself in a sharp battle with the Senate Armed Services Committee over his refusal to sell 39,470 shares of General Motors common stock, which were worth two and a half million dollars.

Although Wilson had agreed to break all other connections with the world's largest private corporation, Senator Harry Byrd had pointed out that retaining such holdings in a company that held nearly $5 billion worth of contracts with the Defense Department was a violation of the section of the United States Code outlawing direct interest between an official and a corporation doing business with the government.[11] Even more embarrassing had been Wilson's high-handed attitude toward the inquiring Senators, as though his position was too exalted for their scrutiny. The hearings had, in fact, produced a Wilson comment that was soon exploited by political opponents. When Senator Robert Hendrickson of New Jersey asked whether Wilson's personal financial holdings would prevent him from making a decision in the interests of the United States government, the business tycoon replied, "I thought what was good for our country was good for General Motors, and vice versa."[12] Opponents of the new Administration, turning his words into a *cause célèbre*, furthered their ends by misrepresenting them as having been "What is good for General Motors is good for our country." It was only the first example of Wilson's tendency to put his "foot in the mouth," a condition that was, according to a source close to the new President, equaled only by "what he did when he took it out again."

Wilson's situation was indeed difficult. As president of General Motors, his salary and bonuses had averaged about $600,000 over the previous two years. Heading the Defense Department would pay him just $22,500. After being pressed by the Armed Services Committee, however, he finally agreed to dispose of his shares in the giant corporation.

But that was not enough to please Harry Byrd and such other conservative Democrats as Lyndon B. Johnson and Richard Russell, the committee's chairman. Since Wilson and his wife had combined holdings of about $5 million worth of stock, Johnson inquired about the magnate's plans for his other holdings and Russell asked what he intended to do with the 1,737 shares of GM stock he was to receive during the next four years under an extended bonus system. Wilson explained that they would also be sold. Russell, still not satisfied, then pointed out that he should, additionally, deny himself the right to those shares because the corporation's profits from government contracts would affect their value.

"I really feel you are giving me quite a pushing around," Wilson protested. "If I had come here to cheat, by God, I wouldn't be here."

When Russell said that he was simply doing his job, Wilson replied, "I understand that. But I am just human, and my God, I am making a great sacrifice to come down here."[13]

Finally, six days after Eisenhower's inauguration, Wilson was confirmed by a Senate vote of seventy-seven to six.

But the other chief Pentagon nominees were also given trouble over potential conflict-of-interest situations. Deputy Secretary Roger M. Kyes, Secretary of the Army Robert Ten Broeck Stevens, Secretary of the Navy Robert Bernerd Anderson and Harold Talbott, the Secretary of the Air Force, were also businessmen whose combined holdings constituted an impressive directory of American corporations. All were associated with several organizations: Kyes principally with GM as a vice-president in charge of procurement and schedules; Stevens with his family's large textile company that sold uniforms to the armed forces; Anderson, a former manager of the vast King Ranch in Texas, with Associated Refineries; and Talbott, who at the age of sixty-four was about twenty years older than the others, with the Chrysler Corporation and the North American Aviation Company. As with Wilson, all eventually agreed to sell most holdings that could lead to embarrassing situations. Accordingly, Wilson's first official act was the barring of Defense Department officials from participating in dealings with firms in which they had a financial stake.[14]

While the Defense Department was a haven for businessmen joining the new Administration, most other top posts came under similar leadership. After all, George Humphrey reached the Treasury Department after heading the Mark Hanna Company, with its vast interests in coal, iron, steel, copper, oil, natural gas, rayon, plastics, shipping and banking. Sidney Weinberg had recommended him to Lucius Clay and Wall Street circles had praised Humphrey as the "ideal choice." Bankers called him a "great financial" figure and one of the country's ablest businessmen.[15] Sinclair Weeks, the new head of Commerce, had been sufficiently familiar with the machinery of Republican politics to be first considered as the party's national chairman to replace Arthur Summerfield; but Weeks, too, was principally a businessman, somewhat of an intermediary between the GOP and big business. He was a loyal organization man who had served for eleven months as an interim Senator from Massachusetts; his principal interests were with the Barton and Reed silverware company and the Carr-Fastener Corporation. Both Summerfield, the new Postmaster General, and the Secretary of the Interior, Governor Douglas McKay of Oregon, owned large automobile agencies. The newly appointed Director of the Budget, Joseph Dodge, was Detroit's most prominent banker as director and president of The Detroit Bank. He had first come to Eisenhower's attention as Financial Adviser and Deputy for Trade and Finance to both Ike and General Clay for the United States Military Government of Germany, where he had supervised the fiscal side of the American occupation.[16]

Neither Brownell, Dulles nor Ezra Taft Benson, the Secretary·of Agriculture, were businessmen. Brownell and Dulles were both lawyers with old and conservative New York firms, Brownell with Lord, Day and Lord, and Dulles with Sullivan and Cromwell, where he was reputedly the highest paid corporation attorney in the country. Benson, a member of the Council of Twelve of the Mormon Church, was a conservative Taftite with a background as an agent of farm cooperatives and agricultural marketing. His appointment had brought immediate praise from the president of the American Farm Bureau Federation.[17]

The carping from liberals, however, did not mirror with much accuracy the public's reaction to the Cabinet, but Eisenhower's determination to install them in key posts was, in fact, viewed with apprehension by some companies. Corporations, mindful of the popular reactions against businessmen after the stock-market crash of 1929 and still haunted by the electoral endorsement of Truman following his castigation of the Eightieth Congress, feared that adverse suspicions would effectively negate attempts to reverse the direction of the economy. The Opinion Research Corporation of Princeton, New Jersey, responded to the anxieties of its industrial clients by surveying the popular reception to the tone of the new Administration.[18]

The organization, which had had long associations with prominent Republicans, polled 1,619 respondents in 155 cities. When asked about the practice of appointing major business leaders to government posts, 78 percent of both Republicans and Democrats approved and just 14 percent were in opposition. Satisfaction was 90 percent among Republicans, 68 percent among Democrats and 79 percent among independents. When pressed further, to determine what they expected the businessmen to achieve for the country, much confidence was expressed in their ability to provide successful leadership in strengthening national defense, making government more efficient and working for world peace. Only somewhat less optimistic, but still in the majority with 54 percent, were expectations about their ability to weed out corruption.

When asked to react to specific individuals, the furor over Wilson's confirmation had resulted in making him the most widely known new member, although Dulles had been prominent far longer. However, when asked which man was expected to perform best, Dulles led the field with 48 percent. Wilson's performance before the Armed Services Committee had apparently impressed more than dismayed the public and he was second in their confidence, scoring only 6 percentage points behind Dulles. No one else came close to their rating. There was, furthermore, little evidence that wealth, such as Wilson's, was considered by most people as a serious handicap. The doubts that were expressed concerned their ability to understand the "little man." A much more common feeling was that accumulated fortunes are more often "taken as an earmark of proven ability." Union members also shared that attitude.[19]

Whatever apprehensions liberals felt about a business-dominated Administration were clearly not shared by the American people. "They have been in the dog house for so long that they frequently fail to realize the tremendous confidence people have in their leadership," Robinson wrote to Weeks. "We have the strong feeling that business leadership is a package which can be merchandised successfully if we would but use our imaginations on it."[20]

The conservatism found by the survey surprised even Weeks's staff. One aide, in digesting the material for the Secretary, noted that "Conservatism is admitted in the report to be almost radical to that of 10 to 20 years ago." Perhaps as probable as the reality of a strong endorsement of businessmen, however, was their benefiting from a popular reaction against leadership by politicians, the reverse of the attitude that had removed GOP rule from Washington twenty years earlier. In the wake of the disillusionment and insecurity, but bolstered by affluence, it had removed Truman and brought in Eisenhower, the "apolitical" man.

CHAPTER 22

The Team

Eisenhower brought to the Presidency the conviction that the country had had its full measure of new programs during the past twenty years and that it wanted consolidation without undermining past achievements. "If I do anything," Eisensower said right after his inauguration, "it's going to be less government and not more government."[1] However, when he faced his Cabinet, with its conservatives eager to begin a counterrevolution, he cautioned them to discard their pet notions about limiting the role of the federal government in public welfare matters because, he explained, whether they liked it or not, the American people had accepted such responsibilities as necessary and proper and the matter had gone beyond any further consideration. Since dismantling would not be considered, attention should be given to new issues.[2]

History had offered little encouragement for believing that Presidents could sell unpopular ideas. Lincoln's attitudes toward Reconstruction had received mounting opposition; Wilson had failed to ignite sufficient support for participation in the League of Nations without diluting reservations; FDR had found that the great popular approval he had received in being re-elected in 1936 could not be recharged for his fight to pack the Supreme Court. Eisenhower, a practitioner of the art of the possible, also dealt with realities in his annual requests to department heads for suggestions about desired legislation. They were sent with reminders about confining ideas to those items with a reasonable chance of success. As he had once written to John Foster Dulles, "There are innumerable instances of method, detail and procedure on which I am always ready to accept almost any revision of my views."[3] Neither a manipulator nor a maneuverer, and a man without much taste for the more mundane aspects of party leadership that normally accrued to the President, Eisenhower was, above everything else, interested in getting a job done.[4] His "crusade" soon became indistinguishable from Eisenhower as a figure of conciliation and paternalism, and his conception of the Chief Executive as the head of a well-organized team diffused the inherited accumulation of Presidential powers. He would take as literal the constitutional powers of the Presidency in foreign affairs and, in domestic matters, the role of the Chief Executive as but one of three coordinate branches of government.

His own emotional development gave him enough security to pursue his chosen course with complete optimism. He was little bothered by those critics who would increasingly point out that he lacked sophistication and political perception. That argument might appeal to the readers of liberal intellectual periodicals, particularly in the more effete centers along the East Coast, but would, he knew, matter little to the voters who liked Ike. If anything, carping from such quarters could actually increase his appeal. He once told Sherman Adams, "If you want to find out how the people feel about things, read the papers, but not the New York or Washington papers."[5]

Publicly, he was careful to preserve his image as a patriotic moral leader eager to preserve traditional American standards of decency and common sense even when coping with the most controversial issues. When dealing within his own official family, as well as with Congressmen and Senators, his method was to convince rather than coerce, charm rather than threaten. That attitude of tolerant understanding, of civilized patience, of even his severest critics, carried over into all public appearances, particularly during his press conferences.

At the same time, those closest to the president, who were in almost daily touch with him, saw a far from naïve Eisenhower—in fact, a most astute man, well aware that his popular following formed the substance of his political strength. As George Humphrey liked to say, his "political battleship drew more water than all the other politicians put together."[6] Those closest to him learned that he was a perceptive barometer of the nation's mood.[7] But he had the skill and personality to perpetuate the image of a man whose demeanor contrasted with the professional politicians who had preceded him. His circumlocutions and lapses of syntax at press conferences, his frequent confessions of ignorance about specific situations were accompanied by an infectious grin that made it impossible for anyone to consider him a shrewd manipulator. Perhaps better than anyone else, he knew that the apparent ignorance, the denial of expertise, was a source of political strength before an American public that was suspicious of experts and "eggheads," as they came to be called, and perhaps still not too far removed from the sentiments found by Alexis de Tocqueville in the 1830s. At one point he defined intellectuals as people who use more words to say more than they know. However, as one of his civilian Pentagon chiefs put it, "If there was any President better informed, I don't know who it could have been."[8]

More than his predecessors, he shared responsibilities with his Cabinet, which met weekly on Friday mornings. Present at such sessions, in addition to the heads of the executive departments, were others who attended by the President's invitation, so that Director of the Budget Joe Dodge, Mutual Security Director Harold Stassen and Federal Security Administrator Oveta Culp Hobby were also present. Frequently, members of the White House staff as well as those present by special invitation were seated along the walls.

As though he were conducting a seminar, the President directed questions to each person around the table. All members were free to contribute their thoughts on every subject, regardless of their own direct responsibilities. The President led and provoked, not hesitating to toss out challenges and even outlandish ideas to solicit reactions, particularly when the sessions were off the record. Jerry Persons, his Congressional liaison man, observed that he would hit "those fungoes out there" just to see what would happen. Ralph Tudor, an Under Secretary of the Interior for eighteen months, reported that "At all times the President is in command. He has tremendous ability to lead people and yet not to push them."[9]

Though businesslike, the President was not above a good laugh with his team. One opportunity resulted from the suggestion that Eisenhower himself had made to Ezra Taft Benson at the Commodore pre-Cabinet session about opening with a silent prayer. Late in January, only a little more than two weeks later, Benson reminded Eisenhower about the importance of such prayers. "The suggestion is made only because of my love for you, members of the Cabinet, and the people of this great Christian nation," Benson wrote. "I know that without God's help we cannot succeed. With His help we cannot fail. . . ."[10] So the procedure was continued. At one meeting, however, Cabinet Secretary Max Rabb dutifully slipped the President a note reminding him that the usual moment of silent prayer had been overlooked. Eisenhower, glancing at the paper, exclaimed to those around the table, "Oh, goddammit, we forgot the silent prayer."[11]

Eisenhower's apparent lack of appetite for power seemed difficult to understand, even to experienced Washington observers. *New Yorker* correspondent Richard Rovere came perhaps closer to the truth than he imagined by suggesting that the President had "organized his office staff and his Cabinet into a kind of conspiracy to perpetuate his unawareness."[12] If it did, as Rovere and others suspected, place Eisenhower at the center of a protective moat, the design was conceived as a filtering process through the White House staff for material that did not require Presidential action. Eisenhower's self confidence permitted extensive delegation of powers. Routine matters were relegated to lower levels with caution to make certain that the President would not be burdened with items that did not require his attention. Each member of the staff, including the department and agency heads as well as the White House aides, was responsible for specific areas. Under these procedures, the complexities of the modern Presidency, it was hoped, would be mitigated by a system that made more efficient use of personnel. Suggestions that the table of organization resembled the military were discouraged; and the man whose role corresponded to the drawbridge over the moat was not called the "chief of staff," which he actually was, but carried the title of Assistant to the President. To Sherman Adams, who had left the governorship of New Hampshire to join Eisenhower and had headed the pre-Inaugural office at the Commodore, went that assignment.

Adams, distantly related to the famous dynasty, was almost the perfect stereotype of the New England moderate conservative. Actually, however, his belief in *Realpolitik* placed him closer to Eisenhower than to any ideological position. Having taken public-opinion soundings in New Hampshire almost a year before the important primary in that state, he had become convinced that there were many potential Eisenhower voters. Furthermore, the New Hampshire Governor reasoned, even though Taft might be more liberal than the General in domestic matters —particularly because of his position on public housing—Ike was in a better position to deal with the nation's most important crises more effectively. And those lay in the realm of international affairs. Not only was Eisenhower a better diplomat, but his credentials for handling foreign relations seemed impeccable. Adams, who continued to feel that Taft's political skill and knowledge would have made him a more outstanding President in domestic affairs, then enlisted in the General's cause. Within the President's official family he became known as one of the more liberal members. Indeed, particularly in the area of racial equality, he was considered among the most enlightened in the Administration.[13]

In Adams, Eisenhower had found a perfect replacement for his wartime chief of staff, General Walter Bedell Smith. Smith, who had served Ike in a comparable capacity at SHAEF, excelled at being Eisenhower's "son of a bitch." He seemed to have much more trouble saying "yes" than "no" and his tyrannical bearing terrorized his office staff. The victim of a painful ulcer, he appeared abrupt, caustic, humorless and impatient with trivia or human weakness. When Eisenhower wrote about his aide in *Crusade in Europe*, he called him "Serious, hard-working, and loyal."[14] However, he also told a British officer to remember that "Beetle," as Smith was called, "is a Prussian and one must make allowances for it."[15] Nevertheless, when Smith, who was leaving the directorship of the Central Intelligence Agency to become Under Secretary of State, was first exposed to Adams in late 1952, even he was dismayed by the taciturn New Englander. "Our first and only conversation so far was not what I call the height of cordiality," Smith wrote to a friend. "You know about my prospective appointment and in this assignment I think it highly important to establish cordial and friendly relations with Governor Adams, if indeed this is possible with one of your chunks of New Hampshire 'granite.' It encourages me to know that he is a trout fisherman."[16]

Adams was, indeed, a conversation piece. He seemed frugal about everything. Associates noted that some of his suits must have dated back to his freshman days at Dartmouth, over three decades ago. While the information media was filling the nation with accounts of how he was "the second most important man in Washington," he was bringing his lunch to work in a cardboard box. Even such amenities as "goodbye," "hello," "thank you" seemed excessive. A typical business discussion with the Assistant to the President began without any of the preliminaries about the weather and health. When questioned about things he preferred to ignore, he would just as soon not reply rather than say "no comment." One of the startling experiences of his subordinates was to receive a telephone call from him at home in the early morning. A crisp voice would make a terse request and suddenly hang up without either having identified itself or waiting for a response. Fred Seaton, after having been named as Douglas McKay's replacement to head the Interior Department, complained, "The Governor is not one iota impressed with my new title. He still doesn't say 'hello' or 'goodbye' on the telephone, and he hangs up when *he* is through."[17] In addition, Adams normally worked from 7:30 A.M. until half past six and expected similar dedication from the rest of the staff. His demands were said to have caused three office girls to cry at the same time. One occasion that must have led to considerable despair resulted from his order to the White House telephone operator to get Sam Pryor, the executive vice-president of Pan American and former Republican national committeeman, at his home in Connecticut. When, a few minutes later, the girl reported that Pryor had left for Guatemala, Adams replied, "They don't have phones in Guatemala?"[18]

While Adams was charged with promoting office efficiency, he soon became a lightning rod for a President too popular to criticize openly. Tom Stephens, an Irish-born house-humorist and Dewey veteran, was in charge of Presidential appointments; but Adams decided who actually got in to the Oval Room for a few minutes with Eisenhower. With members of the White House staff or even Cabinet members, he had to evaluate the validity of the requests. Eisenhower's stated policy that he would be available to his Cabinet if they desired a personal conference did not, however, entitle them to *carte blanche* rights. Adams, at the door, still did the screening. While he served that function, the casual visitor to the White House received the rather obvious impression that Adams decided the President's choices. In reality, the Governor was more simply Eisenhower's "no" man, carrying out the President's desires.

For example, Eisenhower found sessions with Charles Wilson tedious. Wilson's visits invariably dealt with internal problems of running the Defense Department, matters relating to personnel and departmental operating policies. Such details bored Eisenhower, who also felt that Wilson talked too much. Wilson's desires to establish the kind of free-and-easy rapport that Dulles and Humphrey enjoyed were soon frustrated. When Adams consequently acted to bar his free access to the Presidential office, the chief of staff was merely following the President's wishes. Any Wilson complaints that the White House staff stood between him and Mr. Eisenhower were correct, but only in the technical sense that it was they who made the actual denials.[19] Dulles, on the other hand, pretended that Adams did not exist and simply marched into the Oval Room at will, sometimes when the matter was urgent enough, even interrupting a meeting with another visitor. Treasury Secretary Humphrey, who developed the closest personal relationship with the Chief Executive, simply sneaked into the office via a back way. Humphrey, showing his disdain for Adams, decided that the Governor was building his own little "empire" in the White House for his political future.[20]

If Adams harbored that kind of ambition, he could have done better as a private citizen. For his role, combined with his austere personality, made him the Administration's most vulnerable man. Perhaps when he had chosen Adams, just as with his earlier choice of Beetle Smith, Eisenhower had agreed that his own major fault was that he was too tolerant and easygoing toward people and overly patient.[21]

In the fulfillment of his role, Adams was truly indispensable. Once, when a group of Republican industrialists called on him to request his intervention in a case that was about to come before the Federal Communications Commission, they were startled and furious to receive instead a sharp lecture about the ethics of business and government. As they left, they must have wondered whether they had contributed to the wrong party.[22] On another occasion, when Adams received from Commerce Secretary Weeks a memo pointing out ways of effecting further economies in the operation of executive departments, he returned Weeks's paper with the addition of the following handwritten memo: "This would have been more convincing if you had suggested how your department could be cut, instead of the other fellow's."[23] Nor did he believe he should cultivate the press for his own benefit. As he arrived at the White House one day to attend an Eisenhower–Stassen meeting, a band of reporters met to find out what was happening. Despite their obvious curiosity about Adams' role at the session, the Governor ignored them and walked straight ahead. Finally, just before disappearing through the White House door, the chief of staff turned and said, "You bastards haven't paid this much attention to me since I got here."[24]

More serious friction developed over his relations with important Republicans, most of whom, such as Senators Knowland of California and Styles Bridges, who represented Adams's state, were well to the Governor's right. Adams, for example, had been shocked to hear Senator Bridges say that he regarded Knowland as the only Republican fit to be President.[25] Furthermore, there was resentment that so much access to Eisenhower was in the hands of a man who had served only one term in the House and whose position had not required confirmation by the Senate. When Bridges arrived at the Commodore for his pre-Inaugural meeting with the President-elect, he had come determined to straighten out the political novice on the matter of patronage, in the wake of the Durkin appointment, but he had also on that occasion observed the authority that had been given to Adams. When Eisenhower then proceeded to set up his staff system, they foresaw that subsequent appointees would have to come from a lot of different sources. Even though Eisenhower was exasperated by the amount of time he had to spend on patronage matters and said the responsibility would be shifted from Adams's office to the national chairman, he did not remain as aloof as it appeared. When a Nebraska Congressman told Eisenhower that he should fire Philip Young, the Civil Service Commission chairman, the President had to suppress his temper before replying, "Mr. Miller, I love to have your advice, but when it comes to picking my assistants, *I* pick them."[26]

Most often, however, it was Adams who was in the direct line of fire trying to carry out the Administration's personnel policies. When, on one occasion, the FBI report for a man named to become chairman of a regulatory commission seemed to Adams to negate his nomination, the chief of staff had to deal with two irate Senators. In that instance they were Arthur Watkins and Wallace Bennett of Utah. Both, angry, came in for an explanation. That situation was relieved because Adams let them read the reports. But the chief of staff could not go through the same ritual in every case and for every reason. Furthermore, even protests that too many Republicans were being appointed from New York and elsewhere along the Eastern Seaboard, at the expense of the Midwest and Rocky Mountain regions, became Adams's responsibility. Jealousy of his power thus became an important factor among disgruntled Republicans, to whom Adams became a symbol of what Robert Donovan has written was "a small clique of men who have insulated the President from the Republican organization, the 'palace guard,' as McCarthy once called it in attacking Adams."[27]

Another Adams difficulty involved Senator Taft. The Senate Majority Leader and Presidential candidate of the party's stalwarts was, of course, the Administration's most important potential ally in the legislature. Moreover, Taft had taken advantage of the slim Republican ability to organize the Eighty-third Congress by filling the key posts with his allies. Thus, Taftite Eugene Millikin of Colorado became chairman of the Republican Conference, chairman of Finance, Styles Bridges headed the Appropriations Committee, Hugh Butler of Nebraska was chairman of Interior and Insular Affairs; and the Foreign Relations Committee had a considerable dose of such critics of Eisenhower-style internationalism as Taft himself, William Knowland, Homer Ferguson of Michigan and William Langer of North Dakota, although Alexander Wiley, its chairman, had an international outlook often closer to Truman than to Taft.[28] Offending Taft via the Durkin and Humphrey appointments had been clumsy. To antagonize him again, particularly with no significant issue at stake, would be political stupidity. Yet, within days after the Administration was installed, the fury of "Mr. Republican" rocked Adams.

One of the Senator's sons, William Howard Taft III, was a thirty-seven-year-old former professor of Gaelic Culture at Yale University who was currently with the Central Intelligence Agency. The younger Taft, who had received a Ph.D. from Princeton in 1942, had also been in Ireland from 1948 to 1951 as deputy administrator for the Economic Cooperation Administration. In January, with the support of Irish-American groups, he decided that he would like to become an ambassador to Ireland and conveyed that desire to his two Senators from Connecticut, Republicans Prescott Bush and William Purtell. Bush then consulted with Senator Taft, who supported his son's ambition with the comment, "They could look around for a long time without finding a better qualified man."[29] Robert Taft's public statement, however, was that he was keeping hands off his son's campaign for the job. "I have told Bill," he said to the press, "that he is entirely on his own."[30] Bush and Purtell both endorsed the nomination and sent it to Adams.

The matter threatened to become explosive for its political ramifications. Eisenhower's meeting with the senatorial delegation that had visited him in New York after the Durkin appointment had concluded with an agreement for full consultations over all major appointments. Neglecting to include the Senate would, it was clear, threaten the Administration's ability to get confirmation for its nominees.[31] At the same time, since Claire Boothe Luce, also of Connecticut, was slated as ambassador to Italy, Nutmeg State Republicans were apprehensive that the Taft nomination would expend their share of the patronage. If, on the other hand, the Irish post should be classified as a "top level" designation, as was Mrs. Luce's, the Administration's desires to select its own candidates for such diplomatic missions would be compromised. Undoubtedly, such problems delayed any action by Adams's office.

After more than a month had gone by and the story had been given front-page newspaper coverage, Taft's people acted. I. Jack Martin, the Senator's administrative assistant, visited Prescott Bush's executive secretary with the information that Bob Taft was furious. He had been given to understand, he claimed, that the appointment of his son was to go through and he was interpreting the long delay as an indication of uncertainty and that he was regarding it as a personal affront. When that message was relayed to Bush, the Connecticut Senator telephoned Adams.

"You're in deep trouble with our Majority Leader here on this Taft nomination for Ireland," he warned. "This thing has gone too far. Bob Taft is very angry about it and I suggest to you that you get that name down here before noon today or else you're going to be in serious trouble with the Republican Senators, who are strongly behind Bob Taft on this thing. And it's a darn good appointment anyway. It should be made."

All Adams could say was "I think you're right." Before noon on that same day the Assistant to the President called Bush to say that the name was on the way to the Senate and that Taft's office had been notified.[32] William Howard Taft III was nominated on March 18, given final Senate approval on the second of April and sworn in as ambassador to Ireland one week later.[33] Once again, Adams had been the man in the middle.

Ultimately, complaints about Adams became public. In 1955 Republican Congressman Joseph L. Carrigg of Pennsylvania argued that Adams's dealings with GOP legislators had hurt the party and claimed that his "general dislike" for Adams was shared by several other Republican leaders and that Adams was "certainly not the best liaison man" the party could have with the President. Carrigg, as did many others, felt that Adams had failed to give politics enough consideration. He then told the press that either Governor John Lodge of Connecticut or UN Ambassador Henry Cabot Lodge, Jr., his brother, would replace him.

Speaking for Eisenhower, Jim Hagerty was finally compelled to brand the stories as a "lot of nonsense."[34]

As vital as Adams's role was as the logical target for anti-Eisenhower attacks, the Governor's personal prestige with the President could not match the relationship established by some of the Cabinet members. With George Humphrey there was a rapport that included Cabinet and National Security Council sessions as well as the bridge table. Humphrey, for years a leading fund-raiser in Ohio Republican circles and a man whose leadership of the Mark Hanna Company involved him in widespread enterprises, such as the establishment of an iron-ore company in Labrador, could have been equally at home in Washington during the Coolidge years. A self-effacing man with much of the Eisenhower charm who was capable of describing himself as a "hard shell, a non-progressive and everything else" and of acknowledging that he often lacked the foresight of some of the "more forward-looking fellows," Humphrey had been a supporter of his friend Robert Taft until the convention had chosen. He had never met Eisenhower; and Taft had not been the man to influence his selection to head the Treasury Department. That had most likely come from Wall Street financier Sidney Weinberg, who had passed the suggestion along to General Clay. In many ways he typified Eisenhower's Cabinet, and his general attitude toward money and society was remarkably close to the President's. "If you're going to live a good life," Humphrey liked to say, "you've got to live within your income. A good wife can be a helluva good Secretary of the Treasury because that's all she needs to know. The very things she needs to know to run a house are necessary to keep the government's finances in order."[35] Nobody could accuse George Humphrey of holding Keynesian heresies. It is not difficult to understand why he and Eisenhower were compatible from the moment they met.

They first saw each other in Eisenhower's Commodore Hotel office before the Korean trip. The General's opening comment immediately convinced the business magnate that he had found a friend. "Well, George," said Eisenhower, with his usual big grin, "I see you part your hair the same way I do."[36] Their friendship provided Eisenhower with the refuge he often needed to get away from the ordeals of the White House.

Politically, Humphrey admired Eisenhower because, as a businessman, he appreciated the President's desire and ability to "get things done" without engaging in self-seeking. His much quoted reaction to Ernest Hemingway's novel *The Old Man and the Sea* was perhaps only partly facetious. "Why would anybody be interested in some old man who was a failure and never amounted to anything anyway?" he was reported to have said.[37] While it would be difficult to imagine him making that statement without smiling, it nevertheless revealed much about the man.

His special mission consisted of the restoration of "sound money" by balancing the budget. In that crusade he was the most rigid member of the Cabinet about approving additional spending. He was concerned, for example, that the United Nations was perhaps too costly a luxury for the nation.[38] He raised frequent objections to spending for foreign aid and there were consequent conflicts between Dulles and Humphrey over the cost of what the Secretary of State advanced as international obligations.[39] One of his major concerns, which he foresaw as a problem early during the Eisenhower years, was the danger of an excessive outflow of gold.[40]

Whether the discussions concerned international or domestic affairs, Humphrey came to dominate Cabinet sessions, frequently competing with Dulles for the President's ear. Because the Secretary of State often appeared bored or disinterested during discussions of purely domestic matters, Humphrey had a distinct advantage. His authority was further enhanced by his influence over Charlie Wilson. Ultimately, when Humphrey took a stand at meetings of the Cabinet or the National Security Council, there was a tendency for others to withhold contrary views or modify their statements through the belief that Humphrey was stating the President's own opinion, which, on domestic spending, was often true.[41] Yet, whether he was the most influential man in the Cabinet cannot be said with certainty, for Eisenhower's ability to separate men into categories was keen; and while Humphrey was certainly an important influence, the role of John Foster Dulles must also be considered.

The Dulles–Eisenhower relationship, one of the most discussed aspects of the Administration, is generally acknowledged to have warmed up very slowly. There are those who believe that Dulles wanted General Walter Bedell Smith as Under Secretary of State because he had no confidence in his own ability to have a personal relationship with the President.[42] Much has also been made, particularly by Emmet Hughes— although he is not the only one—of the President's impatience with his Secretary's rather ponderous manner of speech. Hughes relates that he "bored" Eisenhower during their earlier days together and that he watched "the all-too-expressive face of the President-elect and the gestures of impatience made almost more plain by the half-successful efforts to suppress them . . . finally, the patient fixing of the eyes on the most distant corner of the ceiling, there to rest till the end of the Dulles dissertation. When the end came, at last, Eisenhower was quite likely to rejoin the conversation with words sharply aimed away from all that had been said, without even acknowledging their utterance."[43] Many years later, Eisenhower's response to that description was a labeling of

Hughes's observations as "a complete distortion of fact" and repudiation of his speech writer's knowledge of their true relationship. However, then the General proceeded to admit that Dulles "had a little habit before he started to talk. Probably in his youth he may have had a little bit of stammering. He waited, sometimes it would be three or four seconds before he'd start to talk. But when he did it was almost like a printed page. He had a very orderly mind."[44]

That Eisenhower should have hastened to defend the memory of his Secretary of State was no surprise to anyone who had experienced their partnership. As some innocent victims discovered, there were times when the President's reaction to complaints about Dulles sounded suspiciously as though he was, in fact, upholding his own ideas and policies.[45] Dulles's emergence as one of the Administration's strongest figures inevitably grew from their mutual view of morality, Eisenhower's view of Dulles's political and diplomatic roles and the Secretary's respect for the President's political acumen. Dulles recognized Eisenhower's superior sensitivity to the feelings of the American public and was impressed with his decency and moral stature.[46] The real debate that ultimately ensued revolved over the question of which of the two men provided the real leadership in the area of foreign policy.

The competition to assess Dulles's role points to his importance. Sherman Adams, in his memoirs, contends with many that "there was never much doubt about who was responsible for the foreign policy of the United States" during Dulles's strong leadership of the State Department.[47] "No Secretary of State in American history ever operated under such a prodigious mandate of authority as Eisenhower gave to Dulles, and which the President continuously renewed," wrote two students of the period.[48] Arthur Larson, however, has maintained that "the main direction and tone of American foreign policy" was Eisenhower's, as "were the first line decisions. If in such a case there was a disagreement between Dulles and Eisenhower, the Dulles view had to yield."[49] Milton Eisenhower also maintains that "nothing can be farther from the truth" than the misconception that the President overdelegated authority to Dulles.[50] Nevertheless, at Cabinet and National Security Council meetings, his dominance can only be compared with that of Humphrey. Their major difference was Dulles's willingness to defer to the Treasury chief during discussions of fiscal matters.

Whenever Dulles took the floor, he always stood out and it was almost impossible to change his position. His legal mind had marshaled all the arguments and synthesized a wide array of facts to overwhelm anybody who tried to dissent. Most people, it was noted, were afraid to stand up to him except in rare instances. During one of Dulles's Cabinet presentations in behalf of foreign aid, he was thoroughly prepared to refute what he had anticipated would be Humphrey's usual opposition to spending. However, after he had gone partly through the talk, Humphrey stopped him and said, "Foster, if I understand your case, you are arguing for continuing foreign aid." Dulles, somewhat startled, replied, "Yes, I surely am." Humphrey smiled and said, "Well, I agree with you." Those in the room could sense Dulles's frustration at being denied an opportunity to use his prepared defense. Nevertheless, he recovered with good humor and remarked that his legal training had taught him that "when you've won your own case, stop talking."[51]

The son of a Watertown, New York, minister, Dulles was a strong Presbyterian and a prominent member of the National Council of Churches. Jim Hagerty said he was a Roundhead, a Puritan, whose ancestors must have been chopping down the Cavaliers in the name of their religious beliefs during Cromwell's days.[52] Eisenhower likened him to "an Old Testament prophet." His trademark was an emphasis on spiritual strength and morality, with the conviction that godly forces, if they adhered to the obligations implicit in such concepts, must ultimately overwhelm atheistic communism. Yet, in a 1949 letter to his son Avery, who had become a Jesuit priest, Dulles wrote, "I know that you have a contempt for 'expediency,' but that is what in fact determines most of people's conduct, and when you ask whether as a practical matter communism can be expected to give up violent methods without first becoming converted to a Christian view of the nature of man, my answer is that all history proves that such a development is quite possible."[53] Perhaps most characteristic of his fusion of morality and *Realpolitik* was his comment to a radio correspondent that "The United States is almost the only country strong enough and powerful enough to be moral."[54]

Dulles was constantly attuned to the political exigencies of the day, just as his considerations in forwarding the ideas about the liberation of captive peoples had been designed to attract ethnic voters to the Republican side. No one was more aware than he of the sources of his predecessor's difficulties. Even though many newsmen considered his first press secretary, Carl McCardle, inept, Dulles in rapid time set out to cultivate the press. Journalists found him lacking the high-handed aristocratic contempt for the working newsmen that Dean Acheson had often exhibited.[55] Conscious, too, of Acheson's incredible difficulties with Congress, Dulles was also careful to mend that relationship. According to the records of the Senate Foreign Relations Committee, he testified as a witness far more frequently than Acheson, who came only when summoned. Dulles, who appeared forty-eight times during his years at the head of the State Department, established a relationship with the Senators that was characterized by "complete frankness and honesty" and was usually responsive to committee suggestions. He always made it a practice to consult with them before and after important international conferences.[56] Dulles, after all, was convinced that political unpopularity had contributed greatly to Acheson's troubles and he thought that Truman's Secretary of State had blundered by pretending that there were no serious problems in the area of internal security. Such doubts that had plagued his predecessor had to be avoided for the successful implementation of foreign policy. The first exposé of disloyalty, Dulles feared, would create a throwback to Acheson's troubles.[57]

Also, every public address made by the Secretary was delivered with concern for its popular response. One of the frequent criticisms of such statements cited their obvious and pious moralizing, but Dulles was more conscious of his audience than were his critics. He carefully avoided complex language and rejected Latin words, which were always removed from the final drafts of his speeches. Such terminology, he held, carried less punch than appropriate Anglo-Saxon language; moreover, foreign phrases brought suspicions of insincerity from his audience. While intellectuals sneered, Dulles's mail usually brought fabulous responses to his speeches from the Midwest. Yet, playing up to the mass audience could not have been easy for John Foster Dulles.

He carried with him an aura of almost foreboding righteousness and, to those outside his immediate circle of trusted aides and advisers, a pompous shell of aloofness. One who was present with Dulles at many meetings used the following words to describe the Secretary:

> When it is time for Dulles to speak or make a reply, he does not look at the person he is addressing but fixes his eyes on the ceiling. This creates an unfortunate impression of conscious superiority on his part, as though the people across the table are not as important as the ideas which represent Eternal Truth, and, therefore, must be addressed to the Cosmos.[58]

Dulles was considered vain and rigid, somewhat of a hangover from the past, "a man who played the fiddle in an age when you have to play the organ." Although he had graduated from Princeton as his class valedictorian, he was not very well known on campus and did not, even then, have the ingredients for personal popularity. He regarded few, if any, as his intellectual equals. Eisenhower had come to respect his great mental capacities and always listened carefully when Dulles spoke. Eisenhower's mentality he considered decidedly inferior to his own, which some likened to a computer. Nevertheless Dulles tended to be intolerant toward any who threatened to get between him and Eisenhower.[59] Whether it was the military or such individuals as Scott McLeod, Nelson Rockefeller, Harold Stassen, General Alfred Gruenther or Emmet Hughes who tried to impinge on his domain, Dulles was quick to guard his prerogatives. Eager to please the President, he arranged to have his brother, Allen Welsh Dulles, who became director of the CIA after Smith, phone Hagerty to find out how Eisenohower regarded Foster. Hagerty explained that the President had had his own difficult period of adjustment and was trying to gear things toward the kind of operation with which he was most familiar. It would be helpful, the press secretary told Allen Dulles, if Foster would not submit memos as they emerged from the State Department but would first go over them himself to tighten the documents by removing all the quibbles because the President would prefer the Secretary's opinion, not that of some Under Secretary. Dulles responded to the advice, and his own assistants believe that the Secretary's relationship with the President became much closer soon afterward.[60]

If the Dulles seen by most people was his only dimension, one would be at a loss to explain his ability to relate to Eisenhower. To his close associates, including the girls in his office, he presented an image never seen by the public. American embassies around the world, for example, soon learned that preparing for possible surprise visits from the most traveled Secretary of State in history required having a plentiful stock of Old Overholt rye, his favorite.[61] Dulles was also capable of spending a dinner hour in his home, during the course of major world problems, discussing batting averages of the teams in the World Series. He was always aware of team standings; but his sporting interest was not confined to baseball. At one particularly momentous and long meeting he buzzed for his secretary, Phyllis Bernau, about every half hour. Whenever she entered the room, he leaned back to hear her whispers. Everytime the ritual was repeated, about eight times times during the conference, all conversation stopped. Those present assumed, of course, that Dulles was getting important messages from the President. When one of his aides later expressed concern about the interruptions, Dulles explained, "Don't you know that the Davis Cup is on today and I kept wanting to know what was happening."[62]

Whereas Dulles could offend as much as impress, Charlie Wilson's approach endeared him with the rest of the Cabinet no more than with the President. His blunt use of words had already caused embarrassment during his confirmation hearings. Later, in 1954, he showed little loss of such talents when he responded to a press conference about the Defense Department's reluctance to plant government contracts as a way of relieving unemployment in certain areas by replying with "I've always liked bird dogs better than kennel dogs myself. You know, one will get out and hunt for food rather than sit on his fanny and yell."[63] Some appreciated his candor; but as a high-ranking government official, his displays of political insensitivity and overbearishness raised wonderment that he had managed to become president of General Motors and, once in that position, had avoided antagonizing the board of directors and stockholders. One White House aide, similarly mystified by Wilson's corporate success, ultimately witnessed an episode that ended such speculation.

While the President had, as usual, developed his State of the Union message with the aid of his Cabinet and was ready to present the final draft for their benefit, he realized that his Secretary of Defense had not participated because of absence from Washington. Since Wilson returned just before the address was scheduled for a reading to the Cabinet, Eisenhower directed that Wilson be shown a draft to enable him to review the contents relating to the Defense Department so any changes he might desire could be incorporated before the meeting. When an aide finally reached Wilson with the typescript, he found the Secretary eager to fine-comb more than his own area. Reminded that it was nearly midnight and that such efforts were not really necessary, Wilson nevertheless persisted. Finally, at about two in the morning, he completed the task. Although he had no complaints about the defense section, he pointed to four minor changes that he felt should be made in the foreign-policy statement. The information that the President had scrutinized that portion of the speech about ten times and Dulles even more often and that they were both happy with the version failed to satisfy him. Tactful suggestions that he, too, should be willing to accept it were also fruitless. He continued to insist on the four changes; and all the frustrated aide could do was to agree politely and promise that the matter would be considered.

When the Cabinet met the next morning, each member followed a copy of the text while the same aide read it to the group. The changes, however, had not been made. Immediately after adjournment, Wilson asked the White House staffer for an explanation and was told that it was too late to make such revisions. Undaunted, Wilson promptly turned to Dulles, who was on his way out of the room. He walked the Secretary of State to the end of the Cabinet table, sat the aide down between them and said, "Now, Foster, there are some changes that struck me on reading this section that I think ought to be made." Dulles, completely unreceptive and eager to leave, was trapped by the aggressive Mr. Wilson. Finally, as Dulles would agree to one change, Wilson went on to the next. Within the next few minutes Dulles had surrendered on all four points. Wilson's tenacity had worn down even the formidable John Foster Dulles and, at the same time, satisfied skeptics about how he had become president of GM.[64]

Although their strong personalities inevitably clashed, such men as Wilson, Dulles, Humphrey and Sherman Adams shared views within the general consensus that supported the Administration. While the plumber among the businessmen-politicians, Martin Durkin, displayed a similar capacity for zealous pursuit of his own ideas, his single-mindedness, unfortunately, was out of place: it would have been considered admirable during the Truman years. Durkin fought, from the outset, for a Labor Department congenial to unionists and for amendments to the controversial Taft-Hartley Labor Relations Act of 1947. Altering the legislation excessively denounced by unionists as a "slave labor law" had become somewhat of a crusade since the legislation's passage over Truman's heated veto message. Durkin, cognizant of Eisenhower's own stated criticisms of some of its provisions, believed that the President had hoped he would fight for such changes.[65] While the President was undoubtedly sincere in saying that certain inequities had to be removed, and, in fact, many Congressmen, including Senator Taft, had proposed changes, Eisenhower's limited experiences had kept him from evolving much of a philosophy toward organized labor and the whole matter of collective bargaining. No other appointment received less of his personal attention. About all that could be determined was his belief that a Secretary should speak for labor on a broad front and not necessarily as a representative of unions.[66] While Eisenhower, at the outset, continued to seem receptive to changing the 1947 law, he blocked Durkin's attempt to choose only unionists as his leading subordinates. Already having named Lloyd Mashburn, who came from the ranks of trade-unionism in California, as his Under Secretary, Durkin wanted men with similar backgrounds as his three assistants. Sherman Adams expressed the Administration's pique over Durkin's ideas by pointing out that almost every nominee recommended by the Secretary was a New Deal Democrat.[67] The clash was not resolved until the late summer when Durkin accepted Eisenhower's desire to have a management man as one of the assistants and they agreed on Rocco Siciliano. As Durkin persisted in his battle to modify the Taft-Hartley Law, he—rather than any of the businessmen in the Administration—was criticized for behaving as though he were a representative of a special interest.[68] One Under Secretary wrote home that Durkin "does not, and I suppose he cannot, have a detached viewpoint of the subject of labor and necessarily must restrict his thinking to one side."[69]

With the additional presence of Sinclair Weeks, who became Durkin's chief obstacle inside the Cabinet, Herbert Brownell, Douglas McKay and Arthur Summerfield, Eisenhower presided over his starting lineup. After having used the reorganization authority that, after a battle, had been extended to the new Administration by Congress, Reorganization Plan I of 1953 had been transmitted to the legislature on March 12 with the provision for the establishment of a new Cabinet-level department, that of Health, Education and Welfare.[70] On April 11, the President announced that his Federal Security Administrator, Mrs. Oveta Culp Hobby of Texas, was being nominated for the HEW job. She fulfilled Eisenhower's vow to give women prominent positions in the Administration; but the attractive conservative made Durkin even more of a misplaced figure.

However active the President was when presiding over his Cabinet seminar, he was even more at home with his National Security Council, which he rejuvenated. Created by the National Security Act of 1947, the NSC was designed as an advisory body to make recommendations to the President on all matters relating to national security. Authorized as statutory members, in addition to the President, were the Vice President, Secretaries of State and Defense, and the director of the Office of Defense Mobilization. Also included as statutory agencies were the Central Intelligence Agency, which had been created by the same legislation, and the Joint Chiefs of Staff. Eisenhower immediately placed great emphasis on the value of the NSC and acted to broaden its representation to include all those with special competence to contribute to its deliberations. Thus, he invited the Secretary of the Treasury and the director of the Bureau of the Budget to sit in on all meetings. On March 23, 1953, announcing the strengthening and improvement of the operations of the NSC, he named Robert (Bobby) Cutler as Special Assistant to the President for National Security Affairs. Cutler thus became the principal executive officer of the National Security Council and the chairman of the newly established Planning Board.[71] The NSC meetings were set for ten o'clock on Thursday mornings, changed on June 4 from Wednesday afternoons, and met much more frequently than had been the practice during the Truman years. Eisenhower usually presided. During the Administration's first 115 weeks, the NSC met exactly 115 times, whereas it had met on an average of only once every two weeks during the five Truman years. Its sessions were even more frequent than those of the Cabinet.[72]

There are those who contend that when the papers of the highly classified Council meetings are ultimately released, they will show the full extent of President Eisenhower's active leadership. Gordon Gray, who served both Truman and Eisenhower, has been quoted as agreeing with such assertions by saying, "The mythical Eisenhower, who left decision-making to subordinates, whose mind was 'lazy' and/or not very bright, cannot be found in these records of the most important business he conducted for the nation." NSC figures also substantiate his personal role, with only illness causing him to miss many meetings. Of the 309 sessions between January 29, 1953, and March 17, 1960, he presided at 280.[73]

That was the place where the President, with the principal assistance of Dulles, was at his most vigorous. There he dealt sharply with the chairman of the Joint Chiefs of Staff and with his department and agency heads. At one such session, when Humphrey opposed a large aid program for India because he felt that nation was going socialistic and a free-enterprise economy should not be taxed to subsidize a socialist country, Eisenhower delivered a vigorous lecture to his outspoken Cabinet officer. "George," he said, "you don't understand the Indian problem. Their situation isn't like our situation. We can operate a free-enterprise economy. . . . But it depends on . . . a whole lot of underpinnings that the Indians simply don't have. If I were the Prime Minister of India, I feel confident that I would have to resort to many measures which you would call socialistic, just by the nature of the situation and conditions in India. So it's quite a mistaken idea that we should judge the Indian situation or the Indian needs or the Indian policies by criteria which may be relevant for us."[74] There were numerous instances of similar assertions of conviction during other deliberations. The President, however, believing that the function of the Council members "should be to search for and seek, with their background and experience, the most statesmanlike answers to the problems of national security," did not announce any decisions during the sessions, but there was no doubt about their value.[75]

Clearly, Eisenhower, although a novice to party politics, operated behind the scenes to move the mechanism of government. Believing in the power of conciliation and guidance and fully mindful of the contending forces within his own party as well as the realities of the Congressional lineup, he acted to preserve the wide public acceptance that had made his election a personal triumph. With Sherman Adams as his drawbridge and a Cabinet designed to his taste, he could be optimistic that the needs posed by politics and national security would be satisfied.

CHAPTER 23

Floating Upstream

THERE WAS NO honeymoon. Less than two weeks after Eisenhower's swearing-in, Senator Wayne Morse remarked scornfully that the country would be better off under Taft; a few days later, the maverick Senator branded the Eisenhower Administration "reactionary" and urged liberals to wake up and marshal their weapons to fight it.[1] Even friendly sources were disenchanted. Henry Luce's *Time* magazine, which had done everything possible to signify the arrival of better days in Washington, recalled the "dry creek" Scripps-Howard editorial of campaign days and noted that the Presidency was in a similar period, "a painful interlude where the objectives were set but the Administration was getting nowhere."[2] And Arthur Krock, who had been praising the qualities of the Eisenhower leadership and style, was forced to admit the validity of the mounting apprehension about the "timorous manner" of the Administration.[3] Some natural friends were finding the need for patience and understanding.

They had to realize that the White House needed to assure conservatives that there had indeed been a change from Truman's ways. Dulles, in a speech interpreted by many as an attempt to regain for the State Department the popular and Congressional support that Dean Acheson had lost, chastised those Europeans who "want to go in their separate ways" in the face of the "deadly serious" threat of encirclement being posed by the Russians and their allies. He warned that the United States, which had invested about $30 billion in Western Europe, would have to re-examine her relationships with those allies if there was "no chance of getting effective unity." Ignoring what he had said earlier about liberating "captive peoples," he nevertheless used vigorous cold-war language by stating that the positive aim of American foreign policy "must be to create in other peoples such a love and respect for freedom that they can never really be absorbed by the despotism, the totalitarian dictatorship of the Communist world." Speaking on TV and standing before a map that was shaded to show the vast areas of Communist control, he enumerated the points on the globe where the enemy was on the offensive and warned, "So far as your Government is concerned you may be sure that it will not be intimidated, subverted or conquered. Our nation must stand as a solid rock in a storm-tossed world. To all those suffering under Communist slavery, to the timid and intimidated peoples of the world, let us say this: you can count upon us."[4]

Just six days after Dulles's pre-recorded speech, Eisenhower went before a joint session of Congress to deliver his first State of the Union message. He spoke with eloquence and with intonations that gave the impression that his mastery of the problems had given him full command of the material. And, while the much praised speech called for such liberalizing measures as extension of old-age and sickness insurance benefits to those not covered by Social Security, the extension of legislation for public school construction and the desegregation of the District of Columbia as well as ending racial separation in the federal government and the armed forces, by far the most dramatic and publicized parts left little doubt that there had indeed been a change in Washington.

The first was of particular interest to the so-called China lobby as well as to the nation's allies. It carried the formal announcement of "instructions that the Seventh Fleet no longer be employed to shield Communist China. This order implies no aggressive intent on our part," he hastened to add, in a section written by Dulles. "But we certainly had no obligation to protect a nation fighting us in Korea."[5] Thus he confirmed what had been known for several days—that the Administration was removing the fleet that had been stationed between Formosa and the Chinese mainland since the early days of the Korean war. The decision, reached jointly by the President, Dulles and the Joint Chiefs of Staff, appeared to contain the essence of military logic. Why, for example, should the Navy "protect" the Chinese Communists when their forces were committed to war against the Americans in Korea? That had not been the case when Truman had first ordered the deployment of the Seventh Fleet to those waters. Furthermore, although neither the President nor the State Department made the admission, it only confirmed what had been happening since shortly after the Chinese had entered the war, as Chiang Kai-shek's Nationalist forces had, despite the presence of the fleet, been striking at the mainland. During the past year such raids had "temporarily occupied," according to the official Nationalist Chinese news service, twenty-one Red cities, 350 villages and nine islands. Furthermore, they had captured or destroyed countless pieces of equipment and many facilities.[6] Nevertheless, President Truman's reversal of the policy had been done quietly, without the overt propaganda threat of a wider war; and, although the Dulles words read by Eisenhower did not say so and had in fact been written to avoid a belligerent tone, the act was commonly referred to as the "unleashing" of Chiang Kai-shek.

Fear that the Administration was contemplating adventurous militarism dominated reactions throughout the Eastern Hemisphere. The Japanese, shocked by Eisenhower's decision and recalling his campaign remarks about turning the Korean war over to Syngman Rhee's soldiers, feared the stimulation of a war of Asians against Asians. The Indian government thought that their worst apprehensions about future Eisenhower-Dulles policies had been confirmed. The French, already upset by Dulles's "brutal" warning to Western Europe, feared that the Seventh Fleet decision contained portents of future policy toward their own continent. In Paris, there was anxiety about how Dulles would explain the new American policy during his scheduled visit. There was, at the same time, obvious uneasiness in England about American policy, which, the British thought, had already blundered tragically by pursuing the Communists above the Thirty-eighth Parallel and into North Korea during October and November of 1950. When Dulles arrived there immediately after the President's speech, he found growing clamor in London.[7] He finally reassured the British government that there would be no real change.

At home, however, the Administration had apparently accomplished its purpose. Although Democratic Senator John Sparkman, who had been Stevenson's running mate in the recent election, asked whether the China policy was "the first step toward global war" and Senators William Fulbright and Albert Gore wanted to probe further, the reception was favorable. And from the right places. General MacArthur, the international military counterpart of Senator McCarthy's domestic anti-Communist zeal, lauded the Seventh Fleet decision and pointed out that it would correct "one of the strangest anomalies known to military history." He also implied that it was a step toward ending the Korean war according to the suggestion he had made to Eisenhower in December. Admiral William D. Leahy called it a "bright idea." Taft considered it a move in the right direction and "about as long a step as we can take at the present time."[8] In the press, while the New York *Herald Tribune* predictably praised the speech, it was more significant that the pro-Taft–MacArthur–McCarthy papers, New York's *Daily News* and *Daily Mirror* and the Chicago *Tribune*, were delighted, as the *Daily Mirror* stated, that the President had rejected the "Marshall–Acheson doctrine" that the United States respond only to Russia's challenges.[9]

But however much Eisenhower Republicans required their party's support and were gratified that they had made a good start, some around the President were not happy at the prospect of alienating their best foreign friends. C. D. Jackson, who had been made the representive of the Secretary of State on the Committee on International Information Activities to report on psychological-warfare matters, had serious reservations about reactions to such moves. Jackson, less than two weeks after the President had announced his rejection of the first clemency appeal of convicted atomic spies Julius' and Ethel Rosenberg, was clearly concerned about what appeared to be the Administration's apparent insensitivity to the opinions of America's allies. Defense of the Rosenbergs against the charges of having passed atomic secrets to the Russians had become an early cold-war cause of left-wing protestants, some of whom worked to rekindle visions of the Dreyfus and Sacco and Vanzetti cases. Their plea to commute the death sentence having been rejected by a federal judge during the last days of Truman's Administration, Eisenhower inherited the problem amid a White House beseiged by picketing protesters and a flood of angry defenders. Even Pope Pius XII was inundated by the outcry and the Vatican had forwarded the messages to Washington. However, less than two weeks earlier, 73 percent of Americans were reported as favoring the death penalty for traitors.[10] Much of the non-Communist left expressed shock when the President finally announced that the lack of new evidence or "mitigating circumstances" justified not changing the sentence. Jackson, analyzing the worldwide consequences of the decision, complained that the Attorney General had "handled this as though it were exclusively an American legal problem, whereas in fact the decision in this case was political warfare raised to the nth power." He noted that American propaganda outlets, particularly the Voice of America, Radio Free Europe and United States Information offices throughout the world were given no advance notice of the decision to enable them to condition popular acceptance of the death penalty. "The fact is," Jackson pointed out, "that the first the Voice knew about it was when it read the President's decision in the newspapers."[11]

The Dulles hard line toward Western Europe and the Eisenhower State of the Union announcement about removal of the Seventh Fleet had created consternation that had been compounded by the handling of the Rosenberg case just a few days later. Additionally, Jackson argued, matters had been exacerbated when the President also informed Congress of his intention to ask them "at a later date to join in an appropriate resolution making clear that this Government recognizes no kind of commitment in secret understandings of the past with foreign governments which permit this kind of enslavement." Jackson complained that that statement, obviously designed to fulfill Republican campaign pledges to condemn the Yalta agreements, had been similarly mishandled. For all the organization that had been established for the operation of the team, there had been inadequate coordination. America's case was not being "sold" abroad. What good, Jackson was really asking, was the acquisition of domestic political strength if accomplished at the expense of America's international interests? A better balance was vital. Dulles, when asked about the matter, explained with his characteristic distaste for details of administration that someone other than the Secretary of State must do such coordinating.[12]

Yet there was no backing away from the promise made in the party's platform to "repudiate all commitments contained in secret understandings such as those of Yalta which aid Communist enslavements." Many believed that grievance resulting from the arrangements made toward the end of the war had been of substantial value to the GOP during the election campaign. Conservatives in particular, then, welcomed the President's State of the Union promise that the United States "shall never acquiesce in the enslavement of any people in order to purchase fancied gain for ourselves" and that he would propose a resolution repudiating unsavory past agreements.[13]

What had really happened at Yalta no longer mattered very much. The Soviet absorption of Eastern Europe was an obvious fact. That Roosevelt had little choice, in the face of Russian military domination over the area during the closing stages of the war, but to rely on Stalin's word that the exiled Poles in London would be permitted to form a coalition government with the Lublin Communist leaders was of little interest to those who viewed the sessions at Yalta as FDR's "sell-out" to international communism. For example, Roosevelt, just eleven days before his death, had been distressed that the Russians were ignoring the agreement and sent the following message to the Soviet dictator: "I cannot conceal from you the concern with which I view the development of events of mutual interest since our fruitful meeting at Yalta. . . . Your government appears to take the position that the new Polish provisional Government of National Unity . . . should be little more than a continuation of the present Warsaw government. . . . I must make it quite plain to you that any such solution which would result in a thinly disguised continuance of the present Warsaw regime would cause the people of the United States to regard the Yalta agreement as having failed."[14] Nevertheless, the extension of Soviet influence in the Far East, amid suspicions that many yet-to-be-revealed concessions had been made by the Democratic wartime leadership, gave what became for many Americans a simple clue to Stalin's postwar successes. Such fears were compounded when the public learned that Alger Hiss had been with FDR at Yalta, which led Senator Tom Connally to observe, "It seems that the only argument some persons can present is to holler about Alger Hiss and refer to Yalta."[15]

If the Republican conservatives thought the election victory had been a mandate to repudiate past agreements, they found little sympathy in either the White House or the State Department. Desires to appease the anti-Communist hysteria by taking jingoistic stances might be fine for Congressmen with bewildered constituencies, but matters were not that simple for the Executive branch. Not only did Eisenhower find scavenger-hunting into the past distasteful, but repudiation could easily haunt American diplomacy for a long time. Germans, for example, feared that the legal status of the West in Berlin might be obliterated if the United States should repudiate the reaffirmation by the Yalta conference of the 1944 London arrangements of the zones of occupation. Furthermore, after such a unilateral abrogation, how could the United States condemn Russian violations? Questions also arose over whether such explicit repudiation was necessary. The ratification of the Japanese Peace Treaty by the Senate on March 30, 1952, had stipulated non-recognition of the Yalta deal on the Kuriles and Sakhalin, which the Japanese had acquired as a result of the Russo-Japanese War and then restored to the Soviets by the agreement. Churchill, who had signed the treaties with Roosevelt and Stalin, had never concurred that they were wrong and, like the Democrats, held that their failure stemmed from Stalin's non-compliance. Moreover, the British Foreign Secretary, Anthony Eden, said that his nation would not participate in any repudiation.[16] The Eisenhower–Dulles objective, therefore, was a resolution condemning diplomacy at the expense of "captive peoples" but avoiding denials of past obligations.

As soon as the Administration's plans for a way to fulfill the campaign pledge were unveiled, however, it became clear that what was favored by the White House and the State Department had little in common with the notions of leading Republicans. At a forty-minute conference with the party's Congressional leaders on February 16, the plan was presented to such leaders as Taft, Joe Martin, Charlie Halleck and House Foreign Relations Committee Chairman Robert Chiperfield. Also in attendance, as the plan was revealed by Dulles, was H. Alexander Smith of New Jersey. Smith, as chairman of the Senate Foreign Relations Subcommittee on the Far East, along with Alexander Wiley and Taft, had a great deal to say about what would be acceptable. And to those gathered that day the Eisenhower plan was a clear disappointment. It was not in any sense a repudiation of the Yalta and Potsdam agreements. No mention was even made of Roosevelt and Truman or of such territorial concessions as involved Poland and China. Instead, it came remarkably close to Democratic defenses of the conferences, similar to those made by Ambassador Averell Harriman. Its thesis was simple: that the Soviet

Union had violated "the clear intent of these agreements or understandings" and had proceeded to subjugate the peoples concerned under the domination of a "totalitarian imperialism." Since that had not been the intention of the American diplomats, the people of the United States, "true to their tradition and heritage of freedom, are never acquiescent in such enslavement of any peoples" and therefore reject any interpretations of the treaties "which have been perverted in order to bring about the subjugation of free peoples."[17] Most of those in the room objected that the plan was too soft, that it should repudiate the actions at Yalta and Potsdam, along with the partition of Poland and the turning over of the Kurile and South Sakhalin Islands to the Soviets. Taft, caught between his desire to avoid an open fight with the Administration on the issue and the demands of his colleagues, was plainly unhappy but expressed his disinclination to oppose the resolution.[18] The others, however, were ready for a fight. Complaints were heard about the Eisenhower version's failure to deliver the kind of repudiation that had been promised at Chicago.[19]

The reaction that followed the President's submission of his resolution to Congress four days later was predictable. Although many Republicans were reluctant to express themselves openly in opposition to the Administration, Wiley called it "disappointing," and Taft, backing away from his initial openmindedness, predicted that there might be "some change in the wording." At least, he told reporters, it was better than the containment policy. He would, however, have preferred a more explicit condemnation.[20] Senator Hickenlooper, also a member of the Foreign Relations Committee, soon went beyond the party's majority leader by calling for much stronger language. He held that any declaration should state that the agreements violated by the Soviets were being regarded by the United States as strictly temporary.[21] On the twenty-third of February, having digested his party's attitude, Taft told President Eisenhower that the resolution would get very little support from Republicans unless it could be revised to avoid any implication of approval for the agreements.[22]

The President's natural allies were on the Democratic side. It was, after all, a matter that implicated their two most recent Presidents as well as their party's handling of the early stages of the cold war. Having fought against repeated accusations that timidity—or even worse—had permitted Russian postwar advances, they were in no mood to help Republicans crucify Roosevelt and Truman. They could even enjoy a good intramural battle within the GOP and come forward as the champions of a bipartisan foreign policy in behalf of the Republican President. Senator James E. Murray of Montana, for example, cautioned that "We shouldn't undertake any move which might embarrass the President in foreign policy." The Democratic minority leader in the Senate, Lyndon Baines Johnson, then spoke for the overwhelming sentiment within his party when he warned that Republican attempts to harden the President's resolution would provoke a major foreign-policy fight. A subsequent statement from the Senate Democratic Policy Committee declared that "The President deserves strong bipartisan support for this effort to preserve the unity of America."[23]

Dulles, who had written the resolution with the President, went to its defense before the foreign-relations committees of both houses. He pleaded with Republicans to forget about the past and to concentrate on the future and warned about the international implications of repudiation. Even some of his critics termed his performance before the House committee as the "greatest advocacy of his career." Repeatedly, he tried to pacify Congressmen eager to impose revisions. Representatives Alvin O'Konski and Charles Kersten, both Republicans from Wisconsin, told him that Eisenhower's text would be an insult rather than an encouragement to enslaved peoples. Republican Senators also proposed amendments. Several days later Dulles, anticipating a move to amend the resolution, notified Chairman Wiley that both he and the President "have no thought whatever that the proposed Resolution would give legislative validation to any of the war-time agreements or undertakings. The President . . . would have expressly disclaimed such a purpose if he or I had had any idea that this interpretation could reasonably be placed upon it."[24]

Two days after Dulles had testified, Taft supported the amendment to satisfy the persistent opponents. Formally introduced on March 3 by Senator Smith of New Jersey, it was in the form of a simple statement: "Resolved, the adoption of this resolution does not constitute any determination by Congress as to the validity or invalidity of any provisions of the said agreements or understandings." The opposition to the change within the committee was led by Democrat Walter George of Georgia and five other Senators from his party. But, with the assistance of the two most powerful Republicans in the upper chamber, Taft and Knowland, the amendment cleared the committee. Democrats, in effect fighting the battle for the Administration against its own Congressional leadership and stung by the latest maneuver, were quick to point out its obvious fallacy. If there was, in fact, nothing legal about the agreements, how could the Russians be charged with violating them? Even more seriously, since negotiations at Yalta and Potsdam had given the Americans occupation rights in West Berlin and Vienna, how could such guarantees be continued if they had been granted by invalid treaties? Democrats immediately warned the White House that failure to issue a public rejection of the amendment would leave them in the lurch and they would muster all their efforts to defeat the repugnant statement on the floor. Meanwhile, the Republican hierarchy vowed complete support for Taft's position. Caught in the dilemma, the Administration began considering abandonment of all efforts to get its resolution through Congress.[25]

Just then help came—and from a totally unexpected source. Word arrived on March 4 that Generalissimo Josef Stalin, the Soviet dictator, was near death. At a meeting of Republican Congressional leaders early the next morning, both sides, weary and frustrated and fearing a fight with the Democrats, agreed that Stalin's condition rendered pressing ahead with the resolution very "inopportune." Diplomatically, the timing would be regarded as particularly callous; moreover, the almost certainty of an early change in Soviet leadership demanded a more cautious assessment rather than a reprobing of old wounds. Yet, at his news conference at about the same time, the President continued to support passage of a resolution, although he told reporters that the final wording was "very definitely" the business of Congress. When he was asked, a few minutes later, to comment on suggestions that the Senate amendment represented "a break between you and Senator Taft," the entire episode received its moment of levity. The President replied, "So far as I know, there is not the slightest sign of a rift or break between Senator Taft and me. And if anyone knows of any, I don't."[26] But a few hours after both Republicans and Democrats had had their laugh, the news of Stalin's death was received.

Whatever the long-run effects of Stalin's passing, the immediate result was the abandonment of attempts to formulate some sort of resolution on the wartime agreements. It was the most expedient solution. After the legislative conference of March 9, Sherman Adams confirmed to Taft that "*Action on the Enslavement Resolution* is to be delayed temporarily pending information from Secretary Dulles as to whether such a resolution is still desirable in view of the situation caused by the death of Premier Stalin."[27] Considerably later, on December 18, the matter was discussed again; but by that time the resolution was as dead as the Soviet leader. Stalin had, for a change, helped an American President out of a dilemma. No resolution was preferable to what his party wanted.

Much less controversial, but more vital for the nation, was another announcement made during that Presidential message of February 2: the decision to permit consumer controls on prices and wages to lapse on April 30.

The Korean war had brought a sharp increase in military spending along with the anticipation of shortages and heavy demand, which resulted in 1950 and early 1951 in sharp upward price and wage pressures. When Truman requested Congress for authorization to combat the economic dislocation, he ran into immediate trouble, particularly from the conservatives. Taft responded with the statement that a domestic economic program "probably means an end to economic freedom in the United States, perhaps forever."[28] But heavy public pressure for action and the testimony of Bernard M. Baruch (the czar of domestic mobilization for war under Woodrow Wilson, who was also prominent in home-front planning during the Second World War) before the Senate Currency and Banking Committee altered the climate for price and wage controls. Nevertheless, Taft, along with John Bricker and Homer Capehart, all Republicans, continued their opposition. Bricker, unable to stop action, did gain the acceptance of an amendment to limit the authority to general rather than selective controls by giving to state regulatory bodies the authority to set ceiling prices on certain goods. Thirty-eight of the forty Republican Senators voting supported him. The final measure, passed overwhelmingly, gave the President permission to, among other things, impose selective or general price-wage controls. An Economic Stabilization Agency was then established to work out voluntary arrangements to implement the goals. The President also created the Office of Defense Production under Charles Edward ("Electric Charlie") Wilson to supervise production, procurement, manpower, stabilization and transport policies and programs.[29] Under the ESA a series of agreements was worked out to achieve voluntary wage-price compliance. Without further Congressional action, such controls were due to expire on April 30, 1953. Truman had already requested their continuation as a necessity for combating inflation.

During his campaign Eisenhower had said little to commit himself on the issue. The matter of controls, however, was clearly contrary to his instinctive attitude toward the economy, with its maximum faith in the ability of unfettered capitalism to fulfill Adam Smith's visions. At his Abilene press conference, after returning from the NATO command, he had made that attitude clear. Acknowledging that a global war might necessitate such measures, he doubted that the Korean situation justified the departure from a free economy.[30] When he took up the issue with his future department heads during the *Helena* voyage, he expressed an almost "religious command" toward getting rid of controls.[31]

The program was not without value, but its course was filled with controversy. A Joint Defense Committee on Defense Production reported in November of 1952 that the action had been significant in ending the dangers of an overheated economy, and the consumer price index rose by less than one percent that year. But the weakening of the Defense Production Act by the inclusion of such provisions as Senator Bricker's amendment had made it more and more difficult to maintain ceilings on many goods, since increases in one commodity would automatically force other businesses still under price ceilings to operate with smaller profits. The Jones and Laughlin Steel Corporation, for example, which had signed an agreement to make no price increases without giving the ESA a twenty-day advance notice, complained that, while only a few of their products had been decontrolled, ceilings had been lifted on prices for most of the services they needed to buy.[32] "It seems all I have done is sign orders increasing prices, and I haven't particularly enjoyed the job," said Tighe Woods, who took over the directorship of the Office of Price Stabilization from Ellis G. Arnall on September 2, 1952. Woods also complained that "it is apparently easy to translate cost increases into price increases, but not cost decreases into price decreases."[33] The turmoil within the Truman Administration over the issue was severe enough to cause Woods's resignation after only three months in office. The day after Woods announced his departure, Edward F. Phelps, Jr., the assistant director of the Office of Price Stabilization, sent him a long memorandum warning that "direct controls represent a drastic and sometimes very painful interference with our kind of enterprise system" and suggested that indirect controls be substituted for price-wage limitations. Their removal would, he advised, be unlikely to bring inflation; but, when dealing with defense-related commodities that were under continuing pressures, controls "should continue for some time after April 30." Wage controls, he pointed out, would also have to be lifted since it was "the view of most experts in the field . . . that selective wage controls cannot be administered successfully."[34] As early as February, Truman's price administrator, Michael V. DiSalle, had established, under Congressional pressures, a seven-man committee to study the possibility of lifting controls over selective consumer goods; and the final report of Truman's Council of Economic Advisers contended that the regulations were doing more harm than good.[35] The chairman of the Senate Banking Committee, Burnet R. Maybank of South Carolina, reported that he had information that Truman was considering abolishing price and wage controls by an executive order.[36]

The outgoing Administration, however, stood pat. While ESA administrator DiSalle and the new OPS director, Joseph Freehill, warned about the dangers of premature discontinuation and leading spokesmen of organized labor, such as AFofL president George Meany, feared the consequences to consumers' pocketbooks, there was little disposition on the part of President Truman to save Eisenhower from the risks of action that was clearly inevitable. DiSalle's fears were undoubtedly genuine. On the day after Eisenhower's inauguration he paid a personal visit to Hauge and Adams to warn against decontrol.[37] Nevertheless, the possibility that their removal would toss an embarrassing inflation into the laps of the Republicans could not have been too far from Truman's mind.

Actually, the question had become less partisan of late and was not one over which labor and capital took distinct sides. After Eisenhower had expressed his misgivings about controls, for example, Bernard Baruch telephoned that such views were "most disturbing" to the General's admirers. Baruch warned that "You cannot mobilize to the extent security requires without priorities over production. You cannot have priorities without price and other⁄controls."³⁸ Still, most business leaders were heartily in favor of decontrol, although the president of one of the nation's largest home-furnishing retail chains voiced favoring the retention of stand-by machinery for the reimposition of emergency ceilings. The businessmen, in taking their stand, were confident that general inflation would not follow because of the large number of items currently selling below the established maximums.³⁹ The *New Republic* also agreed that the threat of inflation was no longer sufficient to warrant controls. While most of organized labor feared its consequences, the lone Democrat and friend of labor within the Administration, Martin Durkin, who served on Weeks's committee to study the issue, also favored abandonment of the program.⁴⁰

Popular opinion seemed unready to push for a rapid change. Dr. Gallup's poll reported in January that 61 percent of the public wanted their continuation. Even the majority of those identifying themselves as Republicans were fearful of letting the controls lapse, although that group did show a distinctly greater hostility toward such regulations than did Democrats. The Republican margin in favor of controls, for example, was only fifty-one to thirty-nine compared with the sixty-eight to twenty-three approval among Democrats.⁴¹

For the new Administration there were other compelling reasons, aside from its economic philosophy. After all, controls were most disliked by the Taft wing of the GOP; their retention would hardly soothe the discontented conservatives. And most Congressional attitudes were generally adverse to the program. To the budget-conscious crew taking over in Washington, there would be another dividend, the reduction of a considerable bureaucracy. As of December 31, the Economic Stabilization Agency had a total staff of 9,313 people, more than half employed by the Office of Price Stabilization. Budgetary expectations for administering the program through fiscal 1954 approximated $50 million, with some $22 million set aside to operate wage and price controls.⁴² That was a minuscule portion of the Truman budget, but any possible soft spot in the effort to reduce its projected deficit seemed attractive. Furthermore, decontrolling would be a dramatic way of announcing the start of the new economic attitude promised during the campaign and would herald an unmistakable shift toward conservatism.

Eisenhower's course, nevertheless, was a model of caution. As Joe

Dodge pointed out, there was the danger of sufficient price rises to increase defense costs, a factor that could very easily negate all the efforts to reduce the budget. On the *Helena*, Eisenhower had listened to all the arguments and had initiated the Weeks committee, which later received hearty endorsement from George Humprey. But the risks, plus the doubts raised by such dissenters as Stassen and Lodge, who cautioned against rapid action, compelled closer scrutiny before advancing. After his swearing-in, one of President Eisenhower's first moves was to call on an academician who knew something about controls, Arthur Flemming, the president of Ohio Wesleyan who had served "Electric Charlie" in the Office of Defense Mobilization and was already involved with Nelson Rockefeller and Dr. Milton Eisenhower in the study of achieving an economic reorganization of the Executive department. Flemming, working on controls with Gabriel Hauge and investment banker James Brownlee, finally brought in a recommendation for a measured, category-by-category decontrol that would be based on the probable inflationary pressures on each commodity.

There was, then, little doubt about the eventual decision. As the time neared for the President to deliver the State of the Union message the chief interest centered around what he would do about rent controls and whether he would request Congress to authorize stand-by legislation to reimpose ceilings in an emergency. While Democrats were fairly together in agreeing on such provisionary legislation as a minimum, the President's own party was split down the middle over the issue. The strongest Republican voice for stand-by controls was Senator Homer E. Capehart of Indiana, the new chairman of the Senate Banking and Currency Committee. Capehart, who had received a warning from the outgoing chairman of the Salary Stabilization Board, Justin Miller, about the necessity for a "stand-by organization in the event of decontrol or suspension of economic controls," was waiting for the President to show his hand.[43] Other Republicans, however, such as Senator Barry Goldwater, who considered controls a way of "tampering" with "America's wonderful free enterprise system," were vehement about jettisoning the whole program. Much more important was the Senate Majority Leader, Taft, who felt that even stand-by authorization was a way of giving "legal recognition to [the] principle of controls."[44]

When the draft of the message was read to the Cabinet on the thirtieth of January, the President promised to take early steps to end controls in an orderly manner. Not only would he permit the relevent portions of the Defense Production Act to expire on April 30 and other sections on June 30, but he said nothing about stand-by controls, except for a statement that failure of the free economy to maintain stability would lead him to "promptly ask Congress to enact such legislation as may be required."[45] He did, however, request the continuation of controls over rents "in those communities in which serious housing shortages exist." When he delivered the speech before a joint session of Congress on the second of February, the first result was the immediate introduction by Capehart of a bill to set up emergency machinery. Fearing a repetition of the inflationary forces that worked during the early days of the Korean war, the chairman of the Senate Banking and Currency Committee declared that it was an "ideal time for Congress to legislate on the subject of controls, free as it is from the stress, strains, and tensions, of a great national emergency."[46] Capehart's efforts ultimately passed the Senate, where the Republicans divided by a vote of twenty-four to twenty-three over Senator Bricker's desperate effort to kill the authorization for a freeze but was finally destroyed in Jesse Wolcott's House Banking and Currency Committee. The President was sustained in the lower chamber.

Then, once his mind had been made up and true to his word, he moved swiftly. The category-by-category plan had been established; now it had to be implemented. With Humphrey continuing to press his argument that rising production combined with tighter credit restrictions would stave off inflation, Eisenhower announced to his Cabinet on February 6, "Let's go," and ordered all wage and some price controls removed at once. The remaining items would be decontrolled within the next few weeks. As he left the Cabinet session, the President stopped Humphrey at the door and said, "I hope, George, that you know what you are doing."[47]

The remaining ceilings were removed in rapid succession. Tires, gas, poultry, eggs, soap, glass, crude rubber and lead were decontrolled on the twelfth, followed the next day by copper, steel and aluminum, until on the seventeenth of March Flemming's Office of Defense Mobilization released all consumer controls that were left. Already obvious by then was the lack of significant upward price movement, although copper, which had been expected to rise, went up to the thirty-cent-per-pound level. During the next twelve months the consumer price index went up only slightly more than a point and the wholesale price index gained fractionally. In September, Sinclair Weeks responded to Eisenhower's request for a report on the status of general price levels and was able to state that "the behavior of prices has been about what we expected. Certainly there has been no such inflationary situation as those opposed to the removal of controls thought would come about. It was alleged that decontrol might result in sharply increased costs for our defense program. This has not happened."[48]

Nevertheless, the President was uneasy. Expressing his misgivings both to his Cabinet and to the party's Congressional leaders during March, he felt that it had been a political mistake to withdraw the government from price stabilization without adopting stand-by controls on consumer credit. Such action, he feared, would substantiate the popular view that his was a "business Administration." While it should be businesslike, he said, in its approach to problems, failure to be responsive to the concerns of "the little man" would hand the Democrats perfect fuel for claiming that only they represented the interests of the people. Taft, however, could not be persuaded; he held that stand-by controls on consumer credit constituted direct rather than indirect controls and he preferred to regulate, instead, bank loans and housing credit.[49] That was where the matter remained, kept firmly in control by the Senate Majority Leader. The President had learned quickly that being torn between his own inclinations and awareness of what the public wanted left little room for maneuvering to satisfy all positions because the ultimate reality was the need to deal with his party's Congressional leadership.

Such conflicts were inevitable. Much more arguable was the wisdom of having the President exploit his own "honeymoon" period by harnessing his enormous popular prestige to "lay down the law" with his party's intransigents. He had, after all, assumed charge of a GOP unaccustomed to govern and much more adept at opposing, to the extent, perhaps, that they had even sold themselves the rhetoric that had accused the Democrats of virtually every political sin from perfidious corruption to intentional assistance to America's real and potential enemies. Thus, with an indecisive Korean war still being waged and with "peace talks" bogging down and with millions willing to tolerate Senator McCarthy's tactics so he could continue his crusade against the Reds and "pinkos," conservatives impatient with the *status quo* had their own notions about what ought to be done. Recalling which Republicans had placed Eisenhower in the White House made them no happier. More and more the General turned President and the Deweyites in his Administration worked to convince the Republican right that they were really red-blooded, nationalistic Americans despite their Establishment clothes.

CHAPTER 24

The Politics of Jobs, Taxes and Oil

THE ADMINISTRATION'S BASIC political realities were the vulnerability of the slight Republican Congressional majority to intraparty dissension and a legislative leadership that was controlled by such conservatives as Robert A. Taft, Styles Bridges, Eugene Milliken, Joe Martin, William Knowland and, dominating the headlines with even greater frequency, Joe McCarthy of Wisconsin. Collectively, they were the most vocal exponents of economy, sound money, lower taxation, reduced domestic and foreign spending, a "get tough" policy toward organized labor and the Western world's most enthusiastic anti-Communist cold warriors.

Their constituents were not at all identical with the party of the New York *Herald Tribune* and those whose economic sphere ranged far beyond the domestic market. Smaller and middle-level proprietors were not equal to the businessmen who bought and sold on a global scale; their more limited assets and holdings rendered them less dominant over vital markets. They were concerned, above all, that a business administration should voice the interests of *their* business. For them, the campaign slogans were not mere rhetoric. Like good businessmen, they had come to believe in their own product.

The politicians, of course, had to satisfy such interests; but since they were impotent without power, the main concern of most Republicans upon their return from the long exile from the White House was patronage. Involved, of course, were jobs ranging from high-level, policy-making positions and diplomatic posts to rural postmasters. But even more important to those already firmly entrenched as policy-makers was the fear that two decades of Democratic rule and deft use of Civil Service protection by the Truman Administration had frozen into posi-

tions a sort of "fifth column" of New Dealers who could be as obstruc-
tive as the "horse and buggy" Supreme Court had been to FDR. Reviv-
ing memories of Jeffersonian complaints about John Adams's "midnight
appointees," Republicans quickly charged Truman with having devised a
"blanketing-in" process to take care of political appointees. Sherman
Adams had to remind impatient Senator Homer Ferguson of Michigan
that the first Republican Administration in two decades could not be
expected to revolutionize the government overnight.[1] A full nine
months after Eisenhower's inauguration, Senator Ralph Flanders worried
that the continuation of Democrats within the Veterans' Administration
resembled "the way in which the Communists got hold of the countries
which are now helpless satellites. They infiltrated the internal security
agencies," he pointed out. "It looks to me as though the Democrats were
infiltrating the vital personnel agencies of the Republican administration."[2]

The perpetuated public image of the President was that of a man
bored by such seekers of personal power. Reporter Robert Donovan,
whose "inside" account of the Eisenhower Presidency was conceived as
a public-relations job by some members of the Administration, relates
Eisenhower's annoyance with the whole question. Donovan, writing
from special access to the Cabinet minutes, has the President telling his
team that he did "not like to have patronage problems brought to him
time after time by individuals in the Republican Party."[3] Sherman
Adams, who did the most to feed such information to Donovan, has
repeated a similar note in his own memoirs. "I'll be darned if I know
how the Republicans ever held a party together all these years," Adams
quotes the President. "This business of patronage all the time—I'm ready
to cooperate, but I want, and we all want, good men."[4] Even Emmet
Hughes's vastly more critical account reports that "Eisenhower tended
always to show his contempt for the power of patronage."[5] Thus was
perpetuated the myth of a politically indifferent Eisenhower, the same
man whose enormous successes had required all the power obtainable
by personal diplomacy.

Dealing with the implementation of a revised Civil Service procedure
that would make certain policy-making positions vulnerable to administrative appointment, Eisenhower was very much concerned about the
political implications that were possible under the plan. On March 18 he
sent a private and confidential personal memorandum to Commerce Secretary Weeks reporting that every protected position in one department
was being held "by an individual who believes in the philosophy of the
preceding administration." Moreover, the President, who was known for
his public avoidance of highly partisan political jargon, pointed out that
they had reached their high offices "through a process of selection *based*

upon their devotion to the socialistic doctrine and bureaucratic controls practiced over the past two decades."[6]

At about the same time, when the Administration had its first scandal, the President was also "above politics" in his public reaction. Wesley Roberts, who had been awarded the national chairmanship of the Republican party to succeed Postmaster General Arthur Summerfield, was revealed as the recipient of an $11,000 legal fee for the purchase of a hospital by the state of Kansas. His 10 percent of the price of the deal, which involved the legislature's granting approval for "acquiring" a facility that obscure records showed the state already owned, was, according to a special committee that had been established to investigate the situation, indiscreet, if not in direct violation of the law requiring lobbyists to register.[7] Eisenhower thus had not a "5 percenter" but a 10 percenter on his hands. Nevertheless, when the story first broke, he appeared unperturbed. After Roberts submitted his resignation, the President told a news conference that finding a replacement would be up to a national committee. Shrewdly, he added a careful qualification: "I am going to try to find a man who commands the highest respect from every way that I can find, as far as my own choice of a person is to be considered."[8]

But the impression that he was above political manipulation had been made. It even fooled one of the party's former Presidential candidates, Alf Landon. Landon, pointing out that recent national chairmen had been disasters, urged Eisenhower not to abdicate his responsibility, to give it the attention it deserved, "for the sake of the Republican Party and of your administration."[9] Eisenhower's response was characteristic. "I completely agree," he assured Landon, "that the selection of the new chairman of the Republican National Committee merits the most careful consideration."[10]

What happened was left neither to chance nor to the national committee. By the time the party's committeemen were actually convened to vote, there were grumblings that they had been assembled to rubber-stamp the one and only candidate.[11] That man was Leonard Hall, a virtual stereotype of the genial politician whose law career on Long Island had propelled him to affluence. He had been Tom Dewey's campaign manager in 1948 and had, from 1939 until 1952, served as a mildly conservative member of the House of Representatives whose principal identity was with the internationalist Eastern Republicans. His Congressional voting record contained little that a Dwight Eisenhower would have found objectionable. Not only was Hall acceptable to the President politically and had, in fact, established a relationship with him on the campaign train in 1952, but Hall's great strength was his standing with the party on Capitol Hill. His chief contribution had been organizing the Republican Campaign Congressional Committee to unify the GOP and strengthen the party's voice in Washington. Such activities had made

Hall familiar to Republicans from all over the country. Moreover, having served as Dewey's campaign manager and having won on his own several times, Hall emerged as the sort of man the party needed for the coming Congressional elections of 1954. With the two parties balanced so evenly, it was natural for Eisenhower's acceptance of Hall to be supported by the House leader, Speaker Joe Martin. Martin did everything he could to promote Hall's candidacy, but the Administration did the rest of the job. Maneuvering was necessary because Hall had two natural sources of opposition, Robert Taft and Tom Dewey.

There was little reason for Taft to be happy with Hall. Except on such issues as labor and government spending they had little in common. Hall had supported Truman's basic foreign programs, including financial assistance through the Mutual Security Act. Where Taft had taken a liberal position, as one of the chief Senate sponsors of the Housing Act of 1949, Hall had been with the conservative opposition. Even more serious from Taft's viewpoint was that Hall's Congressional district had been in a suburb of New York City, and the Empire State was the great bane of Midwestern Republicans. Moreover, it was also Dewey's state. The most compelling way to overcome Taft, who was saying that the GOP should select a "big name" as its head, was to demonstrate with conviction that choosing Hall would serve the party's best interests.

Dewey's opposition, traceable to a falling out over the handling of the disappointing loss in the famous upset election of 1948, had placed the two men in rival positions. Insiders heard that it was Dewey who had vetoed a move to make Hall the national chairman back in 1950. In Hall's home county the Governor's ally was Nassau GOP leader J. Russel Sprague. At the Roney Plaza Hotel in Miami Beach a showdown took place between the forces led by Martin and the opposition organized by Sprague. When the Sprague people found they were unable to outnumber Hall's friends, an expedient reconciliation followed between Hall and the Nassau County leader.[12] Further promotion for Hall came at a testimonial dinner at the Kings Point Merchant Marine Academy that was sponsored by Long Island Republicans on March 28. The Administration's hand was visible in the person of Vice President Nixon, who posed for pictures at the affair with Hall and Joe Martin. Martin forthrightly spoke for Hall as the new national chairman and flatly predicted he would get the necessary fifty-four votes of the national committee.[13] Both the Roney Plaza encounter and the dinner had demonstrated Hall's standing with the party nationally and at home. But the Eisenhower Administration did more for him than sending the Vice President to Kings Point that Saturday night.

The following Wednesday, April 1, Eisenhower's Congressional liaison man, Jerry Persons, met with twenty-eight of the party's House members. Ostensibly, the meeting was to sound out their preferences; in reality, it would serve to convince Taft that the party wanted and needed Hall. Persons informed the group of the President's major aim. That, he said, was to win the 1954 elections. Representative William H. Ayres of Ohio, who had convened the meeting, illustrated their problem by pointing out that in 1952 the party's Congressional incumbents had run ahead of the President in only seventy districts. Twenty seats were won by the thinnest of margins, and Republican strength in twenty other districts was so slender that they could go under very easily. When the President was given his report of the meeting, he was told of their conclusion that the new national chairman must be one with an understanding of campaign problems in different districts, "must not be wealthy, yet not mercenary," not restricted by involvement in party factions, and, most important of all, "must be able to work with women."[14] Furthermore, although a number of other names were mentioned, Hall's had dominated.

Taft, convinced of the party's need and desire, subordinated his own preferences and went along with Hall. As for Dewey, a plea from the White House appealed to his party loyalty. Sprague then made public his own endorsement of Hall and immediately left with his former rival by chartered plane for Albany, where, after a ninety-minute conference, Dewey issued a statement adding his approval.[15]

Then the national committee, after soliciting Hall's assurances that they would get a greater voice in clearing the Administration's patronage requests, made the Hall choice official. The next morning the President explained to his Cabinet that avoiding an open endorsement for any particular candidate had been a way of preventing Hall from being caught in a crossfire between the Taft and Eisenhower factions of the committee, which, Eisenhower pointed out, might be the case if he were marked as "my man."[16] He neglected to add that his own neck had been kept out of the line of fire.

Those who still doubted the President's apolitical posture were given additional contrary evidence by his response to a reporter's question at his April 23 news conference. When Richard L. Wilson of the Cowles Publications pressed Eisenhower about a series of suspicious recent resignations in several federal agencies, he agreed with the inevitability of department heads wanting to get rid of those who did not have their confidence. "But so far as any discharge having taken place in the Government for patronage reasons," he quickly added, "if they have occurred, I am—I tell you flatly—completely unaware of it. That has no appeal to me whatever."[17]

President Eisenhower's overt efforts to avoid partisanship or political controversy shielded the intense efforts to effect an internal revolution of political ideology. Not only did the newcomers generally tend to believe their own propaganda that incredible ineptitude, dishonesty and socialism had overwhelmed Washington during the past twenty years but to a very disturbing degree much of their righteous suspicion was justified. Democrats had, indeed, inundated the federal payrolls. Even worse, there was little the Republicans could do about it. Of the 2,555,-950 who were employed by the federal government as of February 1, few were ripe for Republican plucking. Some 93 percent had job protection under Civil Service provisions. Additional numbers, such as war veterans aided by Truman, were given special coverage. And the ability of Democrats to select from the top three finalists from merit examination lists had discouraged countless Republicans from even trying. The resulting suspicion toward such holdovers was intense; and, as the President's private note to Weeks had shown, he shared that feeling. Nevertheless, overt disassociation was his style, partly through his conviction about the demands of bipartisanship in view of his heavy dependence upon the Congressional Democrats and partly because that role had, from long practice, become his natural response. Just as, in 1956, he denied having persuaded John Sherman Cooper (who was surprised and agitated to hear the President's statement) to leave his ambassadorial post in India to run for the Senate from Kentucky, he gave the appearance of innocence by denying to reporters knowledge of any discharges for political reasons. Yet, just days before the President had taken that detached above-politics position, the Administration had made several highly political moves.

Claude Wickard, who had served as FDR's Secretary of Agriculture from 1940 to 1945 and had then become head of the Rural Electrification Administration, resigned as "anticipated" by Agriculture Secretary Ezra Taft Benson on March 16.[18] Wickard departed with a curt, one-sentence goodbye to become effective that afternoon. Benson said that reports that Wickard had been forced out were "greatly exaggerated."[19] But after noting complaints that strong supporters of the Rural Electrification Program had been embarrassed by the handling of the Wickard resignation, Homer Gruenther informed Jerry Persons that, while it is "generally believed that Wickard was forced out of the department," there was "no quarrel with this except that the REA supporters in Congress feel that the Agriculture Department should not have forced Wickard's resignation before his successor was ready to be announced" and that the resulting impressions of the Administration's hostility toward the Rural Electrification Administration made "a difference to Congressmen and Senators up for election in 1954."[20] Wickard's replacement was the Republican lieutenant governor of Minnesota, Ancher Nelsen, a Benson man. Since the Wickard affair was a normal and understandable political replacement and only the circumstances mattered very much, it was not nearly as controversial as several lower-echelon changes that had been made only days before Eisenhower's statement to the press.

Wickard, of course, was a Democrat; but Dr. Allen V. Astin, a forty-nine-year-old electronics and weapons expert, was a Republican and had been with the National Bureau of Standards since 1932. In June of 1952 he had become head of the bureau, which was under the jurisdiction of the Commerce Department. As a scientist, Dr. Astin was responsible for supervising the fundamental testing of material and equipment for possible use by the government. Failure for a product to gain clearance as a beneficial or worthwhile item had obvious implications for its marketability; and it could also be barred from the mails. On March 31, Commerce Secretary Weeks announced that Astin's resignation had been requested and obtained.

Astin had antagonized a manufacturing outfit called Pioneers, Inc. of Oakland, California. The Bureau of Standards had declared that an additive the company wanted to sell to the government that was designed to prolong the life of storage batteries named AD-X2 was worthless. The California manufacturers charged that the tests had not been conducted properly, and Weeks observed that AD-X2 had been used with success by his own company and that outside tests had also supported the claims of Pioneers, Inc. When the President accepted Astin's resignation on April 2 he said that Weeks was the last person who could be arbitrary or unjust.[21] Dr. Astin, meanwhile, defended the bureau's obligation to adhere to the results of scientific findings regardless of pressures. The nature of his "error" was clear.[22]

What no one in the Administration wanted or apparently expected then resulted. Newspapers and scientific journals featured the story. Weeks was represented as a latter-day Richard Ballinger to Astin's Louis Glavis. The journal of the American Association of Science declared that "scientific work in the government has been placed in jeopardy." Other scientists within the Bureau of Standards threatened to resign if Astin was not reinstated. Congressmen of both parties grumbled that the scientist had not been given a fair hearing. Finally, within hours of the stated termination time for Astin's employment, Weeks announced that the scientist would be asked to stay on at least until the fall, when a specially appointed committee was due to report on the bureau's work. As early as August 21, however, Astin accepted Weeks's request to remain indefinitely.

A similar incident, also occurring before the Eisenhower press conference, had involved Albert M. Day, who had directed the Fish and Wildlife Service since 1946 and had been a career officer since 1918. After Interior Secretary McKay announced in mid-April that he would be replaced by John L. Farley, a former head of the California Fish and Game Commission and currently with the paper-manufacturing firm of

Crown Zellerbach Corporation, Day charged that special interests, Alaska salmon packers and duck hunters who wanted hunting laws eased had forced his ouster. Day was defended vigorously by those aware of his outstanding work, but McKay prevailed.[23]

McKay's Department of the Interior was also involved with the affair of Tom Lyon. Lyon was nominated as a replacement for John J. Forbes, a forty-year career man who had been director of the Bureau of Mines since 1951. Lyon, a retired Utah mining engineer, had been recommended by McKay on March 25. Resembling the recent appointment as administrator of the Housing and Home Finance Agency of Albert M. Cole, who admitted to being opposed to the principle of public housing, and corporation lawyer Edward F. Howrey as chairman of the Federal Trade Commission, the Lyon case encountered immediate obstacles. Vigorous protests came from United Mine Workers chief John L. Lewis. Questioned by the Senate Interior and Insular Affairs Committee, Lyon said that the Mine Safety Law should be administered by the states rather than by the federal government. Furthermore, the hearings also produced the information that the nominee had a pension from the Anaconda Copper Company and that it was revocable at their pleasure, leaving the very clear implication that Lyon's own financial interest was related to the company's desires. Finally, on June 25, the nomination was withdrawn. The next day the President expressed his displeasure at a Cabinet meeting by citing the need for more careful investigation of candidates to determine in advance their philosophies and how they were likely to react.[24]

Then there was the case of Marion Clawson, which also involved McKay. Clawson, director of the Bureau of Land Management since 1948 and a career official since 1929, was pushed out by the Secretary, who said he had resigned. Nine days before the President's news conference of April 23, McKay reported that the job would be filled by his own appointee and that Clawson would be reinstated in a lower-paying position as an adviser on public lands. When the disposed man denied that he had resigned and challenged the Secretary of Interior to give specific reasons for his dismissal, Clawson was charged with insubordination and denied the secondary job.[25] By the summer, Eisenhower insisted that all pending appointments for high-ranking Interior Department posts be given his personal scrutiny.[26]

Expelling New Dealing "fifth columnists" and finding jobs for the loyal continued to agitate the long-time opponents of the Democratic bureaucracy. Executive Order 10440 was issued on March 31 to facilitate the Administration's own revolution. Aiming squarely at Schedule A of the Civil Service lists, which included those office-holders with confidential or policy-making positions normally not protected by the merit system, it singled out those in that category who had nevertheless been given such protection by Truman. The Civil Service Commission was directed to review all Schedule A positions for possible reclassification, and a new category was established. Schedule C was devised for upper-echelon persons for whom job protection would be inimical with the requirements of the new Administration. Vacancies could be filled by the agency and department heads. Eisenhower also moved to nominate as the chairman of the Civil Service Commission Dean Philip Young, of the Columbia Graduate School of Business and the son of Owen D. Young, the prominent Democratic industrialist who was responsible for the de-vising of a new war-reparations scheme in the 1920s. Young, although confirmed without trouble, soon became the bane of patronage-hungry Republicans who wanted what would have been the virtual restoration of the spoils system that would have been achieved by finding that an excessive number of jobs were actually "policy making" and therefore eligible for placement in Schedule C. When Representative Halleck of Indiana wanted to remove Civil Service protection from those who had not taken examinations but had been granted coverage by Truman for wartime service, Young objected. Others argued that it was not entirely a question of who made policy but rather of who wrecked policy.[27]

Still, the Administration needed greater authority over its own personnel. By the early summer of 1953, fewer than twenty-five hundred federal workers had been appointed by Eisenhower and, of the 1,200,000 personnel in the Defense Department, less than twenty reflected the national change. In May, the President directed that the nearly fifty-four thousand Schedule A people who were not veterans could be dismissed at the discretion of their department heads.[28]

For the most part, the main personnel-recruitment task was turned over to one of the original Citizens for Eisenhower founders, Charles F. Willis, Jr. With some fifty-six thousand lower-level appointments to be made, Willis's aim was to siphon all the possibilities through each political channel. Additional thousands were "volunteered" by patronage-seeking Congressmen. Willis's job also involved contacting various leaders in different fields for appropriate appointments. When the number of possibilities for each position had been reduced to two or three, the final choice was left to the President.[29] With the patronage problem still irking national committeemen, who were complaining that Eisenhower was failing to build up the party to support members of Congress by the proper distribution of jobs, Willis finally devised, in 1954, a plan called "Operation People's Mandate." Its objective was to give depart-ment and agency heads efficient knowledge of all key vacancies, thus expediting their staffing by those who were "competent, of high integ-rity and loyal to the program of the agency."[30] But its intricacies and the continuing drive for patronage ultimately led to much dissatisfac-tion. It finally had to be modified so that it did not apply to competitive positions. When the Willis directive found its way into the pages of the Washington *Post* the President described it in a news conference as "an effort to get the best kind of people applying for governmental service that you can get."[31] But neither side was satisfied. Civil Service supporters were unhappy because the Willis plan remained in effect, and several agencies continued to retain political criteria for appointments to Civil Service jobs. Congressmen lamented the shortage of patronage, and some never became convinced that Eisenhower had done enough for them.[32]

Too few jobs and entrenched Democrats had mitigated the spoils of victory, threatening, at the same time, the Administration's efforts to introduce and execute policies consistent with its analysis of national needs. Also troublesome during those first months, and a much more basic indicator of the conflicts within the party, was adhering to a fiscal policy in apparent defiance of the mandate for a change.

Several Korean war-borne taxes were due to expire during Eisenhower's first year. They ranged from a 20 percent excise tax on movie-theater admissions to, more significantly, the Excess Profits Tax of 1950, which, with its higher rates on corporate earnings, was scheduled to end on June 30. Additionally, an 11 percent extra tax on individual incomes had no authorization beyond the end of the calendar year. Permitting those changes and possibly, as a member of Budget Director Joe Dodge's staff had suggested while examining the books of the outgoing Truman Administration, advancing the income revision to June 30 would have been consistent with GOP campaign promises and welcome proof that the old policies were being liquidated.[33]

Equally congenial with those sentiments was the President himself. He wanted to demonstrate that Republicans could rectify New Deal follies. He favored a revenue program that encouraged investments rather than "confiscatory rates" on corporate earnings. While Democrats liked to contemplate increased exemptions to give consumers bigger deductions, Eisenhower's concepts were bound to traditionally conservative, pre-New Deal notions of stimulating the economy from the top for greater productivity. But his most compelling conviction was the continuing concern that potentially inflationary conditions created by large budgetary deficits, as the projected $9.9 billion loss in Truman's budget indicated for fiscal year 1954, had to be rectified before further advances could be made.

Treasury Under Secretary Marion Folsom, who had gone to Washington from the Eastman Kodak Company, had been working on the situation even before he had left Rochester. Together with George Humphrey, he had reached a preliminary decision that gambling on tax reductions to raise needed revenue for budget balancing by stimulating the economy was much too risky. There was, simply, no way to avoid concentrating on trimming Truman's budget. Permitting the excess-profits tax to expire at the end of June would be counter-productive since it would cost the Treasury an estimated $800 million. All the legislated changes together, including the 5 percent reduction in the corporate normal tax rate due to take place on April 1, 1954, could deprive the federal government, it was feared, of $8 billion during fiscal year 1955. Eisenhower, as he had done when he had first received Dodge's bad news on the *Helena*, listened to the analysis with care, reacted with some haziness about corporate taxes but with considerable perception when the other intricacies were discussed and bought the argument.[34]

The battle started early. When the President managed to get away from Washington on February 26, for the first time since his inauguration, he thus took a holiday from not only such matters as the Yalta resolution and the Bohlen nomination but from a battle between the tax-choppers and the budget-balancers. He flew to the Augusta National Golf Club in Georgia, arriving in time to change into golf clothes for some practice tees and then play seven holes until nightfall blackened the well-known course. Sharing the so-called "Bobby Jones" cottage with Mamie, amid tall pines at the edge of the lush green links, he was determined to ignore all but emergencies. By then, however, the battle that had been spurred by his State of the Union message had become intense.

His February 2 speech had stressed the "elimination of the annual deficit" as the first order of business. "Until we can determine the extent to which expenditures can be reduced," he cautioned, "it would not be wise to reduce our revenues."[35] Appearing on television programs the following weekend, both Robert Taft and George Humphrey left no doubt that Eisenhower's words had meant that, as the Senator explained, "I don't think you can cut taxes until you cut the budget." Yet, so ardent for reductions were some Republicans that suggestions were heard that the President's omission of a flat declaration against a tax cut in 1953 was, in effect, an opening for that possibility.[36] Decidedly on record against the President's entire concept was Republican Congressman Daniel Reed, chairman of the House Ways and Means Committee. Reed had taken a position that threatened to cost the Treasury some $3 billion.

An imbroglio had resulted from a combination of the upstate New Yorker's determined fiscal conservatism and inept Congressional relations by White House novices. Reed, a former Cornell football coach, had been offended because the incoming Administration had overlooked inviting him for consultations, although Eugene Millikin, who headed the Senate Finance Committee, had been called in to meet with Eisenhower. By the time the thrifty Congressman was invited to the White House, he had already surprised the Administration by introducing legislation to advance the personal income tax reduction expiration to June 30, which would coincide with the end of the special excess-profits tax.

The White House and the Republican Congressman could not have been at greater odds. Joe Dodge, in his first public statement after having been named Budget Director, had made clear that neither a balanced budget nor tax relief were early possibilities.[37] As Dodge had explained on the *Helena*, the Truman deficit left only a narrow 13 percent in which cuts could be made. Income could, therefore, not be lowered faster than expenditures. But even before Eisenhower's view was given to the nation on February 2, Reed vowed that his measure, HR 1, which had been introduced on the very first day of the Eighty-third Congress, would pass before the end of that month. While Reed undoubtedly spoke for the majority of Republican Congressmen, the President had the loyal support of Taft and Speaker Joe Martin. Martin, primed on the subject during leadership conferences with the President, directed the House Rules Committee to bottle up any tax bill reported out of Reed's group until at least May 1. Earlier action would have preceded the Administration's own revision of the Truman budget. When Ways and Means approved the Reed bill on February 16, it did so by a vote of twenty-one to four and with the complete support of the Republican members. Their report also declared that "tax relief must be the first order of business for this Congress."[38]

By then the Administration was already implementing its own budget-cutting efforts. Dodge had directed, on February 3, all department and agency heads to transmit proposals for budgetary revisions by recognizing the "strictest standards of economy" for all new projects and to "drive for greater efficiency and reduced costs."[39] Charlie Wilson immediately ordered a virtual freeze on civilian employment and a halt to all construction projects by the Defense Department. One month later he ordered the firing of 39,346 civilian employees by May 31.[40] Throughout Washington that winter and spring the economy binge threatened the security of all but the most entrenched and protected. Each department head prepared statements showing how many vacancies he had created, and personnel reductions became an index of economy. By early March all but the Defense Department had submitted proposals for additional ways to slash the Truman budgetary projections. Examining their preliminary reports, Dodge expressed dissatisfaction and indicated that the President might have to order further reductions.[41]

Eisenhower then gave the fight his personal leadership. At Washington's Mayflower Hotel he spoke to the Business Advisory Council of the Commerce Department and pressed the battle. "We must have a balanced budget in sight," he said, "a proved capability, before we can begin to lower revenue—which doesn't mean you may not reform taxes, but you must never lower revenues."[42] At a press conference the next day he proclaimed a similar message. Clearly unable to jar what it regarded as mandatory outlays for national security, the needs of the "great equation" dictated no possibility of a balanced budget but, at least, a reduced deficit was obtainable.

Taft, who had joined the Administration's drive to whip tax-relief-hungry Republicans into obedience, exploded when confronted with Dodge's findings that heavy military burdens would keep expenditures over the $70 billion level. He also heard, at a legislative leaders' conference on April 30, that that was anticipated after a reduction of $7 billion in military outlays and that the projected deficit had been changed from Truman's $9.9 billion figure to $4 billion.* Taft, as he had over the Durkin appointment, lost his temper. As he sat at Eisenhower's left and diagonally across the Cabinet table, his voice rose and his fist banged the surface. "The one primary thing we promised the American people," shouted the Majority Leader, "was reduction of expenditures. Now you're taking us right down the same road Truman traveled. It's a repudiation of everything we promised in the campaign."[43] He wanted to know what had happened to Republican hopes of getting costs below $70 billion.

Eisenhower's consternation was obvious to everybody in the room. The President listened in silence as the Majority Leader warned that spending even on the revised level would defeat Republican House and Senate candidates in the 1954 elections and that, although he was opposing current efforts to cut taxes, he could make no such promise for fiscal year 1955.

There was no reaction from the President even when the Senator finished. The pall of embarrassment was finally ended by George Humphrey, who ventured to support the President's position. Dulles and Dodge also added their comments, enabling the President to compose himself for an impassioned response. Then, in a deliberate, low voice, he reviewed the nation's international commitments, particularly the continuing war in Korea, difficulties with Communist forces in Indochina and the problems presented by the "great equation." He could not, he stressed, accept a balanced budget while endangering national security. When Taft then asked for assurances about improvements for fiscal year 1955, Eisenhower was optimistic but carefully made no promises. Taft had, by then, calmed down and apologized for his outburst.[44]

In a fireside radio talk to the nation on May 19, Eisenhower explained his position to the public. Not only was he opposed to losing the 11 percent additional income tax on June 30, but he added a request for extension of the excess-profits tax until the end of the calendar year. Both would then expire simultaneously. The urgency for continued deficits, he made plain, was the "full nature of the present and future danger before us" in the interests of national security. And that he attributed to the aim of Soviet policy with its announced "hope and purpose—the

* The actual deficit for fiscal year 1954 was $3.117 billion.

destruction of freedom everywhere." Saving more money could only be at the price of national security; and reducing taxes and thus raising deficits would create an inflation that "would cheat every family in America."[45] His proposals then went to Congress.

The President's concern had led to leadership, a display that marshaled the twin forces of his prestige and Congressional lieutenants. Reed, nevertheless determined to fight all the way, announced that his committee would not report out an excess-profits extension as long as the Administration kept HR 1 trapped in the Rules Committee. "When I fight, I fight," said the ex-football coach, who had already failed to get enough signatures to salvage his bill by a discharge petition. As the Administration pressed its case, there were signs, as the New York *Times* reported, that "heat was being used to reinforce prayer" with Republicans being cornered and reminded that Ike's coattails had been valuable in 1952 and his support might be nice to have in 1954.[46] Democrats, meanwhile, chagrined that the President had castigated Truman's spending as the source of all the trouble and delighted, at the same time, with the Republican intramural row, caucused and decided to let the Administration stew in its own predicament. Reed, finally capitulating to pressure, agreed to hold hearings on the President's request.

That brought the Presidency into direct conflict with some of its most natural supporters. Extending the excess-profits tax was denounced by virtually every businessman who testified, including those from the Chamber of Commerce and the National Association of Manfuacturers. George Humphrey, who maintained that it was a necessary evil, afterward made a private observation to NAM president Charles Sligh, Jr. Sligh, who had argued for budget-balancing by reducing federal spending, was told that the NAM's open opposition had been a boon to the Administration. By placing Republicans in the happy role, for a change, as opponents of business interests, the Administration's tax objectives had gained politically. It was so perfect, Humphrey pointed out, that they would never have dared to conspire for that purpose.[47]

Amid extraordinary maneuvering on all sides, the President's legislative success followed. Reed's bill remained dormant in the Rules Committee, while other Ways and Means Republicans responded to White House pressures by overriding his objections and reporting out an excess-profits tax extension. After speedy Senate action, the President, without having denounced any obstructionist by name, signed the measure on July 16. Then, on August 6, he issued his first veto. Representative Noah M. Mason, an Illinois Republican who had warned that continuing the business tax would cost the party forty borderline seats in 1954, had responded to pleas from the Council of Motion Picture Organizations and led a repeal of the 20 percent excise tax on motion-picture admissions. Three days after the Congressional adjournment in early August,

Eisenhower rejected the measure as unfair for having singled out only that industry for relief.[48]

For disappointed conservatives the Eisenhower crusade had marched to Constantinople rather than Jerusalem. The vice-president and treasurer of the Bettinger Corporation protested that taxing excess profits was "a pure and simple discriminatory" act because of the special hardship on small businesses. Just when his company was entering a lucrative period, he contended, the levy threatened to drain off some 65 to 70 percent of the profits.[49] Sinclair Weeks had to explain to the president of the Aeroquip Corporation of Jackson, Michigan, that the Administration also found the tax repugnant but had had no choice.[50] Robert Welch, Jr., a Massachusetts candy manufacturer, Taft supporter and ex-vice-president of the NAM, complained to NAM vice-president Walter Chamblin that the Eisenhower Administration was taking the nation "down the path of socialism" by such actions. Chamblin, after contending that his organization had done its utmost to kill the tax, replied that "I am worried about the attitude of many prominent business leaders like yourself in expecting too much too soon of this administration" and recalled that after FDR's third election he had told the NAM that the only way to "uproot" the New Deal "would be to get a booby-trap gun and take after each department of the government, one by one."[51] Little more than five years later, continuing to find the Administration a disappointment, Welch began to organize the John Birch Society. For the benefit of his own coterie he circulated the manuscript of a tract called *The Politician*. Its thesis was that Eisenhower, the subject of the title, was a shrewd and dangerous politician who, having been "installed in the Presidency" by the Communists, appeared *intentionally* to be carrying forward his Communist aims.[52]

Less doubt about the legitimacy of the change in the White House occurred when, on May 22, the President signed Public Law 31. Better known as the Submerged Lands Act, it granted the states of California, Texas, Louisiana and Florida rights to submerged oil deposits from the low tide line seaward to the three-mile limit. Additionally, it gave them the right to claim, in the Supreme Court, jurisdiction as far out as some contended had been their historical boundaries, a distance of three leagues, or ten and a half miles. Texas, in particular, which had been an independent republic before annexation in 1845, had a strong case for that contention. Yet, as the President signed the measure with a statement that "I deplore and I will always resist Federal encroachment upon rights and affairs of the States," he was completely reversing Truman's position. He was also dismissing claims that the move would constitute, in the words of former Secretary of the Interior Oscar Chapman, the "greatest giveaway program in the history of the world," surpassing the notorious Teapot Dome and Elk Hills raid of federal oil reserves during President Harding's time.[53]

The battle had gone on for thirteen years. More recently, Truman had done everything possible to preserve oil revenue from the potentially rich offshore lands for the entire nation instead of the few states with claims. In 1946, after Congress succumbed to oil lobbyists by voting to grant the extractive rights to the states, a Presidential veto followed. Truman said the Supreme Court had to decide. In decisions pertaining to California in 1947 and to Texas and Louisiana in 1950, the Court reaffirmed federal control. Since the Court had also conceded that Congress had the power, in effect, to nullify those decisions by granting the rights to the states, affirmative action was then passed by the Eighty-second Congress. Once more Truman killed it with a veto. Four days before relinquishing his office to Eisenhower, he left a challenge to the new Administration by issuing an executive order that set aside offshore oil lands as a Navy reserve in the "interest of national defense." Senator Lister Hill of Alabama then spoke for many liberals by suggesting that the revenues be used for federal aid to education.[54]

That was done with complete awareness of Eisenhower's position. The Republican party's platform had denied Truman's assumptions and the General's campaign position had, like Taft, been clear enough on the point to win him the support of the Democratic Governors of Louisiana and Texas, as well as numerous organizations representing oil, banking and corporate attorneys. Jack Porter, who had led the Eisenhower faction during the battle to control the Texas delegation, was an oilman. The valuable substance was also a major factor that aided pro-Eisenhower drives in Texas by such people as Maston Nixon and Oveta Culp Hobby and was ultimately the main reason for Governor Allan Shivers's support of the General. In Louisiana, too, there was much enthusiasm about Eisenhower's position. It was in New Orleans on October 13, 1952, before a responsive crowd in Beauregard Square, that the General denounced as a "shoddy deal" Adlai Stevenson's proposal for the federal government to share the offshore oil revenue with the states. He left no doubt, too, that he favored the states' claims out to their "historic boundaries" and promised to "always resist federal encroachments upon the rights and affairs of the states."[55]

Eisenhower had, by no means, been the Republican candidate of the oil interests. While, in Texas, a majority of the oil-producing counties did back the General, and people like Sid Richardson did contribute generously to the campaign, Oklahoma oil money was almost entirely behind Taft. Persistent rumors held that the Senator, whose position on offshore oil was the same as Eisenhower's, was given more than one hundred thousand dollars for his efforts when he visited Tulsa. Furthermore, observers in the Sooner State noted that Eisenhower's strength was greater in the wheat belt than where oil interests were strongest.[56] Nor did he need the oilmen to convince him of the propriety of the states' claims; they were entirely consistent with his—and the Supreme Court's—view of the Constitution, and furthermore he had been on record with that position since 1948.[57] It was, for Eisenhower, an entirely logical appraisal of the federal government's relationship to the states. That it was, at the same time, a bonanza to the oil interests was no reason for dismay.

The new Administration's call to action came quickly, with Attorney General Brownell denying, on February 16, Truman's designation of the oil as a federal reserve. A battle resulted with the non-oil-interested Southern Democrats, certain conservatives from areas that would realize no gain, particularly in the upper Midwest, and Northern liberals motivated by ideology and a desire for federal money for education and other purposes ultimately staging a filibuster. Somewhat embarrassed by adopting a parliamentary device associated with segregationist tactics to defeat civil-rights legislation, the liberals preferred to characterize their strategy as a long "debate." Since they were clearly outvoted, a logical purpose was to publicize the "giveaway" before a largely apathetic public and thus prepare an issue for the 1954 and 1956 elections. In that effort Wayne Morse set a new filibuster record on April 24 by speaking for twenty-two hours and twenty-six minutes. Clinton P. Anderson, Herbert Lehman, Paul Douglas and Lister Hill all joined in the attack. Brownell, when facing the Senate Interior Committee, had recognized that Congressional action to make outright grants to the states of their claims to the ten-and-a-half-mile limit would precipitate legal challenges and, therefore, prudently recommended letting them claim the property by withholding any titles to the disputed sea bottoms until the Court could decide the merits of each case. That made Louisiana's Governor Kennon comment that he preferred the position Eisenhower had taken during the campaign to the legalistic reasoning of his Attorney General.[58]

The final bill, Public Law 31, followed the Brownell guideline. Its passage was opposed by only nine Republican Senators, a combination of liberals such as John Sherman Cooper of Kentucky, such conservatives as Francis Case, Homer Ferguson and Milton Young, and incorrigible independent and maverick Senators William Langer, Charles Tobey and George Aiken. At the same time, the Congress approved the Outer Continental Shelf Lands Act, giving the federal government jurisdiction from the end of the state claims seaward to the edge of the continental shelf, some 100 to 150 miles out at sea. When the states took their historic claims to the Court, the Administration made very clear that it was an unenthusiastic defender of the government's effort to preserve at least some of the money for the federal government.

In 1958 former Governor Allan Shivers, whose identification with oil interests had become complete by having become chairman of the board of Western Pipe Line Inc., received a reassuring letter from President Eisenhower. The Attorney General, he wrote, had to file a brief in the Supreme Court to settle the disputed area between the three-mile limit and the three-league claims only because "he necessarily has to argue that Texas has no right beyond the three-mile limit . . . but for my own personal satisfaction and so that you may clearly understand that I have never changed my position in this matter, I wanted you to have this in writing."[59] In separate decisions made in 1960, just Texas and Louisiana were granted the old water boundaries.

Only the allocation of "black gold" to the states had completely fulfilled the promises of the Republican Presidential victory; many conservatives had already begun to see confirmation of the consequences of Taft's defeat. Eisenhower had lifted price and wage controls; and there was relatively little dispute about that, but he had demonstrated a rather New Dealish inclination by suggesting the retention of stand-by control authorization and he had acquiesced as Congress later voted to continue ceilings on rent in "critical defense housing areas." The liquidation of holdover snipers from the Roosevelt–Truman era also seemed half-hearted. Furthermore, taxes were not being reduced and no White House spokesman was venturing to promise early budget-balancing. Robert Welch's anger may have been expressed with more vehemence than most, but complaints of inadequacies were plaguing the Administration from others impatient for a conservative revolution. Ernest T. Weir, chairman of the board of the National Steel Corporation, who had wanted legislation to absorb the burden of shipping charges, expressed his grievance to the Secretary of Commerce. "Now we have a Republican Congress, a Republican President, and a favorable Federal Trade Commission, and we apparently get no action," he wrote.[60] And the President himself, in letters to Cabinet officers asking that they consider a program to offer the Congress in 1955, noted that "we have only made a start" toward achieving through legislation the criteria of the domestic program. "Our task is to demonstrate that the goals our people want—in every field—can be achieved by other means than those that result in making Big Government bigger."[61] Gabriel Hauge had also urged that something be done to implement the "Eisenhower Program" instead of dealing with the leftovers and the expediencies of the present.[62] The economist's ideals assumed a readiness for political leadership by the President and his party. By that time the Administration had appeared to have accomplished considerable control over the greatest potential disunifier, the question of "internal security" and the ambitions of Senator McCarthy.

CHAPTER 25

The Holy Crusade

Troubled by racial warfare, burning cities, crime and domestic contention over the most unpopular war in the nation's history, Americans were tempted to recall the Fifties as a "placid" era, a period of great tranquillity presided over by a Dwight D. Eisenhower who, above everything else, ended a war and kept the peace. But, once again, nostalgia merely proved to be seductive and the manufacturer of myths. In reality, perhaps not since the time of the Alien and Sedition Acts and the battles over disunion and Reconstruction had Americans viewed one another with such distrust. The agitation of the era may have seemed less threatening because the leading forces, whether directed toward a modern version of "waving the bloody shirt" against the Democrats or resisting inevitable social and economic changes, were led not by dissenters, racial minorities or non-conformists but by those whose patriotism could never be questioned. The Republican succession brought a messianic drive to eradicate from Washington the corrupt "five percenters," halt the progress of "creeping socialism" and dislodge the disloyal from their sanctuaries along the Potomac.

The popular mood was hardly as disturbed about lingering Democrats in Washington as about disloyalty. That fear of war with the Soviet Union had actually declined since prior to the Korean intervention did not allay apprehensions about internal Communist subversion. The 73 percent in favor of the death penalty for traitors was matched by the number wanting communism taught in the public schools, mainly, of course, to warn about the "Communist menace." Gallup reported that three out of every four respondents opposed permitting even *former* members of the Communist party to teach at the college level, and two-thirds of the sample agreed that Red speakers should be denied access to local forums.[1] FBI director J. Edgar Hoover, who hailed McCarthy for his "Americanism," validated popular fears by declaring that espionage rings were operating more intensively than ever. Earlier, a Republican Congressman from upstate New York, Kenneth Keating, had urged that security agencies be given the right to intercept telephone and other communications. Senator Wiley, the chairman of the Senate Foreign Relations Committee, reacted to soothing tones from Moscow in Stalin's wake by pointing out that his subcommittee was concerned that the "peace offensive" may be simply a cloak for increased spy activity. Maryland's Senator John Marshall Butler, whose election victory over Millard Tydings had been with the industrious aid of Senator McCarthy, urged the ouster from government of all "crypto-Socialists," and Representative James Van Zandt of Pennsylvania wanted the swift deportation to the Soviet Union of all alien Communists and fellow travelers.[2] New York City's Superintendent of Schools reported that the local board of education was investigating 180 teachers suspected of Communist leanings. Furthermore, as the months went by, the hysteria increased. In early 1954 the Veterans of Foreign Wars post in the Connecticut town of Norwalk campaigned to gather the names and addresses of residents "whose record of activities are deemed to be Communistic" by the organization for forwarding to the FBI. When the matter drew widespread attention, the organization's national commander gave the vigilante drive his full support.[3] While accepting an honorary degree at Temple University on June 18, 1953, magazine publisher Henry R. Luce, whose wife was President Eisenhower's ambassador to Italy, warned students and faculty that "we in America have developed a form of brainwashing under the name of anti-communism."[4]

Mr. Luce's observation was not overly strong. An American Civil Liberties survey of the national activities consistent with the crusade reported that twenty-six states had enacted laws designed to bar Communists from running for public office; in many of the remaining states, qualifications had been devised to make such political activity difficult if not impossible. Twenty-eight states had laws denying state or local Civil Service jobs to Communists, and thirty-two of the forty-eight states required their teachers to comply with loyalty oaths. In eleven states Communists were denied the right to meet in school buildings, and hundreds of local boards of education had added similar prohibitions. Furthermore, many private meeting places, such as New York's Madison Square Garden, refused to rent to groups tagged as Communist by the Attorney General's list. Individual suspects were also unable to live in federally aided low-income housing projects, get passports or enter the country even as visitors, hold offices in unions wanting National Labor Relations Board services under the Taft-Hartley Act, or, in Pennsylvania or Ohio, draw unemployment compensation. Many means of livelihood were also out of reach, particularly jobs in radio, television or motion pictures.[5]

Buried under the hysteria, however, was the almost unwelcome reality. The Communist party in America was at a low point in its fortunes, with its total membership at about thirty thousand, little more than one-third of its top strength of pre-Nazi–Soviet pact days in 1939. Confined principally to certain unions, the electrical and furriers, and retaining some strength on the West Coast waterfront, the party was in a state of decay. Its main quarters were in a dingy New York room, over some stores. Its paper, the *Daily Worker*, was languishing with just fourteen thousand subscribers. So few students had enrolled for a Jefferson School course in Marxism-Leninism that each one was practically assured of private attention. Little over four years earlier extreme leftist acceptance by Henry Wallace's third-party campaign for the Presidency had undermined the Progressives by frightening away anti-Truman liberals. More recently, the sensational "Doctor's Plot" in the Soviet Union, with its evidence of blatant anti-Semitism, had further embarrassed the American Communist party. With additional harassment coming from all directions, including the FBI and the Subversive Activities Control Board, only nonexistent evidence of massive financing for front activities from the Soviet Union could dispel the picture of an impotent Communist party.[6] But shock waves of postwar international events, the espionage revelations and the initiation in 1947 in response to Congressional pressures since 1945 of a Loyalty Review Board, had helped to convert a long-standing American fear into a virtual state of panic.

Shaping up right from the start was a battle between Congress and the Administration over control of the internal-security issue. For most Republicans, their organization of the Eighty-third Congress was too good an opportunity to kick away. In the past, Capitol Hill initiative had already been taken by such Democratic committee chairmen as Representative Francis Walter of Pennsylvania and Senator Pat McCarran of Nevada. Now, with the Rosenberg case in the headlines, the opportunity was not about to be missed by the new leadership. Senator McCarthy had taken over the chairmanship of what seemed a rather unpromising vehicle, the Government Operations Committee. Through the brazen use of his arrogance, however, and the exaggerated fear others had of his political power, he soon made it a handy weapon for the McCarthy enterprise and a bane for an Administration already ensnared by the party's right wing.

That McCarthy's ability to terrorize was greater than his real political power has already been demonstrated. In Wisconsin he had run far behind Eisenhower during the 1952 elections, and a county-by-county tabulation made by political analyst Louis Bean showed that he was the low man on the party's ticket and may even have reduced the General's margin of success. Democratic Senatorial candidates who were McCarthy's targets actually gained, on an average, of about 5 percent from his opposition.[7] Only about one-third of the public approved of his activities, and Dr. Gallup's poll never showed his popular esteem higher than 50 percent.

Yet the Senate allowed itself to be pulverized by the unscrupulous freshman from Wisconsin. Such members of the upper chamber as Butler, William A. Purtell, Barry Goldwater, William Jenner and Frank A. Barrett had all won after McCarthy's intervention; and, although there was no way of proving that he had made their victory possible, it was enough to caution many others to remain on his good side the next time around. Additional evidence of his ability to survive was provided by the failure of his colleagues to act on the unanimous report of the Senate Elections subcommittee about his finances.

The result of an eighteen-month investigation was issued on January 2. It questioned many of his financial holdings, particularly his acceptance of ten thousand dollars from a company that had been a constant applicant for funds from the Reconstruction Finance Corporation. Money collected for his anti-Communist crusade had found its way into his personal checking account and was directly tied to his own investments. Nevertheless, it was as though Senator William Benton had never called for an investigation. McCarthy proceeded to hire the youthful son of a New York City Democratic judge, Roy Cohn, as chief counsel to the Permanent Investigating Subcommittee of the Government Operations Committee. And Cohn soon declared that there would be wider, not fewer, probes under the new Administration, a position that McCarthy himself enforced two days later. McCarthy's ally, Jenner, became chairman of the Internal Security Subcommittee that McCarran had led, and Senator Wiley announced that his Foreign Relations Committee had formed a subcommittee on "security affairs" to look into "the impact of totalitarian methods of espionage and subversion on the foreign policy of the United States," particularly the "problem of security in the United Nations and its specialized agencies."[8] Even more ready for action was Representative Harold Velde, the new chairman of the House Un-American Activities Committee. Velde, an ex-FBI agent from Illinois who had been elected in 1948 under the slogan "Get the Reds out of Washington and Washington out of the Red," celebrated his chairmanship by announcing that he preferred to accuse one person unjustly than to allow Communists to escape detection.[9] Before the month of

January had ended, the Senate, ignoring its own demands for economy, had appropriated $714,359 to start investigations under Republican sponsorship of subjects ranging from waterfront rackets to Communists in the Army. Additional requests were yet to come. The total for McCarthy's subcommittee had been doubled over the allocation by the Democratic Eighty-second Congress. Every attempt to economize failed by resounding voice votes, and the resolution boosting the appropriation for Jenner's Internal Security subcommittee was approved by a vote of seventy-three to zero. The Congressional intention, thus, was quite clear.

Eisenhower's State of the Union message of February 2, however, gave such friendly journalists as Arthur Krock an opportunity to proclaim that the President had seized from Congress the leadership of the internal-security issue. Krock, who would repeatedly hail the advent of vigorous Presidential leadership, was happy to hear the Chief Executive state that the "primary responsibility for keeping out the disloyal and the dangerous rests squarely upon the executive branch. When this branch so conducts itself as to require policing by another branch of the Government, it invites its own disorder and confusion." Revealing that all principal new appointees had already been investigated at their own request by the FBI, he stated that the existent powers were sufficient and assured that the cleansing process would have two criteria: "Their first purpose is to make certain that this Nation's security is not jeopardized by false servants. Their second purpose is to clear the atmosphere of that unreasoned suspicion that accepts rumor and gossip as substitutes for evidence."[10]

Within a few weeks, however, the President's words became meaningless as Congressional inquisitors, well funded and certain of being on to a good thing, probed for every conceivable indication of subversion. Not only in Washington, where McCarthy's Permanent Investigating Committee had given the Senator much better leverage than he had seemingly obtained when becoming chairman of the Government Operations Committee, but from throughout the country newspapers carried reports of confrontations with suspected individuals during the late winter months and spring of 1953. Jenner moved his Senate Internal Security subcommittee to New York City to root out any fellow-traveling Americans employed by the United Nations. Later, the Senator went on to Washington and Boston for inquiries about communism in private and public schools; and a score of teachers refused to answer questions under the protection of the Fifth Amendment to the Constitution, which shielded them from possible self-incrimination. While Velde's House Un-American Activities Committee checked into the state of enemy infiltration into education in New York City and went on to expose Communists in the motion-picture industry, a HUAC subcommittee led by

Representative Bernard (Pat) Kearney sought to substantiate its contention that the state government in Albany was infested with subversives. Velde, however, made headlines without his committee when he told a radio audience that HUAC's probes would possibly extend to the clergy, some of whom the investigator charged had been devoting more time to politics than to the ministry.[11]

In a nation of churchgoers and anti-Communists the HUAC chairman's extemporaneous remarks stirred considerable confusion. Within hours, embarrassed members of his committee disavowed the existence of such plans and soon ruled against any investigation of that sort without a vote by their full body. G. Bromley Oxnam, the Methodist Bishop of Washington and a leader of the World Council of Churches, asked whether that was Velde's response to criticisms by clergymen of his committee's methods. Representative Franklin D. Roosevelt, Jr., of New York City, offered a motion to remove Velde from his post. But the American Council of Churches, agreeing that Velde had a good idea, began to circulate a petition among the clergy calling for a probe of religious organizations.[12] The Gallup organization checked into the public's feelings and found that 36 percent agreed with the need for such an investigation.[13] For the most part, however, Velde had become a ridiculous figure.

Inevitably, the President was asked to comment. Before a room full of newsmen at a press conference in the Executive Office Building on March 19, American Broadcasting Company correspondent Martin Agronsky asked if he agreed with the Congressman. After a long thoughtful pause and some careful deliberation, Eisenhower finally replied, "Now, I believe that if our churches—which certainly should be the greatest possible opponents of communism—need investigation, then we had better take a new look and go far beyond investigation in our country, in our combating of this what we consider a disease. Because the church, with its testimony of the existence of an Almighty God is the last thing that it seems to me would be preaching, teaching or tolerating communism. So therefore I can see no possible good to be accomplished by questioning the loyalty of our churches in that regard."[14] But Velde had not been silenced. In May he told churchmen that criticizing his proposal was committing the "sin" of subversion.[15]

Eisenhower was not finished either, for the problem had only begun; and the real crusade was being directed by Joe McCarthy's Permanent Investigating Committee. Two weeks after the President's State of the Union comments on security, the Wisconsin Senator opened public hearings on the operations of a division of the International Information Administration's Voice of America broadcasts. The agency, which was within the jurisdiction of the State Department, was responsible for sending propaganda broadcasts behind the Iron Curtain via a radio operation that was larger than the combined networks of the United States. Day after day the probe made headlines. Many of the sessions were televised. Incompetence or sheer dishonesty was equated with willful subversion. Before a national TV audience the deputy director of the IIA, forty-three-year-old Reid Harris, accused McCarthy of trying to "wring my public neck" by implications that Harris had not altered leftist views he had expressed twenty-two years earlier.[16] Another Voice of America employee committed suicide and left a note stating he feared harassment by the Senator, who then denied that the man had been scheduled for an investigation. Also attacked by McCarthy was a Voice campaign to advertise the advantages of life in America by using the favorable comments of such known Communist or pro-Communist authors as Howard Fast. The State Department responded with a directive severely restricting the use of such material. Voice personnel feared the order had placed a serious limitation on the program's psychological-warfare activities, and steps were taken to work out a compromise. The Administration had also initiated reorganization plans that would remove the IIA from the State Department and place it under an independent agency, known as the United States Information Agency. Dr. Robert L. Johnson, the president of Temple University who had earlier worked on government reorganization, was placed at the head of the IIA, which became the USIA under Reorganization Plan Eight of June 1, 1953.[17] By then, however, McCarthy had followed his familiar practice by shifting his inquiry to more sensational matters. His hunt for culprits within the IIA, however, had been only the most publicized but not the most profound intimidation of the State Department.

No two men in Washington contrasted more sharply than McCarthy and John Foster Dulles. The Senator, from an Irish Catholic background in Wisconsin, had worked his way up through local Democratic politics. Dulles, the patrician from Watertown, New York, whose family had already contributed to American diplomatic history and whose sister, Eleanor Lansing Dulles, was currently a State Department specialist on German affairs, was the Princeton-educated Calvinist with a long-standing devotion to Republicanism. McCarthy, whose ignorance of communism was vouched for by close friends and conservatives who knew him well, had become a subject for Capitol Hill gossip soon after arriving in Washington as a freshman Senator because of his sexual promiscuity and weakness for alcohol. He understood the "internal menace" as the valued issue that lobbyists and zealots like lace-importer Alfred Kohlberg would welcome with appreciative support and which insecure Americans would hasten to accept in lieu of more complex explanations for failures of an international realization of the American dream. Dulles, on the other hand, saw communism as an alien and worldwide force that could be resisted best not by hunting for nonconformists but by material and spiritual strength. He believed, according to one of his closest aides, that there was an evolution in the Communist world that could either be retarded or advanced with intelligent study; at the same time, their possession of military power made them the only contemporary threat to peace. For him, the hunt for internal subversion contained no significance or interest. Once, when standing with Senator Ralph Flanders while both men were overhearing McCarthy delivering one of his tirades, the Secretary of State remarked that such tones were reminiscent of Germany in the 1930s. He feared we were flirting with building an American equivalent.[18]

All of this made it supremely ironic that Dulles should emerge from the nightmare of suspicion as one of the Administration's most willing accomplices of McCarthy and his fellow adventurers. Dulles, ever the pragmatic practitioner of what he considered realism, had every intention of avoiding the pitfalls that had brought upon Dean Acheson such approbrious barbs as "pin-striped diplomacy," suggestive of a snobbish elegance more British than American. Falling out of grace with Congress, as had his predecessor, and lacking the support of the public because of suspicions that he was "soft on communism" would incapacitate his handling of the State Department. The skeleton in his own closet, of which he was self-conscious, had been his endorsement of Alger Hiss as director of the Carnegie Endowment and his subsequent willingness to offer a deposition in behalf of the accused man's character. Further lapses, he knew, could destroy his ability to guide American foreign policy. At best, those considerations were distractions from his real mission. So concerned was he, in fact, about the problem of having to preside over the huge State Department, with all the detail work involved, that in 1952 he had seemed to waver about accepting the top assignment. As a first step, however, once he had been so designated by Eisenhower, he asked that his loyalty be examined by an FBI full field investigation, a procedure that then became standard for all appointees.

Once in office, Dulles attempted to stave off the inquisitors by modifying operations to meet their demands. Speaking from the steps of the State Department building to an outdoor assemblage of departmental personnel, the Secretary spoke with care but no prepared notes and called for their "positive loyalty" to the new Administration. With the term "loyalty" having attained highly significant connotations, with Dulles's own acceptance of the rhetoric that the Department had been packed with the untrustworthy, his remarks were interpreted as establishing a new test. Henceforth, it would no longer be sufficient to be merely loyal but one had to give, as one of Dulles's inner circle of aides has observed, "consistent proof of such fealty." To those to whom it never occurred to be anything but faithful to the new Administration, the unfortunate impact of his talk had a long-standing effect upon morale.[19] Moreover, in notable instances involving such Foreign Service officers as John Carter Vincent and George F. Kennan, and the addition of ex-FBI investigator Scott McLeod as State Department Security Officer, Dulles soon won a reputation that substantiated the most pessimistic interpretations of his request for "positive loyalty."

John Carter Vincent had long been a target of Alfred Kohlberg and his so-called China Lobby, an unofficial conglomeration of businessmen and politicians devoted to the promotion of Chiang Kai-shek and his Nationalists. Though the lobby supported the Generalissimo's cause with much enthusiasm before the conclusive events of 1949, the abandonment of the mainland had actually increased the credibility of its denunciations of all those whose attitudes were suggestive, in the slightest way, that Chiang was corrupt or that Chiang needed to institute economic and social reforms. Equally suspect were those who had had a hand, or who were suspected of having been involved, in the missions to China of General George Marshall and Vice President Henry Wallace. Both had made unsuccessful efforts to reconcile the opposing forces on the Chinese mainland. Explanations for the "loss of China" peddled by the lobby and promoted by numerous Senators and Congressmen followed the general theme that, as at Yalta, such Americans as Johns Hopkins University Professor Owen Lattimore, who had belonged to the much-attacked Institute of Pacific Relations, and a corps of "China Hands" within the State Department had somehow conspired to make Mao Tse-tung's victory possible.

Vincent had served as the American Counselor of Embassy at Chungking from 1941 until 1943 and had then become director of the Office of Far Eastern Affairs. Rapidly he became one of the chief targets of those who failed to understand how Chiang could have lost. As early as the spring of 1947, more than two years before the Nationalists' final collapse, Senator Styles Bridges had suggested Vincent's culpability in a letter to Senator Arthur Vandenberg. The then Acting Secretary of State, Dean Acheson, responded with a massive detailed memorandum that refuted every anti-Vincent charge. Acheson also pointed out that Vincent had been a consistent advocate of the extension of credits to China when conditions there could enable their effective utilization to improve economic conditions and promote a revival of American-Chinese business relations. Furthermore, he was an active supporter of the grant of the Export-Import Bank of a $500 million credit to China in March 1946. As far as his connection with Yalta, Acheson noted, Vincent had known nothing about what had taken place at that conference until he reached Potsdam in July of 1945.[20]

But, as with Lattimore and fellow Foreign Service officers John Paton Davies and John Stewart Service, Vincent remained vulnerable before the vultures. When, on February 20, 1950, Joe McCarthy gave the Senate a list of alleged Communists in the State Department, Vincent was named as the number-two man. The following year the Georgia-born diplomat, who had been with the Foreign Service since 1924, was accused of having been "under Communist discipline" during his World War II service in China. His accuser was Louis Budenz, lately a Fordham University professor; in actuality, however, he was a practitioner of a new specialty, perhaps the only area where Americans were willing, if not eager, to accept the word of ex-Communists—the naming of fellow party members. Budenz, who had been a *Daily Worker* editor and a member of the party's national committee, offered no evidence for his charge. Appearing in 1952, at his own request, before Senator McCarran's subcommittee, Vincent stated under oath, "Gentlemen, anyone, including Budenz, who before this subcommittee or anywhere else, testifies that I was at any time a member of the Communist party is bearing false witness; he is, to put it bluntly, lying."[21] Although he had been cleared by the State Department's Loyalty and Security Board, a three-to-two vote of the President's Loyalty Review Board, in December of 1952, held that there was "reasonable doubt as to Vincent's loyalty to the U. S." Vincent was immediately suspended from active duty in his post as Minister to Morocco; but the fact that the review board's chairman, ex-Senator Hiram Bingham of Connecticut, had ensured the verdict by adding two new members to the board and that Secretary of State Dean Acheson's faith in Vincent was unshaken induced President Truman to set up a board of five men under Judge Learned Hand to review the case.[22]

Thus remained Vincent's status when Eisenhower became President and Dulles took over the State Department. Not content to leave matters to chance, however, Kohlberg, who had always been a prolific letter writer to influential people, bombarded Dulles with correspondence about Vincent. Two days after the outgoing Administration had announced the commission to be led by Judge Hand, the lace importer tried to persuade Secretary of State-designate Dulles that the old Acheson defense of Vincent was fallacious. But even Kohlberg had to admit that "Although I have known of Mr. Budenz's belief about Mr. Vincent for exactly six years, I have never accepted it as conclusive but rather only as a basis for further investigation." Then Kohlberg added: "On the other hand, if Mr. Vincent's testimony before the McCarran Committee exhibits qualities of ignorance, laziness, misunderstanding, lack of interest and lack of study, which if truthful and in the absence of contrary evidence, are so accepted, it would explain all the errors on his part from 1943 to 1947. If this is correct, it would be highly improper to cast doubt on his loyalty."[23]

Once having inherited full responsibility for disposition of the matter,

Dulles accepted the Acheson–Truman interpretation that the loyalty review boards were only advisory and that the head of the State Department had to make the final decision. On January 31 he announced the dissolution of the Hand commission. A few days later the Secretary told Vincent he could choose between retirement or being fired.[24] On the fourth of March Dulles announced that there was no evidence of disloyalty in the case of John Carter Vincent and that the Foreign Service officer was, therefore, entitled to resign with his full pension of $8,100 a year. However, Dulles added, he was being permitted to retire because his professional judgments had not been up to par, which the Secretary failed to define. Even then the critics were not satisfied. Mc-Carran charged Dulles with engaging in "subterfuge," and McCarthy was indignant that Vincent, having been rejected by the loyalty board, was eligible for a pension.[25]

The decision to let George F. Kennan retire, however, had no direct connection with the Red-hunters. Kennan had served Truman as the American ambassador in Moscow until the Soviet government had demanded his recall for "slanderous attacks" on the Russians for having attacked the current "Hate America" propaganda campaign. As a Foreign Service officer Kennan was awaiting reassignment. But the political tides had turned against one of the foremost American experts on the Soviet Union, for it had been Kennan who had written the famous "X" article in *Foreign Affairs* back in 1947 enunciating the containment policy. He was, therefore, far too closely associated with a policy that John Foster Dulles and the Republican party had promised to reverse by having extended hopes of "liberation" to the "captive peoples." Some Washington observers suspected that Dulles could not, in effect, continue Kennan's policy without getting rid of the author of containment.[26] How better to prove that the Truman–Acheson policy was indeed being changed? Moreover, Kennan's own actions had given no evidence that the diplomat intended to accommodate his views to the needs of the new Administration. He remained as outspoken about Republican liberation talk as he had been against the Soviet diatribes.

That January, while awaiting reassignment, he delivered a speech in Scranton, Pennsylvania, warning against any "governmental" action that was designed to interfere with the internal affairs of another country. In a meeting with Dulles shortly afterward Kennan apologized and retracted his statement that, in effect, said foreign policy advocated by Dulles was idiotic.[27] Together they issued a statement discounting any differences between them. But later, at Princeton, Kennan again spoke on the superiority of the containment policy. In March, Dulles took advantage of the automatic retirement provision for any Foreign Service officer, who, after serving as "chief of mission," had not been reassigned within ninety days. Not only did the United States thus lose his diplomatic services but the man perhaps best able to analyze the course of Soviet policy as a result of Stalin's death was not even consulted after the demise of the Russian dictator.[28] Kennan, thus freed, then went on to speak his mind about the mindless anti-Communist crusade of the right-wingers. At the University of Notre Dame, in May, he denounced the zealots.[29] Whatever else may have caused Kennan's retirement, the United States had lost a valued scholar-diplomat. Together with the removal of people like Vincent and such others who had served in Asia as John Paton Davies, who was retired at the end of the year, the politics of suspicion deprived the United States of diplomatic personnel whose experience and wisdom would be missed in the years ahead.

Responsible, too, for the loss of judgment and balance was the damage done to the morale of not only the Foreign Service but of the State Department personnel. More closely identified with that deterioration than any single individual was a former FBI agent and newspaperman, Scott McLeod. McLeod, it was widely assumed, had been brought into government service as a concession by Dulles to McCarthy; hence he was usually referred to as the Senator's agent hunting for subversives. Actually, McLeod got his job through Senator Styles Bridges, whom he had served as an administrative assistant. He had been hired by the Under Secretary of State in charge of administration, Donald Lourie, who had been president of the Quaker Oats Company and a leading fund raiser for the Republican party in the Midwest. McLeod made the most of his mission. Dulles, who had very little patience for such details but was fully cognizant of their political implications, had told McLeod of the need for a security system in the Department. Because of McLeod's FBI experience, Dulles was more than happy to assume his competence in such matters.

Dulles had no illusions about McLeod's political value. Without such scrutiny he knew he could not defend his department before Congress, so the security officer was given free reign. There were those who were convinced that Dulles himself was terrorized by McLeod. For one, he was fully aware of the political ruckus that would be fomented with the right wing by any attempt to get rid of him; and secondly, McLeod's wide-ranging actions stepped on the Secretary's toes. Dulles was not one to brook interference within his area by such associates as Harold Stassen or Henry Cabot Lodge; he certainly had no tolerance for a Scott McLeod. When the nomination of Charles Bohlen as ambassador to the Soviet Union encountered trouble because Bohlen coolly said that he could not agree that there had been a sell-out at Yalta, the "evidence" to be used against the diplomat was gathered by McLeod and taken by him over Dulles's head to the White House. Dulles, who had pressed for

Bohlen, impetuously fired McLeod; but advice from his own Assistant Secretary for Congressional Relations that he was merely stirring up trouble with the Republican Congressional right wing led the Secretary to rescind his order.[30] Edward Corsi, a New Yorker who went to work with the State Department briefly as a consultant concerning immigration, also found that Dulles was virtually pulverized and intimidated by the realization that he needed to remain within McLeod's good graces.[31]

Properly outraged reactions to the witch hunts should not, at the same time, conceal the existence of disloyalty in government agencies. To pretend that such a vast federal bureaucracy, swollen by more than 250,000 persons after the advent of the New Deal, was totally free of those willing and ready to betray the United States would be indeed naïve. For example, the Civil Service Commission, acting under the Hatch Act of 1940, had declared that 448 people were ineligible for government work because of loyalty to the Axis powers, and 563 were denied employment because of pro-Communist sympathies. Ironically, many of the possible subversives who remained in Washington were actually shielded by the incredulity fostered by the irresponsibilities of Congressman Martin Dies's Special Committee on Un-American Activities.[32] The war was still on when more than a thousand classified and "top secret" documents from the files of the Office of Strategic Services and the War, Navy and State Departments were discovered in the offices of a left-wing publication, *Amerasia*. When Truman became President, he also inherited pockets of Communist activity in the National Labor Relations Board, the Board of Economic Warfare and the International Monetary Fund.[33]

Truman's appointment of a commission to deal with employee loyalty was the fulfillment of recommendations of the House Civil Service Committee that had been established during the final days of Roosevelt's Presidency, in January of 1945. The resultant Loyalty Program of 1947, with its Loyalty Review Board, was, therefore, a consequence of a need that had been determined before any popular cold-war passions had arisen.[34] Plagued by the dilemma of how to protect security while safeguarding civil liberties, the program was inevitably attacked for its inadequacy by conservatives and for violations of fundamental rights by civil libertarians. Truman's own concern with democratic procedures intensified the problem. His public statements warned against outlawing any political party and his sharp veto message opposed the Internal Security Act of 1950, which he pointed out "can be the greatest danger to freedom of speech, press and assembly since the alien and sedition laws of 1798."[35] A constant need was to implement security policies so that they avoided totalitarian tendencies while, at the same time, they encouraged sufficient popular confidence in the government.[36] When Dwight Eisenhower and John Foster Dulles arrived in Washington there was little doubt that, despite Truman's tightening of the program in 1951 to provide for dismissal if "there is a reasonable doubt as to the loyalty of the person involved" rather than reasonable ground for belief in disloyalty, the public was more insecure than the nation. And the State Department, which had been greatly expanded since the war by the addition of other agencies, included many who had not been investigated. Hence, in Dulles's view, Scott McLeod had a job to do.

How much power had been placed in McLeod's hands would soon become a debatable matter. Aiding those eager to stress his importance as not only a mere collector of information but as one with the authority to make decisions based upon it was Dulles's press secretary, Carl McCardle. Few could defend McCardle's performance in the service of the Secretary of State. Some would mock his manner of referring to his boss as "Zecredary Dulles." Among the many oral-history contributions to Dulles's record, the most loyal members of the Administration evade the question of Carl McCardle by responding simply that "Andrew Berding [McCardle's successor] was very capable." Why Dulles had chosen McCardle seemed a mystery to the Washington press corps, for he came across as an inarticulate spokesman capable of giving impressions contrary to the Secretary's best interests. Dulles, however, had developed a confidential relationship with him. Long before taking over the State Department he had come to like McCardle and to respect him as a sounding board, for the newspaperman seemed to have an intuitive ability to gauge the response to press releases issued by the department. And that was important to Dulles. Presented with the draft of an announcement, McCardle could advise with accuracy its probable reception. Often, when asked by the Secretary to explain his reasons for such conclusions, the effort overwhelmed him. Yet Dulles virtually tortured McCardle for explanations, and the subordinate, with sweat running down his face, could merely mumble away. One who knew both men has commented that "One of the world's most articulate people made miserable one of the most inarticulate."[37]

When announcing McLeod's appointment, McCardle, zealously trying to promote his boss's concern with security matters, overstated the new officer's responsibility. McCardle, who held the rank of an Assistant Secretary of State, told the press that "If there is anything that needs cleaning up, he will clean it up." Furthermore, McCardle added that McLeod's rank would not merely rival the State Department's Assistant Secretaries but that his appointment had actually given him a *higher* rank. McLeod was thus presented as a house cleaner who would vacuum the State Department with independence.[38]

McLeod went to work with the passion of a defender of public morality. A thorough believer in what most insiders would attribute as the excesses of political rhetoric, he headed a crew of nearly two dozen ex-FBI agents in pursuit of subversives or those whose negligence or vulnerability could be exploited by spies. Of particular concern to McLeod were homosexuals. They and all who were suspected of such deviations in any degree whatsoever were prime McLeod targets. In his first three weeks on the job he was able to take credit for ousting twenty-one employees who allegedly fitted that description.[39] His periodic progress reports were a virtual box score in restoring the masculinity of the State Department, which many of its critics had held needed to reassert some manliness in its foreign policy. One could not have expected such progress under the aegis of a striped-pants diplomat like Dean Acheson, whose British airs were more reminiscent of an Anthony Eden than a Jack Armstrong.

McLeod's agents also conducted regular after-hours checks of offices. Desks, surfaces and drawers, even files that had been left closed but unlocked, received careful scrutiny. The procedure had been instituted by one of Dulles's special aides on the theory that it would be better to have security agents rather than roaming subversives discover precious documents. One man, a well-known author of several books about the United Nations, returned to his office early one evening and was confronted by three strangers who were examining his desk and file drawers. Edward Corsi found the State Department operating under a police-state atmosphere with ubiquitous FBI agents ready to respond to any right-winger's request for action.[40] In November, McLeod, although not having found the need to hold a single hearing, announced that 306 citizen employees and 178 aliens had been separated from the State Department for security reasons.[41] Such figures would continue to pour out, leaving the unthinking with the impression that bands of Communists were thus being unloaded from the confines of the nation's international nerve center. In actuality, there was never any proof that a single subversive had ever been discovered.

However efficacious the security system was, the Administration was clear about two things. Its presence was necessary to convince Americans and their Congressional guardians that something was being done by creating at least the façade of an anti-Communist protective organization. McLeod would, Dulles believed, make possible some means of gauging the validity of McCarthy's charges so he could make a defense against its critics. When, for example, Corsi appealed to Dulles against an effort to sidetrack him by shipping him to South America, the Secretary of State explained that obeying the order would be more expedient than trying to fight the right wing. "I never saw a man so scared of a situation as he was," Corsi later said. "The last thing he wanted was to have the issue of security raised. To be attacked by Congress on that point would sort of 'bring back his own basket of eggs, you know.' "[42] In October, Interior Department officials held an extended discussion about whether announcements of subversives being suspended should be released "in small driblets or all saved up for one big grand slam." Their virtually unanimous decision favored the small-dose approach as a more effective means of convincing the public.[43] Witness after witness has recalled the period as one of shattered morale among the nation's career diplomats and tolerance of an attitude that undoubtedly discouraged untold competent people from such careers and, within the Foreign Service, from providing candid analysis that would have been in the nation's best interests.

The Bohlen affair, which began while the Yalta resolution was still being debated and continued until the end of March, was an example of the use of a routine confirmation by the diehards intent on exploiting New Deal and Truman–Acheson "softness" toward communism. Even more than that, however, was the effort by a small corps of Republican right-wingers, aided by Democrat Pat McCarran, to force the Administration to demonstrate reversal of American foreign policy. New Hampshire's Styles Bridges thus argued on the Senate floor that "one realistic, patriotic, anti-Communist American could handle the Russians better than a boatload of Acheson's holdovers" and that nominating Bohlen "will mean a continuation of the Truman–Acheson foreign policy." Joe McCarthy, who did not initiate that particular controversy but responded at the smell of Red blood, put it more vividly. "One who loves Mr. Acheson must love Mr. Bohlen," he told the Senate on March 23. Two days later he pictured Bohlen as a stooge of Averell Harriman, "a guy who hits only to left field" and whose "admiration for everything Russian is unrivaled outside the confines of the Communist Party." Their policy, McCarthy charged, was containment, "a big word which grew out of the Groton vocabulary of the Hiss-Acheson gang." Echoing the current battles over patronage, the Wisconsin Senator also pointed out that "We do know that many of Mr. Acheson's lieutenants are still in the State Department." McCarthy, still stung by Dulles's clearance of John Carter Vincent's loyalty, had thus capitalized on what had been started and perpetuated by traditional rightists. The affair over the confirmation of Charles E. "Chip" Bohlen had become not the routine matter it should have been, as were the others who were approved by the Foreign Relations Committee at the same time, but an attempt to embarrass the President into withdrawing a nomination they had rendered controversial. Dulles, the author of the promise to liberate the captive peoples and vows to repudiate Yalta, had to suffer the second abuse of his strategy—another attempt to fulfill his promise.[44]

Bohlen was an uncommonly risky choice for the Administration, particularly for the vital Moscow post. His ties with the Roosevelt–Truman foreign policies seemed close, although his presence at both Yalta and Potsdam had been as an interpreter. Robert E. Sherwood's *Roosevelt and Hopkins* had pictured him as far more than a mere technician in that role.[45] Additionally, he was a career Foreign Service officer currently a counselor to the State Department since Acheson's regime. Forty-eight years old, he had already served the American mission in Moscow on several occasions, was fluent in Russian and French, an expert on Russian affairs, and few doubted his credentials as a successor to George Kennan. Before his nomination went to the Senate on February 27 Dulles had several talks with him. The Secretary took care to ask whether anything in his past could prove embarrassing. When Bohlen gave his assurances, Dulles replied, "I'm glad to hear this. I couldn't stand another Alger Hiss."[46]

The tangible opposition to Bohlen was never great, which made the situation even more disturbing; and, as the history of the times had demonstrated, the critics did not have to be numerous, just vocal and persistent. Enough noise, sufficient accusations and the Administration's nominee could become a liability as a choice no different from the Truman–Acheson crowd. Subtly, too, Bohlen could be fused in the frightened public mind with the numerous suspects of either pro-communism or, at best, naïveté toward the "Red menace."

When questioned by the Senate Foreign Relations Commitee at an all-day session on March 2, however, he gave those already rankled by his past associations something else to shout at. Coinciding with the heart of the fight over the Yalta resolution, and coming just before Stalin's death, was Bohlen's statement that he would never join any attempt to condemn the agreements made there with the Russians. Moreover, he held that neither the treaty nor subsequent interpretations had brought Eastern Europeans under Red control. That had resulted purely from Moscow's violations.[47]

The rightists had heard enough. One committee member, Homer Ferguson, wondered whether Bohlen had done more than merely interpret at Yalta. When, after Stalin's death Dulles and Under Secretary of State Walter Bedell Smith pointed out to the committee that Russia's leadership void made swift confirmation essential, they were supported by a Democratic member of the committee, Senator Hubert H. Humphrey of Minnesota. But Ferguson, aided by Senator William Knowland, urged a delay until the transcript of Bohlen's testimony could be obtained and studied. Bohlen, arriving for a scheduled hearing on March 10, waited for ninety minutes in an anteroom only to be excused for the day. When he returned for a hearing with Mr. Dulles the following week, the Secretary of State cautioned against being photographed together lest Bohlen should be rejected as a controversial figure.[48]

It was Styles Bridges who then assumed the key role. He was not a member of the Foreign Relations Committee, but as a prominent conservative and as chairman of the Senate Appropriations Committee, his credentials were sufficient to rally the anti-Bohlen forces. On March 16 he went to request the President's cooperation in withdrawing the appointment; but he learned that Eisenhower was standing by Bohlen.[49] While the President had reasons for confidence, Bridges also had his supporters: Scott McLeod and Joe McCarthy. After Dulles had gone before the committee with a summary of an FBI report that he said left no doubt about Bohlen's loyalty and they subsequently cleared his nomination by a unanimous vote, the anti-Red corps pressed for a fight on the Senate floor. Their new hope was denial of Dulles's rendition of the FBI summary of Bohlen's confidential file and thus portray the nominee not only as a Yalta apologist but as a suspect character.

Pat McCarran took the Senate floor to refute Dulles. The Secretary's testimony, the Nevadan charged, was at variance with Scott McLeod's, as the security officer had concluded from the same FBI report that there were certain matters rendering Bohlen objectionable. McCarran suggested turning the case over to McCarthy's investigating committee. A perturbed Dulles immediately called a press conference to deny any differences with McLeod. McCarthy, however, stressed that the security officer had spent two and a half hours at the White House trying to persuade the President to retreat on Bohlen. McLeod had actually seen only Jerry Persons, the President's Congressional liaison man, but the point had been made.

McLeod's authority to evaluate rather than gather information became an issue. Pat McCarran cited Carl McCardle's introduction of the officer as a vindication of his authority to veto clearances. "If he is not a security officer," McCarran asked, "what is he?"[50] Moreover, confusion about the nature of the charges against Bohlen marked the debate of March 23. Precisely what did McLeod have in mind by going to the White House?

Many were confused about the possible security objections to Bohlen. Senator Francis Case of South Dakota, missing some of the innuendoes, noted that since the file on the nominee, according to Dulles, did not contain derogatory material questioning his security or his loyalty, nor alleged that the Foreign Service officer had a loose tongue, "then to what does it relate?"

Alexander Wiley, the committee chairman who had reported the nomination to the Senate for confirmation, simply replied, "I think I had better take the Senator aside and answer that question."[51]

Senator Flanders brought applause from the gallery by saying, "We have on trial here a Republican Secretary of State, and, by inference, a Republican President. I should like to suggest that the Republican junior

Senator from Wisconsin give this Administration a chance and pin the responsibility on it." But the McCarthy supporters among the spectators also cheered when the crusader denied that the President was on trial and righteously retorted that when "he had made a bad nomination I intend to oppose it on the floor of the Senate or elsewhere."[52]

That day's debate also brought McCarthy into a direct clash with Taft. The Republican leader, who had stated publicly that the matter was of relatively minor importance, contemplated with dread the vision of a party so torn, so incapacitated, so unable to govern that the social-istic leftists would step into the vacuum. Hence, from an earlier willing-ness to capitalize on McCarthy and even encourage him to slay the Democrats, Taft moved into his path, not to thwart the drive against subversives, not to deny the need for his type of investigations, but to support the Administration's choice. "Our Russian ambassador can't do anything," Taft had explained in a statement that avoided outright sup-port of Bohlen. "All he can do is observe and report. He will not influ-ence policy materially."[53]

Therefore, there was an inevitable clash between the forces that wanted to pillory the liberals and the President's supporters. Already the Administration had failed to win acceptance of its own statement on the Yalta agreements. Defeating Bohlen would be a severe psychological blow to Eisenhower's ability to command foreign policy. Even as the debate continued, Senator John Bricker's plan to restrict Presidential treaty-making powers was being considered. Another inevitable inter-pretation, then, was one that saw the Senate taking over from the Presi-dency the direction of the cold war. It was a schism Taft was deter-mined to avoid.

Their clash was brief but sharp. After Knowland, now in support of Bohlen, pointed out that McLeod's responsibility of simply gathering rather than evaluating evidence was no different than the FBI itself, McCarthy stepped in. He said that many other Senators did not share those assumptions about McLeod's limitations. The Knowland statement, McCarthy said, also proved the importance of bringing both Dulles and McLeod before an executive session of the Foreign Relations Committee since the security information was of such a nature "that we cannot discuss it on the floor of the Senate without ourselves violating security." He added that a lie detector ought to be used.[54]

Taft, angered, challenged McCarthy's proposal to use a polygraph device. Didn't McCarthy realize, he asked, that J. Edgar Hoover was absolutely opposed to the instrument as being worthless? Furthermore, the idea of having Dulles confronted by his subordinate before the committee was, in Taft's words, an "un-called-for suggestion."[55]

Clearly, on that March 23, there was a continued challenge to Dulles's interpretation of the FBI's summary of the items in Bohlen's file. Wiley had pointed out that the report had been examined closely by Attorney General Herbert Brownell. Thus, he reminded his colleagues, they had the word of "two lawyers in the highest echelon in Government."[56] Russell Long of Louisiana, a Democrat, however, reminded them that Dulles had endorsed Alger Hiss for his Carnegie Endowment post, so how could the Secretary's word be trusted?[57] When support for Bohlen by Governor Jimmy Byrnes of South Carolina was noted, "Molly" Malone challenged the former Secretary of State's credibility by pointing out that he, too, had been at Yalta and was a defender of the agreements.[58] Finally, Malone's suggestion that the Foreign Relations Committee go *en masse* to examine the FBI reports was streamlined to a request that the committee select one or two of its members to do the job and then to inform the Senate about their findings. Taft and John Sparkman, the Democratic former Vice Presidential candidate, were chosen.

From two until five the next afternoon the pair of Senators, aided by State Department Chief Counsel Herman Phleger, scrutinized the FBI's summary. J. Edgar Hoover had assured Taft that the report contained all relevant materials. The FBI, needing to preserve the anonymity of its informers, had a digest available for such purposes. It was the same material about which Dulles had given the committee his assurances. Taft, in pain from the cancer that would take his life just four months later, not only read the documents but got down to the floor for a more precise hearing of some of the recordings that were included. The men found a scattering of innuendoes that formed no particular pattern. One lady had reported that she could tell by the way Bohlen answered the telephone "that he wouldn't do." A man had been given warnings about his loyalty by his "sixth sense." Others had differed with his political views, but everybody in that category added confidence in the man's loyalty. Taft and Sparkman came away upset that such flimsy evidence could constitute a personal file.[59]

However respected the two Senators were, their report failed to end the battle, and the debate that followed on that Wednesday was one of the most heated in the memory of the participants. McCarran upheld McLeod's right to veto Bohlen. Then he suggested that the summary may have been unreliable because the Justice Department had probably prepared it for the FBI. Shifting the attack to Bohlen's association with the "appeasers," Bridges, taking a cue from his party's platform declaration, called Bohlen's defense of Yalta "a slap across the face of every anti-Communist Pole or citizen of Polish descent in the world." McCarthy then delivered a long speech that accused Dulles of ignoring the "Acheson gang who have been found at every time and place where disaster struck America and success came to Communist Russia." After asserting that we "want no Republican Amerasia," McCarthy pointed out that

"Bohlen was at Roosevelt's left hand at Teheran and Yalta and at Truman's left hand at Potsdam." Other Republicans who continued to attack were Bridges and Everett Dirksen, who, on the final day of the debate, said, "I reject Yalta, so I reject Yalta men."[60]

At his Thursday press conference Eisenhower spoke in warm terms about his personal relationship with Bohlen, recalled that the ambassador had been a guest in his house and that they had played golf together. Furthermore, the President described himself as "deeply and personally concerned" with that appointment and said that Bohlen was "the best qualified man we could find today."[61] Not only did the President sidestep any criticism of the Senators who had attacked Bohlen, after Vance Johnson of the San Francisco *Chronicle* cited McCarthy and McCarran, but nothing was said about—or done to—the overinflated State Department subordinate, Robert Walter Scott McLeod.

The day after the press conference the Senate vote to confirm Bohlen was no surprise. Nor was it close. Of the eighty-seven present and voting only thirteen opposed the nominee. But eleven of them were from the President's party. An additional negative vote would undoubtedly have come from Jenner, but the Senator was off with his traveling investigation. Joining McCarthy were John Bricker, Styles Bridges, Everett Dirksen, Henry Dworshak, Barry Goldwater, Bourke Hickenlooper, "Molly" Malone, Karl Mundt, Andrew Scheoppel and Herman Welker. Pat McCarran and Edwin Johnson of Colorado were the only Democrats.[62] Although the issue had not been engineered by McCarthy or been exclusively his but the party's rightists, the Senator's identification with it was seen as a blow to his prestige. There were even suggestions that the vote against Bohlen would have been larger without McCarthy's intervention.[63] Taft's prestige had also been helpful and, as events that spring showed, his assistance more and more vital. A key concern was the kind of success the Administration could anticipate on an issue that did not have Taft's support, such as foreign aid. Conceivably Eisenhower would then have to be entirely dependent on the Democrats. Furthermore, once the battle over Bohlen ended, Taft's willingness to tolerate McCarthy was demonstrated when he passed word to the White House advising "No more Bohlens."[64]

Nevertheless, although Dulles preserved McLeod, the Administration had backed Bohlen and had succeeded. More important, at the crest of the loyalty and security hysteria, at the height of the condemnations of Yalta, there had been a one-sided victory for a nominee whom opponents had made a symbol of everything they wanted to reverse, from suggestions of dainty diplomats doing dark things in the State Department to appeasement of the Red menace.

CHAPTER 26

The Senator and the President

THE FIRST HALF of 1953 was a critical period in the Administration's coexistence with Joe McCarthy. The Senator, who had complained that the Democrats had given the nation "twenty years of treason," professed his loyalty to the new President at every opportunity. Even on the Senate floor he cited his campaign efforts with vehemence. He gave himself credit for having made more speeches for General Eisenhower than most of his colleagues and glowed about the Administration's early "batting average." Yet, in a series of cases that received wide attention, he had become openly critical. Before the Administration had completed its first six months, speculation had grown about how long Ike would evade a head-on clash with the front-page-grabbing Senator.

McCarthy, of course, was working on a good thing. His personal ambitions were unlimited. Not even the removal of the Democrats from commanding positions could dissuade him from continuing his crusade. Toward Eisenhower his attitude soon became contemptuous. He appraised him as a "political lightweight" who was out of his element in dealing with the Washington infighting. He was, thought McCarthy, essentially a military man whose commanders were now a White House clique that was insinuating its own prejudices and ideas on the President. Eisenhower himself was not dangerous because he was conservative, but "left-wingers" like Sherman Adams and C. D. Jackson could corrupt him with ease. For they were the ones unsympathetic toward "strong patriotism" and Americanism and would "coddle Communists and left-wingers in government and listen to their advice." Of all the important personalities of the Administration, only Vice President Nixon had Mc-

Carthy's high regard. Nixon, he believed, was in the middle; and McCarthy reasoned that "the poor fellow has enough on his hands" and avoided making trouble for him. He was, in short, conscious of Nixon's role in maintaining the delicate balance among the party's several elements. Nixon, for his part, was careful to remain neutral, thereby reserving himself for off-the-record trouble-shooting diplomatic missions with the anti-Eisenhower Republicans.[1]

McCarthy's failure to step aside and let the Administration take over the internal-security process, as when he had been asked by Thruston Morton for the names of the disloyal within the State Department, carried a simple rationale. The Communist issue had been a factor in the Administration's victory and, as the Senator who had done more than anyone else to dramatize the issue by pursuing the suspects, he had every reason to expect the Republican government to act accordingly. Its failure to act, as "proven" by a series of differences with the President over policy, was a signal for the continuation of his own efforts. As for the long-range consequences of his acts, the Senator had not calculated what would happen if Eisenhower should attack him directly.[2]

McCarthy, of course, was correct in believing that he had many enemies in the White House. Jackson, Adams, Bobby Cutler, Gabriel Hauge, Dr. Milton Eisenhower and James Mitchell (who replaced Durkin as Secretary of Labor before the year was over), all thought, as the inevitable conflict evolved, that the President should direct his great prestige and popularity against McCarthy.[3] On May 9, 1953, Eisenhower's friend from the General Mills Corporation, Harry Bullis, warned the President "that the Senator has unlimited personal ambitions, unmitigated gall, and unbounded selfishness. In the opinion of many of us who are your loyal friends, it is a fallacy to assume that McCarthy will kill himself. That can only be accomplished by too much liquor and women. It is our belief that McCarthy should be stopped soon."[4] But the President, who has often been quoted about refusing to "get into the gutter" to battle McCarthy, stated his own position with clarity in a "personal and confidential" reply to Bullis:

> With respect to McCarthy, I continue to believe that the President of the United States cannot afford to name names in opposing procedures, practices and methods in our government. This applies with special force when the individual concerned enjoys the immunity of a United States Senator. This particular individual wants, above all else, publicity. Nothing would probably please him more than to get the publicity that would be generated by public repudiation by the President.
>
> I do not mean that there is no possibility that I shall never change my mind on this point. I merely mean that as of this moment, I consider that the wisest course of action is to continue to pursue a steady, positive policy

in foreign relations, in legal procedures in cleaning out the insecure and the disloyal, and in all other areas where McCarthy seems to take such a specific and personal interest. My friends on the Hill tell me that of course, among other things, he wants to increase his appeal as an after dinner speaker and so raise the fees that he charges.

It is a sorry mess; at times one feels almost like hanging his head in shame when he reads some of the unreasoned, vicious outbursts of demagoguery that appear in our public prints. But whether a Presidential "crack down" would be better, or would actually worsen, the situation, is a moot question.[5]

Just two weeks after Eisenhower's letter, a number of the President's other businessmen friends participated in a secret poll at the exclusive Links Club in New York City. Asked to predict McCarthy's future, forty-three predicted a decline and seventeen went even further. They said he would soon be forgotten. Only twenty-one, or one-fourth of the total, expected his prestige to rise. At the same time, by a vote of seventy-four to eight, they agreed that Ike had "been as good in his job" as they had expected.[6]

Others were more open in their opposition to the Senator. Charles Tobey, a Republican Senator from New Hampshire (who died three months later), appeared on an NBC-TV program and, agreeing that McCarthy was "the bad boy of the Senate," recalled his own grand-mother's advice that "a lie which is half truth is ever the blackest of lies." Dean Francis Sayre of the Washington Cathedral and a prominent Episcopalian spokesman charged McCarthy, among others, with striving to establish "servile patriotism." McCarthy's methods were also attacked by the New York Congregational Christian Conference, which urged the President and Congress to disassociate the Administration from character defamation and irresponsible charges. The leaders of the Americans for Democratic Action, an organization founded in 1947 to provide a liberal response to extremism, urged his repudiation by Eisenhower. In Washington, Mrs. Agnes Meyer of the *Post* scored the Senator's investigative record. At the same time, no public-opinion poll showed anywhere near majority approval for McCarthy by the American people.[7]

Western Europe, still recovering from the great war and much more vulnerable to Russian expansionism and subversion, had become alarmed at what appeared to be the loss of American sanity. In Vienna, the *Arbeiter Zeitung* compared McCarthy's methods with the Nazis and the GPU. A governmental official of West Germany also recalled the anti-Red activities of the Nazis of twenty years earlier. A leading London newspaper asked, "How long will the Americans stand for this?" More and more, informed Europeans were speculating that McCarthy was undermining American leadership of the non-Communist world. Conservative financial circles had even begun to fear that American capitulation to McCarthy and his allies might encourage the inquisitors to imperil commercial and monetary matters that were so consequential to the economies of Western Europe. From Geneva came the possibility that alarmed Continental investors were contemplating divorcing themselves from such irresponsibility by withdrawing their capital from the United States.[8] Thus, when Bullis warned Eisenhower about McCarthy, he expressed concern that the Senator had become "a dangerous and disturbing factor in our economy."[9]

Yet, Eisenhower, pursuing a "strategy" that was, at the same time, most congenial with his own temperament and life style, proceeded to sidestep any direct confrontation with the Senator, while simultaneously tipping off the opponents of McCarthyism that he shared their horror. In the process, instead of exploiting McCarthy's vulnerability and showing the way to a general movement that could exorcise the malignancy from the Republican party, a development awaited eagerly by other frightened men who lacked the President's standing, Eisenhower permitted replenishment for the Senator's recovery from his nadir. By the time he eventually "hung himself," it was less with the rope provided by the President than with the lives of the expendables. One of the victims was the reputation of the United States. The big winner, however, was Eisenhower.

When, with the Bohlen affair hardly out of the way, McCarthy pulled his usual distraction by announcing that the staff of his subcommittee had won commitments from the Greek owners of 242 ships not to carry cargoes to Communist ports, the burden went to Dulles and Harold Stassen. McCarthy gloated over his coup. He claimed to have succeeded where the State Department had failed. In its defense the Department branded McCarthy's claims as phony. He had, charged spokesmen who refused to be identified, attempted to take credit for what they had done. But Harold Stassen, as the Mutual Security Director, was unable to avoid a clash with the Senator. Stassen, complaining that McCarthy was actually undermining the Administration's efforts to stop trade with the Chinese mainland, insisted that such negotiations could be done only through agreements by governments. That brought from McCarthy the politically stinging comment that "I believe if you can keep a gun out of Communist hands, it is good even if you and Dulles don't accomplish it."[10]

Stassen's clash was not, however, appreciated by the Administration. Such encounters could easily jeopardize the administration of foreign aid. Using Vice President Nixon, who was assuming his role as a liaison man with the rightists, Dulles arranged a less publicized method. By having McCarthy at the State Department for a ninety-minute luncheon, he was able to stage a private showdown with the Senator for having usurped the office of the Secretary of State. He spoke in scathing tones that put the usually aggressive crusader on the defensive and explained the dangers of having Congressional committees assume the direction of the nation's foreign affairs. Before the Senator could use the press as a mouthpiece to explain what had taken place, Dulles had Herman Phleger draw up a statement. A subdued Joe McCarthy then signed that he had made no agreements and did not contemplate any. What had been done had merely been voluntary acts by the shipowners.[11] Dulles never had another personal clash with McCarthy.

Then the President had his turn. At his press conference of April 2, when prodded about McCarthy and the shipowners, he staged what one reporter called a "ducking and weaving exhibition."[12] First, when asked whether the Administration's policy had been undermined by McCarthy's actions, he allowed for the possibility of "different kinds of answers" but that since the Executive Department had "the exclusive power of negotiating such agreements," the process could not have undermined its prestige and power. A few minutes later, James Reston, wondering whether he sensed a headline story, renewed the topic by asking if the President had meant to imply a disagreement with Stassen rather than McCarthy. At that point Eisenhower speculated that the Mutual Security Director had probably meant "infringement" rather than "undermining" and added, "I was also trying to make clear that to undermine required a lot more doing than merely making an error, no matter how badly I might consider that error to be."* Furthermore, the statement issued by the Senator after his meeting with Dulles had demonstrated that he "had no idea he was negotiating anything." Therefore, "he is probably in his proper function." But Reston, continuing to pursue his point, wanted to know whether the President realized that McCarthy's original announcement told of having accomplished his feat through negotiations with the ship owners. Again the President responded with agility. "How do you negotiate when there is nothing you can commit?" he asked. Furthermore, since no such group could authorize the United States to take any action, "I would not understand what 'negotiations' means."

The semantic fencing was too much for United Press correspondent Merriman Smith. "Mr. President," he asked, "I am a little confused. Are we to understand, then, that it is your opinion that Senator McCarthy changed his position from the time of his original announcement when he used the word 'negotiate' until the time he met with Secretary Dulles

---

* The following day Stassen came into line by agreeing he should have used "infringed" instead of "undermining."

yesterday?" Ike, however, held firm. McCarthy could not have negotiated, he explained, because he did not have the authority.

Finally, the New York *Post*'s Robert G. Spivack tried to maneuver around the verbal fog by asking, "Mr. President, just to recapitulate all this, are you unhappy with what Mr. Stassen said the other day, or with what Senator McCarthy—"

The President cut him short. "I am not the slightest bit unhappy," he responded. "I think that I know where we are trying to go. I think, by and large, we are developing and getting better cooperation with the Senate and House every day. The mere fact that some little incident arises is not going to disturb me. I have been scared by experts, in war and peace, and I am not frightened by this."[13]

After that performance, some suspected that Eisenhower's conciliatory maneuver had given credence to McCarthy and had raised his prestige. By remaining unopposed despite repeated challenges to the Administration the President was, in effect, encouraging Republican rightists who had no taste for the basic assumptions of the Eisenhower foreign policy.[14] At the same time, lack of strong Presidential leadership could diminish support from not only the party's center, the logical backers of Ike's taxation, defense spending and foreign economic proposals, but also among independent voters who had believed in the need for positive leadership.

Democratic Minority Leader Lyndon B. Johnson was quick to exploit the GOP's dilemma. In a speech before the Gridiron Club on April 11 he ridiculed the failure to control McCarthy by saying:

> They have the Republican Party of President Eisenhower. They have the Republican Party of Senator Taft. They have the Republican Party of Senator Morse. And somewhere—way out behind the Chicago *Tribune* tower—is the Republican Party of Senator McCarthy with one foot heavy in Greece and the other foot in Secretary Dulles' security files.
>
> It makes bipartisanship right difficult. We Democrats need to know which one of the Republican Parties to be bipartisan *with*; and which one of the Republican Parties to be bipartisan *against*.[15]

At about the same time, "Chip" Bohlen confronted Eisenhower with the consequences of the security obsession. Just before leaving Washington for Moscow, while paying his official courtesy visit with the President and with Dulles also present, Bohlen took the opportunity to express himself in his capacity as vice-president of the American Foreign Service Association. The ambassador explained that McLeod's activities were hurting Foreign Service morale. Furthermore, he added, his purpose in making the complaint was to convey the feelings of most of the senior members of the service. Having given their lives to government work, the corps now had to endure suspicion, name-calling and a loss of public confidence.

The President, when questioning Bohlen about his charges, clearly indicated familiarity with the situation. Turning to Dulles, Eisenhower acknowledged that the McLeod appointment had certainly been a mistake. Nevertheless, with Dulles remaining noncommittal, the President concluded that getting rid of McLeod was not a possible solution. He pointed out that it would provoke further troubles.[16] Such conclusions, of course, convinced the Foreign Service that they had been abandoned to the wolves by the Administration, but others argued that thwarting McLeod and McCarthy would provoke incalculable right-wing reactions with even greater consequences for the State Department.

Equally vulnerable was the United Nations delegation. Caught up in the "Four Freedoms" concept, and mindful of Woodrow Wilson's prophecies about the consequences of not joining the League of Nations, there had been surprisingly little resistance to American membership. Praise for the UN and optimism about its ability to safeguard world peace had become a litany for modern liberals. Yet, as the Red scare developed passions and sparked animosities, latent chauvinistic nationalism developed xenophobic reactions. When John D. Rockefeller donated land for the UN's permanent site, for example, the New York *Daily News* editorialized that the deserted wastes of northwestern Mexico would be more suitable than the shores of the East River. Opposition to the Marshall Plan and even to NATO and certainly to the non-military kinds of foreign aid in general expressed such hostility. They were more than just implicit during the condemnations of Yalta. John Bricker's amendment to limit Presidential treaty-making powers conveyed similar feelings.

Henry Cabot Lodge, as an experienced politician and as the new head of the American delegation, was as cautious as Dulles. Taking advantage of the ready cooperation offered by Secretary General Trygve Lie, then in his last months in office, Lodge moved swiftly to leave little room for complaints by the inquisitors. Simultaneous with presenting his own credentials, he gave Lie 1,755 fingerprint questionnaires for distribution to all American employees.[17] Lie did his part by authorizing non-American UN personnel to provide information to the FBI about top-level Americans.[18] Not only did those under Lodge line up for fingerprinting at a special office manned by the FBI, but agents circulated freely throughout UN property to gather data from all who would talk about American personnel. Dr. Ralph Bunche, then a director of the UN Trusteeship Division, was surprised to be confronted by an FBI agent who wanted to know not only about John Foster Dulles's loyalty but how Bunche regarded his fitness to be Secretary of State.[19] Pursuing his role as though he had acquired sudden expertise, McLeod rebutted Dean Acheson's contention that employing Americans of dubious loyalty at the UN could not jeopardize the nation's security; and Lodge told the Jenner committee on April 24 that all those who had refused to answer the loyalty queries had been fired. Nevertheless, when Dag Hammarskjöld replaced Lie that spring as Secretary General, Lie's hospitality to American interrogators was terminated by his successor's vow to maintain the independence of the UN Secretariat in its personnel policy.[20] One of Hammarskjöld's acts was to order FBI agents off UN property.[21]

The Administration then moved to provide machinery to evaluate the loyalty of all American citizens actually employed by the international organization or seeking jobs there. A six-member International Organizations Employees Loyalty Board was established to scrutinize and evaluate their reliability. Most were cleared on the basis of FBI reports. Others, however, were summoned before the board for secret hearings. Despite the usual lack of publicity, in May of 1954 Chairman Pierce J. Geraty was forced by a news leak to confirm that Dr. Bunche himself was being investigated and had been called to a hearing before the board. Geraty's statement, in the midst of an era of endless loyalty probes, cautioned that "no inference should be drawn" from the news.[22]

Bunche was completely prepared for the trial. For one, he was a likely victim of those ready to equate the UN with disloyalty. The liberal positions he had taken throughout the years had made the 1950 Nobel Peace Prize winner a dangerous "leftist" in the eyes of many. When Bunche, a Negro, was nominated for election to Harvard University's Board of Overseers, Archibald Roosevelt had tried to stop him by circulating a harsh forty-page attack among the alumni. (Bunche was then elected with the largest vote as of that date.) On June 6, 1953, Harlem's civil-rights-crusading Congressman, Adam Clayton Powell, Jr., shocked a commencement audience at a Negro college in Baltimore by revealing information that Bunche was about to be investigated by the House Un-American Activities Committee. HUAC never did call him, but Powell was warm. The FBI was gathering information branding Bunche a Communist. Bunche suddenly received a visit from a member of the White House staff, the man who had taken charge of Eisenhower's relations with minority groups and had become Secretary of the Cabinet, Maxwell Rabb. Rabb was on direct orders from the President, who had told him about the FBI reports and of a possible hearing before the IOELB. "Max," said the President, "I feel very strongly about this. Bunche is a superior man, a credit to our country. I can't just stand by and permit a man like that to be chopped to pieces because of McCarthy feeling. This report will kill his public career and I am not going to be a party to this. I am willing to bet he's no more a Communist than I am." When Rabb visited Bunche in New York, he carried the message that the President was ready to support him. Dr. Bunche decided to stand alone and on his own record.[23]

The renowned international mediator found himself confronted by two accusers who were professional witnesses, appearing at loyalty trials throughout the country. Ex-Communists Manning Johnson and Leonard Patterson, who had also testified at HUAC hearings, were, Bunche later learned, on the payroll of the Justice Department.[24] Bunche never learned how the accusations had originated; but, with the aid of his own testimony and of such others as Walter White of the NAACP, the charges were refuted. On May 28, Geraty announced that all six members of the board had been convinced about his undoubted loyalty to the United States.

Curiously, while the hearings were in progress, one session had to be shortened to enable the defendant to make a dinner appointment. Although under investigation as a possible Communist and, therefore, a potential enemy of the United States, he had been invited to dine at the White House with President Eisenhower. The affair was entirely secret.[25] At the United Nations, however, much more exposed and hence more vulnerable than the President, Henry Cabot Lodge kept his distance from the suspected man, as had Dulles with Bohlen before the cameras, until vindication. That took place in Lodge's office.

In other ways, too, the Administration tried to comply with the realities of Washington life in 1953. The State Department capitulated to the demands of the McCarthy committee by agreeing to restore to his former post a security agent named John Matson, who had been transferred to another job after telling the inquiring Senators that reports on homosexuals and suspected Reds had disappeared from the department's files. Although Matson's story had been disputed by others, he was reinstated after a meeting between McCarthy and Donald Lourie.[26] Budget Director Joe Dodge instructed all employees in his agency to report any colleague suspected of conduct "inimical" to the effective operation, security and standing of the bureau. Failure to do so, they were told, "will not be easily excused." Advice that the directive was not intended as "an invitation for snooping or gossiping" was of little comfort.[27] Robert L. Johnson, called to Washington to overhaul the embattled International Information Administration, found it caught in a squeeze play between the economizers led by Representative John Taber and the McCarthyites out to destroy it in the name of security.[28] Martin Merson, a conservative Virginia Democrat who had gone as a consultant to Johnson, found that while the President had effected a public image that implied unhappiness with McCarthy and his methods, his hidden maneuvers "belied the public word." Conferring with Vice President Nixon on April 14, they were told that McCarthy was not a bad guy. He simply had to be understood.[29] In the face of strong GOP pressure from Capitol Hill, they also had to combat the attempt to name as Johnson's principal assistant Orland K. Armstrong. Armstrong had just lost his Congressional seat in Missouri to Dewey Short through redistricting and he was boosting himself for the job by vowing to clean all "pinkos" out of the IIA and thus preserve the agency's appropriations.[30] Johnson, fighting to save the IIA before a capitulating Administration and a frightened State Department, sought help from ex-President Hoover, who spurned the overture by denouncing the IIA as being full of Office of War Information "hangers-on," Communists and left-wingers.[31] Attorney General Herbert Brownell, meanwhile, asked Congress to legalize the use of wiretap evidence.[32] Also that spring, the Administration unveiled its replacement of Truman's loyalty program.

The basic purpose of the new procedures was to tighten loopholes and thereby gain Congressional and public support. Worked out in consultation with Taft and other Republican leaders, the plan abolished having the accused tried by their own friends and colleagues. The Loyalty Review Board and departmental panels were also scuttled. The new plan provided for departmental security officers to investigate and evaluate all federal employees. Adverse findings were reviewed by department heads who were empowered to decide the validity of the charges. Those suspended were entitled to hearings by three-member security boards appointed by the department head from among special officers retained for that purpose by the Attorney General. Colleagues from the accused's department were ineligible to serve on them, but the defendants were granted the right to be represented by their own counsel and to cross-examine witnesses. The department head was free to accept or reject any recommendations by the board. Meanwhile, the accused had to be suspended pending the outcome of the evaluation.[33]

The most significant change, however, was the criteria. The Eisenhower plan, by substituting security for loyalty, broadened the basis for dismissal. With that as a guide, it hoped to remove the stigma of disloyalty so that individuals suspected of homosexuality, gossiping, having radical friends or being in compromising circumstances would, at least theoretically, be dismissed easily and with no further implications to their character.

But, as the Administration had planned, the most important aspects were political. Most of all, it was a Republican procedure, not a holdover from the "Communist-infested" Truman Administration. That, plus the Congressional involvement in its writing, gave it important support on Capitol Hill. Even McCarthy was receptive, praising it as "pretty darn good, if the Administration is sincere."[34] A few days later, on a public-relations TV show, staged by the Madison Avenue advertising firm of Batten, Barton, Durstine and Osborn and billed as a "spontaneous discussion" between the President and four Cabinet officers, Brownell expressed the belief that "without fanfare and steadily over the course of the next few months, we will be able to weed out from the federal payroll every security risk."[35] Eisenhower, who later complained of too much publicity about the rehearsals for the "spontaneous" program and advised that less information about such preparations be made public in the future, addressed his Attorney General as "Herb" and stressed that they would do things out in the open "so that people will know what is going on."[36]

Those fearful of the new code for having adopted broad standards did not have to wait very long for confirmation of their doubts. On July 29, Abraham Chasanow, a civilian hydrographer employed by the Navy Department, was suddenly handed his suspension notification. Chasanow, an apolitical registered Democrat whose ability to vote Republican had enabled him to cast a ballot in his home at Greenbelt, Maryland, for John Marshall Butler over Millard Tydings, had been victimized by disgruntled neighbors. Chasanow had incurred some enemies through his leadership in having the government-built community between Washington and Baltimore taken over and run as an independent cooperative. Some dozen years earlier he had also been a short-term subscriber to George Seldes's left-wing periodical *In Fact*. In 1939 he had also belonged to the now-suspect Lawyers Guild. Although Chasanow's daughter had recently won a countywide contest for the best essay on the meaning of Independence Day, the family was immediately branded as "Communist Jews" by some, avoided as suspected spies by others.

The special three-member hearing board convened in his case had little trouble recommending his reinstatement. But the real shock came when Assistant Secretary of the Navy James H. Smith, Jr., ordered the hydrographer's dismissal after a Security Appeal Board continued to think he was a bad risk. It took a series of Pulitzer Prize-winning articles by Anthony Lewis, then with the Washington *Daily News*, to bring him vindication and restitution. Over a year after the suspension, on September 1, 1954, Smith apologized on behalf of the Navy and conceded that the hydrographer, who had been with the Navy for twenty-three years, was the victim of a "grave injustice."[37]

In 1956, while a special commission headed by Loyd Wright had been appointed to study ways of modifying the security procedures, the Twentieth Century-Fox studio's production of *Three Brave Men*, based on the case as reported by Anthony Lewis, was filmed under the direct supervision of the Navy Department. Its producer, Herbert Bayard

Swope, Jr., apparently worried about proceeding with the project without submitting the film script for approval by the Defense Department, created a dilemma in Washington. Acquiescence would imply agreement with the story's condemnation of what had happened to Chasanow. At the same time, Swope had given the Pentagon little advance notice before the actual start of production. Something, however, had to be done about the planned attack on the security program.[38] Assistant Secretary of the Navy Albert Pratt then acted quickly. He and his aides went to Beverly Hills, California, where they suggested changes to mitigate the criticism. The visiting brass from Washington was received with full cordiality by the studio's president, Spyros P. Skouras, who also entertained them at a Romanoff's Restaurant luncheon. The revised script was, according to Thomas J. Donegan, chairman of President Eisenhower's Personnel Security Advisory Committee, "remarkable inasmuch as it accomplishes the extraordinary feat of creating the impression that the Navy Department should not be blamed for the mistake made in the Chasanow case since they, as much as Chasanow, were victims of the Personnel Security Program."[39] Pratt had also objected to the actor who had been cast in the role of Assistant Secretary Smith and asked that it be given a nobler characterization. The portrayal of Smith should emerge as that of an honest patriot who was acting in the best interests of the nation's security but who, at the same time, was concerned with justice. Frank McCarthy, of Twentieth Century-Fox, mollified Pratt by getting actor Dean Jagger to play the role.[40]

The movie, written by Philip Dunne and starring Ernest Borgnine as "Bernard Goldsmith" (Chasanow), was released in 1957. The government-supervised work, presented without any acknowledgment of such "cooperation," portrayed the victim as a simplistic patriot. Its final scene, where Pratt's role was particularly evident, devoted special attention to allaying fears about the possible misuse of the security program. Reviewers, although unaware of the concessions made by the studio, found the final product more propaganda than a serious attempt to inform the public about the incident. The Roman Catholic magazine *Commonweal* was upset that "such a report on miscarriage of justice in a democracy" had been told with "whitewash" rather than with "irony and bite."[41] The review in the Jesuit publication *America* was particularly perceptive. "For some reason," it said, "Mr. Dunne tried to avoid or soften the particular findings in the Chasanow case."[42] More disturbed was *The New Yorker*, which noted that "what is even more unsettling is that Mr. Dunne bases his whole argument in favor of the hero on the fact that he is absolutely exactly like everyone else in his community."[43]

As in its concept of a security program, the Administration was no better than the mood of the country. When, in June of 1953, Julius and

Ethel Rosenberg, alone among the convicted atomic spies to insist on their innocence, made a final appeal for commutation of their death sentence, the White House was again barraged by protests in the name of humanity. Efforts to spare the lives of the young parents were made by a group of one hundred Protestant clergymen, by Cardinal Feltin and three French bishops, by forty-one members of the British Parliament and by French President Vincent Auriol. In London, the American embassy was surrounded by protestors. Many thousands paraded around the White House. Finally, on the nineteenth of June, the Supreme Court set aside a stay of execution that had been granted by Justice William O. Douglas and thereby upheld the validity of the death sentence under the Espionage Act of 1917.[44] During the thirty-six years of the First World War-inspired law, it had brought no capital punishment.

The Rosenbergs then awaited the President's action on the clemency appeal. At that morning's Cabinet meeting, Attorney General Brownell reviewed the case and said that the government had information corroborating their guilt which could not have been used in the trial. Robert Donovan reported that the President declared that any intervention by him could be justified only, in Donovan's words, "where statecraft dictated in the interests of American public opinion or of the reputation of the United States Government in the eyes of the world."[45]

Jim Hagerty told the press there would be no intervention. Then the President issued a carefully prepared statement designed to counter the anti-American-propaganda use of the case. Noting that the Rosenbergs "have received the benefit of every safeguard which American justice can provide," it recognized the worldwide protests but pointed out that their treachery had "immeasurably" increased the chances of atomic war and "may have condemned to death tens of millions of innocent people all over the world."[46] Even if the Rosenbergs were clearly guilty and not, as Walter and Miriam Schneir have maintained in their recent and careful refutation of the charges, "punished for a crime that never occurred," and even if the Soviet Union would not have perfected atomic weapons within five years after the end of World War II, despite the nearly unanimous estimates of scientists in 1945, it is impossible to disassociate the execution from the contemporary hysteria.[47] A nation that praised its own morality as distinct from the enemies of the "free world" would have been better served by a leader whose humanity matched his reputation.

That was also the spring when McCarthy's young men, Roy Cohn and G. David Schine, barnstormed through Europe in search of additional trouble for the IIA, which had already sustained a barrage of accusations during the Voice of America hearings. Cohn and Schine, operating as a close twosome, swept through American installations in country after country. On a weekend whirlwind stay in Paris they bought large quantities of perfume and silk stockings; although they had, as Congressional staff members, drawn two thousand dollars in counterpart funds, they charged their purchases to the American embassy. The embassy also received bills for their visits to Montmarte night clubs; and they checked out of town on Sunday night without paying their hotel bill, which also had to be picked up by the embassy.[48] They went on to Bonn, Frankfurt, Munich, Vienna, Belgrade, Athens, Rome and London, a sort of grand tour to protect American "interests." Ultimately, their attention centered on the possible presence of "Communist" literature in the overseas libraries operated by the IIA. In Rome, when they visited the apartment of the American minister to Italy, Elbridge Durbrow, they scrutinized his personal library and noted a collection of books on communism. The minister, explaining that they were obviously consistent with his being a Russian specialist, told the McCarthy inspectors that he intended to keep them. But as they continued their romp through Europe, their concern with the contents of the overseas libraries intensified. Cohn, later defending his search, acknowledged that he and his companion were ridiculed as Rover Boys, Innocents Abroad and "junketeering gumshoes." But, he pointed out, those libraries were designed to carry not merely indiscriminate literature but "Cold War products whose purpose was to win friends." Cohn's thinking is best obtainable from his own description of what he found on inspection trips to the American library in Vienna and in the Soviet Sector of the Austrian capital. "We discovered that some of the same books—for example, the works of Howard Fast—were stocked by both," he wrote. "One of us—the United States or the Soviet Union—had to be wrong."[49] On their return to the States they were greeted at the airport with an ostentatious kiss by Frances Knight, who was close to Joe McCarthy and worked for Scott McLeod.

Indeed, McLeod had been one of the trip's promoters. For Dulles, that was another provocation, which, in a less political situation, would have meant an immediate firing. The Secretary reportedly reacted by almost "hitting the roof." But, again, the damage had been done. Yet, that was merely on the level of international lunacy and not the substantive blow to America's international information programs. That had been started before Cohn and Schine had ever emplaned for Europe and had undoubtedly purified the shelves of the libraries in advance of the two inspectors.

It had been Dulles's Assistant Secretary, Carl McCardle, who had first acted to protect the libraries from McCarthy's wrath. The Senator had been displeased to learn of the criteria for stocking books. Their contents, regardless of authorship, was to be the guide. That policy had been based on the findings of an advisory committee under Dr. R. P. Maguire of the Catholic University of America, which had recommended that usefulness to the United States be the only test for books. Furthermore, it would be self-defeating if collections reflected only State Department thinking, according to Maguire's group. Once McCarthy's committee obtained the policy directive, McCardle used his authority over the IIA to rescind the order.[50]

McCarthy's staff had examined the agency's bibliography thoroughly. The Senator soon charged that there were over thirty thousand volumes on the shelves by "Communist" authors. That figure, it later became clear, was obtained by listing individual copies of books by 418 writers. In addition to legitimate Communists or Marxists, it included such writers as Foster Rhea Dulles (a cousin of John Foster Dulles), Arthur Schlesinger, Jr., Brooks Atkinson, W. H. Auden, Edna Ferber, Stephen Vincent Benét, John Dewey, Robert M. Hutchins, Bernard De Voto and Whittaker Chambers.[51] On March 18 the State Department banned "the works of all Communist authors" and "any publication which continuously publishes Communist propaganda," an act that drew McCarthy's praise as a "good, sensible order."[52] When Winston Aldrich, the newly named American ambassador to England, planned to make a Pilgrim's Day address in London, there was serious doubt about whether he could quote from Stalin.

Again, the Administration was pacifying McCarthy. Ostensibly it was Dulles and the State Department that had made the concession. But the Secretary, always conscious of his constitutional limitations, never carried out any policy without careful clearance from the President. Virtually every knowledgeable insider has testified, in interviews and in oral-history records, that the two men not only mapped out broad policy together but that the Secretary scrupulously notified Eisenhower about every move. Even while on his numerous overseas trips he often made several phone calls a day to the White House. There were those who considered Dulles tricky and artful about insinuating his ideas so that Ike would believe they were his own, but even the upholders of the Secretary's dominance thereby recognized that both men came to establish a close working relationship. There is absolutely no doubt that they acted as one toward McCarthy; and Eisenhower, in his own oral history, has made clear that Dulles followed the President's strategy toward the Senator.[53]

Dulles explained the book policy at the Cabinet meeting of June 26; and the next day he wrote a memo to the President that quoted from his directive on the matter. His main point, he wrote, was that "material produced by Communists should be used 'only with great care'; that without carrying the 'matter to the point of absurdity,' we should avoid the buildup of Soviet personalities to such an extent that they command widespread attention. . . . I expressed doubt that works of Communist authors should be made part of these libraries."[54]

A panic of compliance became general at the 189 overseas libraries. It was, in Dulles's view, an overreaction to the policy. Libraries feared being caught by visiting Congressmen with taboo books on their shelves and tended to "play it safe" wherever there were doubts. Others, undoubtedly through anger and a vindictive desire to emphasize the absurdity of the program, complied with vengeance. Where forbidden books were actually burned, the expectation was that such dramatic action would have an appropriate incendiary effect. In June, Dulles disclosed that he knew of eleven books that had been burned in recent weeks.[55]

On June 12 Leonard Hall credited the Administration with stemming a "left-wing tidal wave." Two days later the President appeared at Hanover, New Hampshire, to deliver a commencement address at Dartmouth College. Eisenhower had no prepared speech. While he waited his turn to speak and listened to an address by Canadian Secretary of State for External Affairs Lester B. Pearson, he contemplated what he would say. At the College of William and Mary he had recently talked about freedom. Noting the nation's material abundance and recalling Virginia's Patrick Henry, he advised that "the true way to uproot communism in this country is to understand what freedom means, and thus develop such an impregnable wall that no thought of communism can enter."[56] And just three days before his visit to Dartmouth he had been much more direct. Speaking before the annual convention of the National Young Republicans at the Mount Rushmore National Monument in South Dakota, he had reminded his listeners that his security program for federal employees carried the assumption that working for the government "is not a right but a privilege." But the needs of security, he went on to say, "must be met, without resort to un-American methods; the rights of the innocent and the reputation of the devoted public servant must be militantly defended."[57] At Dartmouth, his turn finally came and he went before the old pine-stump lectern.

He held only an Indian-headed cane that had been presented by the senior class. His notebook, which he had studied while Pearson spoke, was back in his pocket. His talk began slowly and informally, commenting at first about old soldiers who love to reminisce, then about college life, golf and patriotism. Suddenly, about two-thirds of the way through a speech that seemed to be pointless, his manner became serious and he stunned his audience by declaring, "Don't join the book burners. Don't think you are going to conceal faults by concealing evidence that they ever existed. Don't be afraid to go to your library and read every book, as long as that document does not offend your own ideas of decency. That should be the only censorship."[58]

At Dartmouth and throughout the nation there was little doubt about the President's target. Reactions from the public sent to the White House during the next forty-eight hours were not indicative of a massive outpouring, but those telegrams and letters that arrived supported Eisenhower by better than ten to one.[59] In Congress, reaction was mixed along predictable lines. The most interesting response undoubtedly was Senator McCarthy's. "He couldn't very well have been referring to me," he said. "I have burned no books."[60]

When the President held his news conference on the seventeenth, the Senator's opponents awaited a follow-through that would leave no doubt about the meaning of his Dartmouth declaration. What resulted, instead, was confusion. Within the span of the thirty-eight-minute session, the President's responses took the following route: He had not referred to Senator McCarthy. "Now, Merriman, you have been around me long enough to know I never talk personalities." The United States, "strong enough to expose to the world its differing viewpoints," should not fear showing that side. Opposition to book-burning means rejecting suppression of ideas. If, however, the "State Department is banning a book which is an open appeal to everybody in these foreign countries to be a Communist, then I would say that falls outside of the limits in which I was speaking; and they can do as they please to get rid of them, because I see no reason for the Federal Government . . . to be supporting something that advocates its own destruction." On the other hand, "let me point out something to you gentlemen." We were inadequately prepared for World War II "because we had failed to read *Mein Kampf* seriously. . . . Why shouldn't we, today, know what is going on? How many of you have read Stalin's *Problem of Leninism*? How many of you have really studied Karl Marx and looked at the evolution of the Marxian theory down to the present application? . . . So, these things that expose to us right from the original source what is communism, I don't believe we should hide them."[61]

Yet, at the next meeting of the press, the President appeared disturbed that some reports of his June 17 remarks had indicated his approval of burning certain books and challenged a reporter to state where he had specifically said he favored the policy. When Raymond P. Brandt of the St. Louis *Post Dispatch* then observed that part of the controversy had pertained to works by Communists that were not on communism, Eisenhower replied, "I am not going to answer that strictly." But, then told that Dashiell Hammett's detective stories had been discarded, too, the President said, "I think someone got frightened. I don't know why they should. I wouldn't."[62]

The contention that the "essence of his remarks was clear" misses the point.[63] In an open letter to the American Library Association's convention that month, which was drafted for Eisenhower by Emmet Hughes, the President upheld the virtues of free expression and denounced as un-American "zealots" who with "more wrath than wisdom" sought to suppress information and ideas. "Freedom cannot be censored into existence," said the message that was read to the meeting.[64] But in his direct appearance before the press, where he was cornered into responding to the specific situation, his performance had been an artful avoidance of a firm and clear stand on a basic issue. It was no different from his handling of McCarthy and the matter of the Greek shipowners. Once again, when he could have exploited a ludicrous situation by making it seem indefensible, he preferred to have it all ways. If there was an essence to his points it was that his reaction to McCarthy was as fearful as that of the Congressmen and others who had overestimated the Senator's power and then retreated. The Bohlen case, trade with Communist nations and the specter of book-burning had all exposed McCarthy's vulnerability. Almost immediately afterward, the appearance of the July issue of *The American Mercury* pinned the Senator with the guilt-by-association trap he loved to spring for others.

J. B. Matthews, a former "fellow traveler," clergyman and HUAC researcher, had been named staff director of McCarthy's committee a few days earlier. His article in the monthly magazine opened with the sensational assertion that "The largest single group supporting the Communist apparatus in the United States today is composed of Protestant clergymen." Over seven thousand of them, Matthews pointed out, had served Communists. The Stockholm Peace Appeal, originated by anti-American sources, had obtained 253 of their signatures and 528 had even signed a press release of the National Committee to Repeal the McCarran Internal Security Act.[65] Immediately, the Democratic members of McCarthy's committee demanded Matthews's ouster; but the Senator, asserting that he as chairman had control over staff appointments, at first resisted such efforts. Emmet Hughes has described how, as word leaked that McCarthy had decided to free himself by accepting Matthews's resignation, he worked with Deputy Attorney General William Rogers to solicit a telegram protesting Matthews's statement from the National Conference of Christians and Jews; and then, while Richard Nixon co-operated by conversing with McCarthy to delay him, how the White House beat the Senator's statement about Matthews by getting its own response to the ministers (which had been prepared before their telegram had arrived) to the press before McCarthy's announcement. Thus, the statement, agreeably signed by the President, not only blasted "Generalized and irresponsible attacks that sweepingly condemn the whole of any group of citizens," but appeared to have forced Matthews's resignation.[66] Two days after the White House denied having initiated the telegram of protest from the National Conference, one of its three signers, Rabbi Maurice N. Eisendrath, urged Eisenhower to set up a committee of clerics and teachers to draft a program to fight the "specter of McCarthyism."[67]

Eisenhower, however, who had also been pointed in his criticism when Velde had suggested a HUAC probe of the clergy, would go no further. The question of "cracking down" on McCarthy had, by then, begun to plague Eisenhower at virtually every turn. Again, in his news conference of July 22, he refused to mention the Senator's name while rejecting any suggestion that he deal in personalities. He told the reporters that he intended to stand for "what I believe to be right. If that is found to be in opposition to what someone else says, publicly or privately, then that is too bad; but that is what I am going to stand for."[68] Only two days later, however, the issue returned. This time his brother, Arthur Eisenhower, a vice-president of the Commerce Trust Company in Kansas City, was quoted by newspapers as having called McCarthy "the most dangerous man in America." Asked to comment on his brother's remark, the President indicated he would rather not give McCarthy the satisfaction of a reply.[69]

Meanwhile, the McCarthy prestige had lowered sufficiently for the three Democratic members of his subcommittee to resign in protest over his handling of the Matthews affair, and other Senators were encouraged by his new vulnerability, particularly since the assaults on the Protestant ministry. Even such Southern conservatives as Harry Byrd of Virginia and John McClellan of Arkansas delivered pungent rebukes. Earlier, Democrat Mike Monroney called Cohn and Schine "Keystone cops," which brought a televised response from McCarthy charging the Senator from Oklahoma with "a flagrant example of anti-Semitism." That provoked a rejoinder from New York's Herbert Lehman, one of the few who had been speaking out against McCarthy all along. "I—a Jew, sensitive to any religious bias—have," said the Senator, "pointed out that they have been doing our country and the cause of anti-communism great harm both here and abroad. I am very certain that most members of my religious faith, not as Jews, but as Americans, are anything but proud of these two young men." On July 24, when Senator William J. Fulbright of Arkansas took advantage of McCarthy's distress to denounce his interference with the government's information program and to plead for the restoration of funds for the Fulbright program of student exchange, the Senator from Wisconsin responded by referring to the "half-bright program."[70]

In the middle of the uproar, distracting from his embarrassment, Mc-

Carthy suddenly announced he was calling before his committee William P. Bundy, a thirty-five-year-old Washington lawyer. Since 1951 Bundy had been with the Central Intelligence Agency. Ostensibly motivated by the fact that Bundy was slated for liaison work between the Atomic Energy Commission and the National Security Council, McCarthy proceeded to signal his real purpose. He pointed out that Bundy was a son-in-law of Dean Acheson and, moreover, he had also contributed four hundred dollars to the defense fund for Alger Hiss. Three days later the CIA telephoned the McCarthy staff to report that its director, Allen Welsh Dulles, the Secretary of State's younger brother, had forbidden any employee of the top-secret agency to appear before Congressional committees. McCarthy, then meeting with Dulles, advised that his organization was neither sacrosanct nor immune. The director asked for time to contemplate his course before reporting his decision to the McCarthy committee. Once again, however, the Senator was challenging the Chief Executive head on, not only because of the CIA's top-secret position but also because it was responsible to the National Security Council, which was headed by the President. Observers wondered whether the President, if McCarthy persisted, would abandon his detached attitude. But Eisenhower was spared the need for further involvement when Vice President Nixon, now getting considerable attention for his trouble-shooting role, met with McCarthy over lunch and persuaded the crusading Senator that the impingement upon both the agency's secrecy and the Executive Department's responsibility were serious matters.[71]

Robert Donovan has noted McCarthy's predicament during the summer of 1953 by observing that the recent incidents had brought the Senator to a low point, one which marked the start of his decline.[72] It was, however, only a slump. Within the next few months McCarthy had taken the offensive by openly humiliating Secretary of the Army Robert Ten Broeck Stevens and had gone to war against the United States Army, winning for himself enough prestige to raise his Gallup Poll rating to his all-time high of 50 percent by January of 1954, a climb of sixteen points since August.[73] When the Senator had been on the ropes, the President had simply moved to a neutral corner. Correspondent Merriam Smith, taking note of the embarrassment within the Administration, remembered that as the summer when few members of the White House staff would speak frankly about McCarthy.[74]

That Eisenhower thought McCarthy loathsome cannot be doubted. His feelings as expressed to Harry Bullis and as heard by his staff were genuine. If nothing else, McCarthy's style and personality affronted the President's entire system of values. His attitude about the violation of elementary civil liberties represented Eisenhower's notion of fair play and constant readiness to agree that others have the right to be heard. Moreover, the General-President was too often a practitioner of the "art of the possible" to succumb to any kind of rigidity.

Eisenhower's political reluctance to attack McCarthy and thus alienate his own party's right wing—and possibly provoke the Senate to defend one of its own members—was a major consideration. But that was not the only element. The President with the astonishing perception of the public mood was inseparable from his America. He had, during the 1952 campaign, managed to appease McCarthy. More important, however, like most of his countrymen, he was not completely opposed to McCarthy. He shared their sympathy for the crusader's goals. In several campaign speeches in the Midwest and the South, Eisenhower had adopted the McCarthy rhetoric. But, more accurately, it was not the "McCarthy rhetoric" but the neurosis of a nation that had always feared the evils of communism and, trapped in the insecurity and disillusionment of the cold war, had developed a common assumption about the identity of its enemies. Emmet Hughes reports that he was not the man to present the President with the message to the National Conference of Christians and Jews for his signature during the Matthews affair for the very good reason, Hughes writes, that the President "tended by now, to discount the heat of my own feelings about McCarthy."[75] Cyrus Sulzberger, visiting the White House on November 23, 1953, found the President contemplating a forthcoming Big Three conference at Bermuda by considering a proposal to England and France that they join with the United States in outlawing the Communist party. He also told the astonished correspondent that while he detested McCarthy's methods, it was imperative to fight communism hard. "It was silly to think," Sulzberger reported Eisenhower believing, "that the liberties of the United States were being endangered merely because we were trying to squash communism."[76] All the good reasons for acquiescence were embellished by the lack of conviction that the battle was worth fighting.

CHAPTER 27

Redeeming Containment

A<small>MERICA'S</small> <small>MILITARY</small> <small>AND</small> economic dominance over the non-Communist nations failed to make possible the foreign policies that were visualized in the fondest dreams of the anti-containment anti-Communists. The domestic and national interests of the Western allies further restricted the flexibility of American global management; and the continued growth of mutual hostilities and suspicions had rendered East-West relationships as tedious and unwavering as static trench warfare. In pursuance of the American mission to protect freedom from Communist infiltration, the Germans, the French and the British needed cajolery. Maneuvering, however, became most hazardous when the formulation of policies had to satisfy both those concerned with American and "free world" economic progress and those intent on fighting a holy war against the "international Communist conspiracy."

There were, of course, no clear lines that placed such sentiments in simple classifications. Actually, the President and his Secretary of State were fine examples of that overlapping. Usually pictured as one in their international outlook, largely as an explanation of their harmonious relationship, Dulles, nevertheless, was less concerned with using foreign policy as a method of gaining economic advantages, less optimistic than Eisenhower about the value of economic relationships in rectifying moral wrongs, and much more likely than even the General in the White House to emphasize conventional concepts of military power. At the same time, both saw economic progress as an important deterrent of communism wherever lopsided societies made for a tiny ruling class at the apex of a pyramidal structure. Eisenhower, in particular, was also realistic enough to suggest that such nations needed the type of economic planning that was anathema to him at home. On balance, the internationalist, missionary approach was advanced by Eisenhower, while Dulles, carefully deferring to the President when he could not have his own way, preferred to support American desires with the power that made for authenticity, whether economic or military.

Yet, for all of the Secretary's condemnations of containment, there was little to suggest substantive moves beyond the Truman–Acheson lines. The previous Administration had conducted the successful Berlin airlift, had resuscitated precarious regimes in Greece and Turkey, had formed NATO and had responded amid general praise to the invasion of South Korea. Partisan arguments had centered mainly on past issues, on the responsibility for post-Yalta Red gains or the "loss" of Nationalist China or whether Dean Acheson, by openly excluding South Korea from the American defense perimeter, had encouraged the invasion. And, despite the emotional denunciations of Truman for having fired MacArthur in April of 1951, passions had since cooled and there was little evidence of much appetite to extend the war beyond the Yalu River at the risk of widening the conflict a second time. Voters had liked Ike's campaign comments about turning the war over to the Koreans and most people had, for the past two years, come to view the "police action" as a mistake.[1] A MacArthur Presidential victory could have been interpreted as a mandate for a conventional military solution. Had Taft won, the hawkish concept of either going "all out" or "pulling out" might have prevailed. Nothing about Eisenhower, however, particularly after his December visit to the battlefront, indicated any departure from Truman's policies. Even the announced removal of the Seventh Fleet from the Straits of Formosa was more political than military and brought swift denials from Dulles to the British and the French that sponsorship of a Chiang Kai-shek invasion attempt was being contemplated. Approval for the Democratic handling of Western Europe's economic and military recovery, particularly from SHAPE headquarters, had been a principal reason for Eisenhower's candidacy. Therefore, after having romanced the right wing with rhetoric about the immorality of containment, the Eisenhower government, in seeking to perpetuate concepts promoted by James G. Blaine, defended by John Hay and streamlined by Secretaries of State Robert Lansing and Cordell Hull, fought to provide continuity. Republican command merely gave the old product new sponsorship.

Nowhere was the similarity between past Democratic and the new Republican Administrations better demonstrated than by the Eisenhower–Dulles acceptance of the importance of steering the six European countries that had already joined to form the European Coal and Steel

Community—France, West Germany, Italy, Luxemburg, the Netherlands and Belgium—into ratifying the treaty that had been signed on May 27, 1952, to create a European Defense Community. Having spent some $30 billion on Western Europe since the end of World War II, the United States had come to accept the formation of EDC as the keystone of the non-Communist world's ability to resist aggression. Economy-conscious Americans had expressed their feelings about frugality when ousting the Democrats and had long since begun to wonder whether the Europeans would ever be ready to help themselves. Still, few argued against protecting the West.

But NATO, by placing a token force in the path of any Red advance (the so-called "trip-wire" concept) could only discourage or delay aggression until retaliation became possible. To have armed NATO with a separate West German military force was unacceptable to France with her vivid memories of German militarism. Dulles himself, in a speech at the American Club in Paris as early as 1948, had warned that having Germany as a partner in a unified Western Europe carried a high peril: the danger of her future dominance. Agreements "which might be imposed today," he pointed out, cannot be reliable assurances "against that future risk."[2]

Originally conceived by French political economist Jean Monnet, the major fighter for European economic and government unification, it became known as the Pleven Plan upon its introduction by French Defense Minister René Pleven. After the Anglo-American decision to rebuild West Germany as a barrier against Communist expansion, it seemed to hold the most protection against German resurgence. The treaty's military protocol incorporated a vital safeguard by calling for the integration of West German forces with the armies of the other five nations in a single defensive unit. The financial protocol, which was signed along with the basic treaty and the military agreement, also created a common budget for the community.[3]

Eisenhower and his Administration had long since accepted the plan as the only solution that was politically feasible, an argument that was used by Monnet and American ambassador to France David Bruce to remove the General's doubts when Ike was still with SHAPE. But, by the pre-inaugural period, its reality had become increasingly remote. Two weeks before his inauguration, Eisenhower, disturbed that none of the signatories had ratified the treaty, sent a telegram to West German Chancellor Konrad Adenauer. Adenauer, facing a challenge from Social Democrats who feared that EDC would confirm the German separation, was given political support by the President-elect's assurances that EDC would promote the "peace and the security of the free world."[4] Eisenhower and Dulles also decided, at that time, that an early trip to Europe by the Secretary of State and Mutual Security Director Harold Stassen, who would be involved in financial arrangements relating to foreign aid, would, as Ike explained to an old army friend, reaffirm his belief that "only in collective security was there any future in the free world."[5] The mission would, hopefully, allay apprehensions among the proposed participants and aim at encouraging British military support, which seemed necessary to give the French greater assurance. They might gather information that, as Dulles informed Charlie Wilson, would be helpful for "subsequent discussions and for negotiations with our European friends."[6] But what Dulles and Stassen heard was not very reassuring. Domestic politics, coupled with psychological and economic factors, threatened a stillbirth for EDC. In Luxemburg, Italy, Belgium and the Netherlands there was reluctance to act until the Germans and the French had shown the way.

Oddly enough, the French, who had advanced the plan in the first place, had become the most doubtful. The government of Premier René Mayer was dependent on anti-EDC nationalistic followers of General Charles De Gaulle for support, and that group was insisting on special provisions that would retain French freedom to deploy her army in such overseas trouble spots as Indochina, where a battle against Communist Vietminh was in its seventh year, as well as in North Africa. Moreover, the National Assembly was divided almost equally among six different parties, ranging from the Gaullists and the Independents on the right to the Socialists and the Communists on the left. Even within the framework of a defense community with its integrated forces, Frenchmen had begun to fear the consequences of a future deterioration of the alliance that could leave them vulnerable to the army that had invaded their homeland three times within seventy years. Only a strong British commitment to EDC, by becoming "associated" with the community, could possibly provide sufficient guarantees. Furthermore, the Mayer government thought that Washington's desire for EDC might be strong enough for pressure to be exerted on the German Federal Republic to recognize French economic ties with the coal-rich, heavily industrialized Saar. In view of France's other current international burdens, they also wanted increased military aid from the United States, hopefully double the $525 million that was allocated for the current year. From the American point of view, greater assistance to the anti-Vietminh effort in Indochina could keep the Chinese Communists too involved in Southeast Asia to do much more about Korea.

In Britain the outlook was not much brighter. There, Dulles received his poorest reception of the tour. Lord Beaverbrook's conservative *Daily Express*, recalling that the architect of the Japanese Peace Treaty had been somewhat less than honorable by telling Premier Shigeru Yoshida that the United States expected his government to side with Chiang Kai-shek's regime despite his earlier promise to the British that the Japanese would be free to select from among the two Chinese governments, led the British uproar by calling the Secretary of State a "double-dealing" diplomat. British hostility toward Dulles had, in fact, been so great that Foreign Minister Anthony Eden had earlier urged General Eisenhower to name somebody else as Secretary of State.[7] The new American tones of aggression in the Far East, coupled with Dulles's sharp admonition to Western Europe in his January 27 speech, compounded the unfriendly climate. Even as Dulles and Stassen toured the seven capital cities, from January 31 until February 8, they had to reassure Western Europeans that the United States was not about to widen the war in the Far East. As Dulles revealed in a nationwide broadcast after returning home, there was "fear that the United States is not qualified to give the free world the kind of leadership" necessary at that moment.[8]

After having dealt with Democratic Administrations for twenty years, they had to face a party that frequently expressed hostility toward European alliances and, as disturbing, tended to sound jingoistic toward the complex problems of Asia. Furthermore, Republicans were also friends of Senator McCarthy, about whom there was rising apprehension in Europe, with many wondering whether Eisenhower could restrain the Senator.

In London, Dulles gave his assurances, as he had in France, that the Administration's bellicose statements were designed for American domestic consumption. But his real mission was to impress upon the British the need for sufficient support of EDC to convince the French parliament to ratify the treaty.[9] He stressed that without a unified army that included West German contributions, there could be no security for Europe. Failure to unite could force a separate army, with or without French approval. Furthermore, Dulles was reported to have made clear, noting that nine months had passed since the EDC treaty was signed, the American Congress had about exhausted its patience while awaiting European action. He believed that the threat of war was greater, not less, than Europeans supposed, and only with evidence of cooperation from the Western allies could he go before Congress with definite recommendations about the American contributions that France required.[10] Thus, in one huge package, the United States, France and Great Britain were combining requirements of the non-Communist world from Western Europe to North Africa and the Far East.

From the start, however, the Dulles–Eden encounter foreshadowed troubled diplomacy. The British Foreign Minister was fifty-six years old, nine years younger than Dulles, and his experience in guiding his country's international affairs had been substantial. He had first served a

Conservative government as foreign minister from 1935 until 1938, finally resigning in protest against Neville Chamberlain's appeasement policy. During the war, he returned to the head of the Foreign Office, then under Churchill. The subsequent restoration of the Churchill government in 1951 had made Eden the Foreign Minister for the third time.

Both men, Eden and John Foster Dulles, had excellent credentials. They were proud of their accomplishments and abilities, possibly the source of jealousy that some believed caused the friction. Others contend that Dulles considered Eden stupid and vain and thought he epitomized the deviousness the Secretary attributed to the British (a trait, incidentally, often tagged on Dulles). Basically, they were two very different people: Eden was handsome, debonaire and had the vitality of a much younger man, while Dulles was stolid and plodding. But few doubted that Dulles was more self-confident and, despite outward appearances, decisive than his English counterpart. Some who watched both have suggested that Eden's insecurity and uncertainty made Dulles a terrible burden for him. It must, for example, have galled Eden to address Dulles while the American sat calmly and doodled on an ever-present legal-sized yellow pad, only glancing upward occasionally and rather quizzically at the British Foreign Minister, as though the forthcoming words were perfectly predictable.[11] Eden, in his own memoirs, records that Dulles was a "preacher in a world of politics" who sometimes appeared to have "little regard for the consequences of his own words."[12] As Eden saw his role, he was performing the vital task of restraining the more adventurous Americans before they could plunge everybody into a major war. Whether Dulles had any inkling that Eden had attempted, in May of 1952, to prevent his becoming Secretary of State is a moot question; but Eisenhower has recalled that their relationship, particularly in 1953, was "sort of cat and dog watching each other."[13]

After London, Dulles, armed with a letter from Eisenhower giving further support to EDC, went on to Bonn. Chancellor Konrad Adenauer, who had been on very close terms with former American High Commissioner to Germany John McCloy, ultimately became one of Dulles's best foreign friends. Der Alte, as Germans began to call him, was already seventy-seven years old and had become to most Westerners the symbol of an anti-Nazi Germany working toward unification and respectability under a democratic system. Adenauer had been Chancellor since 1945 and, as of 1951, was also his own foreign minister. Thus, Dulles's negotiations in Bonn were directly with the chief of state. And, although they needed an interpreter when they talked, the two men had little trouble relating to each other. Dulles admired Der Alte's strength in guiding postwar Germany and his stern anti-communism, which was closer to American attitudes than he found in most of Europe; and the two men discovered as time went by many other areas of mutual interest, particularly religion. Until Dulles's last visit to West Germany, their closeness increased.

For Adenauer, EDC was completely realistic. All the talk about reunification was quickly becoming a ritualistic hocus-pocus which for many was merely an expected platitude. Adenauer's own zeal for reunification, aside from public gestures, came to be regarded by many as nonexistent.[14] To expect Russian agreement on restoration of the German national state by permitting free elections was more sloganeering than sincerity, for the population of the West was triple that of East Germany. Moreover, the West was Catholic, industrial and dedicated to private enterprise, while the East was Protestant, totalitarian and had been indoctrinated in communism. As Ronald Steel has pointed out, joining the two sectors "might lead to a convulsion that would make the present situation seem idyllic by comparison."[15] With the Russians maintaining one hundred divisions in Eastern Europe, moreover, any other course was impossible; and there was no doubt in Adenauer's mind that a West German contribution of twelve divisions to EDC, thus fusing his republic to the other five nations, was the best hope for security. If it, in the process, would seal the division of his country, that would only bring back the pre-Bismarckian Germany, a conglomeration of virtually independent states. For most Europeans, regardless of what they might mouth about the desirability of reunification, continued partition was really a happy safeguard against the repetition of history.

The claims of Adenauer's opponents that EDC would delay reunification by obviating any hopes of German neutrality between East and West were, of course, correct. In essence, they wanted to repair what had already become a thorough East-West split. Postwar Germany, in a pivotal position between the Communist and the capitalist worlds and feared as much for her military potential by the Soviets as by the Western democracies, had become the main area of conflict between the United States and Russia. Moscow's economic needs, particularly after President Truman had cut her lend-lease allocations in May of 1945 and the rejection by the Americans of a postwar loan or credits, had led to a heavy reparations burden on East Germany and had solidified the Russian hold on all of Eastern Europe. The conflict over Germany, with Russian suspicions confirmed when the Americans proceeded to rebuild the area west of the dividing line, was a major source of the cold war.[16]

When Dulles returned home his cautious optimism was conveyed to the American public. He reported that he and Stassen had concluded that EDC "was not dead but only sleeping" and that the defense community would become the "core" of NATO. "The European Defense Community," he said, "is needed to give the North Atlantic Treaty Organization a stout and dependable heart."[17] His words seemed appropriate when the West German *Bundestag* voted 224–165 to approve EDC together with the military and economic protocols that had formed the treaty. That seemed to have accomplished the first step toward including a half million German soldiers in a unified Western army. Of more significance, however, the British had already rebuffed a personal plea from Premier Mayer and Defense Minister Georges Bidault to keep their existing strength on the Continent and to arrange a political association with EDC.[18] Furthermore, the Eisenhower Administration's ability to respond to the French economic demands in a satisfactory manner would undoubtedly be limited not only by its own concern with reducing costs and working toward an early balanced budget but by pressure from Congress for even greater cuts.

Efforts at achieving European unification were suddenly further endangered by changes in Moscow after Stalin's death. Out of the momentary turmoil that followed the loss of the dictator, the crisis of succession in the totalitarian regime, had come the leadership of Georgi Malenkov, Stalin's ostensible successor. The fifty-one-year-old deputy to the late ruler became Prime Minister. But Malenkov, who was one of Stalin's pawns, had been fortunate enough to survive, along with many of the late ruler's old-time supporters, the behind-the-scenes manipulations to reduce his real power. In the days that followed the succession, Malenkov's price for having taken over the leadership became clear. He gave up the vital post of First Secretary of the Communist party. The struggle provided the checks that prevented a repetition of Stalin's control. Quietly rising to real power, at the same time the Malenkov regime seemed to be consolidating its position, was Nikita Khrushchev, who was the only man to have a seat on both the Secretariat and the Presidium of the Central Committee.[19] At the same time, along with the struggle within the Kremlin was the need for harmony in the face of Russia's international problems, made somewhat more menacing, or so it seemed at the time, by the strident new policies that had only recently been announced by the Americans.[20] Within the next few days the world heard fresh tones, words that offered to the hopeful the possibility that the new rulers might be seeking a *détente* with the West that would enable them to cope with the Soviet Union's intricate domestic inadequacies. Evidence of substance would, to most, come in a display of flexibility toward long-standing problems, particularly in Korea, where the talks at Panmunjom remained stalled, divided Berlin and the whole issue of German unification under free elections, propaganda warfare and other indications that Stalin's policies had been truly liquidated.

Deftly the new leadership threw the West a dilemma that could not be ignored. On the fifteenth of March, Malenkov appeared in the Kremlin's great hall and faced the thirteen hundred delegates who had been convened to give their *pro forma* approval to the organization of the new regime. The event, which also helped to dispel foreign suspicions of a continuing struggle over the succession, featured a long Malenkov speech. While his audience in Moscow cheered without restraint, the Atlantic Alliance nations were suddenly placed in the position of continuing their usual cold-war rhetoric and accepting the onus for the tensions or embracing the new line as a legitimate departure by a regime that wanted to end international conflicts for freedom to cope with Russia's domestic needs. Malenkov, on that day, declared that no existing dispute "cannot be decided by peaceful means, on the basis of mutual understanding by interested countries." And he specifically included the United States. Six days later, after Foreign Minister Vyacheslav M. Molotov agreed to work for an "affirmative" solution to the British request for assistance in obtaining the release from the North Koreans of their former minister in Seoul and nine other citizens, a Moscow radio broadcast recalled the Russian and Anglo-American victorious wartime cooperation. In Korea, there was the first significant Communist concession on the truce problem. Agreement was obtained for an immediate discussion to arrange the exchange of sick and wounded prisoners of war on what seemed to be Western terms, which promised to end the long stalemate at the large tent in Panmunjom. Even in Berlin there was a new face as the Russians negotiated cordially with the West and relaxed their restrictions. The message for new cooperation took longer to reach the Soviet's UN delegation, but there too a shift developed from the hard line as the Russians joined to support the election of Dag Hammarskjöld to replace Lie as Secretary General. One of the most dramatic reversals, however, told more about Russia's internal convulsions than about future cold-war policies. Lavrenti P. Beria, the notorious chief of the secret police and an old Stalinist who was number-two man of the new Presidium, revealed that the "doctor's plot" that had been exposed only three months earlier was a complete fabrication. Evidently designed to prepare for a purge, the scheme had brought forth "confessions" obtained by torture. Nine of the leading Soviet medical specialists, seven of them Jewish, had been accused of plotting against the governmental hierarchy. The arrested doctors were later released, except for two who may have perished in prison. When followed by relaxation on Russia's intellectuals, the change of direction seemed quite emphatic.[21]

The Eisenhower Administration, having attuned itself for psychological warfare, could not afford to appear insensitive to the new attitude. At the same time, conflicting and sometimes contradictory currents posed great dangers. Taking the peaceful overtures at face value could place the President in the untenable position of opposing reduced spending for foreign aid and American military programs, while simultaneously trying to convince the militant anti-Communists that coexistence with the Soviets was possible and even desirable. Yet the domestic dangers were not too great. Few Americans were ready to believe that the Russians had suddenly soured on intentions to "conquer the world"; those opposing liberal foreign economic policies were more likely to deny their efficacy in containing communism and tended to stress, as did Dulles, bolder use of military power.

The real danger, since Americans were so certain about the aims of international communism, was the impact upon the NATO alliance and the efforts to create the European Defense Community. The President began his press conference on March 19 with a statement that referred to the new situation by declaring that any Soviet wish to seek peace was "just as welcome as it is sincere" and by noting the "very direct relationship between the satisfaction of such a thing and the sincerity in which it is meant." He then gave his assurances that such overtures would never "be met less than halfway" and stated that the purpose of his Administration "will forever be to seek peace by every honorable and decent means, and we will do anything that will be promising toward that direction."[22] In early April a three-day Washington visit by Chancellor Adenauer to discuss with Eisenhower and Dulles the implications of the new Soviet line ended with a communiqué reminding the Western allies of the continued need for unity and common strength and then added a challenge. If the Russian leaders were really after peace, that could be demonstrated best by permitting genuinely free elections in the Soviet occupation zone. Adenauer then went on to San Francisco, where he said that West Germany would never give up her place in EDC if the Russians "dangle before her the promise of free elections in East Germany to elect a free, unified—but disarmed—German government."[23] The sparring had begun.

Eisenhower's major response, however, was saved for an April 16 speech in Washington to the American Society of Newspaper Editors. Concern for its circulation almost matched the intensive preparation of the actual contents. The United States Information Agency made the text into a booklet for distribution in Europe and Asia. In India alone, versions were available in eight different languages. The Voice of America and Radio Free Europe also did their best to promote the message. Domestically, businessmen throughout the United States were alerted. The head of one large advertising agency, fulfilling his part of the mission by notifying associates to spread the word among all friendly executives, later estimated that his own efforts may have influenced "perhaps a thousand people" to pay attention to the President's message.[24]

For the President, the speech was a political and personal masterpiece.

Speaking solemnly and slowly, he portrayed a contrast between the postwar behavior of the Communist countries and the democracies, claiming that while the United States and the other "free nations" chose one road the "leaders of the Soviet Union chose another." The upholding of natural rights of all people and the principle of self-determination was unlike the Soviet reliance upon "*force*: huge armies, subversion, rule of neighbor nations. The goal was power superiority at all cost," he said, and their security had to be achieved by "denying it to all others." He went on to cite the material and physical burdens of the cold war and declared that "This is one of those times in the affairs of nations when the gravest choices must be made if there is to be a turning toward a just and lasting peace." Without specifying what had been done by the Russians in recent days to step back from the dangers of atomic warfare, he acknowledged that "Recent statements and gestures of the Soviet leaders give some evidence that they may recognize this critical moment," and he added, "We welcome every honest act of peace. We care nothing for mere rhetoric."[25]

At that point of the address those close to him in the Statler Hotel observed that the President was continuing under great physical difficulty. He was beginning to skip over passages from the prepared text, hoping to manage the important sections despite his discomfort. His voice had already begun to falter and perspiration had beaded his eyebrows and was dripping down his cheeks. Bobby Cutler, moving along the side of the crowded room toward the speaker, saw the President's hands clutching the podium in an effort to keep his stability.[26] He feared he was going to faint. The President and his aides thought he was suffering from abdominal trouble, which had plagued him the night before at Augusta, Georgia, as it had during the campaign, but it was an early manifestation of what was later diagnosed as ileitis.

Nevertheless, he managed to deliver the heart of his prepared speech, which was designed to bolster the "free world" desire for peace with a firm challenge to the Malenkov regime for specific deeds to prove good intentions. A five-point disarmament proposal that involved willingness to reduce "the burden of armaments now weighing upon the world" by limiting the size of all armed forces and the production of strategic material to be devoted to military purposes and the international control of atomic energy and other destructive weapons were cited as the possible basis for future agreements. While negotiations would determine the level of such controls and the suggestions were stated with enough ambiguity to permit agreement in principle, the President challenged the Russians to agree to "a free and united Germany, with a government based upon free and secret elections" as well and the "full independence of East European nations" to end the "present unnatural division of

Europe" and the completion of a peace treaty with Austria. Russia's peaceful intentions could also be proved by willingness to end the Korean war and the restoration of peace throughout Asia. Near the end, barely managing to continue, he added, "These proposals spring, without ulterior purpose or political passion, from our calm conviction that the hunger for peace is in the hearts of all people—those of Russia and China no less than of our own country."[27] The editors and their guests interrupted to applaud five times.

After the speech the President was given sedatives, then had lunch and rested. Unfortunately, the schedule included two other events that day, both ceremonial. At Griffith Stadium he fulfilled a prior commitment by throwing out the first ball of the baseball season, a high heave that was caught by Washington Senator outfielder Ken Wood. He granted the photographers' request for another toss with a ball that hit umpire Bill McKinley on one bounce. Before the Yankees completed their six-to-three defeat of the home team, the President and his party left the ball park after only one and a half innings. His plane then carried him to North Carolina for the two hundredth anniversary festivities of Rowan County. From there he flew back to Augusta to rest from his ordeal.

By that night, while the President recuperated in his cottage at the golf course, worldwide reaction was crowding the news wires. The New York *Times*'s editorial for the next morning praised him for having attempted to "seize the peace initiative from the Soviets and to put their peaceful words to the test." At the United Nations there was interest in Eisenhower's five-point disarmament proposal, which was seen as a revival of the plan that Dean Acheson had submitted to the General Assembly a year and a half earlier. Messages from numerous American embassies and missions overseas reported the most enthusiasm to any statement of high United States policy since General George Marshall outlined his plan for European recovery at Harvard in June of 1947. In Moscow, the ambassador from Burma, who was not considered pro-American, told Chip Bohlen that the President's speech was in the "best tradition of the Founding Fathers of the United States"; and Bohlen found "a favorable reaction" from most of the diplomatic corps in the Russian capital. From Budapest came reports that groups of Hungarians in that satellite nation got together to listen to the radio broadcast of the speech and that many of them wept and prayed during the reading of the Hungarian translation. The Indian ambassador to Egypt told American envoy Jefferson Caffery that the President's speech was wonderful and that it could have been made by no other living man.[28] *Pravda* published the Eisenhower disarmament plan and the call for a "simple and honest" expression by all nations of their intentions, but noted that the President had placed the blame for the international situation on

Soviet policies without having substantiated his contention with factual information. In much the same vein, the Russian UN representative Adrei Vishinsky said the disarmament program was "interesting but not completely accurate," without offering any additional explanation. Nine days after the speech *Pravda* published the complete text and included a page-one statement that the Soviet Union was ready for "serious businesslike discussions" of issues in the world struggle.[29]

At home, the *Times*'s reaction was perhaps the most representative, with many Americans pleased that the President had taken the propaganda initiative away from the Russians. The Congressional response, also positive, included praise from the Democrats. Senator Lyndon Johnson liked Eisenhower's implicit warning to the Russians that the "free nations" will not relax defense preparations as long as there was the slightest risk of war. While the Democrats were happy, politics made them more restrained in their enthusiasm, which was further tempered by reluctance to credit the Republican President for simply restating ideas from the past administration. The chairman of the Republican Senate Policy Committee, William Knowland, and some other members of the President's party discovered warnings that others had overlooked. To them, Eisenhower's words indicated a general hardening of United States policy toward communism in Asia. Knowland was happy it had made clear that "a just peace requires a free and united Korea" and observed that the Administration had made plain that there would be "no more Munichs."[30]

After the early expressions of hope, the differences between the United States and her European allies toward the Soviets began to emerge with greater clarity. In appearances before the Senate Foreign Relations Committee, the newspaper editors and the NATO ministers meeting in Paris, all within the week following the speech, Dulles warned that the United States had to assume that the recent Soviet attitude toward the West was only a tactical shift rather than a basic change in that country's policy. Unless, he told the American Society of Newspaper Editors, the Russians responded promptly, "it will be necessary to move ahead on all fronts, West and East, to develop a strong position." His Paris statement pointed to Soviet history and Communist teaching as offering only a "feeble" hope for a genuine *détente*; and, he said, as much as we must always remain receptive to a change of policy, we must always remember that "the Soviet leaders are to a very large extent the prisoners of their own doctrine which is intensively held by their followers or fanatics" and warned against allowing the "persistence of what may be an illusion which is a design to entrap us into creating what Stalin referred to as a possibility of a renewed offensive under conditions more favorable than those that exist today."[31]

Eisenhower has admitted that his words had been delivered "with little hope they could evoke any immediate response in the Kremlin" and that the proposals were deliberately specific.[32] The state of American public opinion toward the Russians in particular and communism in general and especially the powerful influence of the Republican party's right wing made any substantive concessions by the Eisenhower–Dulles team politically most hazardous. Besides, in their view, what could be yielded? The principle of a unified Germany governed as the result of free elections? Permanent acceptance of the captive condition of Eastern Europe? Settling the Korean war on terms dictated by the enemy and abandoning the United Nations support of Syngman Rhee and his ROK government? Reduction of American arms without firm agreements with the East? A sudden admission that it was possible to deal with the godless Communists who had, as millions believed, "violated every treaty"? Even if the Administration had believed in their feasibility, all would have discarded the entire character of the Republican party's foreign-policy platform and campaign vows. For Western Europeans, lacking a public as fiercely hostile toward communism and not bound by hard-line political commitments, it was much easier for overt expressions of hope that the Soviets were abandoning their truculence in the interest of domestic needs. Thus, on May 11, Prime Minister Churchill rose from his bench in the House of Commons and, with the full attention of the MPs of all three parties, replied to the Eisenhower speech of April 16 by noting what many Europeans had begun to think: that Eisenhower's concern for peace had been welcome but by asking the Russians to yield over basic matters, such as giving up their sphere of influence in Germany and Eastern Europe and, in effect, opening it to the West, he had effectively obviated any chance of acceptance. "It would, I think, be a mistake to assume that nothing can be settled . . . until all has been settled," said the chief wartime promoter of British interests in conflict with Russian aims; "it would be a pity to impede any evolution which may be taking place inside Russia. . . . Russia has a right to feel assured . . . the real events of the Hitler invasion will never be repeated. . . . I believe that a conference on the highest level should take place between the leading powers without long delay."[33]

The State Department immediately issued a release recalling Eisenhower's readiness to meet the other side halfway if there was concrete evidence that personal diplomacy would be productive. The President repeated that sentiment at his Thursday news conference. He had, he said, "no objection whatsoever to Sir Winston's proposal" but merely wanted some tangible evidence of good faith before committing the United States.[34] To the British, with whom Eisenhower had been in constant contact by wire, particularly during the preparation of the speech to the newspaper editors, the President's coyness seemed odd. Had Churchill really pressured him into agreement, despite his own reluctance? There is sufficient evidence that Eisenhower was not only willing to meet with Sir Winston but had actually initiated the conference. Churchill, when he later announced the time and place for the meeting, made that point clear.[35] Eisenhower has since admitted his role with the additional disclosure that Dulles "quietly made necessary inquiries and after a number of difficulties had been overcome, the three governments agreed to meet in Bermuda in June 1953."[36] The President's political caution had obviously made him avoid appearing obsequious toward the new soft talk from the Kremlin.

Churchill's call exposed the basic disagreement among the Western allies, a schism that further jeopardized the European Defense Community Washington had been trying so hard to construct. When Laborite Clement Attlee spoke for his party the following day, he left no doubt that there was full support for Churchill's position. His only concern was with American willingness to depart from Eisenhower's demands. Prefacing his real charge by saying he hoped his words would not label him as anti-American, he noted that "the American Constitution was framed for an isolationist state" and speculated that "one sometimes wonders who is more powerful, the President or Senator McCarthy." Not only were there "elements in the United States" who were opposed to a settlement in Korea, he charged, but there were "people who want an all-out war with China and against communism in general, and there is the strong influence of the Chiang Kai-shek lobby."[37]

Attlee's comments produced the inevitable anger. Senator Knowland said, "We must be prepared to go it alone" since England had joined other UN members in urging a "far western Munich." "This is the thanks we get," said Jenner. "We are told to come to terms with Britain's friend and our deadly enemy even if we must bypass the Constitution to sell out our country." Joe McCarthy virtually declared war on John Bull. "Ships flying the British flag and trading with Communist China are actually owned by Chinese Communists," he said. "Let's sink every accursed ship carrying material to our enemy." At his press conference of May 14, the President did his best to calm the intemperate debate by declaring that "I have met no one in the United States that doesn't want peace."[38] Alexander Wiley spoke for many when he cautioned that the controversy was delighting the Kremlin.

One week later the United States, Great Britain and France announced agreement to hold a Big Three heads-of-state meeting. Afterward scheduled for Bermuda on June 17, its immediate purpose was the resolution of their differences toward the Soviet Union's soft-line policy. News of the meeting immediately led many, particularly Europeans, to assume it would be followed by a Big Four summit conference that would include Russia.[39] Eisenhower denied that inevitability.[40]

But a series of misfortunes finally led to an indefinite postponement. A lack-of-confidence vote that toppled Premier René Mayer's government in late May created the longest parliamentary interregnum in French history as a succession of four deputies failed to form a government. The Bermuda meeting had to be delayed twice during that period until, finally, on June 26 Joseph Laniel, an Independent, had put together a coalition and was elected Premier. Less than twenty-four hours later, however, Churchill announced that his physicians had ordered him to rest and that the Bermuda session would be put off indefinitely. He had managed to arrange, instead, a Big Three foreign ministers meeting to be held in Washington on July 9.[41]

By the time the foreign ministers gathered in Washington for their five-day session, another Soviet development had enhanced the drama behind the continuing struggle for power after Stalin's death. Lavrenti Beria, newly risen to the number-two spot and for so long identified with Russian police-state oppression, became—like Robespierre—a victim of the terror. He had attempted to strengthen his new position *vis-à-vis* the other old Stalinists and had managed the exposé of the "doctors' plot." The reaction was swift. An announcement from Moscow on July 10 revealed his removal and arrest as an agent of the West and a promoter of capitalism. At the end of the year, Beria was tried by a special court and then executed. Such evidence of continued Russian dissension, combined with the embarrassing East German hunger riots in June, further encouraged the foreign ministers to hope that the Kremlin might be eager for a European *rapprochement*.[42]

Their session delineated the European optimism and the American caution. Dulles, confronted with the French mood expressed by Georges Bidault and the Marquess of Salisbury, who substituted for Anthony Eden, then recuperating from complications following the removal of his gall bladder, managed to suppress desires for a full-scale Big Four summit conference. Bidault, asserting French desires to test Russian intransigence before making a commitment to EDC, seconded Salisbury's belief that diplomacy at the highest level was needed. Their compromise, issued as a communiqué on July 14, was virtually effusive in its avoidance of a challenge to the Russians. EDC was cited repeatedly as a step toward a peaceful Europe, "not directed against anyone." A great achievement toward easing tensions, it declared, would be the "early reunification of Germany, in accordance with the legitimate aspirations of the German population. . . ." Dulles's hand at restraining a premature plunge into summitry before the realization of substantive goals, including an Austrian peace treaty, was revealed in its call for a Big Four conference. The Secretary of State wanted to avoid another vodka-and-caviar session at which the Russians and the Western allies sat around a table smiling at each other for photographers. That only served Soviet propaganda by implying that tensions were easing when, actually, the problems were serious. Another meeting must, therefore, deal with such concrete issues as the Far East, Germany and Austria.[43] The communiqué declared that the meeting should convene not the heads of state, as the English and Frénch would have preferred, but the foreign ministers.[44] The Russians, however, insisted that such a conference without Communist China and with the continued demand for a freely elected German government made the invitation unacceptable.

At least as frustrating as the international maneuvering was the process of getting money from economy-minded Republicans and conservative Democrats for foreign economic policies. For many Republicans, foreign aid meant "Democrat"; and while the Marshall Plan's three-year program of providing economic rehabilitation to Western Europe had been of unquestioned success, it had ended. Even before the elections there had been talk among many of the party's Congressional leaders about phasing out the remaining programs in the process of returning to more traditional ways of conducting international relations. Such talk was heard, in the early days of the Eisenhower Presidency, within the Administration itself. The Eisenhower–Dulles leadership, by sending Stassen to Europe and Asia, along with Secretary Dulles, was preparing to justify continued appropriations. Stassen, who was much more enthusiastic than Dulles about granting assistance to even neutral nations, gathered a group of fifty-five American industrial and financial leaders and sent them on survey missions in the fourteen countries that had been accepting the largest grants. Along with suggestions for streamlining its administration, they also showed the urgent need for the Mutual Security Program throughout the non-Communist world.[45]

Foreign aid had been coordinated under the Mutual Security Program since 1951. Actually, it had encompassed previous economic, military and technical assistance programs that had been administered by President Truman under the Marshall Plan, the Defense Assistance Act of 1949 and the Point Four program for underdeveloped areas. However, calling it Mutual Security was a happier political move, one that was easier for Congressmen to justify to their constituents. Nothing about the term indicated a "handout" and the word "security" made its purpose self-evident. Senator Dirksen noted political dangers where people failed to understand the military nature of the assistance and suggested that only by driving home "the fact that this is a program for our own security can we avoid building up of this hostile resistance."[46]

For Eisenhower, battling in behalf of foreign aid, which started during the spring and summer of 1953, ultimately became one of his annual fights. His Administration's initial burden was to convince skeptical conservatives that money and supplies shipped overseas could not only enhance the economies of non-Communist nations but would have significant long-term benefits to the United States. Expanding European economies, propped up with American money and equipment, would become less dependent in the future, for their own domestic recovery would be able to support enlarged military forces. Of immediate benefit to the United States was the need for outlays that would mitigate French objections to the European Defense Community. While the anti-Communist forces in Indochina were already being supplied, on a high-priority basis, with large amounts of military equipment, including airplanes, tanks and ammunition, French pleas for greater help were justified to repel the growing pressure from the Communists. The establishment of a pilot "pacification" project, which would consolidate many small villages into one and so, hopefully, limit the Vietminh's ability to raid the farmers for food and recruits, also increased their expenditures.[47] Appropriations had to be obtained, then, strictly on the basis of bolstering nations against Communist subversion or invasion.

The issue illustrated Eisenhower's dilemma as a party leader. Conservative GOP Congressmen, especially from the Midwest and the Far West, plus their Democratic allies from Dixie, were bent on economizing with little regard for the President's desires. Some businessmen worried that the money would be used to socialize foreign economies. Eisenhower might, because of his background, be particularly difficult to debate in the area of military appropriations, but allocations for other matters, which he thought of equal importance, were far more vulnerable. He tried to satisfy desires for economies by demonstrating improvements over the Truman mutual security request for fiscal 1954 and by arguing that assisting allies would save American dollars in the long run. Hoping to accommodate the critics, Eisenhower requested authorization of $5,828,732,500, $1.8 billion less than Truman's budget had indicated. In justifying a figure that, nevertheless, exceeded the expectations of those out to save money, Eisenhower pointed out America's defensive responsibilities in the absence of "genuinely peaceful purpose on the part of the Soviet Union," and failure to continue the military build-up would threaten to scuttle all that had been accomplished during the past five years. Moreover, the European allocation was necessarily higher. It included more aid to France for Indochina and to Britain's worldwide commitments as well as the expected requirements that would follow German entrance into Western defensive arrangements. Congressmen were also assured that "by far the largest single element in the Mutual Security Program for Europe will be the direct provision of military end items."[48] Once he had said all that, continued resistance forced him to retreat to a $5.5 billion figure.

Such concessions were not enough for the crusaders against foreign aid. On July 7 the President faced the party's legislative leaders with the plea that decimating mutual security would imbalance the whole defensive structure. Cutting one or two billion more might even force other aspects of the security program upward by seven or eight billion dollars. Told that the greatest objections were to non-military appropriations, he pointed out that removing that kind of assistance would be "like ripping one wheel off a wagon."[49] Then, following a typical Eisenhower venture into personal diplomacy that he was pursuing with delegations ranging from women's organizations to politicians, he had a breakfast session with Congressman John Taber, who headed the House Appropriations Committee, to spell out the mutual-security needs with complete clarity. He repeated the tactic at a luncheon conference with the man who headed the Senate's committee, Styles Bridges. Neither made a comment.

When, predictably, Taber's group voted on July 18 to chop more than a billion dollars from Eisenhower's second compromise figure, the President responded at the next press conference to the inevitable query about his reaction to the cut; and he did so by emphatically linking foreign aid with the nation's own enlightened self-interest. Mutual security, he said in essence, meant security for the United States.[50] His personal expression of concern, however, was entirely inadequate; for the final appropriation added only one hundred million to the Taber figure, largely because the Senate passed a slightly higher version—which Democrat Otto Passman of Louisiana was unable to kill—and Eisenhower had to accept a 22.3 percent cut from his original request.* Equally disturbing to the President, and continuing to bother him as the months went by, was continuing evidence that on the foreign-aid issue, as on so many other controversies, the Democrats had been more cooperative than fellow Republicans.[51]

In the annual effort to get foreign-aid money that condition failed to change significantly through the years. For the remainder of Eisenhower's Presidency mutual-security cuts averaged 19 percent, with the largest reduction reaching 28.2 percent for fiscal 1958.[52] If the Democrats continued more amenable, it was largely because, outside the South, their Congressmen came from areas that were less hostile toward spending. Yet, the substantial support given to the President from the opposition was helped by the leadership provided in the Senate by Majority Leader Lyndon Johnson and, in the House, Speaker Sam Rayburn, both from Texas.

In some ways, the history of the mutual-security efforts provide fine examples of the Eisenhower leadership, precisely because it was an area

*Truman suffered a 24 percent cut for fiscal 1953.

in which his personal convictions were strong. At breakfasts, luncheons, at White House evening sessions, he met with both Democrats and Republicans, appealing to their patriotism and sense of duty. But always he was the adviser, not the boss. In that spirit he wrote to Lyndon Johnson on August 1, 1958, "I am deeply sensitive to the fact that the Congress is a coordinate branch of the government and can and must work its own will in regard to this matter; but I would be remiss in my duty should I fail to point out the utter gravity of this situation as it appears to me."[53] Later that month, in an early-evening session at the White House with Congressional leaders, Eisenhower, concerned with restoring deleted funds, suggested that Sam Rayburn improve the prospects of a Senate-House conference committee report by increasing the number of House conferees. Rayburn promptly replied that that was his job. Eisenhower dropped the subject at once, and it was reported as the "one sour note of the conference."[54]

A much more characteristic route for the President was via prominent businessmen, industrialists, publishers and educators. They were often recipients of letters, many of them signed by the President, urging help for mutual security. Working through Harold Boeschenstein, the chairman and president of the Owens-Corning Fiberglas Corporation and an ex-chairman of the Business Advisory Council, Eisenhower used those tactics to secure authorizations in accordance with the Administration's proposals in 1957. But the efforts failed to prevent the mutual-security budget for fiscal 1958 from suffering the largest cuts on record. Eisenhower, acknowledging that Congress had then been in "such a budget cutting frame of mind," hoped that the recent Soviet launching of Sputnik, the first space satellite, "will have convinced a great many people that we cannot afford, at this stage, to neglect our friends in the free world."[55] To improve such attempts at enhancing Congressional attitudes toward foreign aid, the Administration later created a private and nominally independent organization that called itself the "Committee to Strengthen the Frontiers of Freedom." Begun in 1959 and headed by Vannevar Bush, the scientist, the group included such well-placed Democrats and Republicans as William Benton, James B. Conant, Gardner Cowles, Lewis Douglas, Thomas K. Finletter, Leonard K. Firestone, John Gardner, Samuel Goldwyn, W. Averell Harriman, Grayson L. Kirk, Henry R. Luce, Stanley Marcus, Daniel A. Poling, Mrs. Ogden Reid, Dean Rusk, David Sarnoff, Eustace Seligman, Spyros P. Skouras, Mrs. Arthur Hays Sulzberger, William H. Vanderbilt, Sidney Weinberg, William L. White and Henry M. Wriston. When, for example, the President wanted support for Mutual Security while he was going to his encounter with Khrushchev in Paris during May of 1960, he activated their very considerable letter-writing powers.[56] Defense Secretary Thomas Gates did his part as a member of the Cabinet by contacting 130

personal friends, mostly business leaders; and his efforts precipitated letters to the five hundred members of the National Security Industrial
Association, the seven hundred members of the Defense Orientation
Conference Association, plus vigorous lobbying efforts by the Association of the United States Army, the Navy League and the Air Force
Association. The major veterans groups, the Chamber of Commerce and
the AFL-CIO had already helped.[57] The massive effort, if not the decisive factor, certainly did not hurt. Although the President's appropriations request that year was about a billion dollars higher than in each of
the three previous years, the size of the cut, 9 percent, was the smallest
of his Presidency.[58]

Complementing mutual security as part of the nation's foreign economic policy was the stimulation of both foreign trade and American
investments abroad. The value of foreign markets was, of course, highly
appreciated by American localities needing outlets for local production.
In the spring of 1953 Governor Christian Herter of Massachusetts
sought Sinclair Weeks's aid in the expedition of a decision pending before the National Advisory Council on International Financial and Monetary Problems and the Export-Import Bank. His state's economic distress, the Governor pointed out, would be relieved by enabling the
Whitin Machines Works to export machinery to Brazil for making tex-
tiles. Any further delay, Herter feared, would cause the three Brazilian
textile firms that were involved to buy such machinery from Europe.[59]
The Eisenhower Administration, pointing to the need for reciprocity,
maintained that America could not be deprived of access to foreign
sources of copper, lead, zinc, natural rubber, nickel, manganese, crude
petroleum, iron ore and other supplies. Consequently, Congress was informed that "Communist expansion into new areas of the free world
would not only strike at American economic health but would also add
enormously to the military and economic potential of the aggressor."[60]
Encouraging corporate investments throughout the world was a means
of exporting capital far more congenial to a conservative business administration than spending tax dollars. A high enough level in the right
places, with the resultant expansion of foreign economies, might end the
need for public funds. In an early memorandum to the President, Commerce Secretary Weeks expanded at length on the subject of stimulating
the flow of private investment abroad after pointing out that "it is evident that private enterprise and private finances, as well as government
as such, must play a major part in accomplishing the results."[61]

Yet, private enterprise as a basic arm of the nation's foreign economic
policy was not always the answer. In a number of regions, particularly
the underdeveloped countries, the American concept of free enterprise
had little meaning. Hence, the objective of "trade, not aid" hit some
snags. Aware that much public money was available from the United

States, private investments were occasionally suspect and regarded as less desirable.[62] Further, with the expansion of American businesses in foreign countries, by the end of the Eisenhower era domestic producers became concerned that an increasing number of imports were actually the products of overseas American-owned or controlled concerns.[63] In the view of two Cabinet members, John Foster Dulles and George Humphrey, there were other sides to the issue.

Dulles, the fortifier of international resistance against communism, and Humphrey, the businessman concerned with the soundness of investments and money, approached the subject with inevitable differences. In a meeting of the National Advisory Council on International Monetary and Financial Problems on September 30, 1953, Dulles was concerned about the loss of private investments in foreign countries because, as he pointed out, the days of dollar diplomacy were over. Underdeveloped countries, including the United States, had once been developed largely with private capital. Since the same interests were operating both the banks and the government, as in England, foreign policy sought to protect investments. Confiscations of such property were not easily tolerated by the imperial power, as they had not been by the United States in Central America and the Caribbean just before World War I. With current foreign policies unrelated to foreign investments, Dulles said, the added risk was discouraging needed amounts of capital. Losing such money carried the danger of economic chaos with a high risk of communism as a result. The lack of an agency to make political and soft loans on a long-term basis could lose South America to the free world. To Humphrey's reply that a bank can only run on sound banking principles, Dulles's response was "It would be good banking to put South America through the wringer, but it will come out red." Both Dulles and Humphrey, however, dissented from the observation of William McChesney Martin, the chairman of the Federal Reserve Board, that a rigid curtailment of political loans by the government would induce private capital to take up the slack within six months.[64]

As part of the Mutual Security Act of 1957, President Eisenhower got through Congress the Development Loan Fund to promote long-term economic growth in underdeveloped areas as a means of financing "specific projects and programs which give promise of contributing to sound development. This Fund," Eisenhower's message added, "would be used not for short-term emergency requirements but for economic development of long-term benefit to the borrowing country."[65]

The Administration's belief in freer trade was in harmony with most large industrialists and financiers. When seventy-six businessmen were polled at The Links on June 4, 1953, only one said tariffs should be increased. Thirty-four thought they should be left where they were, and a majority, forty-two, were for a general lowering from present levels.[66]

Among the five hundred importers, exporters, representatives of manu-facturing and shipping concerns, and wholesalers and retailers interested in foreign trade, three-fourths expressed a preference for reductions by supporting an informal resolution that also called for the removal of barriers to foreign trade.[67] Industrialist George W. Sloan, advising Eisenhower to reject a higher rate of protection for imported briar pipes, feared that the move "would be interpreted in Western Europe and in other parts of the free world as reflecting a high protectionist attitude on the part of the new administration."[68] Although the United States Tariff Commission recommended the increase, the President blocked it, as he did later when the commission favored limiting wool imports.

The man who ultimately became the businessman most representative of Eisenhower's views toward trade, as well as on the general subject of foreign economic policy, was Clarence Randall, who headed the giant Inland Steel Company. Randall had become familiar with European eco-nomic affairs when Paul Hoffman made him consultant to Averell Har-riman for the administration of the Marshall Plan. He had been trained as a lawyer and was an articulate spokesman as well as a facile writer. The common comparison of Randall with Wendell Willkie was furthered when Randall challenged President Truman's seizure of the strike-bound steel industry by charging that the act was "without the slightest shadow of legal right." The Supreme Court later agreed.

Eisenhower's decision, in the summer of 1953, to establish a commis-sion to study foreign economic policy prompted both Sinclair Weeks and George Humphrey to recommend Randall as its chairman. Dulles, fearing that a major industrialist would be a reactionary trade protec-tionist, was a temporary obstacle to his appointment. To relieve the Secretary of State's fears, Weeks suggested a look at Randall's book, *A Creed for Free Enterprise*, which had been published in 1952. Dulles satisfied himself by reading the chapter on businessmen and foreign pol-icy, which declared, "Once we adopt the hypothesis that American aid to Europe is justified for no other purpose than to advance American security, much that has been confused in our thinking can be cleared up." The importance of trade was also stressed. The steel industry, Ran-dall pointed out, had received much manganese and chrome from Russia and alternative sources had not been easy to find.[69]

The report of Randall's commission became the basic foundation for the Administration's foreign economic policy. It recommended a three-year extension of the Reciprocal Trade Agreements Act, which had already been given an additional year during the first session of the Eighty-third Congress, and granting the President authority to reduce current tariffs by 5 percent a year and to lower to 50 percent of the value of the commodity all rates in excess of that figure.[70] That became the heart of the three-year extension the President obtained in 1955. In 1958 reciprocity was renewed for four additional years. That year Eisenhower and Khrushchev exchanged letters on the possibility of increasing U.S.–Soviet trade.[71]

Nevertheless, protectionists and those who feared that freer trade was aiding Communist nations kept Eisenhower from realizing important commercial objectives. In 1954 Republicans Dan Reed and Richard Simpson, a Congressman from Pennsylvania, who had been dissenting members of the Randall Commission, thwarted the President's attempt to get a long-term extension. Simpson also made persistent moves to attach quotas on the importation of petroleum. Efforts to protect lead and zinc induced Eisenhower finally to agree to a system of subsidies for the mining industry, at the estimated first-year cost of $161 million. When the Administration made repeated efforts to have the nation join the Organization for Trade Cooperation, which had been established in Geneva in 1955 to administer the General Agreement of Tariffs and Trade, two weeks of hearings before the House Ways and Means Committee resulted in a minority report by seven Republican members charging that it would transfer Congressional control over foreign commerce to a "permanent international bureaucracy susceptible to use as a powerful propaganda agency directed against the essential protection of U. S. industry."[72] That helped to kill all hopes of American membership. As he continued to ask for liberalized trade, the President, characteristically, compromised. Thus, he appeased the protectionists in 1958 by agreeing to accept authorization to also *raise* tariff rates up to 50 percent above their 1934 level.

Suggestions that liberalized trade policies would be used to aid Communist countries and, in particular, to open commercial relations with Communist China continued to plague the Administration. Walter Robertson, the Assistant Secretary of State for Far Eastern Affairs and a vigorous supporter of Chiang Kai-shek, advised that trade policies involving removal of the embargo on doing business with the Peking regime might be considered as a long step in the direction of recognition and the seating of Communist China in the United Nations.[73] There were those who also suggested that talk about liberalizing trade with Communist nations was unpatriotic. William G. Sullivan, chief of the research section of the FBI's domestic intelligence division, addressed the Sixth Military Industrial Conference in April of 1960 and advised American businessmen to relinquish thoughts of profitable trade with the Soviet Union and thus avoid becoming pawns of Communist ideology. Referring to the overtures that Khrushchev had been making toward America for increased trade since his exchange of letters with Eisenhower during the summer of 1958, the FBI man said that it was "clearly an attempt to appeal to American business leaders over the heads of our government officials." Clarence Randall read the Chicago *Daily News* account of the Sullivan speech and sent an angry letter to FBI director J. Edgar Hoover. Pointing out that increasing American exports to relieve the nation's balance-of-payments problem would be aided by orderly "trade in peaceful goods with the Russians," Randall, by then a special assistant to the President for foreign economic policy, added that "the reason why our exports to Russia do not increase is the psychological barrier existing in the minds of businessmen that to engage in such trade is unpatriotic, and I have the feeling that what happened in Chicago may make our task more difficult. Coming from the FBI, it will be taken as complete gospel."[74]

Dulles, meanwhile, continued to wage the battle as he understood the requirements of mobilizing the "free world" against the immoral enemy. He was present in Bermuda with Eisenhower when the Big Three leaders finally met. That was in early December of 1953. Eisenhower, having been persuaded that going to the island with his golf clubs could become embarrassing since so many at home were already criticizing his frequent and highly publicized outings to Burning Tree and Augusta, left his clubs in Washington. The British had taken care to determine whether Ike planned to arrive equipped for golf before making the sport taboo for their delegation; and Sir Winston even came without his paints.[75] Fortunately, their foreign ministers were there to do the work. With the Russians having preceded the conference by proposing a five-power meeting to be held in Berlin, Dulles's determination to persuade the allies that Soviet objectives were primarily directed toward blocking EDC was the most important thing about the sessions at Tucker's Town. The British maintained that until the French did something concrete about EDC they could make no further commitment. Additionally, the French received English and American recognition of their Indochina war as of "vital importance" to the "defense of the free world" and agreed that Ho Chi Minh's offer to negotiate a solution should be rejected.[76] As for the Soviet call for a five-power meeting, their final communiqué said that "our hope is that this meeting will make progress towards the unification of Germany in freedom and the conclusion of an Austrian State Treaty and thus towards the solution of other major international problems."[77]

Less than two weeks later, on December 14, Dulles unleashed one of his most sensational bombs. Speaking in Paris before a session of the NATO Council, with the implicit support of American economic and political power, he warned that the failure to achieve a European Defense Community, thus maintaining the French–German schism, would create "grave doubt whether continental Europe can remain a place of safety." As far as his own country, he then said carefully, with a deliberate choice of words, "That would compel an agonizing reappraisal of basic

United States policy."[78] What he had been unable to achieve through negotiations he thus attempted by threatening withdrawal of American and military support for Western Europe.

As Dulles completely anticipated, the reaction was fierce. Several French cabinet ministers called his words "brutal," and others were indignant that, as a visitor to their country, he had been so rude. Yet, even *Le Monde*, a paper that was usually critical of American policy, went beyond attacking the wisdom of Dulles's language to find justification for his attitude. And Paul Reynaud, the Vice Premier, told a secret session of the cabinet that Dulles's admonition had been fully warranted. The Belgian foreign minister agreed that it was "time for a yes or no answer on European unity." The British felt that Dulles had taken a calculated risk.[79] Some have estimated that Dulles's speech may have cost EDC less than a handful of votes in the National Assembly, but there is no way to substantiate the notion that the 319–264 vote that killed EDC in August of 1954 had been conditioned by his bold threat.

A remarkable consequence of the death of EDC was the early restoration of West Germany's full sovereignty and the admission of the Bonn government as an equal partner in the defense of Western Europe. Acting on Anthony Eden's suggestion, the Brussels Treaty of 1948, which had provided for the mutual defense of five nations against a remilitarized Germany, was revised and expanded to create a Western European Union. In agreements signed in Paris and London during October, the occupation of West Germany was ended. The newly independent nation was expected to contribute twelve divisions, 1,300 tactical aircraft and some naval vessels to NATO.[80] With the super-national force originally conceived for EDC no longer a factor, England was free to join the Western European Union; and with the addition of Italy to the Brussels Treaty nations, all the powers that had signed the EDC treaty of 1952 were included. Even before the final French rejection of EDC, the American Senate had approved, by a unanimous vote, a resolution expressing its wish that the President should "take such steps as he deems appropriate . . . to restore sovereignty to Germany and to enable her to contribute to the maintenance of international peace and security."[81] Eisenhower's memoirs recall his agreement with Dulles "that the accomplishment of the transformation was a 'near miracle—a shining chapter in history.' "[82]

Instead of retreating, the United States had found a way of enforcing its military presence in Europe. Ironically, it was through the instrument of NATO, the containment organization created by Truman and Acheson. Similar continuity was achieved through the foreign economic policies. Both the military and economic means were not a denial of containment, but rather a refurbishment.

CHAPTER 28

Ike and the Nationalists

Aт мидмоrning on the tenth of June, the President's Lockheed Constellation lifted out of Washington toward the upper Midwest and the start of a five-day speaking tour. Four hours and twenty-four minutes later, the luxurious transport reached the Wold-Chamberlin Airport at Minneapolis. Ahead lay worshiping crowds, not only those certain to be brought out by efficient local Republican organizations but throngs of ordinary citizens eager for a glimpse of the popular President. As though to substantiate the obvious, the Gallup Poll was reporting that three-fourths of the public liked having him in the White House. The 67 percent that had approved in March had actually climbed seven points by April and was still at that level as he began his journey. Even more emphatic was the Gallup finding released on June 3 showing only one in six critical of his record.[1] And the cheering at the airport provided additional evidence that, although the Korean war was still very much alive and some of the most vigorous fighting was going on, Americans had confidence that their General in the White House would restore peace and tranquillity.

Some were already noting that the golf-playing President, with a staff system that was preventing the White House from becoming his prison, seemed eager to get away from 1600 Pennsylvania Avenue, not only to the links at Burning Tree in Washington, but during less than five months he had vacationed twice at the Augusta National Golf Club, played at Norfolk and Annapolis after speech-making trips to both areas and had gone fishing in Pennsylvania as the weekend guest of Dr. Milton Eisenhower at State College. Staff members ultimately cited the efficiency of the White House team that enabled the Chief Executive to spare both his health and energies for crucial decisions. Thus, in addition to his golf forays, he was able to participate in other delights, such as the camaraderie with good friends around the bridge table or the stag dinners that he enjoyed so much and, one of the best Eisenhower pastimes, cooking various concoctions while working with an apron tied around his waist. He was never happier than the day he personally barbecued, over an outdoor grill at Sinclair Weeks's rural retreat in northern New Hampshire, thirty prime steaks that had been flown to the farm with the compliments of the Omaha Chamber of Commerce.[2] Many suspected that he was happiest away from 1600 Pennsylvania Avenue, but not even the most assiduous President-watchers could deny the legitimacy of a speaking-trip to the hinterlands. Greater public visibility, particularly in the heart of the nation, could be combined with helping to raise money and spirits for loyal party followers, as in his scheduled address at the annual convention of the National Young Republican Organization at the Mount Rushmore National Monument.

Shortly after he had left the airplane, while smiling for the photographers, he heard the latest news from Washington. A reporter informed the President that Senator Taft had turned over his functions as the party's Majority Leader to William Knowland. "I'm very sorry," replied the not too surprised President. "I hadn't heard a word about it." Then a telegram confirmed the story. An announcement released under the name of I. Jack Martin, Taft's administrative assistant, reported that his doctors had advised that his hip condition was "a serious one." It would enable him to continue his work in the Senate but would "prevent his being active as floor leader during the balance of the session."[3] At the end of his speech before the National Junior Chamber of Commerce that afternoon in Municipal Auditorium, where he had received a tumultuous greeting from more than eight thousand delegates, the President noted the development. He told them that he just sent a telegram "saying that as he well knew, that we could not spare such patriotic and devoted service as his, and sent him our prayers for his early recovery."[4]

But the President had already known what even Taft's calculated optimism was failing to hide. In April, while golfing with Eisenhower in Augusta, Taft had mentioned a persistent hip pain. The discomfort continued. The Senator finally entered Walter Reed Hospital, and there, on the twenty-third of May, he learned about his cancer. The President's physician, General Howard Snyder, informed Eisenhower. To the world, however, Taft continued to insist that he only had a "hip lesion." When pressed for a definition of "lesion," he told reporters that the doctors had merely indicated something was wrong with his hip. It was not, he said, fully diagnosed.[5] After leaving Walter Reed he had checked into the Holmes Memorial Hospital in Cincinnati and had emerged a few days later on crutches. Returning to Washington one week before the President's flight to Minneapolis, he appeared drawn and superficially more mellow than the old "Mr. Republican" had ever been. When he visited the White House and tossed his crutches aside while resting in the outer office, President Eisenhower spared the Senator a trip to the Oval Room by meeting him there.

Replacing Taft with Knowland was also a distressing thought. Even more important than the President's thin edge in both houses of Congress and his inability to get much done without Democratic assistance was the fact that of the forty-eight Republican Senators, only thirteen could be counted as ardent supporters of the Administration's foreign policies; and although Taft had been making sounds distressingly close to the dozen or so "Asia Firsters," his demonstrated influence, experience and desire to place party accomplishment above any factional advantage had made him essential. His standing with the President had also been increasing. When, for example, Eisenhower appointed his new chairman of the Joint Chiefs of Staff, the choice of Admiral Arthur Radford, a man strongly committed to reliance on nuclear weapons and known for his advocacy of strong air power, it was made to please Taft.[6] Taft had also chosen Knowland as his successor. Unhappily, where Taft had been a bridge to the party's extremists, Knowland often echoed them. To many, in fact, he had become known as "the Senator from Formosa."

Nevertheless, the President completed that five-day journey amid solid evidence of political strength. At the dedication ceremonies of Garrison Dam, near the center of sparsely populated North Dakota, there were ten thousand people waiting to cheer him. Most, obviously, had traveled great distances. Crowds were also amazingly large in Rapid City, South Dakota; and, as the motorcade passed along the roads of the open plains, farm families gathered to wave enthusiastically. His "don't join the book burners" speech at Dartmouth, on the last day of the trip, drew prominent headlines and much praise from those who feared the unchecked power of Senator McCarthy.

Despite the changed Senate leadership, there was another reason for political optimism. The Korean war, which had been waged since June of 1950 and had been the source of so many animosities, at last looked as though it could actually end within weeks, if not days. The diplomatic stalemate that had discontinued the negotiations in Panmunjom since last October had finally been resolved. United Nations Commander General Mark Clark's letter of February 22 to North Korean Premier Kim Il Sung suggesting that the two sides exchange their sick and wounded prisoners of war had resulted in a reply on March 28 that not only found the American proposal acceptable but actually stated the hope that the move might "lead to the smooth settlement of the entire question of prisoners of war."[7]

Whether or not the response was connected with the recent death of Stalin and the general Communist peace offensive was not clear. There could be no question, though, that it marked a softening of the position taken by the Communists in November when they had rejected Indian Prime Minister Nehru's compromise solution to settle the issue of repatriating prisoners of war. That attempt to end the fighting, which was approved by the United Nations General Assembly after agreement from Secretary of State Dean Acheson, had stipulated that "force shall not be used against prisoners of war to prevent or effect their return to their homelands." It also provided for a neutral-nations repatriation commission to return all POWs, since the UN had discovered that about half of the Korean prisoners and some 80 percent of the Chinese were unwilling to return to Communist control. According to the Indian resolution any POWs still unrepatriated after a ninety-day period following an armistice would be handled by a postwar political conference.[8] An immediate consequence of the termination of the impasse was operation "Little Switch," the first exchange of soldiers. That began on April 20.

Then, after plenary talks resumed on April 26, the United Nations negotiating team rejected a Communist plan that would have assigned all prisoners not desiring repatriation to be sent out of Korea to a neutral nation. They would, in effect, then be incarcerated a minimum of nine months after the end of the fighting while agents were permitted to persuade them to change their minds. A new Communist plan then called for giving custody over the POWs to a five-nation neutral repatriation commission consisting of India, Poland, Switzerland, Czechoslavakia and Sweden. The period during which the POWs would be exposed to the agents was cut by two months and the operation located inside Korea. But the proposal was, nevertheless, rejected by the United Nations command for its failure to guarantee eventual civilian status and freedom for the repatriates, and a counter-proposal was advanced. That made a distinction between the Chinese and the Korean soldiers. The Koreans would be released as civilians with the signing of the armistice, but the Chinese would be placed under the jurisdiction of a neutral-nations repatriation commission. Instead of a cumbersome five-nations custody, the commission's decisions would be supervised by Indian forces and an Indian chairman. All non-repatriates would be given civilian status and freedom after sixty days. The North Korean rejection of that plan threatened to end the negotiations once more.

However, on May 23, General Clark received new instructions. They called for turning all the POWs over to the commission and allowing a ninety- or 120-day period during which the non-repatriates could be convinced to return home. After that, the men would either be given civilian status or their futures decided by the General Assembly of the United Nations.[9] Clark was also told to accept a voting plan for the commission that would decide all disputes by a simple majority. That defied the skeptics who feared that India's Chinese Communist-inclined "neutrality" would give the Reds a three-to-two voting edge. Then, as Clark later reported, if they rejected that "final offer" and made no constructive counter-proposal, "I was authorized to *break off* the truce talks rather than to recess them, and to carry on the war in new ways never yet tried in Korea." On June 4 a real breakthrough resulted with the Communist acceptance with only minor changes of the United Nations command's POW plan. Two days before Eisenhower's trip to the Midwest the detailed arrangements providing for the role each side would play in the disposition of the POWs were signed, and General Clark informed Washington that an armistice was possible as early as June 18.[10]

The President, then, toured the Midwest, New England and New York with virtual assurance that his promise and great determination to end the war was on the verge of fulfillment. Eisenhower had maneuvered the strategy toward peace, so ardently, in fact, that General Clark found that "the Republicans were ready to go further than the Democrats to achieve a truce."[11] His April 16 speech to the newspaper editors calling for the "immediate cessation of hostilities" in Korea had not pleased his Secretary of State. Mr. Dulles, characteristically expressing his disagreement more freely to others than to the President, was asked by Emmet Hughes whether the United States would be glad or sorry to have the Communists suddenly accept the Indian POW compromise for a settlement. "We'd be sorry," Dulles had said. *"I don't think we can get much out of a Korean settlement until we have shown—before all Asia— our clear superiority by giving the Chinese one hell of a licking."*[12] Another member of the Administration has reported that Dulles had also preferred to make any Korean settlement conditional on a prior or simultaneous end to the Indochinese war or, in other words, part of a general solution to the problems in the Far East. On March 24 the Secretary told an Advertising Council conference that "Korea and Indochina are two flanks" and that no satisfactory peace could be achieved as long as forces can be freely shifted from one to the other. He also believed the Administration could not discard the possibility of a Chiang Kai-shek return to the Chinese mainland. On April 3, one day after the President had told a press conference that the United States welcomed "every honest advance, and in this instance, for example, had been trying to arrange this for a long, long time," Dulles took a decidedly harder line by stressing that, despite the Soviet "peace moves," there were dangers to a truce. He also took that opportunity to point out that nothing that had happened justified any relaxation of defense against Communist aggression.[13] Their differences seemed plain.

With Dulles, however, Eisenhower had planned a strategy that later became known as "brinksmanship," to inform the other side of a readiness to use full military power to promote compliance with American demands. Thus accepting a plan remarkably close to what MacArthur had advocated in December, the Administration devised means of going on the offensive in Korea and also unleashing a three-pronged attack against China and, specifically, hitting the Red-held mainland with atomic bombs.[14]

The important step involved relaying the atomic threat to the other side. Eisenhower felt that he had but two choices on how a solution could be achieved and feared that the use of all-out force to unify Korea might involve, as Truman had thought, World War III. He was confident that the Communists would prefer peace. Moreover, brandishing force would minimize bargaining-table concessions. As it was, he was preparing to end the war along the same demarcation line that so many Republicans, including Taft, were considering proof of an unwillingness to win. Even his great prestige might not survive anything less than that; and the POW issue appeared to most Americans a moral responsibility. They wanted no repetition of the World War II forcible repatriation by the Americans to Russia of prisoners who had been captured by the Germans. Therefore, when Dulles and Stassen visited Nehru for two days in May, they told the Indian Prime Minister what the United States was prepared to do if the Chinese attempted to gain a military advantage by using masses of troops to drive the UN forces off the Korean peninsula. Very clearly and very deliberately he advanced the possibility of an atomic bombing of China.[15] As Dulles and Eisenhower had anticipated, the not-so-subtle warning was passed on to Peking by the Indian ambassador, K. M. Panikkar. And General Clark got his orders.

But Syngman Rhee, the seventy-eight-year-old Harvard and Princeton-educated President of South Korea, was a committed nationalist with a very different view of the situation. When he assumed leadership in 1948 his desire to pursue his lifelong goal was as great as the authoritarian powers he wielded against dissenters. Korea had been subjugated by Japan since the Sino-Japanese War of 1894–95 and formally annexed by the Empire in 1910. Nine years later, Rhee became the head of a government in exile that was based in Shanghai with the goal of working for Korean liberation. At the Cairo Conference in 1943, both Roosevelt and Churchill agreed that, "in due course," Korea should become independent. At Yalta, Roosevelt told Stalin that a twenty-five-year trusteeship status for Korea, possibly limited to the United States, China and Russia, was necessary to prepare the country for self-rule. Stalin suggested that only five years would be necessary.[16] Rhee, however, wanted immediate full independence with the ouster of the hated Japanese; but when the Russians entered the war in the Far East as a result of the arrangements made at Yalta and their troops moved into the peninsula from Manchuria just before the Japanese surrender, the Communists were arbitrarily given control of the area above the Thirty-eighth Parallel. Thus, the industrial north was separated from the agricultural south, a division that was sealed by the intensification of the cold war. In 1948 Rhee became President of South Korea, which never accepted the split. His dream of an independent country was only half realized. So his objective was clear: The war must not be stopped along the parallel but pursued to the Yalu River, which separated Korea from Manchuria, and thus rectify an outrage. The intensity of his nationalism was so complete, General Clark discovered, that during the POW negotiations he was indifferent about the fate of Chinese soldiers who refused repatriation but was "sensitive to any tampering with Korean POWs who refused to return to North Korea."[17]

The solution so ardently desired by Eisenhower had to be sold to Rhee. Greatly increasing Rhee's bargaining strength vis-à-vis the United States was that two-thirds of the battle line was controlled by his troops; he could, at any time, upset a truce by starting a drive to the North. He could also provoke an attack by the Communists, which would force American assistance. Moreover, South Korean troops had control of the prisoner compounds, which the United Nations command did not have the troops to man with any semblance of security.[18] Since negotiations had started for "Little Switch," the South Korean position had been vehement. Obedient mobs, distressed as they were about the continuing war, nevertheless demonstrated in the streets of Seoul, as they had when Eisenhower had visited the capital city, against any truce without unification. There could be no truce, Rhee had also warned, unless Chinese troops left all of Korea. In late May, after Eisenhower had sent Clark what became the UN plan, Rhee complained that it had been shown to them just one hour before being transmitted to the Communists. They also threatened to withdraw South Korean troops from the United Nations command and prevent armed guards from any neutral-nations repatriation commission from entering the country. On the thirtieth, Rhee wrote to the American President requesting a United States–South Korean military defense pact or authorization for his government to continue the war alone. Unification was still the American goal, Eisenhower replied one week later, but declared that we "would not be justified in prolonging the war with all the misery it involves in the hope of achieving by force, the unification of Korea." The cessation of hostilities not only would continue that objective but would also be followed not by the kind of military agreement Rhee sought but by a mutual-defense treaty similar to the arrangement with the Philippines and the ANZUS pact with Australia and New Zealand. There would also be economic aid to permit a peaceful restoration of Korea.[19] But the June 8 signing of the Terms of Agreement on the POW exchange sent one hundred thousand South Koreans into the streets in a massive demonstration demanding a march to the North; and, while Rhee was rejecting the Eisenhower reply, his Assembly spurned the truce by a vote of 129–0.[20] Convincing Rhee that any attempt to continue the war would be suicidal had obviously become more sensitive than obtaining an arrangement with the Communists. Unfortunately for Eisenhower, no South Korean version of an atomic threat was possible.

Equally unpleasant was Eisenhower's need to cope with American opponents of his kind of peace. They represented dominant attitudes within the GOP. There were the conservative moralists who, like Ralph Flanders of Vermont, wanted peace sufficiently to work fervently for disarmament but who, at the same time, insisted that there could be no retreat "at the point of a gun" and that ignoring victims of aggression was un-Christian. The Knowlands were more emphatically dedicated "Asia Firsters" to whom American overcommitment to Europe had ignored the continent where the real battle against communism would ultimately have to be fought. Then there were the Tafts, who had, throughout the war, wavered between the logic of avoiding military involvements and the logic of completing such action once undertaken.

Flanders was virtually the stereotype of New England conservative individualism, whose temperament and inclinations were not too remote from the progressives of his youth, William Jennings Bryan, Albert Beveridege, Robert LaFollette and Woodrow Wilson. A successful mechanical engineer who contributed many publications to a profession he never really left, the seventy-two-year-old Senator's political views defied simplistic classifications—except idealism. His interest in disarmament as the best hope for peace, which had made him back the Eisenhower Presidency, later resulted in a book, *Letter to a Generation.* His attitude was expressed to Paul Hoffman when he wrote, "We must align ourselves honestly with moral forces and *draw* the neutral world into support instead of trying to *scare* them into support of our position in a contest for power."[21] Ultimately, he would best be remembered for a speech on the Senate floor denouncing Joe McCarthy. That was in 1954. But his contempt for the Wisconsin terrorist had been of long-standing and his explanation of McCarthyism was unorthodox. "McCarthy would never have had any influence," Flanders explained in 1951, "had it not been for the fact that our late, departed saint, Franklin Delano Roosevelt, was soft as taffy on the subject of Communism and Uncle Joe [Stalin]."[22] Nevertheless, while Truman was President and Stalin still reigned, Flanders suggested the appointment of Dr. Ralph Bunche as ambassador to the Soviet Union. Entirely consistent with his mission of protecting Christian values was his charter membership in the Committee of One Hundred that crusaded against admitting Communist China to the United Nations. He was in complete agreement with ex-ambassador Joseph Grew, who wrote to Mrs. Flanders about the need to maintain that position despite "a vociferous but unenlightened minority which thinks chiefly in terms of the dollar."[23]

The Korean war was, to Flanders, very much of a moral issue. He had held that the American mission was to restore all of the peninsula as a freely elected democratic people. Any armistice perpetuating the division would obviate an "opportunity for obtaining a humane solution" and cannot be "a step toward peace." He told the Senate, on July 1, 1953, that it "was with sickness of heart that we heard anew the proud boast that we had successfully 'resisted aggression' as if the loss of hundreds of thousands of lives and billions of dollars had been well spent in bringing us back to the starting ground of June 25, 1950." Our actions must be "right policies, righteous policies"; any compromises would scuttle the Korean people.[24] Having already proposed aiding a Chinese Nationalist invasion of the mainland to detract from the enemy strength in Korea, Flanders met with Eisenhower in the White House and pressed his plan for a satisfactory end to the war. After sweeping the Reds out of the North, the political unification of the country could be preserved by creating a neutral zone along the Yalu River and the Siberian frontier. Economic rehabilitation should then be promoted.[25]

Although Flanders had pressed his ideas continuously and openly, the President chose to ignore them. Eisenhower heard them personally from the Senator in the White House. Yet, on May 14, when asked to comment on the Senator's solution, Ike reacted at a news conference as though they had been offered on a confidential basis and added that "I find nothing that is different in them from what most of us are working toward, and there is nothing sensational about them."[26] A disturbed Flanders heatedly denied any secrecy and, on May 20 and July 1, he repeated his peace plan on the Senate floor. "There are standards set up by our Bible and by the Declaration of Independence," he reminded the President, "to which we cannot be false."[27] And Eisenhower's attempt to placate the New Englander assured him ambiguously that "Our peace objectives have in no sense been shelved. I could not agree more with your statement that there are certain standards set up by the Bible and our Declaration of Independence to which we must adhere."[28]

While Flanders's sentiments about the American mission in Korea expressed the feelings of most Republican Senators as well as many Democrats[29] and had come from a distinctly "American grain" type, they were not as important as those of Knowland, the newly installed Acting Majority Leader. Knowland was also much more militant. Having become closely identified as the China lobby's chief spokesman in the Senate, he was a firm advocate of overturning the Chou En-lai government and repelling Communist gains throughout Asia. His desire to unify Korea accepted the risk of war with the Soviet Union. Where Flanders talked in terms of a neutral zone that would assure the other side of our peaceful intentions, Knowland said that our military unification of Korea should be accompanied by having the UN brand Russia as "a supporter of aggression." After having accused Great Britain of "urging a Far Eastern Munich" upon the United States and coupling that with a willingness to "go it alone" in the war, he said that, upon the failure of truce negotiations, the war should be expanded even if it brought Russian intervention.[30] Suddenly, however, two days before Taft's announcement that Knowland would take his place temporarily, the Senator from California startled Washington. He delivered a speech warning Rhee against upsetting the truce that had seemed imminent on June 8. Furthermore, after conferences with Eisenhower to discuss the armistice program, he decided that ending the war in that manner was preferable to continuing a stalemate. It seemed as though Taft had not only chosen his successor but had tempered him. Knowland's course, in his new position, finally maneuvered halfway between Eisenhower's and Rhee's; he could not, however, help being pulled toward Seoul.

Taft had moved from an early view that began by questioning Truman's authority to commit American forces in Korea unilaterally and, in January of 1951, by calling for outright withdrawal from the peninsula, to acceptance of MacArthur's plan for bombing China, as well as blockading the Red mainland and using Chiang Kai-shek's forces.[31] Like Flanders, he also favored an invasion of the southern part of China to divert the enemy's Korean deployment. By the spring of 1953, about the time his illness was becoming apparent, his general view was close to the Dulles's, but his position as Majority Leader permitted more freedom than the Secretary of State could enjoy. So he openly depreciated the feasibility of any truce that simply ended the war along the battle line. Fighting could be resumed momentarily, he pointed out. Moreover, to Taft it made little sense to turn off the war near the Thirty-eighth Parallel without settling all the "questions of the Far East in one bite." Communists must be made to lay down arms in Malaya and Indochina as well. His view was clearly not only close to Dulles's but also congenial to most Republicans.[32]

The biggest shock from the Majority Leader, however, came after he had entered the Holmes Memorial Hospital. On May 26, during Taft's confinement, the President released a statement on the armistice negotiations at Panmunjom that followed the "final" UN offer that had been sent to General Clark. After specifically assuring adherence to the rights of those POWs not wishing repatriation and explaining that "our allies are in full accord" with those views, it included the report that "these principles accord also with the prevailing view of a representative bipartisan group of Senators and Congressmen who have been consulted."[33]

The hospitalized Senator had not seen the statement. That evening, in Cincinnati's Netherland Plaza Hotel, before about seven hundred guests at the silver anniversary of the National Conference of Christians and Jews, Taft's thirty-six-year-old son, Robert, Jr., read a speech written by his father while in the hospital. His words had not been shown to the White House. They constituted a throwback to the earlier Taft. "I think we may as well forget the United Nations as far as the Korean war is concerned," his son read. "We should do our best now to negotiate this truce, and if we fail, then let England and our other allies know that we are withdrawing from all further peace negotiations." He also advocated dispensing with any UN involvement in the Far East and leaving the United States with a "completely free hand." He feared that even the best truce obtainable would prove unsatisfactory and make the Korean division as permanent as Germany's. To those shocked by the readiness to dismiss the UN from participating in collective security, he pointed out that he was suggesting nothing that the United States had not already done in Europe through military support under the Truman Doctrine and by establishing NATO. They certainly had not included the UN.[34]

Newspapers immediately ran the story as "Taft Rift with Eisenhower." James Reston's New York *Times* account of their differences was called "Eisenhower-Taft split Bigger than the Men." "The President is a gardener who knows his limitations and believes in cultivating the soil," Reston wrote. "His trouble is that he is trying to lead a covey of mechanics through the wilderness, and being a very human man himself, he too suffers from the hangover of some habits that were more effective in the days of our isolation than they are today. He had been concentrating on the unity of his party rather than leading the country. He had been depending upon the benevolence of nature when a little pruning is indicated."[35] Most Republicans avoided the dispute. Taft later kept to his position but maintained he had not meant that the United States should follow a "go it alone" policy. He even found something good about a truce by saying that limiting American naval action and expendage of ammunition would save two billion dollars a year, an observation that was attacked by AFofL President George Meany, who called for a continued defense program even after a truce until the Russians called off the cold war.[36] Shocked UN delegates, recognizing that dissatisfaction with the Korean war had become the rallying cry for those Americans disillusioned with the world organization, were quick to note the strange similarity between American nationalists and Communist leaders.[37]

The difference, however, was not so much between the President and Taft. Taft, in a showdown, was usually amenable to the requirements of party harmony. It was, rather, the President's need to accept a truce that was more acceptable to Democrats than to Republicans and distasteful to nationalists of both parties. Representative Dewey Short urged the termination of truce talks until the Communists allowed international inspection of POW camps. The American Legion's National Executive Committee, at a convention in Indianapolis, demanded an all-out war in Korea "in the event of failure to reach a satisfactory peace." Senator McCarthy charged that the British sought to blackmail the United States into accepting a Communist peace by threatening to withdraw support. Let them "withdraw and be damned," he declared. H. Alexander Smith of New Jersey, the senior Republican member of the Senate Foreign Relations Committee, expressed his "complete opposition" to any truce that did not settle the prisoner issue first. The President was warned that possibly a dominant faction of the party would break with him if he agreed to what had been widely regarded in Congress as allied "demands" for a Korean settlement too responsive to Communist proposals. Representative Van Zandt of Pennsylvania said that the allies, particularly Great Britain, "prefer war profits drenched with the blood of American youth" to peace in Korea. The President, however, in making his "final offer" had positively rejected an uncompromising stand. His most loyal supporter in the Senate was Alexander Wiley, the Foreign Relations Committee chairman.[38]

Of further distress to the President that June, while Knowland was replacing Taft and he was negotiating to sell both Syngman Rhee and Americans a Korean truce that denied the possibility of a military victory, was the ease with which most people could be persuaded that continued American involvements with other countries, especially those arranged by secret executive agreements, could become greater dangers than Yalta. They could, many believed, subvert domestic constitutional guarantees for international expediencies.

Superficially that had seemed like a real possibility. Unlike the Articles of Confederation, individual states could not negotiate independently with foreign governments. To the President, "by and with the advice of the Senate," went the responsibility for such arrangements. Even more emphatic was the provision in Article VI terming treaties made "under the authority of the United States" the "supreme law of the land." The men so empowered, John Jay had assured in Federalist Paper Sixty-four, would be selected from an electoral system that would choose those most qualified for the role. Jay maintained that he must also be permitted to reach private understandings with other nations that would not be subjected to the process of requiring ratification by two-thirds of the states, since there were those "who would rely on the secrecy of the President, but who would not confide in that of the senate, and still less in that of a large popular assembly." Those who objected to domestic compliance with treaties were reminded of the legitimacy of powers exercised by the judiciary and the executive. Furthermore, Jay pointed out, the objectors "would do well to reflect that a treaty is only another name for a bargain; and that it would be impossible to find a nation who would make any bargain with us, which should be binding on them *absolutely*, but on us only so long and so far as we may think proper to be bound by it."[39] A 1920 Supreme Court decision written by Justice Oliver Wendell Holmes, in the case of *Missouri v. Holland*, upheld the state of Missouri's need to comply with a treaty with Great Britain designed to prevent the extermination of migrating birds that flew annually across Canada and the United States. Yet, for almost three decades after that decision there was little agitation about the matter.

But three years after the end of World War II, President Frank Holman of the American Bar Association began a crusade to save American domestic law, particularly the powers reserved to the states by the Tenth Amendment, from being subverted by internationalism. Holman wanted to amend the treaty-making provisions of the Constitution to protect the states from being governed by laws that could not have been passed by Congress and, further, to make executive agreements subject to the same limitations as treaties. Holman's fight was carried to the Senate by John Bricker.

Bricker, a commandingly handsome, white-haired former Governor of Ohio, first introduced a proposed amendment to the Eighty-second Congress. When the session was stopped by the election recess in 1952, with no action taken, Bricker reintroduced the amendment at the start of the Eighty-third Congress. Presented to the Senate on January 7, 1953, it carried the co-sponsorship of sixty-three other Senators, mostly conservatives and moderates and even a few liberals. Of greater significance to the Eisenhower Administration was its endorsement by forty-four of the forty-seven other Republicans. When Alexander Wiley became the Senate's most important opponent of the amendment, he found himself censured by his home-state Republicans in Wisconsin.[40] A majority of the delegates to a GOP women's rally in Chicago signed pro-Bricker petitions circulated by an organization called Vigilant Women for the Bricker Amendment. After hearings in the spring of 1953, the Judiciary Committee reported out an amendment that was, to many, more objectionable than the one first offered by Bricker.

Generally suspected as Holman's work and introduced by Arthur Watkins of Utah on February 16, the revised version carried the celebrated "which" clause. It declared that "a treaty shall become effective as internal law in the United States only through legislation which would be valid in the absence of a treaty." That led many to fear ratifying treaties would subsequently require approval from each of the forty-eight states, a most cumbersome process, and, moreover, the kind of arrangement that could become an effective deterrent to foreign nations' willingness to make agreements with the United States. Bricker, contending that that would only create a situation similar to what already existed in Canada, denied that interpretation.[41]

The Administration, feeling the overwhelming Republican sympathy with the treaty's objectives, felt that some concessions were necessary. Sherman Adams, for one, complained bitterly because he was under great pressure from the amendment's backers. Warnings were heard of a serious party split resulting from an uncompromising stand.[42] Remove the "which" clause, Bricker was told, and a bargain could be made. Eisenhower was ready to settle for a simple statement saying that no treaty could counter the Constitution. But when Bricker rejected the Administration's compromise draft, which was introduced by Knowland, the first session of the Eighty-third Congress ended without any action. With the President fearing any amendment restricting his conduct of foreign affairs as an attempt to express opposition to international responsibility, such as the stand Bricker had taken in opposition to the Status of Forces Agreements to facilitate NATO troop controls, and with Bricker unwilling to alter his basic position, both sides became more rigid. After much maneuvering and offering of substitutes, a revised version of the Bricker amendment received only fifty out of ninety-two votes cast, far from the required two-thirds majority. Republicans, however, favored it by twenty-nine to seventeen, but it drew only thirteen of the forty-five Democratic votes. Then they voted on a substitute measure offered by Walter George. While dropping the "which" clause, it subjected all international agreements to Senate ratification.[43] The Administration, fearing that its limitation of executive agreements could infringe on the President's war powers and his authority to extend recognition to foreign governments, remained opposed. Its defeat by one vote was made possible partly because Flanders, who had co-sponsored the original Bricker amendment, switched to the opposition on the final roll call.[44] Despite the continued efforts of the American Bar Association, particularly during the next two years, no similar amendment came to another vote.[45]

More significant than the complex maneuvering over phraseology and interpretation was the fact that the issue became, for articulate nationalists, the remedy for the dangers of postwar "un-American" involvements. Its implications far surpassed what might be done about Yalta. The hostility toward the United Nations, scorned additionally for the meager support given to American troops in Korea and for pressures to induce the United States to accept a "soft peace," had also organized the fears of conservatives and states'-righters. Holman, a Seattle lawyer, told a meeting of the Vigilant Women for the Bricker Amendment that his interest stemmed from fear that the rights of Americans could be violated by UN covenants.[46] Pat McCarran, when informed that the Senate would surely block any treaty that threatened to "revolutionize the relationship between the American people and their government," snapped back with "I'm not so sure of that. I voted for the United Nations and I will regret it as long as I live."[47] Bricker himself had introduced the amendment by pointing to the United Nations Covenant on Human Rights. Drafted under the chairmanship of Mrs. Eleanor Roosevelt, it called for an enlargement of governmental powers to provide for such "human rights" as "healthy development of the child," "environmental hygiene," the right of everyone to a job, fair wages, adequate housing, education and "a continuous improvement of living conditions," goals that *Time* magazine declared could be provided for everyone only by making the government "even more totalitarian than, say, the Soviet Union."[48] Bricker said that the covenant was "involved in the whole matter," but maintained that it was only one of the issues. The real need was "to prohibit the use of the treaty as an instrument of domestic legislation."[49] Southerners could agree with Bricker when reading that by ratifying the United Nations Charter, the members had pledged to promote "conditions of economic and social progress" and respect for rights "without distinction as to race." The well-known hate-artist Merwin K. Hart urged members of his National Economic Council to regard the amendment as a safeguard for all American rights. He warned that, without it, the United States could be victimized by the "International Socialists," who have recently *discovered that the Constitution can be amended by the process of ratifying treaties*, which have themselves been drawn up by our own internationalists and those of other countries." Citing the endorsed UN Genocide Convention, he pointed to the danger of a world Fair Employment Practices Commission. "Some force in the world is seeking to destroy America by merging her with other countries," Hart revealed. "The Bricker Amendment is intended to prevent our UN membership from interfering with our

Just before the U-2 incident and the abortive summit conference of 1960, Ike and Prime Minister Harold Macmillan of
Great Britain together at Camp David, Maryland.

The President with two architects of the GOP's immediate future, Senators Barry Goldwater
of Arizona (left) and Everett Dirksen of Illinois, only sixteen days before Ike left the
White House.

The oldest and the youngest Presidents meet as Ike prepares to step down when President-elect John F. Kennedy visits the White House on December 6, 1960.

The President and Sir Winston Churchill (right) visit John Foster Dulles at the Walter Reed Army Hospital on May 5, 1959. Nineteen days later the Secretary was dead.

The nation's foremost amateur tees off on May 27, 1959.

Ike the diplomat in an animated session with United Arab Republic President Nasser in New York City on September 26, 1960.

A study in solemnity: President Eisenhower and Soviet Premier Nikita Khrushchev during the playing of the American and Russian national anthems at Andrews Air Force Base near Washington on September 15, 1959.

The President and his second Secretary of State, Christian Herter, an arthritis victim, at Newport, Rhode Island.

Left to right, former President Harry S Truman, Adlai E. Stevenson, Averell Harriman and Senator Estes Kefauver close the Democratic convention on August 17, 1956, with a display of party unity in behalf of the Stevenson-Kefauver ticket.

Agitated by the outbreak of hostilities in the Middle East, President Eisenhower is flanked on the White House portico by Secretary of State Dulles (left) and Defense Secretary Wilson.

The President, characteristically solicitous toward Mamie, takes her arm after completing his election eve campaign speech on November 5, 195[ ] Looking on in the White House library are Vice President and Mrs. Nixon.

Ike confers in the White House in 1957 with (left to right) Secretary Dulles, Chancellor Conrad Adenauer and Foreign Minister Heinrich von Brentano, both of West Germany.

Eisenhower, the first President to make extensive use of the new medium, as seen by viewers while delivering to the nation a televised report on civil defense on June 15, 1955.

This cheerful view of the recuperating President at the Fitzsimons Army Hospital near Denver did much to calm national apprehensions and also mitigate a struggle for succession within the party.

Ike gives his seven-year-old grandson David a fishing lesson at Fraser, Colorado.

The President and his press secretary, Jim Hagerty, leave the Executive Office Building after a news conference.

After Egyptian seizure of the Suez Canal during the summer of 1956, Secretary of State Dulles (left) is shown during the first of his series of London meetings with Prime Minister Anthony Eden of Great Britain (right) and French Foreign Minister Christian Pineau.

Conferring shortly before the Army-McCarthy hearings began are (left to right) G. David Schine, Roy Cohn, Senator McCarthy and Senator John McClellan (D-Ark.).

The President at the National Airport in Washington in 1953 leaves to inspect the drought area. With him are (left to right) Defense Administrator Val Peterson, Agriculture Secretary Ezra Taft Benson and Lyndon Baines Johnson, of Texas, the Senate's Minority Leader.

Anti-Communists: (from left) Representative Harold Velde (R-Ill.), chairman, House Un-American Activities Committee; Senator William Jenner (R-Ind.), chairman, Senate Internal Security Subcommittee; and Senator Joseph R. McCarthy (R-Wis.), chairman, Senate's Permanent Investigating Committee.

In New York City to dedicate the Simon Baruch housing project in 1953, Ike extends a hearty handshake to financier Bernard Baruch, an ardent admirer of the General.

Former President Herbert Hoover looks on dubiously while a concerned Ike inspects the progress of a steak being barbecued at the Byers Peak Ranch, near Fraser, Colorado.

Three Cabinet appointees pose at the Commodore: (left to right) Postmaster General Arthur E. Summerfield, Secretary of the Treasury George M. Humphrey and Secretary of the Interior Douglas McKay.

Chief Justice Fred Vinson administers the oath of office to President Eisenhower on January 20, 1953.

The President confers with Secretary of State John Foster Dulles (left) and Mutual Security Administrator Harold E. Stassen after both members of the "team" had completed a seven-nation European tour during the early weeks of the Administration.

The President surrounded by his committee to study Defense Department reorganization. Left to right: (front) Dr. Vannevar Bush, David Sarnoff, Eisenhower, Nelson Rockefeller and Dr. Milton Eisenhower; (rear) Robert A. Lovett, Roger M. Kyes, General Omar Bradley, Charles E. Wilson, Arthur S. Flemming and Sherman Adams.

United for victory, Mamie Eisenhower and Senator Joseph
McCarthy enjoy Ike's campaign remarks in Milwaukee.

Governor and Mrs. Thomas E. Dewey (right) welcome the General and Mamie upon their
arrival in Albany, New York. Mrs. Eisenhower's mother, Mrs. John S. Doud, is at the extreme
left.

The General, fulfilling his campaign promise to visit Korea, watches some of President Syngman Rhee's soldiers on the firing range.

The President-elect at his Hotel Commodore headquarters in New York City with Secretary of Defense-designate Charles E. Wilson and his special counsel, Thomas E. Stephens (right).

At John Foster Dulles's home in New York City, Ike faces the press with General Douglas MacArthur, who has just advised the President-elect on how to end the Korean war.

Just back from Europe and campaigning for the nomination, General Eisenhower leaves the Columbia University Men's Faculty Club with Arthur Vandenberg, Jr. (left), and Senator Henry Cabot Lodge.

Eisenhower's convention floor manager, Governor Sherman Adams of New Hampshire (right), confers in Chicago with Governors Douglas McKay of Oregon (left) and Dan Thornton of Colorado.

The GOP's new ticket, Ike and Dick, at Chicago's Blackstone Hotel on July 12, 1952.

Ike and Senator Robert A. Taft pose after their celebrated Morningside Heights conference on September 12, 1952.

sovereignty and our domestic affairs. That is why the internationalists so frantically oppose it."[50] Bill Jenner was equally explicit. He charged that the Constitution was being subverted by a revolutionary group. The movement, according to his analysis, had been started by Harry Hopkins, Alger Hiss, Henry Wallace, Owen Lattimore, Harry Dexter White and others; and its chief agent was none other than ex-Secretary of State Dean Acheson.[51] Robert F. Kennedy, the younger brother of the new Senator from Massachusetts, sent a letter to the New York *Times* contending that Senate scrutiny would have improved the Yalta agreements; but a rebuttal that came from Harvard Professor Arthur Schlesinger, Jr., said that Kennedy's own point illustrated the futility of the amendment for such delicate negotiations.[52]

Many saw the issue as the most significant constitutional debate since FDR's attempt to pack the Supreme Court. Yet, despite all the noise from the interested, there is doubt that the arguments' fine points reached many people. As the disputes continued over the Bricker version, and the variations subsequently offered by a variety of people, particularly Watkins, Knowland, Homer Ferguson and George—and with some local and statewide law groups challenging the American Bar Association—most ordinary citizens were understandably confused. Senator Kenneth Keating of New York, who had earlier offered an amendment of his own, complained jocularly that he could not understand the Bricker amendment. When Gallup's pollsters tried to gauge public opinion, after the Administration and Bricker had reached their first deadlock, they were unable to submit a reliable estimate because the widespread ignorance of the issue had yielded an inadequate sampling.[53]

Much has been made about Eisenhower's lack of firm leadership during the battle which, Robert Donovan has reported, exhausted his patience more than most any other issue.[54] Arthur Krock, who was continuously suspecting that strong Eisenhower leadership was just around the corner, wrote that his willingness to exert stronger influence on the legislative process was being tested.[55]

In a real, if not technical sense, however, Eisenhower was a minority President who, as the battle over treaty-making showed, could get his way on many controversial issues only by fielding a coalition. Furthermore, Eisenhower's talents for conciliation through personal diplomacy seemed particularly vital at that time. Completely appeasing the advocates of constitutional changes was, for many reasons, out of the question; in his view, unyielding opposition from the President risked fragmenting the party. Even more important, perhaps, was his awareness that he was a political leader, and an astute one, whose popularity was largely based on belief that his patriotism would overcome any interest in political warfare. As he told an interviewer in 1964 when questioned about that fight, "I personally had to remember to regard public opinion, because public opinion in this country now became inflamed, to the point where they believed we were going to destroy the Constitution. And I said, 'All right, I'm ready to say that any treaty that violates the Constitution of the United States is null and void. I'll say that much.' " To those, such as lawyer John W. Davis, the Democratic party's 1924 Presidential candidate, who called for more adamant opposition, Eisenhower replied by agreeing to a compromise. "I cannot combat the almost hysterical attitude of so many people."[56]

So the exposure to battle scars was left largely to Dulles. The Secretary of State, who had been embarrassed by those who recalled a speech he had made in Louisville in April of 1952 warning that the treaty-making provisions could empower the President at the expense of the Congress and the states, was not as rigidly opposed to some limitations as many assumed. Bricker, for example, blamed the Secretary for creating Eisenhower's opposition.[57] Yet, although Dulles told the Judiciary Committee hearing that 165 years had offered no evidence that such Presidential powers had been abused, he never really abandoned the attitude he had expressed at Louisville. On January 2, 1953, he conceded to Sherman Adams that "a case can be made for *some* amendment to meet the theoretical possibility that the Executive might negotiate, the Senate might ratify and the Supreme Court might sustain a treaty to deprive the American citizens of their Constitutional rights under the Bill of Rights," but pointed out that the amendment currently at issue "would go far beyond this and might seriously impair the treaty-making power and the ability of the President to deal with current matters, notably U. S. troops abroad, etc. . . through administrative agreements. I think this whole matter needs to be more carefully studied before there is action."[58] More than anyone else, it was Dulles's counsel to the State Department, Herman Phleger, who kept the Secretary of State from accepting the Bricker amendment or its modifications.[59]

Eisenhower, lacking domestic political experience and legal training, quickly became conversant with the issues and plotted the strategy. He consulted, of course, with Dulles and Brownell. He read the Federalist Papers, particularly Jay's No. Sixty-Four; and he decided that weakening the Presidency would be a throwback to the Articles of Confederation, when the inability of the Congress to compel compliance with the peace treaty of 1783 in the matter of restoring confiscated Loyalist properties was used by the British to justify their own violations. In addition to John W. Davis, he requested advice from Judge John Parker, Princeton Professor Edward S. Corwin and Judge Orie Phillips, who favored limitations. "I had convictions of my own," Eisenhower told his interviewer, "and I became very certain that what they wanted to do in the famous 'which' clause would just put us back in the Confederation of 1783."[60] He personally worked over various proposed drafts, showing an ability that amazed Dulles. "Mr. President," said Dulles at the end of a three-and-a-half-hour session on the amendment, "you don't need a lawyer. You can handle this by yourself."[61] When Dulles submitted a requested memorandum on the arguments he would use at the Judiciary Committee hearings, Eisenhower advised against his telling a Congressional group that the Presidency would become subservient to Congress. After all, checking excessive executive powers was an important post-New Deal crusade, as was demonstrated by the adoption of the two-term amendment in 1951. It would be preferable, Eisenhower suggested, to stand on the importance of maintaining maneuverability in diplomacy and to argue that such freedom would be jeopardized. Another objection was to Dulles's plan to tell the hearing that revising the Constitution in that manner was not necessary with a Republican administration in power. If the Secretary believed, Eisenhower pointed out, that such restraint might be necessary for future Presidents, he should support Bricker.[62]

Characteristically, he employed his personality and political astuteness to keep all doors open. Thus he invited Bricker for several personal conferences, one at Dulles's home. Sherman Adams has written that the "warm and sympathetic tone of the talks gave Bricker the impression of more willingness to compromise than Eisenhower intended to give him."[63] Bricker emerged from the conference telling reporters that he and the President had the same objectives. A few weeks later, the same Wisconsin Republicans who had censured Senator Wiley for his vigorous opposition to the amendment lauded Eisenhower for "supporting the principle" of safeguarding constitutional rights.[64]

A masterful performer at his weekly press conferences, the President achieved his purpose adroitly. When first asked about it at his fourth session with the reporters, on March 19, 1953, he reacted as though he were virtually oblivious of the specifics of the issue. "I have to remember the old adage that a man has two ears and one tongue, and I therefore have tried to keep twice as still as I would in other places," he explained. "It is a highly argumentative point." Then he cast the amendment's supporters in a positive light by pointing out that they were not really trying to amend the Constitution but, instead, they were really trying to say, "we are going to make it impossible in the Constitution to break it." And while, he conceded, it might be anomalous to "amend it in order to show that it is going to remain the same," he reminded his listeners that constitutional amendments do not require a Presidential decision. The following week he continued his humility—and, at the same time, threw the onus on Dulles for opposing it—by saying that the amendment, "*as analyzed for me by the Secretary of State*, would, *as I understand it*, in certain ways restrict the authority that the President must have, if he is to conduct the foreign affairs of this Nation effectively."* While retaining charity toward his opponents, he said he feared the possible loss of flexibility needed by a President "in this highly complicated and difficult situation."[65]

Down to the end of the fight he continued to maintain a willingness to relieve apprehensions by agreeing to an amendment that would not upset the constitutional balance between the executive and the legislative branches but would not compromise "one single word" at the expense of altering the relationships—in effect, the façade of a concession.[66] After Bricker refused the final offer, his private reaction was that Frank Holman seemed determined to "save the United States from Eleanor Roosevelt."[67] When, a few days later, Joe Dodge sent the President a copy of Burke's *Reflections on the Revolution in France*, Eisenhower observed that it was a good time to "reread and restudy his [Burke's] philosophy of government." Then, referring to the English statesman, he asked, "Does he say anything about treaty-making functions?"[68]

His patience, however, had failed to place Republicans wholeheartedly on his side. Sixty-three percent of the party's Senators had supported the Bricker amendment, which suffered a one-sided defeat largely because of the Democratic opposition; and the inescapable fact was that the George substitute, which the Administration had rejected, had been stopped by just one vote. While the Democrats also found that less objectionable than the defeated version, and the party's Southerners followed their colleague from Georgia by voting for it in large numbers, among the Republicans alone the approval was thirty-two to fourteen. That represented almost 70 percent of the GOP in the Senate.

Much more upsetting, in view of the party divisions that Eisenhower needed to overcome, was the regional distribution of the fourteen who had voted with the President. Nine were from the Northeast. Joining them were two Border State Republicans, John Sherman Cooper of Kentucky and J. Glenn Beall of Maryland. That left just two others in the entire country, both from the upper Midwest, Edward Thye of Minnesota and Homer Ferguson of Michigan; and Ferguson's defeat for re-election in 1954 was generally attributed to his anti-Bricker position.

Few conflicts had shown a clearer distinction between the insular, largely small-town, rural and nationalistic wing of the party and those who, like the President, were committed to the idea that America's future could not be separated from the rest of the world. The new kind of isolationism, then, as the Korean truce debates were highlighting, was

* Author's italics.

less the Jeffersonian concept of avoiding "entangling alliances" and more of an arrogant indifference to how foreigners viewed the American superpower. Obtaining an armistice in the Far East, therefore, required overcoming both the American advocates of a military victory—who were, to a very great degree, the same forces that had pressed for the Bricker amendment—and President Rhee.

When the Terms of Agreement were signed at Panmunjom on June 8, the obstructions of the ROK government created the greatest concern. Attempting to placate the Korean President at a personal conference, Eisenhower invited him to the White House; but Rhee said he could not leave his country at that critical time and, in turn, suggested that Dulles visit Seoul. When the Secretary of State said he needed to remain in Washington, Assistant Secretary of State for Far Eastern Affairs Walter Robertson arranged to make the trip. But the morning after Rhee agreed to accept Robertson, a plan he had personally prepared with his provost marshal, Lieutenant General Won Yong Duk suddenly challenged both the American and Communist desires to end the war.

On the eighteenth of June the limited number of Americans on hand were helpless as Rhee's guards opened the stockades. The prisoners, both Chinese and North Korean, were fully prepared and fled the compounds, disappearing throughout the countryside, where they were housed and received as heroes by the populace. During the next few days, twenty-seven thousand were released from prisons all over South Korea. Fewer than seven hundred were ever recaptured, and Rhee admitted full responsibility for the act.[69] It would have been perfectly valid for the Communists to have cited Rhee's act as proof that the UN could not force Rhee to adhere to any truce.

But the Communists, whether because of the atomic threat and fear of general American enlargement of the war or because of their own needs, wanted to end the fighting. Cautiously, however, they went through their propaganda rituals. The Americans were charged by Peking radio with having "deliberately connived" with Rhee to violate the accords reached at Panmunjom. Then they made the kind of symbolic gestures that they had been doing throughout the many months of negotiations. A meeting of translators was called off and Communist workmen halted the construction of a new house being built to hold the truce-signing ceremony. Yet, within days, the United Nations command was encouraged when the Peking radio began to concentrate on charging the ROK government, and no other power, with responsibility for the prisoner release. Robertson and General Mark Clark both hastened to Seoul to secure the truce by convincing President Rhee that attempting to drive north without support from the UN would be suicidal. Besides, he needed American oil desperately. Eisenhower, meeting with senior Senators from both parties, indicated that he would make a last appeal to the

Korean President to join in the truce. His refusal would cause General Clark to sign on behalf of his country and the United Nations.[70] Clark also sent a letter to both the North Koreans and the Chinese commanders that guaranteed ROK acceptance of the armistice terms. "Where necessary," it said, "the United Nations Command will, to the limits of its ability, establish military safeguards to insure that the armistice terms are observed."[71]

Most Congressional reaction was cautiously silent; but the outstanding voices were those who did not agree that the Korean mission had been accomplished simply by having kept the Communists out of the South. Ralph Flanders told the Senate that Clark's letter had "put us in the position of threatening the Korean government with an attack from the rear while the ROKs were attacking the Communists at the front." The man from Vermont also declared that "Somewhere along the line the same influence which guided the Truman–Acheson administration got hold of our new administration." We have also, he charged, "retrograded politically and morally in our relations with the brave Korean people, Government and President."[72] Styles Bridges told a New Hampshire American Legion convention that the United States had failed to achieve her goals in Korea, and Joe McCarthy thought that "freedom-loving people" should applaud Rhee's defiance of the truce. Representative Ralph Gwinn of New York offered a resolution commending Rhee for releasing the POWs. And, on July 5, Eisenhower's Acting Majority Leader, William Knowland, resumed his more familiar stance by blaming both Truman and Ike for a "breach" with Rhee. Backing the Korean's demand for unification, he asserted that Rhee had not been sufficiently consulted on the truce terms. H. Alexander Smith supported Knowland's position, but Senator Wiley repudiated the party's new leader and denounced Rhee for having done "infinite damage" to the "free world" and the cause of peace.[73]

Rhee was persuaded by Clark and Robertson that he had only one choice, to accept the truce. The South Koreans were assured of postwar military and economic aid, which would be arranged at conferences after the fighting had stopped. The Communists agreed, on July 7, to resume the plenary talks. They followed that with their heaviest offensive in two years. Fourteen thousand UN troops, mostly Korean, were killed during those few days and southward gains of up to seven miles were registered. Their strategy seemed to avoid American troops, as though they intended to let Syngman Rhee know the futility of trying to resume the war.

The first limited war, which had exacerbated domestic politics for most of its course, had ended in a manner that caused few Americans to cheer, almost along the line where it had begun. Sharply unlike the joy that had greeted the end of World War II, there were no celebrations. New York City's Times Square was quiet, with small knots of people following the Eisenhower announcement on the electric sign. At 10 P.M. on July 26 (EDT), the President announced that the official armistice had been signed almost one hour earlier in Korea. Instead of optimism and joy, he warned about the need for vigilance "against the possibility of untoward developments."[74] Within the White House and the State Department, satisfaction was indeed kept muted with full respect for the widespread skepticism that greeted the peace and as a salve for Syngman Rhee's pride.[75] Some Republicans, such as Dewey Short, still complained that a military victory would have been possible if the armies had not been restricted. Jenner called it the "last tribute to appeasement," and Speaker Joe Martin said, "You cannot go into a military campaign with any hope of success without victory as its objective." Knowland denied the Administration's claims that the Korean campaign had been a victory for collective security by pointing out that the Americans and the ROK together furnished 95 percent of the manpower. Lyndon Johnson, also cautious in not hailing the end of the war, warned that an armistice that "merely releases aggressive armies to attack elsewhere would be a fraud," while other Democrats complained privately that a Truman solution on such terms would have led to impeachment attempts by the Republicans.[76] UN commander Mark Clark expressed the military reaction when he said, "I cannot find it in me to exult in this hour."[77] Eisenhower had fulfilled his promise to restore peace, but only time would decide whether he had achieved a political triumph.

Less than five days after the fighting had ended, just before noon on July 31, Senator Robert A. Taft died in New York Hospital. The President immediately released a statement that "He will be greatly missed on Capitol Hill, where his unimpeachable character and his vast knowledge of the business of good government played such an important part in Congressional decisions over many years." Both he and the American people, the statement added, "have lost a truly great citizen and I have lost a wise counsellor and a valued friend." His loss was generally viewed as a blow to both the Administration and to the party. Not only had he worked closely with both but, as the New York *Times* observed, Taft's absence removed the one real link between the East and the Midwest in the Administration. The paper of the National Association of Manufacturers, noting the consequent burden on the President, said there was no one left with Taft's prestige; and while, it went on to say, there "may be no indispensable man . . . more than one Republican feels that there is such a thing as an irreplaceable man."[78] With Mamie, the President went to Taft's home in Georgetown. Holding Martha Taft's hand in both of his, he murmured, "I don't know what I'll do without him; I don't know what I'll do without him."[79]

CHAPTER 29

The Perils of Moderation

THE INTRAPARTY EXPLOSIONS that had already occurred—the Bohlen dispute, the Yalta resolution, the foreign-aid fund struggles, the internal-security questions and Joe McCarthy, the handling of Rhee and ending the war and, still being argued, the Bricker amendment—had exposed key differences. Additionally, a late Administration appeal for an increased debt ceiling, one that would raise the legal deficit limit from $275 to $290 billion, failed to survive the Senate Finance Committee, and so the Eighty-third Congress's first session ended by emphasizing that it was far more penurious than even the budget-conscious Administration. Even though *Congressional Quarterly* showed that the President had done far better than Truman had ever fared with Congress in getting requested legislation, with a "boxscore mark" of 72.7 percent for that session, it was obvious that Democratic support had been decisive. Moreover, the raw statistics could not show the blandness of the President's eleven-point program that had been presented to the party's leaders on February 9 in comparison with such dramatic innovations as Truman's civil-rights requests.

Losses in the 1954 Congressional elections could cripple Republican rule before the "great crusade" hardly began its salvation of the nation after twenty years of Democratic rule. Opposition jibes about the President being a stranger in his own party were embarrassingly accurate. And, in July, the loss of both Senators Tobey and Taft and the Majority Leader's subsequent replacement by the Democratic mayor of Cleveland, Thomas A. Burke, had ended the Republican one-vote margin in the upper chamber. Recognizing the political realities, three months after his inauguration, the President advised all Cabinet officers to plan their speaking engagements with critical Congressional districts in mind, which meant those areas that had recorded a close two-party vote in 1952.[1] Selecting Leonard Hall as the national chairman had been another step to fortify the GOP for the coming battles.

Eisenhower's preoccupation with his own political base, which rested on his great popularity and prestige and, on the other hand, his role as the party's leader, was evident right from the start. As President, he would lure support through diplomacy and conviviality; and, with the aid of White House staffers working with Congressmen, minds and votes were changed. Bryce Harlow, for example, was instrumental in getting Congressmen Dewey Short, Carl Vinson, Walter Judd and others to alter their opposition to House passage of a defense reorganization act.[2] But Eisenhower was the first to appreciate that his role was more important than merely changing votes and piloting legislation through the two houses. He was the President and, as such, considered himself the national symbol, morally, spiritually and politically, its most important unifying force. Continued public confidence and respect for the President could bridge all partisan interests. Nothing could be more important than that contribution. So while he had to lead his party, his analysis of the situation called for avoiding the controversies that would not only have doubtful results but would render him, like Truman, a partisan rather than a national leader. He must not let political quarrels destroy the President. When fellow Republicans came to discuss viewpoints that could stir controversy, such as Barry Goldwater's insistence that organized labor's denial of "Political Freedom to the union man in certain unions constitutes a threat to our whole concept of liberty," he would find much to his liking. But being congenial with the Senator from Arizona in the Oval Room was far different from exposing the Presidency to the animosity of sizable groups of Americans.[3]

Thus, Eisenhower's caution extended to his Cabinet. Carefully, he pointed out on several occasions that they were free to speak their minds publicly on the issues of the day, and he would back them vigorously *when he could*. At one of his early staff meetings, on March 2, he went beyond that. He cited the furor that had occurred in 1946 when Henry A. Wallace, Truman's Secretary of Commerce, delivered a speech highly critical of America's responsibility for the cold war. When denounced, Wallace explained that he had submitted a draft to the President for clearance. Eisenhower wanted no such risks. His solution was simple. Speeches containing no direct references to himself or the White House would not require prior approval. By giving his subordinates latitude, he provided himself with the real freedom: the ability to react or not as he chose and even to disassociate himself when politic.[4]

Yet, despite all of his efforts, he could become impotent. That would represent a Republican failure, and the party's loss would abdicate the nation to free-spending, centralizing Democrats who just did not understand how a nation's strength required its economic viability and were ready to flout the natural laws that Adam Smith perceived for grubby political gains. During the spring of 1953, his despair had already become visible. At that time he complained to the Cabinet about being "kicked in the shins" by the same party that had worked to elect him. When Charlie Wilson commented that Republicans did not seem to understand that they were no longer in the opposition, he agreed enthusiastically.[5] Reading Roscoe Drummond's newspaper observation that the Republicans had brought a new kind of "mess" to Washington by imposing a government demonstratively "quarrelsome, unproductive and legislatively nearly impotent" moved him to mail the piece to its author with the comment "How right you are!"[6] Then, without Taft, the prospect was for more clashes between the President and Capitol Hill Republicans.

Eisenhower's exposure to the American political party system had awakened him to its inherent contradictions. There he was, he told Sherman Adams, the head of the party that had campaigned for him and had helped to place him in the White House. He, in turn, had supported them, with blanket endorsements, without petty distinctions, McCarthy, Jenner, et al., however much he dissented from their views. And yet they seemed to have no political fealty. Perhaps, he had begun to wonder, there might be a realignment, possibly a third party, one that would be more conducive to positive conservatism or middle-of-the-road thinking. A workable group might even succeed under his popular leadership if, for example, it brought together enlightened Northern Republicans and Southern Democrats. Both were suspicious of federal authority, both were concerned with overzealous spending and both were behind America's international goals. In Georgia, for example, there was no force within the Democratic party more reactionary than the Talmadges —first Eugene and then, after his death in 1946, his son Herman; however, much more than "Ol' Red Galluses Gene," Herman was able to add to the Talmadge rural strength the growing affluent and suburban middle-class voters, the same segment that had gone so heavily for Ike in 1952.[7] The younger Talmadge, when Governor of his state during an Eisenhower visit to Atlanta in 1955, inadvertently expressed what had been in the President's mind. "You know, Governor," Talmadge, impressed with the enthusiastic crowd that had greeted the President, said to Sherman Adams, "We voted for Eisenhower. We believe what he stands for. He's like one of us down here in the South. He understands how the South feels." Then, referring to the Republican eagle insignia on ballots, the Georgian added, "But the thing is we ain't ever gonna put any cross under that bird."[8]

But Eisenhower's thoughts remained in the realm of midnight gossip, the speculations of a general whose life had been spent commanding and being obeyed. He recognized that his own acceptance of the party's support had given him certain obligations and he was too firmly committed to the coordinate powers of the three branches of government to feel that he should, even if the legislature was ripe for subservience, exert strong executive domination like Franklin D. Roosevelt or fight in vain as had Harry Truman. And, of course, one of the realistic considerations in 1953 was the Congressional rebellion against the kind of Presidential power displayed during the past twenty years. American history, furthermore, gave little encouragement to those who really believed, as had Teddy Roosevelt in 1912, they could lead a third party into Washington. He also considered the importance of maintaining the two-party system and rejected the hazards of ideological Balkanization. Even if that were realistic and desirable, could he commit himself within a narrow spectrum?

His usage of "middle of the road" to describe his political position connoted a normal, respectable, democratic creed, similar to the traditional concepts that his West Point textbooks had taught him about American government. It meant, in short, the politics of "Americanism," just as his comment about our government making no sense "unless it is founded in a deeply felt religious faith—and I don't care what it is," inferred to Will Herberg that only Protestantism, Catholicism and Judaism were the legitimate, acceptable faiths for Americans.[9] That provided enough space to observe that "progressive moderates" were preferred by "the great mass of the people of the United States." Or, as he revised his position two months later, it could only mean "dynamic conservatism," which he had stated after Gabriel Hauge's suggestion that he substitute it for his own idea of "conservative dynamism."[10] "I believe we should be conservative," he said. "I believe we should conserve on everything that is basic to our system." He also liked to recall, as he did that same day, Lincoln's advice that government should do only that which people cannot do better for themselves.[11] "Frankly," he wrote to Ralph Flanders, "I believe that liberalism in matters involving people and conservatism in matters economic in nature was a concept tightly held by Abraham Lincoln. Certainly it expresses my own conception of the proper role of government in our time."[12] At a legislative-leaders conference he said that the "line between socialism and social progress is hard to establish—we want one and not the other."[13] Yet, after he met with Norman Thomas and told the Cabinet about his agreement that Socialists should not be excluded from non-policy-making jobs, he countered Dulles's reminder that the Socialist party platform equated capitalism with warmongering by saying that some Socialists were more conservative than middle-of-the-roaders.[14] However vague and unsophisticated his political philosophy was, his creed expressed an Eisenhower who had become for the great majority of Americans the personification of the only meaningful ideology. *The Reporter*, for example, editorialized that the "crusade has become a workaday chore" but that "the President's popularity would not be so great and so enduring had he chosen to lead, rather than to mirror, the nation."[15]

By the fall of 1953 there was growing evidence that the Administration was in trouble. On October 13 Wisconsin's heavily agricultural Ninth Congressional District seated a Democrat for the first time in its history. Seeking to avoid further embarrassment in an attempt to influence voters on the weekend before the General Election Day in November, Jim Hagerty told the press that the President favored all Republican candidates everywhere. "Everywhere" included, as the papers quickly pointed out, the gubernatorial contests in Virginia and New Jersey, a fight to represent the Garden State's Sixth Congressional District, and the mayoralty of New York City. In New Jersey, at least, the Republicans were regarded as clear favorites; and the Virginia election was seen as a test of the future of a two-party system in the Old Dominion. The GOP, however, lost them all. Even before the ballots had been cast, the mood of Dixieland governors gathered at Hot Springs, Virginia, for the Southern Governors' Conference reflected the trend. Their dominant belief was that while Eisenhower was still personally very popular, his party's appeal was waning.[16] The post-mortems in both Wisconsin and the South all agreed that unhappiness among farmers was a major factor.

There was no dispute that, by Election Day, the goat of the Administration's farm problems was clearly the Secretary of Agriculture, Ezra Taft Benson, and not the President. A poll taken by *Wallace's Farmer* showed that, even before the Korean truce, Eisenhower and Benson were regarded as though they were political rivals. Eighty-eight percent, reported the survey, thought the President's performance merited either a good or a fair rating, but the Secretary scored just 59 percent in the same category. More dramatic was the willingness of only 8 percent of the farmers to give the President a "poor" rating, while Benson was disliked by 33 percent.[17]

In attempting to prevent the farm belt from repeating its 1948 desertion to the Democrats, Eisenhower had done his best to calm fears that a Republican Administration would knock down the parity price supports sustaining producers in the face of continuing problems posed by both surplus crops and widespread drought. At his first press conference, immediately after returning from Europe, he dodged the question in Abilene by saying he did not know whether the level should be at 75, 80 or 85 percent. That, of course, was sufficient to create anxieties since the prevailing support had stood at 90 percent of the parity price.[18] But then, repairing whatever trepidations he may have precipitated throughout the farm belt, he made a campaign pledge that went beyond anything contained in the Republican platform. At Kansas City, Kansas, on August 21 and Kasson, Minnesota, on September 6, he told audiences that he favored the retention of "full parity" prices, specifying 90 percent at least until the expiration of the current agriculture law at the end of 1954. His words also left a common impression that he favored permanent retention of price supports.[19]

Nevertheless, his selection of Benson, an idealistic believer in the efficacy of a free economy for agriculture, was a more faithful representation of the President's real views. Benson was not a politician. Eisenhower, however, while still at SHAPE and seeking agricultural advisers in preparation for the issues he would have to handle as a candidate, made his own philosophy known. Thus, he wrote to Paul Hoffman: "While manifestly (assuming that governmental intervention cannot be wholly eliminated) there must be fields in which the broad scope of federal authority must be relied on . . . yet I take it that most of us who oppose governmental interferences have a special fear of bureaucratic federal interferences." He also suggested the possibility of "substituting State Government for Federal in those instances where certain types of controlled group action appear desirable or necessary."[20] Benson, who was later described by a former close aide as having attained his "over-all orientation . . . from two Smiths, Joseph and Adam, and from Thomas Jefferson," went on to receive the President's enthusiastic support during his eight years as head of the Department of Agriculture.[21] Sherman Adams has also recalled that "the so-called Benson farm policies that everybody indignantly called to Eisenhower's attention were actually Eisenhower's own farm policies."[22]

The President's ideas were actually a halfway measure between the advocates of continued support for the farmers, which would do most for the disappearing family or subsistence growers, and those favoring a free market for agriculture. Permitting the laws of supply and demand to govern the situation would inevitably kill off the least efficient producers and, discouraging farm investments, would alleviate the surplus problem. Surviving growers, presumably the more efficient, larger operations, would then have the field to themselves and operate on a competitive, private-enterprise basis. And the government would no longer have to underwrite the industry. Any hints, then, that the Administration might be moving in that direction alarmed the poorer growers and pleased the more affluent operators.

While the President's annual message to Congress was ambiguous on agriculture, merely recognizing the continuing decline of farm prices despite higher production costs and stating an intention to "execute the present act faithfully and thereby seek to mitigate the consequences of the downturn in farm income," his department head assumed the overt crusade to restore the benefits of the free-enterprise system to American farmers. Whatever the merits of reversing the heavy flow of subsidies to farmers, direct and indirect, that had begun during the New Deal, 1953 was a bad time for insensitivity toward agricultural problems.

The decline of the past two years was continuing without much cause for optimism. During the past year alone, the national price index showed a drop of 13 percent; cattle prices, particularly hard hit, fell as much as 32 percent. Wheat was off by some 20 percent and corn about 14. Arid conditions had made soybeans inferior and corn ears smaller than usual. Beef producers were pointing out that their income had fallen to pre-Korean levels, and similar conditions existed among growers of cotton, peanuts and rice, as well as corn. During the past year farm exports had fallen by 35 percent. In large parts of the Southwest, in particular, the drought was especially severe. But even in the Midwest nature had combined with technology to make the farmer feel more vulnerable than at any time since the 1930s. A newspaperman inspecting conditions around Guthrie Center, Iowa, found that the twin uncertainties were rain and the Republican Administration.[23]

Only nine days after the President had indicated the Administration's projected program, Ezra Taft Benson's St. Paul speech kicked up a verbal dust storm. Price supports, he told a large crowd, only lead to uneconomic production practices that would create more surpluses and more subsidies. They should only be used for disaster insurance. When he added the promise that support programs "now in effect or previously announced will be continued," there was little relief from the floor. Nor did he help things much soon afterward by telling people in Des Moines that "price supports are not in themselves adequate to keep agriculture going."[24] He repeated his conviction that continued supports only contributed to continued surpluses.

A minor farm revolt then flared, particularly among the smaller producers. One Oklahoma farmer told a reporter that he, too, believed in free enterprise, but added, "I don't like to see the farmer the only one operating under free enterprise when big industry gets tax favors and tariff protection." And the consternation continued throughout the warm months and into the fall. A tavern keeper observed to visitors that "there ain't as many Republicans around here as there were last winter," and another man reported that "Those that had a good year are still all for Ike, and those who didn't ain't." Then there was the customer who told the proprietor, "You know, Yohnny, the money's all gone; the Dimmycrats ain't in any more."[25] Senator Walter George said the farmers felt neglected in the face of the price declines, and Milton Young of North Dakota called for Benson's resignation. Senator Karl Mundt told Jerry Persons that Congressmen of both parties were "disgusted and mad at the apparent lack of political savvy on the part of the Secretary of Agriculture," and a visit to the growing areas by Homer Gruenther confirmed the bitterness.[26] Those who rushed to the Secretary's defense were the spokesmen of larger, more prosperous farm organizations who were more concerned with reducing inflation and minimizing the federal role. Such Western conservatives as Senator Arthur V. Watkins and Governor J. Bracken Lee, both of Utah, as well as Senator Hugh Butler of Nebraska, vouched for Benson. Watkins applauded Eisenhower for rejecting the "radicals" who wanted to dump Benson and Lee attributed the storm to holdovers within the Department of Agriculture who "merely represent the attitude of insecure job holders."[27] When a delegation of farm-belt Republicans visited the White House in midsummer to discuss the situation they were met not only by the President but also by Leonard Hall. Eisenhower directed the national chairman to forward their findings to Benson.[28]

The President, however, did not remain idle. In October he toured the drought areas and made a major speech to the Future Farmers of America in Kansas City, promising that his Administration would propose no program "that fails to provide solidly for the national interest by continuing prosperity in American agriculture."[29] Without identifying himself more overtly with his Secretary, Eisenhower also sought help from one of his administrative assistants, Fred A. Seaton.

Before joining the White House staff Seaton had been a Senator from Nebraska. But, in this affair, his real value rested on his newspaper and communications powers throughout the Great Plains. He was still, as he had been since 1937, the publisher of the Hastings *Daily Tribune* in Nebraska. But his ability to affect public opinion went beyond that. Seaton also served as president or vice-president of concerns that published papers in Manhattan, Kansas, Lead and Deadwood, South Dakota and Alliance, Nebraska. He also operated radio stations at Hastings and in the Kansas towns of Manhattan and Coffeyville. But the publisher's best outlet was the *Western Farm Life Magazine*, which reached more than 160,000 families in ten states. Seaton, therefore, was in a good position to give Benson some favorable support, and Eisenhower enlisted his assistance. Editorials that appeared in *Western Farm Life* during September, October and November in support of the Administration's policies were a direct result of the President's request.[30] Eisenhower also established, in October, a "non-partisan" eighteen-member National

Agricultural Advisory Commission to help the Administration "to develop a federal farm program that will best meet differing and sometimes diverse interests of the entire farming population and of consumers as well."[31] He was risking little however, since the commission was judiciously overloaded with conservatives hostile toward federal support. Although it was billed as "non-partisan," of the sixteen members who had actually been appointed to the commission by its first meeting date, October 24, only five were listed as Democrats. Of those, four were from the South and the other was associated with the Bank of America in San Francisco.[32]

And Benson remained the idealist and Eisenhower the politician. The day before the Virginia election, despite all the furor, the Secretary addressed the Southern Governors at Hot Springs and reaffirmed that the Administration "is determined that the trend to bigger and bigger Federal Government shall be reversed."[33] While Eisenhower told his Cabinet that his campaign pledge had given him a moral obligation to maintain 90 percent supports for at least one year, Benson cited recommendations of his commission to request an earlier change.[34] Continuously, throughout the formulation of the Administration's farm program, which was finally introduced to Congress on January 11, 1954, as an approach combining gradualism and flexibility while leading toward lowered supports, Eisenhower moderated Benson's desires for quick action by strategically advancing a more cautious approach.[35] Publicly, he defended the Secretary against repeated calls for his resignation, which ultimately came from such people as Joe McCarthy, who blamed the government for singling out the farmer and forcing him to compete "in an otherwise subsidized economy," and Senator Karl Mundt, who was present in 1957 when Benson's appearance before "a sorrowful and sullen crowd" in South Dakota was further marred when five farmers threw eggs at the Secretary.[36] Eisenhower even told his Congressional leaders in early 1958 that if Benson were forced to leave, he would submit his own resignation rather than be known as "a damned coward throughout the country."[37]

The farm problem remained insoluble, economically and politically. Probably the greatest harm done to the farmer by the Administration was in the ending of the Korean war, which reduced demand for commodities and made the surplus situation more serious than ever. Throughout the Eisenhower years there was a tug of war between the Administration and Congress, with the former pushing for sliding-scale supports between 75 and 90 percent of parity and Congressional pressures insisting on the full 90 percent prop. When supports did drop, however, there was no reduction of surplus production because farmers tended to compensate for their losses by enlarging their yield. Therefore, prices remained in a general decline, with such basic crops as corn and wheat lower in 1961 than in 1953. Cattle, which had been worth an average of $179 per head in 1952, remained below the $90 level from 1954 through 1956 and went up only to $134 by 1961.[38]

The one area of general agreement was the need to find additional markets for the enormous amounts of surplus stocks stored in government depositories. President Eisenhower, in 1954, introduced the Agricultural Trade Development and Assistance Act, better known afterward as Public Law 480, which authorized the Commodity Credit Corporation to sell $700 million worth of surplus farm commodities abroad and, utilizing crops as a means of foreign aid, the sending of $300 million of such stocks for famine or relief purposes overseas. Passed and expanded through the years, its major problems were international, as selling countries naturally objected to the interference with their markets. While it may have relieved the situation somewhat, however, it did not solve the basic problem.

Organized labor, always sensitive to evidence of hostility from a Republican Administration, had also created political embarrassment, which left the White House staff somewhere between the wrath of unionists and the indignation of conservatives who felt that, without Taft, their cause was being undermined. On August 31, Eisenhower's Secretary of Labor wrote a letter of resignation which, when publicly accepted by the President on September 10, confirmed the incompatibility of Martin Durkin—the plumber among the millionaires—with the Administration. While the Cabinet officer's loss was understandably regarded by the overwhelmingly Democratic labor establishment as proof of business entrenchment in Washington, there was enough evidence to convince Taft loyalists that the Administration had attempted to appease labor.

Durkin's contention was that Eisenhower's hopes to secure a revision of the 1947 Taft-Hartley law had placed him in the Cabinet.[39] It was, thought Durkin, a position Eisenhower held with sincerity. While rejecting the demands that it be repealed entirely, the General had campaigned in 1952 before the convention of the American Federation of Labor by saying he did favor amending the legislation to eliminate provisions that could be used to "smash" unions. He also singled out for special criticism as an unjust requirement the stipulation that labor leaders alone must take non-Communist oaths. There was no reason, he said, why the "employers with whom they deal" should not be subject "to the same requirement." In his State of the Union message, the theme was consistent: experience with Taft-Hartley "has shown the need for some corrective action, and we should promptly proceed to amend that act." Any changes, he carefully added, should incorporate the views of labor as well as business and the general public, which was also a reiteration of what he had told the AFofL.[40]

Eisenhower, of course, was not ready to write off labor's support.

Accordingly, he made additional moves to win the confidence of traditionally Democratic unionists. Visiting with him at the White House on February 6 were two of the country's more prominent labor leaders, Walter Reuther, the vibrant and articulate United Auto Workers' chief and president of the CIO, and David J. McDonald, the Secretary-Treasurer of the United Steel Workers and a member of the CIO's executive board. Reuther proposed to the President the establishment of an informal commission of six representatives of management, six representatives of labor, several Congressmen and a number of Cabinet members. Their purpose would be to work out areas of common agreement that could form the basis for future labor-management settlements. Reuther was eager to advance his proposal in place of Congressional hearings, where political ambitions often determined the procedures. The President, who was surprised to find Reuther interested in expanding the private-enterprise economy through the settlement of major existing difficulties instead of advocating any "Socialist" ideas, conveyed the labor leader's ideas to the Congressional leaders on February 9. Despite their skepticism about the proposal, they agreed to meet with the labor leader for a further exploration of its possibilities.[41]

While the President then aroused the sensitivities of unionists by not sending Congress any requests for labor legislation, Durkin set up a committee representative of the public, management and of labor. It was in perfect accord with the President's State of the Union proposal for a study of means of perfecting Taft-Hartley. But squabbles over voting procedures soon led Durkin, who was not a participant, to recess the group.[42] Nor did the Reuther idea take hold, as Congressional Republicans continued their initial wariness and the failure of Durkin's group substantiated reasons for skepticism.[43]

For half a year the real clash over changing Taft-Hartley narrowed to a conflict between Durkin's Labor Department and Weeks's people in Commerce, with the New England businessman-politician, although absent from the sessions, strongly represented by his general counsel, Stephen F. Dunn, and the most determined obstacle to Durkin's hopes. Durkin wanted not only what the President had been on record as favoring but also substantial gains that, in the opinion of Commerce, would have exceeded the Chief Executive's commitment. For example, his proposals would have abolished the "right-to-work laws." Not only did he want to drop the need for union leaders to sign non-Communist affidavits, but he also included, along with arguments for giving labor greater control over its membership, a provision that would have required employers to fire those members suspected of being Communists.[44] Durkin's interests also involved liberalizing the freedom to engage in secondary boycotts by making them permissible against farmed-out "struck work," requiring foremen and other minor supervisors to be treated as employees and not as management and having them unionized and, above all, minimizing the jurisdiction of state courts in labor disputes. Commerce, meanwhile, took a basic position that opposed making any concessions beyond what the President had promised and emphasized giving the states clear jurisdiction to enjoin labor violence, illegal conspiracies or boycotts. At the same time, Weeks's people worked to plug the loopholes found by the National Labor Relations Board and the courts in Taft-Hartley.[45] Weeks himself presented that argument to the President, especially in an effort to clarify the authority of the states so there could be no "erroneous" interpretations of the 1947 law.[46] While Durkin made every effort to win liberalizing amendments beyond Eisenhower's expectations, his opponents in Commerce sought to use the opportunity to make the law firmer than the original.

During a series of closed-door meetings in the White House and in Senator Taft's office, Durkin fought as a virtual personal emissary of organized labor; but Weeks left no doubt, as the record shows, that his sympathies and ties were close to the "more conservative business element." The conferences ultimately grew bitter; Commerce's general counsel accused Durkin of being unwilling to make a single concession while offering eight points on which his department was willing to reconcile differences.[47] At one such meeting, held in Sherman Adams's office on June 18, the President walked in while the session was in progress. He said he was interested in the subject and wanted to listen to the discussion. But then, as Durkin argued against increasing the authority of the states, many of which were controlled by strongly anti-labor forces, the President spoke. He said it was imperative that states retain some rights in that field and then added that his Secretary of Labor should be representing the government and not the AFofL.[48] Weeks let Dunn lead the conference battles and waged his own fight outside the meeting room.

Weeks's prime source of frustration was with the third most interested party, the White House. In carrying out the President's direct concern, their purpose was to woo labor support away from the Democrats for the 1954 Congressional elections while, at the same time, retaining the loyalty of the National Association of Manufacturers, the Chamber of Commerce and the followers of Senator Taft both in and out of Congress. With the two executive departments unable to agree, the White House staff took over. The President's special counsels, Bernard Shanley and Gerald Morgan (one of the principal drafters of the Taft-Hartley law), drew up a memorandum containing a suggested position for the Administration to take. That was then further revised with the assistance of Labor Department lawyers. The result was a nineteen point draft of a message for the President to make to Congress.[49] All but three or four of its provisions represented concessions to Durkin, especially the one that could have ended "right-to-work laws." When the White House staffers told the Labor Secretary that they would be disclosed to Weeks, Durkin was assured that the Commerce chief would be unable to stop the message and that, furthermore, he would be advised that they carried the President's approval. The message, Durkin was told, would be sent to Congress on July 31.[50] But, on that same day, Senator Taft died and Durkin was informed that forwarding to Congress amendments to the late Majority Leader's labor law on that very day would be tactless, indeed. He was, however, assured that a public release would follow soon and that there would be no changes.

The coincidence of Taft's death and the efforts to revise the labor law was, perhaps, analogous in its timing with the fight over the Yalta resolution and the demise of Josef Stalin; for, in each case, an opportunity was provided for the postponement, or even solution of a showdown. Weeks had already gone to war against the nineteen changes. Contacting business friends, he asked that prestigious pressure be directed by protesting to Senator H. Alexander Smith, the chairman of the Labor and Public Welfare Committee; Representative Samuel K. McConnell, Jr., chairman of the House Education and Labor Committee; and to Vice President Nixon. Such letters were sent, for example, by Weeks's close friend, Henning W. Prentis, Jr. Prentis, a former president of the National Association of Manufacturers and the chairman of the board of the Armstrong Cork Company of Lancaster, Pennsylvania, responded by sending out letters in August. His message to Senator H. Alexander Smith opened with "Dear Alex" and left no doubt that he expected the Senator's wholehearted opposition.[51] The Vice President, Mr. Nixon, also intervened and was reported by the New York *Times*'s labor correspondent as the man chiefly responsible for preventing the amendments from going to Congress.[52] On August 3 the *Wall Street Journal*, publishing a hitherto "secret" government document under the front-page headline EISENHOWER CIRCULATES HIS IDEAS FOR REVISION; THEY FAVOR THE UNIONS, sounded the alarm that inspired a flood of outraged management complaints.[53] They were particularly incensed at the thought that the provision recognizing the "paramount authority of the Federal law in the interest of uniformity throughout the United States" might nullify the "right-to-work laws." Nixon and Weeks had already convinced the President that alienating business and states'-rightists in one stroke would wipe out the remnants of his support.[54] Any doubt that the nineteen points had been buried for all time was resolved by the *Wall Street Journal*'s exposé.

Agitated, Durkin requested a meeting with the President. But Mr.

Eisenhower, while having set up an office at the United States Air Force's Lowry Field in Denver, was on a "work and play" vacation in Colorado. The press reports, aided by Jim Hagerty's deft distribution of releases with a Denver dateline, enforced the impression that he was doing more than merely golfing and fishing in the Rockies. Durkin, then, had to wait until Eisenhower went to New York City on August 19 to register as a voter in the mayoralty election so that he could support Harold Reigelman against Robert F. Wagner, Jr., for mayor and to dedicate a housing unit honoring Bernard Baruch's father. He asked that Durkin see him alone in his Waldorf-Astoria suite. There, according to the Labor Secretary, the President agreed that the nineteen amendments were still valid, and Durkin returned to Washington still hopeful that the agreement would be honored. When, however, the Secretary called for another meeting at the White House, he found the staff opposed to the plan. After a last-ditch attempt at rectifying their differences was made by the White House staff on September 8, Durkin was called to the President's office two days later. Eisenhower then informed him that, since their New York meeting, his position had changed and that the amendments were no longer acceptable. Durkin was granted his resignation.[55]

Two strong-willed forces had collided, but the Administration's final course—in the absence of a compromise satisfactory to both sides—had to be with the interests that were at the base of its power. Acceptance of amendments diluting Taft-Hartley would have been a surrender to the enemy and, for Durkin, a major coup. He was, simply, in the wrong Administration. As Ralph Tudor wrote home after the resignation, "it is very difficult to have a person so closely identified with a partisan element of the country in the Cabinet"; and he added the additional observation that, as a result, such persons "will ultimately come to clash with the other elements that must consider all the problems of the country."[56] Eisenhower, later reporting that he was disturbed at Durkin's constant use of the expression "collective bargaining," had also, as he had told the labor leader during the session in Adams's office on June 18, come to view the Secretary as a special-interest pleader.[57] But Weeks, whose continued belief that the Secretary of Commerce should, as the *Wall Street Journal* reported on September 29, 1954, "represent the business viewpoint even when that viewpoint is in the minority," was spared that kind of criticism. Durkin's successor, James P. Mitchell, who came to the Administration after having been a vice-president of Bloomingdale Brothers department stores in charge of labor relations and operations, also found reasons to protest Weeks's use of his department to promote interests of business over labor.[58] The stamp of legitimate patriotism was apparently reserved to the true friends of the Administration.

When Vice President Nixon stood before the 1953 AFofL's convention in St. Louis to bring a message from the President, less than two weeks after Durkin had left the Administration and the day after he told his fellow unionists his version of the events that led to his separation, he spoke in earnest about how the government in Washington cared about labor's welfare. He reminded the delegates that the Administration must serve all sixty million working people and read an Eisenhower reiteration of his previous pledge to "always try to be a true friend to labor." The reception was frigid.[59]

However much labor perceived that the "forces around Ike" had caused the President to capitulate, they were convinced that doubts about the Republican Administration had been substantiated. The President was unwilling to use whatever resources he did have to repel the accumulation of anti-labor power centers that were determined to ensure that, unlike during the Truman years, unionists would not have "side door" access to the White House. And yet, as far as Taft Republicans were concerned, the White House—by even suggesting changes that would have threatened the "right-to-work laws"—had been caught, like Louis XVI and Marie Antoinette, in an attempt to consort with the enemy. They, more than labor, were ready to accept Eisenhower's later protestation that "To suggest that I had any prejudice against labor, either as work or a political and social force, was perfectly ridiculous and, from my viewpoint, unthinkable."[60]

Nor was the Administration's standing with conservatives raised when, after Chief Justice Fred M. Vinson died on September 8, Eisenhower made his first Supreme Court appointment. Conservatives viewed the event as the earliest opportunity to return the Court to its pre-1937 tinge. H. L. Hunt, the Texas oil multimillionaire and supporter of reactionary causes, urged Eisenhower to nominate a safe Republican conservative. "If the new Justice were to be a Republican who cannot be accused of Socialist tendencies," wrote Hunt, "his appointment would be a start toward balancing the political complexion of the Court." Eisenhower's noncommittal response said he only wanted to "restore the Court to the position of prestige it formerly held in the eyes of the American people."[61]

The President first offered the appointment to John Foster Dulles, but the Secretary of State never gave it serious consideration. He was too old, he said, to begin a different career and his interest was too firmly involved with international relations.[62] Then in conferences with Attorney General Herbert Brownell, the decision was made to offer the seat to Earl Warren. Warren, Governor of what was then the nation's second largest state, had many virtues, in Eisenhower's view. He had a reputation for integrity; he was a former Republican Vice Presidential candidate and a leading GOP figure who was also a lawyer with experience as his state's attorney general (when he helped to place the Japanese-Americans in "detention centers" during World War II); and, moreover, he was well known as a middle-of-the-road moderate who had drawn formal bipartisan endorsements in California. Since he had held the California delegation for himself in Chicago and Nixon had done the real job for Ike with that group, the Warren appointment was no political debt.[63] The complaints of most lawyers that Warren lacked judicial experience and that many eminent jurists had been bypassed overlooked his peculiar ability to dramatize Eisenhower's desire to give the Court a moderate tinge.[64] After Brownell flew to Sacramento and obtained Warren's approval, the selection was announced as a recess appointment during the Congressional break. That enabled Warren to join the Court while it was hearing arguments brought by the National Association for the Advancement of Colored People against the public school segregation practices of Topeka, Kansas.

The choice was not a widely popular one. In addition to the questions about Warren's qualifications, the selection came under heavy attack from conservatives. Fulton Lewis, Jr., and David Lawrence led radio and newspaper denunciations and their followers took up the cause. By October 13 almost 75 percent of the White House mail disapproved of the new Chief Justice.[65] While his confirmation was being considered by a Senate Judiciary Subcommittee, Warren was the target of two hundred documents that were filed with the group charging him with being "under the domination of a notorious liquor lobbyist" while Governor to having a record of "100 percent" adherence to the "Marxist line." From his vacation spot in Palm Springs, California, the President came to his defense by calling Warren "one of the finest public servants this country has produced."[66] His confirmation on March 1, 1954, was unanimous.

Burns's report in September that the Council of Economic Advisers expected a "readjustment" in the economy during the coming months threatened to compound the Administration's troubles. Reduced military spending after the Korean truce and the high levels of recent production had left inventories higher than demand. Industrial setbacks had begun to cause concern in many localities. Senator John F. Kennedy of Massachusetts, citing the labor surplus in his area, had asked for better tariff protection for the woolen textile industry in New England.[67] While the Cabinet minimized the need for a public-works program to stimulate the economy, the President recalled that the party's campaign pledge had included promises to use the full power of government, if necessary, to prevent "another 1929." The first Republican Administration since the

Great Depression was the most vulnerable to anxieties about widespread unemployment and business failures. When George Humphrey said that rising unemployment could be tolerated for perhaps six or seven months, the President pointed out that countering the cycle with public-works spending should be regarded as investing in the nation's economic future. While the recession continued and brought a level of unemployment more than double the 2.5 percent figure for 1952, the Administration managed to retain its reins on spending by tax reductions and consumer credits. Organized efforts were also made to promote confidence that the economy's recovery would be rapid.

But when the voters went to the polls on November 3, 1953, the recession was just starting to deepen. In retrospect, the statement issued by Hagerty saying that Eisenhower endorsed all Republican candidates was, of course, a blunder, one that was attributed to the President's having capitulated to the judgment of his staff rather than following his own instincts that told him to remain neutral. Those around him had yet to appreciate his political sagacity.[68] Anticipating the inevitable question about the results on the day after the elections, Eisenhower brought laughter by saying, "I have lost skirmishes before." After dodging questions about whether he would, in the future, support even those Republicans who opposed him, he said that victory will come not by having "party machinery turning out the vote or anything of that kind," but by attracting independent voters with "something solid, progressive, and real on which to base your argument."[69]

Meeting with a number of his Cabinet members and Republican political leaders—a group that included Humphrey, Adams, Summerfield, Lodge, Hall and Thomas E. Stephens—the President stressed the need to promote the Administration's public relationships as though they were selling a product. As Mr. Eisenhower wrote in an *aide memoire* following the session, "It is up to the Administration and to the Republican leadership in the Congress to produce the product—*a product composed of legislative and executive measures that operate for the general welfare of the United States as a whole, in both foreign and domestic fields.* Of course, a well organized highly efficient machinery within the Republican Party is *one* element in the necessary selling organization. However, there is involved also a broader promotional and sales program than can be effectively accomplished solely through a political organization."[70] Chairman Hall acted to invite several professional advertising men to submit ideas about carrying out the job. Such aid then came from The Advertising Council. During the 1953-1954 recession, the council conducted a "Future of America" campaign to spur confidence in the recovery from the recession.[71] At the same time Hollywood movie star Robert Montgomery was enlisted to enhance the President's television appearances.[72]

By that time, however, Eisenhower had already reached out for political mileage on another front, one that was rapidly proving itself reliable in American politics: communism. Richard Nixon was, of course, the Administration's chief crusader against domestic subversion. He was, as Eisenhower had anticipated when selecting him as his running mate, the team's answer to McCarthy. Once installed as Vice President, the young California Quaker was more than merely a member of the Administration but the main liaison between right and left in the Republican party, a role that became much more important after Taft's death. On another level, however, the Vice President took care to preserve his own sources of strength. He could then be not only a line of communication for Eisenhower but, at the same time, would preserve his credentials for some future and perhaps inevitable triumph of conservatives. Even before Senator Taft's death the Vice President had won his credits by trouble-shooting in several incidents, particularly the Greek shipowners affair and when McCarthy had attempted to call the CIA to account over William Bundy. At the Cabinet meeting of April 24, when Attorney General Brownell revealed that the new security program would be released the following week, Nixon was the one to point out that McCarthy and Velde should be informed in advance.[73] Nixon had also been instrumental in helping to sell the Korean truce to the conservatives. After McCarthy had gotten himself hung up over the Matthews affair, in which Nixon's credentials with "Tail Gunner Joe" had helped to achieve the prearranged letter from the National Conference of Christians and Jews, it was Nixon who was encouraging the Senator to cast his accusations at Truman Administration corruption instead of plaguing an Eisenhower who feared giving the Wisconsin crusader additional publicity.[74] The junior Senator might yet be brought around to cooperating with the Administration.

McCarthy ignored Nixon's request that his fire be turned on Truman, but the Eisenhower people opened a campaign to offer new evidence as proof that they were not apathetic about Communists in government. Three days after the elections, at a luncheon meeting of the Executive Club of Chicago in the Palmer House, Herbert Brownell opened the way for a series of events that inevitably involved the Administration, McCarthy and Nixon. He made sensational headlines by referring to an incident that had taken place in 1946 and involved a man who had died two years later. The key figure was Harry Dexter White, an economist and an Assistant Secretary of the Treasury whom Truman had appointed as the executive director for the United States of the International Monetary Fund. Truman's move, Brownell told the businessmen, was made despite FBI reports that White was spying for the Soviet Union. The most recent description of White's activities had gone to the Executive Mansion in early December. But that had not stopped Truman from nominating the economist on the twenty-third of the following month. "The case of Harry Dexter White and the manner in which it was treated by the Truman Administration is illustrative of why the present Administration is faced with the problem of disloyalty in government," Brownell explained. "The manner in which the established facts concerning White's disloyalty were disregarded is typical of the blindness which inflicted the former Administration on this matter."[75]

Sharp exchanges with Truman and hearings before William Jenner's Senate Internal Security Subcommittee substantiated much of Brownell's claim. Despite Truman's immediate retort that he knew nothing about the report on the man and that he was fired as soon as his disloyalty was discovered, the ex-President had to retreat when making his formal reply, which he did in a television speech to the nation on November 16. Acknowledging, finally, having received confidential information about White's activities, Truman explained that a decision had then been made to proceed with the White appointment because intercepting it would have hindered the FBI by tipping off the many others under surveillance. He explained that J. Edgar Hoover had agreed with the strategy. His additional point cited the failure of a federal grand jury, the same one that had "indicted the twelve top Communists in the country," to return an indictment against White after having heard him testify. White's eventual "dismissal" in 1947, Truman then admitted, had come only after poor health had forced him to resign.[76] The former President, however, failed to explain why he had written an effusive letter accepting White's departure. While Truman supported the prerogatives of the Presidency by refusing Jenner's flamboyant move to subpoena him to testify, Brownell went before the committee and presented an impressively documented case. Truman's former Secretary of State, James F. Byrnes, then agreed that his chief had been aware of the charges against White, and J. Edgar Hoover denied having approved any plan to permit the accused to remain in office. Although nobody could say that White had actually been found guilty of spying (he had denied, until his death, any association with the Russians), the best that could be said for the Truman Administration was that the promotion of a man under such serious charges had resulted from slipshod work—unless Truman could ultimately be supported in his claim that the move carried the strategic approval of the FBI.

Eisenhower's handling of the controversy illustrated the distinction he was able to make between the Administration's political needs and his own role. Even before his formal response to Brownell, Truman had criticized what he called the "fake crusaders who dig up and distort records of the past to distract the attention of the people from political failures of the present"; and, on television, the furious former President said that the Eisenhower Administration had "fully embraced, for political advantage, McCarthyism," which he called "this evil at every level of our national life."[77] But listening to Eisenhower gave the distinct impression that he had been sucked into a situation that was both embarrassing and beyond his control. He told a press conference on November 11 that Brownell had been advised to follow his conscience as to his duty and, when asked about the legal ramifications, pleaded that he was no lawyer and referred the reporters to his Attorney General. As the newspapermen directed question after question at the revelation, the President avoided any statement that his predecessor had been disloyal or even in error. His declarative sentences were confined to the need to combat communism in government and stating that he himself was vague about White's identity.[78] Facing his Cabinet the next day, he expressed bewilderment that newspaper accounts said he was not supporting his Attorney General. He then stressed that Cabinet members had extensive authority both in their own right and to act for him and that he was determined to stand behind them, unless there were "obvious necessary exceptions."[79] As the press reaction continued to be highly critical of the Administration, the White House released a statement on November 16 further emphasizing that, although Brownell had notified the President about what he planned to say, no "advance copy" of the speech had been submitted for clearance.

Nevertheless, Eisenhower's purpose had been achieved. Brownell had told both Hagerty and Adams about his impending speech. Eisenhower has written that he had been notified by his Attorney General via telephone the night before. With both his press secretary and his chief of staff fully aware, and with what Brownell personally told him, the President could have had no doubt about the sensational nature of the charge. Indeed, Sherman Adams has written that Brownell's advisory to Eisenhower made the point that it was "justified political criticism and that it would take away some of the glamour of the McCarthy stage play."[80] The President had accepted, for the Administration, the attempt to counter the demagogic Senator not by disavowing him but by offering sensational competition. There was no other reason to delve into the intrigues of the past, especially when the need to safeguard the secrecy of FBI records continued to make the circumstances unclear. But, at the same time, Eisenhower was keeping sufficiently aloof from personal responsibility. After Len Hall joined the cause a few days later by declaring that communism in government would be "one of the main issues" in the 1954 Congressional election campaign, Eisenhower again stepped back. He told his next press conference about his hope that "the whole thing will be a matter of history and of memory by the time the next election comes around."[81]

But even after the President had spoken, House Majority Leader Charles Halleck also expressed Hall's sentiments, and the Administration's loyal foreign-policy supporter, Alexander Wiley, stridently vowed that Congressional investigations of espionage and subversion would continue "whether or not foreign relations improve or worsen."[82]

Near the end of the Presidential news conference of November 18, an International News Service correspondent, Robert E. Clark, called for a comment on the Truman charge that McCarthyism had been "embraced." Eisenhower first paraphrased the question deftly to indicate it had referred to "whether this Administration has embraced something called McCarthyism." Then he pointed out in beginning his reply, McCarthyism was a term "I don't particularly understand, but I said I was ready to take the judgment of this body whether there is any truth in such a statement."[83] Promptly, the New York *Times*'s Washington bureau polled eighty of the newspapermen and women, or close to one half of those who had attended the conference, and discovered that they were eager to make an important distinction. Eisenhower, they felt, was innocent of that charge, but his Administration was another matter. Brownell and those around the President had been guilty of accepting the Senator's tactics.[84]

McCarthy, however, was not about to be overshadowed. Charging that Truman had maligned him, he was granted a request for radio and TV time to reply to the ex-President. "McCarthyism," he told the nation that night, had been concocted by the Communist party and Truman had accepted their definition. The real issue should be "Trumanism," the coddling of Communists in government and the "placing of your political party above the interests of the country, regardless of how much the country is damaged thereby." All that was fine, as he proceeded to refute Truman's defense of his handling of the White case; but then, after noting that the present Administration had "gotten rid of 1,456 Truman holdovers who were all security risks" and was thus compiling a superior record in cleaning out "the Augean stables," he offered proof that the Communist issue would continue to be a valid concern as long as such people as old "China Hand" John Paton Davies, Jr., were still in the State Department after "eleven months of the Eisenhower Administration." Davies, McCarthy maintained, was "part and parcel of the old Acheson–Lattimore–Vincent–White–Hiss group which did so much toward delivering our Chinese friends into Communist hands." Furthermore, by not moving to force the Chinese Communists to account for the nine hundred missing Americans known to have been their prisoners in Korea, our "nation has allowed itself to be reduced to a state of whimpering appeasement" rather than fighting to "regain our national honor regardless of what it costs." We are still afraid to stop "this trading in blood money" by our allies doing business with the enemy.[85]

There were sufficient reasons for viewing the speech as his most direct attack upon the Republican Administration. C. D. Jackson, the next day, sent a confidential note to Sherman Adams saying that the speech was a "horrible experience" that, in effect, marked "an open declaration of war on the Republican President of the United States by a Republican Senator." It should serve, he wrote, to enlighten those "of the President's advisers who seem to think that the Senator is really a good fellow at heart." Then referring to Eisenhower's oft-repeated comment that he would not get "into the gutter" with the Senator, Jackson added, "Obviously, the President cannot get down in the same gutter—but neither can he avoid a question, if not several questions, at the next press conference. Would it not be better to arrange to have the *right* question asked?" Jackson also wanted to know why, if every egghead in the country could rise to a fever pitch when Brownell talked about Truman, a single Republican Senator couldn't work up some temperature when McCarthy referred to Eisenhower as he did.[86] Stanley M. Rumbough, Jr., and Charles Masterson, both special assistants in the Administration, responded to a request for suggestions on how the President should react to McCarthy by urging a dramatic, televised press conference during which Eisenhower and Dulles would stage a counterattack. The image "of the President as an inspirational leader is important to the Independent voter, who provided the margin of victory in the last election," they argued. "These men and women did not vote for the Republican party; they voted for Eisenhower. If their image of the President becomes clouded and if they do not vote again as they did in the last election, no amount of effort by the Republican Party will bring success."[87]

But the President was unmoved. He still harbored the hope that McCarthy could be persuaded to join his "team." When he faced the press on December 2, he began with a statement about the impending Big Three conference at Bermuda and then reiterated his hope that communism in government would have evaporated as an issue by the 1954 elections. Dulles had already repeated his rejection of McCarthy's ideas about impeding trade with America's allies, but Eisenhower stayed clear of even an allusion to the Senator. He was not abandoning those Republicans who continued to regard McCarthy as an asset. When the anti-Communist crusader launched a "write-to-Ike" campaign by telling his followers to make their views on trading with the Reds known to the President by writing to the White House, and some fifty to sixty thousand letters and telegrams swamped the White House and supported McCarthy by two to one, the Republican Congressional leadership continued to espouse his—and not the President's—hopes for 1954. Some were so enthusiastic about continuing the issue that they predicted it would be alive through the Presidential elections in 1956, and Senator Knowland promised even more extensive investigations, beyond the Truman era and into FDR's time. The Majority Leader also agreed with ending all "free world" trade with Red China.[88] Speaker Joe Martin predicted failure for all the "desperate efforts" to force a McCarthy–Eisenhower rift. When, on December 18, *U.S. News & World Report* published the results of its survey of what Senators and Congressmen regarded as "the big political issues" today, Republicans were shown placing communism first. Eighty-two percent said it was the leading concern. Democrats, however, placed the issue fifth on their list, as only 40 percent gave it prominence.[89] At the Cabinet meeting of December 15, Nixon suggested that Australia's banning of the Communist party might serve as a useful precedent for America, and Brownell called for accelerating the hunt against subversion by legalizing in federal courts wiretapping evidence and permitting the Attorney General to grant immunity to witnesses.[90]

Every indication shows that, by the end of 1953, the Administration was ready to exploit the domestic subversion issue as the best means of keeping the party together and moving onward successfully through the 1954 Congressional elections. On the third of a three-day legislative leadership conference in mid-December, Jenner, McCarthy and Velde joined Brownell to formulate possible new legislation to deal with the Communists, including wiretapping.[91] The meeting brought Eisenhower face to face with McCarthy. How to make that a permanent working partnership had been the concern of the Eisenhower staff, which, in the absence of any Presidential willingness to mar his political image by taking forthright action against the Senator, became the means of keeping the President from being tarnished.

Attempts to bring the energetic crusader from Wisconsin into a mood of greater cooperation dated from just days after the Administration had taken office. Roy Cohn has since written that Dr. Milton Eisenhower lunched with pro-McCarthy columnist George Sokolsky to explore the possibility of an "accommodation with Senator McCarthy." Not only has the younger Eisenhower denied this, but the President's brother was a most unlikely party to such an arrangement. He was among those who had urged the General to oppose the Senator openly, and he would have been a poor choice to confer with so reactionary a man as Sokolsky.[92] The work was left to those with better conservative credentials. I. Jack Martin, Taft's administrative assistant until his death and afterward a member of the White House staff, conferred with McCarthy and Cohn at the home of Mrs. Ruth McCormick Tankersley, who published the Washington *Times-Herald*. Martin's proposal that the McCarthy subcommittee confine its hearings to executive sessions while permitting

Eisenhower to take "appropriate action" against people named in the testimony was dismissed as totally unacceptable.[93]

More serious ventures at coralling the Senator for the Administration were made by Nixon and Deputy Attorney General William P. Rogers, whose association with the Alger Hiss investigation had brought him close to both the future Vice President and McCarthy. Nixon's sympathetic biographer, Earl Mazo, has reported that the Vice President never shared the views of some members of the Administration that "Communism to McCarthy was a racket" and that he "believed what he was doing very deeply," which is substantiated by those who observed how carefully he avoided any criticisms of the Senator. Nixon feared that an Eisenhower–McCarthy split would damage the party and place it in poor shape for the 1954 elections. Those trying to goad the President into an open fight with McCarthy, Nixon argued, were mostly unfriendly to both. In his role as the Administration's liaison with McCarthy, the Vice President made overtures to the Wisconsinite at Rogers's home shortly after the inauguration and at a private dinner for McCarthy during the summer of 1953. By the time of their most important meeting, on December 30 at Key Biscayne, Florida, those managing the President's relations with the Senator had much more serious problems.

Neither Nixon nor Rogers could have known on that December day the real significance of their mission, although the tension had been rising steadily. Nor could they have anticipated that failure would, in the long run, become the Administration's success; for McCarthy's course would inevitably lead to his downfall, not because Eisenhower had set the trap but, rather, because the President's agents were unable to win his cooperation. Their efforts were directed toward dissuading McCarthy from continuing to pressure the Administration, particularly the Defense Department and Secretary of the Army Robert T. B. Stevens, into granting him access to the Army's confidential files on loyalty and security. Since late summer the McCarthy committee had been investigating subversion in the armed forces. In mid-October, closed-door hearings were held on espionage activities allegedly still occurring at the Army's Signal Corps Radar Center at Fort Monmouth, New Jersey, where Julius Rosenberg had worked.

Robert Stevens, who had joined the Administration from his family's well-established textile firm, was a mild and courteous gentleman with insufficient experience in dealing with the likes of a Joe McCarthy. As McCarthy kept pressing him to turn over documents to facilitate his investigation, Stevens took the position that he could not permit the executive branch's records to become the prey of any Congressional investigation. Furthermore, under a Truman executive order, much of what McCarthy demanded was classified. When Rogers asked Stevens on

September 9, after the Secretary's most recent encounter with Mc-Carthy, how he managed to deal with "Jumping Joe," Stevens explained that he was succeeding by yielding on minor items but holding the line on highly classified papers. Stevens telephoned the Fort Monmouth commanding general on October 2 and told him that he was "working with the committee" and wanted to facilitate the appearance before McCarthy's group of people who had come "under a cloud." Not only should those called to testify be given authorization to appear because, as Stevens explained, "As long as it is a committee of the Congress I am sure nothing but good will come of it," but Stevens extended the courtesy to include the turning over of files being requested. The Secretary, by working with McCarthy in that manner, was hoping to get the Senator to turn the investigation over to the army. McCarthy must be made to understand, the Army Secretary said, that "executive orders prevent our giving this stuff out." "Of course," he added, "Joe may make an issue by asking the President for it," but McCarthy would be urged to keep it out of the White House, "where anything gets out of hand."[94]

The Nixon and Rogers session with McCarthy at Key Biscayne took place against that background. There, Nixon encouraged the Senator to go after all Communists in government but asked him to remember that "the people in this Administration, including Bob Stevens, are just as dedicated as you are to cleaning out people who are subversive. Give them a chance to do the job." Progress had apparently been made when McCarthy, while still in Florida, told the press that his committee would enlarge its field to include questionable tax settlements made during the Truman Administration. But shortly afterward, when Nixon was reported to have said that McCarthy would investigate matters other than communism, the Senator hotly denied that he was giving up his favorite subject.[95]

The Administration was also eager to have McCarthy become amenable for other reasons. The growing rift, particularly since the Senator's speech of November 24, had aggravated a difficult political situation. Right-wingers were being made indignant about allied shipping with Communist nations, the Administration had been caught wooing labor, farmers were bitter, and the economy was still moving downhill. All autumn, Gallup had revealed, the President's popularity had been dropping; by Christmas it had reached an uncustomary low of 60 percent.[96] McCarthy's popularity, meanwhile, was headed toward its highest level. Claude Robinson's survey of public opinion had also begun to show that "the public is becoming increasingly critical of the Eisenhower Administration for failing to produce what was expected of it," and *Business Week* suggested that it was "only natural for people to ask themselves whether Republicans are equal to the responsibilities of power."[97] *U.S.*

News & World Report, criticizing from the Republican right, warned the President that it was going to be difficult to get votes "from grandiose world plans," a reference to the Atoms-for-Peace speech made by Eisenhower before the United Nations in early December.[98] *The Reporter* thought it incredible that little "over a year ago a large majority of Americans used to chant 'I like Ike,' but, the magazine noted, in many of those same circles "to be liked by Ike is almost seditious."[99] The Chicago *Tribune* seemed to agree. Since the "New Dealers have captured the Democratic and Republican parties," said Colonel McCormick's paper, a new national party was needed. Five months later the Colonel joined with Clarence Manion, who had broken with the Administration over the Bricker amendment, Burton K. Wheeler, Hamilton Fish and John T. Flynn to form a group called For America. Their formation had been foreshadowed by a *Tribune* writer who had declared that "All over America people are talking about 'another political party'—something to vote for which really represents their views. Thousands who are 'fed up' with Republican national leadership after more than a year of President Eisenhower's rule—who claim that the change from internationalism and New Dealism they voted for has not taken place—are making their voices heard." The McCormick staff writer, Frank Hughes, went on to say that the most frequent complaint of the disenchanted "is against internationalism—against foreign aid spending, high taxes, continued military conscription, the 'uneasy truce' in Korea, the unbalanced budget, the 30 cent dollars, and the fact that Eisenhower Republicans are carrying on the same foreign policy that was voted out with Truman and Acheson in 1952."[100]

The middle of the road, as Eric Goldman has observed, was indeed getting bumpy. The President's desperate desire to retain his moderation was becoming increasingly difficult. McCarthy, convinced that weak Presidential leadership could be exploited as he had the national hysteria, was already bullying the supine Administration with arrogant contempt. The "sensational" exposure of a Red dentist at Camp Kilmer would soon provide more headlines for his investigation as well as an additional weapon for Roy Cohn to demand preferential treatment from the Army for the recently drafted special aide, G. David Schine. And while these events were threatening the President with the showdown he feared, he and Dulles were watching the accelerating dissolution of French Indochinese colonialism. That, too, might require a response from Washington.

CHAPTER 30

The Crises of 1954

THE NIXON-ROGERS MEETING with Senator McCarthy at Key Biscayne was of such limited value that the differences between the Administration and the Senator from Wisconsin moved toward the inevitable open clash. His continuing prestige among influential Republicans, along with an ability to draw financial support from affluent contributors, certainly encouraged his activities. Of great advantage, of course, were the conditions created by popular fears of communism that gave virtually any anti-Red crusader significant advantages. Political death was feared by any public figure accused of "softness" toward the enemies of "free world" values. A race had already begun for credit as author of legislation to outlaw the Communist party, with liberals like Hubert H. Humphrey seeking to place themselves on the "right" side of the issue while secure anti-Reds, most prominently J. Edgar Hoover and Attorney General Brownell, pointed out the dangers of driving the party underground. In the House, Harley O. Staggers of West Virginia submitted a bill urging the establishment of a commission to study the question of making such membership illegal.[1] When McCarthy's subcommittee applied for new appropriations in January, it received the support of every Senator except J. William Fulbright of Arkansas.

While people like C. D. Jackson and Masterson and Rumbough were urging the President to take the offensive against McCarthy, the President moved, on December 3, to initiate an investigation of allegations made about the country's most respected nuclear physicist, J. Robert Oppenheimer. The man who had only recently appeared before the President at a National Security Council meeting to state his position on armaments and American policy, as part of a process that ultimately led to Eisenhower's atoms-for-peace proposals on December 8, was thus en route toward becoming a prominent symbolic victim of the national delusion. The President thus wrote in his diary:

> I directed a memorandum to the Attorney General instructing him to procure from the Director of the FBI an entire file in the case of Dr. Oppenheimer and to make of it a thorough study. I assured them that I did want a thorough and prompt recommendation from him as to what further action should be taken. . . .
>
> It is reported to me that this same [security] information, or at least the vast bulk of it, has been constantly reviewed and re-examined over a number of years, and that the over-all conclusion has always been that there is no evidence that implies disloyalty on the part of Dr. Oppenheimer. *However, this does not mean that he might not be a security risk.**

Extensive hearings were then held during the spring of 1954 before the Personnel Security Board of the Atomic Energy Commission. Meanwhile, Eisenhower minimized his news-conference comments about Oppenheimer but emphasized he "certainly admired and respected his very great professional and technical attainments. . . ."[2] By a vote of two to one, the board revealed on May 27, Oppenheimer was not disloyal but was, nevertheless, guilty of "conduct and associations" contrary to the "requirements of the security system" and was, therefore, susceptible "to influence which could have serious implications for the security interests of the country." Moreover, he had opposed the development of a hydrogen-bomb program and had tried to so influence his fellow scientists even before Truman's order to go ahead with the project. The majority opinion, signed by Gordon Gray and Thomas A. Morgan, was disputed by Dr. Ward A. Evans. Evans agreed that Oppenheimer's testimony contained inaccuracies. But he was ready to believe that bad memory rather than duplicity was at fault. Indeed, the scientist had matter-of-factly acknowledged his continuing friendship with a French Communist intellectual, Haakon Chevalier. At worst, Evans wrote, the physicist had been politically naïve. But, he pointed out, Oppenheimer was being charged with derogatory material, as Eisenhower had observed, that had been available to the Atomic Energy Commission when he had first received his clearance in 1947. "All people," Dr. Evans declared, "are somewhat of a security risk. I don't think we have to go out of our way to point out how this man might be a security risk." He also feared that "our failure to clear Dr. Oppenheimer will be a black mark on the escutcheon of our country."[3] Amid rumors on Capitol Hill that the Joint Atomic Energy Committee was prepared to haul before

---

* Author's italics.

it the members of the Atomic Energy Commission if the AEC ruled contrary to the board, the executive agency headed by Admiral Lewis Strauss upheld the denial of Oppenheimer's security clearance by a vote of four to one.[4]

Oppenheimer's associations were damning. He had contributed to numerous West Coast leftist organizations. He had admitted to having been a "fellow traveler" from 1937 until 1942. He still considered Chevalier a friend and had visited him as recently as the previous December. He even confirmed the investigators' knowledge that he had gone to bed with a Communist, Dr. Jean Tatlock, a member of the party in San Francisco. His wife had been married to one until his death in 1937 while fighting for the Spanish Republic. His brother and sister-in-law were also Communists. All of his affiliations that were cited as subversive had been so designated by the House Un-American Activities Committee years *after* he had joined. In the existing climate of American anti-Communist paranoia, plus the Administration's fervent need to demonstrate its own purity, the evidence that had been accepted earlier and the people who had once endorsed and recommended him, such as Admiral Lewis Strauss, suddenly became the axes that struck him down.

The price for public confidence meant getting rid of Oppenheimer, just as surely as it had led to the separation from the Foreign Service of John Carter Vincent and would, at the end of 1954, lead to the retirement of a constant McCarthy target within the State Department, John Paton Davies. Davies had to wait until 1969 to regain his security clearance. Oppenheimer, who died in 1967, was a guest at a White House dinner in 1962 given by President John F. Kennedy for Nobel Prize winners. In December of 1963, the same Atomic Energy Commission that had lifted his clearance in 1954 gave him its highest prize, the $50 thousand Fermi award for "his outstanding contribution to theoretical physics and his scientific and administrative leadership."[5] Coinciding precisely with the Oppenheimer hearings, the long-delayed showdown with Senator McCarthy and the deterioration of the French position in Indochina gave the Eisenhower Administration twin dilemmas.

When McCarthy continued to be frustrated by Secretary Stevens in his efforts to gain access to the Army's loyalty files, his new vow to subpoena the members of the Loyalty and Security Appeals Board that had cleared the Fort Monmouth scientists went beyond a mere challenge to the Chief Executive and the military in their control of the security program. It also, as Sherman Adams noted, threatened "to widen the breach within the Republican party." Henry Cabot Lodge, continuing a concern for GOP stability that had placed him behind General Eisenhower in the first place, urged a meeting to explore the implications of the Senator's challenge and threat to the party. On the day after their meeting, McCarthy, who had also come under pressure from the majority members of his subcommittee and by Army counsel John G. Adams, announced he would defer the subpoenas.[6]

But that same meeting, held on January 21, also revealed the incredible affair that had been going on between the Army versus the team of G. David Schine, Roy Cohn and McCarthy. John Adams told those gathered in Herbert Brownell's office that while McCarthy was railing against the Army, Cohn was haranguing the service for special treatment for Schine. Cohn and Schine, who had made a foray through Europe in search of subversion between hard covers, had become almost inseparable. Privately, however, McCarthy had begun to view Schine as an embarrassment and a publicity-seeker and had confided to Stevens that he hoped the Army would help him out by sending the young man far away. Frequently, when Cohn was not present, the Senator was critical of the brash heir of hotel and motion-picture fortunes. McCarthy did join with Cohn, after Schine's draft board had called him in July, in efforts to get him a commission; but they failed.

And once Schine was finally inducted on November 3, Cohn waged a war against the Army on behalf of his friend. Schine had even requested appointment as a special assistant to the Secretary of the Army, but Cohn made his own contributions. When told, at one point, that Schine could be sent overseas, Cohn replied that such boldness by the military would get Stevens tossed out as Secretary of the Army. Numerous phone calls to Fort Dix, where Schine was stationed, helped win the celebrated trainee four times as many passes as any other soldier in his outfit. Once Cohn even called John Adams, while the Army counsel was on a speaking engagement at Amherst College, to demand that his friend be removed from the KP roster for the next day. In pressuring for a favorable permanent Army assignment for Schine, Cohn also asked that he be stationed at West Point, where he could scrutinize the academy textbooks for subversive material, or, perhaps, there might be a good plainclothes spot for him in New York City. While driving up Park Avenue and arguing the issue with John Adams, Cohn became so impassioned that he ordered the Army lawyer out of his car. Privately, McCarthy sympathized with Adams and agreed that, on the matter of Schine, Cohn was unreasonable. When the account was revealed at the meeting of the twenty-first, Sherman Adams suggested that a chronology of the pressure campaign be prepared.

Schine, however, was only incidental to the subsequent eruption. The McCarthy committee, with the three Democrats who had quit during the Matthews affair returning on January 25, came up with evidence that an Army officer at Camp Kilmer had been promoted despite his refusal to answer questions about alleged Communist activities. He was Major Irving Peress, a dentist at the reception center for inductees. After his promotion, which had been routine under the automatic provisions of the Doctor Draft Law, discovery of his failure to comply with regulations probing for subversive affiliations resulted in an order by the First Army's adjutant general for his discharge within ninety days. But McCarthy, finally spotting a "real" Communist (who belonged to the left-wing American Labor Party in New York City), pounced on the case with zest. After questioning Peress in a closed session on January 30, the Senator said the major had refused to respond to questions about alleged Communist activities and demanded that he be court-martialed. Peress countered by requesting the immediate granting of his discharge. The Army, happy to get rid of the dentist, returned him to civilian life with an honorable discharge.

McCarthy's real headlines were still ahead. "Who promoted Peress?" he demanded to know. On February 18, acting as a one-man subcommittee, McCarthy interrogated Brigadier General Ralph W. Zwicker, Camp Kilmer's commanding officer. Until that day the general had been a McCarthy sympathizer. But the Senator proceeded to subject him to a brutal inquisition, as though Zwicker's responsibilities had given him personal jurisdiction over the Army's security process. Finally, after having badgered the general with hypothetical problems, McCarthy turned on him and said, "Any man who has been given the honor of being promoted to general and who says, 'I will protect another general who protected Communists,' is not fit to wear that uniform, General."

This time McCarthy had gone too far. Even the Chicago *Tribune* editorialized that the general had deserved better treatment and that the Senator had thereby "injured his cause of driving the disloyal from the Government service."[7] He had also, it was reported, implied that the high-ranking officer did not have "the brains of a five-year-old." Moreover, his order that Zwicker return for another session offered no other interpretation than that McCarthy wanted some more righteous indignation at the general's expense.

Until that point, for almost half a year, Secretary Stevens had handled McCarthy with the caution that was consistent with the White House's attitude. But the Zwicker affair brought the Army chief to his general's defense. He denounced the "unwarranted abuse" of the soldier and prohibited him from testifying any further. All other officers, to their delight, were also instructed to ignore summonses from the McCarthy subcommittee. Stevens added that he would be happy to testify in the general's place to answer questions about the Peress case, but he could not tolerate such conduct toward Army officers.[8] No member of the Administration had defied McCarthy so openly, and Stevens's chances of surviving his stand seemed more questionable than any consequences to the Senator. In fact, McCarthy then contacted Stevens with a warning. "Just go ahead and try it, Robert," he said over the telephone. "I am going to kick the brains out of anyone who protects Communists! . . . You just go ahead. I will guarantee that you will live to regret it."[9]

All of McCarthy's recent actions indicated he had indeed become more brazen than ever, and the lack of willing challengers had been most encouraging. In the Peress case, however unimportant the dentist seemed to the interests of national security, McCarthy had found what was generally accepted as a blunder. It was bad enough that the doctor's original unwillingness to answer questions about his affiliations had been overlooked, but how could Zwicker or Stevens, or anybody, explain why he had been granted an honorable discharge once the case had been exposed? Enjoying his new heights, then, before his castigation of Zwicker, McCarthy delivered a series of Lincoln Day fund-raising speeches before Republican gatherings and responded to their enthusiasm with commensurate ferocity by charging that the Democratic Administrations that had preceded Eisenhower's had given the country "twenty years of treason." Then, on the Sunday after the Peress case had made front-page headlines, Leonard Hall appeared on television and said he considered McCarthy an "asset" to the party's 1954 campaign efforts and substantiated his point by citing the heavy demand for the Senator to make additional speeches. His travels, moreover, were being underwritten by the Republican National Committee.[10] At his next press conference, Eisenhower, who had just called for an end to extreme partisanship, was asked whether he approved of such sponsorship by the party for the man who, along with Senator Jenner, was the greatest practitioner of those tactics. "I don't think my approval or disapproval here is needed," explained the President very carefully, "and I am not going to comment any further on that." He also recalled his vows to avoid "anything where personalities are involved."[11]

With the President continuing to remain immune from the upheaval—as some thought the Zwicker situation recalled Eisenhower's famous capitulation to McCarthy in Wisconsin over the Marshall speech—and with most of the Republican Congressional leaders and several White House insiders unwilling to sacrifice the Senator's home-run bat from their lineup, Stevens understandably needed new sources of support. A logical group were the three Democratic members of the subcommittee; and the word in Washington was that they were receptive. Why not? They had everything to gain from the spectacle of an open clash between the Secretary—and, hopefully, the whole Administration—and McCarthy. But from within the Administration, under the leadership of Vice President Nixon and Jerry Persons, new plans were laid to deprive the Democrats of a feast. They urged Stevens to appear in Senator Dirksen's office, room P-54—just off the Capitol Building's Rotunda—for a meeting with McCarthy on February 24.

It would, they suggested, be a secret session. In addition to the two principals, only Dirksen, Karl Mundt and Charles Potter, the three Republicans on the subcommittee, were invited. The President, who on that day was returning to Washington from a one-week golfing vacation in Palm Springs, California, was not informed about it either. Until the moment he left his office in the Pentagon, where he had been rehearsing for his scheduled appearance before the subcommittee, Stevens did not say where he was going.[12]

When he reached the meeting place for the scheduled luncheon, he found what should have been a clue to the plans that had been laid: Some fifty reporters and a battery of photographers were waiting to record the big news. Inside the room Stevens first engaged in an acrimonious exchange with McCarthy. When the Secretary declared he would not tolerate having his officers browbeaten, the subcommittee's chairman replied, "I'm not going to sit there and see a supercilious bastard sit there and smirk." But as the session progressed, and with Stevens assuming that a *rapprochement* had been desired by the "highest level" of the Administration, Karl Mundt was able to type a "Memorandum of Understanding" to be announced at the close of the meeting. When the photographers were admitted to room P-54, McCarthy had a satisfied smile and was eager to pose. Stevens, much less enthusiastic, could manage only a feeble grin as the flashbulbs went off.

The Secretary, then returning to his Pentagon office, was not in a festive mood. He explained to those in his office that he had done his best. And that had not been too bad. The scheduled confrontation of Stevens before the McCarthy committee that was due for the next day, before television cameras, had been called off. More important, Stevens explained, was McCarthy's agreement that there would be no intimidation of officers appearing before the subcommittee in the future. A face-saving arrangement, in which both parties could claim victory, had been accomplished. He was congratulated.[13]

As the afternoon progressed, however, the Secretary fell into a deep despair. During the evening Senators who spoke to him on the telephone heard his sobbing voice say he would have to resign because he had "lost standing" at the Pentagon. In the intervening hours, the "Memorandum of Understanding" had been circulated and widely interpreted as a meek surrender to everything McCarthy had demanded. There was not a word about the respectful treatment Stevens claimed to have been promised for his people. Instead, the four-point release announced that the Secretary of the Army had agreed to furnish the subcommittee with the names of "everyone involved in the promotion and honorable discharge of Peress." Such individuals would also be made available before the committee, including, at a later date, General Zwicker. Then, adding considerable distress to Stevens's condition, came word that McCarthy had gloated to reporters that the Secretary could not have given in "more abjectly if he had got down on his knees."[14]

The press compounded the defeat. The New York *Times* ran a banner headline saying STEVENS BOWS TO MC CARTHY AT ADMINISTRATION BEHEST; WILL YIELD DATA ON PERESS and carried a front-page blow-up of a photo showing both men in an amiable conversation. Even the Administration-supporting New York *Herald Tribune* ran an editorial saying that "Compromise is always desirable—except when compromise means giving away what is essential to the maintenance of basic principles." Overseas, the *Times* of London announced, "Senator McCarthy this afternoon achieved what General Burgoyne and General Cornwallis never achieved—the surrender of the American Army." In Washington, particularly within the Pentagon, there was shock. One "distinguished observer" was quoted as explaining "The Secretary didn't mean to surrender to Senators McCarthy, Dirksen and Mundt yesterday, he merely thought they wanted to look at his sword."[15]

The one man in Washington who did not act perturbed was Dwight D. Eisenhower. On the afternoon of the twenty-fifth, the day after he had returned from California, he changed out of his brown business suit and donned gold slacks and went out to the south lawn of the White House with a number 8 iron to practice his pitch shots. Perhaps he was hitting the ball in frustration at having to suffer the humiliation of first General Zwicker, with whom he had been familiar from European command days, and then Secretary Stevens. But the President, while ostensibly detached from the affair, had already initiated a counterattack that was being devised at that very moment in the White House's East Wing.[16]

Something had to be done to repair the situation, particularly since Stevens's threats to resign raised the possibility of additional embarrassment. Reportedly at the suggestion of the Vice President, Eisenhower had called Dirksen to request that he join with the other three Republican Senators on the subcommittee in the drafting of a statement that Stevens could approve as a way of mitigating the situation. But finding language satisfactory to both the Secretary and McCarthy was, they found, an impossible job. The great danger, in McCarthy's view, was acceptance of anything that might imply past misconduct by his subcommittee. Unable to accomplish that task, a large group gathered in the East Wing to prepare a statement that would save face for Stevens by being released from the White House. Finally, Sherman Adams went out to the President on the south lawn and informed him that a draft of the counterstatement had been prepared. Eisenhower listened, hit the ball several more times, and then asked that Stevens, Nixon and Persons meet with him in the Presidential study on the second floor.[17] After the President sat in on a half-hour conference, the statement was released by Stevens from Jim Hagerty's office at 6:15 P.M.

Eisenhower was not present. Stevens read to reporters his determination to "never accede to the abuse of Army personnel under any circumstances, including committee hearings." He added, "I shall never accede to them being browbeaten or humiliated" and then concluded by saying that assurances received from members of the subcommittee made him confident that such conditions would no longer be permitted. As soon as Stevens finished, Hagerty added, "On behalf of the President, he has seen the statement. He approves and endorses it 100 per cent." McCarthy promptly replied, "If it will be unpleasant to tell the truth, I can't be responsible."[18]

The following Monday was March 1, and Eisenhower met with his party's Congressional leaders. Almost casually he observed that questions at his next news conference would center around McCarthy and Stevens and he expressed the hope that the legislators would enable the Administration to get "a better handling of things like this." Stevens, the President said, had informed him he was playing the game and trying to cooperate with the Republican Senators. He explained that the Secretary had attended the fried-chicken luncheon in Dirksen's office under a vow of secrecy and even he had not been told about it. Charlie Halleck expressed disturbance that the "boys had fixed up a statement without any regard to protecting Stevens's good name" and said that a reading of the transcript convinced him that there had been "browbeating in the hearings." He was relieved, however, that a televised fight among Republicans had been averted. George Humphrey, who was also present, agreed that Stevens should have been protected. Knowland, however, tried to absolve the Republican subcommittee members from full responsibility by saying that their interests were also in protecting Stevens from a bad situation but that side remarks "made as a result of needling by the press" had created most of the damage. The President, stating the public position he would take, informed the leaders that at his March 3 conference he would probably not challenge the right of Congress to investigate but would rest his case on pointing out that we can't defeat communism "by destroying the things in which we believe."[19]

When he faced the press two days later there was nothing casual about his preparation. Before any questions could be asked, he read an opening statement that admitted serious errors in the Army's handling of the Peress case and announced improvements were being made in the procedures. After reaffirming that no subordinate is expected to "violate his convictions or principles or submit to any kind of personal humiliation when testifying before Congressional committees or elsewhere," he listed three additional observations. First, he stated, "We must be unceasingly vigilant in every phase of governmental activity to make certain that there is no subversive penetration." Secondly, in "opposing communism, we are defeating ourselves if either by design or through carelessness we use methods that do not conform to the American sense of justice and fair play." Finally, he offered reassurance that the "conscience of America" is "reflected in the body of the United States Congress." Then he added a vigorous reaffirmation of the President's responsibility for all parts of the executive branch and lauded General Zwicker, who, he pointed out, "was decorated for gallantry in the field." Not once did the President mention either Stevens or McCarthy by name.[20]

The well-publicized Senator was on virtually everybody else's tongue during those days, even more during the month of March than in April. On the night following the news conference, a stag dinner was held at the White House. After the meal the President and his guests went into the Red Room, where they engaged in an evening of wide-ranging conversation. For the most part, the men directed their questions at the President, who led the discussion. Many subjects were covered, but no one was tactless enough to mention McCarthy.[21]

By March there were many indications that McCarthy had overreached himself. At a dinner for the Neiman Fellows on March 4, the members of the journalism group goaded Herbert Brownell in an attempt to get his admission that the President's statement of principles had been wishy-washy. The Attorney General, holding his ground, insisted that it was too early to tell the true effects of the President's words. Still, whether or not directly attributable to the counterattack or to the Senator's own excesses, there was an unmistakable shift in what the American public was willing to tolerate. An ex-New York *Herald Tribune* correspondent, John Metcalfe, completed a five-thousand-mile lecture tour of the country and reported an "amazing" change in public sentiment toward McCarthy. One year earlier, he pointed out, it had been unsafe to suggest the Senator had any shortcomings; but now audience after audience had questioned Metcalfe about what should be done with "this fellow, McCarthy," and their attitudes provided evidence that he had blundered by getting too rough with someone whose popularity was greater than his own. A former assistant to Oveta Culp Hobby, Jack Bearwood, found Southern Californians beginning to resent the Senator's "bombastic and dictatorial actions." *Fortune* magazine revealed that business executives were becoming exasperated with the Red-hunter, and the Gallup Poll that was released in mid-March confirmed McCarthy's troubles by gauging his acceptance as four points below the high level of 50 percent reached in January. Apparently sensing the trend, Leonard Hall reversed his recent position by telling a Republican conference in

Omaha that McCarthy had been hurting the party. In Kansas City, Harry Truman commented that Eisenhower should send his "great investigator to hunt spies in Siberia."[22]

McCarthy's new vulnerability encouraged his critics. At Miami Beach, on the first Saturday night of a month in which the Senator's name hardly ever left the headlines, Adlai Stevenson addressed a Democratic fund-raising dinner and charged that the descendants of Lincoln had created a "political party divided against itself, half McCarthy and half Eisenhower." The following Tuesday, Ralph Flanders, having exhausted his own patience, rose on the Senate floor to deliver the most outspoken attack yet made on McCarthy by a colleague. The Vermonter accused him of having become a "one-man party" who was "doing his best to shatter" the GOP. "In this battle of the age-long war," Flanders continued, "what is the part played by the junior Senator from Wisconsin? He dons his war paint, he goes into his war dance, he emits his war whoops. He goes forth to battle and proudly returns with the scalp of a pink Army dentist."[23]

As soon as the news from the Senate reached the President, he quietly sent a simple personal note to Flanders which read, "I was very much interested in reading the comments you made in the Senate today. I think America needs to hear from more Republican voices like yours."[24] Publicly, in his news conference the following day, Eisenhower commended the New Englander for pointing up "the danger of us engaging in internecine warfare" for the sake of personal aggrandizement at the risk of dividing the party.[25] A quieter response received by Flanders was from the President's closest social associate in the Cabinet. George Humphrey visited the Senator's office to warn that the continued well-being of the Republican party was being jeopardized by continuing such attacks. The GOP, Humphrey pointed out, was vital for the good of the country and disunity would be counter-productive.[26] Knowland, Homer Ferguson and Styles Bridges gave additional warnings about the consequences of such statements.

At the March 10 news conference, when Eisenhower defended Flanders, the President was also asked about a new controversy over McCarthy. The Republican National Committee had received free radio and TV time to respond to the Stevenson attack. The Chief Executive admitted that he had been present at a conference that had decided to give Vice President Nixon the job of handling the accusation by the Democrat. That decision, made in conjunction with Jim Hagerty, Len Hall, Sherman Adams and Republican press director James Bassett, gave the Vice President his most uncomfortable role after one year as a peacemaker with McCarthy. Nixon, who considered the assignment as one of his toughest writing jobs, had to cope with the dilemma of at once rebutting the Stevenson assertion about the McCarthy influence over the party and not offending the Senator. He confined himself to his hotel room and there worked out the delicate balance to minimize his own alienation from McCarthy. Before going on the air that March 13, he spent forty-five minutes discussing the speech with the President, who then departed to his Catoctin Mountain retreat, Camp David.[27]

Nixon's efforts were insufficient to prevent a wedge between himself and the Senator. Carefully, he avoided mentioning his name. Nixon's target was unmistakable, however, when he criticized those whose efforts to expose communism in America "not only have diverted attention from the danger of communism but have diverted that attention to themselves." He said that Congressional investigators who indulge in "reckless talk and questionable methods" divide the United States on the great issue and divert attention from the program of Dwight D. Eisenhower, who, he emphatically asserted, was the unquestioned leader of the party.[28] McCarthy, who was also the victim of a half-hour televised documentary attack on CBS that was delivered by the prestigious newscaster and commentator, Edward R. Murrow, went on to score Murrow's "left wing" affiliations and denied he had provoked a fight with Eisenhower, blaming the press for creating that impression. He also charged the Democratic party with twenty counts of "treason or gross stupidity" and named Stevenson as their "defense attorney."[29]

By then, however, the big showdown had already been arranged. On March 11 the Army submitted its chronology with the members of the Senate Permanent Investigations Subcommittee on the McCarthy–Cohn attempts to win preferential treatment for Schine. McCarthy replied by charging that it was "blackmail" to force the termination of the Army probe. But the subcommittee then voted to hold hearings. Normally, the Armed Forces Committee would have been the appropriate body, but its chairman was Leverett Saltonstall of Massachusetts. Up for re-election that year, Saltonstall ducked such involvement in view of McCarthy's heavy following among the Catholic voters of his state.[30] The Administration then fought to have McCarthy step down temporarily as chairman while his group conducted the hearings and finally won that battle when, with the support of the party's national committee and Congressional leaders, Karl Mundt was designated temporary chairman.[31] With the drama finally set to begin on April 22, Republicans faced the prospect of a bitter internecine fight before TV cameras.

Only four days after the subcommittee's vote to hold hearings in the Army–McCarthy affair, the Administration was confronted with the impending realization of a major fear: the communization of Indochina. The arrival in Washington on March 20 of a highly respected French general, Paul Ely, provided the unsettling confirmation that military developments were deteriorating for the Associated States of Indochina and the French Union Forces. Ely, already known in Washington for his previous service as his country's representative to the NATO Standing Group and regarded as pro-American, had been sent by Minister of Defense René Pleven to avoid any misunderstanding with the United States. His mission touched off apprehension within the Eisenhower Administration about the nature of his request. What he had to say relieved those fearful about American intervention but dismayed optimists who had banked on the feasibility of a military victory by the Union forces. His basic message was that, without additional matériel supplies and American aviation technicians, there was little hope for the survival of the garrison at Dien Bien Phu. Located in a valley in northeastern Vietnam, the town's natural limitations as a military bastion had been further weakened in recent days by the Communist capture of key surrounding hills and artillery fire that was making its airfield useless. However more symbolic than significant that outpost was, it was also becoming plainer—despite wishful thinking in Washington—that the Navarre Plan (which had projected enlarging French Union Forces with promises of greater autonomy for the Associated States of Cambodia, Laos and Vietnam) was about to fail. Ely, in several days of discussions, including with the President, forced key American evaluations of its course in the crisis.[32]

For the inheritors of the cold war there was no mystery about American policy toward Southeast Asia. After the British helped the French return to Indochina at the end of World War II, the ideal of complete independence and the termination of colonialism that was the hope of such Americans as Franklin D. Roosevelt became secondary to the containment of communism. Supporting the French presence defied nationalist aims; and overlooked by Americans was the Vietnamese regard for Ho Chi Minh as the epitome of their aspirations. Deemed much more important was the need to support the French presence as the best way of preventing a Communist takeover.

As the Pentagon Papers that were revealed in 1971 demonstrated, Ho's appeals for American support were ignored. Washington's fears of his communism blinded the United States to any concept that he would emerge as an independent force, as did Tito in Yugoslavia. While it would, perhaps, be asking too much in retrospect to have expected such perspicacity among American policy-makers, additional information reveals that the anti-Communist mania at home—and the swallowing of their own propaganda—kept the Truman–Acheson formulators from seeing the situation with any sense of reality. When the fighting for independence began in earnest in late 1946, the French colonial forces were already using American military equipment and Washington had, in addition, arranged the extension of credit for them to buy $160 million worth of vehicles and miscellaneous industrial equipment for use against Ho's followers. A State Department Office of Intelligence Research survey of Communist influence in Southeast Asia in 1948 that found evidence of Kremlin-directed conspiracy in virtually all countries but Vietnam, which noted that the real anti-Americanism was being expressed in the French colonial press rather than by Ho Chi Minh's government, was disregarded. The subsequent Pentagon study that was ordered by Defense Secretary Robert McNamara in 1967 concluded that the "U. S. insistence on Ho's being a doctrinaire Communist may have been a self-fulfilling prophecy."[33]

Subsequently, despite the French monopolization of Vietnamese government and business, which virtually excluded indigenous participation in the area's economic life, fear of communism and concern for French participation in the European Western Alliance led to American recognition of the puppet government Paris established in Vietnam to counter the claims of Ho Chi Minh. American economic and military aid was also sent to the government led by Emperor Bao Dai, who could never convince his countrymen that he was anything but a French lackey. Washington, during those days, was only too happy to leave the area to French responsibility. Preoccupied with European recovery, Indochina was seen as one region "in which the U. S. might enjoy the luxury of abstention."[34]

After the French tried to appease nationalistic desires by enthroning Bao Dai as the head of a new Associated State of Vietnam and by giving that country as well as Cambodia and Laos the façade of independence within the French Union, American recognition followed. The American commitment was also reaffirmed in December of 1949, when the National Security Council formally adopted a policy of aid to Asians opposed to communism. The Russians and Chinese Communists then recognized the claims of Ho's government, which led Dean Acheson to declare that Moscow's action "should remove any illusions as to the 'nationalist' nature of Ho Chi Minh's aims."[35] Until the end of the French involvement in the spring of 1954, the subsequent flow of American aid totaled 78 percent of the entire effort, which came to $2.6 billion in military matériel. That did not include $126 million given to the Bao Dai government in direct economic, military and technical assistance. Chester Cooper aptly concluded that "to Ho Chi Minh and his colleagues the Viet Minh victory in 1954 was not only against the French armies but also against the arsenal and treasury of the United States."[36]

The statement of policy drawn up by the National Security Council in early 1952, entitled "United States Objectives and Course of Action with Respect to Southeast Asia," clarified American interests. Implying the so-called infamous "domino theory" well in advance of its public usage, the document ignored the realities of nationalistic communism and social and economic factors by warning that, in Southeast Asia, "the loss of any single country would probably lead to relatively swift submission to or an alignment with communism by the remaining countries of this group." That development was directly related to the interests of American "security" because of United States holdings in the Pacific and vital sources of natural rubber and tin, as well as petroleum and "other strategically important commodities." All of that made the French effort "essential to the security of 'the free world, not only in the Far East but in the Middle East and Europe as well." Adding to the terror by 1952 was the existence of the Peoples Republic of China. Especially after their intervention in Korea, via "volunteers," it was easier to regard the Peking regime as a threat to the entire area, almost as though American policy-makers were applying to Asia the lessons of pre-World War II Europe. Therefore, the paper decided, "The danger of an overt military attack against Southeast Asia is inherent in the existence of a hostile and aggressive Communist China," although it then admitted that "such an attack is less probable than continued communist efforts to achieve domination through subversion." While assistance to the French would be necessary and, if possible, efforts should be made to "bring to bear on the policies and actions of the French and Indochinese authorities to the end of directing the course of events toward the objectives we seek," open military intervention should not be undertaken except in the unlikely event of an overt attack by Communist China. Meanwhile, the United States should furnish "appropriate military, economic and financial aid to France and the Associated States." Should the French lose the will to continue their fight, the report went on to say, or should they seek an accommodation with other interests, the United States ought to "oppose a French withdrawal and consult with the French and British concerning further measures to be taken to safeguard the area from communist domination." Emphasized in every discussion of the possibility of American intervention was the need to determine "jointly with the UK and France that expanded military action against Communist China is rendered necessary by the situation. . . ." Almost lost in the report was the greatest single factor that doomed the French cause: colonialism. It merely called for "reorganization of French administration and representation in Indochina as will be conducive to an increased feeling of responsibility on the part of the Associated States."[37]

No evidence shows that either Eisenhower or his Secretary of State were primarily concerned with anything other than assumptions about stopping the spread of monolithic world communism in Asia. Eisenhower himself has revealed the advice he gave to the French while he commanded the NATO forces in Europe in 1951. "Look, you people are making one very bad error," he recalled having said. "You're letting the world and particularly the people in Indochina believe that you're still fighting a colonial war. You've got to make this thing a matter between freedom and communism . . . for some reason or other, they didn't want to come right on the spot and make the Vietnamese people understand 'We're fighting for you and when we win this war, you people are going to have the right of self-determination.' "[38] In his memoirs he has added that immediately after his inauguration in 1953, "recognizing the necessity of stopping Communist advances" in Vietnam, "we started immediately . . . to devise plans for strengthening the defenders politically and militarily within the proper limits."[39] Dulles, too, was disturbed by any suggestion that communism—and hence what he considered American interests—was not the overriding consideration. In his 1950 book *War or Peace*, he declared that the defeat of the government we back, "coming after the reverses suffered by the Nationalist Government of China, would have further serious repercussions on the whole situation in Asia and the Pacific. It would make even more people in the East feel that friendship with the United States is a liability rather than an asset."[40]

By the time General Ely came to Washington, however, the options available to the Administration were far fewer. If the Korean war had never taken place, a Truman-like commitment of American power could have been viewed as a gallant gesture to save the "free world." But with the end of that war along the Thirty-eighth Parallel, the Administration was in no mood to forfeit credit for what was obviously becoming its most popular accomplishment by, less than one year later, sending fresh American troops to a new Asian battlefield. Furthermore, the French desire for money and matériel and technicians made them no more receptive to tolerating the humiliation before their subjects that would be implicit by acceptance of overt American assumption of the war. Even Washington's offer to send training missions was turned down. Yet, the Administration feared, the same wing of the Republican party that was still defending Joe McCarthy, and a public that was anxious about the advance of "international communism," would not tolerate the abdication of still more territory to the Reds, especially by a government that had come into power vowing a tougher policy after having attributed previous enemy gains to the Democrats. Not one member of Congress or the Administration questioned the assumption that further Communist expansion would threaten American security. And, in May of 1953, Senator Knowland, shortly before succeeding to Taft's position, urged all-out aid for the French.[41]

Administration sympathy with ending colonialism in the area, even as only an instrument of the anti-Communist cause, was increasingly played down in public. Privately, however, there was little question about where the President stood. Dwight Eisenhower sent a personal response note to Senator Flanders's July 1 remarks on Capitol Hill, expressing complete agreement "that France should announce a firm intention of establishing self-government and independence in the Associated States of Indo-China" and then made an additional disclosure. "I have personally urged this upon the French authorities and secured their agreement in principle," he wrote. "So far the trouble has been that they have made such announcements only in an obscure and round-about fashion—instead of boldly, forthrightly and repeatedly."[42]

Eisenhower had to be cautious with the French. Like Truman, he was not only trying to entice the NATO allies into EDC but feared a move by a harried government in Paris to negotiate with the Viet Minh. Any settlement through such means was ominous to Washington, as it had been since the early days of the long war, for it could only weaken the anti-Communist position, virtually by definition. Having inherited the situation from the previous Administration, and adhering to the 1952 statement of American objectives in the area, his Administration could not afford to tolerate the communization of the area, let alone be an overt accomplice.

Yet, as was recognized from the start, it was a different kind of war. As a frustrated Dulles was to tell the Cabinet during the critical days of May 1954, the problem of calling attention to the need to draw a line against aggression in Asia was much more difficult than in Europe. Instead of a clear invasion across frontiers, there was subversion and "burrowing under fire" but with no visible evidence. "It is easy to marshal world opinion against aggression," he pointed out, "but not easy in regard to internal change. If we take the position that we will fight the Communist bloc if it gets hold of any country, we would have to act alone. Most countries do not share our view. They do not regard Communist control as a serious question." The President agreed. "People have to understand," he said, "that there is something better in the world than just giving up to the Commies. It's a long hard road."[43]

The prescription had to be public "education," which meant selling the crisis as the Administration understood it. Tone down the issue of colonialism, as Ike had earlier advised the French, and stress the morality of defending the "free world" against Red aggression. In Asia, having just come through a war in Korea that involved many thousands of so-called "volunteers" contributed by Peking, it was relatively simple to stress the Chinese Communist role as one of expansionism. Their contributions to the Viet Minh, in the form of training personnel and other assorted non-military personnel and equipment, plus continued anti-American propaganda coming from Chou En-lai's government, simplified the task. And, as feared by Dulles at the time of the Korean truce, the end of fighting on that peninsula did release greater Peoples Republic of China contributions. Observers in Hanoi could see an immediate enlargement in the supply of instructors and matériel from the north.[44] The increased availability of American goods that also resulted from the change in Korea probably more than matched what the Chinese could do and, in retrospect, marked a new plateau in the process of what was eventually recognized as the escalation of American presence in Vietnam.

Dulles, like Eisenhower, never had any doubt that the situation called for the determined response historians were writing should have been given to the German and Japanese assaults during the 1930s. Colonialism was an issue which, however much it may serve to weaken the defenses, must not be allowed to detract from the real fight. The French government under Joseph Laniel, Dulles told the Cabinet on July 10, 1953, could very well be the last one willing to hold on in Indochina. When Dulles spoke to the public the following week via radio and TV, in a speech primarily devoted to the pending armistice in Korea, he deemphasized colonialism by stressing that the three Associated States had, "with France, strong bonds of a cultural, economic and military nature." They were capable of being preserved "consistent with full independence, within the French Union," in a "free association of wholly independent and sovereign states" that would resemble the British Commonwealth of Nations.[45]

The Administration's effort to condition public opinion continued to accelerate. Eight months before he made his reference to falling dominoes when describing the consequences of losing in Vietnam, Eisenhower conveyed the spirit of the National Security Council paper of 1952 by addressing a Governors' Conference in Seattle and invoking the specter of having all of Southeast Asia succumb if "we lose Indochina." Gone, said Eisenhower, would be the "tin and tungsten that we so greatly value from that area." "All of that weakening position around there is very ominous for the United States," he explained, "because finally if we lost all that, how long would the free world hold the rich empire of Indonesia? So you see, somewhere along the line, this must be blocked. It must be blocked now. That is what the French are doing."[46] Less than one month later Dulles told the American Legion that the Chinese Communists were not only helping the Viet Minh but were capable of repeating the Korean experience by sending armies into the country. They should consider the danger, he warned, that "such a second aggression could not occur without grave consequences which might not be confined to Indochina."[47] Two weeks later, the Secretary of State addressed the UN and designated the Russians as the ones whose cooperation was needed for the achievement of peaceful independence in Indochina.[48]

Nixon, then giving evidence of becoming more than just another innocuous Vice President, traveled to the Far East. The 38,000-mile tour was conceived by Eisenhower via an impromptu remark during a Cabinet session. Ike's purpose, Nixon explained, was to dramatize that American foreign policy was aimed at putting Asia on a par with Europe. In Saigon, he linked French, American and anti-Communist Vietnamese objectives with the cause of "freedom and independence." He also warned against attempting to force the exit of French expeditionary forces or quitting the French Union. To have real independence, he advised Emperor Bao Dai, "you must destroy the Communists on your soil." Just before concluding his trip, he added that the United States would oppose any negotiated peace because victory must be complete. The New York *Times* promptly applauded the Vice President for having clarified that the United States "could not be a party to a compromise or settlement that would sacrifice the liberties of the Indo-Chinese peoples."[49]

At the same time, post-Korean war American military aid began to mount. During the summer, General John W. ("Iron Mike") O'Daniel had been sent to Saigon to supervise the use of American supplies. Later, he was made chief of MAAG, the United States Military Advisory and Assistance Group working with the Vietnamese. After the State Department reported that over three hundred shiploads of military aid had been supplied to the French and native forces, the National Security Council recommended an additional $385 million, which was then granted. Greater consultation between France and the United States, stressed in an exchange of correspondence between Washington and Paris on September 29, was also regarded by Prime Minister Laniel's parliament to mean that they could not negotiate an Indochina cease-fire with the Viet Minh or with China without prior American approval.[50]

Such moves were attempting to counter the serious French domestic pressures for extrication from the Far East. Even Laniel directly contradicted Nixon by saying his country did not seek unconditional surrender and would accept an honorable peace. François Mitterand, who had resigned from Laniel's cabinet because of the continuation of the war, was building up his following by leading National Assembly protests against trying to hold on in Indochina. A new Ho Chi Minh peace appeal, made through the Stockholm *Express* late in November, in which the Vietnamese leader blamed the American "imperialists" for keeping the war alive, was received with considerable interest. But, caught between their own right-wing business interests and the needs of the U.S. leadership, the French were not free. Dulles remarked that he doubted the sincerity of the Communist peace feelers and the French were assured of continued aid.[51] The American "education" campaign was then aided by Vice President Nixon saying on radio and television that the "free world owes a debt of gratitude to the French and to the forces of the Associated States for the great sacrifices they are making in the cause of freedom against Communist aggression in Indochina."[52]

The special *ad hoc* committee that Eisenhower then established was not concerned with studying future policy toward Indochina but, instead, means of supporting the Navarre Plan to keep the French in the fight. The group included Bedell Smith, Roger Kyes, the Joint Chiefs of Staff, Colonel Edward G. Lansdale and CIA Director Allen Dulles and, at a meeting in Kyes's office on January 29, agreed to recommend meeting French requests for more assistance by sending two hundred uniformed Air Force technicians to augment MAAG and Civil Air Patrol pilots. Admiral Radford told the group that ten B-26 bombers that were then en route to the Far East would bring the total up to the twenty-five operational aircraft requested by the French. Significantly, upon a request by the CIA director, it was agreed that Colonel Lansdale, "an unconventional warfare officer," would later be attached to MAAG.[53] Lansdale's exploits had already included helping Philippine President Ramon Magsaysay suppress the Hukbalahap insurgents.

While the Administration was assuming a larger share of the war's economic burden, the President had already initiated efforts to revamp military defense forces in a manner that would have important implications for the American response to the Indochinese situation. From the days when the "Great Equation" was discussed aboard the *Helena*, the General had continued his efforts to provide a military New Look as a more effective deterrent while, at the same time, contributing toward economic soundness. Excessive spending for obsolete and unrealistic numbers of ground forces could, he held, undermine the nation's economy. That would be self-defeating. During the campaign he had called for "security with solvency." Much later, as ex-President, he would feature that consideration in a speech before the Naval War College. He reminded the officers at Annapolis that "we know that the Communists seek to break the economy of the United States—an economy that is based on free enterprise and a sound currency. If we, therefore, put one more dollar into a weapons system than we should, we are weakening the defense of the United States." He cautioned that the way of life we are defending "can be destroyed in more ways than one."[54] Hence, Reorganization Plan 6 of 1953 concerning the Department of Defense, which the President had submitted to Congress on April 30, emphasized civilian authority over the military to reduce interservice competition for appropriations. Minimizing standing armies that have been the mainstay of conventional warfare and relying instead upon swift and powerful retaliatory power to discourage aggression would, the Administration contended, accomplish that purpose. Dulles pointed out that a potential enemy would be left "in no doubt that he would be certain to suffer damage outweighing any possible gains from aggression."[55] Consistent with such planning to achieve a "bigger bang for a buck" was a National

Security Council paper, NSC 162/2, which Eisenhower approved in October. The major reliance was placed on a strategic retaliatory Air Force and tactical nuclear weapons. Planning for limited war, such as the Korean conflict had been, was not given prominence.

When Dulles went before the Council of Foreign Relations in mid-January of 1954, even while the *ad hoc* committee was evaluating French needs in Vietnam, he gave his interpretation of the program. After saying that the Administration was after an international security system that would provide "for ourselves and the other free nations, a maximum deterrent at a bearable cost," he added that "Local defenses must be reinforced by the further deterrent of massive retaliatory power."[56] His position was promptly described by critics as "massive retaliation." Worse, there was a common assumption of an implicit threat to use nuclear weapons wherever a local crisis got out of hand, with or without consultation with America's allies.[57] Thus, although the President subsequently told a news conference that there was nothing new about taking retaliatory measures and responded with force whenever critical questions were raised, both Dulles and Defense Secretary Wilson were the ones most closely identified with the reshaping taking place.

Yet, the issue was one that Eisenhower supported with deep conviction. Such critics as General Ridgway, Adlai Stevenson and Chester Bowles, the former ambassador to India, voiced the common complaint that the country would be left helpless in the event of limited wars and indirect aggression. Without adequate conventional arms, they charged, even minor conflicts might require a nuclear response. But, as such resistance continued, the President became more agitated about their unwillingness to accept what seemed so obvious to him. He lectured his Congressional leaders about the fallacies of merely continuing to enlarge standing armies beyond what he called "the law of diminishing returns" and for ignoring the very real and immediate need in the face of a greater danger, the importance of improving means of evacuating cities in case of attack from the air. Recalling that the SHAPE planners had regarded the continued availability of American resources as one of their greatest concerns, he concluded that enemy bombing of American population centers required more attention than merely adding numbers to the uniformed ranks.[58] "How much defense do they think we can *buy?*" he asked about his critics at another point. An enormous army would virtually be useless because no one seemed to have a clear idea of what should be done with it. A much more valuable asset, then, was a good reserve program. In exasperation, he exclaimed one day, "I get a little bit tired of having to defend myself against the charge of 'being out to wreck the Army'!" Both in public and in private he reasserted his excellent credentials for making such judgments. "You have got to learn who you are protecting—not the generals but the American people," he later told Charlie Wilson.[59]

Since the economy and streamlining program was already under way by the spring of 1954, any move toward active American participation in Vietnam with ground forces would have fed the arguments of those contending that the New Look ignored the reality that fighting limited wars was bound to be the greatest need. Any overt commitment more substantial than MAAG, and of a more forthright military nature, would have caught the Administration in a contradiction. At the same time, fear that Eisenhower's announcement about sending technicians meant a foreshadowing of more substantial aid was in evidence when the President met with the Congressional leaders on February 8. He told them that while it was not a completely desirable thing to do, the French had been notified that their own people would have to fill the need by June 15 because Americans would then be withdrawn.[60] He also said at a news conference that any American involvement in Indochina would have to be sanctioned by Congress. "Now, let us have that clear; and that is the answer," he added emphatically.[61]

The French, however, had already given up any hopes of a military victory in Indochina but were turning to the Americans with the hope of further matériel aid that would enable them to hold out with sufficient strength to retain a bargaining hand by the opening of the conference scheduled to begin in Geneva on April 26. When the Big Four met in Berlin in January and February, an international meeting to reach a political settlement in Korea was approved. Dulles, who had declared on the second day of the session that the United States would not join in a five-power conference with the "Chinese Communist aggressors for the purpose of dealing generally with the peace of the world," soon found that the sensitivities of the French alliance led him to accept two politically dangerous arrangements that had been demanded by Prime Minister Laniel: meeting face to face with the Chinese and acquiescence to pressures from Paris to include Indochina on the agenda. The United States could not become vulnerable to charges of sacrificing French soldiers while refusing even to discuss the possibility of peace. Furthermore, as Eisenhower has written, if the American government was responsible for blocking such a conference, the "moral obligation to carry on the war . . . might be shifted from French shoulders to ours."[62]

Just as Dulles had anticipated, American hard-liners were shocked. They feared two ominous prospects: opening the way for recognition of the Peoples Republic of China and a commitment of troops for the war. When the Secretary returned to Washington he was quizzed by sixteen Republican and Democratic Congressional leaders. Republicans, led by Knowland, were the most concerned. The Senator from California warned that the Administration would be held accountable for any "slips" at Geneva—or diplomatic recognition of China—and for anything that might lead to American intervention in the war.[63] Ralph Flanders was so worried that China's admission to the United Nations would follow that he was ready to take some comfort in any vote on that issue that might reveal "an inevitable and sharp decline of interest on the part of the people of the United States in the support of the United Nations." Flanders also suggested that Henry Cabot Lodge remind the other members that defying American desires on that matter meant disregarding the country that was absorbing one-third of the UN's costs.[64] The criticism within the party of the Dulles agreement soon led to hints that the Administration was planning to downgrade the conference by having Under Secretary Walter Bedell Smith do most of the actual negotiating at Geneva.[65]

General Ely found that the man most receptive to requests for military aid at Dien Bien Phu was Admiral Radford. His meeting with the full JCS had brought only suggestions that the program for training pilots for Indochina taking place in the Philippines might be stepped up and, what he was still unwilling to accept, sending of an American mission to help improve Vietnamese capability. In a session with Eisenhower and Radford on the following day, the French general was told by the President that the admiral would do everything possible to fulfill his requests. Dulles had already told Ely, during their meeting on the twenty-third, that the United States could not afford to risk her prestige in a military operation "and suffer defeat which would have world-wide repercussions." Only overt aggression by the Chinese Communists would be sufficient provocation.

Therefore, after an additional session Ely had with the full JCS, during which they agreed to send twenty-five more B-26 bombers, Radford made a dramatic proposal. He was ready to convince the President to contribute massive American air strikes from about sixty B-29 bombers stationed at Clark Field in the Philippines and 150 fighter escorts from the carriers *Essex* and *Boxer* that were in the Gulf of Tonkin. Three small tactical atomic bombs would be used. Without such efforts to destroy the Viet Minh positions around Dien Bien Phu, Radford said, the garrison's chances were hopeless. After General Navarre's approval, the French agreed to request what became known as Operation Vulture.[66]

But the American position, as the Joint Chiefs of Staff had recommended back in 1952, was opposed to unilateral intervention. Dulles, in fact, even while Radford's offer was being relayed to Paris, spoke before the Overseas Press Club on the twenty-ninth and, after terming the extension of Soviet and Red Chinese power in Southeast Asia "a grave threat to the whole free community," stated that such a possibility "should not be passively accepted but should be met by united action."[67] Although he maintained in public, during the next few days, that Chinese assistance had created the situation—including at Dien Bien Phu—his word to the Cabinet on March 26 was that the main situation in Indochina was not a military one but an outgrowth of the disintegration of French colonial capability, a position in harmony with the large numbers of Americans and Europeans who were less alarmed than he about Communist aggrandizement. He thought the Navarre plan remained sound and that there was "no *military* disaster foreseeable."[68]

Of greater importance, in view of what he heard about Operation Vulture from Radford the next day, was his opinion regarding the consequences of the collapse at Dien Bien Phu. He could not consider that a military disaster. The location was not of sufficient importance, he said, to alter the balance of the rival military forces. Its loss would be much more important as a psychological setback. What General Ely and Radford were concerned about was, in Dulles's view, hardly sufficient to warrant all the risks and political hazards of open intervention. "The main thing to realize," Dulles told the Cabinet, as Eisenhower listened, "is the existence of an extremely serious situation which may require us to go to the Congress for approval of some more extensive action. A number of alternatives are being considered but there is no decision yet made."[69]

Military involvement would also place the United States in the position of openly supporting French colonialism. Since the war was, primarily, a French affair, such a move would have been a great blunder. Furthermore, as the legally minded Dulles was well aware, unilateral belligerency would be regarded internationally as an act of unlawful aggression. Then, too, the New Look refinement would have to be resolved to meet that situation, and it was encountering enough political difficulties without the complication of new ones. Finally, perhaps, neither Dulles nor Eisenhower thought that highly about blatant military force as the proper solution for the problems in Indochina.[70]

Nor did the President have much faith in American involvement. He told those around the table that he deplored the complications caused by "that colonial factor" and observed that if we could sit down and talk about it without having to use force, we could get something done. He could only be certain about one thing: that—again as the National Security Council had urged in 1952—there be no action without allied support. That, of course, meant the assistance of France and the United Kingdom. After Radford told Dulles about Vulture the next day, the Secretary of State and the President discussed the matter several times during the week.[71] At no point did they waver from the belief in "united action" that Dulles had described on the twenty-ninth.

Eisenhower, of course, also had his perceptive antennae tuned in to popular opinion. The constant efforts made by Nixon and Dulles to point to Chinese misbehavior in Asia had stressed the communism factor;

but, as much as a deterioration of "free world" positions was not wanted, few were ready to go to war again. And any such move, both Eisenhower and Dulles told Radford, required Congressional approval. The difficulties that move would encounter were demonstrated on April 3, when, acting on the President's suggestion, Dulles convened a secret meeting of members of Congress: Under Secretary of Defense Roger Kyes, Navy Secretary Robert B. Anderson and Dulles's assistant for Congressional Relations, Thruston B. Morton. They gathered at the State Department that Saturday morning to hear Admiral Radford describe his plan.

Dulles introduced Radford by saying the Administration wanted a joint Congressional resolution authorizing the use of air and naval power in Indochina. He said that the President, who was not at the meeting, had asked for its consideration, although he hinted its passage might make implementation unnecessary. Radford then took the floor. After he described before the silent Representatives and Senators, including Minority Leader Lyndon B. Johnson, how the planes from Clark Field and the *Essex* and the *Boxer* would be used to relieve Dien Bien Phu, sharp questioning followed. The admiral was forced to admit that he was the only member of the Joint Chiefs who favored the plan and left open the possibility that its failure might require American ground forces to finish the job. When the possibility of thereby provoking the Peking regime was raised, Dulles aided Radford by suggesting that the Russians did not want a general war and could be counted on to restrain the Chinese. As Eisenhower had expected when suggesting the meeting, which took place while he was at Camp David, Radford got a firsthand demonstration of their unwillingness to agree to Operation Vulture without the support of America's allies.[72]

The reaction of the Congressmen was taken up the next night at a White House meeting. Radford and Dulles were present. There, President Eisenhower in effect reaffirmed what had been obvious to him all along: that, as the eight Senators and Representatives had demanded, a recommendation sent to Congress for intervention required French willingness to continue the fight and to relieve the United States from any hint of supporting colonialism by taking "decisive steps" to grant full independence to the Associated States. Great Britain, Australia and New Zealand must also join in the arrangement for the establishing of collective defense.[73]

Nor did the debates on the Senate floor offer much encouragement for open involvement. The resolution discussed at the April 3 meeting and at the White House the next day was not requested, nor did anybody argue for it; but concern about Indochina dominated their remarks. Both Paul Douglas of Illinois, a supporter of swift response to foil Communist aggression, and his Democratic colleague from Mississippi, John Stennis,

feared the allies would stand by and permit the United States to repeat
its Korean assumption of the overwhelming burden of the war. Stennis
also said he could not "agree that under any circumstances I can now
think of our land troops should go into Indochina and be committed in
this war area."[74] Foreign Relations Committee Chairman Wiley feared
that "if war comes under this Administration, it would well end the
Republican Party."

Most of their plaudits, both from liberals and conservatives, were paid,
however, to a long speech on April 6 by freshman John F. Kennedy of
Massachusetts. Kennedy's comments, especially interesting in view of his
own subsequent Presidential escalation of American participation in that
area, at a different stage, were directed to the thesis that nothing could
overcome the adverse effects of French colonialism short of outright,
unquestioned independence. He warned that pouring "money, matériel,
and men into the jungles . . . without at least a remote prospect of
victory would be dangerously futile and self-destructive." Describing a
country in which French commercial interests continued to monopolize
its economic life, which "flies in the face of repeated assurances to the
American people by our own officials that complete independence has
been or will be granted" by such spokesmen as Assistant Secretary of
State Dean Rusk in 1951, he surmised that "no amount of American
military assistance in Indochina can conquer an enemy which is everywhere and at the same time nowhere, 'an enemy of the people' which has
the sympathy and covert support of the people." A military victory in
that area, he concluded, "is difficult if not impossible, of achievement . . .
without a change in the contractual relationships which presently exist
between the Associated States and the French Union." Knowland complimented Kennedy, as he agreed with the basic premises of the speech,
and added that it pointed to the wisdom of collective action should overt
aggression develop, and Stennis called it "the finest statement I have
heard on this subject."[75] Continued reactions, during the following
week, pointed out the contradictions between more extensive commitments and the New Look policy, with Albert Gore of Tennessee suggesting it might be time to reconsider the Administration's 30 percent
reduction in the budget for the Army.[76]

But by far the most common criticism was the charge that the Administration had not taken Congress into its confidence by explaining its
position. What, for example, did Dulles mean by "united action"? Why
had the President said there would be no American involvement without
Congressional approval? Although there had been a secret briefing on
the third of April that had included five Senators and three Representatives, some thought it would be more appropriate for the President
himself to go before them to outline what was needed. Hubert Humphrey observed that there "seems to be a reluctance on the part of the

executive branch of the Government, in the present critical situation, to fully inform the responsible committees of the Congress."[77]

Humphrey, of course, was right. But barring any such folly as Radford had suggested and fully recognizing the disaster created by the French did not mean that Eisenhower and Dulles were ready to signal to any would-be Chinese Communist invasion force, as the United States had by its pre-World War II neutrality laws, that America would remain on the sidelines. At the same time, the Administration's domestic supporters who were eager to see Republicans improve upon their predecessors' ability to contain the Reds in the Far East and those who had been disappointed by the Korean truce could be assured that the Secretary of State's warnings about the Chinese and call for "united action" meant that Asian policy had indeed been hardened. When Eisenhower at his press conference of April 17 applied the "falling domino" principle ("You have a row of dominoes set up, you knock over the first one, and what will happen to the last one is the certainty that it will go over very quickly.") to project the possible loss of all Southeast Asia, he was being no clearer about his intentions. Nor could he know what future options might be available. But the *possibilities* were there.[78]

Perhaps the most controversial comment made during the policy of obfuscation came on April 16. Richard Nixon said that he "hoped the United States will not have to send troops there, but if this Government cannot avoid it, the Administration must face up to the situation and dispatch forces."[79] Was that really a "trial balloon" as many suspected? The Vice President and those close to him later denied that he had spoken with any authority other than his own, that he had merely given that possibility to emphasize his belief in the importance of stopping the Chinese in Indochina. The surrounding circumstances, however, were intriguing. It was supposedly an off-the-record talk, not for attribution; but attempting secrecy before the full convention of—of all groups—the American Society of Newspaper Editors by the Vice President of the United States seemed tailor-made to enliven the mystique about the Administration's intentions. Jim Hagerty has since said that he was not aware of any prior arrangement between Dulles or the President and Nixon but he has agreed that it is "almost inconceivable" that it could have been done without the knowledge of the White House.[80]

The real drive consisted of American initiative for "united action" in the form of announced readiness to retaliate against any potential Communist invasion and, at the same time, the establishment of a regional collective defense barrier in Southeast Asia. Dulles in his *Foreign Affairs* article that appeared in April described the need for "community" response. Furthermore, overcoming French objections would have permitted covert American intervention to, as Eisenhower wrote to General

Gruenther, "get a good guerrilla organization started in the region" and "to take over a great part of the burden of training native troops, and numerous offers of help in the logistic field."[81]

On Sunday afternoon, April 4, Dulles entertained Australia's Percy Spender and Sir Leslie Munro of New Zealand, as well as Radford, Charlie Wilson and Walter Robertson, at the Secretary's Washington home on Thirty-second Street. He urged the Australian to contribute an aircraft carrier. He then removed from his bookcase the first volume of Sir Winston Churchill's *The Second World War*. Turning to page eighty-seven, he read to the group how the failure of the British and Americans to act collectively in 1931 and 1932 had permitted Japanese conquest of Manchuria. With evident triumph, he read the most pointed sentence: "The British Government on their part showed no desire to act with the United States alone; nor did they wish to be drawn into antagonism with Japan further than their obligations under the League of Nations required."[82] By the time that lesson was recalled for Dulles's guests, the United Kingdom, France, South Korea, Formosa, the Philippines and Thailand, as well as Australia and New Zealand, had all been asked to form a coalition.[83]

But, as Anthony Eden has explained, the British were not ready to be "hustled into injudicious military decisions." Unlike the United States, they had recognized the Peoples Republic of China and were reluctant to foreclose any opportunities for peace in the area. The safety of their colony at Hong Kong was another consideration.[84]

The French also opposed "united action." Their purpose in calling for a conference on Indochina had been to end the war in a way that would still preserve their economic concessions, not to refuel it. That would, of course, happen if the Chinese Communists intervened to oppose an allied move. Surviving on the battlefield long enough for a political settlement was one matter, but enlarging what was already unpopular in France could bring down the Laniel government and even provide Peking with an excuse to scuttle the conference.[85]

When, in the face of a rapidly deteriorating position at Dien Bein Phu, they asked Washington to implement Operation Vulture, Dulles replied that the United States could not act without British participation and Congressional approval.[86] Nevertheless, within the next few days, two American aircraft carriers sailed toward the Indochina coast from Manila with atomic weapons in a display of force. Meeting with the Cabinet on the ninth of April, Dulles explained that efforts were being made, despite the disappointing reaction of the two vital allies, to "build a strong position in advance of the Geneva meeting so as to protect against the imminent possibility of the French giving in."[87]

As far as the United States was concerned, the diplomatic frustrations of the next two weeks guaranteed failure at Geneva. Seeking to repair the situation, Eisenhower arranged for a Dulles visit to London again to air the American position. Eden, Dulles then found, was still adamant about any kind of pre-conference declaration proclaiming readiness for a joint military strike to protect the Associated States from outside intervention. He worried that it would be a "bigger affair than Korea."[88] But the American was pleased by what seemed to be an improved outlook toward a coalition for collective security. Their communiqué, issued on April 13, after two days of talks, represented to Dulles a fine starting point. It stated their agreement to join with the other countries "in an examination of the possibility of establishing" such a coalition "to assure the peace, security and freedom of Southeast Asia and the Western Pacific."[89] Dulles assumed he had approval to convene a nine-power conference to form the coalition. Accordingly, right after returning home, he arranged for a meeting to take place in Washington on April 20. But on the morning of Easter Sunday, two days before the start of the first session, the British ambassador, Sir Roger Makins, called at the Secretary's home with devastating news. Eden had forbidden his attendance for that purpose.

Dulles would always feel Eden had reneged. He attributed the reversal —which he was certain it was—to opposition by Prime Minister Nehru of India. The English Foreign Secretary had suggested, during his discussions with Dulles, that India be invited to join any NATO-like organization that might be concocted for Southeast Asia; but his American visitor contended that a distasteful controversy would thereby be unleashed, led by the same elements in the United States that had objected to the positions he had accepted at the Berlin Conference. Republicans, like Knowland, would then insist on the inclusion of Formosa and South Korea. Instead of extending it both westward and eastward, Dulles explained, it would be best to limit membership to the nine nations already designated. Nehru, Dulles was convinced, under the heavy influence of his pro-Chinese special envoy, Krishna Menon, had forced Eden into his new position. Through Menon's influence, then, as the Secretary analyzed the situation, the net effect was a veto by Red China over American policy.[90]

There were other possible explanations, however. Eden was under heavy opposition pressure. The day after the Eden–Dulles communiqué, Aneurin Bevan quit the Labor party's "shadow cabinet" in protest against his party's support of a government that was backing American policy in Southeast Asia. Sir Winston, then eighty years old, could be expected to step down within a year or two and his Foreign Minister would be foolish to do anything that could hinder his becoming the new Prime Minister. Eden would, therefore, be safer to make no commitment until after Geneva. Those familiar with Dulles's persuasiveness surmised that he had left London convinced that Eden's agreement was clear. But even their communiqué had been ambiguous. Nothing definite had been said about a coalition; the Foreign Minister had approved a statement calling only for an "examination" of such united action as a "possibility." And that was hardly firm. It was, therefore, easy for Eden to regard Dulles's call for a pre-Geneva nine-power conference as a precipitous American move.

The British position then gave Dulles an opportunity to *appear* amenable to a last-minute French request to reconsider his April 5 rejection of an air strike to save Dien Bien Phu. The appeal was made on April 23, while the Secretary of State was in Paris en route to Geneva. In Dulles's presence that next morning, Admiral Radford tried to convince Eden about the importance of bombing to keep the entire military situation in Indochina from getting out of control. A report subsequently published in the Washington *Post* by Chalmers Roberts on June 7, 1954, described Dulles as revealing that President Eisenhower was then prepared, upon British agreement, to go before Congress to request a resolution authorizing such action.

Eden's account, however, shows that Radford and not Dulles dominated the conversation. Furthermore, on the thirtieth, Dulles stressed that nobody was advocating military intervention in Indochina, "though he understood that perhaps some remarks of Admiral Radford, whom he was inclined to criticize, had caused us to draw back in our attitude towards the pact." Dulles then emphasized that the admiral "was not the spokesman of the United States. Only the President and himself could express that opinion."[91] Furthermore, there is no evidence that the draft of a letter the British observed Dulles hand to French Foreign Minister Bidault offering to respond to their second request for air intervention, if the British also agreed, was anything but a tactful way of sidetracking the issue. Bidault approved the sending of an official American offer; but Dulles, after his very recent conversations with Eden and London's consistently negative attitude, could have had no doubt that their response would enable him to avoid being put on the spot. When the British cabinet met the next day, both Churchill and Eden opposed the second American proposal and it was given a final rejection. The news was cheered in the House of Commons.[92]

Nixon, Radford and Dulles emerged from those critical weeks as the "warriors," but Eisenhower's image as a keeper of the peace was unmarred. When *Look* magazine carried an article by Fletcher Knebel revealing how close the nation had come to war, it ran a subtitle claiming ". . . but Ike Said No." Still, to believe in the existence of any substantive difference on that issue between the President and his Secretary of State is fallacious. Their outlook toward the Far East was in harmony. Ten years later, Eisenhower was asked privately whether he and Dulles were together on that issue. "All the way," Eisenhower replied, "Oh yes, yes, absolutely."[93]

On April 26, as the conference was starting in Geneva, Eisenhower told his legislative leaders about the high future cost of not helping the French in Indochina. "Doing unpleasant things when they are not properly understood is not easy," he explained and observed that the alternative of no action would perhaps be much worse. When Congressman Halleck worried about committing American troops, the President again stressed that any involvement should be in concert with the "free world —and the free world must realize that our effective role does not lie in furnishing ground troops."[94] Moreover, Eden's own description of his discussion with Dulles in Geneva on April 30 is strikingly in harmony with Eisenhower's, who later portrayed the Secretary of State as explaining that "no matter what the British might have inferred from strong statements by any of our officials . . . the United States was not seeking *large-scale intervention** in Indochina or war with China. We were earnestly trying to avoid such developments—but they could best be avoided by a show of Western firmness."[95]

On Thursday, April 22, Dulles was in Paris before going on to Geneva. In Washington, Karl Mundt was conducting the first session of the Army–McCarthy hearings before a television audience that would even exceed the twenty million estimated viewers of Senator Kefauver's committee investigation of the underworld in 1951. Dwight Eisenhower, on that same day, was interrupting his latest vacation at Augusta, where he had played golf with brother Edgar on Wednesday, to deliver an evening speech at the Waldorf-Astoria Hotel in New York before the American Newspaper Publishers Association. He urged "most earnestly" that attention be given by the press "to the things that united the American people equal to that it gives the things that divide them."[96]

Through thirty-five days of hearings, the Republican party underwent the agony of having its most flamboyant and controversial Senator demonstrate before the millions of viewers an arrogance and ruthlessness that had not been properly understood before, even after his treatment of General Zwicker. Now, however, with his young lawyer, Roy Cohn, he took on the Army and its special counsel, a gentle, mild-mannered Boston attorney named Joseph Welch. The Administration's position, of course, was the Army's; and after Secretary Robert Stevens and John G. Adams testified in detail about the abuse they had taken from McCarthy and Cohn, the hearings moved on to a chronicle of monitored telephone calls, cropped photographs, charges of blackmail and claims by Cohn that the Army was holding Schine as a "hostage" to force the subcom-

* Author's italics.

mittee to halt its investigations of subversion in the military. McCarthy himself, beginning his testimony on the ninth of June, offered his own charges about the Army's role in getting him to end the probes. He called Stevens "a very honest individual—with no experience in politics" who had gotten "mouse-trapped in the very rough politics being played" in Washington.

On June 9, also, McCarthy drew the most emotional outburst of the thirty-five days. He suddenly charged that Welch's prominent law firm had a thirty-two-year-old attorney who "had been for a number of years" a member of the National Lawyers Guild, which, the Senator added, had been "named by various committees, named by the Attorney General, as I recall . . . as the legal bulwark of the Communist party." Welch, composing himself carefully, trembled and then said, in a voice that only barely suppressed bitterness, "Until this moment, I think I never really gauged your cruelty or your recklessness." He explained that the man who had been attacked, Frederick G. Fisher, had belonged to the Guild while at Harvard Law School and for a "period of months" after that and, at present, was secretary of the Young Republican League in Newton, Massachusetts. Turning to McCarthy again, Welch added, "Little did I dream you could be so reckless and so cruel as to do an injury to that lad. I fear he shall always bear a scar needlessly inflicted by you." When McCarthy tried to continue, Welch stopped him by saying, "Let us not assassinate this lad further, Senator. . . . Have you no sense of decency?"[97]

By that stage of the hearings, Republicans had long since been on edge and the President had come under increasing pressure to intervene, as he had been throughout his encounters with the Senator from Wisconsin. Not long after its start he referred to it before his Congressional leaders as "this shameful inquiry" and asked whether some particularly appealing legislative items could be found to distract from the show.[98] The dangers to the party were finally confirmed on May 28 when, responding to the Administration's challenge to McCarthy's request for federal employees to provide him with classified information regardless of security regulations, he stretched his previous "twenty years of treason" charge to "twenty-one," thus including the Eisenhower period.[99] The President had also barred John Adams from testifying about the private meeting and telephone calls involving the executive branch. Cautiously, however, he told the Congressional leaders that while he hoped his action would not be viewed as needlessly stirring up a struggle with the legislature, there was some virtue in continuing a struggle between both branches of government so long as respect and mutual confidence were maintained.[100]

But other Republicans were far more agitated about the public proceedings. Harry Bullis reported that at business meetings in New York,

Washington and Toledo he had found "no one who was not utterly disgusted" with the hearings and that their unanimous opinion was that they should be ended immediately. Many of the businessmen wondered, he wrote, whether the President realized to what extent "public opinion among businessmen is mobilizing against McCarthy, even though some of these businessmen do not have the courage to express their opinions publicly." A banker from Wichita Falls, Texas, suggested that McCarthy had been hurting the Republicans so much he may even be "in the employ of the New Dealers. He has done more to destroy morale and create fear and doubt than the Russians could ever do."[101] Senator Dirksen tried a gambit to cool things off by asking for a week's recess to study the situation created by the President's order keeping John Adams from testifying about the meeting of January 21. But his motion was accepted along blatantly political lines. Avoiding further embarrassment, Eisenhower asked that the hearings be continued.[102] Then, on the first of June, Ralph Flanders again attacked McCarthy on the Senate floor, this time comparing him to Hitler and accusing the junior Senator of spreading fear and confusion. Flanders also denounced him for hurting the Republican party in an election year.[103]

Most of all, his TV performance accelerated the downward slide that had begun even before the start of the hearings. Well in advance of the subcommittee's verdict, which was released on August 31, the public had come to its own conclusion. The basic charges made by each side, they felt, had been substantiated; but the weight of the sympathy, Gallup reported, was with Stevens and the Army.[104] At last, little controversy remained about the Senator's value to the party. Further losses in his popularity were reported from his home state of Wisconsin, where the strength of a "Joe Must Go" recall movement was regarded as significant. McCarthy's attack on Welch's young lawyer had been, according to observers in his home state, his single most damaging blunder. Reports from throughout the country confirmed the trend. In a primary election held in Tennessee in August, the renomination of progressive Democratic Senator Estes Kefauver against a challenger identified with McCarthy's tactics was also thought significant.[105] The majority report of the subcommittee held that while there had been no substantiation of the charges that McCarthy had used improper influence, McCarthy should have disciplined Cohn, who was "unduly aggressive and persistent" on behalf of Schine and had used "an inordinate amount of Committee time in his efforts." The majority, consisting of the Republicans, also agreed that Stevens and John Adams had tried to interfere with the investigations at Fort Monmouth, while the Democratic minority came down harder on both sides.[106] However, even before the hearings had concluded, Flanders had called for a resolution to remove McCarthy from his chairmanship of the Government Operations Committee; later, after

Knowland objected that debating the motion could block "the Administration's legislative program," Flanders substituted a call for censure. In early August the issue was referred to a select bipartisan committee, which came under the chairmanship of Senator Arthur V. Watkins, a Utah Republican. The months before the Congressional elections was a particularly sensitive time for Senators to be forced into taking positions on the still controversial McCarthy. The committee's recommendation in favor of censure came out on September 27, but the adjournment of Congress to permit campaigning avoided that problem.

Eisenhower's caution had enabled him to weather the McCarthy crisis. Even the Senator would not blame the President nearly as much as those around him in the White House who had done the "misleading." Yet, if the issue of McCarthy had been blunted for the forthcoming elections, especially with the censure vote scheduled for after November 2, the issue of communism was still very much alive. Having stumbled into a fight against McCarthy and his followers at home, with the consequences to the party that Eisenhower worried so much about, the Administration could not simultaneously preside over a Communist victory in Indochina. Since no headway had been made in getting agreement for "united action" before the start of the Geneva Conference—for a collective security coalition and a joint willingness to use force to protect the French Union positions, and the French were resisting covert guerrilla-warfare assistance—Eisenhower and Dulles had to do everything possible to keep the battle from being lost at the bargaining table.

To the Administration, the session at Geneva could easily become an opening wedge for Communist domination of all Southeast Asia. British rejection of American overtures and French reluctance to "internationalize" the conflict had apparently doomed the outlook. Even more importantly, the dark situation on the battlefield, with the fall of Dien Bien Phu becoming imminent, gave the Communists the upper hand. Republican agreement with anything leading to the Western loss of Indochina could someday become their Yalta. As he had decided earlier, when he had been defensive about justifying his agreement to participate with Communist China and to include the Associated States in a conference originally set to cope with the problems of unifying Korea, Dulles would not give the proceedings the dignity of his prolonged presence and Under Secretary Walter Bedell Smith would replace him early.

At the first session a number of statesmen took advantage of a break in the proceedings to lounge in the reception hall. Chou En-lai, Eden and Molotov were already there together when Dulles appeared. When he spotted the Secretary of State, the Chinese leader approached him in an obvious bid to shake his hand. Photographers were present, however. Visions of the group pictures of Roosevelt, Churchill and Stalin seated together amicably at the famous Black Sea resort probably flashed through Dulles's mind. Just as Chou En-lai extended his hand, the Secretary "quite brusquely"—according to a member of the American delegation standing nearby—turned his back. For many years afterward, the Chinese premier delighted in recounting the incident.[107]

After he returned to Washington, the Secretary conveyed to Smith the President's instructions confirming the attitude to be taken by the American delegation. There should be no dealings with the Chinese Communists that would "imply political recognition" and the United States should be at the conference as "an interested nation which, however, is neither a belligerent nor a principal in the negotiation." There was not to be American approval of "any cease-fire, armistice, or other settlement which would have the effect of subverting the existing lawful governments of the three aforementioned states or of permanently impairing their territorial integrity or of placing in jeopardy the forces of the French Union in Indochina, or which otherwise contravened the principles stated above."[108]

The Korean question ended early and in a deadlock. Disagreement over holding elections to reunify that country, with the West contending that the more sparsely populated North wanted to make free elections impossible by guaranteeing for itself a disproportionate share of the power, left the boundary near the Thirty-eighth Parallel, where the fighting had stopped.[109] Creating a similar partition in Indochina would just as surely write off territory to the Communists. And with every indication showing that Ho Chi Minh was by all odds the most popular leader in Viet Nam, agreement to hold elections in the near future guaranteed that he would be in control. A National Security Council report dated April 5 had urged the United States to take "all affirmative and practical steps, with or without its European allies," to demonstrate determination to stop communism. American policy should "accept nothing short of military victory in Indo-China" and should oppose at Geneva any move by the French to compromise that position. Even the lack of French support should not deter the United States from keeping the war going. The "free world strategic position," it stated, was too important to permit fears about jeopardizing the ratification of EDC to prevent even the "most extraordinary efforts" to save Southeast Asia from Communist domination.[110] Nevertheless, the actual implementation of such measures was, of course, up to the President.

He was determined to use every *show* of force, every *covert* method and every *credible threat* to attack, as a means of deterring a Chinese invasion even while the conference was taking place and to encourage the French to remain in the war. His and Dulles's trepidations about large-scale intervention, with or without allies, had already been supported by the recommendation filed by Army Chief of Staff Matthew Ridgway. The general had sent a team of experts to survey Indochina and found the area completely uncongenial for modern warfare and best for guerrilla fighting, which would give the Chinese a great advantage. The cost of a war there, Ridgway later wrote, "would have eventually been as great as, or greater than, that we paid in Korea." When his report reached the President its military "implications were immediately clear" to him.[111] As to striking from the air, Eisenhower considered such plans to be "just silly." "After these people are deployed, and secreted all around in the jungle," he asked, "how are we, in a few air strikes, to defeat them?" He also wanted no part of a "war that has, as its only purpose, the re-establishing of colonial power over Indochina."[112] When Dien Bien Phu was on the verge of collapse, he met his Congressional leaders and recalled having favored, at one point, sending a message to the French suggesting they issue a statement of determination to fight on even if Dien Bien Phu should fall, but he changed his mind through fear it might demoralize the beleaguered garrison. Furthermore, he told them, the British had not stopped any proposed American action because we had never considered going in independently.[113]

When Dulles turned over the American delegation to Under Secretary Bedell Smith and reached Washington on May 5, he was prepared to inform Congress that Dien Bien Phu could not be saved but that it was still advisable to press ahead for a collective defense system. Two days later, at the same time the Viet Minh captured the town, Dulles made a televised report to the nation in which he said that "The present conditions there do not provide a suitable basis for the United States now to participate with its armed forces." We would, however, be upset at any armistice in Geneva that "would provide a road to a Communist takeover and further Communist aggression. If this occurs, or if hostilities continue, then the need will be more urgent to create the condition for a united action in defense of the area." He repeated that any commitment would require Congressional approval and would only be undertaken in the absence of an "adequate collective effort."[114]

That clearly spelled out the real question at that point: What to do if an honorable cease-fire were impossible? The National Security Council's Planning Board pointed out, as Bobby Cutler reported the next day, that the "mere proposal of the cease-fire at the Geneva Conference would destroy the will to fight of French forces and make fence sitters jump to the Viet Minh side." Cutler, participating in a meeting with Eisenhower and Dulles just before the Secretary's TV speech, recorded the President's emphasis that the French must be told that we would never intervene alone and without an invitation "by the indigenous people, and that there must be some kind of regional and collective action." Cutler pointed out that American willingness to ask Congress to authorize intervention had only been hinted at in the past but not made clear. Dulles, who was about to meet with the French ambassador that afternoon, said he would mention that point to M. Bonnet, "perhaps making a more broad hint than heretofore."[115]

Three days later, Prime Minister Laniel asked Ambassador Douglas Dillon about the conditions for American intervention. After the President discussed the latest development with Dulles, Wilson and Radford, the Secretary of State was directed to prepare a resolution requesting authority to commit American troops for Indochina that he could present before a joint meeting of Congress. The draft was prepared and subsequently circulated in the State, Justice and Defense departments.

Nevertheless, on the fifteenth of May, although Eisenhower later admitted that the French were well aware of the "bulk of these conditions" for intervention, Dulles sent a secret note to Ambassador Dillon in Paris, spelling out formidable prerequisites. As Eisenhower has recounted them, they requested that

1. France and the Associated States make a formal request for American military participation.
2. Australia and New Zealand must also be invited to help.
3. The United Nations be brought in to form a peace-observation commission.
4. France "guarantee complete independence to the Associated States, including an 'unqualified option to withdraw from the French forces at any time'; that France keep its forces in action, with the American assistance—'principally air and sea'—as supplements, not substitutes."
5. Agreement be reached on American participation in training native troops and working out a command structure for united action.
6. Both the French cabinet and National Assembly must accept all of the decisions.[116]

British participation was no longer mentioned. But the conditions listed did require extensive internationalization and involvement, including the United Nations, in addition to assurances that all French forces would continue to fight; that guaranteed rejection by the cabinet in Paris and could only precipitate violent protest in the National Assembly. It was, in short, a plan to intervene on purely American terms and one that contained the greatest degree of caution. The United States clearly preferred to step aside and tolerate the consequences of the French-created disaster than assume any risks unilaterally.[117] Indeed, on May 26, a Joint Chiefs of Staff memorandum to Defense Secretary Wilson urged that any American intervention should be limited to "air and naval support directed from outside Indochina." And then it pointed out that "*Indochina is devoid of decisive military objectives and the allocation of more than token* [the covert support Eisenhower had been pressing for all along] U. S. armed forces in *Indochina would be a diversion* of limited U. S. capabilities." Concern was also expressed about extensive deployment that would leave the United States unprepared in other parts of the Far East, particularly in Korea.[118]

The French Cabinet, moreover, still wanted a settlement and not an extension of the fighting. There were strong fears that the anti-war sentiment within the National Assembly would topple the shaky government, which, in fact, did fall in mid-June, bringing Radical deputy Pierre Mendès-France to power. Finally, on the fifteenth of June, Dulles told Henry Bonnet that the deterioration of the military situation had negated any possibility of intervention. The Viet Minh, with the aid of guerrillas, had gained control of the Red River delta near Hanoi.[119]

Such activity has been described as taking the United States to the brink of war for a second time during that crisis. In actuality, however, it was hardly more substantive than the first, the maneuvering in April. Eisenhower's resolution never went to Congress. Had he decided to act, as both past and future experiences illustrated, impossible obstacles would not have been imposed and he would have moved swiftly, possibly with more power than the NSC recommendation of May 26 suggested. That was especially true where the enemy could negate the advisability of such action within a few days. The President's response, at almost precisely the same time, to a concern about communism elsewhere was in sharp contrast.

In Guatemala, the government under Jacobo Arbenz Guzmán, reformist and tolerant of its Communist supporters, had been expropriating American business interests, especially the United Fruit Company. A Dulles-sponsored resolution at the Organization of American States conference in March at Caracas, Venezuela, had agreed that the control of any country in the Western Hemisphere by the "international communist movement" was justification for "the adoption of appropriate action in accordance with existing treaties." Arbenz, lacking support from his army and being undermined among his people by pastoral letters from Archbishop Mariano Rossele y Arellano, head of the country's Catholic hierarchy, was insecure in any case. But then, while most eyes were on Indochina, American covert assistance, arms, pilots and airplanes, including United States personnel bombing the capital city of the tiny Central American nation, assisted an invasion force from Nicaragua. When President Arbenz asked the UN Security Council to investigate charges of aggression, Dulles was fortunate enough to be able to talk with two distinguished visitors to Washington, Churchill and Eden, while all three were being driven from the airport to the White House, and persuaded them to switch from a pro-Guatemala vote to abstention. The French followed suit and the Russian-backed request failed. With the help of the CIA, which took the major role, and the enthusiastic supervision of Bedell Smith in Washington, Colonel Castillo Armas was able to oust Arbenz and head a military junta. Eisenhower, informed at the last minute that additional planes were needed, helped seal the overthrow. When he was told that some of his aides were having second thoughts about the operation, the President pointed out that there was no time for such hesitations once a commitment to support violence had been made and that all possible consequences should be considered beforehand and not while the project was being executed.[120]

Indochina, however, could not be controlled that easily. At a Cabinet meeting on May 14, four days after Laniel had requested American intervention, the complexities were discussed. Dulles talked about the frustrating job of bolstering the country to prevent its complete collapse and pointed out the liabilities inherent in the French attitude toward colonialism and the difficulties of getting united action, which, he said, were made much worse by British "backsliding." Lacking the "moral judgment" of the UN and "clear support" in Asia, he said, it was "doubtful if we can arrange to save Indochina." Whatever hopes remained would depend on French negotiations in the days ahead. That, in turn, would require stronger backing than the Laniel government was getting.

Eisenhower said he had been told by two or three advisers that he should speak to the people on the Indochinese situation. How did Dulles feel about that and what could be accomplished in "fourteen minutes?" The Secretary replied that it would be "premature until French conversations clarify." That, of course, indicated a lack of finality about Laniel's reported "request" of the tenth. Then, deploring Eden's position and attributing desire to preserve relations with Communist China a reason for his attitude, President Eisenhower said for all to hear, "Man known by company he keeps; man known by excuses he makes."[121]

While the National Security Council and the Pentagon were preparing their papers on the means of intervention, Dulles and his wife, Janet, spent a relaxed Sunday afternoon at the home of his sister, Eleanor Lansing Dulles. The Secretary of State defied the fifty-eight-degree temperature of the water in the pool and took a long dip. Then he mixed a six-to-one martini and ate a large lunch that included a rich cake. He topped that off with two brandies. Sitting there in the afternoon wearing a tweed suit that had been made for him in 1936, he seemed to be in a fine mood. He was unusually inclined to joke and talk about trivia. Also present was Richard Harkness, an NBC radio and television news commentator who was particularly close to the Secretary.

Harkness turned the conversation to Geneva. There was, Dulles said, no outlook for any kind of a truce in Indochina or a settlement of the

Korean unification issue or anything else unless the French surrendered completely. Since the British had openly announced the allied division on united action, the West was without diplomatic cards to play against the Reds in Asia. Harkness then wanted to know whether Congress and the American public would support intervention.

The Administration, Dulles explained, was "caught in the horns of a dilemma." We had not made a firm commitment on military action and, without that decision, there was no chance to bring in the British. Further, as far as the public was concerned, "we cannot begin an educational campaign for a war in Indochina until we are sure that we want to go in." And that could not be done until the American people had been rallied to its support. Calling the French weak and describing the Associated States in a condition of disintegration, he was most discouraged about the outlook. The people of Indochina had nothing to fight for, he explained, and were deserting the French in large numbers. He was convinced that the communization of that area would lead to a Red Thailand in "one or two years."[122] Less than three weeks after their conversation, the Gallup Poll upheld the Administration's view of popular attitudes by showing a marked aversion among Americans toward intervention. As was indicated by party affiliation, 76 percent of Republicans and 70 percent of the Democrats opposed sending troops.[123]

Thus, the Eisenhower Administration stayed clear of the final agreement, which was signed on July 21. The President had already said he would not be a party to a treaty that made "everybody a slave."[124] In a separate statement issued on that date, he announced that the United States, which "has not been a belligerent in the war" and which "has not itself been party to or bound by the decisions taken by the Conference," would not sign the Geneva declarations. Having ended the war in Indochina and brought independence to the three Associated States, the agreement divided Vietnam at the Seventeenth Parallel. Perhaps even more obnoxious to the United States was the provision calling for free elections to be held in July of 1956. It also called attention to the prohibition of "the introduction into Vietnam of foreign troops and military personnel as well as of all kinds of arms and munitions."[125]

With the Administration absolved of any responsibility for agreeing to establish Ho Chi Minh in control over North Vietnam and with the final showdown over McCarthy set for the Senate in November, more attention could be paid to the mid-term elections. Eisenhower, unusually active for a President during such campaigns, traveled extensively by air and asked the voters for a Republican Congress that would continue the "great work" his Administration had "begun so well." On one day in late October he flew 1,521 miles to address crowds in Cleveland, Detroit,

Louisville and Wilmington, Delaware, an unprecedented feat.[126] Meanwhile, his Vice President concentrated on the heavily Republican areas, particularly along the West Coast and the Mountain States. There, he lashed at the Democrats for their "softness" toward communism. He charged that liberal Democratic Senate candidates were "almost without exception members of the Democratic party's left-wing clique which . . . has tolerated the Communist conspiracy in the United States." On September 18, in Huron, South Dakota, he said, "We're kicking the Communists and fellow travelers and security risks out of government . . . by the thousands."[127] In Cheyenne, Wyoming, the Vice President contended there was an alliance between the Communist party and the left-wing Democrats to defeat Republican Congressional candidates. In Pocatello, Idaho, two days later, he charged that five Western Democratic Senate candidates, including Samuel W. Yorty in California, were "all from the left wing of their party," which meant "they are sincerely but enthusiastically dedicated to the Socialist left-wing policies of the ADA and the Truman Administration." Stevenson retorted that Nixon was engaging in "McCarthyism in a white collar."[128] The Democrats charged Republicans with responsibility for the unemployment rate that was still rising in many parts of the country and with indifference to the small farmer. When the results were tabulated, the Democrats had taken over the Senate by a one-vote margin and, in the House, a gain of nineteen over the Eighty-third Congress gave them a 232 to 203 edge. Moreover, Republicans lost heavily in gubernatorial contests. Democrats won eight state executive offices, including the victory of Edmund S. Muskie in traditionally GOP Maine, while the Republicans failed to remove a single Democrat from a state house.[129]

With the elections out of the way, the roll-call vote on McCarthy came on December 2. After those who favored the resolution had carefully stressed their own anti-communism, the Republican from Wisconsin became the third Senator ever censured. The "condemnation," as it was actually called, was supported by a vote of sixty-seven to twenty-two. All forty-four Democrats went with the majority. The President's own party, however, was perfectly divided, twenty-two to twenty-two.

The vote seemed to expose Republican internal differences in its most obvious form. For example, among the party's Congressional leaders, only Leverett Saltonstall voted with the Watkins Committee's recommendations. The others, Dirksen, Bridges and Millikin, all supported McCarthy; but the most dramatic defiance of the White House was by William Knowland, who announced his opposition to the censure move in a speech on the Senate floor. Newspaper accounts noted that it was the most important break with an Administration by a party's leader within memory.[130] More significant than even the Majority Leader's defection, at least for the long-term interests of the Republican party, was the geographic split, once again. McCarthy was supported by most Republicans from the Midwest and Far West—Goldwater, Knowland, Tom Kuchel, Millikin, Henry Dworshak, Herman Welker, Dirksen, Jenner, Hickenlooper, Andrew Schoeppel, Hugh Butler, Langer, Milton Young, Guy Cordon, Karl Mundt, Frank Barrett—and only William Purtell, Styles Bridges and Ed Martin of Pennsylvania from the East. Eisenhower had been careful to praise the procedures of the Watkins Committee without judging its conclusions. Reacting, however, to the Senate vote, he faced the press on December 3 and rebuked Knowland and the right wing and said the party could not remain as a force in American life without recognizing the needs of progressivism. Carefully, he explained he could be hard on communism and still be progressive.[131]

What happened next made the party, still upset at the most recent election returns, fear what might occur in 1956. At the subcommittee hearings on December 7, McCarthy charged the President with tolerance of Communist China and with having encouraged those opposed to him. Furthermore, McCarthy then "apologized" to the American people for having supported Ike in 1952 and admitted to having been mistaken in believing that Eisenhower would launch a vigorous fight against communism.[132] McCarthy loyalists, in breaking openly with the Administration, compounded the dilemma. Hundreds of thousands of petitions protesting the treatment of the Wisconsin Senator were collected by a group calling itself the Ten Million Americans Mobilizing for Justice. Retired Rear Admiral John G. Crommelin said he could not say his group would be the nucleus of a third party but claimed that its leaders felt they were riding a "grass roots movement" that is "interested in restoring and maintaining the right of the Legislative Branch to investigate the Executive." Even before the actual censure vote, Crommelin's group had compiled over 350,000 names.[133] In Oklahoma, GOP workers organized a "Constitutional Party" along pro-McCarthy and anti-Eisenhower lines. The executive committee of the Wisconsin Republican party, reacting more cautiously, praised both McCarthy and Eisenhower for their fight against communism.[134] Another group of McCarthy diehards called themselves the Abraham Lincoln National Republican Club and began a drive throughout the country to wrest control of the party from "New Dealers and Internationalists." In Chicago, on Lincoln's Birthday, a group called the Committee of One Thousand Republicans, resembling For America, staged an enthusiastic meeting of 1,700 conservatives. The leading speakers included General Robert Wood, Governor J. Bracken Lee and Republican Senators Dirksen, Malone and McCarthy, who was cheered lustily when introduced. Red, white and blue "I'm for McCarthy" buttons were sold outside the ballroom. The audience cheered every attack on the Administration, which, among other things, was charged with having subverted the party's 1952 victory. Still other McCarthy loyalists formed the nucleus of an organization that called itself Americans for American Action.[135]

By November of 1955 disgruntled conservatives had a new publication that aimed at becoming a *Nation* or *New Republic* of the right. William F. Buckley, Jr., a thirty-year-old heir to oil millions, whose *God and Man at Yale* had upset his former professors in 1951 by charging irreverence and ultra-liberalism with having driven Jesus from the campus and whose recent book, *McCarthy and His Enemies*, had been the first important full-length apologia for the Senator, introduced the *National Review*. In an opening statement, Buckley explained that "energetic social innovators," particularly on college campuses, have been "plugging their grand designs, succeeding over the years in capturing the liberal intellectual imagination." He was offering, instead, "a position that has not grown old under the weight of a gigantic parasitic bureaucracy, a position untempered by the doctoral dissertations of a generation of PhDs in social architecture, unattenuated by a thousand vulgar promises to a thousand different pressure groups, uncorroded by a cynical contempt for human freedom. . . ." Its "Credenda" held that coexistence with communism was "neither desirable nor possible, nor honorable" and promised opposition to "any substitute for victory." Both parties, the magazine complained, had been taken over by "Fabian operators" under "such fatuous and unreasoned slogans as 'national unity,' 'middle-of-the-road,' 'progressivism,' and 'bipartisanship'. . . . No superstition has more effectively bewitched America's Liberal elite than the fashionable concepts of world government, the United Nations, internationalism, international atomic pools, etc." Perhaps the best remaining hope within the Republican party, declared the *National Review*, was Vice President Nixon. As a member of the Eisenhower team, he could remain in the public eye and yet emerge as "the only refuge for a disgruntled and disorganized right."[136]

When Dwight Eisenhower was asked, on December 8, 1954, for his evaluation of the possible consequences to the party of the McCarthy censure, he continued to avoid using the Senator's name and said he was working in behalf of the "progressive moderates." All speculation about the party's future was referred to Leonard Hall.[137]

"Two Scorpions in a Bottle"

W<small>ITH A CROWD OF</small> about three thousand on hand that afternoon, the Presidential party, marked by a long fleet of limousines, pulled up at the north esplanade of the United Nations. The Chief Executive, tanned from the Bermuda sun, emerged from his car. He waved his gray hat and grinned toward those behind the police barricades and walked to the entrance, where he shook hands with Dag Hammarskjöld. Then, before entering the Hall of Assembly, he went to the Meditation Room, better known at the UN as the "prayer room," in accordance with his special request that the schedule permit additional time for a brief visit to the small chamber. Then, stepping to the lectern before an audience of 3,500, he received a notably warm reception.[1]

For those few hours on December 8, 1953, the President was neither the leader of a political party nor a conciliator. More truly he represented the morality of mankind appealing to the aspirations of the "free world." His mission had thus given him the kind of opportunity he had long anticipated. With the British and the French still at Bermuda, the *Columbine* had taken him to New York City's La Guardia Field.

In August the Russians had detonated a hydrogen bomb. That news increased the urgency of the President's desire to respond to demands that he show what the United States was willing to do about the dangerous atomic race. Even before the unsettling development, during the early days of the Administration, an advisory group headed by Dr. Oppenheimer (who, by December 8, was being separated from security information by a "blank wall") reported that some solution had to be found for the possible consequences of the mindless drive toward nuclear destruction. In an article that summer the physicist warned that atomic weaponry had advanced far since Hiroshima and that conventional thinking about building bigger and bigger stockpiles was already becoming obsolete. Continued competition with the Soviet Union would be foolhardy, he maintained, because of the inevitable conclusion that "our twenty-thousandth bomb, useful as it may be in filling the vast munitions pipelines of a great war, will not in any deep strategic sense offset their two-thousandth." Of much more important military relevance in the future would be "the art of delivery and the art of defense." He warned of a "state of affairs in which two Great Powers will each be in a position to put an end to the civilization and life of the other, though not without risking its own" and compared the United States and the Soviet Union to "two scorpions in a bottle, each capable of killing the other, but only at the risk of his own life." For a democracy to make vital decisions about so important a matter, he argued, the public must be informed about the realities of the situation. "As a first step," he wrote, "but a great one, we need the courage and the wisdom to make public at least what, in all reason, the enemy must now know: to describe in rough but authoritive and quantitive terms what the atomic armaments race is. . . . When the American people are responsibly informed, we may not have solved, but we shall have a new freedom to face, some of the tough problems that are now before us." The first step, then, is candor, "candor on the part of the officials, the representatives, of the people of their country."[2]

What came to be known as Operation Candor analyzed and debated the extent of the information to be revealed. C. D. Jackson, the psychological-warfare man, joined Oppenheimer in advocating a frank report to promote awareness of the dangers and problems. At the other extreme stood Admiral Lewis Strauss. A Wall Street investment banker with close ties to the Republican right wing who had also served as secretary to Herbert Hoover, Strauss was wary of divulging more than the public needed to know. He was also emphatic about the needs of security. Later, in his memoirs, he recalled that "The President had been urged to disclose the extent of our weapon stockpiles and be candid in a number of other particulars which would not have advantaged the American public but certainly would have relieved the Soviets the trouble in their espionage activities."[3]

As chairman of the Atomic Energy Commission and Eisenhower's adviser on nuclear matters, Strauss's influence was naturally great. Although he had been credited with thwarting the initial purposes of Operation Candor, and Eisenhower has been described as being somewhere between Jackson and Strauss in his thinking—"encouraging both without offending either"—it was the President who viewed the so-called "Bang! Bang!" papers with their descriptions of atomic horrors and the vulnerability of retaliation as leaving "everybody dead on both sides, with no hope anywhere." He asked, "Can't we find some hope?" and had observed that "We don't want to scare the country to death."[4] Moreover, if the American people were told the full truth, including the ease with which they could be incinerated, what would be the consequences of such disclosures? What could be done at that point? Might it trigger a panicky demand for outlandish and largely ineffectual defense appropriations?

In September, at the funeral of Chief Justice Fred Vinson, Eisenhower told Bobby Cutler about an idea he had been contemplating while in Denver. Each nation, he explained, should provide the UN with specified amounts of fissionable material to form an atomic-energy pool for constructive peaceful purposes throughout the world. Soviet willingness to join the United States, which would be essential to the project, might also reverse the trend toward atomic warfare. Once a method had been devised to thwart possible thefts of uranium from the international body that would be set up, the agency could be established.

Many American scientists, at the same time, like Oppenheimer, were interested in using the alarm over nuclear fears to effectuate some means of disarmament. Their major fear was atomic proliferation. Ultimately, half a dozen or more nations might obtain such weapons. Their solution would not continue atomic stockpiles, as the Eisenhower plan permitted, but would achieve a "reduction of national forces so drastic that no nation will be able to wage aggressive war; the substitution of the rule of law for the arbitrament of force."[5] Concerned scientists at the Argonne National Laboratory were already working on a proposal for a balanced disarmament and control plan. Senator Flanders, hoping to take advantage of the White House desires to do something about the atomic situation, forwarded their proposals to the President. "The problem of disarmament and the international control of atomic weapons is one that must be solved," Eisenhower replied agreeably, "and we can all be thankful for all thoughtful contributions to its solution."[6]

It was, of course, the Eisenhower concept that finally prevailed. The aims of Operation Candor dissolved. Plans for frank revelations yielded to preference for a public display of dramatic boldness. The inherent problems became the subject of numerous breakfast discussions between Jackson and Strauss, at Washington's Metropolitan Club, which the insiders began to call "Operation Wheaties." Once the biggest obstacle, how to safeguard the international uranium stockpiles from illegal seizure, had been overcome, the President asked Henry Cabot Lodge to arrange with Dag Hammarskjöld to take advantage of the standing invitation Eisenhower had to address the United Nations so he could introduce the plan as a major proposal.

Every effort was then made to publicize it throughout the world, in advance of the President's speech. In the subsequent propaganda campaign, Eisenhower took a close personal interest. Jackson brought together all the agencies that were involved and, with the basic outline of the proposal, worked out a worldwide campaign that utilized the Voice of America and international press services.[7]

The speech was planned /to follow the Bermuda Conference. That would give the President an opportunity to have an advance consultation with Sir Winston Churchill. After the Prime Minister's atomic adviser, Lord Cherwell, had read and approved the draft, Sir Winston suggested the deletion of one passage that could be regarded as a belligerent threat inconsistent with its purpose. Other refinements were also needed.

Fortunately, there were two typewriters and a mimeograph machine aboard the *Columbine*. The plane's cabin became a busy office during that flight from Bermuda to New York. The President took personal charge of the final rewriting. Ann Whitman, his secretary, worked at the large-print typewriter that produced the giant-sized letters Eisenhower always used to read speeches. Strauss, Jackson and John Foster Dulles contributed their clerical manpower by proofreading and operating the duplicating machine as well as collating and stapling. When the plane came down on the runway at La Guardia, all was ready.[8]

The next few minutes were clearly among Eisenhower's most satisfying occasions. Before him was no political party, no Congress, no McCarthy, no need to maneuver around contending factions; he could face the world as the leader of the most powerful democracy, appealing to the international forum in terms of high moral purpose to inspire mankind.

He told about the Bermuda decision to meet with the Russians in a four-power session at Berlin. "We will bend every effort of our minds to the single purpose of emerging from that conference with tangible results toward peace—the only true way of lessening international tension," he declared. The peoples of Russia could not be considered "an enemy with whom we have no desire ever to deal or mingle in friendly and fruitful relationship." The great hope for the conference, he continued, lay in the establishment of a new relationship with the Soviet Union that will lead to a "harmonious family of free European nations."

Then he got to the heart of the message, the area he labeled an unexplored avenue of peace, the willingness of the atomic powers to reverse the armaments race overshadowing "the very life of the world." To vanquish fear of the atom, he proposed the establishment of an International Atomic Energy Agency. The United States, he announced, was willing to make contributions from its stockpiles of normal uranium and fissionable materials. Kept under ingeniously secure conditions to make them immune from theft, "this fissionable material would be allocated to serve the peaceful pursuits of mankind." Scientists could then study its usefulness for a wide variety of peaceful purposes, so "the contributing powers would be dedicating some of their strength to serve the needs rather than the fears of mankind." And, of course, the Soviet Union must be willing to agree for the plan to work. As for his own country, the President said, "the United States pledges before you—and therefore before the world—its determination to help solve the fearful atomic dilemma—to devote its entire heart and mind to find the way by which the miraculous inventiveness of man shall not be dedicated to his death, but consecrated to his life."[9]

Until his final words there was no applause. Thirty-five hundred people sat in silence. When the twenty-minute speech ended, however, they responded with enthusiasm that was unprecedented in UN history. Even the five Soviet-bloc delegations joined in the acclaim. It seemed, at that moment, that the burden of proof was on those who carped that he could make no political headway with the American people by advocating "grandiose world plans." Atoms-for-peace was soon seen as the "one real crusade of General Eisenhower's period of the Presidency."[10]

Its major contribution toward mitigating the arms race was in showing the way to an international agreement that could be begun immediately and without awaiting progress on general disarmament proposals. Soon after World War II the Russians had rejected Bernard Baruch's plan for atomic energy because of their fear that the Western anti-Soviet powers would dominate the international organization that would have been created to control fissionable material. The late Senator Brien McMahon of Connecticut, whose advocacy of increasing atomic production to reduce eventual defense spending anticipated the New Look policy introduced by Eisenhower, had offered a plan in 1950 calling for total atomic disarmament in exchange for American economic aid to all countries, including the Soviet Union. The Eisenhower offer, then, was a challenge to the Russians that contained none of the earlier strategic advantages for the United States.

But the Russians, not as advanced in atomic capability as the Americans and newly a hydrogen power, were in no hurry to retard accumulating their own stockpiles. Even if they were ready to make such sacrifices, the prospects of acquiescing to the President's grand overture could hardly have seemed very attractive to the Kremlin, any more than would the United States have succumbed to a similar Soviet initiative, as was demonstrated on several future occasions. Furthermore, assumptions that the Americans were ready to reverse the military trend and forgo their belief in security through strength would have had to accept the argument that President Eisenhower and his Secretary of State were publicly heading in different directions on one of the most vital of international issues.

Dulles, as he had indicated to Ralph Flanders even before the Eisenhower candidacy had become official, considered disarmament totally unrealistic. The concept contradicted his faith in power as the most efficacious means of dealing with the Soviets. When he contemplated the subject at all, as his aides noticed, he tended to treat the question as a technical matter. Any desire by the Russians for arms reduction, he held, had to be viewed as part of a Communist scheme to slacken Western defenses and, in particular, to prevent the formation of a European Defense Community as well as weakening NATO. Only a few weeks before the President's speech he had warned the Cabinet that a summit conference by the four major powers, including the Soviet Union, was undesirable because it could create "false hopes" that might jeopardize the not-yet-dead EDC.[11] At a staff meeting in late 1955, Dulles explained that he wanted disarmament "closed out quietly."[12]

That nothing substantial resulted from the Eisenhower atoms-for-peace gesture, except for some momentary hope that sanity would finally dominate, surprised no one familiar with the situation. Yet an international agency did evolve; and when it appeared that the Soviets might, in 1955, be willing to contribute to the sort of pool envisioned by the President, the *Wall Street Journal* greeted the prospect by declaring that "History may very well record that it was the most important single service that Mr. Eisenhower has performed for his country."[13] Although the International Atomic Energy Agency finally did materialize and met for the first time in Vienna in October 1957, it had "lost some of its bloom," as Lewis Strauss has written; and the Eisenhower years were to end without any significant reduction of fissionable material available for weapons.[14]

For more than three years the American disarmament position rested on the so-called "Six Principles" that had been presented to the United Nations Disarmament Commission on April 24, 1952. Stating the making of war inherently impossible rather than its mere prevention as its goal, the proposals visualized the reduction of armed forces to levels necessary for internal security and whatever peace-keeping obligations might be imposed by the UN armed forces and legal armaments would then be reduced to "fixed maximum levels, radically less than present levels and balanced throughout the process of reduction, thereby eliminating mass armies and preventing any disequilibrium of power dangerous to peace," as well as "the elimination of all instruments adaptable of mass destruction." There must be, to ascertain the carrying out of all phases of the disarmament program, "an effective system of international control of atomic energy to ensure that atomic energy is used for peaceful purposes only." The final point emphasized the need for "an effective system of progressive and continuing disclosure and verification of all armed forces and armaments, including atomic, to achieve the open world in which alone there can be effective disarmament."[15] But Russian obstruction created a deadlock in the commission, and an Anglo-French memorandum placed before the UN's Disarmament Subcommittee in London on June 11, 1954, that called for a bold first step brought agreement no closer.

For Dulles, that was neither surprising nor undesirable. Continuing East-West tension, in Europe, the Far East and the Middle East, in particular, made the ability to respond with power absolutely vital, as he had explained in his "massive retaliation" speech. It was, as he told the fifteenth meeting of the NATO council in Paris in December of 1954, no time to drop our guard. The Soviet Union, he contended, was maintaining and developing her armed forces and increasing nuclear and atomic capabilities as rapidly as possible. The Russians were also refusing to contribute to the President's plan for creating a world bank of fissionable materials and were remaining unresponsive to "continuing efforts being made in the disarmament subcommittee of the UN to limit control effectively of both atomic and conventional armaments." Their main aim was to promote disunity in the Western world, he warned his NATO colleagues, and recalled that the most fervent Russian denunciation had always been provoked by instances of anti-Communist cooperation. Conciliatory gestures by the Russians might be expected to induce a false sense of security to reduce such solidarity. The Chinese Communists were also following the same pattern, he said; and everywhere outside of the Russian-Chinese orbit, they were pressing subversion as instruments of policy, a maneuver of particular efficacy in colonial and dependent areas. As ever, both Communist giants were remaining devoted to the basic Stalin and Lenin thesis that the road to victory lay through alliance with the liberation movement of the colonies and dependent countries of imperialism. At the same time, it would also be foolhardy to respond provocatively. Such moves would be ill-considered and would weaken the ties binding the anti-Communist alliance. President Eisenhower had wisely advised on December 2 against permitting ourselves to be "goaded into actions" that would be foolish. A much better approach, and a much harder one, would be patience that would enable us to "tirelessly . . . seek out every single avenue open to us in the hope of even finally leading the other side to a little better understanding of the honesty of our intentions." Such advice, Dulles pointed out, should not be lost even in the midst of crisis.[16]

That kind of pressure, said Dulles, was currently being applied to the United States in the Far East. The planning was deliberate, done with the hope of enticing an overreaction that America's European friends would regard as ill-advised. An inevitable result of American military retaliation would shake Western unity just when it should be strengthened. Therefore, he emphasized, the United States did not intend to become reckless.

While European problems remained unsolved, although a Western European Union had been established to replace the dead EDC, the Far East had become the most sensitive cold-war front for the United States. With the signing of the Geneva agreements on July 21, American power was left to fill what Washington considered a vacuum that had to be filled to contain the ambitions of the Peoples Republic of China. Every effort had to be made to salvage the wrecked situation in Vietnam. Not having signed at Geneva, the United States assumed a new two-part commitment, in addition to its continuing responsibility toward Chiang Kai-shek and Syngman Rhee in the Far East.

The first consisted of saving the southern part of Vietnam and thus preventing what Washington regarded as a partial surrender at Geneva from becoming complete. As Dulles told the Congressional leaders at their briefing of June 28, it would be making the best of a bad situation, as in Korea.[17] The National Security Council concluded, in August, that the settlement was a "disaster" that "completed a major forward strike of Communism which may lead to the loss of Southeast Asia." Adding to their chagrin were the equally pessimistic CIA reports, which offered little hope that any post-Geneva transformation of French policy, during the period of transition to complete independence, would attract much popular support. On August 20, the President approved an NSC paper that visualized a program of extending military, economic and political assistance to the anti-Communist nationalists in South Vietnam. The commitment was confirmed on October 1, when Eisenhower wrote to Diem offering to "assist the Government . . . in developing and maintaining a strong, viable state, capable of resisting attempted subversion or aggression through military means."[18]

Unless Washington was prepared to write off the area, there was no answer but covert operations to keep the Communists from completing their triumph. Not only was the Administration's own political future at stake, particularly with the persistence of the China lobby and the Committee of One Million, which included such people as Paul Douglas, Hubert H. Humphrey, General Clay, Jay Lovestone and Congressmen Jacob Javits and Eugene McCarthy, but it firmly believed in the danger of the subsequent loss of all of Southeast Asia with its raw materials and markets. The latter was held as particularly vital for Japan. That bastion of capitalism formed, with South Korea, Formosa and the Philippines, an economic and military girdle containing the very considerable Russian and Chinese-supported indigenous aspirations aiming at the overthrow of colonial and exploitative regimes. Resistance had already been achieved in the Philippines and the British were still hanging on in Malaya. Colonel Lansdale, who learned his lessons from those two battlegrounds, noted that victory was not possible in either country without their people believing in "a heartfelt *cause* to which the legitimate government is pledged, a cause which makes a stronger appeal to the people than the Communist cause, a cause which is used in a dedicated way by the legitimate government to polarize and guide all actions—psychological, military, social and economic—with participation by the people themselves, in order to bring victory."[19] The United States, in 1954, with all its loathing of becoming associated with colonialism, felt it had no choice but to inherit the French debacle.

Lansdale has described how, on June 1, 1954, he arrived in Saigon "with a small box of files and clothes and a borrowed typewriter" and, rooming at first with General O'Daniel, went to work. As head of the still skeleton Saigon Military Mission, his job was to "enter into Vietnam quietly and assist the Vietnamese, rather than the French, in unconventional warfare."[20] After the French had signed the Geneva agreements, he was directed to pursue paramilitary operations in Communist areas instead of unconventional warfare. Since the agreements had stipulated a ceiling on the number of foreign military personnel in Vietnam, part of the personnel assigned to the Saigon Military Mission were placed under MAAG cover. All worked through Lansdale and the CIA headquarters in Saigon.[21] Later, President Eisenhower sent General J. Lawton Collins to Vietnam as his personal representative, and Collins paved the way for the French withdrawal by arranging with them for the American assumption of something the Administration had not been able to achieve before Geneva, the direction of all military-training activities. Hence, the United States was in full sponsorship of the means of maintaining a viable anti-Communist government below the Seventeenth Parallel.

One of General Collins's most important tasks was strengthening the Saigon government of Prime Minister Ngo Dinh Diem. As a fervent anti-Communist nationalist, Diem's reputation for honesty and energy had been rewarded as early as 1933, when, after having served with distinction as governor of Phan Thiet Province, Emperor Bao Dai selected him as Minister of the Interior. A member of a prominent aristocratic Vietnamese Catholic family, Diem visited the United States in 1950. During a two-month period he met a number of American anti-Communists who were concerned about Vietnam. Among them was Cardinal Spellman of New York, to whom Diem had been introduced by his brother, Bishop Ngo Dinh Thuc of Hué. With such credentials Diem was able, upon his return to America in 1951, to reside at the Maryknoll seminaries at Lakewood, New Jersey, and Ossining, New York, both within Cardinal Spellman's diocese. It is also clear that during that period in the United States, in which he was active as a lecturer on Vietnam, he won the confidence of such prominent Americans as Supreme Court Justice William O. Douglas and Senators Mike Mansfield and John F. Kennedy. All were looking for a liberal alternative to communism in Vietnam. The reserved and scholarly little nationalist then left for Paris in 1953. Suddenly, on June 16, 1954, Bao Dai asked him to become Prime Minister. He arrived in Saigon on June 26.[22]

The reasons for his rise to power are not clear. Angry Americans have attributed his selection to the CIA and to Cardinal Spellman, who was supposed to have used his standing to influence the Eisenhower Administration. More recently, Chester Cooper has described the activities of French "bankers, shipping magnates, and owners of the rubber plantations and tin mines" in South Vietnam as a pressure group to induce the weakening and dependent Laniel government to install Diem as the best guardian of their interests.[23] According to this version, the American role was limited to acceptance of the French choice, with the hope that he could form a strong coalition to oppose the Communists from among the various factions and religious sects.[24] Furthermore, a subsequent ambassador to Saigon has also speculated that the United States did not choose Diem but merely helped him remain in power, a view coinciding with the analysis of a prominent American journalist with good connections in South Vietnam.[25]

Nevertheless, one of Dulles's closest confidants has revealed that the Prime Minister was, in fact, "discovered" by the CIA and then backed almost solely by the Secretary of State, who "rammed" him through objections of the British and the French. At a Cabinet session on October 19, 1954, Dulles himself referred to Diem as someone the Americans and the French had agreed to support and pointed out that the French endorsement was "halfhearted."[26] A French delegate at Geneva, who later became his country's foreign minister, has claimed that both he and his government were convinced from the start that American support of Diem was a mistake. That is consistent with the claims of Dulles's associate that the French were contemptuous of Diem and expected him to be impotent in Saigon. Moreover, peeved that the Americans could possibly succeed where they had failed, they exploited their slow evacuation to undermine Diem's ability to succeed.[27]

The subsequent tragedy of the Diem regime was, indeed, evident from the earliest days of the American commitment. Dulles's report to the Cabinet that fall stressed that South Vietnam still lacked a strong government although the situation in newly independent Laos and Cambodia looked much better; it could not be said with certainty, he pointed out, that the Diem government would not follow the route of the country's northern half.[28] General Collins also saw little progress in anything the Prime Minister was doing to broaden the government for greater representation. Even then it was apparent to the American general that Diem's brother and sister-in-law, who would ultimately do so much to infuriate the Buddhist opposition, were having a great influence on him. The "sad fact of the case," Collins reported to Washington, was that nobody of any real ability without entrée to the family was going to have any part in the government.[29]

On April 26, when Eisenhower met with his Congressional leaders, the President prepared for his disposal of Diem. He revealed Collins's disturbance and noted the general's reports that the Prime Minister was losing the support of his own people. The situation was so serious, in fact, that only Collins's intervention kept some of Diem's supposed followers from quitting the cabinet. His move had at least maintained the façade of harmony. In reality, however, the President told the Congressmen, Diem's only support seemed to be coming from his own brothers. Particularly menacing to the regime's stability was the Binh Xuyen sect, which, Eisenhower explained, was an Al Capone sort of gang that sold vice and made payments to the government for their concessions.[30]

When Dulles met with Collins the next day, he came to the reluctant agreement that there was no other choice. Diem had to go. An order to the American embassy in Saigon to find a replacement was then sent out. Within the next few hours, however, Diem moved swiftly and successfully in repressing Hoa Hao and Cao Dai sects, which had united with the Binh Xuyen; and the order was revoked. In 1955, a 98 percent sweep in a national referendum made Diem President and dethroned Bao Dai. By that time, acting on his own but also satisfying Washington's apprehensions about the consequences of all-Vietnam elections, Diem had already indicated that he had no intention of complying with the Geneva Accords' provision for voting to take place in 1956.

The second part of the commitment was made in September. With Dulles continuing to provide the initiative for the "united action" he had been unable to achieve before and during the Geneva Conference, eight nations signed a treaty at Manila to provide for the collective defense of Southeast Asia. The Southeast Asia Treaty Organization, which included the Philippines, Australia, New Zealand, Thailand, Pakistan, France, the United Kingdom and the United States, pledged the signatories individually and collectively to meet armed attack and "prevent any counter subversive activities directed from without against their territorial and political stability." The Pacific Charter, which was signed on the same day, September 8, defined the protected area as Southeast Asia and the Southwest Pacific; and, it specified, the existence of a threat would be determined by the unanimous agreement of the members with any resultant action requiring the consent of the government concerned.[31]

Unlike NATO, there was no provision for an integrated military command for instant responses to aggression. A firmer commitment, closer to the European alliance, was the hope of the Asian members, particularly the Philippines. England, however, was opposed to a stronger, NATO-like obligation; and the French, then in the process of liquidating their interests in the area, would have preferred something less than even the SEATO agreement that emerged, something more akin to neutralization. Dulles, happy to get a treaty that he explained was directed specifically and only against Communist aggression, opposed the concept of neutrality, holding it essentially negative and basically immoral.[32]

American involvement along the Pacific's western perimeter was thus firm, from north to south, with a regional treaty added to unilateral obligations. At no time since Secretary of State John Hay first sent the Open Door notes in 1899 had United States presence in the area been so complete. Except for active sponsorship of a Chiang Kai-shek "return to the mainland" and a northward drive by President Rhee, there was nothing else the Administration could do to please its Asia Firsters, at least in the absence of direct provocation.

But the challenge had already begun even before SEATO had been signed and Dulles could leave Manila. The President had started a Denver vacation only a few days earlier when, on the third of September, he received a message from Robert B. Anderson, then the Deputy Secretary of Defense, that Chinese Communist shore batteries were shelling the island of Quemoy. Located only two miles from the mainland port of Amoy, the island had never been yielded by Chiang Kai-shek, who, at that moment, still garrisoned nearly fifty thousand troops there. Like the Matsu Islands to the north, which had some nine thousand Nationalists, Quemoy was in the Formosa Straits opposite from Taiwan. Both islands, unlike Formosa and the nearby Pescadores, had always been part of China. Since they were so close to the mainland their military value was confined mainly to radar facilities and perhaps impeding any attempted Communist invasion of Chiang Kai-shek's stronghold. Mostly, however, the Nationalist troops situated almost in Amoy Harbor lent Quemoy a symbolic and psychological importance, as they gave the Taiwan government the appearance of verging on a return to the mainland. For the Communists, the continued enemy presence on Quemoy and Matsu, as well as on the Tachen Island group to the north, was a reminder of an unfinished "liberation." The word that reached the President from Anderson was that the Joint Chiefs could not agree on whether the United States should defend the islands. They did, however, conclude that they were not essential for the security of Formosa and that the Nationalists could not hold them without American assistance.[33] When Dulles rushed back to Washington from Manila, he urged the President to convene the National Security Council.

At Denver's Lowry Air Force Base, the 214th meeting of the National Security Council deliberated the American response. Unlike the other military men, General Matthew Ridgway, as he had during the Indochina crisis, warned against intervention. Even if such conflict resulted in our devastation of Communist China's military might, the Chief of Staff said, that would merely create a power vacuum that would have to be filled with hundreds of thousands of our men; we would then be face to face with Russia along a seven-thousand-mile border; lacking the desire to send in such troops would merely encourage the Soviets to enter the area.[34] Ridgway's thesis, which also opposed Admiral Radford's arguments in favor of fighting to hold the offshore islands, impressed General Eisenhower. He also disagreed completely with suggestions that the United States should aid the Nationalists in bombing the mainland. Their conclusion that Sunday, moved forcibly by Dulles, was that the American defense line should be limited to Formosa and the Pescadores and that the offshore islands were not intrinsically vital. But no definite decision was taken about a direct military response. The President also approved Dulles's suggestion that the issue be submitted to the UN Security Council with the hope of getting an injunction for a cease-fire and the maintenance of the *status quo* in the Straits of Formosa.[35]

The UN move, however, was thwarted when Chiang Kai-shek refused to tolerate any precedent under which the world organization might decide the legitimate ownership of Formosa. There were also those who, such as England's ex-Prime Minister Clement Attlee, thought the United States should reduce the provocation by removing the Seventh Fleet from the area around Formosa. Fears of general war in the area widened when the Chinese Communists bombed the Tachen Islands on November 1 and, three weeks later, announced that thirteen American airmen who had been shot down during the Korean war were being imprisoned for espionage under terms that ranged from four years to life.

As Eisenhower had anticipated—and warned against—Senator Knowland then demanded vigorous action. Taking the Senate floor in November, he demanded American action in the form of a blockade of the Chinese coast whether or not the United Nations approved. But the President preferred flexibility rather than any specific statements about what the United States would do in the event of an attempted overthrow of the offshore islands.[36] That provided maneuverability between prudence and firmness.

American action then revealed the response. A mutual defense treaty was signed between the United States and the Republic of China. Chiang then promised he would not attempt an invasion of the mainland without prior consultation with the United States. Dulles also persuaded the Nationalist leader to reduce his large garrison on Quemoy to about one-third of his forward forces so it would become more of an outpost and less of a large commitment of their forces. In return, the United States agreed to boost the fortifications by adding 240mm. howitzer batteries.[37] After numerous appeals from Admiral Arleigh Burke to Dulles that muscle be displayed to support Chiang, the Secretary finally agreed and won the President's approval to use the Seventh Fleet to deliver LSTs to within three miles of Quemoy and Matsu, to demonstrate with clarity American willingness to help. Dulles, after the Communists overran one of the Tachen Islands, also convinced Chiang Kai-shek to abandon the outpost, located to the north of Formosa, in exchange for the Secretary's promise that the United States would defend the Nationalists' right to remain on Quemoy and Matsu.[38]

On January 24 the President, citing Communist claims that the attacks were a prelude to an invasion of Taiwan, asked Congress for authorization to aid the Republic of China to repel actions "which are recognizable as parts of, or definite preliminaries to, an attack against the main positions of Formosa and the Pescadores."[39] Identical resolutions were then introduced in each house of Congress. In the consultations that took place between the Senate Foreign Relations Committee and the State Department, the question of a commitment to the defense of Quemoy and Matsu was purposely left vague to keep the other side guessing.

The President had finally proposed something of more general appeal to Republicans than to Democrats. The House passed the resolution swiftly, by a vote of 410–3, after Speaker Sam Rayburn had assured his colleagues that it gave the President no constitutional powers that he did not already have. But among Senate Democrats, in particular, there was fear that the ambiguity of the Formosa resolution could be used by Chiang Kai-shek to involve the United States in a way that was unforeseen by the President. Senators Morse and Flanders both feared the consequences of "preventive war," and Kefauver, Humphrey and Lehman expressed unhappiness over the loose wording. Three amendments were then proposed: William Langer's to prohibit the United States from intervening within twelve miles of the Chinese mainland; Kefauver's to emphasize UN responsibility for Formosa; and Lehman's to limit the President's authority to Formosa and the Pescadores. All were defeated overwhelmingly. Only Morse, Langer and Lehman opposed the final resolution when it passed on January 28.[40] It authorized the President to use military action "as he deems necessary for the specific purpose of securing and protecting Formosa and the Pescadores against armed attack, this authority to include the securing and protection of such related positions and territories of that area now in friendly hands and the taking of such other measures as he judges to be required or appropriate in assuring the defense of Formosa and the Pescadores."[41]

While all that was taking place, however, Dulles had moved on another front. Along with Anthony Eden, he believed that New Zealand should take the initiative in getting the United Nations to effectuate a cease-fire in the Formosa Straits. Subsequently, extensive negotiations were carried out between the three governments, both in Washington and New York. Sir Leslie K. Munro, the New Zealand representative to the United Nations, met with Dulles in secret sessions. Within the State Department there were few who were aware of what Dulles was up to; indeed, the entire episode remained one of the most closely guarded secrets, one that never leaked.[42] On the same day that the Senate passed the Formosa Resolution, January 28, Sir Leslie asked the Security Council for a cease-fire resolution, with the Americans and the British promptly concurring. When the Peoples Republic of China was invited to join in the discussion, however, Chou En-lai refused. He held, as Chiang Kai-shek had earlier, that the UN could not intervene in China's internal affairs.

Personally, Dulles was convinced that Quemoy and Matsu were of little value. They could be sacrificed; but that would be foolhardy because there was no indication that Chou would then be satisfied. His real aim was to take over Formosa. However futile Chiang's cause might seem—and he made it sound even more ludicrous by his annual vows to "return to the mainland"—it could suddenly be salvaged by a big break —not by launching an invasion with his three hundred thousand soldiers against three million under arms on the mainland but by waiting for a revolution to oust the Peoples Republic of China. Chiang must, therefore, be preserved for that possibility. "As things stand today," Dulles said, "if the Chinese Nationalists are unable to defend those outposts, we would probably help."[43]

By May the crisis had dissipated. An informal cease-fire was in effect on the Formosa Straits. To Eisenhower and Dulles there was little doubt that their policy of cautious firmness had paid dividends. With the domestic economy staging an encouraging recovery and going on to what would become the most productive year in American history, and with a Western European Union being established, the Administration had every reason for confidence that things were getting better after the disappointing mid-term elections in 1954. The Gallup Poll also reported that month that the President was winning the approval of 68 percent of the public. Possibly of even greater significance, an April report had shown voters more certain than they had been during the winter that he would run again in 1956.[44]

On the tenth day of that same month, at a meeting of the UN's disarmament subcommittee, the Russians made a startling move. The session in London was amazed to hear the Soviet delegation announce substantial acceptance of the Western proposals for nuclear and general disarmament. Basically, what had been approved were the Six Principles of 1952. Not only would Russia lift the Iron Curtain for inspection in compliance with the provisions, but they also proposed their own plan for ground supervision, which included "Control Posts" at large ports, railway junctions, highways and at airports. They were to protect against surprise attack by nuclear weapons and would precede the implementation of actual disarmament measures. The French delegate responded by saying, "The whole thing looks too good to be true." The American delegate, reacting forty-eight hours later after consulting with Washington, said, "We have been gratified to find that the concepts which we have put forward over a considerable length of time, and which we have repeated many times during this past two months, have been accepted in large measure by the Soviet Union."[45]

Then surprising things began to happen. When President Eisenhower was asked for his opinion, on the day after the Russian announcement, he said he had only been able to glance at it. "Would you care to comment on it, sir?" asked Walter Kerr of the New York *Herald Tribune*. And he replied, "No, not at the moment. The whole question is so confused. It has still some of the elements they have always had in it. They want to get rid of one kind; we would like to get rid of everything. It is something that has to be studied before you can really comment on it."[46] Thus began an American turn-about; now that the Russians had shown that they did not merely want to "ban the bomb" without inspection and were in basic accord with the Six Principles, the requirements were being changed. When the President was drawn into further comment on the situation at his news conference of July 6, he complained not about the lack of provisions for inspection but about "How do you enforce such things?" His subsequent response was curious for one who had complained about the secrecy of the Iron Curtain. "What kind of inspection are we ready to accept?" he asked. "Are we ready to open up every one of our factories, every place where something might be going on that could be inimical to the interests of somebody else? . . . This question of inspection, what we will accept and what, therefore, we would expect others to accept, is a very serious one; consequently, there is just nothing today that I could say that is positive beyond that point."[47] On September 6 Harold Stassen told the Disarmament Subcommittee that the United States was withdrawing the Six Principles. The reason given was that, as the Russians themselves had pointed out on May 10, a secret stock of nuclear weapons could be hidden from UN inspectors and thereby retained by a disloyal power. As Philip Noel-Baker has pointed out, that argument was an old one and had been used as recently as May 5 by the French delegate to *justify* the Six Principles on the grounds that it was "better to have an imperfect

plan of nuclear disarmament and control than to have no plan at all."
Nevertheless, that problem was used as an excuse for withdrawing the
same proposals that had been urged upon the Russians for three years,
just after they had finally given their acceptance.[48]

To Dulles, as he had predicted all along, there was nothing surprising
about seeing the Russians weave one way and then the other, forever
trying to throw the Western alliance off guard. A peace offensive had
followed Stalin's death and Western disharmony had resulted, particularly after Churchill's speech of May 11, 1953, suggesting a Big Four get-
together. Now, with Malenkov out as chairman of the council of ministers as of February and replaced by Marshal Bulganin, and with Khrushchev obviously rising to a position of real power within the hierarchy,
Moscow was on a new campaign to throw the West off guard. They
had already agreed to sign an Austrian State Treaty on May 15 to end
the postwar joint occupation of that country, and arrangements were
being made for a Big Four summit conference at Geneva. Military resistance was doing too well in both Asia and Europe, where the Western
European Union was replacing the unborn EDC, to permit the Soviets to
use deception to slacken defenses. "Under these circumstances," a biographer has quoted Dulles as having mused, "we and our allies might not
take the necessary steps to keep the free world together." Moscow was
simply trying to promote "false euphoria."[49] To Eisenhower the Secretary of State pointed out his belief that "one of the major Soviet desires
is to relieve itself of the economic burden of the present arms race." His
advice on the matter, in preparation for a meeting with the Russians at
Geneva, was to "keep this discussion within the narrow and confidential
confines of the UN Disarmament Subcommittee" rather than to accede
to their hopes of exposing the issue before the public. "They believe,"
Dulles explained, "that if world opinion can be aroused and focused
upon us we may accept disarmament under hastily devised and perhaps
imprudent conditions."[50]

That, indeed, was a major reason for reluctance to participate with the
Russians in a top-level meeting. Other discouraging factors were the
problem of having to reject, in that kind of forum, Soviet insistence on a
regional security system covering all of Europe, a plan that would, by
definition, replace NATO and the Western European Union and remove
American troops from the Continent; the dismal prospect of being able
to accomplish nothing toward German unification, if that was anybody's
desire; and the fear that, as Dulles advised Eisenhower, "the Soviets will
probably gain a considerable degree of relaxing on the part of the West,
particularly in terms of NATO level of forces and German disarmament."[51] Also a formidable obstacle was the American political climate.
Unlike popular sentiment in Europe, where hopes were rising for the

eventual fulfillment of Sir Winston's call for a meeting that might reduce international tensions, the Administration represented the party
that had made too much of such conferences in the past, particularly
Yalta, and was reminding voters continuously of the evils of Munich.
How could they accept participation without trepidations? Yet, the
President had never ruled out willingness to attend a top-level conference. He had only asked that the other side demonstrate by deed evidence of a sincere desire to clear the atmosphere of suspicion and fear.
Recent events suddenly seemed to fulfill that prerequisite.

Besides, other pressures were building toward a conference. Walter
George, the new chairman of the Senate Foreign Relations Committee in
the Democratic Eighty-fourth Congress, joined French Premier Edgar
Faure in suggesting that a meeting take place. A greater pressure developed from England that April. With the resignation of Sir Winston as
Prime Minister and the appointment of Anthony Eden as his replacement, the Conservative party's foreign policy began a determined drive
to bring the four nations together. With general elections called for in
Great Britain to take place on May 26, it was politically wise for the
incumbents to gain popular favor by arranging a summit conference.[52]

A widely accepted interpretation was that the Eisenhower agreement
to go to Geneva in July for a face-to-face meeting with Marshal Bulganin and Khrushchev was in defiance of his Secretary of State's advice.
The General himself later promoted that idea in his memoirs by explicitly stating that Dulles was "emphatically" skeptical that anything useful
could come from a "Summit."[53] Thus, Eisenhower's confidence in the
powers of personal diplomacy prevailed. Once again the impression created was of a President seeking peace with open sincerity while his
Secretary of State, more consistent with the party's right wing, held out
for the hard line. In reality, however, both were strongly opposed to the
affair; and Dulles may even have been at the end somewhat less reluctant
than the President. Eisenhower, forced into it by circumstances, planned
a propaganda coup to counter the opposition and thereby salvage some
gains but finally went "very, very reluctantly to the first summit meeting."[54]

Real pressures had yet to be applied when Eisenhower faced the legislative leaders on March 22 and noted that Senator George's advocacy of
a Four Power meeting had promoted discussions between himself and his
Secretary of State. But both had concluded that there were more disadvantages than advantages. At the same time the President assured Senators Knowland and Bridges, who were strongly opposed to any confrontation with the Russians at a bargaining table, that they would be the
first on the Hill to be informed about any affirmative decision.[55] Within
the next few weeks the pre-election pleas from the new Eden government, with Harold Macmillan as Foreign Minister, began to reach Wash-

ington with growing intensity. Macmillan discussed the idea with the American ambassador in London, Winthrop Aldrich, who guessed that the President would be cool toward the idea. Telegrams from Eden to both Dulles and Eisenhower then followed. Eisenhower's reply, according to Macmillan, was not "altogether discouraging." Although he expressed surprise that a definite proposal had been formulated, he understood why it would be helpful to the Conservatives. But his own situation was different, the President pointed out, and American public opinion also had to be considered.[56]

Macmillan then flew to Washington to convince the Secretary of State. Dulles had not yet made a recommendation to the President, the Foreign Minister learned, but he had begun to see the point. Much more concerned at that time over the continuing problem of the offshore islands, Dulles was looking for a solution. He had long since been convinced that the best way to solve that was by getting Chiang to evacuate them. That would remove them from contention and give the Chinese Communists a hollow, unheralded "victory" and a few square miles that were basically worthless. But the Generalissimo would not consider such abdication, not even when Dulles sent Walter Robertson and Admiral Radford to Formosa to plead his case. Dulles, then, was more troubled by a Far Eastern predicament that could re-explode at any moment. Macmillan even observed that the Secretary would like to be flexible in his approach to that situation "if he were not the prisoner of a public opinion which had been largely formed by his own party." With the British proposing a session that would leave the real work of negotiating the intricacies to a foreign-ministers conference that would follow at a subsequent date, Dulles saw an advantage. Believing, as he did, in the closeness of the Russians and the Chinese Communists, he thought a summit meeting would soothe tensions at least sufficiently to give the United States more time to pressure the Nationalists to evacuate the islands. On the ninth of May Macmillan was able to note in his diary that "The President had now moved, under Dulles' advice, almost to full acceptance of our plan."[57]

But Eisenhower was still full of doubts. He was not ready to plunge into an affair that would certainly provoke the indignation of his right wing. In Paris, on May 10, Dulles had to confront Macmillan with a counter-suggestion from the President. Perhaps the United States could be represented by Vice President Nixon. Macmillan, believing the Secretary was joking, recalled an old story about the "terrible thing" that had happened to poor "Mrs. Jones," who had two fine sons. "One of them went down in the *Titanic*, the other became Vice President of the United States. Neither of them was ever heard of again." Dulles laughed and agreed, saying, "I guess poor Nixon wouldn't like that."[58]

The Russians soon accepted a joint Anglo-American-French note calling for "a new effort to resolve the great problems" that divide us to remove the "sources of conflict."[59] The foreign ministers of the four powers then met on May 15 to sign the Austrian treaty; and after the Conservative triumph in the elections on May 26, the conference was scheduled to open in Geneva on July 18.

Eisenhower had first to pacify disturbed Republicans. His acceptance brought heated objections on the Senate floor. Styles Bridges warned that all international conferences contained seeds of "appeasement, compromise and weakness." Joe McCarthy, no longer given much attention by the newspapers, proposed a resolution requiring the President to condition his going to Geneva on Russian agreement to have the conference discuss the satellite nations of Eastern Europe. The Democratic Majority Leader, Lyndon Johnson, promptly came to Eisenhower's side by charging that McCarthy's proposal had "placed a loaded gun at the President's head." Then Johnson and Walter George maneuvered to further the Republican embarrassment. They kept it alive in the Foreign Relations Committee by having the eight Democrats outvote the seven Republicans and brought it to the floor. Homer Capehart complained that Johnson was having a field day out of something that "should have been thrown into the trash can," and McCarthy began to have doubts about his own measure and wanted it withdrawn; but the Majority Leader denied the unanimous consent needed for withdrawal, and it was defeated by seventy-seven to four.[60] When the President convened a bipartisan session of Congressional leaders on July 12, he assured them that Geneva would not be another Yalta. With the Bricker amendment still being pressed by the American Bar Association and interested individuals, he told the legislators that no decision would be made without their approval. Most of all, there would be no appeasement.[61]

Eisenhower and Dulles, having been drawn in against their own inclinations, quickly prepared for the big meeting. One pitfall to avoid, Dulles advised, was the Russian desire to exploit the conference to establish moral and social equality with the West. "These gains can be minimized by the President avoiding social meetings where he will be photographed with Bulganin and Khrushchev, etc., while maintaining an austere countenance on occasions where photographing together is inevitable," the Secretary wrote in a secret memorandum. Soviet gains could also be limited by publicizing the fact that the United States was using the occasion to "push for satellite liberation and liquidation of international communism."[62] Then fearing the Communists would bring the disarmament issue into the open, the President readied his own propaganda challenge. He assembled a group that included Nelson Rockefeller, Robert B. Anderson, Harold Stassen, Gordon Gray, General Alfred Gruenther and Admiral Radford and had them work in seclusion at the Marine base at Quantico, Virginia. Several proposals were considered. While the dignitaries were assembling in Geneva, the Quantico Panel—as it was called—met in Paris. The group selected Anderson as their spokesman to review the various possibilities. The idea and the final decision were both Eisenhower's. Dulles, fearing that the question of disarmament or arms limitation would be brought up by the Russians, liked the plan.[63]

For Geneva, the occasion was a festive one. Everybody seemed to be there. Fifteen hundred or so correspondents from all over the world, lobbyists and ordinary sightseers jammed the beautiful city. Even the Reverend Billy Graham was on hand and held a revival meeting that drew thirty-five thousand worshipers. Khrushchev, from the moment he walked down the ramp of the airplane with Bulganin, left no doubt about who was the real mover on the team. But their arrival, as that of the others, was simple when compared with the landing of the *Columbine* on Saturday, July 16. The security precautions were much more elaborate for the President, whose plane was guarded by circling helicopters as it came down and whose limousine was protected by Secret Service men who trotted along at either side as it moved down streets that were lined with enthusiastic crowds eager for a glimpse of General Eisenhower.[64] Few seemed to care that progress in resolving such momentous issues as German unification, disarmament, East-West trade and European security would determine the success of the conference. The very fact that they were present together and meeting cordially was, as Dulles had feared, sufficient to signify a turning point in the cold war.

When Bulganin proposed agreements on "armaments and the prohibition of atomic weapons," Eisenhower directed Rockefeller and Stassen to leave Paris and join him in Geneva. Then, after evaluating what he wanted to propose, he directed Stassen to draft a message that he could deliver in addition to his previously prepared statement.

There was no advance warning as the President prepared to speak on the afternoon of the twenty-first. The lake and the city outside the Palais des Nations were darkened by heavy clouds. Rain was falling. The atmosphere, despite the elaborate decor of the conference room, was gloomy. The President began with a recitation of the complexities of disarmament and the need to find a better way to safeguard peace while maintaining security. "We have not," he stressed, in response to the position the Russians had been taking since May 10, "as yet been able to discover any scientific or other inspection method which would make certain of the elimination of nuclear weapons" and said that, nevertheless, the United States had not abandoned the possibility of finding some solution.

"Gentlemen," he then said, "since I have been working on this memorandum to present to this Conference, I have been searching my heart and mind for something that I could say here that could convince everyone of the great sincerity of the United States in approaching this problem of disarmament." Addressing himself across the four-sided table directly to the Russians, he proposed that both nations exchange a "complete blueprint of our military establishments, from beginning to end, from one end of our countries to the other; lay out the establishments and provide the blueprints to each other." The United States was also willing, he announced, to make itself completely open for aerial photography, if the Russians were ready to reciprocate, so that each nation could scrutinize the other to reduce the "possibility of great surprise attack, thus lessening danger and relaxing tension." "A sound peace—with security, justice, well-being, and freedom for the people of the world—*can* be achieved," he concluded, "but only by patiently and thoughtfully following a hard and sure and tested road."[65]

At that instant, as if by a prearranged signal, a tremendous flash of lightning filled the hall and all lights in the building went out. There was darkness and, for a moment, total silence. Suddenly, the President chuckled and said, "Gentlemen, I did not intend to turn out the lights."[66]

At the coffee break after the session, the President sought out Bulganin and asked for his informal reaction, but the Premier was noncommittal. Seeing his old friend Marshal Zhukov, he tried again for a response. Just then, however, Khrushchev interrupted them. The rotund First Secretary of the Communist party's central committee said the plan was unacceptable. It would, he explained, merely give American strategic forces the chance to accumulate target information and to zero in. He thereby left no doubt who really headed the Soviet Union.[67]

The Open Skies proposal was a grand gesture. Eisenhower has claimed that it was presented because he wanted to show "the dedication of the United States to world peace and disarmament and our sincerity in offering a concrete way in which we would participate."[68] To most of the European journalists present in Geneva it was indeed a genuine offer. But, as Richard Rovere wrote from Geneva, "The Americans . . . could not put out of their minds the long detours our civil aircraft must make to avoid flying over the atomic proving grounds in the Southwest, or the elaborate security checks that must be run on our own nationals before they are made privy to the facts about our installations that Mr. Eisenhower was proposing to hand over to the Russians."[69] Eisenhower himself has told an interviewer, "We knew the Soviets wouldn't accept it. We were sure of that. But we took a look and thought it was a good move."[70]

Reports that the opposing leaders had been civil toward each other and that desires for peace were genuine gave the "spirit of Geneva" the aura of a new era in foreign relations. Stories of conviviality and toasts and tales of congenial Russians raised hopes that the world was retreating from the prospect of nuclear war. With the domestic economy well out of the recession, corporate profits at new levels and pay envelopes having greater purchasing power, declining international tensions seemed particularly appropriate. America, in the days following the Geneva conference, experienced the first substantial relaxation since the start of the cold war. The thaw was serious enough for FBI director Hoover to warn a closed session of the House Appropriations subcommittee that the "Geneva spirit" was encouraging the Communists to leave their hiding places and make distinct gains among naïve Americans who were playing the Red game innocently. For each hard-core Communist, he declared—estimating a total of 22,280 in the country—there were ten or more loyal citizens being duped.[71]

Although actual negotiations on all the good intentions were scheduled for a foreign ministers' conference in October, Eisenhower's open-skies proposal became the big news and deprived the Soviets of the boldest headlines. The man who had offered atoms for peace eighteen months earlier won new acclaim for being an anti-war soldier. The press reported that even the Russians were convinced that he, unlike his Secretary of State, was against aggression. The best that Khrushchev's alleged memoirs could later say about Dulles, after observing him at Geneva, was that "he knew how far he could push us, and he never pushed us too far."[72] When Eisenhower returned home his TV report to the people told about one substantive area in which agreement seemed near. That was the possibility of "increased visits by the citizens of one country into the territory of another, doing this in such a way as to give each the fullest possible opportunity to learn about the people of the other nation."[73]

The optimism was refreshing. The Fund for the Republic made its annual report and declared that the domestic atmosphere was better than it had been five years ago. Senator Norris Cotton of New Hampshire said that Eisenhower's re-election in 1956 could make the Republicans the dominant party, and Leonard Hall exulted that Truman was "bitter, frustrated, and jealous of Eisenhower's accomplishments and popularity." The August Gallup Poll showed the President's popularity at a record high of 79 percent.[74] Not unreasonably euphoric was James Reston's observation that "The popularity of President Eisenhower has got beyond the bounds of reasonable calculation and will have to be put down as a national phenomenon, like baseball. The thing is no longer just a remarkable political fact but a kind of national love affair, which cannot be analyzed satisfactorily by the political scientists and will probably have to be turned over to the head-shrinkers."[75]

Not surprisingly, at that high point, the politicos began increasing their pressure for the President to run again in 1956. With Mamie's encouragement, he had always entertained hopes that all his designs for the country could be accomplished during one term; for, considering the relatively late age at which he had begun his Presidency, he thought he could then step down and turn over the executive office to a younger successor. That idea had been in his mind even before Inauguration Day. He had contemplated saying as much at his swearing-in but had been talked out of it at the last minute, reminded perhaps how such vows had plagued the incumbencies of Rutherford B. Hayes and Theodore Roosevelt. Now, Cotton's hopeful statement was joined by a steady flow of new pleas.

On August 14 he left Washington for a long-awaited fishing-and-golf vacation in Colorado. With the Summer White House operating in Denver, at Lowry Air Force Base, he could stay at his mother-in-law's home and also enjoy the out-of-doors at Aksel Neilson's ranch. But the party needed him and there were constant reminders, even during that work-and-play vacation. When Leonard Hall visited Eisenhower in Denver and repeated the importuning, the President turned to him with some exasperation and reminded the national chairman that he had already given "all of my adult life to the country."[76] He had also warned a group of visiting Ohio politicians that his obligation to serve was not endless.[77] Such reactions were merely restatements of what he had told close associates many times, but they were easily dismissed as the weary comments of a man who seemed to enjoy freedom more than his power. But he was emphatic when addressing a breakfast meeting of Republican state chairmen at Denver. He lectured about the responsibilities of party organization and said he refused to believe that the GOP was "so lacking in inspiration, high quality personnel, and leadership that we are dependent on one man. We don't believe it for a minute." Human beings, he reminded them, "are frail—and they are mortal." The flag should never be pinned "so tightly to one mast that if a ship sinks you cannot rip it off and nail it to another. It is sometimes good to remember that."[78]

That was on the tenth of September.

Fifteen days later, at the Hotel Alperzhof in the town of Garmisch-Partenkirchen, Germany, a former member of Truman's State Department, Dean Rusk, was seated across a conference table from Dr. Gabriel Hauge. Rusk scrawled a message on a scrap of paper and passed it to Eisenhower's economic adviser and speech writer. It read:

Hauge:
Jack Heintz has heard an unconfirmed report from Geneva that the President has had a coronary. It's in a Geneva paper. This group, of course, would be deeply affected. Should you phone for clarification?

Dean R.[79]

PART THREE

"Modern Republicanism"

CHAPTER 32

The Crisis of the GOP

FROM SEPTEMBER 24 UNTIL November 11, the President of the
United States was a patient at the Fitzsimons Army Hospital near Denver, Colorado. Although the critical period was of relatively brief duration, the Republican party and the nation could not be certain until the
last day of February that the popular general would succeed himself.
The GOP's loss of Congress in 1954, together with the enhanced political power of the President during the post-Geneva glow, made his retention on the ticket a matter of desperation. To most observers, during
those dark days while the President lay under an oxygen tent, even his
complete recovery would not reverse his own and his family's hopes for
his retirement after the 1956 elections.

The greatest irony was the timing of the coronary. Only six days
earlier the Gallup Poll had reported that 61 percent of the voters were
prepared to favor him in another contest with Stevenson, a margin that
could mean the difference between recapturing control of Congress for
the GOP or defaulting to the Democrats.[1] Nationally, the domestic
economy was booming; only farmers among all major groups were failing to participate in the record-breaking prosperity. Internationally,
with the Geneva Conference widely depicted as a personal triumph for
the President and the meeting of foreign ministers not scheduled until
late October, the prospects for peace had not seemed as great since the
start of the cold war. Indeed, when the startling news came from the
Summer White House that weekend, the deployment of leading members of the team furthered the aura of relaxation. While the President
had already spent six weeks in the Rockies, combining some routine

duties with hunting, fishing and painting, Herb Brownell vacationed in Spain and Sherman Adams toured NATO installations in Europe. If anyone saw as much of the President on a day-to-day basis as Adams, it was Jim Hagerty; but the press secretary, too, was enjoying some time off, vacationing in Washington while assistant press secretary Murray Snyder handled the dispatches from the Summer White House. It was, in fact, Snyder who telephoned Hagerty on September 24 with the news that what had been widely reported as another one of Eisenhower's bouts of indigestion was far more serious. Before the general public was informed, Hagerty relayed the message to the Vice President.

Nixon had also permitted himself a change of pace. Unlike most Saturdays in Washington, he had not gone to his office. He and his wife Pat had just returned from a wedding that afternoon of Senator Henry Dworshak's son and a stenographer from the Vice President's office, and Nixon was settling down with the evening paper, not taking seriously the report about the President's stomach ache and moving on, instead, to inspect the latest baseball average listings. Then Hagerty gave him the news.

Suddenly, the ever-present but usually remote possibility of his succession to the Presidency became very real. Not since Woodrow Wilson's stroke had a Vice President been so close to the top as Nixon was at that moment. The news that Eisenhower had suffered from a coronary thrombosis, just twenty days before his sixty-fifth birthday, had placed the still young politician from Whittier, California, in a proximity to the White House that was dependent on no human effort. Only the day before had marked the third anniversary of his "Checkers" speech, which had salvaged him from political demise. Since then, as Vice President, his career had advanced quickly, proving to all observers his disinclination to become another Throttlebottom. Far from the pathetic cipher of the musical comedy *Of Thee I Sing*, who could get into the White House only with the tourists, Nixon was already the best publicized and most active of those who had held his position. His trip to the Far East in late 1953 had earned compliments from even some who normally regarded him with distaste, if not skepticism. Another tour, this time to the Near and Middle East, was already planned for early November. His activities during the 1954 Congressional election campaign had infuriated Democrats resentful of his liberal association of the opposition with softness toward communism, if not with treason, as Harry Truman later charged. He had also been the Administration's liaison man with McCarthy and took on, rather unhappily, the assignment of replying to Stevenson's charge that Eisenhower's leadership reflected the Senator's influence. Moreover, Nixon served as an active participant at Cabinet and National Security Council sessions, remaining at all times close to the decision-making process in a manner far removed from Franklin D. Roosevelt's cavalier treatment of Truman. With a President unrepresentative of the party's mainstream and serving their interests mainly by drawing voters to the GOP line, Nixon was highly regarded by the party's professionals, particularly the national committeemen and Congressmen still sulking over the Eastern and Dewey influence in the White House. Without Taft, Nixon was the best hope of the conservatives and many moderates who viewed his identification with Eisenhower an added strength. More than anything else, the heart attack placed him in the position of either being made or totally destroyed, just as had his talk to the American people of September 23, 1952. Fully realizing, during those first minutes of living with the news, that "many eyes would be watching to see whether I become brash or timid in meeting the emergency" and that the only safe recourse was in avoiding reporters and cameras, he slipped out through the side door of his home and went into temporary seclusion at the Bethesda residence of his good friend, Deputy Attorney General William P. Rogers.

In Denver, meanwhile, the situation was being clarified. On Friday afternoon, while playing twenty-seven holes at the Cherry Hills Country Club, the President had interrupted his golfing with a hamburger and large slices of raw onion. Then, at the home of Mrs. John S. Doud, his mother-in-law, he spent an hour working in the basement painting a copy of a *Life* photograph of an Argentine woman praying at a desecrated shrine. After dinner with Mamie, Mrs. Doud and his friends Mr. and Mrs. George E. Allen, he complained about some indigestion, probably from the raw onion, and went to bed at ten o'clock.

Mamie slept in an adjoining bedroom; but, at around two-thirty in the morning, she was awakened by the sound of her husband moving about in his room. To combat what he said was indigestion, she gave him the standard dose of milk of magnesia and water and they both returned to bed. But, a few minutes later, a terrible pain seared his chest. Mrs. Eisenhower quickly phoned Major General Howard Snyder, the President's personal physician, who arrived within fifteen minutes. That was at 3 A.M.

Dr. Snyder administered by hypodermic one grain of papaverine followed by one-fourth grain of morphine sulphate, then a dose of heparin. To control the symptoms, about forty-five minutes later, he gave the President a second hypodermic of one-fourth grain of morphine. The patient slept comfortably for seven hours. A cardiogram taken at 1 P.M. located a moderate lesion in the anterior wall of the heart. But mindful of Mamie's own valvular heart condition and the possible shock to Eisenhower, Dr. Snyder delayed diagnosing the attack as a coronary. Twelve hours after the first pains, with the news wires carrying stories about indigestion, the President walked from the Doud home to his own car at the curb and was driven to the Fitzsimons Army Hospital, about seven miles from Denver. Then Dr. Snyder revealed that Eisenhower had experienced a "mild" heart attack.[2] A team of three doctors working over the stricken President was later joined by a noted heart specialist from Boston, Dr. Paul Dudley White. Early Monday morning the four physicians issued a bulletin saying there had been no complications from Saturday's "moderate" coronary thrombosis. The President, still in an oxygen tent, was cut off entirely from official business while the medicos worked to repair the heart damage.[3]

The country was without a functioning President, but the greatest personal dilemma was the Vice President's. Constitutionally, of course, he was the number-two man and since John Tyler's time sufficient precedent had been established to empower an accidental President with the full authority of the office. But the President was not dead, just incapacitated, and the first two weeks were regarded as the most critical period. For a while, at least, there could be a repetition of the situation that had followed President Wilson's stroke, when the Chief Executive lay in seclusion for months after his collapse in 1919. Yet, at that time, there was no provision in the Constitution covering Presidential incapacity.* Any precipitate rush to take over Eisenhower's duties, or even an overt eagerness to become his chief's successor, would instantly confirm allegations that Nixon was inordinately ambitious and ruthless. Instead of easing him into the White House, the coronary could do what the exposure of his secret fund had failed to accomplish. Yet, he was the Vice President and had to demonstrate responsible leadership in a time of crisis. Less than two weeks before the heart attack, a Gallup Poll had shown him the leading GOP candidate for 1956 if Ike should withdraw.[4]

For the party, of course, the situation verged on the catastrophic. Coming at the height of the President's popularity, it seemed, at first glance, to seal his previously expressed reluctance against running for a second term. With the general conviction that another four years could be his for the asking, particularly since the 1954 elections had confirmed the Republicans' minority status, it would be a great loss if only because his pulling power offered a chance at recapturing Congress. The Gallup Poll released on September 18 had reported that Eisenhower was favored by 61 percent if he ran against Stevenson again.[5] However, the family's opposition to another term was well known. Mamie would have gladly abandoned the White House for the Gettysburg farm. Even with a full recovery, the illness seemed certain to resolve any doubts. That was the

---

* The Twenty-fifth Amendment, providing for Presidential incapacity and succession, was ratified in 1967.

widespread impression during the weeks of the President's confinement at Fitzsimons.

Most of the general public assumed he would not run again, despite the optimistic reports that began to flow from the hospital; and, the day after his return to Washington on November 11, the publication of a poll taken among capital newspaper correspondents showed that the 88 percent of the White House press corps believed that the Republicans would field somebody else at the head of the ticket in 1956. The Associated Press's Managing Editors Association followed that up by saying the odds were four to one against his running. All agreed that Richard Nixon was the most likely replacement.[6]

But the Administration had its own ideas. Of vital importance was the need to demonstrate that, despite the continued immobilization of the President at the edge of the Rockies, the "team" established by a leader who knew how to delegate authority would now prove its value. The Administration, ignoring the contradiction inherent in trying to prove Presidential leadership with or without Eisenhower's presence, made every effort to deny any hints of disruption or panic within the staff. The President had, after all, Nixon told the press upon emerging from seclusion, "set up the Administration in such a way that policies, which are well defined, will be carried out in his absence" and emphasized that there was no reason to suspect any interference with the normal business of government. His own role would be confined to presiding over National Security Council and Cabinet meetings; when asked whether it would be enlarged, he wisely refused to comment. Calling off his Middle East trip was his most substantial change. Then, with the absentees back from Europe, the Vice President conferred over lunch with the staff and announced that, in addition to an NSC meeting scheduled for Thursday, the Cabinet would meet on Friday, September 30. In a press release, the Vice President pointedly observed that "the subjects on the agenda for these meetings were of a normal routine nature." To let the public observe the harmony within the "family," photographers were invited to record how teamwork was enabling the government to function "as usual."[7]

When the Cabinet met that Friday, however, the superficiality of the unity was demonstrated before a helpless Vice President. Mr. Nixon opened the session by calling for silent prayer and then reported that the President spent an excellent night. He also stressed the need to carry out the policies already established by the President and to delay any new initiatives. Humphrey, voicing a commanding concern, mentioned the importance of avoiding the "appearance" of controversy. Dulles then complimented the Vice President for the wonderful way he had been reacting under the stress. In view of the Administration's other main concern, however, the Dulles remark was a concession to Nixon's pride.[8]

For, in reality, the Secretary of State was the quarterback, directing the plays and making certain the Administration's major objectives were being carried out. Others were more in the public eye, but, as a prominent member of the team has observed, he "was the general above everybody else." Acting for the President, he deployed the others. Nothing was done without his approval.[9]

And, at that Cabinet meeting, before his complimentary words for Nixon, Dulles helped to win ratification of a plan that he had guided through at the preceding day's NSC meeting. It was simple but significant. Not the Vice President but Governor Adams was directed to go to Denver as the President's principal assistant. All business for the convalescing leader's attention was to be cleared by the chief of staff. After Herb Brownell read the formal statement stipulating the arrangements, which also confined Nixon to presiding over NSC and Cabinet meetings and being available for consultations on matters before departments for action, the Vice President demurred. Speaking from a position weakened by circumstances, he questioned the arrangements. Adams, he had assumed, would continue to man the White House staff during Eisenhower's absence. At that point Dulles, as Adams has reported, "came out firmly and emphatically for stationing me with Eisenhower in Denver as the liaison officer who would handle all matters concerning government business coming to and from the President." He summarized all the reasons for the arrangement, stating that others might exploit the opportunity to set themselves up as authoritive spokesmen for the President on various issues. With the Secretary's well-known aversion to infringements upon his own authority in the formulation of foreign affairs, his conern seemed clear. Moreover, he pointed out that Adams's place was in Denver because the chief of staff had become recognized nationally as a public figure closely identified with the President, as though Nixon were not. At that point the Vice President, attuned to the sensitivity of the situation, had no choice but to second the Secretary's remarks.[10] The statement given to the press after that meeting also stressed that the Administration had rejected considering any further delegation of powers by the President.

Under the guise of efficient teamwork, then, had come tacit confirmation of rumors that were circulating through Washington. Given the real chance that the President could not or would not run again, there was no desire by his closest adherents, including Dulles, to deliver political power into the hands of Richard Nixon. Whatever hopes had been entertained of converting the Old Guard-dominated party into a middle-of-the-road concept of "Modern Republicanism" would thereby be lost. It would have meant abdication to the right wing and final abandonment of the rationale that, in 1952, had convinced the General to run. There was, also, little confidence that the Vice President could command enough appeal to win election in 1956, despite his acknowledged popularity among Republicans. A Gallup Poll in October showed Nixon losing to Stevenson but indicated that Chief Justice Earl Warren, a liberal Republican, could defeat the Democrat.[11] Furthermore, with Joe McCarthy's political career all but shattered, Nixon was the country's most controversial politician, quite the antithesis of Eisenhower and the man Democrats were most eager to demolish before the electorate.

Thus, within twenty-four hours after the news of the heart attack had reached Washington, perceptive journalists were noting the Washington power play. James Reston reported that Eisenhower Republicans were eager to keep control in the hands of Sherman Adams and away from Nixon. Political correspondent Richard Rovere also observed, in a *New Yorker* "Letter from Washington" column dated September 29, that Sherman Adams "regards himself as the President's appointed caretaker and is doing everything he can to cut Mr. Nixon down to size."[12] With Dulles manipulating the strategy, the efficient and taciturn Assistant to the President emerged more truly than ever before as the "second most important man in Washington," in a role that guaranteed his damnation by the party's right wing. Nixon himself has revealed his own supporters' frustration that he was not doing enough during that period to assert power. As an example, he cites a telegram from Senator Styles Bridges, Adams's colleague from New Hampshire and political foe. It advised: "You are the constitutional second-in-command and you ought to assume the leadership. Don't let the White House clique take command."[13]

To attribute the anti-Nixon maneuver solely to Dulles's plotting, however, would ignore that the Secretary of State was the quarterback but not the coach. Both the purpose and the method constituted the purest possible example of Eisenhower's style of accomplishing the desired through indirection, a way of getting results while minimizing personal risks. "Dwight D. Eisenhower," as William S. White wrote one year later, "is a master politician, far from learned in its lore, still comparatively a newcomer to its techniques—but a master, nevertheless."[14] Troubled over the conditon of the party in the hands of a successor, the President was understandably reluctant to relinquish his leadership to Nixon. One week before the start of the foreign ministers' conference at Geneva, he sent the Vice President a polite but firm note reminding him that Dulles was going to Europe with "my complete confidence" and that they had reached a "close understanding." Hinting that Nixon must not use the new meeting with the Russians for one of his well-known anti-Communist attacks, and also striving to retain his Secretary of

State's authority without interference, he explained that "He must be the one who both at the conference table and before the world speaks for me with authority for our country."[15] Similarly, he had strong reservations about retaining Nixon in a second campaign. He had "watched Dick a long time, and he just hasn't grown," Eisenhower told Emmet Hughes. "So I just haven't honestly been able to believe that he *is* Presidential timber."[16] In searching for some "younger blood" to rehabilitate the party, as he had been advising others to do, he did not view his Vice President as more than a political instrument. Much more to his liking, and the man he wanted as his running mate in 1956, was Robert B. Anderson.[17]

Lean, bespectacled, scholarly-looking, deeply religious and mild-mannered, Anderson struck Eisenhower as the man who could be trusted to implement his own ideas of what America needed. The Texan, however, argued that he was politically inexperienced, that he had never engaged in partisan politics, even back home. Nevertheless, beginning in 1955, the President worked to change his mind. He tried to persuade the Deputy Secretary of Defense that he would be one of the few qualified men acceptable to the various elements within the party. As a Southerner and a Democrat, he might be effective in preserving and even extending the GOP's Dixie gains. Additionally, Anderson's most conservative side coincided with Eisenhower's. As Anderson was a fiscal authority and an expert in international finances, economic integrity and currency soundness were among his greatest concerns. His approach to money matters was comparable to George Humphrey, whom Anderson later succeeded as Treasury Secretary. As though to prove his attractions to the right wing, as well as to the President, the Texan was wooed by such people as General Robert Wood, the former head of Sears, Roebuck and chairman of the America First Committee.[18] Those solicitations, Anderson suspected, were sponsored by Eisenhower. Also concerned that lack of exposure was Anderon's greatest weakness, the President urged that he make himself better known by accepting as many speaking engagements as possible and by broadening his base of operations.[19]

Particularly impressive to the President was Anderson's management, early in the Administration, of racial desegregation within his department. Eisenhower had hardly adjusted to the White House when Anderson rescued the Administration from embarrassment posed by a challenge from Harlem Congressman Adam Clayton Powell, Jr. The wife of the New York City Democrat, popular pianist Hazel Scott, had reported that her concert tour of veterans' hospitals revealed the continued segregation of patients at two installations in Tennessee, despite Truman's military integration order of 1948.

Immediately, with his usual instinct for publicity, Powell sent letters to the President and the Veterans Administration calling for an investigation and an explanation.[20] Others then joined his demands for equality within the armed services. News-conference questions by Alice A. Dunnigan of the Associated Negro Press provoked a Presidential inquiry into the existence of segregated schools on military posts in Virginia, Oklahoma and Texas.[21] The NAACP promptly charged that Anderson's subordinate, Under Secretary Francis P. Whitehair, had approved "rigid racial segregation" at the large Charleston and Norfolk naval yards.[22] Powell, also seeing non-compliance at those installations, then notified the White House that Secretary of the Navy Anderson was guilty of "insubordination" for continuing segregation at the bases by blocking federal efforts to end their traditional accommodation with local customs. He also included the charge that Oveta Culp Hobby had "virtually countermanded" the President's policy on segregation in schools for dependents on Army posts.[23] Robert Donovan has reported that "No other newspaper story at the time ever caused such commotion in the White House so quickly."[24] The President's personal outrage shocked his staff into action. Nobody could deny the existence of such practices or dispute the willingness of most of the military brass to emulate regional racial separation on their posts.

Upset by Powell's headline-making blast, Eisenhower sent trouble-shooter Max Rabb to see the Congressman. Confronting Powell, Rabb explained that such statements could only create a schism between Negroes and the new Republican leadership. He pleaded that the Eisenhower people needed more time to deal with complaints. Rabb then won Powell's agreement to reciprocate in a friendly manner with a conciliatory letter to be written to him by the President.[25]

Less than one week later an accommodation took place between the Republican President and the Democratic civil-rights crusader. Powell summoned the press and revealed a letter from Eisenhower pledging to take not a "single backward step" and agreeing that there must be "no second-class citizens in this country." It also revealed that those Powell had called obstructionists were now "pursuing the purpose of eliminating segregation in Federally supported institutions." Powell, complying with his part of the bargain, hailed the Presidential statement as a "Magna Carta for minorities and a second Emancipation Proclamation."[26] In his Mount Rushmore speech, the next day, Eisenhower cited the "substantial steps" being taken to remove "terrible injustices . . . wherever the authority of the Federal Government extends."[27] At the start of July, Powell referred to Eisenhower's revival of the President's Committee on Government Contracts and revealed that the Chief Executive would act within a few days to ban racial discrimination in work being done under government sponsorship.[28]

Sparing the President any further criticism but still pursuing his cause, Powell then attacked the Navy Department for having defied Eisenhower's orders. The service, he claimed, was harboring a "modernized, twentieth-century form of slavery," with Negroes being used as nothing more than "man-servants to the admiral clique."[29] Moreover, Powell inferred that the racist attitude of the Texan at the head of the department was responsible for continuing segregation. But Anderson had already interpreted as an order the President's suggestion that something be done about the situation and, with tact and caution, had acted to remove the last official vestige of segregation.

The Secretary's uniformed and civilian assistants had been almost unanimous in their apprehension about the consequences of such a change, if not its wisdom. The installations, they argued, employed civilian residents of the states in which they were located and, therefore, each unit commander should continue to adhere to local custom. Anderson, however, decided that the change had to be made, that the installations were federal property and that the government could not condone anything less than equal treatment for all personnel. Convening all members of the naval districts involved, the Secretary informed them of his decision. Each commander was directed to develop a program that would be appropriate in his own district and to submit written reports every thirty days, directly to Anderson, detailing the exact plans and progress. Not only would the means necessarily vary from place to place, but the whole operation was to be done without any resistance-provoking publicity. At the same time, each commander would explain the situation to local civic leaders and members of such influential organizations as the chambers of commerce or veterans groups and explain the determination to effect the change quietly but effectively.

Without fanfare, then, and without notification, the traditional paraphernalia of military Jim Crow was carefully dismantled. Quietly, offering no reasons, segregated busses were removed, then unostentatiously replaced by vehicles that contained one difference: no signs directed separate seating. Where bathrooms were segregated, they were simply closed for a few days while notices explained that the facilities were being modernized. Meanwhile, they were painted and overhauled; when reopened, there were no racial distinctions. Lunchrooms were similarly refurbished and opened in a few days as though Jim Crowism had never existed. The greatest danger of ugly clashes occurred at the Charleston yard, where local Negroes—on the first day the cafeteria was reopened on a desegregated basis—deployed themselves at the various tables in a bold pronouncement of the change. Immediately, the eating place was closed down for three more days. Lester Granger, the director of the Urban League who had been appointed by Anderson as a consultant to advise on problems connected with the new policy, met with the leaders of the black community and explained with care the disadvantages of direct confrontation and pointed out that their interests could be served much better if they simply went about their business in a routine manner without provocative gestures that seemed to say, "See here, we now sit where we couldn't sit before." When the cafeteria was reopened, the waiting members of the news media were prepared to record a clash, but none occurred. Instead, only about a fifth of the former users returned. Each day, however, brought additional numbers until only the seating pattern was different. On November 11, 1953, President Eisenhower was able to announce the elimination of segregation at forty-three naval shore stations in the South and to declare that the policy was "completely effective." Congressman Powell sent Anderson an apology for his earlier inferences about the Secretary's racial attitude. The problem had been handled by the Secretary in characteristically Eisenhower style.[30]

Anderson's personal qualities and political potentialities were very clear to Eisenhower, but the Texan could not be persuaded to undertake the preparations that would make him acceptable to the party and known to the voters. Still, the President had others in mind, all of whom would do more justice to his concept of moderation than the Vice President. In his memoirs he revealed that "the necessary qualities for successful administration and leadership" could be found in a number of other men; and, along with naming Anderson, he listed Herbert Brownell, Cabot Lodge, Gabriel Hauge, Milton Eisenhower and Generals Clay and Gruenther.[31]

Fortunately, Eisenhower's convalescence and gradual resumption of a normal work schedule coincided with a lull in international and domestic relations, a period that required few decisions that were beyond the competence or authority of the NSC and the Cabinet and permitted a situation that almost—but not quite—rendered plausible the claim that the team could carry on without the President. The most significant event, the foreign ministers' sequel to the summit conference, opened in Geneva on October 27 and lasted for three weeks. In August the Soviets had foreshadowed the disarmament impasse by rejecting the Open Skies proposal; and, as effectively as the United States opposed the holding of elections in South Vietnam, the Kremlin continued to be adamant about voting in Germany, so, as usual, no progress was made on reunification. Even the third item on the foreign ministers' agenda, increased East-West contacts, was stalemated. So the most important residue of the "spirit of Geneva" remained the peaceful intentions of the American President rather than any real mitigation of the cold war. Simultaneously, as newspapers pictured a steady flow of visitors to the Eisenhower bedside and optimistic medical bulletins kept coming from Denver, domestic tensions began to relax. The stock market, which had slumped badly after the original news from Fitzsimons Army Hospital—with 7,720,000 shares traded on September 26 alone—more than made up the losses by November.

The calm enabled Nixon to plot his own course. Remaining pre-eminent as a possible successor, his friends advised, meant attention to two considerations. First, he had to convince the nation that he was no longer the harsh, intensely partisan young man who was despised by many for having waged scurrilous campaigns in California against Jerry Voorhis and Helen Gahagan Douglas and had done the dirty work for Eisenhower on the anti-Communist issue with such zest in 1954. As long as that image remained, it would be impossible for non-Republicans to find him a credible heir to the General's politics of moderation, and the party's minority status made election impossible without the votes of substantial numbers of independents and Democrats. Secondly, as much as with the general public, the Vice President had to dissipate the substantial opposition from the Eisenhower loyalists. Only by demonstrating his conversion to "Modern Republicanism" and by sounding unifying rather than divisive themes could both liabilities be repaired.

On the night of October 17, while delivering the closing speech of the annual forum sponsored by the New York *Herald Tribune*, Richard Nixon made his conversion most notable. Rejecting the strident, sweeping condemnations of the past, his speech contained no hint of the usual charges of "softness" toward communism or blame for the "loss" of China or for turning the "captive peoples" over to the Soviet Union. Nor was there anything about how many concessions the Russians would have to make to substantiate the "spirit of Geneva." Indeed, the tone was more Eisenhower than Nixon. Democratic leaders Lyndon Johnson and Walter George were thanked for their "magnificent" support of the Administration's foreign policy. Americans were urged to emphasize the United Nation's "successes rather than its deficiencies." He called for lowering trade barriers and criticized those wanting to restrict foreign-aid programs. And the man who had built his reputation among the party's conservatives by belligerent anti-communism opposed the idea of reducing contacts with the East.[32] Beyond that particular speech, in attempting to broaden his appeal within the party, the Vice President managed to win general praise for his conduct during the difficult period. While his strongest constituency continued to be Republican politicians, his fortunes were, to them, distinctly secondary to their major consideration—convincing the President to run for a second term.

The President walked out of Fitzsimons Hospital on November 11 and flew to the capital, where a crowd of well-wishers cheered his arrival at the Washington National Airport and thousands lined the route as the Presidential motorcade crossed the Memorial Bridge and entered the city. In a statement welcoming his return, twenty-nine Republican Senators immediately pledged their support. Four days later he went on to Gettysburg, where his farm was set up as a White House during his convalescence. The local post office became a temporary office. More than ever before, Eisenhower seemed in complete command of the loyalties of his party and the nation. Significantly, too, his increased prestige coincided with a Gallup Poll, released on the sixteenth of that month, that showed three out of every five Americans favoring a "Man who usually follows middle-of-the-road policy."[33] When Adlai Stevenson announced, during that same week, his candidacy for a second nomination by the Democratic party, he asserted that "wisdom and responsibility" did not reappear in national affairs until his party had regained control of Congress. But, carefully, he avoided any criticism of the President.[34] On the twenty-first, Eisenhower was driven the twenty-five miles to Camp David so he could preside over a National Security Council meeting and, the next day, the Catoctin Mountain retreat became the site of the first Cabinet session since his return. Democratic suggestions that the Republicans were deceiving the public by pretending that the President had regained full charge of the Administration were belied by the photographs and stories from Gettysburg.

Then came renewed pressures to run again. David Lawrence suggested that both parties endorse his candidacy because "the American people ought not to be deprived of the services of President Eisenhower in a world crisis"—to which William F. Buckley, Jr., replied, "There is abroad in the land a spirit of blind submission whose political expression is the attempt to Caesarize Dwight Eisenhower, with or without his cooperation. There seems to be a deep yearning in some quarters of America for a benevolent monarch or, *mutatis mutandis*, a reigning chairman-of-the-board."[35] Leonard Hall visited Eisenhower at Gettysburg on November 28 and found a depressed Sherman Adams and Jim Hagerty awaiting him with the news that the outlook for a second term was bleak. During his subsequent visit with the President, the national chairman at least got permission to say whatever he desired publicly and promptly told reporters that "Ike and Dick" would head the ticket again in 1956.[36] Three weeks later, Dr. White announced that the President's recovery was "excellent and encouraging" and declared him "out of danger." The gradually increasing activity had left no symptoms of heart strain.[37] With such medical reports apparently removing the major obstacle and a Gallup Poll showing Ike's lead over Stevenson the same as before his illness, many influential Republicans, including General Lucius Clay, assumed the task of convincing the reluctant President.

Generally, their arguments stressed that the team organization would minimize the burdens of a second term, that he could resign if the strain became too severe and that the party and the country could not afford to be placed in the hands of the right wing. That the politicians would almost surely replace him with Nixon was, it may be safely deduced, an argument that was pressed with great force. For a while Nixon was trapped between the party's two main wings. The Vice President's identification with Eisenhower had made him anathema to the more extreme conservatives, some of whom hoped to form a coalition around Styles Bridges.[38] Greater numbers watched Bill Knowland, who pointedly challenged Presidential hopefuls of both parties to declare whether they would fight the admission of Red China to the UN and indicated his own availability unless Eisenhower announced a willingness to run by the end of January. A non-partisan organization, the National Committee for an Effective Congress, announced in its publication that "The illness of President Eisenhower has given extremist elements and leaders their first real opportunity for a comeback since the censure of McCarthy." Undeterred by defeats in 1954, the committee warned, such groups were "launching an intensive effort to re-create an atmopshere for fear and suspicion" in which they "might once again become a dominating political factor."[39] Since the leading moderate alternatives to Eisenhower, Chief Justice Earl Warren and Dr. Milton Eisenhower, were both beyond persuasion, a clash between the party's various elements would unquestionably lead to Nixon's emergence.

Any doubts Nixon may have had about the origin of the movement to thwart his ambitions were resolved not long after the President had returned to Gettysburg and before he left for a recuperative stay at Key West. On the day after Christmas the younger man heard Eisenhower's observation that his political base needed bolstering, that a recent Gallup Poll showing Warren three percentage points stronger indicated that the Vice President might serve himself better in some other post. Distraught, Nixon heard Eisenhower say he could have any Cabinet position he wanted, except of course that of Secretary of State, where Under Secretary Herbert Hoover, Jr., had the inside track if Dulles retired; nor could he become Attorney General because his legal experience was insufficient. Charlie Wilson's spot, heading the Defense Department, might serve well, however, and it would be a good idea for Nixon to consider that possibility. The suggestion reappeared during five or six of their private conversations; but never, even when the Vice President prodded him for a direct statement of his belief that the Republican ticket and leadership would be better with somebody else, did Eisenhower make a flat declaration that Nixon should step down.[40] However, Eisenhower intimates have maintained that the President's motivation concerned improving Nixon's position for the top spot in 1960 and was actually being done with his best interest in mind.[41]

More important, however, was the President's decision about his own future. During that period perhaps the most significant factor remained the clear possibility of the triumph of moderation. Eisenhower's Presidency had, undeniably, brought relaxation from the strident rhetoric of the past few years. The general mood, with prosperity and reduced fear of war predominant, reflected the sudden absence of sharp contention. When, for example, the *Democratic Digest*, the official organ of the opposition, reported in its December issue the ten areas of greatest discontent with the Republicans, the survey of their own party leaders conspicuously omitted foreign policy. The only item with substantial voter attraction, falling farm income, headed the list. What followed resembled typical Democratic complaints, of the sort that meant little to the average voter enjoying a comfortable livelihood in a time of peace: tax breaks for the rich, public power "give-away" programs, favoritism to big business, misconduct in government, rising cost of living, small-business failures, anti-labor policies, inadequate schools and the growth of monopolies, reported in that order.[42] In Congress, the President's program contained little to arouse the passions of those fearful that the Republicans were about to return to the past. Indeed, it continued to the left of the party's legislators. No substantiation could be seen for Mr. Eisenhower's own gloomy campaign rhetoric, made before the 1954 elections, that a "cold war of partisan politics" would result if the Democrats controlled Capitol Hill. On such issues as public housing, reciprocal trade, mutual security and the extension of corporate and excise taxes for another year, the Administration, in each case, achieved results that fell somewhere between the desires of both parties. On the farm bill, which did not come to a vote in the Senate before the session ended, House Democrats defeated flexible supports and, in a test that provided one of the few good examples of partisan balloting, achieved by the narrow margin of 206–201 the restoration of 90 percent of parity. All in all Eisenhower's own position, usually on the side of moderating the cost of any new programs, had come to represent a balance between the divergent views rather than an orthodox identification with either a liberal or a conservative position. Little had been accomplished without the Democratic votes and, when preparing for the President's third annual message on the State of the Union, every effort was made to continue the politics of moderation that would, in effect, appeal to a bipartisan constituency. When the President retired to Key West, Florida, for a period of recuperation, such aides as Gabriel Hauge, Sherman Adams and Gerald Morgan joined him for continued labor on the speech to be delivered at the start of the Eighty-fourth Congress's second session. As the blueprint for an election-year legislative program, with the President being wooed to run for a second term and more firmly in command of his party than ever, the audience was the American public rather than Republicans or Democrats. There was little the GOP could do about it. As in 1952, they were certain only Ike could bring victory.

President Eisenhower's seventy-sixth news conference took place far from the usual location—in the lobby of the Bachelor Officers quarters at the U.S. naval base in Key West. There, on January 8, virtually the entire session was devoted to the second-term decision. Parrying questions about his health and intentions, the President kept his guard with skill; but, nevertheless, specks of optimism were visible. He agreed, for example, with Dr. White's observation that "hard work is not only a very, very fine thing for most humans but it keeps them healthy." He also told them he was "as ready to go to work as a person could be, after the physical experience I have been through." Lest anyone feel, however, that any conclusions had been reached, he warned that he had not fixed his mind "in such and such an extent that it can't be changed."[43] As the reporters themselves observed, no final judgment could be made until the President had been given the thorough check-up scheduled by his doctors for mid-February. As the whole panoply of Republicans awaited the outcome, from Knowland to Nixon to the guardians of the Eastern Establishment, few party stalwarts quarreled over Eisenhower's importance to the future of the GOP.

CHAPTER 33

Before San Francisco

Vacationing at Key West, with plenty of golf and walking, had left the President optimistic about resuming regular routines, which would further test his physical reactions. Two days after Eisenhower returned to the White House, Hagerty announced that the latest medical examination had, indeed, shown no sign of overwork and fatigue. Republican morale climbed.

Had it all been up to Mamie, however, there would have been nothing left to decide. Like her husband, she had assumed that the White House period would constitute simply a four-year delay of an idyllic, stable and financially comfortable retirement at Gettysburg. The farm, purchased with their hope of taking up permanent residency there in 1957, was the only real home they had ever had. Until then, life in the White House was, for Mamie Eisenhower, something tolerable only as a temporary inconvenience, not unlike the past sacrifices of a loyal Army wife following her husband to various bases. While visitors to the mansion inevitably raved about her warmth and charm, at heart she resented the public nature of life at 1600 Pennsylvania Avenue. Those responsible for arranging receptions for various groups, such as teas for Republican women, discovered her reluctance to compromise with her longing for privacy. Only persuasion that argued about Ike's interest requiring such amenability dissolved such resistance.[1]

Milton, too, had doubts about his brother's future course. Torn between worry over Ike's health and the nation's needs, he could not be happy about a possible replacement. His own aversion to Nixon was greater than his brother's. His desires for world peace were at least equal to the President's and, as one who had been bitterly affronted by what McCarthy and his followers had done to the Republican party and the nation, keeping the extremists from power remained an important objective. When contemplating a Democratic succession, however, he could only visualize a confused and divided leadership under Stevenson and a party immobilized by its formidable Southern wing on the increasingly important matter of civil rights. They had also, since New Deal days, engaged in irresponsible deception, constantly offering, in exchange for votes, expensive programs that ignored economic realities. Only a Republican party, free from the suspicion of "softness" toward international communism and concerned with reconciling the public need with the public till, could prevent such distortions. And only his brother's candidacy could ensure moderately progressive leadership. Nevertheless, "Little Ike" found it difficult to persuade himself that Ike Eisenhower had not already given more of himself than his country could rightfully expect and that his own health and happiness should not now be primary considerations. With such feelings, Milton had to face an assignment, on the night of January 13, requiring him to summarize the sentiments of eleven others on the question of a second term.

They gathered that Friday night in complete secrecy—having, in fact, canceled an earlier session because word had leaked—in the Trophy Room on the second floor of the White House. Dinner was over and Mamie had left them alone. Lively flames filled the fireplace. Seated on two parallel couches, they faced each other and took turns offering opinions. Dulles, whom much of the opposition press and general public viewed as the most militaristic Cabinet member, emphasized the importance of avoiding nuclear war and talked about the President's unique talent for reconciling differences as the best way to preserve peace. Lodge and Summerfield both offered the unification theme, with the UN ambassador repeating his concerns of 1951 and 1952 and stressing accomplishments in repairing divisions among the American people. The Postmaster General and ex-party chairman admitted that Mr. Eisenhower had forced many Old Guardsmen to reconsider their long-cherished negative views toward government responsibility. Each voice was another vote for a second term.

As planned, Milton's turn came last; but the one-sided consensus had left him with little to summarize. Still, he pointed out that his brother's public contributions had been sufficient for one man and that he should not be denied the long-delayed opportunity for a private existence. Those in the room, aware that Milton had been left with only his own forebodings, came away sensing the President's determination to accept the challenge of his responsibility. But the final medical report had yet to be considered.

Eisenhower's third message on the State of the Union, delivered to

Congress *in absentia* the week before the Trophy Room conference, expressed his determination to continue, at least, his own brand of Republicanism. It conveyed his reliance on what Arthur Krock noted were merely "prudent laws" to regulate the social economy without impairing New and Fair Deal concepts. Actually, in such matters as federal aid for school construction, extending Social Security coverage, immigration and strengthening eight-hour laws for government workers, he adopted the substance of what many liberals thought possible during that period of conservative retrenchment. For agriculture, conceded as the more severe domestic economic problem, he advocated means of relieving overproduction by using the old New Deal soil-bank idea and providing stronger activities to dispose of surplus crops. Farmers alone, he pointed out, "of all major groups have seen their incomes decline rather than rise."[2]

Near the end of the message, civil rights received attention. For the first time the President budged from his insistence that federal laws could not resolve national racial troubles. Legislatively, at least, such impotence had been confirmed repeatedly. Every bill for racial equality had been beaten back. The Senate's retention of Rule XXII, which provided for the continuation of debates in the absence of a two-thirds closure vote, had ensured the filibustered death of all proposals. More basic, however, remained the deeply ingrained political conflicts. The Democratic party, containing Northerners with large liberal constituencies and black newcomers from the technologically advancing agricultural South, was at an impasse on the issue that constantly threatened to rekindle the Dixiecrat movement. And the GOP, which had urban representatives like Hugh Scott, Kenneth Keating and Jacob Javits demanding action, had yet to decide whether it wanted to expand its influence in the Old Confederacy by appealing to the most rigid segregationists or by offering moderate alternatives. That course would also attract Northerners repelled by Southern domination of Democratic Congressional leadership.[3] In December, led by Attorney General Brownell, the Justice Department had already begun to draft proposals; and so the President's State of the Union message told of "allegations" that, in some localities, "Negro citizens are being deprived of their right to vote and are likewise being subjected to unwarranted economic pressures," which should be investigated by a bipartisan commission that would soon be recommended to Congress.[4]

Any assumption by the Eighty-fourth Congress that Eisenhower would not run again implied a commitment by Republicans to minimize their opposition to his programs. Another course would open the possibility of a contest for power that, inevitably, would create internal competition. Such splits threatened even more the success of other GOP Presidential candidates in the fall and certainly the need to regain control of Congress. Therefore, after holding a morning conference with the President on January 10, the party's Congressional leaders invited every Republican Senator to attend the weekly sessions of the Senate Republican Policy Committee. Viewed in another way, it was a step toward preserving the President's program even if he chose to step down. Although most of the committee's twenty-three members were Eisenhower men, orthodox Republicans like Styles Bridges, its chairman, and Bill Knowland had kept control.[5]

While contingency plans were important, nothing overshadowed desires to preserve the Eisenhower–Nixon ticket. Publisher Mike Cowles, among those contributors and long-time friends of the GOP pushing Nixon's prospects, gave a dinner for the Vice President. Before a select group of influential businessmen, the potential heir gave what one participant called "the best apologia for the Administration I've heard yet." Stressing that Ike had kept the country out of war, he contrasted the Democratic record. If the party would only run on the Administration's record, Nixon told them, victory could be achieved. If Ike should head the ticket, of course, it would be a pushover. And the impression that the President would run "was subtly conveyed," the observer reported to Sinclair Weeks, "with ineffable charm and very obvious and engaging sincerity." The Commerce Secretary relayed those comments to Nixon with the wish that they "may bring you a ray of light on a dark morning."[6]

The Vice President's gloom and that of party stalwarts desiring to keep the ticket intact had been deepened by what the President told his news conference on the morning of January 25. Correspondent Marvin Arrowsmith had asked whether he would favor Nixon as his running mate. "Well," he replied, "my admiration, respect and deep affection for Mr. Nixon I think are well known." Then, with an absence of candor, he added, "Now I have never talked to him under any circumstances as to what his future is to be or what he wants it to be, and until I confer with him I wouldn't have anything to say."[7]

On the night of January 20, the third anniversary of the inauguration became a gigantic fund-raising occasion for the party. In fifty-one cities and thirty-six states, "Salute to Eisenhower" dinners catered to one-hundred-dollar-a-plate contributors. In New York's Madison Square Garden, that price bought a box supper featuring half a cold lobster cut into bites for convenient eating while seated around the indoor arena. In some of the smaller centers, however, adjustments to local conditions reduced the tab to just twenty-five dollars; and in Kansas City, one-hundred-dollar tickets could be obtained for a down payment of twenty-five dollars and three additional installments to be paid later. In almost all the cities, the celebrants received the President's image via closed-circuit television and heard him pledge that "in whatever capacity I shall serve,

I shall support with all my strength the foreign and domestic programs for America that have been the guide of all of us for these past three years."[8]

But the most vigorous speech at any of the dinners was delivered in person by the Vice President in Chicago's International Amphitheater. There, Richard Nixon denied complaints that the Administration's domestic program was too liberal and "New Dealish" and insisted that "The choice is not between the Eisenhower program and something more radical. The American people are not going to stand still," said the conservative Vice President. "They want progress." Republicans, he told them, must assure another term for the President's policies whether or not he decides to run.[9]

Winning the President's redesignation of Nixon had become more difficult than convincing him about a second term. White House callers were noticing his conversation being enlivened by talk about running again.[10] The main problem, he had told the press right after refusing to commit himself about Nixon, was whether he would have the "zip and zest" required by the Presidency to "get something done for the good of the United States."[11] At the same time, his earlier apprehensions about his Vice President were enhanced when a Gallup Poll trial heat showed Stevenson widening his lead over Nixon. Matched against Eisenhower, however, the Democrat had no chance. Even in the South, the President held a substantial lead.[12]

Yet there were good reasons for believing that any departure from the Eisenhower–Nixon combination might aid attempts to breach the middle-of-the-road leadership. Unless the President tolerated an even more conservative replacement, dropping the Vice President would offend the right wing. Knowland warned that such a move would offend the Taft Republicans, who would then feel disfranchised. Such conservatives, the party's Senate leader warned on March 1, "now feel that they have not been made so much a part of the team as their long service in the party warrants."[13] Harry Truman himself aided the process of keeping Nixon respectable in right-wing eyes by charging that, during the 1952 campaign, the Vice President had called him a traitor. For several months thereafter, a controversy persisted between partisans over whether Nixon's words at Texarkana, Texas, on October 27, 1952, justified Truman's complaint. As reported by the Associated Press, Nixon had said that the Democratic President, Acheson and Stevenson were "traitors to the high principles in which many of the nation's Democrats believe" and added that "real Democrats" were "outraged by the Truman–Acheson–Stevenson's gang's toleration and defense of communism in high places."[14] That hardly lowered Nixon's standing with the For America group. Meeting at New York's Carnegie Hall on February 22, the right-wing radicals heard Joe McCarthy hail Douglas MacArthur as the "contemporary George Washington" and declare that "traitors" retained high Defense and State Department posts.[15] Others at a series of meetings in Chicago under the sponsorship of the Abraham Lincoln National Republican Club, which had a declared objective of wresting the party's control from the Eisenhower "liberals," heard Senator Jenner accuse the executive branch of "collectivism" and "one-worldism." The clear-cut issue facing Americans was "the American system versus international socialism," Senator Malone told them, and added that "The American system means keeping the American markets for Americans."[16] At the same time, liberal discontent with Nixon continued, despite his congeniality toward the Eisenhower program. The mere mention of the Vice President's name "outside of one's own household," Fred Morrow wrote in his diary, "is like throwing gasoline on a smoldering fire." The "black man in the White House" had come to respect Nixon and speculated that the "terrific anti-Nixon feeling in this country—even among Republicans" must be a residue from the 1952 campaign.[17] All such remonstrations made clear that any attempt to dump him could only jar the consensus that had been achieved; but his retention required Eisenhower at the head of the ticket.

The final medical report, announced on February 14, made a negative decision almost impossible. Dr. White reported that all indications showed no reason why the President could not carry on "his present life satisfactorily" for another five or ten years. With that out of the way, Eisenhower gave himself still another test of his stamina by leaving for a ten-day vacation of golf and quail hunting at George Humphrey's Georgia plantation.

When he returned, General Lucius Clay received a telegram from the White House. He and his wife Marjorie were requested to join the President and Mamie for dinner. Clay, who had been among the leading non-politicians trying to persuade Eisenhower for a second term, thereby got the first report of the President's decision. After the two couples had finished dinner and gone to the second floor of the White House, Eisenhower said to his old friend, "Tonight's the night I'm going to make my decision as to whether I'm going to run again."

"It's your decision, not mine," said Mamie. "I'm not going to have anything to do with it."

"Well," said the President, "I've made up my mind. I'm going to run again."[18]

The nation learned the news via a morning press conference and then an evening television talk that he delivered on February 29. At the same time he continued to embarrass his Vice President. To prodding reporters Eisenhower said, "I think we will have to wait to see who the Republican convention nominates, and then it will be proper to give an expression on that point."[19]

The next time he met the press, Marvin Arrowsmith began the interrogation by recalling the reports that some of the President's own advisers had been urging him to dump the Vice President and that he himself had suggested Nixon shift to a Cabinet post. Eisenhower appeared indignant. He told them that "if anyone ever has the effrontery to come in and urge me to dump somebody that I respect as I do Vice President Nixon, there will be more commotion around my office than you have noticed yet." Furthermore, Eisenhower said, he had not "presumed" to offer advice about his future. "The only thing I have asked him to do is to chart out his own course and tell me what he would like to do. I have never gone beyond that."[20]

Nixon continued on tenterhooks. The President had embarrassed him and, at the same time, provoked national apprehensions about the quality of an emergency successor. Republicans, confused and concerned that Nixon's presence on the ticket would hinder their attempts to recover Congress, resembled anxious Democrats. The Administration's opponents, unable to challenge the President on the issue of war and peace and vainly trying to convince Americans that the Republican prosperity ignored unhappy social and economic realities, concentrated on portraying the President as a frustrated and reluctant man; and, turning an old vote-getter to their own partisan advantage—now that domestic communsim had lost its potency as an issue—charged that Dulles's ideas about "going to the brink" to avoid war, as James Shepley had described in a *Life* article that January, was irresponsible diplomacy, frightening to our allies and counter-productive. International insensitivity, obsession with trimming defense budgets and standing armies, insufficient attention to guided-missile development and space satellite research and myopia about the appeal of communism to backward and exploited peoples, they charged, were furthering Russian gains and weakening American prestige. As William V. Shannon wrote in *Commonweal*, a liberal Catholic weekly, "the country is in growing danger because it has not summoned up the reserves of vigor and initiative, or imagination and sacrifice, which the Russian menace demands."[21] Adlai Stevenson spoke in Hartford and charged that the President was only a "coach" who has "missed most of the plays" and was not "too sure of the score." In a major foreign-policy address he delivered in April, in which he also first mentioned the idea of suspending nuclear-bomb tests, the Democratic titular head asked, "Do you think we are winning or losing ground in the competition with the Communist world?" The United States, he declared, was merely standing pat on a system of alliances while the Soviets, exploiting our inertia toward change, were bent on their stated goal of "a Communist world."[22] Continuing a government by "regency," as Wayne Morse charged, and duping the public that all was well were to Democratic partisans the only expectations from four more years with Eisenhower. Retaining him with his vulnerable heart was bad enough, but the prospect of going on with Nixon as Vice President received, that March, anxious attention.

At the start of the month, a New York *Times* dispatch claimed that Republican leaders had been notified that he would receive the President's support for the nomination. Those closer to Mr. Eisenhower, however, understood its real meaning: If necessary, rather than fight for a change, the President would capitulate to the desires of the national committee and Len Hall. Both publicly and privately, Eisenhower talked about an "open" convention, usually couching his position behind the observation that it would be inappropriate for him to say anything about a running mate until after the Presidential nomination. But Knowland's warning about keeping Nixon for conservative representation coincided with the *Times*'s story and made front-page headlines; and the next day, the Vice President himself attempted a self-fulfilling prophecy by telling the Cabinet about the great cooperation evident among Congressional Republicans and the accuracy of Eisenhower's belief that references to a Taft or an Eisenhower wing of the party was an "unreality."[23] Six days later, at a Thursday-night White House stag dinner given by the President for some old friends and advisers, including Nixon, Dewey, Paul Hoffman, Lucius Clay, Tom Stephens, Harold Stassen, Sherman Adams, Bobby Cutler and Herb Brownell, Eisenhower kept the issue wide open.

For the President, such stag dinners were liberations from the oppressiveness of the White House. There, without newsmen or routine pressures, he could relax with congenial company and enjoy informality. With an evidently light mood that evening, he led the conversation as he and his guests enjoyed a loin-of-beef dinner. Of the many items mentioned, the Vice Presidency received few words but much attention as those around the table listened for any hints about his thinking. But he simply repeated his determination to avoid making a choice until after the Presidential nomination and added, "I don't understand why they don't believe that I mean just what I say. I have tried to make my position clear." The Vice President heard that remark and the other guests discreetly let the subject end without further comment. Later, however, the President told one of the guests that stating a preference before the convention would be "improper."[24]

Almost immediately afterward, Nixon's fortunes rose. He astonished most observers by receiving a demonstration of grass-roots Republican support in drawing twenty-two thousand write-in ballots in the New Hampshire primary. That achievement won Eisenhower's comment that he "would be happy to be on any political ticket in which I was a candidate with him," which proved to be the closest he ever came to an endorsement.[25] Leonard Hall, who had masterminded the drive to preserve the "Ike and Dick" ticket since the heart attack, calculated that the time had come for Nixon to strike. All that time, too, an old Republican professional hand named Victor Johnston had been working hard rounding up pro-Nixon signatures from more than eight hundred delegates or prospective delegates, a number far beyond what would be needed at San Francisco. Also working behind the scenes for the Vice President, along with such people as Mike Cowles, was financier Sidney Weinberg. At one point, Weinberg tried to add Nixon's name to the Citizens for Eisenhower title. His effort, however, was blocked by one of the President's close friends and Nixon opponents, General Clay. However, with the signatures as evidence of strong support, Hall urged the Vice President to confront the President with his desire to be retained.

He did that on April 26. The President expressed his delight and directed Jim Hagerty to call in the press. Nixon told them he had informed the Chief Executive of his decision that "it is in the best interest of the Republican party and this Administration for me to continue in my present office" and that he would be "honored to accept that nomination again as I was and as I did in 1952." At the next Cabinet meeting, Dulles exulted that "Ike and Dick" would lead the "team" once more, a sentiment the others applauded warmly.[26]

That seemed to leave the Democrats with all the problems. With a Gallup Poll showing that even their own partisans liked Eisenhower better than Truman, they appeared to have been undercut by the President's illness and fine recovery. Since the shock of his near death, the popular figure in the White House had acquired an additional glow, a spell sufficient to overwhelm skeptics about his fitness for a second term. Opponents foolish enough to question the widely publicized medical opinions also risked provoking more sympathy. That left the Democrats largely issueless and, led by National Chairman Paul Butler, reduced to exploiting the unproductive theme of a "nice guy" but "part-time" President ensconced in the White House, in Grant and Harding fashion, by knots of conniving "big businessmen" designing new get-rich schemes while a docile puppet played golf, smiled, waved and assured the nation that life had never been better. Indeed, popular association of Republicans with the wealthy offered the most lucrative campaign fodder for desperate Democrats.

But while Americans continued, in every survey of public opinion, to brand the GOP as the "party of the rich," Eisenhower's own monopolization of the political center also compounded Democratic difficulties. Their three main contenders, Stevenson, Averell Harriman and Estes Kefauver, debated over occupying Eisenhower's ground or appealing to more liberal views. Moderation, Harriman told the Atlantic City convention of the newly merged AFL-CIO, was no place for Democrats. Later, the man who had succeeded Dewey as New York's Governor boasted that he alone among the contenders could not be accused of softness toward communism. Kefauver had antagonized Southern segregationists and lacked general organizational support throughout the country. He worked to demonstrate the popularity of progressivism by besting his rivals in primaries and went on to defeat Stevenson in New Hampshire and almost fatally damaged the titular leader's chances in Minnesota. Continuing to do well, but working against Stevenson's fight to recover, Kefauver lost in Oregon. Finally, opposed by even the head of his own state's delegation and failing to generate enough enthusiasm to impress the party's establishment, he withdrew and urged his followers to back Stevenson.

The articulate former Governor of Illinois remained in the race against Harriman. Both looked to Truman to abandon his neutrality and grant an endorsement. But the ex-President, closer to the New Yorker's people and still piqued over Stevenson's 1952 aloofness from him, was preparing a dramatic move to stop the political "egghead" of the 1950s.

Hardly less perplexing than opposing an Eisenhower-led ticket was the civil-rights issue. As the primaries had demonstrated, the question had acquired considerable passion. Democrats, by not including the matter among the ten "issues" listed in their magazine, appeared desirous of burying the problem. Still, racial equality had emerged as a major factor in several contests for state delegates. Especially during the Florida campaign, Kefauver's liberal approach rankled traditionalists, while Stevenson continued as a moderate.[27] With two clearly disparate wings, party unification seemed incompatible with the desires of crusaders for equality and those fighting for states' rights.

In the White House, where virtually every view was represented, the developing conflict received careful attention. In addition to Fred Morrow, Max Rabb, Sherman Adams, Jim Hagerty and Jim Mitchell were sympathetic. Conservatives like Jerry Persons and George Humphrey remained less comfortable with the accelerating rate of change, and many of the others viewed the trend mainly for its political implications, a consideration common to all the Eisenhower aides before civil rights became an intense issue. During the 1952 campaign, for example, Fred Morrow, the staff member who had worked with both the Urban League and the NAACP and had a personal commitment to racial justice, suggested that an anti-FEPC newspaper column by ultra-conservative black journalist George Schuyler be exploited by having thousands of reprints circulated in densely populated Negro communities.[28]

Still, before the Supreme Court's 1954 desegregation decision provoked greater national controversy, the Administration had moved to undertake small but significant measures in opposition to Jim Crowism. Desegregation in Army post schools and Anderson's success with civilian

Navy yard workers corresponded with the President's moves to update racial relations in the District of Columbia, with Attorney General Brownell winning in the Supreme Court an overturning of an earlier decision by the Federal Court of Appeals that upheld segregation in Washington's restaurants.[29] When the American Friends Service Committee worked with the city's leading business executives to end inequality, the Administration gave its support. "In this attempt," wrote a leader of the Quaker group, "we have been greatly aided by the President and his staff. It has been our hope that a general attitude of support for the President's pronouncement may be encouraged at all levels within the agencies of the federal government." Eisenhower was particularly pleased by such progress in the nation's capital because, as he wrote to the District of Columbia's Board of Commissioners' president, it was "an area of exclusive federal jurisdiction."[30] Additionally, although Morrow remained the only black special assistant on the White House staff, efforts were made to hire Negroes in all Executive departments and agencies. The appointment of John W. Mitchell by Ezra Taft Benson in October of 1953 to lead Negro agricultural extension work resulted from a personal suggestion by the President to the Secretary that at least one black aide should be given a position of responsibility in that department.[31] After the Court had rendered its opinion, on August 13, 1954, an Executive Order established the President's Committee on Government Contracts. A revitalization of the old Committee on Government Contract Compliance, its prestige was enhanced by being placed under the chairmanship of Vice President Nixon. Under its guidance, which was designed to ensure private industry's adherence with the non-discrimination clause in government contracts, additional gains were made in Washington. Job opportunities opened for Negro bus drivers and streetcar operators, and segregation ended in the offices of the Chesapeake & Potomac Telephone Company.[32]

Such advances, except when Adam Clayton Powell called attention to what remained to be done, were implemented with as little publicity as possible. While the Administration worked to avoid conflicts, however, Negro papers and spokesmen noted the gains with favorable comments. NAACP Executive Director Walter White distributed, in November, a complimentary review of the Eisenhower record.[33] At the same time they also responded with anger when Ezra Taft Benson capitulated to Southern demands that non-discrimination clauses be dropped from agreements with lending agencies making farm price support loans.[34] The President, when asked about Labor Secretary Mitchell's endorsement of the Humphrey–Ives Equal Employment Opportunity Bill, reiterated his displeasure with "punitive or compulsory federal law."[35] In April, he fielded a question about FEPC by saying he expected that "states will move on this in an enlightened and forward-looking way."[36] The Administration's moves had been confined to areas outside of the jursidiction of individual states.

On May 17, 1954, the Supreme Court's unanimous ruling in the case of *Brown v. Topeka* reversed the *Plessy v. Ferguson* "separate but equal" decision of 1896 and called school segregation in violation of the Fourteenth Amendment. Holding that separation was inherently unequal, the Court utilized sociological and psychological arguments. The following day, President Eisenhower called to the White House the commissioners of the District of Columbia to tell them about his hopes that Washington would become a model for the rest of the country in integrating Negro and white public school children.[37]

But whether he welcomed its application to the states was another matter. At his press conference of May 19, the President only hinted at his reaction to the first significant decision by the Warren Court. When reporter Harry C. Dent of the Columbia (South Carolina) *State and Record* asked whether he had any advice for the South, Eisenhower's first words were "Not in the slightest." He then noted that the Court had spoken, however, "and I am sworn to uphold the constitutional process in this country; and I will obey." When Mr. Dent observed that the decision was made "under the Republican Administration," the President countered with "The Supreme Court, as I understand it, is not under my Administration."[38] In August, when asked whether he had given any thought to requesting any legislation for the enforcement of the required integration, his terse reply was "The subject has not even been mentioned to me."[39]

Eisenhower's own past record, in addition to his opposition to an FEPC, had been given some attention during the 1952 campaign. Harlem voters were reminded that the Republican candidate was the same soldier who had gone before the Senate Armed Services Committee in 1948 and testified against military desegregation by saying, "I do not believe that if we attempt merely by passing a lot of laws to force someone to take someone else, we are just going to get into trouble."[40] He would, however, permit Negro platoons to be part of white companies, but warned that complete integration would place blacks at a disadvantage for promotions to higher non-commissioned ranks.[41] Roy Wilkins met with the General during the summer of 1952 and found him clinging to a typical "West Point, Old Guard view of race relations." The NAACP leader's session with Eisenhower turned out to be a carefully structured thirty-minute affair in which the candidate was flanked by public-relations men and politicians. That contrasted with the congenial two-hour talk he had with Stevenson. While the Republican candidate had prepared Wilkins to expect little civil-rights leadership from any Administration he would head, the Governor agreed that Rule XXII should be changed to facilitate ending filibusters and even offered to support the Humphrey–Ives bill for an FEPC.[42] Eisenhower, on the other hand, approved passage of FEPC laws by individual states.

White House staff members concerned with improving the lives of American Negroes found the President humanely sympathetic, aware of the increasing gravity of the problem and emphatic about eliminating discrimination among federal employees.[43] Yet he found it difficult to comprehend the full impact of bias upon the abused. Fred Morrow's attempts to describe the situation brought resistance to belief that things could really be so bad.[44] To Morrow's distress, when the President finally did seem to absorb the pressing needs, a few days of socializing with George Humphrey negated those efforts.[45]

Eisenhower never did go beyond the simple acknowledgment that, as President, he was bound to uphold the Court's decision. For many, his position *vis-à-vis* the South placed him in a particularly difficult spot and his displeasure with the ruling was noted by some; others even hinted that he regretted the Warren appointment, but no confirmation of that ever became available. Arthur Larson, then Eisenhower's Under Secretary of Labor, has reported more forthrightly that the President flatly disagreed with the Court.[46]

The public was never told about his own serious doubts concerning *Brown v. Topeka*. Racial separation, he believed, was deeply ingrained within most Americans and no attempt to force white acceptance of unacculturated blacks could change feeling or assuage fears. Negro children were being raised under standards offensive to most of society and whites were not ready to expose their own children to such classrooms. Only a slow process of education could rectify the injustices of the past and must precede gains.[47] While he agreed that school integration was inevitable, as did even so traditional a Southerner as Harry Byrd of Virginia, Eisenhower thought that the correct procedure would be to start the process at the college and university level and eventually win its approval at the lowest elementary grades.[48] At heart, the President was too imbued with states'-rights concepts to welcome such federal leadership.[49] Subsequently, the Court's 1955 direction that desegregation should be implemented "with all deliberate speed" did nothing to satisfy the apprehensions of either the President, proponents of effective civil-rights enforcement or conservative resistance. Publicly, the President maintained his neutrality and even regarded comments on Supreme Court decisions as violations of judicial authority.

But, as the 1956 campaign mounted, sufficient evidence accumulated that traditional *laissez faire* would no longer suffice. The forces of massive resistance had already organized. As early as the summer of 1954, in the home county of Mississippi's Senator James Eastland, the most influential citizens formed the first White Citizens Council chapter to unify the new "fire-eaters" in defense of traditional social and economic patterns. At the same time, Governor Thomas B. Stanley of Virginia promised to "use every means at my command to continue segregated schools in Virginia." By October of that year, respectable Old Dominion businessmen and lawyers were represented by the Defenders of State Sovereignty and Individual Liberties.[50]

Within the following two years, or by the time the 1956 campaign was nearing the convention stage, some fifty segregationist groups formed throughout the South. Largely a middle-class response that attracted local business and service groups, state farm bureau federations and fraternal organizations, the White Citizens Councils became unifiers of resistance and, as such, more potent than the primitive and considerably less respectable Ku Klux Klan. Also significant was formulation of the so-called Southern Manifesto. Conceived by South Carolina's J. Strom Thurmond (then still a Democrat), the document declared "political war against the Court's decision" and won the signatures of 101 of the 128 Southern Senators and Representatives. Kefauver's rejection of their demand did considerable damage to the Tennesseean's attempt to gain his party's Presidential nomination. Later, a manifesto with the names of eighty-three Dixie Congressmen was called "Warning of Grave Dangers" and advanced the proposition that protecting civil rights by legislation constituted a threat to liberty. Others resurrected the old concept of interposition as a legal buffer against federal action. By interposing the sovereignty of the states, their goal was the nullification of laws from Washington. State legislatures and Citizens Councils both adopted that constitutional shelter.[51]

Economic and physical reprisals flared. When NAACP chapters sponsored petitions for school desegregation, the Councils published lists of the signatories. More than half of the Negroes who endorsed a petition in Selma, Alabama, lost their jobs.[52] In August of 1955 the Negro leader of a voter registration campaign was killed on the lawn of the Lincoln County, Mississippi, courthouse. None of the many witnesses were called by state authorities. Two weeks later, in the most sensational case, fourteen-year-old Emmett Till, a Chicago Negro visiting in the Sunflower State, was accused of whistling at a white woman and paid for his indiscretion by ending up floating face down in a river. Such murders violated no federal laws; left to the states, there were no convictions.

The Till case strained the Administration's policy of silence. "If Washington had made a move and been rebuffed it could have collected some kudos for effort," wrote Roy Wilkins to Valores Washington, the Republican party's director of Minorities. "But it said nothing and did nothing."[53] To Morrow, the Negro special assistant on the White House staff, Wilkins pointed out the Administration's responsibility to avoid "what could be an ugly racial conflict."[54] As early as the summer of 1955, Morrow, Rabb and Sherman Adams had been upset when Gallup polls reported that criticism of the President as one who "encourages segregation" was high among the public's evaluation of his leadership and that, despite the Democratic party's phalanx of rigid Southern segregationists, Northern Negroes were still loyal to the party of FDR. Morrow warned Rabb of a coming "dangerous social conflagration" and soon learned that, despite the Gallup findings, suggestions that some leading Administration spokesman, if not the President himself, denounce the breakdown of law and order evoked "complete fright" among people closest to Mr. Eisenhower.[55]

Becoming increasingly disturbed by his role as a black man in an Administration stressing morality while trying to pacify unreconstructed Southerners, Morrow sent a long, passionate memorandum to Sherman Adams on December 16 that could not have left any reader ignorant about what Negroes were experiencing. Morrow also proposed the convening of "a dozen or more of the leading ministers, white and Negro in this country . . . under the auspices of the Administration to discuss what can be done to allay the fears and despair of Negroes in Mississippi as a result of the recent wave of terrorism that has swept through that state."[56] That suggestion appealed to Max Rabb, and Sherman Adams thought it worthy of further consideration, but the idea was resisted by the President.[57] Three days after Morrow's statement, Rabb conferred with all black staff members and told them of the difficulty being experienced in getting the President's close associates to agree to subordinate their fears of alienating the South by taking a forthright stand.[58] Val Washington, receiving reports at his headquarters from throughout the country, reported to Sherman Adams that most Negroes were already convinced that the "Administration has had nothing to say on this subject for political reasons and are catering to the Southern wing of the party."[59] During that same month, Charlie Masterson commented in a long interoffice memorandum on the Negro vote situation and observed that "Confusion seems to exist among Republicans as to whether or not the Civil Rights accomplishments of the Administration should be told."[60]

The Administration's timidity did not stop Senator Eastland from complaining that left-wing pressure groups were controlling the government.[61] The Mississippi segregationist also joined with Georgia's Governor Marvin Griffin, Herman Talmadge and others to organize the Federation for Constitutional Government, which, said the Mississippi Senator, wanted to "fight the Supreme Court, fight the CIO, fight the NAACP and pressure groups who are attempting our destruction."[62] In Montgomery, Alabama, at the same time, the Reverend Dr. Martin Luther King, a young Baptist minister, was taking over the leadership of a bus boycott organized in retaliation for the arrest of a Negro woman,

Mrs. Rosa Parks. Tired after a day's work, she had refused to transfer to a rear seat in the black section of the bus. In February, two days of rioting at the University of Alabama defied a court order and prevented Miss Autherine Lucy from enrolling as a student and thus desegregating that institution. The university's officials aided the disrupters.[63] Yet, when Eisenhower was confronted with that situation at his February news conference, he said, "I would certainly hope that we could avoid any interference with anybody else as long as that state, from its governor on down, will do its best to straighten it out."[64] The President failed to point out that the ouster of the young black woman violated several Supreme Court decisions. Asked about interposition soon afterward, he said little except to point out that the matter was "filled with argument on both sides."[65] The Eastland group would have had to acknowledge that the "left-wing pressure groups" had not moved the President very much.

Two days after the President stated his attitude, the White Citizens Council sponsored a meeting at the State Coliseum in Montgomery, Alabama. Handbills circulated among the audience were called "A PRE-VIEW OF THE DECLARATION OF SEGREGATION" and contained the following message for fellow crusaders in behalf of white America:

> When in the course of human events it becomes necessary to abolish the Negro race, proper methods should be used. Among these are guns, bows and arrows, sling shots and knives.
>
> We hold these truths to be self evident, that all whites are created equal with certain rights: among these are life, liberty and the pursuit of dead niggers.
>
> In every stage of the bus boycott we have been oppressed and degraded because of black, slimy, juicy, unbearably stinking niggers. Their conduct should not be dwelt upon because behind them they have an ancestral background of Pigmies, head hunters and snot suckers.
>
> My friends, it is time we wised up to these black devils. I tell you they are a group of two legged agitators who persist in walking up and down our streets protruding their black lips. If we don't stop helping these African flesh eaters, we will soon wake up and find Rev. King in the White House.

LET'S GET ON THE BALL WHITE CITIZENS[66]

Also furthering the impression of the President's insensitivity that winter were Congressman Powell's tactics. The old watchdog against permitting federal funds to sanction discrimination employed what came to be known as "Powell Amendments." Designed specifically to bar allocations in such circumstances, anti-bias amendments had already been offered, all without success, for public housing and military reserve bills. Twice the President had told news conferences that the measures were "extraneous" and could only kill needed programs. There was no sense, he maintained, in outlawing what was already illegal.

But on the matter of getting a school construction bill through, such maneuvers suited the Administration's pre-election strategy, which was to permit if not provoke a grand clash among the vehemently opposing Democratic wings. Neither Northerners nor Southerners could fail to rise as expected to their cause when confronted with federal legislation against racial discrimination. Accordingly, on the tenth of January, Republican Congressional leaders met and agreed that, despite the Administration's repeated and well-known opposition to "Powell Amendments," they would remain silent. Two weeks later, after the Congressman had done the anticipated by introducing his addition to the school construction bill that Eisenhower's State of the Union message had requested, they reaffirmed that decision.[67]

Anticipating interest in the matter at that day's news conference, a White House staff session early on the morning of the twenty-fifth discussed possible means of treating the question. Recognizing sharply critical reactions to his past statement, they advised the President against repeating that such amendments were "extraneous." Gerald Morgan cautioned that endorsement of Powell's desire might bring accusations of insincerity because of his past stated concern over the national shortage of classrooms. Others, agreeing that it was an explosive situation, speculated it might pass the House but would be filibustered to death in the Senate. Jim Hagerty, however, could not see how the "party of Lincoln" could turn its back on a matter that should be enforced in every aspect of American life.[68]

When Eisenhower met the press and the inevitable question arose, he made an extended effort to deal with it by pointing out that two separate issues were involved. "Now," he concluded, "if Congress wants to put the other on, and does it, I will understand why they are doing it. But I just simply say, let's get the school bill; that is what I want."[69] With only the House acting by the end of the session, the Powell amendment passed. The Administration's request to provide aid to the states for school construction went down to defeat, as did a Democratic-backed measure calling for $1.6 billion in grants over a four-year period.[70] On the more delicate issue, however, Eisenhower remained safe.

A mid-February Gallup report showed the President still far ahead of Stevenson in the South.[71]

On March 2, only two weeks after having praised Eisenhower for making "the greatest contribution to civil rights in the history of the United States," Powell accused the President of dodging the civil-rights issue, for "passing the buck, trying to wash his hands like Pilate in the blood of innocent men and women in the southland."[72] Then, after accusing Stevenson of similar "pussyfooting," the Congressman cited the possibility of a third party if the existing ones continued to lag on civil rights.[73] That brought him into line with a view held by Morrow, who, only five days later, lamented in a White House memorandum the abdication of Southern Negroes by an Administration that was leaving the blacks "to the mercy of state governments that have manifested their intention to violate all laws, human and Divine. . . ." Val Washington also advised Republicans to "make up their minds as to whether they desire the colored vote."[74]

Republicans and the Administration, however, wanted it both ways, preferring a larger share of the Northern black electorate without, simultaneously, sacrificing recent Dixieland converts. After Clarence Mitchell of the NAACP had threatened that Negroes might abandon the Democrats because of continued committee control by Deep South segregationists, Rowland Evans, Jr., of the New York *Herald Tribune* asked the President for his reaction. And the reply was masterful. Mr. Eisenhower stood squarely on the proposition that "it is anybody's judgment as to whether I am doing my job well or not doing it well" and also revealed that, whatever that was, it was being done for all "166 million people, not for any group." And, he pointed out, regardless of whether "you define them" or "you separate them geographically or racially or religiously, I am for America. . . . So if they want to come in under that umbrella, I welcome them with open arms."[75] That placed the President in the dead center of his own Administration.

With the Vice President presiding in place of the recuperating Mr. Eisenhower, on December 2, 1955, the Cabinet met and reviewed the civil-rights portion of the forthcoming message to Congress on the State of the Union. Brownell appeared disturbed at some of the language in the draft. Threatening to investigate the White Citizens Councils while suggesting, with no firm evidence, the existence of organized efforts to keep Negroes from voting, he held unnecessarily inflammatory. Instead of "waving the red flag," said the Attorney General, the Administration should rest on a simple statement supporting the Court's integration decision; that, he predicted, would be the nation's most prominent social issue for some time to come. He also informed the group that the Justice Department was under great pressure to investigate the mounting violence in the South, particularly since the Till murder.

Dulles listened sympathetically. Agreeing that the Till murder was rather tragic, he nevertheless wondered whether the Administration should, for political and constitutional reasons, get involved in that situation.

The Vice President had a possible solution. Probably better than doing nothing, he suggested, would be throwing the problem to Congressional investigation procedures and keeping the Justice Department aloof. Any legislation that might then emerge would undoubtedly be blocked by the powerful Southern Democrats with their filibuster weapon. The idea appealed to both Brownell and Dulles, and Nixon continued with his thoughts.

It would be best, he suggested, to drop the proposed preliminary statement repeating the President's constitutional authority to act. Keeping it would only highlight the innumerable contradictions stemming from withholding action in certain areas while advocating federal intervention in others, such as poll taxes and lynching. Furthermore, he pointed out, parts of the South were doing a good job despite their difficulties. Bringing black teachers into formerly all-white schools presented severe difficulties and such efforts deserved a "pat on the back." Wisdom and discretion might be better served by having the message trust evolutionary progress while advocating compliance in those "isolated areas" where correction lagged. Then, by dropping the clause calling for the initiation of "Congressional study," the entire matter could be turned to political profit. Northern Republicans would ultimately benefit if a "seed might be planted" with "two or three aggressive fellows" in the House, to move for a Congressional committee investigation in that field. That, Nixon added, would be most appropriate because the legislature would probe into the violation of federal laws and the Administration would not be responsible for having stirred up the whole issue. Then, with nothing substantial emerging from the Democratic-controlled Congress, Republicans would gain a good "talking point" during the campaign.[76]

Instead of that more devious route, the Justice Department's draft favored the establishment by Congress of a bipartisan commission to investigate "allegations" about lawlessness in the South. Not lost to the legal minds on the White House staff, however, was an intriguing possibility. Congressional designation of the Vice President as the commission's chairman would constitute a political coup against the Democrats. How could a party with important civil-rights supporters in its Northern cities afford to elect a Southerner for second place on the ticket if he would automatically head the Civil Rights Commission? In recent years, only Henry A. Wallace had been selected by the Democrats despite an absence of Southern or Border State ties. John Sparkman of Alabama had been their Vice Presidential candidate in 1952, and Estes Kefauver, certain to be prominent at the 1956 convention, came from Tennessee.[77] Brownell and his staff then began work on a civil-rights message for legislation to implement the President's report to Congress.

A session of the Cabinet on March 9 considered the proposals. Composed of three main parts, it called for a commission to "investigate allegations of deprivations of voting rights," an additional Assistant Attorney General to handle civil-rights cases and sufficient authority for him to use civil suits for injunctions to enforce federal guarantees of non-discriminatory voting and other civil rights. In a draft statement distributed among the Cabinet members, Brownell rejected asking Congress to designate the commission's membership and asked that it be left up to the President. "Such a commission," he assured, "will not engage in witchhunts nor will it become the tool of any private pressure groups." Nor was it "contemplated that extensive use of civil remedies by the Department of Justice will be made in civil areas other than voting," he added.[78]

Marion Folsom, Secretary of Health, Education and Welfare, demurred. Increased tensions since the State of the Union message, he contended, had reduced rather than increased the desirability for doing anything more than establishing a new commission and a new division within the Justice Department. Desires for more extensive measures should be trimmed to "realistic" consideration of "the practical circumstances which exist as of this moment." Regardless of how the proposals may be presented, and despite their modesty, the South would inevitably consider them as further efforts to extend federal legal authority to bring about fundamental social changes. Definite recommendations, therefore, should await the findings and suggestions of the proposed Civil Rights Commission.[79]

Eisenhower, too, just five days after that Cabinet session, commented to reporters in a way that appeared to place him in line with Folsom rather than with his Attorney General. He called for patience without complacency and urged "understanding of other people's deep emotions as well as our own. . . . We are not talking here about coercing, using force in a general way; we are simply going to uphold the Constitution of the United States, see that the progress as ordered by them is carried out." Those in rebellion, he recalled, were still adhering to the 1896 *Plessy v. Ferguson* decision, a sentiment that must be understood because those still holding to that interpretation were "acting in compliance with the law" as understood at that time. They would require time to adjust their ideas to the new requirements.[80] His concern differed little from Folsom's; and, as Max Rabb pointed out to Sherman Adams a few days later, whatever gains the administration had achieved have "been done so quietly and with so little publicity that, in circles where it has come to general attention, Administration civil rights policy has come to be known as 'the Eisenhower Approach'; i.e., calm, without fanfare, and effective."[81]

Several weeks later, in early May, Presidential administrative assistant Bryce Harlow's attention lit on a *Congressional Quarterly* article that made some interesting points. In the 1954 Congressional elections, it said, Negro voters exceeded the margin of the winning candidates in sixty-one districts outside the South. Thirty-two had chosen Democrats and twenty-nine Republicans, many by close votes. Therefore, especially in the ten districts that had been lost to the party by close calls in 1954, a sizable shift of the Negro electorate would strengthen the GOP and weaken the opposition. Very helpful to that goal would be a Southern Democratic filibuster, which "could be the signal for a stampede by Negroes to the GOP banner." Harlow passed the article on to Max Rabb. Both Rabb and Sherman Adams used it to instruct a Young Republican Leadership meeting.[82]

By planning his strategy carefully, Brownell, an adept political tactician, moved to accomplish that shift while minimizing any injury to the GOP's Southern flank. Timing the proposed legislation to languish without enthusiastic support from the White House and to gather momentum late in the session, when both parties were eager to adjourn to their national nominating conventions, would leave it up to Southern Democrats to deliver the final blow in the Senate. Democrats could then be blamed for its death. When, in late March, the Administration had still failed to forward its specific proposals, some House members were prepared to introduce their own bills.[83]

By advancing such legislation in the first place, Brownell was, in that instance, violating the President's annual reminder against pushing for anything that seemed hopeless. Even the "Powell Amendment" had not been expected to clear the Senate. After the President's State of the Union message had given the bill official but unenthusiastic endorsement, Senator Knowland told the legislative leaders at the White House on March 20 that there was little chance that a civil-rights bill could pass that session. Only the provision for establishing a bipartisan commission and adding an Assistant Attorney General for civil rights had any prospects for surviving.[84] The President himself narrowed to just those items his list of "must" measures.[85] Rejecting a suggestion by Florida's moderate chief executive, LeRoy Collins, for a conference of Southern Governors, Eisenhower said he preferred to see how his proposed Civil Rights Commission would handle the problem.[86] On April 9, the proposals finally reached Congress.

That summer, in the midst of a debate on the various civil-rights recommendations that were before the House, Congressman Kenneth Keating of New York was astonished to hear James Roosevelt of California read on the floor a letter from Bryce Harlow. Dated May 3, the day Harlow forwarded the *Congressional Digest* article to Rabb, it stated that the President had approved the Attorney General's requests and offered assurances that he desired their enactment.[87] Keating, agitated that a Democrat had obtained a letter that was unknown to the Republicans, complained that Roosevelt's action on the floor made him the Administration's spokesman, "to the great irritation of all Republican members." One of their own, Keating insisted, should read a similar letter but one that would carry the President's own signature. Harlow transmitted Keating's angry telephone message to General Andrew Goodpaster, Eisenhower's staff secretary, with a suggested draft of a Presidential letter placing the Chief Executive in full support of the civil-rights requests.[88] Nothing ever came from the top.

The House passed the Administration's civil-rights proposals comfortably on July 23, with only twenty-four recalcitrant Republicans joining in the heavy bloc of Southern Democrats in opposition. Joseph Alsop noted in his newspaper column that, "if the Eisenhower Administration had had the faintest serious desire to pass a civil rights bill, the bill would have been introduced at the beginning of the session and pushed with maximum power thereafter. . . . The sole intention . . . was to encourage the Democrats to stage an intraparty Donnybrook Fair."[89] As early as April 27 the New York *Times* had editorialized that "the sudden flurry of interest so late in the Congressional session is enough to make one wonder."[90]

Nor did the Democratic-led Senate entirely disappoint the Administration. Majority Leader Lyndon B. Johnson, although later denying there were such motivations, kept all civil-rights bills confined within the Judiciary Committee to avoid the need for a filibuster, until the race between the snail and the sloth ended with the inevitable adjournment.[91] "There is a great reluctance on the part of the staff even to talk about civil rights legislation," Morrow wrote in his diary. "It is one of the most disturbing notes in the whole situation here, and I am greatly pained when the matter comes up and there is an immediate effort to squelch all discussion or turn the talk to something else."[92]

Judging from what the President said before and after the Congressional fiasco, a determined push for legislation would have questioned the sincerity of his attitude toward civil rights and the federal government, not only the states'-rights concept but his conviction that progress could not be achieved without first correcting popular attitudes. In a Hollywood Bowl campaign speech on October 19, more than half a year after his prescriptions had been submitted to Congress, he stated his position very clearly. "And we have always been aware of this great truth: the final battle against intolerance is to be fought—not in the chambers of any legislature—but in the hearts of men," he said. That popularization of what William Graham Sumner had written in his influential 1907 book, *Folkways*, also appeared in a thought the President expressed during a question-and-answer telecast on October 12, when he stated that "every true American does want to see progress proceeding until finally the equality is not only known by all, it's felt by all, right down deep within them."[93] Conventional conservative doctrine, it failed to account for the ability of legislation to sanction social and moral progress, which subsequent experience demonstrated.

Even while the civil-rights battle continued in the House, questions about Eisenhower's physical fitness recurred. On June 8 what at first appeared to be a routine stomach disorder was diagnosed as ileitis, an inflamation of the lower portion of the small intenstine. Taken to Walter Reed Hospital, the President underwent an emergency operation for the correction of a problem that, it was finally realized, probably accounted for his chronic stomach trouble, including the one that persisted during his "Chance for Peace" speech on April 16, 1953.

Fortunately, as the public learned almost immediately, no further heart trouble developed. The surgeons, in performing an operation delicate for a man of his age, provided a bypass around the obstructed area, and the President's condition improved remarkably within twenty-four hours. As the nation awaited the outcome of the latest health crisis, the New York *Times* proclaimed in a banner headline: PRESIDENT WALKS 30 FEET WITH AID AND SITS IN CHAIR. Unlike the heart-attack emergency, once surgery had been pronounced successful, the President gave no consideration to retiring. And again, as during the previous illness, Sherman Adams emerged as "captain of the team."[94]

Doubters, however, noted newspaper pictures of the convalescent President and saw evidence that the latest ordeal had marked his face. Certainly age seemed to have advanced suddenly. New questions arose about his ability to serve with full capacity. Congressional concern with providing a constitutional solution for the problem of Presidential disability, prompted by the heart attack and then neglected, received new attention. Others worried again about a possible Nixon succession. Still only forty-three and, to many, of doubtful maturity for the Presidency, the Vice President might serve both his nation and the party better by stepping aside in favor of a less controversial and more acceptable possible President. Leonard Hall, determined to keep the ticket intact, visited Gettysburg again and once more told reporters Eisenhower had reaffirmed his desire for Nixon.[95] Nevertheless, the question remained alive even as the President completed his five-week convalesence. At nine-thirty on Friday morning, July 20, as Mr. Eisenhower prepared to fly to Panama the next day for a delayed meeting with Latin American Presidents, a visitor arrived at the White House. Harold E. Stassen, the disarmament adviser, wanted to reveal his plan.

CHAPTER 34

The Travail of Childe Harold

In MANY WAYS, the man who entered the President's office that morning embodied the kind of Republicanism Dwight Eisenhower hoped would revitalize the party. Long convinced that the GOP's lost progressivism had to be replenished, he became Governor of Minnesota at the age of thirty-one and visualized himself among the vanguard of those desiring to rectify the loss that had followed Teddy Roosevelt's 1912 revolt. As early as 1939 Harold Stassen had advised the party to select a liberal candidate and platform and learn to live with the social reforms of the New Deal. Rejecting the fashionable isolationism of his region, he led Wendell Willkie's fight on the convention floor in Philadelphia in 1940 and then, after serving in the South Pacific on the staff of Admiral William F. Halsey during World War II, he became one of the American delegates at the UN's charter session in San Francisco in 1945. The following year he delivered the Godkind lectures on Human Rights at Harvard University. After his own chances for the nomination had disappeared in 1948, he favored Arthur Vandenberg, with whom he had worked closely.

As a member of Eisenhower's team he remained the idealist. Where Dulles scorned neutralism, Stassen emphasized the need of the underdeveloped nations for food, technical skills and literacy as prerequisites for ideological compatability. Where Dulles thought in terms of the deterrent uses of power, Stassen looked toward breaking the nuclear deadlock and reducing the arms race. As Mutual Security Administrator and director of the Foreign Operations Administration he worked with the kind of zeal that often conflicted with Dulles's carefully protected domain. During the controversy with McCarthy over the Greek shipowners he denounced the Senator's methods only to have the President leave him standing with his accusation. Later, Stassen's concern with world peace—part of what became a long-standing dedication to making the United Nations work—involved him with disarmament. As a member of the Quantico Panel and present when the group assembled in Paris while Eisenhower went to Geneva in 1955, he became one of the principal drafters of the Open Skies speech; earlier, he worked with C. D. Jackson on the atoms-for-peace proposal. In March of 1955, with the President unable to get any arms-reduction proposals out of the existing deadlock among the State and Defense departments and Lewis Strauss's Atomic Energy Commission, Stassen was given Cabinet rank as Special Assistant to the President for Disarmament Studies, a post immediately dubbed by the press as "Secretary of Peace." Concerned also with the domestic economy, he objected to high-interest policies, calling them detrimental to the needs for "long-term construction and development of the future production capabilities of the country, and for housing, and for the financing of schools and public improvements." He decried its tendency toward "high profits by banks, more bankruptcies in small business, great centralization by the corporations with strongest national resources and an increasingly unhealthy aspect to our high level of overall economic activity which could turn in a very unfortunate manner."[1] Tall, attractive and soft-spoken, with an intelligence respected even by opponents, he was only forty-nine years old that summer and convincing to some as a man with a political future capable of exceeding his past. But what he had to say made him the most villified man in the Republican party.[2]

The President heard a familiar thesis. Having Nixon on the ticket would cost enough votes to minimize the party's chances of winning control of the Congress. Stassen substantiated his point by advancing the findings of a private poll showing Nixon as a running mate retarding the Eisenhower popularity by 6 percent. Furthermore, and in contrast with all other advice about getting rid of Nixon, Stassen stated his intention to make a public statement of support for Governor Christian Herter of Massachusetts as the party's Vice Presidential nominee. Having Herter on the ticket would, he contended, attract rather than repel the independent and Democratic votes needed for a Republican victory.

Precisely what transpired during that session has never been clarified. Nobody, however, has ever suggested that the President demurred in the slightest way, and Stassen interpreted his reaction as a green light for the project. Sherman Adams, whom Stassen saw before entering the President's office, has said that Eisenhower simply repeated his desire for an "open convention," and Stassen noted his request that any announcement about Herter must be made as an individual decision and not as his spokesman.[3] James Reston's report of the visit, written three days later, told of his "personal knowledge that if the President had told Mr. Stassen that he was determined to have Mr. Nixon on the ticket . . . today's announcement would not have been made."[4] Eisenhower's own account contended that preoccupation with the forthcoming Panama trip deflected his interest in Stassen's proposal and prompted his dismissal of the overture by saying, "You are an American citizen, Harold, and free to follow your own judgment in such matters."[5]

While in Panama the President heard that, at an afternoon press conference on July 23, Stassen had called upon the Republican party to replace Nixon. "I am confident," the disarmament adviser told the newsmen, "that if the Republican national convention nominates Governor Christian Herter for Vice President, President Eisenhower will be pleased to have him on the ticket." In the chief's absence, Jim Hagerty immediately issued a press release confirming the Stassen visit with the President and distinguishing his right to speak as an individual from his authority to be a spokesman in his capacity as "a member of the President's official family."[6]

The resulting furor virtually overlooked the reality that, as Sherman Adams has written, "the choice of Nixon in 1956 had really been made long ago by Hall and the Republican National Committee."[7] To sympathetic realists, Stassen was Lord Byron's Childe Harold, having concluded that he had "better sink beneath the shock/ than moulder piecemeal on the rock." But to most Republicans, even to Tom Dewey, who saw no reason for breaking up a winning team, the former "boy wonder" was little less than a traitor. How could he, Sinclair Weeks asked a friend, participate with the Cabinet for three and a half years as though he were a legitimate member of the team and then turn upon the Vice President?[8] Twenty members of the House, immediately after Stassen made his announcement, signed a public message telling the dissenter they were "amazed and shocked" and suggested he submit his resignation. Senator Barry Goldwater declared that he ought to be given to the Democrats the way "we gave them Wayne Morse." "Harold," said Governor Robert E. Smylie of Iowa, "this is a pipe dream." A California protégé of Richard Nixon, Congressman Pat Hillings, circulated a petition among the 203 House Republicans and got 180 endorsements for the Vice President. David Lawrence retorted that Stassen's pollsters had failed to consider that, among faithful Republicans, Ike's 6 percent gain would be overwhelmed by a 20 percent loss. Len Hall, remaining as firm as he had since the heart attack, "predicted" that "the ticket will again be Eisenhower and Nixon"; the next day, the national chairman announced Governor Herter's willingness to nominate Nixon at the convention.

Nevertheless, the Eisenhower reputation for action by indirection left others not quite sure about Stassen's sponsorship, so that people like Governor Victor E. Anderson of Nebraska reached San Francisco without being certain what the President really wanted.[9] A former Republican national chairman, John D. M. Miller, was upset at rumors that Eisenhower's hand had activated Stassen in a design to gauge Nixon's real strength and the potency of the opposition. Others gossiped that Stassen would not have acted without knowing that the President could not survive another four years.[10]

During those pre-convention weeks the President's role remained detached. Not a hint reached the public that he had in any way modified his desire for an open convention or had actively sought a replacement for his Vice President. Shaking Nixon's hand longer than Stassen's upon arriving at Washington from Panama was less significant than sharp-eyed journalists quickly claimed: Nixon was his Vice President and protocol could hardly have had it any other way. Indeed, an ostentatious hello to Stassen at Nixon's expense would have said much more than the President desired. Then, upon Stassen's request, he granted his disarmament adviser a four-week leave to pursue the anti-Nixon campaign, while maintaining that his aide was acting as an individual. On August 1, while continuing to insist that the issue should be settled at San Francisco, Eisenhower told the press that Stassen "had stirred up more of a storm than he had anticipated." Asked to comment about the thesis that Nixon would detract from the ticket, the President replied that "he certainly didn't seem to in 1952, and I can't believe that the United States does not consider that Mr. Nixon has made a splendid record as Vice President in these past four years."[11] Meanwhile, Stassen remained undeterred and claimed that telegrams reaching him were giving his position a seventeen-to-five margin of support, in sharp contrast to what most Republicans believed was a one-man crusade. He also repeated his call for Nixon to support Herter. After eating breakfast with Hall on the twenty-sixth, he stressed that no commitments had been made and promised a new poll, more representative than the earlier ones.[12] As each day passed, Stassen's loneliness became more obvious.

Perhaps more than any other event since the heart attack, the move only provoked a rush toward the Vice President. Conservative displeasure with Nixon's recent moderation yielded as he became a cause for their support.[13] Tipped off by the national committee's chief spokesman that Nixon remained their man and lacking any direct word from the President to the contrary, others prudently associated themselves more faithfully with the source of power. Unhesitatingly, then, Republicans proclaimed their loyalty to Nixon, while Stassen became more like Don Quixote than Childe Harold. Only when the Democrats met in Chicago, the week before the Republican convention at San Francisco's Cow Palace, and renominated Adlai Stevenson (despite Truman's dramatic endorsement of Harriman and last-minute denunciation of his former choice) did the Republicans have any trepidations about locking up matters for Nixon. Stevenson proclaimed the choice of his running mate by staging an exciting clash of power that, rare for a Vice Presidential nomination, lasted through two ballots. Senator John F. Kennedy, actually far ahead of his Tennessee opponent after completion of the second roll call but before the result was announced, suddenly succumbed to a tide of switches after Albert Gore withdrew in favor of his colleague, Estes Kefauver. Democrats thus chose a ticket more liberal at the bottom than at the top; but for anxious Republicans, Stevenson's gamble offered a contrast with the ratification ceremony about to be staged by the GOP.[14]

Desperately, Harold Stassen did not give up. He sent a seven-page letter to all Republican delegates explaining the reasons for his move. Reiterating the importance of wooing Democrats and independents, he told about a Republican labor leader, an AFL-CIO man, who refused to vote for the ticket as long as it contained the Vice President's name. His own privately financed poll, he reported in some detail, had shown the public becoming increasingly concerned over the number-two man, especially since the ileitis operation. Simultaneous with that interest, Nixon's popular support had declined. In Michigan, it fell four percentage points within four weeks. His loss, moreover, was particularly great along the West Coast, where, as Stassen pointedly reminded the delegates, the Vice President was best known. He explained, also, his frustrated attempts to meet with Nixon just prior to making his own statement public and accounted for the tardiness of his move by recalling that he had not returned from the disarmament talks in London until May and his absence from the country had kept him unaware of the latest developments. In contrast with the Vice President, he concluded, Governor Herter could unite the "entire range of Eisenhower supporters from the most conservative businessmen to the independents, labor, minority voters, and Eisenhower Democrats throughout the nation."[15] In San Francisco, where he arrived on August 17, he gave reporters a careful, sophisticated analysis of his latest private poll. Its upshot was that *any* additional name on the ballot detracted from Eisenhower's but that Herter's involved a smaller loss than Nixon's.[16]

Instant rebuttal came from Styles Bridges. His figures utilized findings by Robert Maheu Associates of Washington, D.C., who employed only former FBI agents throughout the country in a "Fair and Square Attempt to Attain the Facts." Financed entirely by Manchester, New Hampshire, publisher and right-wing supporter William Loeb, the poll stressed Herter's identity problem. Of those questioned, 47.47 percent could not recognize Herter's name and more than twice as many preferred an Eisenhower–Nixon ticket to one with Eisenhower and the Governor. While reporting extravagantly high figures on pro-Republican party preferences, such as stating that 98 percent of Connecticut voters and 78 percent of Texans were ready to vote for the GOP, the poll made an amazingly accurate prediction when it showed that 57.7 percent of the people would vote for Eisenhower and Nixon.[17] In support of his clear advantage, Nixon came to San Francisco in full pursuit of the delegations. His efforts were gratuitous, as anyone could have predicted.

Conceivably, Stassen could have been acting as detractors suspected, to further personal ambitions. But closer analysis renders that improbable. As to the possibility of his own nomination, not a chance existed—and that despite a Gallup Poll released two days after he had made his original announcement showing him 5 percent stronger than Nixon among independents and the third most popular Republican in the country.[18] He had, after all, suggested an entirely plausible candidate in Christian Herter, and it would have been inconceivable for the fruition of the Stassen suggestion to have resulted in the choice of the man who had created the furor. His past reputation as a schemer, particularly during the 1952 campaign and lingering feeling among still others that he had "double-crossed" Wendell Willkie during the Wisconsin primary contest in 1944, left an aura not unlike existing attitudes toward Mr. Nixon.[19] Moreover, in bucking the national committee, he was more than tilting at windmills, he was trying to lead the GOP's heartland through parted waters of the Red Sea. The only logical explanation must link Stassen's effort with his long fight to liberalize Republican leadership.

The President, confronted on July 20 with Stassen's proposal, in no way resembled the man who had promised to greet such boldness with a "commotion" unprecedented in his office; more likely, he welcomed the opportunity to resolve an unsettled situation. Either the national committee would, as a result, be convinced that opposition to the Vice President warranted serious attention and might be resolved by substituting any one of several possible replacements, from the reluctant Robert Anderson to the more frequently mentioned names, or the support for Nixon would make him an obvious necessity.

As the party gathered in the Cow Palace for the GOP's one hundredth anniversary convention, Eisenhower's enviable position became more evident. He was the undisputed boss. Unlike Chicago in 1952, when a Taft-dominated party, embarrassingly defeated on the delegate-seating issue, had to compromise for the sake of victory, the President's middle-of-the-road theme set the tone. Eisenhower's own tactical suggestions, dictated from Washington on August 18 by Ann Whitman, urged a note of welcome for "all independents and all 'straight-thinking' or intelligent Democrats," and, by all means, "No long and dreary speeches."[20] Consequently, Emmet Hughes spoke to the convention and was presented as an "independent." Although Governor Arthur Langlie of Washington spiced his keynote address with a strongly partisan line that made Eisenhower wince and Representative Joe Martin, the convention chairman, failed to resist striking at "those forces bent on creating an alien, socialistic state in America . . . despoiling our heritage with indelible stains of corruption and Communism," the tone remained amiable and moderate; and, as the *New Republic* noted, the new theme running through the speeches indicated they had passed through the same hands of the national committee and the White House.[21] Roy Wilkins, present at San Francisco to press for a civil-rights platform plank that would have supported a vigorous federal role to end all forms of racial abuse by the states, observed that a distinctly more tepid, inoffensive version was dictated by the White House.[22] Nevertheless, even the more cautious approach gave strong support to the Supreme Court's edict that desegregation be accomplished "with all deliberate speed" and recognized the constitutional grant of citizenship as "an unqualified right, regardless of race, creed or color." Neither tampered with the filibuster nor with FEPC laws, but even the moderate Eisenhower version was stronger than the generalizations accepted by the Democrats.[23] Publicly, however, Eisenhower had already remained aloof from the issue; he had told the press that he had no idea of how the civil-rights plank would be stated and said he had not given "any thought" about whether it should contain a specific endorsement of the decision voiding public school desegregation.[24] On communism, the Democratic platform continued recent charges that budget-conscious Republicans were yielding military superiority to the Russians, and the GOP again concentrated on the internal menace—but with the assurance that the loyalty-security program would respect the rights of the individual. Generally, however, even the platform conveyed the spirit of the President's State of the Union message and presented a striking contrast with such statements as the 1950 "Declaration of Principles" and the vindictive accusations of four years earlier.[25]

Indeed, except for Nixon, Stassen and his followers found little to dislike in San Francisco. A century removed from that original band of rebellious Northern Whigs, Free Soilers, Know-Nothings and abolitionists who fell in line behind John Fremont in 1856, the Republican party had moved through the hundred years of close identification with the rise of American corporate capitalism without entirely divesting itself of its Protestant "mug-wump" reformers, people like *Harper's Weekly* editor George William Curtis, a "gentleman in politics" unable to fulfill the more sordid demands of the profession. Hitching their theme to the public responsibility of the better bred, better educated and financially secure, they stressed notions of morality and service rather than the spoils of power. Eisenhower's own scholarly Under Secretary of Labor, Arthur Larson, a "house intellectual" usually regarded as somewhat of a "lone wolf" within the Administration, had just published *A Republican Looks at His Party*, an elucidation of what he called the "New Republicanism." Rather than a business- or labor-dominated force, Larson suggested sustaining private enterprise through a better balanced relationship between economic and political interests. Government, he contended, existed mainly to "avoid extremes in the business cycle" and for protecting the public "against harmful practices, and to ensure adequate protections against the human hazards of a risk economy."[26] Federal-state relationships would be accommodated to a satisfactory balance between the hazards of overcentralization while preserving individual rights on the local level. The New Deal's failures would thus be corrected and its goals streamlined in a sweeping national consensus. When Eisenhower was asked whether Larson's ideas were compatible with his own, he agreed that the author had "expressed my philosophy of government as well as I have seen it in a book of that size."[27]

But in much the same way Eisenhower had continually subordinated ideals to the pragmatic, in fulfillment of "getting the job done," he accepted the final surrender of Harold Stassen. After a long talk with Sherman Adams and Leonard Hall, during which he was informed he could see the President only if he agreed to second the Vice President's nomination, Stassen conferred with Eisenhower at the St. Francis Hotel for eleven minutes. About forty minutes later, the President faced the press and said that his disarmament adviser had become absolutely convinced "the the majority of the delegates want Mr. Nixon," so his effort to stop the Vice President had been abandoned. He would also second his nomination before the convention. Thus the Stassen rebellion came to an end, having taken with it very few of the quiet malcontents. Missouri's national committeeman Elroy Bromwich, who disassociated himself from the subsequent campaign because of Hall's treatment of Stassen, had very little company.[28]

Except for one individualistic expression of discontent with the proceedings, everything else followed the script. After Eisenhower's renomination by acclamation on the twenty-second, the afternoon of the day Stassen capitulated, the convention went on to the routine process of naming his running mate. But Terry Carpenter, a delegate from Nebraska, startled everybody and provoked a rush from reporters by announcing his nomination of "Joe Smith." Perplexed, Joe Martin never-theless digested the little rebellion and declared, "Nebraska reserves the right to nominate Joe Smith, whoever he is." Asked for an explanation, Carpenter said that Joe Smith was a "real person, a symbol of an open convention" and a stimulant for a dull affair.[29]

Recovering from that deviation, Herter nominated Nixon in the best interest of perserving a winning team. Harold Stassen then seconded the nomination, for which Nixon said he was "deeply appreciative"; and the Eisenhower Convention, the only one that could be so regarded, had completed its mission.

The President faced the convention the following evening and deliv-ered his acceptance address. Throughout the nation, radio and television sets were tuned in to the final event of the efficiently dreary program at the Cow Palace. His words seemed to present a challenge to those al-ready predicting that, as the first President to serve a second term under the two-term restriction mandated by the Twenty-second Amendment, his authority would evaporate during a four year "lame duck" period. After disposing of the obligatory homage to Abraham Lincoln, he dwelt on the theme that "what is past is prologue" and urged his fellow Repub-licans to "quit fighting the battles of the past" and shift attention to the problems of the "present and future, on which the long-term well-being of our people so urgently depends." There was, he maintained, no desire for ignoring the uses of government for the public good; but while "warm, sensitive concern" for the everyday needs of people must be continued, the "Big Brother is watching you" kind of interference can-not be tolerated. "The individual—and especially the idealistic young person," he argued, "has no faith in a tight federal monopoly on problem-solving." But that was no excuse for smugness. "There are still needless sufferings to be cured, enough injustices to be erased, to provide careers for all the crusaders we can produce or find." For that fight he called upon Republicans, independents, "discerning Democrats—come on in and help!" Yet, when he went on to civil rights, in the very next paragraph, other than acknowledging what had been accomplished in the Armed Forces and the District of Columbia, and after singling out the Vice President's work as chairman of the Committee on Contracts, he ob-served that "in all existing kinds of discrimination there is much to do"; and, lest fearful interpretations jolt the South, he enumerated the elderly, the physically handicapped, migrant farm workers, American Indians, low-income farmers, women, small businessmen "and employers and workers in areas which need special assistance for redevelopment" as the ones needing such help.[30] When asked at his subsequent news confer-ence whether he was satisfied with the school-segregation plank of the party's civil-rights platform, his comment was no more specific than the acceptance speech. "Here is a problem," he replied, "as I have said a thousand times, that is charged with emotionalism, where everybody has got to work hard with all of the strength he has; and I think that the more that that work is done privately and behind the scenes rather than charging up on the platform and hammering desks, the better and more effective it will be."[31] He never gave a clearer public exposition of his thinking on that subject; and its spirit continued his acceptance-speech attempt to depict the GOP as the "Party of the Future" and the true conveyer of American progress by compromise and conciliation of divergent views. For moderate Democrats and the millions of non-partisans, Ike's speech had said it all.

CHAPTER 35

Trust Ike

How can anyone defeat a candidate who was not only first in peace and prosperity but, as events soon reaffirmed, first in war? Additionally, the public agreed that the GOP had been more adept than the Democrats in preserving peace, a point stressed repeatedly by Republican speakers. At the same time, despite organized labor's overwhelming opposition to the Eisenhower–Nixon ticket, the unprecedented prosperity of American workers, with suburban homes, automobiles, television sets and clothing selling at record levels, had created little dissatisfaction. No union efforts to "educate" the membership could dispel what seemed obvious to most workers. Wage earners had never been so attracted to a Republican Presidential candidate. Only in the farm belt, North and South, did the President face difficulties; but even there the party and not Eisenhower received most of the blame. Despite Stevenson and Kefauver's fast early start, exploiting the momentum provided by the more exciting Democratic convention, the early September Gallup Poll showed the GOP's ticket ahead by 11 percent of the popular vote and, what was more significant, a two-to-one edge among independents.[1]

Such advantages required a simple strategy. Aside from the national well-being, Eisenhower's personal fitness had to be stressed. The public must believe that they were not simply choosing a figurehead who would enable Nixon to wield the real power. Eisenhower's televised appearances, closely supervised by Robert Montgomery, were so successful that the President actually appeared younger and more fit than Stevenson.[2]

The over-all selling aspect of the strategy was, as in 1952, placed with the professional talents of the prominent New York advertising firm of

Batten, Barton, Durstine & Osborne. Meeting with the BBD&O representative in early September, Eisenhower was told of the need to emphasize himself as President "of all the people" and to stress his fine physical condition. The advertising man recalled that at Gettysburg on September 12, when the party held its kick-off festivities on the Eisenhower farm, his simple declaration that "I feel fine" received by far the most enthusiastic response. He was also advised to exploit his favorable personal image. The picture of him shaking hands with his little grandson, David, was cited by the BBD&O man as "one of the best vote-getters we have at our command." When the President showed apprehension at displaying signs of anger in public, he was reassured that such reactions made him more believably human, particularly when discussing a subject of "special interest."[3]

Tom Dewey sent the White House suggestions from a friend that Republicans should not forget how successful running against Truman had been in 1952 and that reminders of why they had voted for Ike would reinspire them to do likewise in 1956. "I think the main job of the party in office in getting re-elected," said Dewey's friend, "is to scare hell out of the voters—about war, about income taxes, high prices, and about business depression." Moreover, a successful issue from a previous campaign could easily be revived. "Everyone who has ever dealt with the public knows that you can repeat a campaign two or three times before it runs out," so that Republicans "should not miss the opportunity of running against Truman again."[4] Then, with Nixon inspiring more partisan Republican audiences and with reassurances about states' rights for the South, the winning combination of 1952 could be repeated. Under the general slogan of "Peace, Prosperity and Progress," how could the ticket fail?

Moreover, even within the severely fractured GOP, significant campaign unity formed behind Eisenhower's popularity. Much like Franklin Delano Roosevelt's decimation of the Socialist vote in 1936, old Taftites and others of an ultraconservative stripe, perjoratively called the "Old Guard," could not ignore the need to identify with the President. Eisenhower's ability as his party's main unifying factor had never been as pronounced. The far right, the extreme malcontents, could only take refuge with an assortment of splinter groups that endorsed an Independent States' Rights ticket headed by Eisenhower's first Director of Internal Revenue, T. Coleman Andrews, and ex-Republican Congressman from California, Thomas H. Werdel as his running mate. Resisting appeals from conservatives to work through the established parties, they adopted a platform endorsing, along with states' rights, the Bricker amendment and the "creation of permanent, overwhelming American air superiority, supported by adequate modern surface forces." They opposed the income tax, the "dangerous trend toward socialism," communism, and the "Atlantic union and world government." Numbered among their supporters were For America's co-chairman, Clarence E. Manion, the man who had fallen out with the Eisenhower Administration over the Bricker amendment; Vivien Kellums, the anti-income-tax industrialist from Connecticut who had formed a group called the Liberty Belles; Facts Forum moderator Dan Smoot; Lieutenant General George E. Stratemeyer, retired from the Air Force and former chairman of a drive opposing Senator McCarthy's censure; and the For America organization. Significantly, however, the group remained largely impotent. Only in six states, Wisconsin alone outside of the South, did it appear on ballots; and in Mississippi and South Carolina, the Andrews–Werdel combination was replaced by one consisting of Senator Harry F. Byrd and Representative John Bell Williams of Mississippi. But, with the exception of Governor James F. Byrnes of South Carolina, prominent politicians found the "third party" eminently resistible. Andrews's offer to "certain Republicans" to find a home with the new group went largely unanswered.[5] Motivated by notions of Republican responsibility for the *Brown v. Topeka* decision, the movement attracted little enthusiasm outside of Mississippi and South Carolina. And Eisenhower, in refuting a Nixon statement that the desegregation verdict had been issued by a "Republican Chief Justice," had continued his efforts to cement the coalition of conservatives, middle-of-the-roaders and moderate progressives.

Embarrassment, however, soon came from a friend of Republican liberals, Paul Hoffman. His article in *Collier's* that October described the President's concern with making over the GOP, a process, Hoffman contended, that could be encouraged by giving Eisenhower four more years to enable him to "achieve something unique in American politics, a party that is fundamentally pressureproof; something profoundly superior to its great rival, the Democratic party, whose irreconcilable differences leaves it permanently open to the pressures of contending narrow-interest groups."[6] Finding that the "nature of the party in 1956 is almost totally different from what it was in 1952," both in personalities and in the philosophies of Republicans who learned to accept Eisenhower's course, Hoffman nevertheless concluded that the party still contained too many "senators claiming the label Republican who embrace none or very little of the Eisenhower program and philosophy." Separating them into two categories, the "unappeasables" and the "faint-hope" group, he identified Joe McCarthy, William Jenner, Herman Welker and George Malone with the first and, as not quite beyond salvation, Henry Dworshak, Andrew Schoeppel and Barry Goldwater. The President, Hoffman wrote, "still hopes to bring these men over."[7]

One of the most sensitive predicaments of the campaign required tact and reassurance. Upset that he had been named, Goldwater sent a personal appeal for a clarification of his own standing with the President. Directing it to Sherman Adams, he wanted to know whether he was considered guilty of "dangerous thinking and reckless conduct." Was he also among those, Goldwater wanted to know, whom the President thought should be avoided? Positive replies would indicate he wanted mere puppets in the Senate, a departure from his earlier positions. Fellow Republicans in Arizona required prompt answers, he warned. Adams responded by observing that Hoffman and not the President had mentioned the Senator's name and, after an expression of appreciation for Goldwater's support and encouragement, itemized the Senator's questions in the manner of a parent reassuring a child and answered each in turn with a simple "No," except for the last one, which received an "Of course not."[8] Reporters aboard Nixon's plane heard the Vice President explain that he, for one, did not think certain people should be read out of the party. He added that he had not given up trying to convert such recalcitrants as McCarthy and Jenner to the President's views.[9] Eisenhower, confronted with the Hoffman account at his press conference, denied the existence of any such thing as "national parties" in the United States and said that the membership must be determined within each of the forty-eight state organizations. "There is nothing I can do to say so-and-so is Republican and so-and-so is not a Republican," he explained, although he did add his desire to have as "many Republicans as I can possibly get going down the line with me, because time is short."[10] Calmly, Eisenhower recognized long since as a skillful employer of press conferences, which had been televised nationally since early 1955, thus managed to preserve harmony for the remaining days of the battle.

His Democratic opponent, however, did not have Eisenhower's respect as a candidate. His well-delivered and finely written speeches were, the President knew, not convincing to the average American's desire for a more pragmatic and less pessimistic outlook. "Most Republican leaders were convinced," Eisenhower has written, "that the team finally selected by the Democrats was probably the weakest they could have named . . ."; and his own view was that a ticket led by Senator Lyndon B. Johnson and either Hubert H. Humphrey or John F. Kennedy would have had a better chance of winning by its appeal "to both wings of their party."[11]

Stevenson, however, experienced the inherent frustration of trying to prevent a second term for a popular incumbent whose thinking pleased most Americans. Without a recession, depression or domestic strife, international disgrace or highly partisan issues, all reasons for ousting the Administration were unconvincing. They had, after all, ended the Korean war and, with the exception of a slight increase in consumer prices, the unprecedented prosperity of 1955 had continued into 1956. The only emotional issue, civil rights, had yet to have a strong impact on most Americans, and even those concerned about the Administration's delicate balancing act could not present the Democrats as a believable alternative. Years of Congressional delay, filibustering and torpedoing legislation within committees were, after all, acts committed mainly by Southern Democrats, and thus anti-Administration liberals had no partisan justification for credible criticism. Moreover, by the fall of 1956, resistance to the Supreme Court's decision, aside from the notable accomplishments in a few Border areas—as in the District of Columbia and the public schools of Louisville, Kentucky—had not become as patently obvious as it became later. The nation, it may also be said, was still within the time span of whatever was meant by "with all deliberate speed." Stevenson's party, under the leadership of Lyndon Johnson in the Senate and Speaker Sam Rayburn in the House had also followed a policy of accommodation with the middle-of-the-road Eisenhower policies that substantiated the basic consensus that the Administration represented. And, as with all incumbents, especially during FDR's battle in 1940 for a third term, any Presidential action was politically potent, whatever the motivation asserted by the White House.

In short, Stevenson could do nothing right. He listened to the professionals by adopting a hard-hitting and less cerebral approach, and thus annoyed and disappointed the intellectual admirers of his 1952 efforts to achieve a high-level dialogue with the American people. Never a civil-rights crusader, he nevertheless went deep into the South, to Miami, New Orleans and Little Rock and urged acceptance of the Court's desegregation decision. But Eisenhower, carefully preserving his Southern strength, reaffirmed any doubts that his "great crusade" did not include federal government protection for the basic rights of all Americans, despite the Supreme Court. Even though Texas Rangers had been sent to both Texarkana Junior College and Mansfield High School by Governor Allan Shivers to keep the institutions segregated as white mobs had demanded, the President implicitly upheld the Governor's use of interposition by telling reporters that the "responsibility and authority in carrying out police functions to preserve law and order and to make certain that no one is injured" was a state matter. His moral outrage rested with a statement that "the youngsters that are indulging in violence are not being counseled properly at home."[12] Then, making a late campaign foray into the South, he assured Dixie that racial injustice ought to be handled at the local level and also told a Richmond, Virginia, crowd that he was proud to pay his respects to Senator Harry Byrd for upholding the "great heritage for efficiency in government, elimination of extravagance, strong local government. . . ."[13] Still, Adam Clayton Powell, Jr. emerged from a White House conference with the President on October 11 and announced he would campaign for Eisenhower and do his best to sway Harlem's traditionally Democratic vote to the GOP; and in such places as Chicago's South Side the Congressman became the prime force attracting increasing numbers of blacks to the Republican ticket.[14] Adding to Stevenson's woes, the majority of Negro newspapers, including such important weeklies as the New York *Amsterdam News* and the Pittsburgh *Courier*, joined their white brethren by endorsing the President.[15] Stevenson's pro-labor appeal carried the usual Democratic charge that the Republicans ran the government by and for big business and, going beyond the usual rhetoric, specified via five elaborate papers, averaging some ten thousand words each, what his plans for a "new America" offered in the fields of aid for senior citizens, education, economics, natural resources and national wealth. But, although they were designed mainly as ammunition for his loyal supporters, their effect never redeemed the personal attention he gave to their contents. Continuing the Democratic line, he tried to accuse the Administration of shortchanging national defense despite increasing Soviet strength and urged the growth of America's output to meet Communist expansion. At Portland, Oregon, alluding to the "New Look" program, he charged that defense spending had been cut without consultation with the military establishment.[16] While thereby exploiting international fears of communism, in contrast with the Republican concentration on its domestic dangers, he puzzled many by renewing and pushing his earlier advocacy of a unilateral halt to hydrogen-bomb tests and then embellished that with an appeal for an all-volunteer Army instead of the draft. Both were juicy fast balls grooved down the middle for a batter like Ike, who had only to tell the American public, as he did, that Stevenson's ideas were a "design for disaster."[17] The Democrat never did win public support on either issue.[18] He worked hard appealing to farmers and tried to exploit Gallup Poll evidence that the GOP's popularity had fallen some fifteen points in the Midwest by blaming Benson's policies; and the Democrats did achieve their greatest gains through the upper Great Plains but provoked a reaction that was still too feeble to withhold their electoral votes from Ike.[19]

Nor was there much attraction for the voters when the Democrats and Stevenson attacked the Administration's bias in behalf of private over public power. In numerous projects throughout the country, mainly in the South and the Far West, the Eisenhower people had begun the process of reversing Democratic-initiated federally constructed and operated systems to provide for flood control, inland waterway navigation, electric power and land reclamation. As Interior Under Secretary Ralph Tudor commented in the summer of 1953, "The Democrats and the demagogues are trying to say that we are selling out to the private power interests. Well, of course, there is no such thing as a private power interest. They just happen to represent a lot of stockholders like you and me."[20] To such people as Tudor and particularly to his boss, Douglas McKay, government had no business usurping a function that could be performed by private enterprise. Further, Eisenhower consistently maintained that federal assumption for such responsibility in one area could not be done without similar attention "with respect to every other area and region and corner of the United States of America."[21]

In the most blatant reversal of New Deal policy, therefore, and in pursuit of a program most acceptable to conservatives, every feasible project attractive to private companies was taken out of federal hands. Work on the John Jay Dam, an authorized project on the Columbia River in Oregon, was abandoned, as were the Priest Rapids and the Coosa River projects. The latter was given over to the Alabama Power Company, a rival of the Tennessee Valley Authority. Much greater controversy was aroused, with the Administration nevertheless finally prevailing, when they abandoned earlier plans for a high federal dam in Hell's Canyon on the Snake River along the Idaho–Oregon border and, in line with recommendations made by the previous Interior Department at a Cabinet meeting on April 24, 1953, withdrew previous objections to permitting the Idaho Power Company to build three dams at the site.[22] It was probably Eisenhower's deft removal from another and much more widely publicized and extended situation, the proposal by the Atomic Energy Commission to sign a long-term contract with a corporation to be formed by Edgar H. Dixon, the president of Middle South Utilities, and Eugene A. Yates, chairman of the board of the Southern Company, that vitiated a potential campaign issue for Stevenson.

The plan proposed to have the AEC purchase power from the Dixon and Yates-organized Mississippi Valley Generating Company that it would otherwise have obtained from TVA. "The fact is," Eisenhower wrote to Senator John Sherman Cooper, "that the proposal will allow time to determine what changes, if any, are needed. Such a study is an essential prerequisite to the evaluation of your suggestion that TVA be authorized to issue bonds for the construction of steam plants. As the study proceeds, the Dixon-Yates proposal will meet the area's immediate needs." Characteristically, he reassured the Kentucky Senator that the solution was "reasonable and practical."[23] To his friend Judge Orie Phillips, whose support he received, he observed that "it is gratifying to know that we are thinking along the same lines insofar as we fear the encroachment of socialistic tendencies that would inevitably hinder our free democratic processes."[24] Estimates showing that the AEC would be forced actually to pay more for its power from the Dixon-Yates company than it had been paying to TVA, even taking into consideration the government's ability to collect taxes from the private organization, did not deter Messrs. Joseph Dodge, Roland Hughes and Lewis Strauss, all of whom were normally preoccupied with reducing the cost of government. Finally, the arrangements approved by the Securities and Exchange Commission required the Dixon and Yates combine to put up only five and a half million of the needed \$105,415,000.[25] The real battle began when, over the objections of TVA Chairman Gordon Clapp, the request for appropriations for a steam plant at Fulton, forty miles north of Memphis, was omitted from the 1954 budget.[26]

On another level, the Administration wasted little time preparing to replace Clapp with a more compatible thinker. Three directors comprised the agency's board. Each served a nine-year term and could not be removed without special cause. Yet, on May 13, 1953, Sherman Adams solicited from Charlie Willis the status of each commission member and asked whether they could be removed by law.[27] When Adams heard that appointments were for a specific length of time and not revokable, he turned to Dodge with the suggestion that perhaps some of them might be induced to resign.[28] While Clapp, whose term was due to expire on May 18, 1954, continued to protest denial of funds for the steam plant, efforts were started to find a "very strong business person" who, at the same time, would not be vulnerable to political opposition because of past involvements with the utility industry.[29] Joe Dodge, in describing the prerequisite for a new chairman, informed Adams that "it is particularly essential that the individual have a high personal public standing, an appropriate background of experience, recognition as an executive, complete sympathy with the objectives of the Administration, and, above all, an ability to step into, and handle and represent the Administration as the head of an agency that is highly sensitive politically." Furthermore, Dodge warned, "he cannot be subject to attack on account of past or present relationships to the utility industry."[30]

Meanwhile, Clapp's reappointment for another nine-year term became a public power *cause célèbre*, with the newspapers of the TVA region, including the Scripps-Howard Memphis *Press-Scimitar*, taking up the fight. On March 16, a visit to the President by the Citizens for TVA Committee brought signatures for Clapp's reappointment from over sixty thousand citizens of the Tennessee Valley. The group's chairman, named States Rights Finley, pressed the fight as the chief grass-roots spokesman.[31]

Another political battle soon threatened when sentiment developed within the Administration for the appointment of Harry C. Carbaugh. Carbaugh had absolutely no qualifications for the post other than his closeness to Republican Representatives Carrol Reece and Howard Baker, both of Tennessee. A successful, self-made businessman from Chattanooga, he was president of the Tennessee Egg Company and one of the directors of the Hamilton National Bank. Carbaugh was described by one of his bank's vice-presidents as "a sound conservative individual without any New Deal tendencies." When the story about his possible appointment reached Chattanooga, local Democrats began a movement to write to Eisenhower in protest and in favor of Clapp.[32] The most important objection came from Senator Cooper. His own past principles would be overturned if he supported Carbaugh, he informed the White House, and warned that he would have to oppose the blatantly political appointment rather than risk any harm to his own re-election prospects.[33] Cooper soon received assurances from Adams that his protest would not be in vain, and the Administration avoided further embarrassment and examined a series of other possible candidates until finally nominating Brig. Gen. Herbert Davis Vogel, a fifty-four-year-old civil engineer then heading the Arkansas White and Red River Basins Interagency Committee and a member of the Mississippi River Commission.

Thus, Eisenhower had begun to accomplish with the commission what he was trying to achieve with TVA's facilities; but an unexpected fight had been provoked. The efforts to retain Clapp despite the Administration's persistence and the flare-up surrounding the possible nomination of Carbaugh, whose appointment would mainly have pleased Reece and Baker, had fortified any doubts that TVA needed to be defended from the Republicans. Roy Howard, of the Scripps-Howard newspaper chain, moved into the picture to quell the rebellion and finally notified the White House that "his boys down there" had been "converted back to private enterprise."[34]

However, what finally led to Mr. Eisenhower's order of July 11, 1955, to withdraw from the Dixon–Yates contract was a genuine business conflict, one that supported Arthur Krock's contention about the dangers businessmen themselves posed to a business Administration. Adolphe H. Wenzell, a vice-president of the First Boston Corporation, had been called to Washington by Joe Dodge as a consultant on the technical arrangements of the contract. What nobody in the Administration knew until the information came out during the Congressional hearings was that Wenzell was simultaneously consulting with Messrs. Dixon and Yates on behalf of the First Boston Corporation. His own banking house was preparing to become the financial agent for the contract between the AEC and the Mississippi Valley Generating Company. And, as if to arouse suspicions even more, a detailed chronology of the history of the negotiations omitted mentioning Wenzell, as though to hide his participation, while, in fact, he was involved in numerous sessions between May 1953 and April 1954.[35] The affair thus came to a rather dismal end. The city of Memphis undertook to construct its own steam plant, leaving the President satisfied that, at least, the government had not contributed to TVA's proliferation.[36] With little choice but to cancel the contract, the President probably avoided what Senator Gore had warned would be an extended debate over the issue; mostly, he deprived the Democrats of the luxury of being able to denounce an act rather than an attempt.

Stevenson had promised to avoid the President's health as a campaign issue. But, as his prospects for victory became more and more remote, he delighted the pros by aiming at the Vice President with increasingly personal salvos, attacking Nixon before a lukewarm audience in the automotive center of Flint, Michigan, as a "man of many masks" who was unfit for office. While never quite adopting Truman's language that a vote for Eisenhower was a vote for "tricky Dicky," he nevertheless departed from his 1952 level by hitting hard and in the language of the "common man," hardly above some of Nixon's own past performances. During the campaign's closing days, Stevenson told a friendly crowd in Los Angeles that a sick Eisenhower would be unable to lead if re-elected and that Nixon, the "beloved of the Old Guard reactionaries," awaited the opportunity to step into the "vacuum." How, he asked, could Nixon be trusted with America's destiny?[37] Pounding even more, during the campaign's waning days, on the specter of Nixon as the "heir-anointed" and the "heir apparent," he warned that Eisenhower's age, health and the effects of the Twenty-second Amendment would enable his understudy to dominate the party in a second Administration. Finally, desperately, Stevenson faced the Democrats last campaign rally in Boston on election eve and grasped at the health issue by predicting that a Republican victory would probably install Nixon in the White House "within the next four years."[38] Only a few days earlier, however, the newspapers told the public that Dwight D. Eisenhower had undergone a new physical checkup at Walter Reed and was pronounced in "excellent health."[39] Once again, a smiling, confident-looking President graced the front pages.

Still, as in every campaign, anxieties tempered complacency. Weak and "defensive" campaigning reportedly created dissatisfaction in Iowa, where the number of voters switching to Stevenson discouraged Republican workers. *Wallace's Farmer's* mid-September poll showed the Democratic candidate pulling into the lead for the first time.[40] Polls by the Des Moines *Register and Tribune* and the Minneapolis *Star Tribune* showed similar trends.[41] Maine's traditionally early election brought an ominous foreshadowing with the comfortable re-election of Edmund Muskie, the state's first Democratic Governor since the Civil War. White House aides, getting jittery, received disturbing reports that even Cincinnati, that usually reliable Republican stronghold, could become a toss-up by Election Day.[42] Industrialist Henning W. Prentis, Jr., precipitated further concern among businessmen and politicians. After the Republican National Committee circulated a Washington *Daily News* article headlined "A Debt Owed Reuther" containing a picture of United Automobile Workers President Walter Reuther in a close huddle with Stevenson, Prentis panicked about the possibility that Reuther's support foreshadowed labor domination of the Democratic party and took his concern about widespread unionist activities against Eisenhower to Tom Dewey, Senator James Duff of Pennsylvania and Ben Duffy of BBD&O. At the White House, letters supporting Prentis came in from a number of leading businessmen, including the chairman and president of the Westinghouse Electric Corporation, the chairman of the Aluminum Company of America and the leading officers of Alco Products, Inc., formerly the American Locomotive Company. All agreed with Prentis's urging for Ike to denounce Stevenson's labor friends by warning that "a vote for Stevenson is a vote for the CIO and Walter Reuther." Bobby Cutler, however, attempted to cool their demands by citing the President's aversion toward mentioning his political opponents by name. Besides, he pointed out, wisdom dictated blasting Reuther as a man avaricious for political power rather than as a labor leader.[43]

Suddenly, nothing seemed secure. Having already decided to step up his television campaign "to please my many good friends," Eisenhower had continued to rule out barnstorming or whistle-stopping. But then fear of trouble spots, particularly in a number of Congressional contests, and the need to demonstrate without doubt his own physical fitness led him to a hard-hitting foray into various parts of the country. In Seattle, the President accused the Democrats of "half truths" and "hit-and-run statements" and reaffirmed the nation's good health despite his critics. Facing a conservation-conscious audience, he took pride in the Administration's initiative in getting the St. Lawrence Seaway project started, the Upper Colorado River storage project and the recently passed interstate highway program, but ignored Dixon–Yates and Hell's Canyon.[44] At Portland, Oregon, he continued to laud his Administration's accomplishments in the field of natural resources by claiming that his policies "reflect our partnership policy—joining Federal, State, local and private effort in our great common endeavor," reversing the "tight centralization of control in Washington—a virtual Federal monopoly of construction of water and power projects."[45] Moving on to the Hollywood Bowl, he revived the 1952 corruption charges against the Democrats and rebutted Stevenson's charges of corruption in his own Administration.

As the campaign reached its final phase, fear suddenly developed that another Stevenson charge—one that the Democrat had been pursuing with increasing acidity—might be confirmed. The challenger, questioning GOP peace claims, repeatedly contended that the tense developments surrounding President Gamal Abdel Nasser's seizure of the Suez Canal for the Egyptian government on July 26 reaffirmed the failure of American diplomacy. Assuredly, efforts made by the United States, Great Britain and France, plus fifteen other users of the vital waterway, had brought Nasser's rejection of any plan for internationalization. Privately and publicly, America's two major European allies had left no room to doubt how gravely they viewed the situation. And the tiny state of Israel remained at the edge of a full-scale war with either Jordan or

Egypt, or both, while *fedayeen* commandos struck from the Gaza Strip and terrorized the new nation that had been created in what had been Palestine. How, under such threats, could the Administration in Washington afford optimism? Stevenson's favorite taunt, that the President had deceived the nation by saying he had "good news from Suez," was based on the opening words of the Presidential news conference of October 12. Announcing that the allies had reached a set of principles for negotiations, Eisenhower had judged that "it looks like here is a very great crisis that is behind us. I don't mean to say that we are completely out of the woods, but I talked to the Secretary of State just before I came over here tonight and I will tell you that in both his heart and mine, at least, there is a very great prayer of thanksgiving."[46] The very next day the Soviet Union used her Security Council veto at the United Nations to kill an American-sponsored resolution to place the canal under the operation of an international body, to be known as the Suez Canal Users' Association.[47]

Since mid-October, in fact, right after the UN veto, Eisenhower's efforts to stabilize the Middle East and prevent war had taken an ominous turn. C. Douglas Dillon, the American ambassador in Paris, received confidential information from a member of the French government that an attempt to topple Nasser's regime would be made. The effort, Dillon learned, would take place right after the American election, and corroboration that plans were being made came from CIA operatives in France. Soon afterward, newly operative U-2 reconnaissance planes, designed for photographic surveillance high above the range of anti-aircraft fire, flew over the eastern Mediterranean island of Cyprus and observed military preparations. Dulles also noted that a week had lapsed without any high-level communications having come from either London or Paris. Telegrams to Dillon and to Winthrop Aldrich, the American ambassador in England, confirmed the silence.[48] Together, with a sudden embargo on any kind of exchanges about the Middle East and reconnaissance reports given to Eisenhower as early as October 15, that the Israelis had sixty French Mystère planes—far more than the twelve that Dulles had arranged surreptitiously to be sent from aircraft that had been designated for NATO—there seemed little reason to doubt Dillon's information about a post-Election Day move.[49] As American reconnaissance increased, both in the air and through the CIA in various capitals, intelligence noted an unusually heavy flow of electronic communications filling the airways between Tel Aviv and Paris.[50] Although the British claimed no knowledge of such preparations, White House aides drafted a Presidential statement, planned for immediately after Eisenhower's victory had become evident, calling upon all nations to hold their fire while the United States attempted new diplomatic efforts.[51]

On Thursday, October 25, the President of the United States went to New York to deliver the traditional big speech at Madison Square Garden. His visit coincided with the increasing White House trepidations. Far more than just the Middle East threatened disaster. Behind the Iron Curtain, uprisings against Russian domination had already exceeded the importance of the East Berlin upheavals. Early-summer rioting that had begun with a general strike of industrial workers in Poznań, Poland, had continued into August, finally bringing to power Władysław Gomułka under a government more representative of Polish nationalism than the Kremlin. Then it spread into Hungary. By the twenty-second and twenty-third, demonstrating students in Budapest were being joined by soldiers and workers; when Eisenhower reached New York, he learned that Parliament Square in the capital had become a battlefield when a Soviet tank fired on several thousand peaceful, flag-carrying demonstrators. Before his speech the President issued a statement deploring the use of Soviet troops "to continue an occupation of Hungary by the forces of an alien government for its own purposes."[52] But such statements, along with resolutions in the United Nations, had to suffice; nothing was more evident than that any real attempt to "liberate" the captive peoples would, virtually by definition, force a military showdown with the Russians and the start of World War III. And, at that moment, the Administration feared any outbreak of fighting, no matter how local, that could negate their campaign slogan and give further credence to Democratic charges. So when the President spoke in New York that night, he repeated the theme that had been emphasized since the start of the crisis in July: the preservation of peace. Twenty thousand enthusiastic loyalists, each one sure of victory on November 6, applauded, whistled and cheered, interrupting his thirty-minute speech forty-eight times. Peace, he told them, will be achieved not by simply discontinuing nuclear tests but by "making impossible their use in any nuclear war." From that "mission of peace," he said with assurance, "we shall never rest—nor ever retreat." Rather than the "illusion" of disarmament, the road should lead toward "the reality of disarmament." Toward that noble end "We shall go steadfastly seeking safe and sound means of disarmament—so that history can never say that this generation left humanity crucified upon a cross of iron."[53]

But, within a few hours, reports from the Middle East indicated the mobilization of the Israeli Army. After conferring with Dulles, Eisenhower sent Israel's Prime Minister, David Ben-Gurion, a cable expressing his "concern at reports of heavy mobilization on your side" and urged "that there be no forceable initiative on the part of your Government which would endanger the peace."[54] Then, with Dulles already off to Dallas for a speech before the Council of World Affairs, the President entered Walter Reed Hospital for his scheduled overnight pre-Election Day physical.

Earlier plans called for the Chief Executive to make a quick campaign foray on Monday into the South, via the *Columbine*, to speak in Miami, Jacksonville and Richmond, Virginia. Additional speeches for later that week were due to be made in Texas, Oklahoma and Tennessee. But each hour jeopardized Mr. Eisenhower's schedule, most seriously when Under Secretary of State Herbert Hoover, Jr., acting as his department's chief in Dulles's absence, arrived at Walter Reed that Sunday with a cable from the American ambassador in Tel Aviv, Edward B. Lawson, reporting total mobilization. Moreover, CIA reports also being received removed doubts about their objective—not Jordan, it was clear, but Egypt through the Sinai Peninsula.[55] From the hospital, the President sent Ben-Gurion another peace appeal.[56]

Meanwhile, no advisories, let alone consultations, reached Washington from either Tel Aviv, Paris or London. Only information gathered by Intelligence reached the State Department. Dulles, returning from Dallas late Sunday afternoon and confronted with Ambassador Lawson's message, made a desperate search for details. Were they really preparing to strike immediately, without even waiting until after the elections? He called in Ambassador Abba Eban, who had mystified the Americans by complacently playing golf at a country club; but the Israeli, finding Dulles and his aides poring over a huge map of his country's frontier with Jordan, merely maintained that Tel Aviv's moves represented defensive preparations against Egyptian and Jordanian aggression. Desperately, Dulles telephoned the chairman of the board of the Chase Manhattan Bank, John J. McCloy. Reached at the home of his mother-in-law in Hastings-on-Hudson, New York, the former American High Commissioner for Germany was asked whether he had observed any extraordinary flow of funds from New York banks toward Israel or any of the European powers. Despite the late Sunday hour, McCloy managed to telephone the foreign department heads of some half dozen large New York banks. When the banker reported no significant movement occurring, he learned that Dulles was simply searching for any strands of information.

Eisenhower, having been discharged from Walter Reed that Sunday with a perfect physical report, kept to his determination to follow Monday's schedule. Before departing for Florida, he met with several staff members and provided for the deployment of the Sixth Fleet for possible evacuation of American citizens from any trouble in the eastern Mediterranean. At 8:30 A.M. he left Washington for his speaking engagements at airports near Miami and Jacksonville, and then the *Columbine* flew northward toward Richmond. In mid-afternoon news arrived of an Israeli land and air strike across the sands of the Sinai and toward the Suez Canal. Paratroopers had been dropped from sixteen Dakota transports at Mitla Pass, thirty miles east of Suez, and twelve Mystères patroled the canal itself. Their military dispatches claimed progress only twenty miles from the canal, where they said their soldiers had dug in.[57] Receiving the news before his plane landed at Richmond, the President coolly decided against disappointing the waiting crowd in Virginia's capital and thus made his speech. Noting the developments in the Middle East briefly, he repeated his pledge to work for peace.[58] By the time his limousine pulled into the White House driveway at seven that evening, the Dulles brothers, Admiral Radford, Sherman Adams and Jerry Persons were waiting to confer with him.

Foster Dulles, noting the importance of preserving the canal as a pipe line for Middle Eastern oil, guessed that the French and British were ready to intervene, and Radford suggested that Nasser could be toppled easily, while Allen Dulles expressed bewilderment about the eventual disposition of the British and French forces on Cyprus because of the allied information blackout.[59] They agreed to take the issue to the UN Security Council the next morning and urged British and French cooperation in implementing the Tripartite Declaration of May 25, 1950, which pledged all three nations to maintain a balance of forces in the Middle East and to go to the aid of any victim of aggression.[60] As recently as April 9 Eisenhower himself had renewed that commitment by saying in Augusta that the United States would protect the victim of aggression "within constitutional means."[61]

Political "flack," as Eisenhower well understood, could come from all sides. American Jews, claiming that the Ben-Gurion government had tolerated many years of outrageous attacks upon her territory—especially recent *fedayeen* raids from the Gaza Strip that had left no part of the country safe—would instinctively rush to Israel's defense. Israel, defending herself since her creation in 1948, from hostile neighbors who ringed her boundaries with arms and threatened to push her into the sea, had never been recognized by the Arab states. Since 1950, in direct violation of the Constantinople Convention of 1888, providing for the operation of the canal by an international corporation and the unrestricted use by ships of all nations, the Egyptian government had closed its waters to Israeli vessels. The emotional identification, then, for American Jews concerned with maintaining some safe haven for survivors of Hitler was understandable. But, unlike the Democrats, Republican strength was not as dependent on the large Eastern cities that had significant numbers of Jewish voters; furthermore, the Eisenhower margin in 1952 had been considered large enough to make him virtually immune from the relatively few Jews who did support the GOP. On the other hand, Eisenhower, more than any Republican since the New Deal, was proving himself attractive to American Jews just as he appealed to others, and nobody deprecated the importance of keeping New York State's forty-five electoral votes safe for the Republican party. Recognition of that very factor had inspired Jack Porter, the leader of the Eisenhower delegates from Texas during the 1952 convention fight over seating, to urge the President to make life easier for American oil interests in the Middle East by supporting current proposals to change the electoral system. Either of the changes then before the Congress, Porter advised, whether the Lodge-Gossett amendment to divide the electoral college in proportion to the actual popular vote or the Mundt-Coudert proposal to have each Congressional district select one elector, "would simplify the handling of our foreign relations problem as it concerns Israel and the Arab states."[62] But siding with Egypt, on the other hand, after Nasser's arms purchases from the Soviet-bloc nations and recognition of Red China, had placed the Egyptian President in a class with Marshal Tito of Yugoslavia and Premier Nehru of India, as far as American right-wingers were concerned. Support for him was clearly no way to please Republican conservatives.

Yet, for most of the world, and particularly for American liberals, the road to the Middle East disaster had been paved by Dulles. As during the Indochina crisis, the Secretary of State was the villain. He had provoked Nasser. He had mishandled America's two most important allies. Whatever breakdown occurred was his responsibility. Dulles, the man vulnerable, had pressured the British to evacuate their eighty thousand troops from the Suez Canal. Dulles, moral and proud, had provoked Nasser's announcement of July 26 about the seizure of the canal. Dulles, furthermore, in a meeting at the start of August and in two subsequent London conferences, had placed obstacles in the way of quick action to overthrow the Egyptian leader while extending the bait of possible American assistance in any overt attempt to depose him that remained as the only possible alternative. "But the net result was that in some ways the final peak of tragedy in October was Dulles's doing almost as much as Eden's and Mollet's," an English biographer of the American Secretary of State has written. "And in his record at the State Department it marks by far his most humiliating failure."[63] An American historian of the Suez affair, Herbert Finer, has been even harsher in his condemnation of the Secretary of State. "Dulles's intellectual and spiritual pride and colossal self-righteousness drove him into a morally indefensible role," he has written, "for he evoked the Rule of Law as the world's hope while he and the President (the latter soon with some reluctance) clandestinely subdued Britain, France, and Israel with moral economic sanctions."[64] Much clearer, however, is the simple truth that on Middle Eastern policy, as on everything else, Dulles and the President worked together and the Secretary, as carefully as in all other matters, deferred to Eisenhower's constitutional role.

For more than three years the Administration had been trying to maneuver an approach to the region that would at once preserve the state of Israel and maintain American influence with the Arab countries. Nothing in the policy deviated from the 1950 Tripartite Declaration. If anything, they were more determined than Truman to preserve relations with the Moslem lands, the most important of which was Egypt. American interests, particularly at the crest of the cold war, viewed as disastrous any policy encouraging Arab nationalism to seek Soviet assistance. Continued Western colonialism could, in Washington's view, exacerbate that condition. Britain's efforts to retain her Iranian oilfields and military base at Suez and the French opposition to nationalism in Algeria presented perfect opportunities for exploitation by anti-Western interests. The Eisenhower and Dulles policy, therefore, feared a blatantly pro-Israel American position as fraught with negative implications. Israel's value hardly went beyond the implicit moral need to support the only European-style democracy in the area; to offend her government jeopardized few economic interests and, if anything, could improve American influence with the Arab League, which, after all, sat squarely on the oil needed by most of Western Europe.

Egypt, since the overthrow of King Farouk's dissipated regime in 1952 and after an interim stewardship under General Mohammed Naguib, had been dominated by the forceful and compelling personality of Colonel Gamal Abdel Nasser. Even before he rose to official power in 1954 as that ancient land's President, the CIA appraised him as a man of "vanity, obstinacy, suspicion, avidity for power. His strengths are complete self-confidence, great resilience, courage and nervous control, willingness to take great risks, great tactical skill and stubborn attachment to initial aims." Furthermore, added the confidential analysis, "He gets boyish pleasure out of conspiratorial doings. Has a real streak of self pity. While a patient, subtle organizer, he can lose his head."[65] Others, such as French Prime Minister Guy Mollet, thought his unlimited ambitions depended upon getting control of the oil supply. Mollet supported his view by showing visitors a copy of Nasser's *Philosophy of the Revolution*. Far from the decadence of a King Farouk, however, Nasser's concern with improving the longevity of his own people seemed genuine. The life expectancy of Egypt's twenty-two million people, mostly crowded into the narrow strip of fertile land formed by the Nile Valley, was only thirty-five years and their average annual income approximated sixty dollars. For Nasser, then, as head of the key nation of the region, reverence from his own masses and respectful treatment from the major powers could go a long way toward establishing his dominance.

Eisenhower's determination to keep the Egyptian leader within the

American orbit soon became evident. Dulles presented him with a personal gift from the President, an ivory-handled Colt .38 revolver, to symbolize the new American friendship, an unfortunate gesture that provoked Sir Winston Churchill's apprehensions about American hints of readiness to arm Egypt.[66] Anthony Eden also expressed fears, in a conversation with Cyrus Sulzberger, that the Egyptians were about to play the Americans off against the British while harboring the "delusion" that they could expel the British from Suez and then get American military and economic aid to promote themselves.[67] Eden's worries materialized far more than his expectations had thought possible. After the presence of some eighty thousand British troops along the canal, there under the terms of the Anglo-Egyptian Treaty of 1936, had provoked open hostility among the people during the Naguib era, the eventual agreement for their removal was prompted by heavy American pressure.[68]

Perhaps, too, as has been suggested, the Eisenhower Administration, more than its predecessors, was more responsive to pressure from American oil interests. Unlike during most of the Truman period, however, such companies had valid reasons to feel insecure. They lived under the shadow of the British experience in Iran, where Premier Mossadegh nationalized the Anglo-Iranian Oil Company in 1951 until his own overthrow in August of 1953 with the aid of the CIA. Shortly after Eisenhower's election, a representative of Consolidated Brokerage of Sixty Wall Street, which dealt with crude oil, petroleum products and petroleum transportation, called the President-elect's attention to Iranian nationalization as a potential "prairie fire which would spread throughout the Middle East to the detriment of American oil interests in other countries. We have good reason to believe that, unless a prompt solution is obtained to avoid Iran going to the Communists, the prairie fire of Communism will consume all the strategic interests of the United States and the West throughout the Middle East."[69] More even than mere nationalism, such groups also feared having oil poured into the world exchanges without the safeguards of the industry's international marketing controls. Eisenhower himself, in July of 1953, touched upon that problem by noting that "many American citizens would be deeply opposed to the purchase by the United States Government of Iranian oil in the absence of an oil settlement."[70]

To protect the Middle East from a Russian southward thrust toward the Mediterranean, in continuation of a drive for warm-water ports dating back to the days of Peter the Great, Dulles suggested the formation of a mutual-defense pact along the region's so-called Northern Tier, an anti-Soviet infiltration concept that had been discussed since 1951. Never visualizing a NATO-type of force in the area, Dulles sought some kind of unification, particularly among Turkey, Iran and Pakistan, to minimize divisive rivalries. Great Britain, however, fearful of not being able to renew her own expiring alliance with Iraq, and desiring to maintain her two air bases in that country, suggested Iraq's inclusion and then also joined what became known as the Baghdad Pact. Although American participation had been assumed, the United States feared that joining would hinder her flexibility to respond to sensitive Egyptian–Israeli relations.[71]

Unfortunately, the Baghdad Pact helped to provoke a new chain of competition. Egypt feared Iraqi dominance through the new position of the Baghdad government, and the Soviet Union was presented with a challenge to find new routes into the region. The most discommoded was Israel. The only nation in the area not linked with one another or with the West by a treaty felt increasingly vulnerable. Thus Abba Eban began overtures to Dulles in 1954 and 1955 concerning the possibility of a treaty between Washington and Tel Aviv. Through Arthur Dean, Dulles's former law partner, Eban sent a memo to the Secretary arguing that Israel needed a counterbalance to the existing network of treaties with their hostile implications. Throughout those months Dulles appeared sympathetic but, in his view, the United States could not go along without a prior Egyptian–Israeli agreement guaranteeing their frontiers. Eban's retort that such an achievement would obviate the need for a security treaty failed to dissuade Dulles from his basic avoidance of offending the Arabs. Short of sponsoring a two-year-long effort by Eric Johnston to arrange a division of the Jordan River's waters between Israel and Syria, which failed largely because of pressure on the latter from Egypt, and continuing to uphold the sanctity of the Tripartite Declaration, the Administration shied away from overt friendship toward the Jewish state. Tel Aviv's attempts to compensate through the only possible alternative, the construction of a superior military arm, met with similar difficulty when Washington repeatedly limited her desire to make military purchases, particularly aircraft. Covertly, however, Dulles did render some assistance. He arranged for the Canadians to provide Israel with F-86 jets and for France to send Mystère fighters that had been designated for NATO. Although both supplying nations urged the United States to share with them the blame before the Arab world, Dulles prudently refused to go beyond saying the deal had American acquiescence.[72]

Furthermore, the closer Egypt drew to the Soviet Union, the more Washington feared Cairo's power. Even as the Big Four were meeting in Geneva, Nasser and the Soviets arranged a barter deal. Thought at first by the West to be limited to Czechoslovakia and not to Russia herself, the arrangement to exchange cotton for Communist arms was publicly confirmed by Nasser on September 27, 1955, a development considered by Dulles as the most serious one "since Korea, if not since World War

II."[73] That threat to the Middle Eastern balance of power, with its prospects of Russia hurdling over the Northern Tier, precipitated a chain of events that ultimately worked both for and against Nasser's appeal for American assistance in the construction of a High Dam at Aswan on the Nile River.

Eugene Black, the American president of the World Bank, had been told by General Naguib that building a dam to create new arable land for a population that increased by some half million per year was the most important thing that could be done for Egypt. The plan involved the building of coffer dams, then the High Dam, followed by a series of irrigation canals, a large power plant and transmission lines. Projected to take twelve to sixteen years to construct, the Aswan Dam, it was agreed, could be financed through a four-way arrangement. The dam was expected to cost $1.3 billion. The World Bank would lend Egypt $200 million, and both the United States and Great Britain would make initial grants of $54 million and $14 million respectively, while Cairo provided $900 million in local currency.

Black reported the plan to Eisenhower, who seemed agreeable and said he would see what could be done if the undertaking proved feasible. When the President arrived at Camp David for a Cabinet meeting on December 8, 1955, while still recuperating from his heart attack, he carried a cablegram from Anthony Eden. The Prime Minister, agitated that the Russians had offered to help with the job at attractive terms and concerned about the spreading of their influence in Africa, had sent a blunt warning. American rejection of assistance for the dam, he said, would free the British from any obligation to restrict their trade with the Russians.[74] Dulles, strolling through the woods of Camp David with Eisenhower, added his feelings that the project would help to improve American-Arab relations. Then, after a series of negotiations with the British and Eugene Black, with George Humphrey and Herbert Hoover, Jr., playing leading roles, agreement on the terms was reached that month.

For the next half year tortuous maneuvering made the Aswan proposition far from certain. Hoping that Nasser could be persuaded to concentrate on the project rather than continue his anti-Israeli objectives, Eisenhower expected that Nasser and Ben-Gurion might yet be brought to a reasonable understanding. To carry out top-secret negotiations with both governments, the President selected as his personal emissary his trusted friend who had, only recently, temporarily left government for private business, Robert B. Anderson. Even today, the mission remains as highly classified information.[75] Nevertheless, some indication of Anderson's difficulties have already been gleaned. Journeying back and forth between Cairo and Tel Aviv, while keeping the President closely informed via a flood of telegrams, he found Ben-Gurion insistent upon direct negotiations with Nasser and not through any intermediary, while the Egyptian President pointed to the political dangers of his undertaking such personal discussions with the Israeli leader. Unknown to Anderson at that point, Ben-Gurion had already been urging his cabinet to accept Major General Moshe Dayan's plan to seize the eastern part of the Sinai Peninsula.[76] At the same time, Nasser, objecting to conditions attached to the financing of the Aswan project to limit his undertaking of other enterprises, which was deemed necessary to ensure his ability to provide the needed local currency, was urged by Black to understand that they were not only reasonable but vital for the successful realization of the High Dam. Finally persuaded personally by Black, Nasser then decided to attempt getting some amelioration of the terms offered by the United States and Great Britain. Sparring developed, with Nasser contending that provisions limiting Egyptian expenditures for other major enterprises consisted of an infringement upon his nation's sovereignty. Eugene Black visited with the Egyptian leader and argued that the World Bank had made reasonable conditions, but those efforts failed to dissuade Nasser from writing to Washington and London with requests for changes.[77]

But, in both Western capitals, deep misgivings had begun to develop. The British, caught up with their Baghdad Pact involvements, found Egypt's Moslem rival, Nuri-es-Said of Iraq, complaining that his nation's cooperation with the allies was less fruitful than Nasser's independence. As Eden's memoirs have recorded, "The Iraqis had got £3 million and a few tanks; the Egyptians seemed about to get the Aswan Dam. If there was to be charity, then friendly Arab countries had the right to apply."[78] Egyptian agents throughout the Middle East plotted against existing regimes in Libya, Lebanon, Jordan, Iraq and Saudi Arabia. Radio Cairo, calling itself "The Voice of the Arabs," fulminated against Western inperialists. Gradually, Prime Minister Eden and Foreign Secretary Selwyn Lloyd decided, in Eden's words, that they "could not go on with a project likely to become increasingly onerous in finance and unsatisfactory in practice," another way of saying they wished to undermine Nasser.[79]

Washington also found the prospective grant of money for Aswan becoming a distinct burden. In May, Nasser recognized Communist China. That was soon followed by a new purchase of weapons from the Soviet bloc and rumors that the Russians had offered a large interest-free loan. Coming on top of the anti-Western propaganda already flowing from Cairo, plus the earlier dallying with Communist supplies, rendered him no more palatable to American conservatives than such "neutralists" as Marshal Tito or Nehru. Particularly in the House, sentiment strengthened against sending large amounts of money to Egypt while that country was, in effect, pledging its future revenues from abroad to the Russian bloc to pay for arms purchases.[80] At a meeting of the House Committee on Appropriations, while considering the Administration's request for a new $5 billion mutual-security bill, Chairman Clarence Cannon privately warned Dulles that his group would not approve one cent for a dam in Egypt and advised in strong terms that no such measure could clear the House.[81] Adding to the growing antipathy, although never a major factor, was a largely unwarranted fear about the prospects of newly irrigated lands near the Nile eventually producing long-staple cotton in competition with American growers, a factor brought up by Herman Talmadge in his successful primary-election victory to succeed Walter George in the Senate from Georgia.[82] Like the British, Dulles, hitherto eager to keep the proposal alive to bind the Egyptian economy, and particularly its cotton crop, to inhibit further spending for arms, began to have new doubts, qualms that Eden encouraged.[83]

So did the President. Nasser, increasingly anti-Western despite the prospects of financing for the dam, and encouraging stories about Soviet readiness to do the job, had been demonstrating the futility of expecting such assistance to produce peace in the Middle East. Further, as the Anderson mission had discovered, Nasser felt in no position to make any overt conciliatory gesture toward Israel. More realistically, the existence of the Jewish state had become a powerful emotional issue to enable him to rally the Arab world. Politically, especially in an election year, little could be gained and much lost by completing the arrangements. His own party, his own Secretary of State, had, after all, taken the most vehement positions against those leaders willing to play with both the East and the West. All of the other factors may yet have been overcome, in the President's mind, until Nasser's most recent deals with the Soviet Union.

Clearly, then, the President and not his Secretary of State, encouraged by the revised British attitude, shifted gears. At Camp David just before the middle of July, the National Security Council met and heard President Eisenhower express his doubts. Dulles, citing Nasser's continued pro-Communist position, agreed that the negotiations over the dam, which had been suspended after Eugene Black had been given a series of totally unacceptable counter-proposals in Cairo on June 20, should be terminated. During the long discussion that took place that day, support for the project received no strong backing, with the possible exception of Harold Stassen. When, shortly after that session, the President revealed his decision, the members were relieved.[84]

When word reached Washington that Nasser had decided to accept the offer, after all, and was sending his ambassador, Ahmed Hussein, to see the Secretary of State, Dulles had a statement prepared in advance. Senator Prescott Bush of Connecticut, one of those given a preview of the document, asked if Dulles really thought the move was the right thing to do. "If I didn't think so I wouldn't do it," Dulles replied.[85] The

President also approved the statement. The British were similarly advised.[86]

Mr. Hussein confronted Dulles in the presence of diplomat George V. Allen and Herbert Hoover, Jr. The ambassador, considered strongly pro-American, stated his concern about the implications of possible Egyptian acceptance of Russian offers to build the dam at Aswan. After reasserting that he preferred the United States to do the job, he added, "We've got the Soviet offers right in our pocket." Then, according to Allen, Dulles spoke gently but frankly and took advantage of the opening given to him by Hussein and paraphrased the prepared statement's point that the United States no longer found the loan economically feasible.[87] Egyptian economic commitments elsewhere had, as the statement said, placed in doubt her "readiness and ability to concentrate its economic resources upon this vast program."[88]

Although, as some have noted, the events of the preceding weeks should have indicated to Nasser that the money would be denied and, as Dulles later revealed, monitored telephone calls showed that the Egyptian government knew that the reply would be negative, the abruptness of the final move, it is still fair to say, played into Nasser's hands. Dulles, of course, like Eisenhower, had been infuriated by Egyptian talk about going to Russia for the money and agreed with the President's feeling that ambitious foreign leaders could not be encouraged to believe that the route to Washington was by way of Moscow. Yet, even granting the validity of George V. Allen's personal observation that Dulles's manner was gentle, for much of the world, and particularly American critics, the deed was a pure example of the Secretary's personal outrage. Hussein had obviously left the office in distress, his face ashen. Viewing the move as one motivated by Dulles's "moral righteousness," Herman Finer has cited a comment that "Mr. Dulles kicked Nasser in the teeth, with a missionary twist."[89] When the Egyptians finally dedicated the Aswan High Dam, on January 15, 1971, in a ceremony attended by Soviet President Nikolai V. Podgorny, whose country had extended more than $300 million in loans for that purpose, American academic and government personnel agreed that the rebuff had hurt the United States more than Egypt.[90] But the public never did learn that the move had reflected National Security Council deliberations and the President's own decision. Just as naïvely, public-opinion analyst Gerard B. Lambert, then working for the CIA, suggested to Eisenhower one day shortly afterward that the move had been a mistake and, moreover, that "Foster pulled the rug out from" the Egyptian ambassador abruptly. The President suddenly reddened and dismissed Lambert curtly.[91] Eugene Black, the man whose negotiations with Nasser in behalf of the World Bank had kept the arrangement viable as long as possible, considered the rejection a terrible blunder.[92]

When French ambassador Couve de Murville told the State Department that Egypt would retaliate by seizing the Suez Canal, his words drew laughter. Not one American official anticipated Nasser's move of July 26. Nor is there any present evidence that it was even considered during the NSC deliberations. Nasser himself told a press conference on August 12, 1956, that he had been discussing the move for two years but made the decision after the offer was withdrawn.[93] The possibility that he used or even provoked the incident for his own purpose must remain worth considering. His dramatic announcement of that date, made at the end of a speech delivered in Alexandria, astonished Eisenhower, as it did almost everyone else.[94] Nasser's hands held the canal on which three-fourths of the NATO countries were dependent. Its total income in 1955, when 14,666 ships passed through, was $100 million. By nationalizing Suez, he thus removed it from the hands of the Suez Canal Company, an Egyptian organization that had mostly Englishmen and Frenchmen as shareholders. Operated under a concession granted by the Cairo government, it had rights only until 1968, when Egypt was scheduled to attain ownership. Although its rights could be abrogated by Nasser, the Treaty of Constantinople of 1888 had guaranteed its use as an international waterway, which had already been violated by denial of its facilities to Israeli shipping. In Egyptian hands, the vital supply line to the West could be snapped by one additional capricious act.[95]

The dilemma confronting the President on that Monday, October 30, with the Anglo-French memorandum calling for a cease-fire and announcing their movement toward the canal, represented the failure of a three-month American effort to do virtually anything that might thwart Eden's determination to use force, a situation virtually the reverse of American attempts to win England's commitment during the Indochina crisis before and during the Geneva Conference of 1954. Immediately after Nasser's takeover, Eden's determination to use force was communicated to Eisenhower, pending, of course, the failure of political means.[96] But from the outset the American President informed the Prime Minister of the folly of impetuous action and pointed out that public opinion in America and elsewhere "would be outraged" without prior efforts to find other ways to resolve the crisis.[97] After sending Dulles to London for emergency meetings at the start of August, Eisenhower continued to encourage the belief that efforts to find a peaceful solution must be completely exhausted before any force could be contemplated. Clearly, the Administration meant to deny military action unless Nasser actually closed the canal to Western shipping.

But the British and the French needed more hope than that. Thus, Dulles worked in London to delay hasty action, even to provide a cooling-off period. First, however, Eden and the French needed to believe that the Americans would use force if all else failed, which Dulles indicated.[98] Almost immediately he told Eden that a "way had to be found to make Nasser disgorge what he was attempting to swallow. . . . Then if a military operation had to be undertaken it would be more apt to succeed and have less grave repercussions than if it had been undertaken precipitately."[99] When all three agreed to convene a conference of maritime nations, and the British and French wanted to act as soon as possible, Dulles asked more time for preparations, and the selection of August 16 came as a compromise. After eighteen nations had decided on a plan to internationalize the canal and a five-man committee had attempted in vain to sell the idea to Nasser, Eisenhower and Dulles together devised a plan that the Secretary presented at the Second London Conference, the Suez Canal Users' Association. When asked at one point by an American diplomat what inducements would be offered to the Egyptian leader to accept the idea, Dulles simply replied, "We are just going to argue that it's the best way for Egypt as for the users to operate the canal effectively."[100] Some of Dulles's closest associates failed to understand how the SCUA could be made to overcome Nasser's objections, but the British and French, at least, were hopeful about it as a means of keeping the United States involved. When Dulles told Eden that the President would need Congressional approval for any American commitment, the Prime Minister found it encouraging that the United States should be thinking in the context of military action at all."[101] Appearing with the President on a radio-TV address on the Suez crisis in early August, Dulles stressed that we "have given no commitments at any time as to what the United States would do" if conferences should fail and promised to "invoke moral forces which are bound to prevail."[102]

Certainly, during the election campaign that autumn, the President's public statements made fewer concessions to the possibility of military involvement. During a news conference on August 8 he said he could not "conceive of military force being a good solution, certainly under conditions as we know them now and in view of our hopes that things are going to be settled peacefully."[103] Eisenhower's statement of hope "not to give up, even if we do run into other obstacles," was viewed by Eden as damaging to efforts at winning Nasser's acceptance of international control.[104]

With everything else having failed, the European powers believed that the Americans, faced with a *fait accompli*, would have no choice but to aid them. Careful plans were worked out between Tel Aviv and Paris; Great Britain, sensitive about her relations with the rest of the Arab world, kept her distance from collusion with the Jewish state. The Israelis, possibly learning that Eisenhower planned to appeal against the use of force right after his election, decided to move at once, before the balloting, hoping that Administration concern with the Jewish vote would at least prevent interference. A false communiqué that Israeli troops were near the canal, when her concern was actually with the Gaza Strip, the source of the *fedayeen* raiders, would signal the prearranged Anglo-French action.

Eisenhower, personally thwarted just before Election Day, would have no part of the fighting. The American response, more than was ever realized, was his. Dulles, who had labored at the conference tables and had extended the encouraging possibility of United States intervention, received the burden of the blame for having deceived Eden. But, as General Andrew Goodpaster, then Eisenhower's staff secretary, has observed, the Secretary of State merely worked within the perimeter established by the President.[105] "We'll do what we think is right regardless of how it affects the election," Eisenhower told Dulles. "If they don't want me, let them get someone else."[106] One of Dulles's top legal aides has also testified that the policy came from the President and was followed by Dulles from beginning to end without deviation. Eisenhower, not Dulles, reacted with fury and insisted the United States go to the Security Council immediately and stop the invasion. He never accepted the notion of waiting until the canal had been captured.[107] The President could not help but recall how in 1955 he had aided Eden's election by his willingness to announce readiness to attend a summit conference. The English were not, it seemed, equally cooperative. One of the President's close White House aides has also offered the view that British and French blame should have been reserved for Eisenhower rather than the Secretary of State, for it was *his* decision. Dulles served as the scapegoat.

Aside from pressing for a cease-fire within the Security Council, Eisenhower's policy was simple. The United States would not become involved in the Middle East. The United States, unlike England and France, adhered to the Tripartite Declaration of 1950 as applicable to the situation and would continue to work for peace.

The final seven days before the elections demonstrated the inherent advantages of an incumbent, an asset, as it turned out, that Eisenhower did not need. But, as the Israelis continued their swift occupation of the Sinai and overran the Gaza Strip, with General Moshe Dayan's troops routing over thirty thousand Egyptians east of the canal, and the Anglo-French air attacks prepared for landings at key canal posts, the President resolved to fulfill his peace-keeping promises. Going before the nation via television on October 31, he declared American opposition to aggression even if, sadly, the act had been committed by the nation's best friends. "There can be no peace—without law," he said. "And there can be no law—if we were to invoke one code of international conduct for those who oppose us—and another for our friends."[108] In Philadelphia's Convention Hall, the next day, he abandoned the campaigner's role to speak of "great things" and announced his rejection of international justice that distinguished between the weak and the strong.[109] Forsaking the scheduled second Southern swing, he remained close to the White House and kept in close touch with the efforts of Dulles and Henry Cabot Lodge to press the anti-invasion case before the United Nations. Transcending the advantage of his official position, before the American public, was the national trust in Dwight Eisenhower as a military expert who would reject any impetuous response that could bring further calamity, factors that helped transform any of the Administration's responsibility for the series of events into, instead, positive political assets. A quick New York *Times* survey reported general agreement that he was the best man in time of trouble.[110]

While siding with the American attitude toward the Middle East, as the British and French landed in Egypt, the Russians took advantage of the preoccupation to rectify another problem. Having, in effect, acknowledged the brutality of the Red Army's response to the Hungarian revolt and withdrawn their forces to allow Imre Nagy greater freedom for changes, they suddenly reversed themselves. Nagy's desire to break with the Warsaw Pact nations and embrace cold-war neutrality could not be tolerated. The Hungarians had carried their rebellion far beyond the Polish example; such blatant defiance of Moscow's firm hold over the satellites threatened to disintegrate the entire bloc. Suddenly and more brutally than before, Soviet tanks and troops swept back into the country with a powerful display of steel and bullets. Rebel "freedom fighters" desperately radioed pleas for Western help, especially from the United States, whose CIA-sponsored Radio Free Europe propaganda broadcasts had been promising aid for attempts to break the Soviet hold. Eisenhower, faced with another challenge to his peace-keeping skill—as well as to the Republican campaign promises of 1952—worked through the United Nations, which approved an American resolution deploring the use of force and calling for a withdrawal; in a personal note to Marshal Bulganin, the President urged, "in the name of humanity and in the cause of peace," the granting of Hungarian self-determination.[111] Such futile gestures succeeded mainly in directing additional attention to the tragedy. With ease, the Russians digested their propaganda loss, obliterated the resistance and jailed Nagy and his followers and quickly installed a reliable puppet, Janos Kadar.

At about ten o'clock on the night of November 2, John Foster Dulles, weary after an all-night UN debate, was back in his Washington home and tried to get some sleep. Twice, sharp stomach pains awakened him; finally, during the early-morning hours, he was rushed to Walter Reed Hospital. At first suspecting either kidney stones or appendicitis, surgeons found, during a two-and-a-half-hour-long operation, that the pains had been caused by cancerous growth protruding into his abdomen.[112] The localized malignancy removed, the operation's success was then pronounced, without public acknowledgment of the findings. Eisenhower then told the nation that Herbert Hoover, Jr., would act in Dulles's place.

Not stated, however, was the extent of the President's personal direction of the turbulent diplomacy. Extended telephone conversations between the White House and New York determined Henry Cabot Lodge's actions in the UN. The President also telephoned several direct calls to 10 Downing Street in efforts to persuade Eden to call off his project and order a withdrawal.[113] But a public call by the Russians for American participation in a joint effort to stop the invasion provoked Eisenhower's scorn. However much the Russians might fulminate, Eisenhower thought that military logistics rendered Moscow just as helpless to intervene in Egypt as the Americans were in Hungary.

But, while the allies occupied Port Said, at the northern end of the canal, the Egyptians, who had already blocked the waterway with sunken ships, appealed for foreign volunteer assistance. Moscow reported scores of Russians ready to respond. Then, just as Americans prepared to vote, Soviet notes to Paris and London warned about Russian intervention and carried reminders about the efficacy of long-range rockets.

After both sides had made their final speeches on election eve, Americans went to the polls on November 6 in the midst of an unresolved crisis. Anthony Eden, panicking at the prospect of Russian intervention even though the goal of seizing the canal had not been realized, telephoned Guy Mollet to say he was stopping the invasion, and the French, assuming that their forces had captured the canal, had little choice but to agree.[114] Their announcement reached the United States at 7 P.M., EST, while the polls were still open. All the allies had achieved for their trouble, however, was a calamitous blockage of the Western European supply line that depended upon Suez. Within several hours, even the early fragmentary returns revealed that Eisenhower and Nixon had exceeded their 1952 majorities. Eastern Jewish big-city voters, however, had favored Stevenson more than they had in 1952, although Eisenhower's over-all total in New York City rose by 5 percent.[115] Eisenhower, much more jubilant than four years earlier—and with much more reason to regard the victory as his own—rushed to Dulles's bedside at Walter Reed the next day. His boyish grin told the story.

Ten days later, Dulles, still hospitalized, received two British visitors, Selwyn Lloyd and Sir Harold Caccia, Whitehall's new ambassador to Washington. The Secretary of State had a question. "Once you started, why didn't you go through with it and get Nasser down?" he asked.

"Foster," said Lloyd, "why didn't you give us a wink?"

"Oh!" answered Dulles. "I couldn't do anything like *that*!"[116]

CHAPTER 36

Patience and Moderation

Nine months after his second inauguration, Dwight Eisenhower, following a usual late-night routine, sat at his White House bedroom desk answering some of the accumulated correspondence. "Someday, if the opportunity ever presents itself," he wrote to a friend, "I shall tell you the story of how I developed the characteristics of patience and moderation that some of our people find so objectionable. For a man of my temperament, as you can readily understand, it wasn't easy."[1]

The route from November of 1956 to the following October had indeed seemed long and puzzling. Never before in his brief political career, even during the days of McCarthy's greatest strength and his early battles against the Republican rightists, had those attributes seemed so vital. Never before, further, had their limitations upon the application of Presidential power become so apparent to both professional and lay observers of the man in the White House. Far from the pattern of the first four years, the personal characteristics of the first President legally restricted from running again by virtue of the Twenty-second Amendment received challenges that were blunt and sometimes not far from contemptuous; moreover, Republicans had begun to tolerate and even second Democratic barbs. Nothing reflected the changed mood better than the temper of his press conferences. One week before confiding to his friend about patience and moderation, Eisenhower felt compelled to respond to a reporter's question about the harsh things being said about him by recalling that the "greatest human the English-speaking race has produced," George Washington, had endured far harsher criticism.[2]

The immunity of his great prestige no longer seemed to protect him from journalistic barbecues. After five years of being called a "lucky" President, commented the conservative *U.S. News & World Report*, things have suddenly changed.[3] As early as March television viewers saw a flushed and angry Eisenhower snap at a reporter and turn away abruptly. Chicago *Daily News* correspondent William McGaffin, pursuing the already hot issue of economy in government, asked about the President's willingness "to do without that pair of helicopters that have been proposed for getting you to the golf course a little faster than you can make it in a car?" Reddening, Eisenhower replied that he did not "think much of the question, because no helicopters have been procured for me to go to a golf course," and then cut off the journalist's attempt to continue.[4] It was, wrote a much cooler President Eisenhower to a man who had sent him a newspaper editorial upholding his right to reach Burning Tree by helicopter, "the silly season for reporters and there is nothing at all to be done about it."[5]

The conference of July 31 proved particularly trying. Not only did the President hear loaded questions about his failure to give energetic support for the school-construction bill as having been responsible for its death in the House, but two other insinuations provoked his anger. Maxwell Gluck, a dapper and amiable little man with a fine pencil-thin mustache, was the multimillionaire board chairman of the Darling Stores Corporation, a chain operation with 140 retail outlets and eighty-five subsidiary concerns. Dividing his time between homes in New York City and Lexington, Kentucky, where he bred and raced thoroughbreds, Gluck had another ambition. He wanted to be an ambassador. For that post he had one qualification: In 1952 he had contributed "around $10,000" to the Republican campaign and, four years later, had given generously to both the party and its Senatorial candidate in New York, Jacob Javits, an amount that fell somewhere between twenty and thirty thousand dollars.[6] Javits, a "modern Republican," had sponsored Gluck's diplomatic appointment. With the Democrats in control of the Senate by just two votes and with the Senator having warned the national committee that he would fight for his man, Gluck's name reached the Senate in late June for confirmation as ambassador to Ceylon.[7]

Secretary Dulles asked the former ambassador to that country, Philip K. Crowe, to prepare Gluck for the post. Crowe found the ambassador-designate likable enough, all right, but nothing about the man's background prepared him for any kind of government work, let alone a diplomatic assignment to an Asian country. He had not even graduated from high school and virtually all his information was limited to what he read in *Women's Wear Daily*. Distressed about his own shortcomings, he explained that the Ceylon assignment resulted from Javits's persuasion that service there would be a valuable contribution to his country.

Crowe, warming up to Gluck's sincerity, voluntarily provided him with all the information he could conceivably need about Ceylon, including a directory of its most important people. During subsequent briefing sessions, the name of the country's Prime Minister, S. W. R. D. Bandaranaike, figured prominently.

But Gluck, insecure and nervous as he appeared before the Foreign Relations Committee, suffered from stage fright when Senator Fulbright asked him about Bandaranaike. Challenged that way before the formidable group, during a closed hearing, Gluck found the pronunciation of the Prime Minister's name beyond his ability. Using an idiomatic expression that was natural for him, he replied, "His name is a bit unfamiliar now, I cannot call it off," which was generally understood as "I can't recall it." He had similar difficulty with Prime Minister Nehru's first name and, under direct questioning from Fulbright, confessed to total ignorance about the United Nations special report condemning the Soviet Union for the Hungarian intervention, although Ceylon had been a member of the commission that had prepared the document. Nor could he tell anything about NATO or SEATO, or anything not directly pertaining to Ceylon. Nevertheless, his confirmation went through.[8]

Eisenhower's patience was tested when confronted with the Gluck situation by Chalmers Roberts during that press conference. Roberts asked whether he knew about the ambassador's ignorance and the extent of his contributions to the party. Angered, Ike said he would never consider any man recommended solely on that basis and expressed confidence in Gluck's ability to learn. A few minutes later, while discussing ways of improving conflict-of-interest laws, the President was told that a current series of articles described his personal holdings as worth about a million dollars. "Could you tell us, perhaps as a guide to other persons entering government service," asked Robert E. Clark of the International News Service, "how you assure that the conflict-of-interest problem never arises in your own case?" Obviously annoyed, Mr. Eisenhower responded that "If that man who knows so much about my business will offer me a million dollars to sell out, he is going to make a sale in a hurry." That provoked a roar of laughter from everybody but the President. When the twenty-seven-minute conference ended, he was overheard saying as he left the room, "My goodness, it gets hot in here."[9] At his next session with the reporters he defended himself against charges of flabby leadership and "self-righteous moralizing," calling them "weak and inconsequential" when compared with the abuse directed at George Washington.[10]

The deterioration had resulted from a combination of circumstances, only partially within the control of the Administration. Oddly, a major contributing factor had been Eisenhower's personal success during the

1956 elections. In a way that had been largely unforeseen, those results, plus the Twenty-second Amendment and the internal dynamics of the Republican party, had combined to make an unsuspecting Dwight Eisenhower a national President rather than the leader of his party.

During those first few post-midnight hours on November 7, Republicans cheered for the GOP. In Washington's Sheraton Park Hotel, as the results showing an Eisenhower landslide held consistent all night, a restive but happy crowd in the huge ballroom awaited the President's appearance. Chants for "Ike" and "Dick" went unanswered. In an upstairs suite, meanwhile, the President waited patiently for a Stevenson concession statement. Finally, 1:25 A.M., television sets showed the Democrat before his own workers in Chicago's Conrad Hilton Hotel reading the text of a telegram to Eisenhower. "You have won not only the election, but also an expression of the great confidence of the American people," it began. "Tonight we are not Republicans and Democrats, but Americans."[11] In Washington, both Eisenhower and the Vice President made their appearance together.

Leonard Hall introduced Nixon, who then yielded to the President, whose arms rose over his head in his famous victory salute. Facing the microphones and cameras, he declared that "modern Republicanism has now proved itself. And America has approved of modern Republicanism." The GOP, he added, through its ability to adhere to the "ideals and the aspirations of America," will "continue to increase in power and influence for decades to come." For the victory he thanked "Republicans, friendly Democrats and Independents."[12]

A four-minute ovation followed. Eisenhower and Nixon wrapped their arms around each other's waists and thrust one-arm victory salutes into the air, as cameras recorded the ebullience. When shouts of "Mamie" and "Pat" came from the crowd, the First Lady waved and Mrs. Nixon bowed gently. At that moment few would have disagreed with Len Hall that the occasion marked a great triumph for the Republican party.[13]

By the next day, however, the national chairman had to change his analysis. The victory, he conceded, was mainly Eisenhower's. Most startling, although the President had drawn close to 58 percent of the popular vote, better than in 1952, for the first time in 108 years a victorious Presidential candidate had failed to place his party in control of either house of Congress. The Senate remained the same, with the Democrats holding a forty-nine to forty-seven vote edge, and the House was virtually unchanged. Moreover, defeated Republican Senatorial candidates included such Eisenhower stalwarts as Dan Thornton, Jim Duff and Arthur Langlie. Possibly most ominous for the party's chances to win in 1960, the President's 457–74 electoral-vote triumph had not stemmed an actual GOP loss of governorships. Only nineteen Republicans remained in state executive offices. George Docking became Kansas's first Democratic Governor. Even Douglas McKay, who had been encouraged by the Administration to leave the Cabinet so he could regain his old governorship in Oregon, lost out to Robert D. Holmes. Furthermore, almost everywhere one turned, figures showed Eisenhower's popular percentage well ahead of the party's statewide and local tickets. In seven Southern states, despite either token or nonexistent GOP candidates at the local level, Eisenhower's percentage was higher than in 1952. In Texas, for example, where he improved by 2.5 percent, his 55.7 percent compared with 15.9 percent for the Republican gubernatorial candidate. Nor did ultraconservatives have much to cheer about. J. Bracken Lee, Herman Welker and George Bender were all defeated; and a right-wing Republican effort in Wisconsin to deny re-election to Alexander Wiley had failed. Only in agricultural districts did the Eisenhower margin slip.

The Negro vote, too, proved interesting. For the first time since the New Deal had diverted blacks from their old loyalty to the GOP, a Republican Presidential candidate had reversed the trend. Stevenson's own civil-rights position lacked sufficient strength to compensate for his party's sorry national record and pusillanimous platform plank, and Negroes were wooed to the President's name for much the same reason as other Americans. Adam Clayton Powell's Harlem constituency turned in an Eisenhower gain of 16.5 percent, and Chicago's largest Negro district went up almost 11 percent. While Eisenhower's national percentage gained 2.2 percent, his standing among blacks climbed by five points to 47 percent.[14]

"The old and once powerful orthodox Taft wing," proclaimed William S. White in the New York *Times* on November 11, "once predominant in Congress, lies in ruins . . . [because of] its failure to preserve the lives of many orthodox Republicans." Considering that Len Hall had gradually installed Eisenhower Republicans in party posts throughout the country, including the national committee, the President's optimism about the triumph of modern Republicanism seemed warranted. Venturing the hope, at his news conference one week after the elections, that Old Guard "doubters" would be convinced by the results, Eisenhower boldly defined his political creed. It was, he said, the type of "political philosophy that recognizes clearly the responsibility of the Federal Government to take the lead in making certain that the productivity of our great economic machine is distributed so that no one will suffer disaster, privation, through no fault of his own. Now," he added, "this covers the wide field of education and health, and so on." Asked, then, whether he intended to exert leadership when working with Congress, he explained that "I am not one of the desk-pounding type that likes to stick out his jaw and look like he is bossing the show." The reporters laughed when he added, "I would rather try to persuade a man to go along, because once I have persuaded him he will stick. If I scare him, he will stay just as long as he is scared, and then he is gone."[15]

Thus, the politics of conciliation between the White House and Congress showed no sign of abatement; and the President, speaking from the top of his strength, appeared to have mastered the situation. During the next two months, prior to the second inauguration, his ability to lead the way with ease seemed secure. Despite his weariness and longing for some golf and relaxation at Augusta, Dulles's continued hospitalization kept Ike in Washington, where, working together with Herbert Hoover, Jr., he filled the vacuum in the State Department. When Prime Minister Eden, harried by the turn of events that left his foray into Egypt a shambles and with the Laborites clamoring for his hide, telephoned early in the morning of November 7—only some seven hours after Eisenhower's victorious appearance at the Park Sheraton—to suggest a quick flight to Washington by both he and Mollet for intensive discussions of the situation, the President's instinctive reaction was positive, even enthusiastic. Any opportunity to mitigate the sudden breach in the Western alliance seemed like good sense. Unhappily, that evening he had to call back Eden to inform the Briton of the State Department's counsel against having the United States risk giving any appearance of having been a participant in the Middle Eastern affair, a matter of particular urgency since the allies had yet to comply with the UN resolution to withdraw and permit an international emergency force to maintain the cease-fire.[16] On November 14, having already dispatched U-2 reconnaissance planes to patrol the Syrian skies to monitor the southward movement of any Russian planes, Eisenhower warned the Kremlin that their entry into the area would again compel American opposition to aggression within the UN. He did not exclude other possible alternatives.[17] Many additional hours were spent deliberating the release of an emergency supply of oil, in accordance with a plan drawn up by Arthur Flemming's Office of Defense Mobilization, the Interior and Justice Departments, to relieve the critical shortage in Western Europe. Should England and France be aided before they had agreed to a troop withdrawal? Despite the desperate situation created by the blockage of the canal by more than forty sunken vessels, the Administration was reluctant to release the additional two hundred thousand barrels a day. Both the UN and Nasser would be undercut. Finally, Washington's pressure and threats to hold back the oil impressed London sufficiently to achieve compliance.[18] At last, getting away to Augusta on November 26, after telling a friend that any additional engagement "merely constitutes another nail in the coffin of my hopes," Eisenhower nevertheless fortified himself by taking an unusually large staff for the heavier work load required along with golf, bridge and hunting.[19] His plan to remain about ten days, however, extended so that about half of December was spent at the course. On January 5, one week after returning to Washington from a second stay at Augusta, the President addressed a joint session of Congress to request what, when finally passed in March, became known as the "Eisenhower Doctrine": legislative authorization to send American military forces into the Middle East "against overt aggression from any nation controlled by International Communism," to be used only "at the desire of the nation attacked," as a means of discouraging miscalculation. Thus, the lessons of Korea and memories of Bricker amendment debates continued to mold the President's international responses, for he already had whatever constitutional authority he needed to deploy troops.[20] The President, therefore, had fulfilled the desires of the American people by first ending the war and then moving to maintain the peace, an act that gave him high popular endorsement. The Gallup Poll also showed, in January, his standing with the public reached its highest point, 79 percent expressing approval of his handling of the Presidency.[21] Comparing Eisenhower's position with four years earlier, the New York *Times* noted that he "fully enjoys the prestige, the emoluments and the stimulus of living in the White House." The professionals, the paper added, were rating him as "the greatest instinctive politician since FDR."[22]

The President's most talented speech writer, Emmet Hughes, has recalled that Ike spent most of three days with him in patient preparation of the Inaugural Address. "He never seemed more quick and expedient or more deeply committed to vigorous action," wrote Hughes.[23] Since the twentieth coincided with a Sunday, the actual swearing-in of both the President and the Vice President took place at a private White House ceremony, with only a Navy photographer recording the event for history. "Swede" Hazlett was the one outsider present. At the public ceremony on Monday, an overcast day in Washington with the temperature in the low forties, a somewhat smaller crowd than the festive throngs of 1953 watched the President being given the oath of office by Chief Justice Warren. Nixon was sworn in by Senator Knowland, his rival at the political right. Wearing a black Homburg and looking remarkably fit, considering his two recent illnesses, the President paid tribute to the Hungarian martyrs and, in a thirteen-and-a-half-minute address, delivered a somber message that gave the audience little opportunity to applaud. Sounding as though Taft and the isolationists had never existed, he described America's responsibility to all nations as including the need "to help others rise from misery, however far the scene of suffering may be from our shores." As the crowd listened intently, he said, "No people can live to itself alone. The economic need of all nations—in mutual dependence—makes isolation an impossibility; not even America's prosperity could long survive if other nations did not also prosper. No nation," he reminded his listeners, "can be a fortress, lone and strong and safe."[24]

Thus was the international profile of modern Republicanism elucidated. Domestically, too, while emphasizing prudent fiscal policies for a strong economy, nothing had been done to upset the past. The Eighty-fourth Congress had granted a further expansion of Social Security coverage, and the Administration had also gone on record in favor of civil-rights legislation, aid for public housing and school construction, a boost in the minimum-wage rate and an interstate highway program financed by new taxes to help to meet the over $30 billion outlay expected in federal and state funds. The Administration's major difference with the Democrats usually involved its desire to minimize the cost of such programs. Eisenhower, too, had preserved the character of the Supreme Court, which had first been so dramatically altered by FDR. If anything, the first three appointments Eisenhower had already made were on the average more liberal than Truman's choices. After Earl Warren, mildly conservative—although not on civil rights—and scholarly John Marshall Harlan received a seat in 1955 and, in 1956, the President chose a liberal Democrat from New Jersey, William Brennan. Consistently, the President's fifth State of the Union message to Congress, delivered on the tenth of January, stressed goals consistent with the Administration's more liberal tone. He called for resubmission of the defeated civil-rights legislation and the school construction bill ("uncomplicated by provisions dealing with the complex problems of integration"), membership in the proposed Organization for Trade Cooperation to facilitate the export of American commerce, and expressed a willingness "to enter any reliable agreement which would reverse the trend toward ever more devastating nuclear weapons." In dealing with the problem posed by the current inflationary trend, he appealed to both business and labor to hold the line, for business to be content with "reasonable" profits and for wage increases to be "reasonably related to improvements in productivity." Only in his appeal for the need to halt the "steady depreciation of the value of our money" did he express conservative thinking.[25]

Then, when Leonard Hall announced his coming return to private law practice, Eisenhower made clear his choice for successor more directly than his original support for Hall. Following the Chief Executive's desires, the national committee chose Meade Alcorn, a moderate politician from Connecticut, who defined modern Republicanism as "enlightened conservatism." The President, acting as though he had been liberated from the restraints of the right wing, seemed ready and eager to move forward. Still, even during the height of his great political prestige, familiar noises were returning.

The party's ultraconservatives had begun to act as though they, too, had scored a personal victory and had not, only weeks earlier, fallen into line behind the President thankful he had chosen to run again and dependent upon him for success. But the Eisenhower triumph had, after all, done nothing for them; his popularity had not been transferred; as a lame-duck President, what influence could he have over 1960? The more he talked about modern Republicanism, the more the rebellion simmered, although the validity of all their old suspicions about the man who had snatched the nomination from Taft had been substantiated. Thus, within two weeks after Election Day and the President's tribute to the success of modern Republicanism, Joe McCarthy announced he would run for re-election to the Senate in 1958 under the battle cry: "Get the US out of the UN and the UN out of the US."[26] In early January the ultraconservatives' best hope, Senator Knowland, announced his retirement at the expiration of his term. That immediately opened the likelihood that his attempt to salvage the party from the Eastern "liberals" might come via the governorship of California. On January 18, Representative Richard Simpson of Pennsylvania, upon his third election as chairman of the Republican Congressional Committee, urged the GOP to "sell" the party and not Eisenhower. They had, he warned, spent too much time under the "warm glow" of the President's name. "We 'Iked' the American people," he declared, "and neglected to include the Republican party label."[27] After the submission of the Administration's proposed budget for fiscal year 1958, a record-breaking $71.8 billion, Representative Clare Hoffman, a Michigan Republican, charged that Ike and "his left-wing, free-spending, international one-world advisers propose to disinfect, fumigate, purify, renovate, unify and remake the Republican party." Describing himself as one of Eisenhower's "loyal supporters, one who keeps him from going too far," Hoffman suggested that it might be possible, even under the Twenty-second Amendment, for the President to run as a Democrat in 1960.[28] In Chicago, the Abraham Lincoln National Republican Club sponsored a seminar on "real Republicanism" versus "modern Republicanism," and 1,300 people in the Sheraton Hotel ballroom cheered as Joe McCarthy attacked atoms-for-peace as an " 'Atoms for War' program." Wouldn't it be easier, asked the Senator, "if we were just to send a shipload of atom bombs to the Communist empire and be done with it?" Other prominent speakers included J. Bracken Lee, William Jenner and Herman Welker, as the President's foreign-aid program and the "executive's accumulation of power" were denounced.[29]

While only a nascent revolt, it contained the elements of a wide-ranging movement that had the tacit support of many silent Republicans who desired to return the party to "orthodox Republicanism."[30] The challenge to the President could render his patience and moderation incompatible with the needs of leadership. By early 1957, the Administration suddenly found itself besieged by conservative anger about spending and growing racial violence that threatened to jeopardize the feasibility of moderation.

A long time in the making, the great budget battle of 1957 could not have been avoided. As early as March 30, 1956, the outgoing Director of the Budget, Rowland Hughes, sent a memorandum to the President warning that the initial zeal for reducing expenditures, "the zest for this crusade," which helped to bring the Administration into power, had been mitigated by the claims of various interest groups. "Special pleaders for particular expenditures," Hughes called them, who wanted allocations "regardless of the impact on the budget as a whole." Pressure to satisfy such demands was undermining that initial zeal. Cabinet and agency heads had become convinced, "equally sincerely," that their own budgets could not be reduced. Therefore, Hughes pointed out, the record of the past three years, while one of "progressively reduced expenditure totals," had shown that "the majority of the pressures for the future will be in the contrary direction." Should that continue, the Administration's opponents would be justified in claiming that the spending proclivities of the New Deal had been matched. The principal violator, the Budget Director maintained, was Defense Secretary Charles Wilson, who stubbornly held to successive increases that amounted to several percent each year. All were related to new programs; but, as Hughes pointed out, they were additive rather than replacements for lesser priority projects.[31]

Therefore, when the Administration advanced a budget for fiscal 1958 that totaled $71.8 billions and also included an additional $73 billion for the authorization of current and future federal programs, the storm began. Exacerbating the situation however, was the President's continued faith in the stature and reasonableness of Congress to work with him even if he did not "pound the desk" in order to grant the appraisal of the country's needs. Convinced by George Humphrey that spending had to be cut, but still frustrated after long and determined sessions spent with Wilson and the new Director of the Budget, Percival Brundage, Eisenhower, at the same time, showed his readiness to accept all reasonable suggestions for possible cuts. In fact, during a New Year's Day meeting with Congressional leaders from both parties, he urged their cooperation in a mutual effort to pare costs.[32]

That 1958 budget approximated Eisenhower's vision of the sad necessity rather than his ideal. All the bright hopes of economy had been waylaid by a combination of factors, largely beyond the scope of any Administration's efforts, that included an inflationary trend, the need to raise salaries of government workers and military personnel, interest payments on the federal debt, foreign-aid commitments and rising defense requirements. The latter, it was pointed out, proved the demise of the "spirit of Geneva." But, as Eisenhower said about the military, "This country can choke itself to death piling up military expenditures just as surely as it can defeat itself by not spending itself for protection," a sentiment, of course, that had motivated the "New Look" program.[33]

The President's own dilemma and desire to effectuate economies while paying for what he held necessary led to the creation of the popular impression that he and his Secretary of the Treasury were at vigorous odds about the Administration's request. Humphrey, who was delaying his return to the Mark Hanna Company until the fiscal 1958 program could be secured, had been engaged in a running clash with Charlie Wilson over Defense Department spending. He had hoped for a $3 to $4 billion budgetary surplus that could be used to reduce the national debt; subsequent stabilization of federal expenditures might then make possible a long-delayed tax cut by the 1959 budget. Total expenditures would thereby be kept below the $70 billion mark. Wilson, however, held that, although Defense claimed well more than half of the total budget, it could be reduced no further. He had wrestled with the figures over and over again and brought them down "billion by painful billion," and nobody in government could be more rigid than he when the time came to take a stand.[34] Reviewing the whole situation with Wilson and Brundage during his Augusta stay in December, the President reluctantly yielded to the Secretary's $38 billion defense figure. Wilson's argument that Russian desires for disarmament negotiations made American ability to bargain from a "position of strength" all the more important helped to persuade Mr. Eisenhower. Yet, within the councils of the Administration, as well as with the President, remained the feeling that Wilson had become unable to control the military's thirst for more money. The civilian businessmen brought to Washington by the Republicans were themselves continually amazed by the tendency of seemingly modest incipient programs to blossom fantastically into major expenditures as they progressed through the Pentagon.[35] Humphrey's subsequent public critique of spending policies provoked the impression of a split between the President and his most influential Cabinet officer.

But, however differently it seemed, there was nothing inconsistent about Eisenhower in the affair. When, at a Cabinet meeting before Congress received the budget, Humphrey suggested that he send an open letter to the press to demonstrate the Administration's concern with a budget that had gotten out of hand, that not only failed to make a pretense of moving toward the famous Morningside Heights agreement with Taft to lower spending to $60 billion—a foolishly stated objective in view of inflationary realities—but one that actually pierced the seemingly sacred $70 billion ceiling, Eisenhower agreed that it would be a good idea. He preferred Humphrey to make a statement before the press, however, rather than send a letter. The statement was revised many times and scrutinized before the entire Cabinet. Eisenhower himself helped in its preparation.[36] Yet, when Humphrey faced the reporters on January 15, ostensible dissent from Eisenhower's own ideas captivated the media.

Its purpose, of course, suited Eisenhower's own goal. Humphrey's opening statement acknowledging the difficulty of preparing that budget and the stress that all pressures for increased federal spending were responsible for a situation that threatened the soundness of the dollar were fine. "It just kept creeping up on us," he explained. "Everybody from the public all the way through have just been looking to the federal government for more and more and more and we have not controlled it." Strict economies, he urged, were necessary during the next eighteen months, particularly because $40 billion for military goods and services tended to stimulate demand without increasing the number of consumer goods, creating a perfect climate for inflation. His call for "substantial reductions" during that period, however, permitted the appearance of a break with the President. But most startling, and tending to obscure everything else, he said, was a colorful comment made during the last minute and a half of the long conference. "If we fail to economize over a long period of time," he warned, "I will predict that you will have a depression that will curl your hair, because we are just taking too much money out of this economy that we need to make the jobs that you have to have as time goes by."[37] Quickly, word spread that Humphrey had predicted the inevitability of a "hair-curling depression."

Nothing could have publicized the situation more effectively. At the President's own next session with the press, the first question asked for his reaction to the statement that, in the words of the Associated Press reporter, "we are going to have a hair-curling depression if spending isn't cut." Immediately and clearly, the Chief Executive pointed out that the Secretary's comment did not pertain to the immediate future but, rather, to the effects of a "long-term continuation of spending of the order of which we are now doing." Carefully, too, he tried to place Humphrey's position in its correct perspective by revealing his own role in the writing of the statement that had led to the sensational comment. At that point, however, the President, still trying to have it both ways, unwittingly opened the gates to the budget-slashers. Assuming his own regard of Congress as a coordinate branch of government would be reciprocated, he invited all critics of the budget "to find some place where he might save another dollar." If "Congress can," he added, "it is their duty to do it."[38]

That marked an open-hunting season on the budget. Both parties, with the Democrats especially delighted at the development, pounced on the invitation as though the President had admitted to the extravagance of many expenditures. With conservatives leading the way, a tide of predictions came from Capitol Hill, all the way from the claims of Styles Bridges and William Knowland that from two to two and a half billions could be reduced, to Virginia's old Democratic boss and Senator, Harry Byrd, the chairman of the Senate Finance Committee, who topped them all by claiming he could personally lop off six and a half billion dollars. Joe Martin, the GOP's House leader, aimed at "three billion or so" and his Democratic counterpart, Speaker Sam Rayburn, figured that somewhere between three to five billion could be pared. When the House then passed a resolution asking the President to indicate where he thought substantial cuts might be made, Eisenhower's fellow Republicans attacked what they considered an abdication of legislative authority.[39] The heavy volume of anti-budget mail reaching the White House that spring forced Sinclair Weeks to compose a form letter defending the Administration's accomplishments. At the head of his list was the statement that "Peace was gained and for four years has been kept."[40]

On the defensive, the President appealed to Congress to avoid decimating his requests by recalling the Administration's past fiscal accomplishments, the dropping of a quarter of a million employees from the federal payroll, the $7.4 billion tax cut in 1954 and three consecutive balanced budgets.[41] Then, hearing that he would take his case before the public, Democratic Majority Leader Lyndon Johnson delivered a barbed "welcome" of such appeals by suggesting that they might be more effectively directed toward members of the President's official family. But the President, abandoning his past relationship with Congress, fought back. On May 14, in a televised "fireside chat," he failed so badly to state his case with conviction and urgency that the White House quickly summoned Emmet Hughes back from New York to prepare the following week's public defense of the mutual-security portion of the budget. That second appeal, in contrast with Eisenhower's first appearance, suddenly led to acclamations that the man who only the day before was accused of being a pathetically weak, vacillating leader had regained the initiative over both Republicans and Democrats.[42] The President and the White House staff also directed the full pressure of the Executive Branch, by telephone and in person, for the party to unite in support of the Administration.

But, as Charles Murphy pointed out in *Fortune*, the President had found "his lines of communication with his own party snarled and himself, for a while at least, in confused retreat." Had it not been for the budget, Murphy wrote, the schism would have been provoked by something else.[43] With its denial of the old $60 billion promise, the budget did lend itself to suspicions that "modern Republicanism" was "New Dealism" decorated in more respectable clothing. Senators Cooper, Javits and Prescott Bush all charged that right-wingers dominating their own party were exploiting the controversy to attack Eisenhower's "modern Republicanism."[44] Both the National Association of Manufacturers and the Chamber of Commerce were brought into open opposition against a Republican "big business" administration. The *Wall Street Journal*, becoming more indignant than at any time since the New Deal, accused the conservatives in Washington of recommending "a whole slew of new legislation designed to take the people's money and spend it for them on things they are better able to provide for themselves." *Commonweal* observed that the President was having less success than with the country at large in selling his brand of moderation and that "anti-Eisenhower whispers inside the GOP have been growing louder and louder. . . ."[45]

The final result was, as Sherman Adams has admitted, "a serious and disturbing personal defeat" for the President.[46] Four billion dollars finally came off the total budget, and the President's hopes for mutual security fell $1 billion short of his initial request. Ironically, however, a sudden spur in the arms race, motivated by the Russian launching of the first space satellite. Sputnik, on October 4, 1957, led to such increased demands for military and scientific spending that the economizers were overwhelmed. "These potential new weapons are not toys," urged the American Aviation Publishers in newspaper display advertising under the heading "An open letter to President Eisenhower." "The nation that first controls space will control the world. The choice is democracy or slavery. The launching of their first Sputniks and space rockets are much, much more than 'neat scientific tricks.' . . . And the American people expect you to do something about it."[47] That push, coinciding with a serious recession, left George Humphrey's successor, Robert B. Anderson, with the embarrassment, in fiscal 1959, of a deficit in excess of $12 billion, the largest ever during peacetime.

CHAPTER 37

The Shrinking Center

In 1957, A COMBINATION of forces helped to ensure the success of the first post-Reconstruction civil-rights act. The Administration and Congressional Republicans had interpreted the 1956 Negro vote as promising its possible reconversion to the GOP. As early as December, Republican Congressional leaders were told by Attorney General Brownell that the President and the Department of Justice were going to resubmit the requests that had failed before; the President himself, meeting with them on December 31, stressed the importance of moderate civil-rights legislation.[1]

Vice President Nixon, in his role as President of the Senate, furthered the Administration's goal by deciding that Senate Rule XXII, which had been used to protect repeated filibusters, was not binding without re-affirmation by the new session.[2] Although a two-thirds vote for cloture was retained, Democratic liberals agreed that the Vice President had strengthened his own position as a potential Presidential candidate. At the same time, Majority Leader Johnson, similarly ambitious and seeking to rectify his own image as an anti-civil-rights Southerner, informed his colleagues at the start of the year that some sort of legislation would pass. No filibuster did develop. But extensive debates took place, mostly over granting the Attorney General power to initiate suits seeking court injunctions against those depriving individuals of any civil right which Southerners feared would, with the retention of an 1866 statute empowering the President to use armed forces to "aid in the execution of the provisions," bring about integration at bayonet point. Ultimately, that was discarded, as was the 1866 statue. But the bill did grant the federal government the right to seek injunctions against the obstruction or deprivation of voting rights. Claims by conservatives, including Johnson, that jury trials should be guaranteed led to a compromise that left that decision up to the judges in voting-rights cases. The act also established a six-member bipartisan Civil Rights Commission with legal powers to investigate violations of voting and equal-rights laws. Thus, what had been the victim of mutual scuttling by both parties prior to the 1956 elections won wide bipartisan endorsement, by 279–97 in the House and 72–18 in the Senate, largely in preparation for 1960. Although the President was reportedly "bitterly disappointed" at the inclusion of the jury-trial device—which liberals feared Southerners would use to exonerate violators—and convinced those who met with him privately, including Senator Richard Russell, that he considered legislation imperative, his public attitude continued to display indifference, remoteness and even ignorance about what was happening.[3] The result carried the brand of Congress and the Administration rather than the enthusiasm of a determined President. The continuing civil-rights controversy, however, challenged his neutrality.

By early 1957 the militant segregationists had dropped all pretenses of confining resistance to mere constitutional challenges. Governor LeRoy Collins of Georgia, faced with a violent eruption when Negroes occupied the front seats of busses, suspended service in Tallahassee. Montgomery's newly integrated busses drew repeated sniper fire and, after the midnight bombings of four Negro churches in the city, suspended all operations.[4] On February 14, dynamite ripped the heart of the Negro district in Clinton, Tennessee. A KKK cross burned at the U.S. Marine Corps base at Camp Lejeune, North Carolina, touching off a race riot between groups of servicemen, and explosions jolted two black sections of Bessemer, Alabama.[5] Near Americus, Georgia, Koinonia Farm, a biracial communal group of some sixty people that had existed since 1942 in fulfillment of their concept of brotherhood, suddenly became the target for dynamite and rifle fire that threatened to eradicate the community. Appeals to President Eisenhower by its founder, Dr. Clarence Jordan, simply brought an explanation from the Attorney General that the matter was outside the reach of federal jurisdiction.[6] Although Brownell then reminded Governor Marvin Griffin about the state's responsibility, the attacks continued.[7]

Predictably, Negro anger deepened. When the Administration moved to expand immigration authorization and to extend mutual-security funds to provide for admission to the country of refugees from the Hungarian disaster, obvious contrasts were drawn. Fred Morrow, himself involved in helping to set up the Hungarian Relief Committee, was surprised by the depth of black bitterness about the American role in going all out to provide the survivors with housing, clothing, food and jobs. In Chicago, the White House administrative assistant found that "Negro clients in dire need of relief often experienced great difficulty in having their needs met and in finding benevolent and sympathetic treatment" despite the recent action of those agencies in bending "over backward to administer to the needs of Hungarian aliens."[8] When Eisenhower dispatched Vice President Nixon to Austria just before Christmas to act as his "personal representative" to study Hungarian refugee problems, additional bitterness jelled. The Reverend Fred Shuttlesworth, pastor of the Bethel Baptist Church in Birmingham, Alabama, suggested that Nixon travel instead one thousand miles to study problems at home instead of eight thousand miles abroad to spread Americanism.[9]

On January 11, the day after the Montgomery bombings, Dr. Martin Luther King, Jr., convened a conference in Atlanta of Negro leaders from ten states, a meeting that resulted in an urgent request for the President to "come immediately" to a Southern city and utter words of "wise counsel" on the disorders. Their telegrams suggested that he make a "major speech in a major Southern city asking all persons to abide by the Supreme Court's decisions as the law of the land."[10] A telegram to Brownell also demanded a meeting with the Attorney General.

The next day the President announced travel plans—a three-day tour to the Southwest drought country to dramatize the plight of the land and its farms and rangers, a trip he had not made since July of 1953. His expedition, he hoped, would spur regional efforts to solve the problem.[11] Immediately, Harlem's *Amsterdam News* ran a front-page "bulletin" announcing that their efforts to get a reply to the black leaders' request "brought the comment that the White House press secretaries were on tour of the drought areas with the President."[12]

When asked on January 23 about the appeal made by Dr. King and the others, the President seemed unfamiliar with the events. Apparently as unaware as the public that Warren Olney III, the Assistant Attorney General in charge of the Criminal Division, had already replied to King and Shuttlesworth rejecting their invitations to make a major speech in the South on civil rights, Eisenhower turned to Jim Hagerty and exchanged whispers with his press secretary. Turning back to the reporter, the President merely explained that Governor Adams had turned the issue over for study by the Justice Department. Questioned again about his response on February 6, the President explained that he had "a pretty good and sizable agenda" on his desk every day and "as you know, I insist on going for a bit of recreation every once in a while, and I do that because I think it is necessary to keep up to the state of fitness essential to this job." While he had often discussed the subject in both North and South, he added, "I don't know what another speech would do about the thing right now." He did not, however, offer a single word of condemnation about the violence.[13]

Clearly, the Administration was not movable without militancy. A. Philip Randolph had used the threat of a "March on Washington" to push FDR into granting an FEPC for federal employees in 1941. Again, in 1946, such a threat was renewed. Now the Southern Negro Leaders Conference met for two days in New Orleans in mid-February and then Dr. King held a press conference. Continued Presidential stubbornness, he warned, would cause thousands of whites and Negroes to march to Washington. "This will not be a political march," he said. "It will be rooted in deep spiritual faith." Joining King in formulating such plans were Randolph as the reviver of his old project, the Reverend Ralph Abernathy, Shuttlesworth, Roy Wilkins and King's secretary, Bayard Rustin.[14]

Plans were made and pressure was put on Washington. Abernathy warned that Presidential silence would provoke a half million blacks and whites to march. In Brooklyn, a few days later, his projected demonstration strength rose to one million. The Southern Presbyterian Church, representing 850,000 members in sixteen Southern states, supported their black brethren by issuing the most sweeping indictment of segregation ever made by a major Southern church group. While they were both in Ghana that March for the inauguration of the newly independent African nation, Dr. King personally urged Vice President Nixon to travel to Dixie after his trip to Africa to speak out in behalf of Negroes being bombed and persecuted. The Vice President responded by inviting King to meet with him privately in Washington.[15]

There was still no real advocacy of militant action by the blacks. By giving their "march" a spiritual overtone and calling it a Prayer Pilgrimage for Freedom—a concept that emerged early in the planning—they hoped to arouse the nation's conscience and so provoke the President and Congress into action. But standing apart from the planning and yet thoroughly interested was Adam Clayton Powell, Jr.

Powell, increasingly criticized for having aided the Administration's re-election, was watching the movement's leadership pass over his head. In her newspaper column, Eleanor Roosevelt accused him of deserting sincere reformers by seeking publicity with amendments that had no chance of passage. She clearly implied that he was among those who "try to gain personal power and a personal following through methods they know must fail."[16]

An attack from Mrs. Roosevelt was a serious matter. The widow of FDR was perhaps the most admired white American woman among

Powell's people. In New York City, her column was carried by the *Post*, an afternoon paper of militant liberalism and with a wide Harlem readership. Powell, assessing the situation, appealed to the Administration for aid. On March 28 he asked Sherman Adams to forward a letter that Powell had written to the President. A proper reply from the White House, Powell pointed out in his note to Adams, "would help tremendously" in view of the criticism.[17]

Powell's letter informed the President that he had opposed efforts to persuade Ike to speak in the South. But, he wrote, a "word spoken now with continuing emphasis by you would not only have an impact for good, but would bring hope to millions of Americans that the Chief Executive of our land is concerned with this problem."[18]

In short, Powell wanted to regain his prestige as a civil-rights fighter. With virtually every other prominent black leader issuing public calls for the President to travel to the South and deliver a vigorous condemnation of anti-Negro lawlessness, the President's continued silence was becoming more obvious. Powell was offering him a compromise. Speak out, he was saying, but do it from Washington. Some kind of statement seemed inevitable. Conscious of retaining credits for having supported the Administration's re-election, Powell was in effect asking that such a concession be made as a public reply to his request, in much the same way a local politician becomes the funnel for patronage that is passed down from the top. It would dramatize that Adam Clayton Powell, Jr., alone among the civil-rights crusaders, could bring the Administration into the fight. It would also vindicate Powell for having supported Eisenhower in 1956.

After Powell's letter was circulated through the White House staff, Assistant Attorney General Olney advised Max Rabb that such an exchange of correspondence between the Harlem Congressman and the President would not "serve any useful purpose" and that whatever might be said should be directed to the entire Congress. Olney's memo was written on April 15.[19]

Powell, unaware of the eventual disposition of his request but hopeful, now made renewed efforts to ingratiate himself with the Administration by informing the White House about the Pilgrimage planning activities of the Negro leadership. He also told them in clear terms that, unlike the black activists, he was very much opposed to such a "March on Washington" and would do what he could to stop it.[20] At the same time he told that to Rabb, Powell telephoned Adams to relay the news that Wilkins, Randolph and King had called a conference of key Negroes to meet on April 5 to plan the march. Powell's message, left with Adams's secretary, said the event would occur in May and contained Powell's offer to talk to the Assistant to the President about it at any time before

April 5.[21] Adams, however, instructed Rabb to keep a close watch over the conference.[22] Powell, in turn, assured Rabb that he would attend the session and report its proceedings. "He is still a little fearful," Rabb wrote to Adams, that "Martin Luther King may still try to make a march on Washington." He advised that Powell would do his best to "keep the meeting under control."[23] Powell had volunteered to spy on the black leaders for the Administration.

The conference met at the Metropolitan Baptist Church in Washington. May 17, the third anniversary of the Court's school-desegregation decision, was chosen as the most appropriate date for a gathering of an expected 50,000 people at the Lincoln Memorial. Powell dutifully conveyed this information to Rabb, along with the report that, while the march idea had been accepted, he and a few others had kept Dr. King from planning it as a protest of the President's failure to speak out in a Southern city.[24] The Prayer Pilgrimage concept had, therefore, prevailed. Giving himself credit for what the black leaders had been planning to do all along, Powell assured Rabb that the resultant non-political but spiritual occasion would not embarrass the President.[25]

A few days later, on April 14, Powell spoke in Atlanta, Georgia. Rather than attempt to defend his support of the Administration in 1956, Powell's statement ignored the Republican record and concentrated on a safer target. "Under creeping Eastlandism," he declared, "moderation, go slow and gradualism mean stop, stand still, do nothing." His public denunciation of "gradualism" and "moderation" contrasted with private assurances to the Administration that he was doing his best to head off a militant demonstration by the black leadership. Nor did he yet see fit to take advantage of the opportunity to attack the Republicans for having frustrated the Administration's Negro supporters.[26]

Powell's March 28 request to the President was, at that time, still alive. From Powell's point of view there was every reason to believe that it would succeed. His White House meeting of the previous October had been with the man known throughout the world as the Ike whose smile and warmth could charm the most sophisticated. Of Eisenhower's willingness to cooperate with Powell's little compromise, the Congressman must have been very confident. After all, Powell had engaged in a public exchange of statements with the President after his 1953 meeting with Rabb over desegregating the naval bases. Again in 1956 mutual interests had brought them together. Why not once more? But, as Olney's memo had advised, no such word came.

The Prayer Pilgrimage for Freedom was, in effect, the first civil-rights "March on Washington," foreshadowing the major one that occurred six years later. The crowd estimate was fifteen thousand, according to the local police and, in the view of the Pilgrimage planners, twenty-seven thousand. Coretta King, in her 1969 reminiscence of her martyred husband, elevated the figure fondly to thirty-seven thousand.[27]

Not only did the Pilgrimage disappoint the sponsors, but it received scant attention from the press. The New York *Times* ran a simple article with only two and a half paragraphs at the bottom of the front page and less than a column on page twenty-three. Neither additional background informational stories nor editorial comment appeared. The editorial page, instead, was devoted to gratitude for the safe recovery of a little boy from a well in Manorville, Long Island, Nasser, the Gross National Product, taxes, labor reform and Armed Forces Day. In the national news magazines, neither *Newsweek* nor *Time* carried a single word. Only *The Nation*, with a sympathetic article by Dan Wakefield, and *The Christian Century* noted that it had occurred. Even *Ebony*, the popular Negro magazine, ignored it altogether.

But the *Amsterdam News*, in its full account of the occasion, reported to its Harlem readers that Adam Clayton Powell had drawn "little raves" by blasting both parties for inaction and calling for a "third force" of Negro ministers in the fight for civil rights. "We are meeting here today," he told the Lincoln Memorial crowd, "because we are getting more from a dead Republican than from live Democrats and Republicans."[28]

With the national impact of the Prayer Pilgrimage nil and the event forgotten almost as soon as the crusading vanguard disbanded from the steps of the Lincoln Memorial, its sponsors were left with no choice but to implement available means of dramatizing their need before the public, the Congress and the President. And to them, Eisenhower, the man Americans trusted above anyone else, was the key to their ability to demonstrate their need. Nobody else, they believed, could create a more congenial climate for better racial relations. There was no substitute for his moral leadership.[29] But, with the White House watching the progress of its civil-rights legislation with one eye and the Southern reaction with the other, their request—far more than when first proposed—had become a matter of much greater sensitivity than a routine visit to the President's office by a delegation of spokesmen.

The burden of the black demands funneling into the White House centered on Fred Morrow, the closest Negro to the President. Accordingly, pressure for him to move the White House staff in their direction became increasingly intense. Failure meant excoriation as an "Uncle Tom" working to promote the fortunes of a "racist" Administration.[30] Within the White House, Morrow, noting that more than a year had passed since the first suggestions had been made, reported that the apparent apathy had convinced rank-and-file Negroes of their abandonment by the President. Unrest, he warned, was high; tensions had reached a new peak. "If the President will consent to see Messrs. King, Randolph and Wilkins at the same time," he advised, he and Max Rabb could work out the details and take care of protocol briefings.[31] Meanwhile, Rabb had told Dr. King that he and one or two others would be able to speak with the President in the near future, but he had to have patience. It could not be arranged until either the Congressional debate on civil rights had subsided or the session on Capitol Hill had ended. King seemed agreeable.[32]

But the pressure continued. A. Philip Randolph wanted a larger session, one that included sixteen black leaders who would represent various religious, civic, fraternal and labor organizations. Advancing a request that had originated at a "State of the Race Conference" that had been held in the capital on April 24, 1956, Randolph explained that such a group would like to discuss with the President the "basic socio-economic problems that are of vital concern to millions of American Negro citizens and which have a fundamental impact on the general welfare of our nation." All seventy-three participants at that 1956 session had agreed on the importance of seeing the President.[33] Morrow approved of the Randolph plan; and Assistant Attorney General William Rogers, soon to replace the retiring Herbert Brownell, Jr., had overcome his previous doubts about the value of such a session.

The Reverend Dr. King, seemingly mollified by Rabb, nevertheless met with Vice President Nixon in June. Accompanied by the Reverend Ralph Abernathy, King explained his endorsement of even compromise legislation that appeared about to emerge from Congress as better than nothing at all and, anticipating assistance from its provisions, informed the Vice President that "a crusade for citizenship" to get at least two million Negroes registered for the 1960 elections had been started. He also asked Nixon to help apply pressure on the President to agree to a meeting.[34]

By September, with the end of the Congressional battle over the Civil Rights Act of 1957, final arrangements were being made. In Newport, Rhode Island, the President signed the new law on September 9. The White House had agreed to invite a delegation that would include Roy Wilkins, A. Philip Randolph, Martin Luther King, Jr., Jackie Robinson and Dr. Frederick Douglass Patterson, the president emeritus of Tuskegee Institute. One unresolved matter pertained to the site of the conference. Would it take place in Washington or at the naval base in Newport, Rhode Island, where the President had gone for a vacation?[35]

Ironically, however, Newport became, instead, the site of another conference, one of ultimately greater importance for both the progress of racial equality in America and the exercise of the President's constitutional powers. The events leading to that session, the effective obstruction by Governor Orval Faubus of the integration of Central High School in Little Rock, Arkansas, had also killed for the duration all plans to have the President confer with the black delegation.[36] On the same day Morrow sent a memorandum to Sherman Adams about completing arrangements for the Presidential meeting with the Negroes, Faubus wired that he would arrive at Eisenhower's vacation headquarters on Saturday, September 14.[37]

Governor Faubus, with a reputation as a racial moderate that had, in fact, been the target of a rough primary campaign conducted by the leader of the Arkansas White Citizens Council, had taken the first step toward permanent enshrinement in the scrolls of resistors of integration. Defying both a federal court order and its compliance by Little Rock's Board of Education, Faubus had used the state's National Guard to block the entry into the school of nine Negro students. The resistance that September 3, after integration had already been effectuated elsewhere in the state, marked a bold defiance of federal law. Unhappily for the President, Faubus had also shaken his determination to avoid implementing integration by force of arms.

As Faubus arrived at Newport on that Saturday morning, via helicopter from Providence, he had reason to believe his position would be understood. Only on July 17 Eisenhower's dislike for using federal troops was stated clearly and publicly in response to a press-conference question about the powers that would be available under the original draft of Part III of the civil-rights legislation currently being debated in Congress. "I can't imagine any set of circumstances," he declared, "that would ever induce me to send federal troops into a federal court and into any area to enforce the orders of a federal court, because I believe that [the] common sense of America will never require it."[38]

As recently as eleven days before Faubus's arrival, hours before leaving Washington for Newport, he responded to the Governor's move by ignoring the obvious constitutional issue. He repeated, instead, his caution about the fallacies of changing "people's hearts merely by laws" and, seeming very sensitive to the sentiments behind Southern resistance, noted their strong emotional opposition to what they called the "mongrelization of the race."[39] Additionally, what Faubus did not know but later suspected, Eisenhower and Herbert Brownell differed on whether a meeting with the Governor could be productive and, moreover, sympathized more than the Attorney General with the Governor's need to comply while retaining his newly won credentials with the segregationists.[40] Yet, on September 5, in replying to a telegram from Faubus requesting understanding of his action and asking removal of FBI investigators from the scene, the President offered a direct reminder of his own responsibility to uphold the Constitution "by every legal means at my command."[41]

But Eisenhower's continued faith in his personal diplomacy won out. Meeting alone with the President at the naval base, Faubus stressed, as he had earlier, the rioting that had been avoided by his act and probably hoped, as Sherman Adams suspected, to convince the President to co-operate in rescinding the federal court order. The President stood by the need to comply, however, and to achieve desegregation gradually. Faubus found their conference encouraging until the conversation included Attorney General Brownell. When the Governor left Newport, he gave no hint about his ultimate course. Whether he would withdraw the National Guard remained unanswered.[42]

The Arkansas troops remained at Central High throughout the following week. Then, after federal judge Ronald Davies ordered their removal, Faubus complied. Monday, September 23, brought the greatest turmoil since the *Brown v. Topeka* decision as an angry mob, inflated by trouble-seekers from the neighboring countryside, despite the presence of local and state police, forced the nine students from the building. That same evening the President issued a statement denouncing the "disgraceful occurrences" and warned that continued obstruction would bring out "whatever force may be necessary" to implement the court's order.[43]

Little changed by the next morning. Mayor Woodrow Wilson Mann of Little Rock sent a frantic telegram to Newport that told the story:

THE IMMEDIATE NEED FOR FEDERAL TROOPS IS URGENT. THE MOB IS MUCH LARGER IN NUMBERS AT 8 AM THAN AT ANY TIME YESTERDAY. PEOPLE ARE CONVERGING ON THE SCENE FROM ALL DIRECTIONS. MOB IS ARMED AND ENGAGING IN FISTICUFFS AND OTHER ACTS OF VIOLENCE. SITUATION IS OUT OF CONTROL AND POLICE CANNOT DISPERSE THE MOB. I AM PLEADING TO YOU AS PRESIDENT OF THE UNITED STATES IN THE INTEREST OF HUMANITY LAW AND ORDER AND BECAUSE OF DEMOCRACY WORLD WIDE TO PROVIDE THE NECESSARY FEDERAL TROOPS WITHIN SEVERAL HOURS. ACTION BY YOU WILL RESTORE PEACE AND ORDER AND COMPLIANCE WITH YOUR PROCLAMATION.[44]

The Constitution, the Presidency and Eisenhower had all been defied. Sherman Adams has written that his subsequent deployment of a massive force, consistent with his belief in the discreet but effective use of the military, was the most repugnant move he ever had to make as President.[45] But, in that state of anarchy, lives were at stake and the right of children to go to school never more clearly denied before a watchful world. Thus, the circumstances he could not have imagined just a short time ago had forced him to act.

Ten thousand Arkansas National Guardsmen were nationalized, thereby giving responsibility for implementing integration to the same forces that had been turning the students back, and one thousand paratroopers from the 101st Airborne Division were also rushed into the area. All were placed under the command of Major General Edwin A. Walker, whose name, ironically, later became associated with the most extreme right-wing groups that began to emerge with the close of the Eisenhower era. The integration of Central High was consequently accomplished, but under an armed guard for the rest of the school year. After having been closed by Faubus for the 1958–1959 session, reopening came in August of 1959 under a federal court order.

Finally, after all the politic delays, Eisenhower met with four Negro leaders in the White House on June 23, 1958. Dr. King, Roy Wilkins and Lester Granger were there with A. Philip Randolph, who was their spokesman. The carefully planned conference, which lasted nearly one hour, consisted largely of having Randolph read a nine-point program that called on the President to establish a "clear national policy" against racial discrimination that would include more vigorous enforcement by the Justice Department of black rights to life, property and voting. Mostly, the President listened and seemed sympathetic. At one point he included integration as but one of many major problems. When the four leaders left and had the usual post-White House conference with the press, they reported that he had been gracious and also felt their cause had been "advanced."[46]

But the Little Rock episode, exploding as it did during the fall of 1957, combined with other events to throw the President and his Administration into deep gloom. On the surface, Americans polled by the Gallup people expressed approval for the President's move. Sixty-four percent said he had done the "right thing." Even many Southerners, a surprisingly high 36 percent, agreed, but mostly through the belief that inaction would have encouraged further rioting and even bloodshed. Interestingly, all regions agreed that the President had acted wisely in not sending troops any sooner.[47] One Little Rock School Board member, in a personal note to Mr. Eisenhower, praised him for having made an appropriate response to a correct analysis of the situation.[48] Martin Luther King, Jr., rejoiced over what he told the President was "of great benefit to our nation and to the Christian traditions of fair play and brotherhood."[49] Indeed, thoughts about the precedent that would have been created by failure to support integration against mob rule left little question about the future importance of the President's decision.

At the same time, however, Little Rock immediately threatened to destroy whatever hopes the GOP retained of wooing the South. When the Southern Governors met at Sea Island, Georgia, for their annual conference on the day the troops moved in, they could talk about nothing else.[50] Congressman Billy Matthews of Gainesville, Florida, complained bitterly that the South had been cheated, that Part III of the Civil Rights Act had in effect been used although its obnoxious provisions had been eliminated. The move, he wrote to the President, had "placed federal troops, our own troops, with bayonets in their hand, to enforce integration."[51]

The reaction to Herbert Brownell's resignation as Attorney General to return to his private law practice with the firm of Lord, Day and Lord in New York showed that he was regarded generally throughout the South as a major culprit. "From Harper's Ferry to the Rio Grande, and in all the land between," proclaimed the Richmond *Times-Dispatch*, "no tears are being shed for the retirement of Herbert Brownell, Jr. as Attorney General. The frightful mess the South, and the country, are in is probably as much his responsibility as that of any living man."[52] Others blamed him directly for having turned the President's ear against the South and its traditions.[53]

On October 4, while the Administration already grappled with the advent of a serious recession, the Russians orbited their Sputnik which millions of incredulous Americans, so certain of their own technological superiority, at first refused to believe had ever taken place. The Administration soon found itself on the defensive about losing the missile race to the Soviets. John Foster Dulles told the President about the State Department's concern that Sputnik would cause "Congress to be liberal with military appropriations, perhaps even with the military aspects of mutual security, but will offset this by cutting down on the economic aid," which, Dulles pointed out, was at least equally important.[54] Assistant Secretary of Defense Donald Quarles acknowledged to the Cabinet on October 18 that the Russians had indeed displayed the great competence of their scientists and attributed their work as an integral part of the Soviet military program, an arrangement which we, "for good reasons," had "deliberately not pursued." At the same time, he cautioned that, while the Russian competence must not be minimized, there was not enough justification for regarding them as ahead of the United States. He reaffirmed that the American satellite program would proceed on schedule.[55] Eisenhower then appointed Dr. James R. Killian of the Massachusetts Institute of Technology as a Special Assistant to the President for Science and Technology. Only a few days after Sputnik, irate farmers at the National Corn Picking Contest near Sioux Falls, South Dakota, incensed by the continued agricultural price decline, threw eggs at Secretary Ezra Taft Benson. Five men were arrested, sentenced to thirty days and fined one hundred dollars, but the judge then suspended all except half of the fine for each man on the condition of future good behavior.[56]

All through the spring and summer of 1957, during the budget and civil-rights battles, and while the cost of living continued to rise and the

President's personal popularity slipped from month to month, the party revolt gained momentum. "Rising population, rising prices and rising criticism are the order of the day at home," wrote James Reston.[57] There was talk about the "erosion of the Presidency" and the discrediting of whatever was meant by "modern Republicanism." Senator George Aiken, an independent moderate, warned that the GOP belonged to Republicans and not solely to Eisenhower. Meade Alcorn, too, moving along with the rightward drift, began to describe "modern Republicanism" in ways that sounded indistinguishable from the traditional variety. He told a Nebraska audience that the "Government should be the people's servant and not their master" and then, in a speech the following month, renewed old charges that Democrats had "coddled Communists" and brought a climate for corruption.[58] Faced with a question at his May 15 news conference about charges being made by Congressional Republicans that he had "moved somewhat to the left" since 1952, Eisenhower responded by saying, "Far from it. If anything, I think I have grown more conservative."[59] Coincidentally, with Eisenhower's new vulnerability, rumors spread about his physical condition. He even had to refute as the "worst rot that I have heard since I have been in this office" reports that he was contemplating resigning and turning over the reigns of government to Vice President Nixon.[60] Never before had the absence of a clear constitutional provision covering Presidential disability received such widespread attention.

In early May, after a short stay at the Naval Medical Hospital in Bethesda, Maryland, hepatitis, aggravated by his continued drinking, killed Senator Joe McCarthy at the age of forty-seven. His loss came as a shock to those on the right still hopeful that he could lead the growing revolt. The vacancy thus created in the Senate then led to a special election that, instead of demoralizing the ultraconservatives, encouraged their cause.

The election, held that August, placed ex-Governor Walter J. Kohler against a forty-one-year-old liberal Democrat, William Proxmire. Kohler campaigned as an "Eisenhower Republican." But Proxmire, rated as the underdog, nevertheless won a sensational upset victory, carrying fifty-six of the state's seventy-one counties, including several rock-ribbed Republican farm centers. Instead of reading the results as a boost for liberalism, conservatives immediately attributed the Proxmire victory to a protest against "modern Republicanism." The President himself had to concede that he had taken a "bad licking" in Wisconsin. No test since the 1956 elections produced as much concern in Washington. The Negro vote, too, which had shown promising signs of reverting to the GOP in 1956, went heavily for the Democrat, despite the Administration's role in obtaining the Civil Rights Act of 1957. Suddenly, Republican hopes of recapturing Congress in 1958 were deflated.

The Vice President, meanwhile, regarded by almost everybody as the insider heading for the top spot at the party's 1960 convention, had been continuing the alteration of his reputation for greater acceptability. He was no longer the anti-Communist "hatchet man" who had roared through the West excoriating the Democrats in 1952 and 1954 and had linked Truman with the word "traitor." His concern was with the continuation of the Eisenhower Administration and the party's welfare. He also adopted the tone of greater moderation to prove his increased "maturity" that independents, in particular, might find attractive in a Presidential candidate. Therefore, to rekindle GOP morale and fuse its cracks, the President turned to Sherman Adams to deliver the partisan blows.

Adams's position, of course, had always been sensitive. As floor manager in the 1952 convention, he had played a prominent role against the Taftites over the seating issue. Then, with the unique position given to him by the President, many Republicans regarded him as the key obstacle, the major explanation for the lack of sufficient patronage and for the continuation of hold-over Democrats and the assignment of moderate and liberal Republicans in key positions. Furthermore, during the crisis following the heart attack in 1955, and even after the ileitis scare the following year, Adams emerged as the central figure in blocking the rise of Nixon to a position of greater power, an affair that also damned him among the conservatives, particularly Styles Bridges. Democrats, too, with their reluctance to attack the popular President personally, found it easier to pick on Adams as a man with inordinate power and no constitutional responsibility. Moreover, the Assistant to the President had also, by the sheer difficulty of his personality, antagonized numerous individuals within both parties. His situation could ill afford the additional burden of partisan controversy.

Yet, by accepting the President's request as loyally as he did, he marched himself directly toward disaster. In Trenton, on May 24, while conceding that a "little breach" had occurred within his party, he charged the Democrats with being "schizophrenic." The Republicans, he said, had the "liberals, the liberal conservatives, the conservative-progressives, the plain and simple conservatives and the reactionaries . . . the moderns and the un- or anti-moderns, the old fashioned and the traditionalists—each resoundingly the oracle of the true meaning of Republicanism." But unless some mending is done, he warned, "by our own huffing and puffing, we blow our house down."[61] Ten days after Sputnik he appeared before the San Francisco Republican Finance Committee in the Cow Palace and delivered a line that became widely quoted as an example of insensitivity to the significance of the Soviet space achievement. Denying any American participation in any race with the Russians, Adams said, "The serving of science, not high score in an outer-space basketball game, has been and still is our country's goal."[62] In November, after defending the White House staff against charges that a "palace guard" actually ran the Executive Office, Adams's plea for party unity that would give Republicans a fighting chance in the coming elections included the warning against the possible return to office of "confused, irresponsible stumblers who might bring us into another war—and that war the last one."[63] By then, however, undermining Adams's requests to end anti-Administration carping, the President's Gallup rating had fallen to its lowest point since the 1954 Congressional elections, 57 percent. In the South, significantly, where the party had held so many hopes for real gains, the aftermath of Little Rock had dropped it to 36 percent, precisely *one half* of where it had stood in January.[64]

At that unfortunate moment, on November 26, President Eisenhower suffered his third major illness, a mild cerebral stroke. A small blood clot or blood-vessel spasm of the brain did not require his hospitalization, nor did it impair his reading, writing or reasoning abilities, although it resulted in a slight, often completely unnoticeable hesitation in his speech, as though reaching for the proper word had become far more difficult. A team of physicians found his temperature, blood pressure and pulse all normal.[65] At worst, a short period of recovery was necessary.

The reaction to that scare had its similarities and contrasts with the previous two illnesses, both of which occurred before the 1956 elections. Again, Adams resumed his "caretaker" role, while Senator Bridges once more called upon Nixon to assume some Presidential duties. The emergency, however uncertain its consequences, was less serious than before, since the President was hardly at all out of touch and capable of making emergency decisions; so Attorney General Rogers explained that no delegation of powers was needed. Still, by then, Nixon had emerged as the irrefutable heir apparent. Even Dulles acquiesced to have the Vice President represent Eisenhower at the December 16 meeting of NATO in Paris. Throughout the many concerns then plaguing the Administration, Nixon proceeded to play a greater role, emerging as the Administration's spokesman.[66] While he had no additional responsibility, his prominence was seen as preparation for any sudden advent to the Presidency either by death or retirement. In many ways, the old image of him as "Tricky Dicky" had been largely mitigated.[67]

Combining with conservative desires to see Nixon as President—and, of course, as the incumbent in the 1960 election—the specter of Eisenhower suffering a possible mental impairment with over three years left in office stimulated calls for his retirement. Even the liberal New York *Post*, with its great distaste for the Vice President, joined in the call, as did Congressman Emmanuel Celler. The *Harper's* "Easy Chair" column by John Fischer maintained that there was one "last great service which President Eisenhower can perform for his country. He can resign."

Nixon "would at least give us somebody in full charge of the government."[68]

To such suggestions Eisenhower had reportedly said that the Presidency is a "job you may die from but it's not a job you resign from."[69] Amid suspicions that talk about his resignation had hurt him deeply, he proceeded to stage a swift resurgence of physical presence and active leadership. Within two days after the stroke he resumed a limited work schedule, signing twelve papers and conferring with Adams and Nixon. On the second of December he met with the full Cabinet for one hour and then practiced golf shots on the White House lawn for fifteen minutes. After also spending about one hour conferring with Dulles about foreign-policy problems, an examination at the end of the day by Dr. Howard Snyder pronounced his condition as "excellent" and without signs of fatigue. The next day, at a White House briefing for Congressional leaders in which the Administration revealed its plans for meeting the Soviet military and scientific challenges in the new space age, he personally presided over half the session. Putting in his hardest day's work since the stroke, he looked perfectly fit. Sinclair Weeks, writing to George Humphrey that night, noted that "The boss is back in harness—he was with the Cabinet yesterday for an hour and a half and with the Leadership meeting today. He was in and out and didn't talk too much because he still claims some speech difficulty, although it doesn't show up much—if at all. He looks just as well as he ever did and he is cheerful and really amazing."[70] After an examination by six doctors on December 10, he announced his intention to go to Paris, after all, for the NATO meeting and delivered the session's opening address on December 16. He faced both houses of Congress on January 9 to deliver his State of the Union message, which concerned itself largely with international relations and emphasized the development of long-range ballistic missles to overcome the Soviet lead. His presentation was both clear and forceful.[71] Shortly afterward, he revealed the details of a plan he and Nixon had arranged to cope with any future Presidential inability to perform the functions of his office. Nixon would become Acting President with the powers and duties of the office after any determination by Eisenhower that his own ability to act had become impaired. Lacking even that power, the Vice President, after proper consultation with the Secretary of State, Sherman Adams and the physicians, would determine the start and termination of any such period of emergency.[72] Then, commenting on a statement by Senator Schoeppel that some Republican Congressional candidates would be unable to win by running on the Administration's record, the President warned he would not back candidates in 1960 who failed to share his own views on the "big issues."[73]

By early 1958, then, despite the frustrations created by an intensifying recession, the President had recovered ground from the earlier laxity of leadership charges and, aside from dispelling talk about his resignation, had begun to defy the supposed hindrances imposed by the Twenty-second Amendment. Despite the economic decline, his own popularity began to rise. On the fifth anniversary of his first inauguration, Eisenhower spoke in Chicago and urged the election of a Republican Congress. Calling for party unity, he also advised against continuing to criticize Democrats for security failures.[74]

That very day, his Assistant to the President addressed a Minnesota United Republicans dinner at the Leamington Hotel in Minneapolis. Reading a speech written for him by Bryce Harlow, he revived the standard charges that became so familiar during the 1952 campaign: the "loss" of China, the Korean war, the loss of atomic secrets, and even added their culpability for Pearl Harbor and turned the blame for the missile "lag" on the Democratic Congress. He also blamed the Democrats with hindering the Administration's efforts to heal the North-South split over civil rights.[75] The speech, which had been shown to the White House staff beforehand, stirred up controversy along the very lines the President cautioned against at Chicago. Confronted with the inconsistency, Jim Hagerty admitted that the President and Adams were both aware of what the other was going to say.

Adams, however, in accepting the old Nixon assignment, lacked the kind of political backing that strengthened the Vice President. Consequently, he found himself vulnerable before angry Republicans already dissatisfied by the inevitable disappointments over patronage and "modern Republicansim" and Democrats eager to expose feet of clay right under the President's nose. Overtly, Lyndon Johnson advised colleagues on his side of the Senate to ignore the abuse. In the House, Sam Rayburn's anger intensified.[76]

Three weeks later, Dr. Bernard Schwartz, a crusading professor of law serving as special counsel to the House Interstate and Foreign Commerce Legislative Oversight Subcommittee, released a salvo that landed in the office of the Assistant to the President. Schwartz, just fired for defying his subcommittee's investigative inertia, made certain that the probe that had been first suggested by "Mr. Sam" in early 1957 would not result in Congressional "whitewash." He first cited Adams for having intervened with the Civil Aeronautics Board to help Murray Chotiner. The California lawyer and Nixon's 1952 campaign manager had been accused in 1956 of having used influence with the Justice Department to help other clients. Now, in a matter involving North American Airlines, Schwartz displayed letters between Adams and Chotiner in which the Assistant to the President not only took up the matter with the Acting Chairman of the CAB but generously offered to do "anything further in this matter" that might be helpful.[77] In June, however, after that revelation had been glossed over and treated contemptuously by the President, an investigator for the committee produced evidence that Adams had received substantial gifts and favors from Bernard Goldfine, a New England textile manufacturer.

As the investigation proceeded, the evidence became firmer. Adams had not only accepted a "gift" from Goldfine of a $2,400 Oriental rug and an expensive vicuna coat, but Adams and his family had also occupied hotel rooms in Boston, New York and Plymouth, Massachusetts, that were paid for by the industrialist. The hotel bills totaled more than three thousand dollars. Also named as having been Goldfine's guest was Senator Frederick G. Payne of Maine, who was up for re-election in September. Goldfine had also sent checks at Christmas "to some of the poor workers" in the government.

Adams and Goldfine had been friends for eighteen years. Goldfine had not only maintained his New Hampshire textile mills while competitors had transferred their operations to the South but had also made political contributions to Adams in the past. Their families had socialized frequently and had weekended together in Plymouth.[78]

Not surprisingly, as the evidence developed, Goldfine took advantage of his friendship with the man called by the press the "second most powerful man in Washington" to help his cause in several difficulties with regulatory agencies. In 1954, when one of the Goldfine companies was charged with violating the Wool Labeling Act by producing fabrics with substantial amounts of nylon fibers despite labels that read "90% wool, 10% vicuna," Adams, upon request, took up the matter with Federal Trade Commission chairman Edward F. Howrey. Responding to the Presidential assistant's telephone call, Howrey obtained from his staff a full report on the matter, which he then sent to Adams. Adams forwarded the document to Goldfine. When Adams's secretary inquired about the case one month later, she was told the matter had been closed. But, the following year, similar charges were made against Goldfine. Obligingly, Adams arranged an appointment for his friend with Howrey. After the session with the Commissioner and the FTC staff, Goldfine ostentatiously, in the presence of everybody in the office, told Howrey's secretary to "get Sherman Adams on the phone." Then, again so that no one could fail to hear what was going on, he said, "Sherm, I'm over at the Federal Trade Commission. I have been well received over here."[79] In 1956, Adams asked Eisenhower special counsel Gerald Morgan to find out from the Securities and Exchange Commission about the status of a complaint that Goldfine's East Boston Company and its subsidiary, The Boston Port Development Corporation, had failed to file required annual financial reports over an eight-year period.[80]

Adams protested that he had neither sought nor won any special favors for his friend, that his inquiries were common in Washington and that such dealings resulted from his friendship with Goldfine, a relationship between the two families that did not lend itself to insinuations.[81] Appearing before the committee on June 17, upon his own request, Adams acknowledged he had made mistakes in judgment in the Goldfine case and delivered convincing testimony that he had never used his White House position to influence government agencies for any individual or company.[82]

But the committee's chairman, Representative Oren Harris, an Arkansas Democrat whom Dr. Schwartz had earlier accused of having tried to hinder any legitimate investigation of regulatory agencies, had, for some reason, worked up enthusiasm for the task. Turning to Adams, he asked, "Have you in your position found it necessary to ask any Commissioners of these agencies to hand in their resignations?" The normally frigid Adams, who found it easy to remain silent when avoiding a question, was stunned. After a brief conference with his attorney, Gerald Morgan, he replied, "If you insist on the question, I should have to answer in the affirmative."[83]

That, of course, was the point. Only someone naïve—and Adams was not—could have thought that anyone in his position could make inquiries as though he were a neutral party. Particularly with the well-known fact that he performed so much of the detail work for the President, made so many decisions in matters not requiring the Chief Executive's attention, a phone call from him expressing interest in a case was virtually equivalent to a Presidential request.

Still, to place his misdeeds in perspective, Adams had done what was—and is—routine in Washington, where, as he said, such acts were "legion." And gifts ranging from simple tokens of appreciation to costly items are far from rare. In addition to Senator Payne, for example, Goldfine had also picked up hotel bills for Styles Bridges and Senator Norris Cotton of New Hampshire.[84] Eisenhower himself received some vicuna cloth from Goldfine, although not a complete garment; but estimates indicate that the President, in fact, got more personal gifts than any Chief Executive in history, mostly for his Gettysburg farm. Costly machinery and, among other livestock, several dozen Aberdeen Angus cattle, each valued as high as two thousand dollars, came from friends. After he had been in office less than three years, *Newsweek* magazine estimated that gifts to Mr. Eisenhower totaled some forty thousand dollars, and muckraking journalist Drew Pearson figured that, by 1960, contributions to his farm alone were worth over three hundred thousand dollars.[85] Moreover, when Adams's name came up, the following month, in connection with alleged pressure to influence $40,382 in penalty refund payments to the defunct Raylaine Worsteds Corporation—a case that was dropped for lack of evidence—two other men were involved —Senators Irving Ives and Styles Bridges.[86] While Adams was not as pure as Caesar's wife, despite the fact that, as Dr. Schwartz has written, he "pictured himself as the very paragon of rectangular rectitude," he in no sense deserved to be singled out as an example of official corruption in Washington.

For Eisenhower and the Republican party, however, the situation could hardly have been more embarrassing. National Chairman Wesley Roberts's Kansas real-estate transactions had been an early setback, and, in 1955, Secretary of the Air Force Harold Talbott was forced to resign after evidence had been produced that showed his position had been used to promote business for a private company. Then, that same year had come the revelation about the dual role played by Adolphe Wenzell in the abortive Dixon–Yates contract. The Adams affair, however, while less unsavory than the others, had hit closest to the throne. For Democrats, like Sam Rayburn and Lyndon Johnson, watching Oren Harris roast the Presidential assistant must have been a joyous sight. Charges that the Democrats had made a "mess in Washington" could not be replayed so easily for yet another election.

Adams had suddenly become Washington's most expendable man. For the Republican Old Guard, who disliked everything Adams stood for and blamed him for their predicament, the "chickens had come home to roost." "Here was an opportunity for them to remove me from the President's staff and they intended to take advantage of it," Adams later wrote. "I kicked myself for having given it to them."[87] Virtually everybody up for re-election that fall demanded his resignation, but conservatives shouted the loudest. Sinclair Weeks, after complaining that Adams was "the most whip-lashed . . . individual in our generation," found himself the target of angry rejoinders, 90 percent of which recalled that Joe McCarthy had been similarly victimized.[88] Across the country, GOP state chairmen joined the outcry. Vice President Nixon, meeting with them on June 20, cautioned them to stick together and not panic and doubted that the matter would "have much effect" on the Congressional elections in November.[89] General Robert Wood, however, informed the Vice President that Republicans could not achieve unity while Adams remained.[90]

Resisting the tide were Eisenhower and the Eisenhower loyalists, particularly those not up for re-election. Hence, Senators Aiken, Carlson, Flanders and Javits lauded him for not being "stampeded" by the demands. Ogden Reid, while running *Herald Tribune* editorials defending the chief of staff, urged that the "error of judgment" not be permitted to distract the American people from getting on with the real "life and death problems to confront," pointing out that while that distraction was taking place, the Communists executed ex-Premier Imre Nagy of Hungary, committing "a crime which signaled the onset of a new age of barbarism."[91] Harold Stassen, who had resigned from the Administration in February to seek election as Governor of Pennsylvania, suggested that the President ask the American people to forgive Adams for his error. Hopefully, Eisenhower replied, "the statement I made in the press conference today will serve to clear away most of the confusion and quiet some of the uproar."[92] From that three-hundred-word statement, however, one which opened the conference with a reminder that "a gift is not necessarily a bribe" and restated his faith in Adams's integrity, three dominated the headlines: "I need him." But his closing line was "Admitting the lack of that careful prudence in this incident . . . I believe with my whole heart that he is an invaluable public servant doing a difficult job efficiently, honestly and tirelessly."[93] For critics of the staff system and for those who liked to picture the President as a boob being led by the rock from the Granite State, Eisenhower's three sincere words became the ultimate confirmation of their suspicions.

The real blow fell in September. Governor Edmund Muskie, not surprisingly, defeated Senator Payne in the early election held in Maine, with the size of the Democratic vote in what had been regarded as a thoroughly Republican state astonishing almost everybody. Fifty-three percent of the ballots for seats in the state house had gone to the Democrats, and the GOP held on to just one of the five principal offices that were at stake. Immediately, the fact that Payne, like Adams, had admitted to having received gifts from Goldfine became, for Republicans everywhere, *the* explanation.[94] Payne had accepted a $3,500 interest-free loan, which had not been repaid. Horace A. Hildreth, a former two-term Governor of the state, protested to Sinclair Weeks that "it was Fred Payne's dealings with Goldfine and his failure to pay off his debt to Goldfine and not Adams that had the bearing and influence in the Maine election."[95] Nevertheless, realizing that they had lost the corruption issue and fearful of what the Maine results foreshadowed for the Congressional races throughout the country, in the face of all the other ominous signs that fall, Republican pressure to dump Adams revived.

But the verdict had actually been reached before the voting in Maine. Meade Alcorn's report to the President was glum. Politicians and big contributors both wanted no part of the tarnished New Englander. "When Adams used the word 'imprudent' regarding his conduct," said financier Sidney Weinberg, "he was using a word meaning 'stupid.' " Eisenhower then asked Alcorn to conduct a secret survey of the national committee. Wherever he turned, particularly during the party's meeting in Chicago on August 26 and 27, the reaction was the same. Representative Simpson and Senator Andrew Schoeppel, the GOP's Congressional finance men, threatened to issue a public ultimatum to the President calling for Adams's head. When Alcorn reported his findings immediately afterward, Eisenhower told him, "You've got to handle it. It's your job. The dirtiest job I could give to you."[96] While neither Eisenhower nor Adams subsequently admitted that Alcorn revealed the information that left him with no choice, the President himself has agreed that, even before the Maine results were known, he had concluded that Adams's "retention of his office would be a mistake both for him and the office."[97] On September 22 Adams flew to Newport, where the President was vacationing, and had his resignation accepted.

Perhaps, after Eisenhower, the loss of Adams was felt most deeply by Fred Morrow. In May, Max Rabb had left the White House. Despite their occasional policy disagreements, Morrow had regarded Rabb as "perhaps the only one in the White House staff who showed deep personal concern about the plight of the Negro and other minorities in the country." Now, with Adams gone, there was real distress. "From this point on," Morrow predicted, "it will be difficult to get through to the President any observation, suggestion, or counsel on the matter of racial problems and particularly in the present delicate field of civil rights and desegregation."[98]

The Republicans, therefore, faced the crucial Congressional elections without Adams. And Nixon, campaigning as a moderate for GOP candidates, chose to castigate the "radicals" in the opposition instead of their entire party. In New York City on October 23, moving far from his 1952 comments, he praised Truman and declared that the Communist party was the only "party of treason."[99] But after balloting ended on November 4, the returns demonstrated that, as Maine had warned, the party had suffered a disaster, a Democratic landslide unmatched since the 1930s. The GOP lost forty-seven House seats and thirteen in the Senate. Furthermore, a shift of an additional 5 percent of the vote in some districts would have cost sixty-one other seats. Throughout the country, Democratic Congressmen received 5,877,311 votes more than did the Republicans, compared with 2,330,000 in 1954 and 1,600,000 in 1956. Nor did any regional success offer much consolation. The Democratic success extended through traditionally Republican New England and carried along 53 percent of the Middle West vote. A general rout of Republican conservatives by Democratic liberals completed the pattern. In New York State, however, a left-of-center Republican and former Under Secretary of Health, Education and Welfare in the Eisenhower Administration, Nelson Rockefeller, moved into Albany behind a half-million-vote plurality.

CHAPTER 38

Voyages of the Lame Duck

On the morning after the elections, 195 reporters in the Executive Office Building awaited the President's reaction to the GOP's latest disaster. Since both he and Nixon had argued that "radicals" had become dominant in the Democratic party, did he believe, as newsman Ed Folliard asked, that "the people yesterday chose left-wing government rather than sensible government?"

The President had no trouble making an analysis. "I know this," he said, "that they obviously voted for people that I would class among the spenders, and that is what I say is going to be the real trouble. And I promise this: for the next two years, the Lord sparing me, I am going to fight this as hard as I know how." Then, in response to a follow-up question, he warned that "if the Republicans don't start fighting this morning, this very day, for the next election, they're going to be in a bad way. I believe this is true throughout the country."[1]

The dilemma was plain. Where did the responsibility lay, with the President or with Congressional Republicans? Had the President really led the party, or was he merely pontificating before the public and preserving his own apolitical image? In short, Eisenhower had long since become to many observers somewhat of an enigma, one apt to draw praise for decisive action and leadership for bold, definitive moves and, at almost the same time, condemnation for passiveness and caution that yielded Presidential prerogatives to the loudest voices on Capitol Hill. To many critics, the "great crusade" that he had promised in 1952 had been dissipated by the politics of conciliation and appeasement—or, even worse, lethargy. William V. Shannon, in a *Commentary* article that month, viewed the Administration as a "time of great postponement" that merely presided over the preservation of past gains.[2] Others saw the President as a bitter and disappointed old man who had become resigned to political compromises and had lost what many claimed he never had— enthusiasm for the job. He was, they concluded, merely serving out his remaining months, playing golf, bridge, hunting for quail and leaving as much as possible to his staff.[3] Arthur Krock, however, who had rejected most of the adverse views of Eisenhower, confounded critics of Presidential inertia by writing in January that party leaders and White House aides were making a concerted effort to restore to its peak the old image of the General as a national leader.[4] And the events that had already taken place in 1958, a series of international crises—in the wake of Little Rock—and a combined inflation and recession had provided ample grist for critics to paint with colors of their choice. In the wake of defeat, of course, the harshest accusations emerged most freely.

Eisenhower himself, after having the post-mortem press session on November 5, seemed to vanish from prominence, as though confirming the debilitating effect of the Twenty-second Amendment. He got away for a hunting vacation with his former Treasury Secretary, George Humphrey, then went on to Tacoma, Washington, for a brief visit with his brother Edgar, soon to become a trustee of the Americans for Constitutional Action, a new ultraconservative organization dedicated to opposing "spendthrift and inflationary" government policies.[5] Then, after ten days in the White House, the President left for a golfing vacation in Augusta. With old friends Bob Woodruff and Bill Robinson, he watched the Army-Navy football game on television. Not until December 2 did he return to Washington. He met with the press on the tenth and, in response to questions about a national right-wing trend, reaffirmed his personal conservatism, again holding fast to the principles he had described in St. Louis back in 1949. "So far as philosophy is concerned," he said, he had not undergone "one single change."[6] On Christmas Day he drove to the Gettysburg farm and went shopping for clothes with his little grandson, David, and played bridge with an old partner, General Alfred Gruenther, a real master of the game.

At the same time, a congenital condition of the American Presidency had also afflicted the Administration. Except for such notable survivors as Ezra Taft Benson and John Foster Dulles—as well as Postmaster General Arthur Summerfield—the starting team had been largely replaced. Jerry Persons, taking over from Sherman Adams, was welcomed by some as a liberator of the flow of information to the President; but to others, such as Fred Morrow, the workings of the White House machine had largely stalled in Adams's absence and an "atmosphere of indecision and fear" seemed to have permeated the "attitude and morale of the entire staff."[7] Gone, too, was Gabe Hauge, the economist and speech writer regarded by many as a leading purveyor of "modern Republicanism." Sinclair Weeks, returning to private business in Boston, was replaced by former Atomic Energy Commission chairman Admiral Lewis Strauss, who received an interim appointment by the President pending confirmation by the Senate. Charlie Wilson, rated a considerable disappointment for his inability to control the Pentagon, had yielded the Defense Department to Neil McElroy, the efficient and attractive president of the Procter and Gamble soap company. Maurice Stans had already become the fourth Director of the Budget. William Rogers, Jim Mitchell and Fred Seaton all remained after having replaced members of the starting lineup.

But, in substituting for George Humphrey, President Eisenhower had found a man able to provide continuity over the management of money. To Eisenhower, Anderson was the ideal man. Matching Humphrey's fiscal conservatism, the former Navy Secretary and special emissary to the Middle East became, in effect, the architect of the President's domestic program. He worked to counter the twin evils of inflation and recession by restricting both credit and spending in a massive effort to restore a balanced budget after the $12.5 billion deficit created in fiscal 1959 by the post-Sputnik panic. In 1959 alone the President and his Secretary's compatibility in fiscal matters became evident when Mr. Eisenhower vetoed two Housing and Urban Renewal bills and two Public Works Appropriations measures. All four attempts, products of the Democratic-controlled Eighty-sixth Congress, brought Presidential complaints of financial extravagance. In returning the first of the housing bills, Eisenhower also observed that it would tend to "substitute federal spending for private enterprise."[8] Urged by corporation executive Owen Cheatham to approve the housing bill because the economy needed such stimulation to ensure prosperity through 1960, the President replied that with "this thief and robber" called inflation "stalking across the country, we can easily have an apparent prosperity for a time, but not for long. Inflation must be avoided, and this means that the federal government must not only live within its means but must, in times of prosperity, begin reducing the nation's debt."[9] Anderson, finally noting the achievement of an improved federal budgetary position and finding the outlook "very encouraging" because of the Administration's fiscal management, continued to urge the pursuit of "sound tested fiscal and monetary policies that are the very foundation of sustained, noninflationary economic growth."[10] His influence over Eisenhower had exceeded even Humphrey's.[11]

"If the President could choose his successor," commented a Cabinet member, "it would not be Nixon or Rockefeller, but the Secretary of the Treasury."[12] In a conversation with Emmet Hughes, Eisenhower was explicit. "Of all these fellows," he said, "the one who had the broadest gauge—best in experience and sense and the right age—it's that Bob

Anderson. Boy, I'd like to fight for him in 1960!"[13] Furthermore, despite Anderson's continued reluctance to seek elective office—an attitude that he had maintained since 1955—the President did not hesitate, in his typically discreet manner, to make known his real preference. Adopting, during his last months in office, the practice of inviting White House correspondents in for informal, "off-the-record" sessions, he gave a dinner at which Anderson was the only other Administration official present. While the reticent Texan listened in silence, he heard the President proclaim his virtues.[14]

Every Republican in the country, of course, had his eyes fixed on the succession. The President's possible influence over the forthcoming convention, indeed, became a test of whether he had become paralyzed by the Twenty-second Amendment. Harold Stassen, defeated in a primary contest for Pennsylvania's gubernatorial nomination, conferred with Eisenhower on November 12 in a new attempt to save the party from Richard Nixon.[15] The Vice President, having worked hard in behalf of many defeated candidates, had apparently marred his reputation as a campaigner. Moreover, his efforts to embrace the Eisenhower wing of the party as well as his old right-wing base, which ultimately led him to advocate "progressive-conservatism,"[16] risked his credibility with the Old Guard. As the Administration's final two years progressed and as the party moved toward the 1960 convention in Chicago, it became more apparent that traditionalists were becoming enchanted by a Southwesterner who, in the 1958 Congressional defeat, had defied the general collapse of the right wing.

Barry Goldwater, hitherto best known as a staunch opponent of organized labor—and, particularly, of the United Auto Workers' chief, Walter Reuther—had brought off a significant coup. Having taken his Senate seat in 1952 from Ernest McFarland by getting 51.3 percent of the vote, Goldwater's achievement in winning a second term, despite the national trend, came by attracting 56.1 percent of the Arizona electorate. Personally popular, an Air Force reserve officer and jet-plane enthusiast and a talented amateur photographer, the forty-nine-year-old Senator and ex-retail businessman appealed to conservatives of both parties as a Taft with warmth and charm. Moreover, he spoke plainly and with candor. Appearing on a television interview program in January, without mentioning Nelson Rockefeller or Tom Dewey by name, he warned about an effort within the party to "stifle all conservative voices" and charged the responsibility to "some king-makers in New York."[17] Within the next three months Goldwater declared the party must move to the right because it had gone as far to the left as possible, urged the GOP to return to Taft's principles to win election and, in a speech at Jackson, Mississippi, upheld Nixon as a legitimate conservative and told the South it would do much better under a Republican Administration than under Democrats. Chief Justice Earl Warren, he told his receptive audience, was a "socialist" and unqualified to head the high court. "The general feeling among Republicans is to let the states handle desegregation," he said. "If there is any violence, of course, that is another matter."[18] Requests for the Senator to address local Republican groups mounted sharply.

For Richard Nixon, aside from the elections, 1958 had already been a trying year. Sent by Eisenhower on a good-will tour of Latin America that spring, he became the victim of the Administration's friendship toward such local reactionary dictators as Odría of Peru and Pérez Jiménez of Venezuela (both recipients of Legion of Merit awards from Eisenhower) and his own reputation as a warlike militant anti-Communist. Unlike the earlier receptions for Dr. Milton Eisenhower and the one given later to the President himself, as well as other prominent Americans, Nixon encountered well-organized and bitter massive protests. In Lima, he was surrounded by angry crowds shouting, "Nixon, go home!" and "Yankee warmonger" and pelted with rocks. When he appeared in Caracas, the danger increased. Not only were both he and his wife spat upon, but his limousine was ambushed, trapped and pounded with rocks. President Eisenhower had to order paratroopers to prepare for a possible rescue mission.[19] While most of the American press conveniently attributed the ugliness to South American Communists, the Administration's subsequent bolstering of economic assistance to that continent constituted recognition of the need to repair relations. Such moves to toughen the region against the appeals of communism ultimately became the genesis of President John F. Kennedy's Alliance for Progress.[20] For Nixon, however, his close brush with disaster undoubtedly achieved a political plus at home, with applause for his bravery and coolness under fire dominating the reaction.

As the months went by, despite the Congressional defeat, he was the obvious leader for the party's nomination in 1960. Every sampling of GOP popular opinion showed him monopolizing the potential Republican vote. Additionally, the party's national committee had become particularly eager to accord him equal billing with the Administration so that, even if his role remained the same, the appearance of greater responsibilities and experience would be enhanced.

Only six days after the Republicans had suffered their election defeat, attention once more shifted to a cold-war crisis, the third major one that year. In Moscow, Nikita Khrushchev, undisputed boss of the regime since displacing Bulganin as Prime Minister in March but clearly lacking Stalin's old grip, delivered a speech which, in a year that had seen East and West go to the brink of war in both the Middle and the Far East, carried the ominous possibility of a direct Soviet-American clash. Khrushchev, needing a grand coup for his own prestige and feeling emboldened that Russian means of delivering nuclear weapons had reached parity with the West, chose that day to initiate a new crisis over divided Berlin. Russia, he announced, was prepared to sign a "peace treaty" with East Germany at an early date. That immediately constituted a threat to Allied rights in West Berlin, an island of capitalism and democracy 110 miles east of the border between the two Germanys. Long intolerable to the Russians as a bastion of the West, the escape from the East of more than two million East Germans since 1949—many of them skilled and highly trained professional people—had made the city become what Khrushchev called a bone in his throat. Anthony Eden, in Geneva in 1955, and Polish Foreign Minister Adam Rapacki in several statements during 1957 and 1958, had urged that the goal of German unification be negotiated with the possibility of accepting neutralization, demilitarization and disengagement in Central Europe.

On November 27, in a formal note to Washington, Khrushchev's position was further clarified. The three Western powers, he charged, had turned West Berlin "into a kind of state within a state and using it as a center" for subversive operations against the German Democratic Government. Continuing such occupation rights, declared the note, was "tantamount to recognizing something like a privileged position of the NATO countries" and, therefore, steps had to be taken to convert West Berlin into a free and demilitarized city. The Soviet Union was prepared to negotiate with the West for the revised status. While such efforts were being made, Allied traffic into the city would be undisturbed. But that period would end in six months. Failure to reach an agreement would necessitate a settlement between the Soviet Union and the East German government which would enable the satellite regime to control the access routes, an effort that would be assisted by Moscow's military power.[21]

As Khruschev well knew, there were ample reasons why West Berlin would be one of the last places on the globe for an American retreat; and the Eisenhower Administration had shown not the slightest proclivity for yielding along any of the numerous fronts the superpowers controlled even if the Berlin airlift of 1948 and 1949 had to be repeated. The President, opening his news conference on December 10, reaffirmed the American "responsibility" and "duty" to maintain the "freedom of the western part of Berlin."[22] Any agreement for a free city, he maintained in discussions with Dulles, would have to apply to *all* of Berlin and not just the West.[23] The Secretary of State, convinced that the Russians were not merely saber-rattling but were presenting the United States with a new test of its courage, conveyed the American resolve to Khrushchev through First Deputy Premier Anastas Mikoyan, who arrived in the United States for a "private visit" in early January.[24]

Berlin, the most dangerous of all the trouble spots, thus threatened to destroy Eisenhower's hopes of thawing out the cold war. If the Soviets were truly serious about their six-month timetable, May 27 could see the start of a crisis in the form of a challenge to the continued presence of American troops in the western sector of the city. Harassment on a grand scale by the East German government might easily cripple all land access routes across the 110 miles from the border. Such renewed tension, even if Allied troops could be maintained and provisioned, would, of course, kill whatever hopes the President had for a thaw that would permit increased trade with the East. Even without that kind of challenge, the American people would not tolerate any deviation from containment. Of that Eisenhower was sure; and at every public opportunity he voiced their sentiment. In private, too, dining at Bermuda's Mid-Ocean Club with Prime Minister Macmillan and British Foreign Secretary Selwyn Lloyd during the evening of March 23, 1957, the President stressed that point. He referred to the strong domestic sentiment against admitting Communist China to the United Nations and declared that the entry of Peking might force American withdrawal. Macmillan was sardonic. Having recently replaced Anthony Eden in the aftermath of the Suez affair, in which the United States had defended moral righteousness rather than the allies, the Prime Minister observed that the Americans apparently liked the UN only as long as it remained amenable. Eisenhower, softening his original statement, explained that he was only expressing the view of the American people; continuing membership, despite a seat for Red China, he added, would require considerable effort on his part.[25] Certainly, the Administration could be no less rigid about Berlin. Joining with England and France, and supported by the NATO Council, Moscow was notified on the last day of the year that they would refuse to negotiate with the Soviets "under menace or ultimatum." Also reaffirmed were the "rights of the Three Powers to remain in Berlin with unhindered communications by surface and air between that city and the Federal Republic of Germany . . . under existing conditions essential to the discharge of that right and responsibility."[26] Dulles, pressing that point with Mikoyan a few days later, was assured by the Russian that the six-month reference did not constitute an ultimatum; and, although May 27 was considered a reasonable date by which to expect some progress, they were more interested in beginning negotiations than in a deadline. On January 10 the Soviets also responded affirmatively to Western requests to discuss Berlin within the context of German reunification.[27] Consistent with the Russian policy of waxing first hot and then cold, it also became clear that the Mikoyan trip was also designed to move the Big Four toward another summit conference, a theme Khrushchev began to stress. In contrast with the British, Eisenhower and Dulles felt that only Russian propaganda purposes would be served. General Charles De Gaulle, who had just assumed the Presidency of France's newly formed Fifth Republic, was also cool to the proposal. Chancellor Adenauer of West Germany was positively hostile to any move that might result in detaching his country from NATO. During 1958, even before the latest crisis, containment had already received two challenges.

The first, in the Middle East, threatened the ultimate domination of the entire region through the extended influence of Nasser's United Arab Republic, a union of Egypt, Syria and Yemen that had been formed the previous year. American desires for keeping the *status quo* in the area, in the wake of the Suez Canal debacle of 1956, had finally induced the Israelis to follow the British and French withdrawal and permit the assumption of peace-keeping forces by an international army sponsored by the United Nations. Eisenhower, at that point, also sent a South Carolina Democrat and former chairman of the House Committee on Foreign Affairs, James P. Richards, on a thirty-thousand-mile tour of the Middle East that included fifteen countries. With a retinue of USIA, Defense, State and International Cooperation Administration officials, the Richards mission accomplished agreements in principle for the extension of $118.7 million in American economic assistance, slightly over half for the development of over-all economic strength. After having been assured of the intentions behind the Eisenhower Doctrine and told that the President himself would retain discretion to determine when direct American military assistance might be required, thirteen of the countries visited subsequently issued statements endorsing the resolution that Congress had approved in March of 1957.[28]

Lebanon, divided between Moslems and Christians and under the leadership of President Camille Chamoun, a Maronite Christian, had followed a strongly pro-Western course. The Moslem rebels seemed more than merely inspired by the United Arab Republic. Not only were they receiving money and supplies but American intelligence reported that their instructions were coming over open telephone lines from Damascus.[29] Chamoun, convinced his departure from the Presidency would turn the nation over to Nasserite successors, attempted to amend the constitution to permit himself to run for another term, a move that helped to precipitate an armed uprising in Beirut. Yet, despite six pleas from Chamoun to Washington for assistance, Eisenhower failed to invoke the military provisions of the Middle East doctrine. The American President preferred, instead, to await the findings of a UN observer corps, headed by Secretary General Dag Hammarskjöld, which went to Lebanon in June.[30]

Suddenly, a well-executed but bloody overthrow in Iraq, just when the Lebanese situation seemed capable of resolving itself, tested whether the Eisenhower Doctrine was, as its critics were claiming, mere paper.

By dawn on July 14, the Iraqi Third Army Division, after an all-night action that besieged the royal palace, completed the sweep to power of a military corps headed by General Karim Kassim. Both King Faisal and Prime Minister Nuri es-Said, along with Crown Prince Emir Abdul Illah, were murdered. The Baghdad Pact had suddenly lost its keystone member, a reality Kassim confirmed the following March.

To Chamoun, the danger was clear. An invasion from Syria, after the Nasserite success in Iraq, could easily trigger a bloody civil war in Lebanon. Three hours after hearing what had happened in Baghdad, at nine o'clock on the morning of July 14, he met with the American, British and French ambassadors and stressed the imminent danger to his country. Turning to the American, Robert M. McClintock, Chamoun requested immediate assistance—"not by words but by action"—and a reply within twenty-four hours.[31]

At two-thirty that afternoon, Washington time, the President, after having reviewed the situation in the morning with CIA director Allen Dulles, met in his office with twenty-two leaders of both houses of Congress. Also present, in addition to the CIA chief, were John Foster Dulles and General Nathan Twining, the chairman of the Joint Chiefs of Staff. The legal ramifications were discussed, including United Nations Charter Article 51, which permitted emergency action until the UN could take over. Speaker Rayburn feared involvement in what might be primarily a civil war, and Senator Fulbright questioned whether communism was really a factor. Allen Dulles's function, undoubtedly, was to convey the evidence of Syrian and Egyptian support for the Lebanese rebels and to describe the pattern under which Nasser, having effectuated a *coup d'état* in Iraq, would move to absorb Lebanon next. Clearly, Eisenhower had by that time decided that the United States had no other choice. Lebanon had accepted the Eisenhower Doctrine; failure to act, failure to support American friends in the area, could be fatal and only confirm weakness in the face of Soviet threats.[32] Turning to General Twining, the President asked how many Marines were available and was told that three battalions were in the Mediterranean ready to move at any time. Then he looked at Secretary Dulles.

"Foster," asked the President, "what will we do? Send in the Marines or the Boy Scouts?"

Dulles looked perplexed. Finally, he said, "What do you mean, Mr. President?"

Eisenhower did not answer. He had, of course, made his decision, one that Sherman Adams has recalled was with as much regret as his Little Rock move but a course that, nevertheless, had to be taken. "We're going to send in the Marines," he announced. And then, in typical Eisenhower fashion, he added, "We're going to send in everything we've got, and this thing will be over in forty-eight hours if we do."[33]

He ordered the first battalion to land at 3 P.M. the next day, Lebanon time, or 9 A.M., July 15, Washington time, when Jim Hagerty could also release the news to the public. By August 8, 114,357 American soldiers and Marines reached the little country at the eastern edge of the Mediterranean. Great Britain then dispatched troops to Jordan. While there were some mild reservations at home about the provocative nature of the move, both ex-Presidents Hoover and Truman declared that Eisenhower had had no other choice. The foreign reaction was predictable. Moscow denounced it as an "act of aggression against the Arab world" and left-wing European opinion, including the British Laborites, were hostile. Bitterness came from Arab nationalists. While it carried the very real danger of Soviet counter-reaction as a demonstration that they, too, could not be intimidated, the passing days—with Robert Murphy in Lebanon to handle diplomatic relations there and with the Kassim regime in Iraq—brought the controversy into the United Nations. Finally, the passage by the General Assembly of an Arab-sponsored resolution pledging non-interference in each other's affairs and providing for the withdrawal of Western troops led to final departure of American forces on October 25. In 1959, the dead Baghdad Pact was replaced by the Central Treaty Organization, or CENTO. Including Iran, Pakistan, Turkey, Great Britain and the United States, it was designed to fill the geographic gap between NATO and SEATO.[34]

By then, however, most attention was aimed on the Straits of Formosa where, once again, after a three-year lull, Chinese Communist shore batteries had opened fire against Chiang Kai-shek's emplacements on Quemoy and Matsu. The shelling, which began on August 23, may have evolved from calculations to coincide with the Western distraction in the Middle East and from the growing tensions between Peking and Moscow.[35] Thus, the new call for the "liberation" of Formosa, without any real design for an actual invasion of the offshore islands, was a brazen attempt at the "brinkmanship" popularly associated with Dulles's name. The Americans would be forced either to commit themselves to the defense of Quemoy and Matsu and thereby risk the condemnation of those outraged by the thought of going to war over such minor objectives or have to admit that Chiang Kai-shek could not depend upon their support. Khrushchev, too, who had visited Peking on July 31, would be placed on the spot. Failure to supply the nuclear weapons requested by the Chinese Communists would expose him to charges of timidity.

The American dilemma was equally severe. Publicly to write off Quemoy and Matsu would mean abandonment of the Chinese Nationalists. On the other hand, Dulles and Eisenhower feared offering Chiang Kai-shek anything that would encourage him to attack the mainland and force American assistance. Dulles, despite severe opposition within the

State Department and liberal demands that the islands be abandoned, stood firm. The Administration's policy could only be to keep all sides guessing while, at the same time, reaffirming support for the Taiwan regime. From Newport, Rhode Island, on September 4, where he had gone to confer with the President, Dulles issued a statement saying that any judgment indicating steps to invade the island of Formosa itself would, in accordance with the resolution of 1955, require the use of American troops. "The President," it said, "would not . . . hesitate to make such a finding if he judged that the circumstances made this necessary to accomplish the purpose of the Joint Resolution. In this connection, we have recognized that the securing and protecting of Quemoy and Matsu have increasingly become related to the defense of Taiwan (Formosa)."[36] Eisenhower also tacitly let the Communists know that the Seventh Fleet, patrolling the Formosa Straits, was being reinforced and all American arms in the area were on a "readiness alert."[37] After numerous appeals from Admiral Arleigh Burke to Dulles that muscle be displayed to support Chiang, the Secretary finally agreed and then won the President's approval to use the fleet for the delivery of medium landing ships and other equipment to within three miles of Quemoy and Matsu.

The Russian influence over Peking seems to have been significant. Khrushchev, in a maneuver characteristic of Soviet retreat from the brink of war, sent Eisenhower a belligerent letter on September 7 warning that an attack on the Peoples Republic would be regarded as war against Russia. Only the day before the Chinese Reds themselves announced willingness to reopen the suspended talks with American ambassador Jacob Beam at Warsaw.[38] On the eleventh, right after having been told by Defense Secretary Neil McElroy that the Joint Chiefs of Staff thought the islands should be vacated because Chiang was hoping to use the situation to provoke a war that would enable him to invade the mainland, the President spoke on radio and television and stressed his intent to remain firm in the face of Communist pressure. "I must say to you very frankly and soberly, my friends, the United States cannot accept the result that the Communists seek," he explained. "Neither can we show, now, a weakness of purpose—a timidity—which would surely lead them to move more aggressively against us and our friends in the Western Pacific area." Adopting the language of the "China lobby," he declared that "a Western Pacific 'Munich' would not buy us peace or security" but would merely encourage aggression and "dismay our friends and allies there. If history teaches us anything, appeasement would make it more likely that we would have to fight a major war."[39] As though to enforce his words, side-winder air-to-air missiles were sent to the Nationalists. Russian and Peoples Republic reaction showed little desire to make much of an issue of the American weapons, which were instrumental in the downing of ten Chinese Communist MIGs during an air battle on September 24. The Russians had evidently refused to supply Peking with similar missiles, thus further diminishing their threat. Finally, on October 6, the Minister of Defense of the Peoples Republic of China announced a one-week suspension of the bombardment to permit the provisioning of the garrisons without American escort. Then, after a suspension for an additional two weeks, they announced that firing would resume on only odd days of the month. And so the crisis was permitted to peter out without any final solution.

The problem of missiles had also become a domestic political issue. Until 1957, American superiority not only in nuclear weapons but also delivery systems had been taken for granted, affording comfort that the so-called "nuclear stalemate" had created a situation in which neither superpower would dare to strike first. Dr. Henry Kissinger of Harvard, in a 1957 book that gained wide circulation, observed that "The power of the new weapons is said to have brought about a tacit nonaggression treaty: a recognition that war is no longer a conceivable instrument of policy and that for this reason international disputes can be settled only by means of diplomacy." But, suddenly, after relative complacency, Kissinger warned that increased Russian capability to "inflict a catastrophic blow on the United States" was becoming a real prospect for the future.[40] Khrushchev's threat of June 2, 1957, to Americans that their grandchildren would live under "socialism" and his promise to "bury you" sounded like more than another rocket-waving, saber-rattling speech. When Sputnik orbited on October 4, 1957, it followed by little over a month the Soviet test-firing of an intercontinental ballistic missile, a development that American intelligence had been tracing since 1956 with the use of Lockheed's high-altitude U-2 planes. When, on November 3, the Russians followed that by launching Sputnik II, a half-ton space vehicle that required much stronger thrust and also carried a live dog, the upsetting of the "balance of terror" became a nightmarish prospect. Russian technology, hitherto regarded by the West as relatively primitive, quickly won the kind of excessive respect that often accompanies surprise and shock. Sherman Adams's comment about "outer-space basketball" received derisive treatment. Within the next six months, half of the nation's high schools had undergone curriculum changes in recognition of the importance of scientific studies.[41] Even the launching, in rapid succession, of three American satellites in early 1958 failed to allay apprehensions as their weight continued to render as superior the Soviet achievement. Finally, the orbiting of an Atlas missile in September of 1958, with a recorded Christmas peace message from President Eisenhower to the world, relieved worries about the existence of a "missile lag." Those making projections about future Soviet capability, however, were virtually unanimous in acknowledging the problem of what had become known as the "missile gap." Indeed, the new bellicosity over Berlin encouraged suspicions that Moscow's plunge had been reinforced by her newly developed brawn.

In effect, the Administration itself created worries about a "missile gap" and then had to survive its ramifications while insisting on moderating defense spending. First of all, the furor originated from leakage of the contents of the highly classified so-called "Gaither Report." Officially known as "The Security Resources Panel of the Office of Defense Mobilization Science Advisory Committee" and consisting of a group of private citizens originally under the leadership of H. Rowan Gaither, Jr., Chairman of the Board of the Ford Foundation, the panel had been appointed by the President in April of 1957 to conduct an independent examination of how to provide for civil defense in case of nuclear attack. Moving from that launching point into a much broader inquiry, they examined the relative position of the "two scorpions in a bottle." What the American people were soon able to read, despite the official restrictions maintained by the President, were that the Russians were increasing their gross national product at a much more rapid rate than was the United States and that, given the present Soviet rate of military spending and capability, they might be able to hit the United States by late 1959 with one hundred ICBMs carrying megaton nuclear warheads. In short, it might soon become possible for them to launch a massive single-strike knock-out blow.[42] Delivered to the National Security Council shortly before the Russians launched their Sputnik and calling for substantial increases in the defense budget to improve America's strategic position in view of the Soviet capability, its contents were largely leaked to the press. Despite divided counsel over whether to divulge the entire report since so much of the information had become public knowledge, Eisenhower held firm. Replying to a request from Senator Lyndon Johnson for its release, Eisenhower took a position similar to one he had taken during the Army-McCarthy hearings, that it was a purely Executive matter that did not have to be revealed to the Congress. Additionally, he wrote, "I consider it improper and unwise for me to violate the confidence of the advisory relationship that has existed between me and these Panels or to make public the highly secret facts contained in their reports. I believe we must all be sensitive to the added consideration that these reports are documents of the National Security Council."[43] He also wanted to avoid, it is clear, public exposure of the panel's recommendation of the need to start massive construction of fallout shelters. He agreed with Dulles, who pointed out that for the United States to commence that kind of program, while her allies could not afford to do the same thing, would mean "writing off our friends in Europe."[44]

Nevertheless, Khrushchev's threats and the Russian technological gains seemed to confirm the danger.

Secondly, Eisenhower himself was far from alarmed by the Gaither report. His faith remained with the importance of the "great equation" and maintaining the "New Look" policy. At a meeting with the National Security Council on October 10, 1957, he reached back to his World War II experience and recalled that "when you have worked out a good sound plan at a time you were able to be calm, the soundest policy is to stand by it."[45] Furthermore, as he reminded the Gaither panel, American installations around the periphery of the Soviet Union, in addition to intelligence-gathering radar bases—helped out since 1956 by photographs from the U-2 overflights—made possible immediate retaliation. Confidence also remained in the superiority of the American strategic bomber force. The Administration also ordered the deployment at advance NATO bases of Thor and Jupiter liquid-fueled intermediate-range ballistic missiles (IRBMs). Both he and Dulles agreed, moreover, that the cold war had to be waged by other than purely military means. Substantial expenditures for mutual security would, for example, pay more dividends in the long run.

But, during the post-Sputnik period, with the projections of a certain missile lag accepted by just about everybody, his position seemed harder and harder to defend without giving the impression that the President was underestimating—or ignoring—the threat. A *Newsweek* article in December claimed that Allen Dulles thought the Russians would have operational ICBMs in about two years. Subsequent national intelligence estimates indicated that the USSR could have as many as ten by early 1959, one hundred by early 1960 and five hundred by mid-1961. Figures presented by the Alsop brothers were many times higher, claiming a possible two thousand by 1963. One study reported to the Senate Foreign Relations Committee suggested that "The military position of the United States has declined in the short span of 15 years from one of unchallenged security to that of a nation both open and vulnerable to direct and devastating attack."[46] Senator Stuart Symington, who had been shown by Allen Dulles that there would, indeed, be a substantial and growing gap, thought the Soviets would have a four-to-one advantage by 1962.[47] After hearings conducted by his Preparedness Investigating Subcommittee, Senator Johnson agreed that the Soviet Union's ballistic-missile development far exceeded the American rate.[48] Later, his close associate from Texas, Sam Rayburn, said what a lot of other people were thinking. "What good are a sound economy and a balanced budget if we lose our national lives and Russian rubles become the coin of the land?"[49] Then, Albert Wohlstetter, in a significant and highly disturbing article appearing in *Foreign Affairs*, questioned the assumption that deterrence dependent upon first-strike ability would necessarily prevent surprise attack. We have, he wrote, been "confusing deterrence with matching or exceeding the enemy's ability to strike first." Far more important for discouraging and from being tempted to deliver a swift knock-out blow would be to guarantee the ability to inflict great damage to an aggressor after having suffered the first attack. Furthermore, he warned, the widespread dispersion of IRBMs with nuclear warheads "raises measurably the possibility of accidental war." The importance of a protected retaliatory capacity would then be not only its ability to deter rational attack but also "in offering every inducement to both powers to reduce the chance of accidental war." Assuming the disadvantages inherent in every weapon, ICBMs would certainly increase the ability to retaliate.[50]

But the President stubbornly refused to panic. Undoubtedly, he had access to data supplied by sources that could not be shared with many others, making it impossible to refute the prophecies about what the Russians were about to achieve. The test ICBM firings in 1957, for example, had been monitored from radar sets in Turkey.[51] Additionally, information was either gathered or verified by the U-2 overflights, to which the President had given his personal consent despite the inherent dangers. While Dulles maintained that the Russians would not admit to having detected their presence, Eisenhower viewed that probability differently. "Well, boys," he later recalled having said, "I believe the country needs this information, and I'm going to approve it. But I'll tell you one thing. Some day one of these machines is going to be caught, and we're going to have a storm."[52] From the vast intelligence array undoubtedly came information that the Russians themselves were lagging, were not keeping pace with estimates of their capability.[53]

As pressure continued to mount, Eisenhower took a calculated risk. Braving continued American alarm about the opening of a serious "gap" by the early 1960s was one thing, but gambling with having the Russians deceived into *thinking* they *were* well ahead was quite another. Given a choice between having operational at an early date liquid-fuel missiles and waiting considerably longer for cheaper, more efficient solid-fuel models, the President chose to develop both. But his decision was to produce only a limited number of the more costly and less responsive liquid-fuel missiles and to concentrate on solid-fuel Minuteman and Polaris weapons although they would not become operational until 1963 and 1964.[54] Until they were added to the American arsenal, the expected Russian ICBM advantage constituted the mythical "missile gap," which was gleefully used by the Democrats during the 1960 Presidential election campaign and then laid to rest when the figures were gradually adjusted in mid-1961. But coming as it did amidst the fears of an imbalanced nuclear capability, Russian contumacy over Berlin found considerable credence.

Dwight Eisenhower picked up a pencil and wrote a message to his Secretary of State. "This morning I learned from my panel of doctors that you are *now* going out for routine checkups. For your sake—and ours—please do not neglect this, in spite of rebellions, wars, and what have you. D"[55] John Foster Dulles had kept up with his periodic check-ups, not so much, it often seemed, despite his rigorous schedule and frequent absences from Washington but often because his duties demanded his presence wherever and whenever necessary. He had a function to perform and his body was merely part of the mechanism that helped to make everything else possible. With some discipline and self-control, one could manage to overcome debilitations that might make lesser men surrender. At his Duck Island retreat on Lake Ontario one day, relaxing with his wife Janet, he bent down to get into his little sailboat. At that second his back went out. He remained rigid for about twenty seconds, mesmerized with pain. Then, as though nothing had happened, he got into the boat and sailed away. To his sister Eleanor, standing on the nearby dock, his excruciating pain was obvious.[56] That he suffered from a slipped disk was, to Foster, just another of the liabilities one had to live with. The cancer, fortunately, had been removed; and the passage of time prompted encouragement that it would never return. That still left him, in addition to his painful back, with serious allergies, bad eyes, malaria, gout, a thromboid flebitis and diverticulitis. When he entered Walter Reed again for a checkup and almost a week of rest on December 6, after the start of the Berlin crisis and before going on to the NATO foreign ministers' conference in Paris, he learned to his relief that there was still no sign of the cancer. But he had developed a large and severe inguinal hernia; an operation was clearly the only solution, but first, he pleaded, there were urgent matters to be taken care of during the next few weeks.[57] During that two-day session in mid-December, during which the United States joined with the other NATO members in upholding the Western position in Berlin, Dulles hardly ate or slept. Functioning only by his own will power, he paced the floor at night in pain and even tried using the bathroom floor for a bed. Looking for a quiet retreat for Janet and himself when the sessions ended, he went to spend almost two weeks at Round Hill, the home that C. Douglas Dillon owned on the island of Jamaica.

There, he and Janet spent their days taking long walks, which usually made him feel better, and playing backgammon. They kept a running score of each day's game, usually played during the afternoons and some evenings. Careful about his diet, finding it hard to hold down most food, he pretty much supervised his own menus and the food preparation. The Dillons had frozen salmon shipped down to him from New York and he delighted in chicken stewed in broth. Though he was isolated from the world's problems during those few restful days, his intense physical discomfort ruled out any visitors. He did, one day at Jamaica, receive a cable telling him that Fidel Castro, who had long headed the "Twenty-sixth of July" movement from Cuba's Sierra Maestra, had entered Havana in triumph, displacing President Fulgencio Batista. Dulles, reacting to the news, remarked, "I don't know whether this is good for us or bad for us."[58]

As soon as he returned to Washington in early January, just before the Mikoyan visit, he called in Dr. Leonard Heaton, the surgeon who had operated on him in 1956. He told Dr. Heaton that he had to keep going because there were critical matters to attend to, including a trip abroad to see Prime Minister Macmillan and Chancellor Adenauer. He resisted the doctor's plea that he submit to a hernia operation at once. Heaton, who found Dulles in a poorer state than at any time since the removal of the cancer, prescribed a truss for his patient and extracted a promise that he would enter Walter Reed immediately upon returning from Europe.[59]

The European trip, of course, resulted from the tense circumstances surrounding the Berlin situation. The British, appearing receptive to Russian overtures for a summit conference, feared American rigidity could abandon them and all of Europe to the prospects of a nuclear war brought on by Khrushchev's impatience and ambitions. Chancellor Adenauer, meanwhile, worried that Western submission to Communist threats would completely deprive the Bonn regime of its NATO role and position with the democracies. Dulles himself appeared to add to the worries of his German friend when he told the press that free elections might not be the only way to achieve reunification. The very next day, President Eisenhower appeared at the National Press Club and also seemed to offer some flexibility. He voiced the possibility that the Mikoyan trip did have legitimate peaceful intentions and wondered whether both superpowers were "really so sick of the burdens that we have to carry in the armament field that we want to find with some intelligence and some common approach a way out of this dilemma?" And, while pointing out that stripping the Germans completely of their sovereignty and military arm would be impossible, he appeared sensitive to Russian fears of a nuclearized bastion in Bonn by adding that "we would say we don't believe in the free arming of Germany in the sense that Hitler tried to rearm it." Germany might be so completely integrated in Europe's economy and defenses that any fears about revived militarism should be obviated.[60] Two days later Dulles had a second meeting with Mikoyan and the following day talked with both the President and the visitor from Moscow. The Russian, having already depreciated the significance of a six-month deadline, apparently left Washington convinced that the Americans meant further business.[61] On

February 2 Dulles left for London, Paris and Bonn. America's European allies had to be reassured.

When the Secretary reached the airport at the West German city, his reception by Adenauer resembled a reunion of old school chums. During their meetings at Schaumberg Palace, despite Dulles's attempts to minimize his physical condition, Adenauer did everything he could to mitigate the pain. At one point he offered Dulles a small bowl of warm gruel and urged his friend to try it. It was the only liquid Dulles consumed thereafter during those sessions. As they returned to the aiport, the Secretary of State attempted to allay Adenauer's apprehensions by telling him about the forthcoming hernia operation. "I mention it to you," he said, "so that you won't be shocked when you hear about the operation and so you won't think it was because of a return of cancer."[62]

Dulles returned to Washington on the ninth of February and entered Walter Reed at ten the next morning, occupying the President's own suite, which Eisenhower made available to him. The operation, on the thirteenth, was disturbingly long for a mere inguinal hernia. As he explored further, Dr. Heaton's fears were confirmed. Cancer implants were in the hernial sac. Upon palpitation through the hernial ring, implants could be felt on the peritoneal surface as well. Much fluid was also removed from Dulles's abdomen.

Upon hearing the truth, Dulles and Janet accepted the news with their usual Puritan stoicism. Dulles, eager to attend that spring's NATO sessions, pressed the surgeon for an estimate about how much time was left and Dr. Heaton replied that the operation had left room for optimism and that subsequent X-ray therapy might well remove the danger. Dulles, then, feeling responsible for having misled the elderly statesman in Bonn, immediately communicated to Adenauer the truth about his condition. President Eisenhower made his first post-operative visit to the hospital and issued a statement expressing satisfaction with the outcome of the hernia operation. When fluid reappeared in Dulles's abdomen, radioactive gold implants were made. With his condition improving and his weight returning, Dulles left for Hobe Sound, Florida, at the end of March to get some rest. As pain began to attack his back, however, he returned to the hospital with renewed fluid and a deteriorating general condition. Only drugs could relieve his suffering. On April 16, President Eisenhower announced that Dulles's resignation had been offered and accepted. One week later, at the hospital, Dulles was sworn in as a "Special Assistant to the President with Cabinet Rank." But the downhill course accelerated.

During the early-morning hours of May 24, Dr. Heaton, Janet and the two Dulles sons, Brother Avery and John, were at his bedside. Suddenly, at 7:49, Foster took Janet's hand and said he was leaving. "Is he gone?"

Janet asked the doctor, who replied, "Yes, Mrs. Dulles. I'm very sorry."[63]

Before his death, Dulles received a secret message from Ambassador David E. Bruce. Henry Cabot Lodge had reported a statement made by Khrushchev during a conversation the Russian leader had with Dag Hammarskjöld. "I feel very sorry for Dulles," he said. "I admire his intelligence, his wide knowledge, his integrity and his courage. Dulles invented brinkmanship but he would never step over the brink."[64]

Christian Herter, Under Secretary of State since 1957, having succeeded Herbert Hoover, Jr., was sworn in to replace Dulles at a brief and solemn ceremony on April 22. The President's demeanor expressed far more his loss than enthusiasm for the new State Department head.

Scarcely a month after Dulles's death, the President suffered another loss, this time a political setback that observers of his Administration called his most severe personal rebuke. For the first time since 1925, and only the eighth in American history, a Cabinet nominee failed to win confirmation from the Senate. Just after midnight on June 19, a vote of forty-nine to forty-six turned back Eisenhower's effort to seat Admiral Lewis L. Strauss to succeed Sinclair Weeks as Secretary of Commerce. Only the day before, Eisenhower had declared publicly his determination to have Strauss confirmed. He already held the position on an interim appointment. "There are a number of things that I have recommended to the Congress, and when my conscience tells me they are right, I'm going to use every single influence that I can from the executive department to get the Congress to see the light. If that's lobbying," he added, "I'm guilty, but I don't think there's anything else to do about it."[65]

Strauss, by the age of sixty-three, had incurred many enemies during his long and often distinguished public career. By his own admission he had an "unfortunate trait of stubbornness in refusing to conciliate by conceding error where error had not occurred," a most vulnerable characteristic for a traditional old conservative whose service dated back to Hoover's years. Not a pleasant adversary, he had taken strong stands. While a member of the Atomic Energy Commission he submitted a minority report urging a "crash" program for construction of the hydrogen bomb. Later, while AEC chairman, his position in the Oppenheimer case made him even more anathema to liberals, as did his subsequent role in negotiating—at the President's direction—the Dixon–Yates contract. Both public-power advocates and those concerned about the radiation fallout hazards from continued nuclear testing considered Strauss a firm enemy. Oddly enough, the fervent anti-Communist also drew fire from anti-Semites and right-wing fanatics for having been associated with a banking firm that had "financed the Bolshevik Revolution" and for caring more about the plight of Central Europe's Jews than his primary duties with the American Relief Administration during the First World War.[66] As controversial as he had become, however, no enemy deprecated his integrity. Nevertheless, when the Administration contemplated, in early 1958, reappointing him for a second five-year term with the AEC, Bryce Harlow received the following prognosis from Senate Majority Leader Lyndon Baines Johnson:

> If the President would send Admiral Strauss' name up now, there would be a knockdown, drag-out fight. Some of my people are very upset about him. They consider him arrogant and resent his statements that they have tried to socialize the power industry through the use of nuclear reactors, whereas the Administration is represented as the only true friend of free enterprise in the field of power. However, if there is good progress in connection with the Scientific Information Exchange bill, and if the Congress gets some good AEC reports on various pending bills relating to atomic energy, things might improve a bit. In such an event Clint Anderson might be able to get the matter through despite the general feeling that Strauss has been "high and mighty" in his statements and in his attitudes toward the Congress. The feeling, though, is pretty strong and bitter.[67]

After that, Strauss was permitted to retire and the job went to John McCone. But what the Administration did not count on was Clinton Anderson's personal fury. Anderson, the ranking Democrat in the Joint Atomic Energy Committee, opposed everything Strauss represented. Moreover, those who knew both men recognized the passion of what had become a bitter personal feud, fanned perhaps through a clash of personalities. Anderson tried to block the appointment within the Interstate and Foreign Commerce Committee. He accused Strauss of "substantial defects of character," of telling an "unqualified falsehood," of withholding information about Dixon–Yates, and of issuing a press release on a "clean bomb" to "create myths about his accomplishments," most of which Strauss refuted in a two-day appearance before the committee.[68] After the committee approved the nomination by the narrow margin of nine to eight, Anderson took his fight to the floor and behind the scenes. Embodying the conservatism of the Administration, Strauss's personal reputation made him a perfect target for those who not only wanted to stop the admiral but for those desiring to embarrass Eisenhower and the Republicans. The battle against Strauss, then, fought against a Presidential choice of a nominee to a position within his own department, became one of politics and personal pique that ignored the overwhelming editorial persuasion, from both Democratic and Republican newspapers, that the Chief Executive was entitled to leeway in choosing his own Cabinet.[69]

Anderson set it up and Lyndon Johnson, despite a public statement that his party's leadership would take no stand on the nomination, outmaneuvered the opposition. After assuring his colleagues that no vote would be taken on Strauss during the coming week and telling them to consider themselves free to keep speaking engagements, Johnson found that all sixty-four Democratic Senators were on hand while three Republicans—Thruston Morton,* Wallace Bennett and Milton Young—had left Washington. Suddenly, on the eighteenth of June, Johnson declared that the Senate would remain in session "today, tonight and possibly early tomorrow" until a vote had been taken.[70] The White House acted immediately by sending out calls—and Air Force planes—to retrieve the absent members. Morton and Bennett returned, and, while Young's plane was over the Midwest and not due in until 3 A.M., Senators Javits and Keating of New York led a filibuster to delay the roll call. Barry Goldwater took the Senate floor to read some of the thousands of messages praising Strauss. At that point Johnson asked Goldwater to yield and announced that an agreement had been reached to "pair" Young with Senator Mike Mansfield and that would enable a roll-call vote to begin at 12:30 A.M. Since early that evening Republicans figured they might get Strauss through by three votes and, at the very least, by a tie, which Vice President Nixon would break.[71]

With the Vice President in his chair, the Senate came to order. The reluctance of many Senators to announce their intentions had helped to increase the tension. The galleries were crowded. The roll call began. Fulbright's name brought no response; the Senator, unable to decide either way, had left the chamber. William Langer's "nay" was the only deviation from Republican ranks, but that caused little surprise. More disappointing to Strauss supporters was the "nay" from Edmund Muskie, whose approval was considered possible. But the biggest shock came from Muskie's colleague, the senior Senator from Maine, Mrs. Margaret Chase Smith. In a low but firm voice she delivered a negative vote. Some suggested that both Smith and Muskie were responding to the influence of Maine state legislator Sumner T. Pike. Pike, who had opposed Strauss on the H-bomb "crash" program back in 1949 and had then become chairman of the AEC, was a known opponent of the admiral.[72] Anderson won his fight. "The Senate's rejection of Lewis was shocking and shameful," Eisenhower wrote to Joe Dodge. "I cannot fail to believe that the American people as a whole so consider it."[73]

Those gleeful of the President's wound, however, were overly optimistic. While politics had determined the final outcome, with every possible Democratic contender for the party's 1960 nomination, including Johnson and John F. Kennedy, opposing Strauss, Eisenhower had not surrendered his initiative to the fever of the "lame duck." Already,

*Morton had replaced Mead Alcorn as GOP National Chairman that spring, a move heartily endorsed by the President.

at the outset of the Eighty-sixth Congress, he had, by his usual indirection, altered the GOP's House leadership. Ever since 1954 Charlie Halleck had wanted to oppose Joe Martin. Each time, however, the White House pointed out the liabilities of an internal fight. Martin himself, holding down the position as Minority Leader, left some dissatisfaction with his strength. Moreover, he was overconfident. When Bob Humphries, his closest friend, tried to persuade him to bolster his position by appointing Congressman Gerald Ford of Michigan as his assistant, he refused because he figured he had the votes. Eisenhower himself let Halleck know that, unlike in past years, he would not stand in his way. Thus, the "hands off" that the General's memoirs relate that he took actually became a signal for the change, which was accomplished when the House Republicans caucused and, by a secret ballot of seventy-four to seventy on January 6, replaced a bitterly disappointed Joe Martin with Charles Halleck.[74] Halleck's leadership was generally regarded as more effective, but he himself has said that it was made easier by the President's frequent personal conversations with Speaker Sam Rayburn and Lyndon Johnson, who, as many liberals complained, admired and frequently aided the bipartisanship offered by Eisenhower.[75] Moreover, despite such rebukes as the President sustained over the Strauss affair and the slump following the Congressional elections of 1958, it had become apparent by the spring of 1959, to the Majority Leader and to most observers, that Eisenhower's popular appeal was not receding but gaining momentum, defying what seemed to be the more logical course.

Like their President, the American people were not ready to concede to communism any ground within the Western sphere. The lessons learned during the 1930s were, in fact, being practiced during the 1950s. Rather than yield or appease over West Berlin, most people were confident that a firm stand would assure peace. Khrushchev, they seemed to be saying, was sufficiently prudent to withdraw before the possibility of nuclear devastation, and any talk to effectuate that outcome was better than war. Facing the reporters in mid-August, during a conference held in an improvised old gymnasium off Gettysburg's main street, the President himself voiced that sentiment as he expressed the "hope for a bettering of the atmosphere between the East and the West."[76]

Already, on August 3, Eisenhower had confirmed what he called "one of the worst kept secrets of a long time," that he and the Soviet leader had agreed to exchange visits. Khrushchev was scheduled to reach the United States in September and the President would go to Russia later. Suddenly, as though the arrangement itself had found a solution for the incendiary problem of Berlin and German reunification, both powers seemed to have retreated from the threat of disaster.

Without Dulles heading the State Department, it became easy to explain the new venture into personal diplomacy as proof of the President's sudden leadership over foreign policy. The President himself, at the Gettysburg gymnasium, denied that he had reversed "Dulles's policy" and pointed out that the matter had been considered with the late Secretary and others in the State Department for some time.[77] Moreover, at that point, he was in no position to explain the truth about his own reluctance.

Conservatives, of course, thought they had been abandoned. As early as January a Democratic Senator, Thomas Dodd of Connecticut, urged the President to resist a bilateral conference with the Russians lest it become a way for them to divide the United States from the free world by playing upon "the fears and resentments of our allies."[78] On April 2, Styles Bridges, satisfied with the President's objections to meeting with the Russians, expressed his pleasure to Eisenhower that "this Government is not going to be bluffed or blackmailed into a summit conference" and offered support for the Chief Executive's view that "we need some prior assurance that a summit conference will produce real achievement."[79] Upon hearing the news about the forthcoming exchange of visits, the Archbishop of Philadelphia immediately offered a mass for the welfare of the President and America and cabled the White House that "Today's announcement leaves a deep wound."[80] The President considered it politic personally to telephone Francis Cardinal Spellman of New York to assure him that the personal diplomacy would involve no "surrender" and that the firm stand on Berlin would continue.[81]

Influential segments of the press, however, which had only recently viewed the President as virtually planning a premature retirement, suddenly saw a new man in the White House. To James Reston he was the reincarnation of the "old" or pre-political Ike, the man of action, "moving and planning and speaking out with new serenity," out of the shadows and at center stage. A magazine article entitled "The 'New Look' of the President" observed that, despite the Twenty-second Amendment, "by virtually every measure of public opinion polls and personal soundings, President Eisenhower's standing with the public at large remains high. The latest Gallup poll shows 62 percent of the voters approving the way he is handling his job," a level of support which, if translated into votes, would constitute a major landslide. Additionally, it observed that the President's "stature, as he nears the end of his White House tenure, is growing rather than shrinking—his heroic image has almost as much luster in the public eye as it had six and one-half years ago, and in the *techniques* of the Presidency his hand is steadier than it ever has been."[82]

In reality, however, the initiative had been undertaken by Prime Minister Harold Macmillan, Khrushchev and the State Department itself, and the final plans were the product of a simple but significant misunderstanding. Ever since the winter the British leader had been displaying a willingness, even anxiety, to arrange a summit conference to break the Berlin impasse. While Chancellor Adenauer fumed at the thought of a settlement that would compromise the maintenance of Western forces in Berlin, Macmillan went to Moscow for a twelve-day exploratory trip. Finding Khrushchev determined to fulfill his plan to hand over authority to the East German government, with all the consequences that portended, the Prime Minister agreed to press for a conference.[83] He then went to Washington. Meeting with Eisenhower at Camp David, he found the President adhering to his public and private position, that surrender on "the installment plan" was no way to avoid war.[84] American agreement to a meeting hinged completely on substantial evidence, in advance, that it would be productive and not another hollow "spirit of Geneva." Khrushchev, for his part, pressed for the summit by agreeing to the foreign ministers' conference (with his assumption that it would automatically lead to a summit conference). Two sessions were held at Geneva that spring and summer and, as one newspaperman wrote, the "spirit of Geneva" of 1959 was "nine-tenths cynicism and one-tenth hope."[85] Even that 10 percent was dashed on June 19 when Soviet Foreign Minister Andrei Gromyko presented a plan that would have left West Berlin as a free and demilitarized city and extended for one year the "provisional maintenance of certain occupation rights of the Western Powers." After six weeks of discussions, Secretary of State Christian Herter reported to the American people via radio and television that "no significant progress was made toward settlement of the problem of the continued division of Germany and of Berlin."[86] The second session was also doomed to futility, but even before it began Eisenhower was asked at a news conference on July 8 about a story that Premier Khrushchev had told some American Governors traveling in Russia that he would like to visit the United States.[87] Under Secretary of State Robert Murphy has revealed how he and some colleagues at the State Department conceived of the plan to exchange visits. It was then submitted to the President and transmitted to Khrushchev through First Deputy Premier Frol R. Kozlov, who returned to Moscow on July 13 after having toured the United States. "I must say for Eisenhower," Murphy has written, "that he agreed very reluctantly."[88]

Murphy might have been more emphatic. The President was not only reluctant but dismayed. When he received acceptance from the Soviet Premier despite the failure of the second session at Geneva, he learned from the Under Secretary that his instructions had been misunderstood. The invitation conveyed by Murphy via Kozlov had been unqualified, whereas the President's understanding conditioned it on the *success* of the foreign ministers' meeting. "After a bit of cool reflection," Eisenhower wrote in his memoirs, "I realized that the cause of the difficulty lay more in my own failure to make myself unmistakably clear than in the failure of others to understand me."[89]

Two days after the impending visits were announced, Vice President Nixon returned from his own trip to Russia. Some have suggested that Eisenhower deliberately revealed the news early to deprive the ambitious Nixon of apparent credit for having negotiated the journey, although the President had already denied, most emphatically, that the Vice President had been given any authority to arrange for a visit.[90] More pertinently, however, Nixon's return coincided with the close of the Geneva conference. Linking the news with the official announcement of the failure at Geneva, which was made by Christian Herter on that August 5, was precisely what Eisenhower had wanted to avoid all along.

But Nixon, who had traveled as the American half of a cultural exchange with the Russians, which had seen Frol Kozlov open a Soviet exhibit at the New York Coliseum, had nevertheless gained important political mileage. Standing with Khrushchev at the model of a kitchen at the American exhibit in Moscow's Sokolniki Park, the Vice President debated with the Premier the relative merits of life under capitalism and communism and, more importantly, widely circulated pictures of the two men in action showed Nixon pointing a menacing-looking finger at the Russian's face. But the fact that elections lay ahead for the following year had also given the Vice President some additional burden and embarrassment. Resurrecting an old battle cry, both houses of Congress had passed a resolution directing the President to designate the third week in July as "Captive Nations Week" and to "issue a similar proclamation each year until such time as freedom and independence shall have been achieved for all the captive nations of the world." Dutifully, the President complied, signing the proclamation on July 17, five days before Nixon's departure.[91] In Moscow, Khrushchev found it hard to get off the subject, telling Nixon he regarded the resolution as a very serious "provocation." But, chagrined as he was, the Premier nevertheless looked forward to the trip his diplomacy had worked to achieve. His arrival in Washington was set for September 15.

Seeking to repair his predicament, the President preceded the Khrushchev trip with one of his own. Making what turned out to be the first in a series of four "good-will" tours, he devoted himself to some real Eisenhower-initiated personal diplomacy. His mission was designed to reassure the other NATO powers that his private sessions with the Russian leader would neither infringe upon their interests nor weaken the American contribution to the defense of Western Europe. From August 26 to September 7 he went to Bonn, London and Paris. Conversations with Adenauer, Macmillan and De Gaulle included not only Berlin and Germany but such global problems as the revolt in Algeria, the status of the underdeveloped nations and the situation in the Far East, particularly Indochina, where the stability of the Royal Laotian Government was being threatened by Pathet Lao rebels invading from Communist North Vietnam. Mostly, however, NATO unity received the first priority.

At the popular level, the trip's success was obvious. The man who, to millions of Europeans, was still the hero of World War II got a warm and often enthusiastic reception wherever he went. In England and Scotland, responding to the hospitality, he resembled an energetic freshman Congressman running for re-election in a doubtful district. His obvious good health and stamina did much to quell apprehensions that his illness had induced him merely to coast toward his retirement. Not least of all, his activity at last matched the exuberance of the active and earthy Khrushchev. Returning to Washington on September 7, he prepared to await the Russian leader. Accordingly, too, in preparation for the significant visit, U-2 overflights over the Soviet Union were ordered suspended from September 15 to 28 lest any mishap mar the occasion.[92]

Nikita Khrushchev stepped down from the Soviet plane at Andrews Air Force Base on September 15 as gleefully as a child devouring a long-awaited treat. Moreover, he had something to boast about. Only three days before his departure, obviously timed for the occasion, a Soviet rocket had been fired to the moon. He immediately referred to the feat at his airport reply to the President's greeting and later presented General Eisenhower with a model of the projectile. At a White House dinner that evening they were entertained by the music of Fred Waring and his Pennsylvanians. "We must depend upon truth and fact," said the President in his toast. "And we must make it our common purpose, as I see it, that we develop for each other the maximum of fact and truth, so that we may better lead—between us—this world into a better opportunity for peace and prosperity." Khrushchev, replying, held that "our countries are much too strong and we cannot quarrel with each other." When the weak fight, he said, "they are just scratching each other's faces and it takes just a couple of days for a cosmetician and everything comes out all right again. But if we quarrel, then not only our countries can suffer colossal damage but the other countries of the world will also be involved in a world shambles."[93] The dinner, to which many businessmen and other leaders were invited, was an undoubted success and closed with Fred Waring's rendition of "The Battle Hymn of the Republic."[94]

After a round of visits with members of the Senate Foreign Relations Committee, an appearance at the National Press Club and a talk at the Soviet Embassy, where he declared that the cold war had begun to thaw out, he was given a cool but polite welcome in New York City. There, on the eighteenth, he addressed the United Nations and dramatically proposed a four-year plan for "total disarmament," involving the complete elimination of all armed forces, weapons, general staffs, foreign bases and even military training schools.[95] His sudden and unilateral suspension of nuclear-bomb tests in March of 1958 had caused the Administration to follow suit seven months later. Subsequent talks at Geneva for a permanent ban had, however, since become deadlocked. As unachievable as his proposal was, Khrushchev nevertheless encouraged the seekers of "peaceful coexistence" that a very un-Stalin-like ruler, indeed, led the Soviet Union.

With his peasant origins still very evident, and escorted by an American patrician, Ambassador Henry Cabot Lodge, Khrushchev then toured the country. Angered when told that security complications would prevent him from visiting Disneyland, at Anaheim, California, and derisive at the "immorality" of dancers at the Hollywood set of *Can-Can*, he nevertheless proceeded with boisterous enthusiasm. While on the West Coast, however, he encountered open hostility from prominent men whose need to demonstrate their antipathy toward the Soviet Union made him a captive victim. At a civic dinner given for Khrushchev at the Ambassador Hotel in Los Angeles, he was sufficiently offended to threaten the immediate termination of his trip.

Ambassador Lodge had advised that city's mayor, Norris Poulson, against throwing back at the visiting Premier his comment that "we shall bury you," a remark that was made in connection with his claim about the inevitable superiority of the Soviet economic system. Nevertheless, the mayor chose to demonstrate that he, too, like the other Californian who had debated with Khrushchev at Sokolniki Park, was a tough anti-Communist. The context of Poulson's "welcome" address was not belligerent. "Now, Mr. Chairman," he said, "I want to make this statement in the most friendly fashion. We do not agree with your widely quoted phrase 'We shall bury you.' You shall not bury us and we shall not bury you. We are happy with our way of life. We recognize its shortcomings and are always trying to improve it. But if challenged, we shall fight to the death to preserve it. . . . I tell you these things not to boast or to threaten, but to give you a picture of what the people of Southern California feel in their hearts. . . . we are planning no funerals, yours *or* our own. There never will be a funeral for the free spirit that lives in every man." Considering the circumstances, however, Mayor Poulson's comment was in very questionable taste and, for the Eisenhower Administration, an embarrassment, particularly when the incensed Premier appeared on the verge of disrupting his tour.[96] Later, when learning that mayors were independent of any control from Washington, Khrushchev remarked, "Now I begin to understand some of the problems of President Eisenhower."[97]

Poulson, however, spoke for most Americans. While in San Francisco the Russian was given a hard time in a closed session by seven labor

leaders. Led by Walter Reuther, they seemed eager to exonerate themselves from suspicions of trade-union "softness" toward communism.
Their approach offered a significant contrast with the cordial reception
given by businessmen who were eager for commercial relations with
Russia.[98] Others also expressed their doubts about the value of Khrushchev's visit. In a report to the Senate Internal Security subcommittee,
the following January, FBI director J. Edgar Hoover held that the Premier's presence had created an "atmosphere favorable to communism
among Americans" and an opportunity for the Communist Party to
enhance its influence.[99]

But, at a Camp David session on Sunday, September 27, the second day
of Khrushchev's final weekend in America, substantive progress did appear. Eisenhower had maintained with firmness his position against
agreeing to a summit conference without any prior evidence of progress
and reiterated the importance of Western rights in Berlin to peaceful
coexistence. Finally, on that day, Khrushchev agreed that the time limit
would be withdrawn. Significantly, he asked that the return to the *status
quo ante*—and, of course, the end of the crisis—be delayed until he
returned to Moscow and had explained his concession. So the final communiqué of the Camp David discussions merely hinted at the development by saying an "understanding was reached."[100] The "spirit of
Camp David" thus replaced the illusion of Geneva.

Eisenhower's place as a man of peace was firmer than ever before.
Popular confidence in his leadership rose to 66 percent by November
and, at the outset of 1960, to 71 percent, its highest point in nearly
three years.[101] After a round of negotiations among the Western allies,
with De Gaulle clearly in no hurry for an early meeting, a summit
conference with the Russians at Paris was set for May 16, and Eisenhower's visit to the Soviet Union was scheduled for June. Meanwhile,
the man who, more than anyone alive, had come to symbolize peace
concluded 1959 with an ambitious and triumphant eleven-nation "good-
will tour" that took him to Europe, Asia and Africa.[102] Indeed, peace
had begun to seem less illusory, if, of course, the Russians really meant
to be reasonable about West Berlin.

On Sunday evenings in most American towns and cities, snack counters at railway and bus terminals become the only places in the downtown area where one can buy a sandwich and a cup of coffee. Joseph
McNeill, a freshman at the all-Negro North Carolina Agricultural and
Technical College, tried to do just that on January 31, 1960. McNeill
was hungry; but he was also black. That, he was promptly told, made
him ineligible to be served. Returning to his dormitory, he conferred
with a roommate and other students in search of what could be done
about the local ordinance. At ten o'clock that next morning, McNeill

and three friends entered the Woolworth's five-and-dime store and took seats at the lunch counter. Ignored, they nevertheless remained. After two and a half hours they walked out and recited the Lord's Prayer on the sidewalk of the busy downtown district and vowed to send shifts of other students to continue the sitting-in until the barrier had been removed.[103] Within a few days the protest spread to the local S. H. Kress store. On February 5, Klansmen came to assist the local whites. A bomb threat closed both stores, and the Negroes agreed to withdraw their protest for two weeks while service policies were being re-evaluated.

Before the month had ended, sit-ins had spread throughout the South. Charlotte, Durham and Winston-Salem experienced similar tactics, and the idea spread into Virginia, where Negro students demonstrated at lunch counters in Richmond, Hampton and Portsmouth. The largest department stores in Nashville, Tennessee, were also affected. Thirty black students descended upon two Chattanooga stores, forcing them to close. When the lunch counter in Hampton opened its services to Negroes, they found themselves faced with premium prices.[104] Assistance soon came from the Congress of Racial Equality, or CORE, and Dr. Martin Luther King. Restraint by the peaceful demonstrators, in the face of KKK and other opponents, became more difficult. At his press conference Eisenhower defended the right to demonstrate as long as the protestors were peaceful.[105]

Thus the South began to experience the counterattack against segregation. Spurred by the series of court decisions rejecting racial separation and encouraged by the example of Dr. King's Montgomery bus boycott and the mounting conviction that change required direct action, the movement spread to eating places throughout the region. Even before Greensboro, organized assaults had been made on discrimination in Wichita, Kansas, and Oklahoma City. In Wichita, sit-ins began at the huge Katz Drug Company outlet on August 19, 1958. Four other establishments were also chosen, and, at the end of two weeks, all but one had changed their policies. Before the end of the month, activists were also operating in Oklahoma City, where a church mediation committee worked closely with the proprietors so that by early 1960 more than thirty establishments were open to customers of both races.[106]

That year, too, the Student Non-Violent Coordinating Committee was born to guide the protest movement. The incredibly slow pace of school desegregation, with only a tiny percentage of black children attending integrated schools six years after the *Brown v. Topeka* decision—and then mostly in the Border states—and the massive resistance led by the Citizens Councils and other groups had sparked the counterattack. Despite the Administration's role in the Civil Rights Act of 1957, or perhaps because of its complicity in striking out the provision to allow the Attorney General to seek court injunctions where voters were deprived of their rights, and regardless of the President's move in the Little Rock affair, Negro confidence in the leadership from Washington had continued to diminish.[107]

One month before he met with the black leaders in the White House, President Eisenhower, much to his surprise, provoked anguish from prominent Negroes. Finally persuaded, for the first time, to address an all-black group, Eisenhower, on May 12, 1958, appeared at a luncheon in Washington's Presidential Arms sponsored by the National Newspaper Publishers Association. Every seat was taken and there were many standees. When he entered the room, the man who had recently defied Governor Faubus received a tumultuous ovation. Speaking from notes supplied by Max Rabb, he talked on his favorite theme, the relationship of the economy to national defense and the importance of mutual-aid programs. Then pushing his papers aside, he began to ad-lib. "No one is more anxious than I am to see Negroes receive first-class citizenship in this country," he said; and then came the words that stunned his audience—"but you must be patient."[108]

When he finished, there were few cheers but much hissing. Three hundred years of waiting, most of his listeners thought, had been long enough. Jackie Robinson felt like standing up and shouting, "Oh no! Not again." For the next few weeks the White House received scores of indignant letters and telephone calls. "When you said we must have self-respect," Robinson wrote to the President, "I wondered how we could have self-respect and remain patient considering the treatment accorded us through the years."[109] In a reply to the ex-Brooklyn Dodger baseball star, the President denied that he had meant the use of patience and forbearance as "substitutes of constructive action or progress."[110]

That the Administration was appeasing the South had become the conviction of both moderate and militant leaders. Dr. King, who was active in desegregation drives during the summer of 1958, had attempted to maintain an attitude of respectful cooperation toward the Administration. Meeting with the other black leaders on the night before their conference at the White House with the President, the reverend who continually preached the need for non-violence even objected to using the word "angry" to inform Mr. Eisenhower how Negroes felt toward the leadership in Washington. Later that summer Dr. King was arrested by Montgomery, Alabama, police. Roy Wilkins, on an airplane stopover at Chicago while en route to San Francisco, saw an early-morning newspaper with a picture of two policemen twisting the minister's arm behind his back. Reaching the West Coast, Wilkins saw a second photograph, one taken at the police station afterward. The NAACP leader was horrified to see King still being held in the same manner. Expressing his agitation to Fred Morrow, Wilkins warned that "It will be a dangerous and rueful day when Negro Americans became convinced that local, state and federal governments have turned their backs and delivered them to unrestrained persecution."[111]

Just a week before the King incident, the President had dismayed civil-rights leaders by acknowledging in a news conference that, while he did not think he should comment about a Supreme Court decision, he believed that caution, accompanied by "reason and sense and education," had to "go hand in hand if this process is going to have any real acceptance in the United States."[112] On Sunday, October 5, five weeks later, three heavy dynamite explosions ripped the newly integrated Clinton High School in Tennessee, inflicting an estimated two or three hundred thousand dollars in damages.[113] Furthermore, the GOP had suffered serious loses in state after state where the number of Negro voters could easily have made the difference for the party. Not only were they offended by the Administration, but local Republicans were obviously either indifferent or even hostile toward their needs.[114]

The Civil Rights Commission, established slowly under the provisions of the 1957 act, spent much of 1959 investigating the status of black voting. Holding hearings in several cities, both North and South, the group found evidence of serious interference with suffrage rights. Although, in Alabama, almost 30 percent of the voting-age population was black, only 8.1 percent were actually registered. In Mississippi, only 3.9 percent could vote, although Negroes comprised 41 percent of the state's total population. Sixteen Southern counties, in which a majority of voting-age citizens were black, had not a single non-white voter.[115] "In terms of securing and protecting the right to vote," stated the commission's report, "the record of the Department of Justice's Civil Rights Division under the Civil Rights Act of 1957 is hardly more encouraging than it was before."[116] The department was far more zealous in other fields, such as in anti-monopoly matters. To recify the situation, the commission urged the establishment of registrars to deal with substantiated instances of the denial of the right to vote by administering state election laws "in connection with the election of Federal officers until the President determines that such procedures are no longer necessary."[117]

A new civil-rights law did emerge in 1960, finally, for the first time despite a filibuster and after an eight-week debate. The product, although stronger than the 1957 legislation, passed largely through the maneuvering of Majority Leader Lyndon B. Johnson, who was shedding his "Southern" legislative record with a careful eye upon his party's Presidential nomination. Instead of registrars, as the commission had urged, provision was made for the Administration's concept of "referees," who would be empowered to report to courts interference with voting rights. The courts could, however, authorize the referees to supervise the casting and counting of ballots by the disfranchised. Not only did the Administration fail to revive the defeated 1957 plan enabling the Attorney General to obtain injunctions, but Southern opposition kept both the President and his party's leadership from pressing the Administration's original call to establish a permanent Commission of Job Equality Under Government Contracts and to give federal technical assistance to school agencies going through the process of desegregation. Furthermore, although it had been an Administration request, and despite the almost solid opposition by Southern Democrats, the desegregation assistance amendment was tabled in the Senate with the votes of 70 percent of the Republicans and 65 percent of the Democrats. The final version did win the support of all GOP Senators, however, while eighteen Democrats, all from the South, voted nay.[118]

In signing the Civil Rights Act of 1960 into law on May 6, the President regretted that two of his recommendations had been deleted but labeled it "an historic step forward in the field of civil rights."[119] While an improvement over the earlier law, which was, after all, not bad for the first legislation in that field since 1875, wide areas of racial inequality, including stronger enforcement of voting rights and discrimination in employment and accommodations, were untouched. A. Philip Randolph soon threatened to stage demonstrations outside the conventions of both parties to protest their joint "failure to enact a meaningful rights bill," and Dr. King formulated plans for a march to the site of the Democratic convention in Los Angeles.[120] What had been accomplished, far from preserving the President's cautious middle-of-the-road approach, had only convinced the black leaders that real gains required meeting stiff conservative resistance with bolder means, a course that would take them far from the conscience appeal of the 1957 Prayer Pilgrimage.

On May Day, Francis Gary Powers was in an odd place for a thirty-one-year-old flyer from the village of Pound, Virginia. His U-2 high-altitude Lockheed plane, virtually a motorized glider, was on a course that would take him across the heart of the Soviet Union and toward where another U-2, on April 9, had detected the possible location of an operational ICBM base. Taking pictures had to be accomplished quickly, before the construction at the site could be camouflaged and further obscured by the heavy fog that rolls over the northern part of the Soviet Union with the coming of warm summer weather. Also near his route, some thirty miles east of the Aral Sea (or Aral'skoye More), was the launching installation for the long-range missile shots.

Powers, already under close observation from American radar situated in Turkey, where his flight had originated, crossed the Russian border at an altitude of sixty thousand feet—and still climbing—with the Communist tracking scopes also locking in on him. Despite the heavy cloud cover, he switched on his camera with its rotating 944.7 millimeter lens and began photographing everything possible. Four hours out of Adana, Turkey, and over thirteen hundred miles into Soviet territory, the U-2 approached the regional metropolis of Sverdlovsk, at the eastern edge of the Urals. Suddenly, an exterior blast rocked the plane and Powers saw a great orange flash light up the cockpit and the sky. After a long downward spin, he finally climbed clear of the aircraft, and his automatic parachute opened at fifteen thousand feet and landed him with a painful crash on a field. Two startled men waited to greet the mysterious stranger.[121]

In Moscow, a May Day parade was already under way. Before the reviewing stand in Red Square, loaded with Khrushchev and the rest of the hierarchy, Russian military might passed in a long procession. While an American correspondent had his eyes on the Kremlin's bosses, the chief of the Soviet Air Force, arriving late, at about 10:45 Moscow time, whispered something into Premier Khrushchev's ear.[122]

President Eisenhower had spent the morning of May 1 at Camp David, where persistent rain frustrated hopes of driving back up to Gettysburg for some more golf. That afternoon a telephone call from General Goodpaster told him that the U-2 from Adana was overdue and had disappeared from radar screens. Its significance was immediately clear. Instead of driving back to Washington, as he had planned, the President quickly returned by helicopter.[123]

The next few days made intelligence history. A story about a missing "weather" plane had already circulated from Turkey. Therefore, on May 3, the National Aeronautics and Space Administration released a report that a "NASA U-2 research airplane" on a joint NASA-USAF Weather Service mission was missing after apparently having gone down on Sunday morning in the area of Lake Van, Turkey. The pilot, an "employee" of Lockheed Aircraft engaged in making "high altitude weather studies," had radioed about oxygen trouble.[124]

Had Dulles been right about the Russians? Or would they, as Eisenhower feared, admit that they had been the victim of U-2 overflights? That question was answered by Khrushchev himself. Speaking in Moscow on May 5, he revealed that a flight by an American plane had violated Soviet air space, just as one had done on April 9. "Just imagine," he said, "what would have happened if a Soviet aircraft were to appear, say, over New York, Chicago or Detroit. . . . How would the United States react? United States officials have repeatedly declared that they keep A-bomb and H-bomb planes on the alert, and that with the approach of a foreign aircraft they would take off and head for their designated bombing targets. That would mean the outbreak of war."[125]

Khrushchev revealed nothing else. His information seemed to have come from mere radar detection. Eisenhower agreed, in view of the story coming out of Moscow, that he should stay out of the picture and went along with a decision to have the State Department handle the matter. Secretary Herter, just back from a conference in Istanbul, approved a new statement. The information was given to the reporters by press officer Lincoln White, who, like almost all Washington officials, was ignorant about the real nature of the flight. It restated the original cover story. The next day White also assured the press that "there was absolutely no—no—no deliberate attempt to violate Soviet air space, and there never has been."[126] The Americans had entered Khrushchev's trap.

On the seventh, facing the Supreme Soviet, the Russian leader gleefully announced that "We have parts of the plane and we also have the pilot, who is quite alive and kicking. The pilot is in Moscow and so are parts of the plane." He displayed pictures of Francis Gary Powers. That evening, after hours of uneasy silence from Washington, the President took a step unprecedented in the annals of espionage. He authorized a State Department statement that an intelligence-gathering aircraft had "probably" flown over Soviet territory.[127]

The incident left many puzzled, angry and deeply perplexed about the Administration's course. The United States government had been caught in a lie and, moreover, had admitted that the original account had been fictitious. With the State Department still taking full responsibility, Herter then issued an ambiguous statement justifying the overflights and seeming to say, without actually doing so, that they must continue. Soviet secrecy, and their unwillingness to accept such proposals for mutual aerial inspection as the President had offered at Geneva in 1955, had made such security measures necessary.[128] The next Sunday night the Vice President appeared on David Susskind's evening TV talk show and declared that they were needed to prevent "surprise attacks" and would continue, thus putting the other side on notice that the Americans, having been caught redhanded, had no intention of stopping.[129]

But what Herter and Nixon said or implied was one thing; the President's responsibility was another. Khrushchev himself indicated that Eisenhower probably had no personal knowledge about the policy. That implied confirmation of what the President's critics were saying all along, that he was the unknowing prisoner of a staff system that did pretty much as it wanted and withheld the unpleasant. Yet, on the eleventh, after telling a group of Congressmen at breakfast that he intended to say nothing further about the U-2, he reversed his course by the time he met the press at 10:27 and opened with a statement directly defending such intelligence-gathering. "No one wants another Pearl Harbor," he said. "This means that we must have knowledge of military forces and preparations around the world, especially those capable of massive surprise attacks." His own responsibility and knowledge of what was going on was clear, as it should have been, since his role with the flights had been intimate since their inception.[130] To the widespread, almost universal anger about the timing of the Powers mission, just two weeks before the Paris conference, Eisenhower was hinting at his real concern, a worry he would express to confidants over and over again later while waiting for his successor to be inaugurated—that the Soviets, like the Japanese in 1941, might use overtures toward negotiations and periods of distraction to launch a surprise attack upon the United States.[131] For the United States to attempt to hide its responsibility, furthermore, he held completely unrealistic in an age when spies were being sent into enemy air space with, as Eisenhower said, the evidence "strapped on their backs." For him to deny knowledge of the situation would constitute an admission that he did not run his own government, a position that would create a serious disadvantage during personal diplomacy with Khrushchev.[132] Senator Francis Case was only one of the many who questioned the wisdom of Eisenhower's candor. Perhaps, suggested the South Dakota Republican, national interest would have been better protected by having the "heat" borne by lesser officials. "While I understand your concern," replied the President, "I nevertheless feel that the course of action with respect to the U-2 matter was the proper one. I assure you my decision was my own; I felt it only fair to all concerned to get the whole story accurately told."[133]

He did not, however, rule out going to Paris and attempting the summit conference, or even the later visit to Moscow. Khrushchev, faced with American guilt and defiance, fulminated righteously in Paris on May 16 and demanded an apology from the President and a promise that such flights would not continue. Temperamentally and politically, just as the Russian had to storm about his grievance, that was impossible. Demanding it was an ultimatum. Eisenhower, in a statement that evening, did announce that the flights had been halted and accused the Russian of wrecking the conference.[134] The invitation to visit Russia was also canceled. On May 19, after further conversations with Prime Minister Macmillan and President De Gaulle, Eisenhower left Paris.

For those not irrevocably tied to American thinking, Khrushchev had, of course, scored a great propaganda coup. Leftist opinion throughout the world applauded his actions, while, even at home, liberals attributed the outcome to a President who had no control over his government. But Khrushchev's move, at the same time, satisfied many needs. Chancellor Adenauer, all along, dreaded what might result from an agreement over Berlin and Germany. De Gaulle, too, was extremely wary; his desires had delayed the session until May 16 in the hope that something might happen before then to remove the problem.

And Khrushchev himself had obtained a means for extricating his own position. Going on to Peking after his Camp David concession to Eisenhower, the Premier found the rift with the Chinese Communists widened. Not only had he failed to accommodate them with nuclear weapons during the offshore-island crisis, but now he had displayed weakness before the West. Furthermore, unlike the President, who had traveled to consult with his allies before the bipartite meeting, the Russian did so only after the fact. The friction that resulted at Peking was sufficient for both sides to forgo issuing the usual joint communiqué about their talks, and Khrushchev, upon departing, made the barbed point that "we Communists of the Soviet Union consider it our sacred duty, our primary task . . . to utilize all possibilities in order to liquidate the cold war."[135] The Red Chinese press continued their accusations that he was more intested in appeasing the West. As May Day approached and Powers prepared to take off from Adana, Khrushchev reverted to his old statements about Russian dictation of a German settlement. An angry exchange then developed between the Premier and Under Secretary of State Douglas Dillon, who vowed to reject any arrangement that would compromise German freedom. On April 26 Khrushchev retorted that when "hotheads" begin to invoke "force and not right and justice, it is but natural that this force will be countered with the force of the other side."[136]

The summit was lost as much for political and diplomatic reasons as for the handy justification provided by American intelligence operations. Khrushchev later said he could not agree to another conference until six or eight months hence, pointedly fixing his date to coincide with the presence of Eisenhower's successor in the White House. In the United States, public opinion showed little sign of blaming the President for the U-2 or the events at Paris; in fact, confidence in his leadership rose.[137]

In June he set out for another extensive "good-will trip," this time to the Far East. En route to Japan after visiting Manila and Formosa, he was told by the government in Tokyo that the great upheavals stirred up by leftists over American "imperialism," particularly because of the U-2 incident, had made his visit inadvisable. A few weeks later the Russians shot down an American RB-47 reconnaissance plane, which, they charged, had been used for espionage over their territory.

The arrival of summer in 1960 found Americans in a new state of shock and uncertainty, unlike anything since one decade earlier when the collapse of Chiang Kai-shek, Russia's acquisition of nuclear power and entrenchment in Eastern Europe, spies and spy-hunters and a frustrating war in Korea ultimately convinced the electorate to ignore party labels and turn to the General who symbolized peace, patriotism and honor. In June, Jim Hagerty, Tom Stephens and Douglas MacArthur II, together in a limosine at Tokyo's Haneda International Airport, experienced a harrowing situation. Rock-throwing anti-American demonstrators, their hatred recharged by the U-2 incident and the events in Paris, trapped them in their car for one hour and twenty minutes. Together in the Japanese capital to prepare for the Eisenhower visit, they had to be rescued by a United States Marine helicopter and then only with a great deal of difficulty.[138] The subsequent cancellation of the President's visit, marring the final leg of his fourth good-will tour within a year (he had also gone to South America in February) and so soon after the rejection of his trip to Moscow, seemed to recall the darkest days of the cold war. The "spirit of Camp David" had joined the "spirit of Geneva" in mythology.

Elsewhere, too, events were moving so rapidly that it became legitimate to speculate about the wisdom of having Vice President Nixon—certain to be nominated at Chicago—run for the White House as "Ike's boy." Bloody turbulence in the Republic of the Congo, after its independence on June 30, threatened to become a new East-West battleground. Swiftly the Soviet Union exploited the anti-colonialist impulse and attempted, in the Security Council, to condemn the presence of Belgian troops as an act of aggression. While the rebellion of the Province of Katanga against becoming federated under Patrice Lumumba's central government in Leopoldville began to win sympathy from conservatives, Russia became increasingly identified with the newly independent regime. As UN troops rushed in to restore order, Moscow's aid went directly to Lumumba. All summer and into the fall, fighting raged in the African country and the United Nations debated the issue. In September, Eisenhower spoke before the General Assembly to urge support of the UN's efforts to resolve the Congo dilemma.

More important to Americans, however, the course of Fidel Castro's new regime in Havana had become unsettling. On July 6, President Eisenhower, signing Public Law 86–592 authorizing him to determine the Cuban sugar quota, proclaimed a drastic reduction of tonnage to be purchased. Noting that the Castro government had "embarked upon a deliberate policy of hostility toward the United States," he complained that Havana "has committed itself to purchase substantial quantities of goods from the Soviet Union under barter arrangements."[139] Three days later, from his vacation site at Newport, he denounced Premier Khrushchev's support of Castro as an attempt by "international communism to intervene in the affairs of the Western Hemisphere."[140] While Ambassador Philip Bonsal, who had replaced Earl T. Smith along with Batista in Havana, regretted the act of "perhaps the rising pressures of an election year in our own country," most Americans approved penalizing what appeared to be a Russian satellite ninety miles off the Florida coast.[141] Castro retaliated by nationalizing the American sugar mills and confiscating the remaining Yankee investments.

The new Prime Minister and hero of the 26th of July Movement had entered Havana in triumph on January 1, 1959, after ousting dictator Fulgencio Batista. Many Americans, even those skeptical about his revolutionary zeal, were ready to welcome him as a potential democratic liberator. Eisenhower, too, long anticipating Batista's overthrow, was sympathetic to the aspirations of the new leadership. Voicing the concern of American businessmen who had dominated large segments of the country's economy under Batista's benevolent treatment, the President equated their legitimacy with the protection of the contractual rights of the investors.[142]

Shortly after his installation, however, Castro showed distinct signs of a leftward movement. The bearded young middle-class lawyer announced that it would be in the public interest to delay elections "till political parties are full developed and their programme clearly defined."[143] A wave of executions then followed, against both real and alleged *Batistianos*, and the regime began to move leftward and to acquire a suspiciously pro-Communist tinge. His rising anti-Yankee rhetoric re-evoked the old hatred toward the "colossus of the North." On March 26, Allen Dulles informed the President that CIA information indicated a steady movement toward complete dictatorship on the island, with Communists "operating openly and legally in Cuba," although Castro's government was not Communist.

Alarmed when the American Society of Newspaper Editors invited the flamboyant leader to speak at the National Press Club in Washington on April 17, the President considered refusing to grant him a visa.[144] Pointedly, Eisenhower greeted Castro's presence by going to Augusta for some golf, although it is questionable whether the Cuban himself would have considered an invitation to the White House as politic. But he did confer with Vice President Nixon. During their three-hour session, Nixon showed Castro files indicating the extent of communism among his supporters; but the Prime Minister showed no interest and tried to explain the necessity for the executions that had brought so much condemnation. Disturbed, Nixon afterward sent a memorandum to the CIA, the State Department and the White House advising against trying to "get along with" and "understand" Castro. He also suggested that the United States organize a force of Cuban exiles to overthrow the revolutionary leader.[145] Such an attack, mounted at that early stage, would inevitably have depended upon *Batistianos*, for the anti-Batista, anti-Castro Cubans had yet to flee from the regime.

On March 17, 1960, four months before the sugar-quota proclamation and Castro's retaliations, the President ordered the CIA to, as his memoirs report, "begin to organize the training of Cuban exiles, mainly in Guatemala, against a possible future day when they might return to their homeland."[146] Characteristically, however, Eisenhower was cautious and did not make a specific commitment for an invasion. That decision would depend upon the estimates of the likelihood of success as gauged by the strength of the indigenous opposition to Castro.[147]

July's economic warfare made turning back seem impossible. Relations between the two countries continued to deteriorate, bringing the cold war much closer to home. After Democratic Presidential candidate John F. Kennedy put out a statement that called for strengthening the Cuban counter-revolutionaries, Richard Nixon became upset. Assuming that Kennedy had been briefed about the activities taking place in Guatemala, during his fourth televised pre-election debate with his opponent, he accused Kennedy of advocating a course that would probably cost the United States all her friends in Latin America and "we would probably be condemned in the United Nations, and we would not accomplish our objective."[148] Not until the seventeenth and twenty-ninth of November, however, did Kennedy learn about the actual plans for a possible invasion.[149] While Kennedy's information came from Allen Dulles and Richard Bissell, word about the training of the brigade in Central America spread throughout the Caribbean. Finally, Castro ordered the reduction in staff of the United States Embassy and consulate in Havana to just eleven and the departure from Cuba of all other personnel within forty-eight hours. Seventeen days before the end of his Presidency, Eisenhower responded by breaking diplomatic relations with the revolutionary regime.

The situation in Indochina, as if to complete the picture of global deterioration of the American position, provided the outgoing Administration with mounting concern. Rural violence had become endemic. Land reforms instituted by President Diem, such as they were, left most of the holdings in the hands of the few, many of them directly in control of the government. Two percent of the population still held 45 percent of the countryside.[150] Both Communist and non-Communist opposition to the American-assisted government increased, and the terrorism that accelerated in mid-1959 was accompanied by a marked upsurge in Vietcong activity.[151] In April, eighteen Vietnamese dissenting politicians gathered at the Caravelle Hotel in Saigon and drew up a "manifesto" of grievances against the government. They complained that "the people do not know a better life or more freedom under the republican regime which you have created" and that official tyranny was filling "the jails and prisons to the rafters."[152] They urged the modification of policies "so as to remedy the situation, to defend the republican regime, and to safeguard the existence of the nation. We hold firm hope that the Vietnamese people shall know a brilliant future in which it will enjoy peace and prosperity in freedom and progress."[153]

Ambassador Elbridge Durbrow agreed that something had to be done. The danger to Diem's regime was serious, he cabled Secretary Herter in September. And while he recognized that support for Diem had to continue because he was the *"best available Vietnamese leader,"* Durbrow recommended recognition that the American objective required a *"strongly anti-communist Vietnamese government which can command loyal and enthusiastic support of widest possible segments of Vietnamese people, and is able to carry on effective fight against communist guerrillas."*[154] Two months later, as though in confirmation of the ambassador's fears, bursts of heavy machine-gun fire poured into Diem's bedroom at three o'clock on the morning of November 11. The attempted *coup d'état*, staged by three paratroop battalions stationed in Saigon that were considered by Diem among his most faithful, was led by a small group of civilians and military officers. Government troops quickly subdued the insurgents. Consequently, all eighteen members of the "Caravelle Group" were arrested and jailed.[155] In December, the National Liberation Front, although in existence informally since 1954, was established to lead the insurgent forces and become the political arm of the rebellion.[156] A long memorandum from Brigadier General Lansdale, dated January 17, 1961, warned that the "free Vietnamese, and their government, probably will be able to do no more than postpone eventual defeat—unless they find a Vietnamese way of mobilizing their total resources and then utilizing them with spirit."[157]

Two days after the Lansdale communication, the President of the United States, in his last full day in office, conducted a meeting in the Cabinet Room. Present were Secretary Herter, Secretary of Defense Thomas Gates, Treasury Secretary Robert Anderson, as well as three emissaries from the incoming Administration, Dean Rusk, Robert McNamara and Douglas Dillon. Clark Clifford was also there and, at President-elect Kennedy's suggestion, took notes. While the discussion centered around the events in Southeast Asia, the President's main concern was with the ominous situation in Laos, where the American-supported government was losing to the pro-Communist neutralists backed by the Soviet Union. After the flight into exile in Cambodia by Prince Suvanna Phuma in December, the Pathet Lao displayed increased strength. Eisenhower's anxiety was obvious. Laos, he warned, had to be defended. It was the key to all of Southeast Asia. Permitting a Communist takeover would mean writing off the entire region. The best course would be to persuade America's allies of the need to defend Laos. If they refuse, he added, "Our unilateral intervention would be our last desperate hope in the event we were unable to prevail upon the other signatories to join us."[158]

During those last White House months it became fashionable to characterize its occupant as a man who had become more conservative during the course of his eight years. He fought against large budgets with a zeal that he displayed for few other causes. He insisted on the need to maintain "sound money," a favorite theme of conservatives. Even when additional spending was prescribed as an antidote to the 1958 recession, which had been caused by large inventories and reduced investments, he and Robert Anderson emphasized "tight money" and prudent expenditures to halt inflation. Stability did come, but at the cost of an unemployment level that temporarily topped five million and included 7 percent of the labor force.[159] By the next year, however, the economy once more resembled 1955; but recovery had been promoted by the increased spending that the President had resisted and, contrary to George Humphrey's old theory, a grossly unbalanced budget did not discourage private investments. Moreover, passage of the Landrum-Griffin bill in 1959 (the Labor-Management Reporting and Disclosure Act), inspired by the McClellan Committee's revelations about corrupt union practices and containing stricter provisions than the Taft-Hartley Act to police labor spending, was considered a major victory for both the President and the House Republican leadership under Charlie Hallek. Also, as the 1960 elections neared, General Eisenhower stuck to his position that, despite complaints about a slowing down of the Gross National Product, the nation's strength and economy had never been as sound. The battle over Strauss and the President's tepid attitude toward stringent legislation to protect civil rights, including an admonition in 1959 against expecting too much from laws, seemed to complete the impression that the old cry of "modern Republicanism" was indistinguishable from traditional conservatism.

Yet, facing a breakfast session of the Republican National Committee in Chicago on the day after he had addressed the convention, the President warned that those who "insist on marching in the gutters of the extreme right and left are, in the long run, always defeated. . . . You must find the broad highway and you must ignore the gutters."[160] All year he fought hard for mutual-security funds. Before leaving for the abortive summit conference in Paris he dictated a letter to be sent to two hundred friends warning of the ominous consequences that would befall the "free world" by acceding to conservative demands to effectuate reported cuts of over a billion dollars. "It is incomprehensible to me that at this point in world affairs," he wrote, "we should face the possibility of undermining, by our own hand, our buttressing of free nations and our partnerships in defense against Communist imperialism."[161] When the Democratic leadership maneuvered Congress into a special post-convention and pre-election session in August, Eisenhower sent a special message urging full restoration of the over half-billion-dollar cut. He also called for enactment of a moderate though broad range of social legislation, including provisions for helping older people meet serious illnesses, expansion of the Fair Labor Standards coverage, an increase in the minimum wage and a "sound area assistance program directed specifically to the areas in need."[162] As political as they were, challenging the Democrats—who, after all, were in firm control of Congress—not one item represented anything the Administration had not advocated earlier.

Moreover, the nomination of Richard Nixon at Chicago in July gave the GOP a candidate who had moved to the center. While there is no evidence to show that the Vice President was the General's first choice, and plenty to indicate a preference for Anderson or possibly some others, neither can anybody argue that Eisenhower put up any resistance once the national committee and the overwhelming choice of Republican voters had centered on Nixon. A challenge to the Vice President from Governor Rockefeller of New York provided opposition from the left.

Rockefeller's own Presidential ambitions appeared to have become subordinated to reality as far back as December. After touring the country to assess whether he could command enough backing to get the nomination, he finally announced his "definite and final" decision not to try because of his finding that "the great majority of those who control the Republican convention stand opposed to any contest for the nomination."[163] In early June, however, he took advantage of the Vice President's tactic of deliberate caution not to upset his obvious lead by challenging Nixon to make his views known before and not after the nomination. Neither the nation nor the GOP, declared the Governor, could afford to march to meet the future holding aloft a banner "whose only emblem is a question mark."[164] During the subsequent sparring, Eisenhower, given an opportunity to support a more liberal candidate, would do no more than call him a "dedicated, honest, hard-working man," with whose conclusions, however, he disagreed.[165]

At Nixon's right were the conservatives, most of them his former allies. They were among those who had regarded the Eisenhower Presidency as a mere interlude, a holding action against the "socialistic" Democrats, one that would at least restrain spending, government control, bureaucracy and internationalism until the return to Washington of genuine conservatism. Others, however, were more bitter. They had waited through twenty years of Democratic Administrations and then, having finally cleaned them out of the White House, had had to endure a Republican who often sounded like a New Dealer. By the opening of the convention, those no longer certain about Nixon's conservatism were already looking toward Goldwater for leadership.

That spring the Senator's manifesto, *The Conscience of a Conservative*, issued by an obscure Kentucky publisher, told them what they had been waiting to hear from a Republican leader. Sounding a Lockean theme in an industrial age, it also appealed to traditional nationalism. Both parties, Goldwater wrote, citing Arthur Larson's *A Republican Looks at His Party*, have surrendered the constitutional "system of restraints" by permitting the federal government to usurp the rights of the states. Washington's involvement in social and economic programs violated true conservative principles. The foreign-aid programs were called "unconstitutional" and the national leadership was accused of not having "made *victory* the goal of American policy." Goldwater also declared that "The central strategic fact of the Cold War is that the Communists are on the offensive and we are on the defensive." During the Berlin crisis the President should have called the entire matter non-negotiable and the Soviets would have backed down.[166] The little book soon became required reading for a new generation of youthful rightists.

Although Nixon had the nomination as thoroughly clinched as though he were an incumbent, Goldwater had already attracted a substantial minority of the delegates. As the South Carolina state chairman explained, he was the only GOP candidate who could carry the independent vote and capture "the stay-at-home voter who doesn't go for this metooism."[167] While Nixon had the delegates, the Senator had their enthusiasm. After asking that his name be withdrawn, he nevertheless received ten votes, all from Louisiana. In his dramatic convention appearance, during which he was cheered lustily, Goldwater called upon all conservatives to back Nixon and avoid a split that would only help Democrats "dedicated to the destruction of this country." If they would only "grow up" and get back to work, he said, they would be able to "take this party back some day—and I think we can."[168]

Other rightists, having become disenchanted with both parties and convinced that the battle against international communism and domestic socialism was being lost, stirred without waiting for Election Day. During the March primary contest in New Hampshire, the manager of the state committee for Nixon, Governor Wesley Powell, charged Senator John F. Kennedy with being "soft" on communism. Nixon's prompt repudiation failed to deter the Governor from pressing his point.[169] The Americans for Constitutional Action, formed in 1958 as a right-wing antidote to Americans for Democratic Action, charged in August that both political parties were "being steadily pulled closer together by the strong panaceas offered through all-powerful, centralized government." Its chairman, Admiral Moreell, called for the election of Congressmen "who show by their deeds that they are dedicated to constitutional principles of government."[170] At the same time, Robert Welch's John Birch Society was reported by both the Chicago *Daily News* and *Time* to be gaining followers as an ultraconservative and semi-secret group throughout the country. Their appeal was largely to middle-of-the-road and conservative Republicans.[171] Others on the right, assured by party loyalist Goldwater in October that Nixon was a true conservative, awaited the outcome of the election.

Nixon, running with Henry Cabot Lodge, an old Taftite nemesis, soon encountered trouble, reversing the early Gallup figures indicating a 6 percent lead for the Republican ticket.[172] The Democrats had an attractive and dynamic young candidate, Senator John F. Kennedy. Moreover, as a Roman Catholic, he threatened to appeal to many of his co-religionists who had voted for Eisenhower in dismay over their party's weakness before Communist gains. Furthermore, Kennedy's running mate, Majority Leader Lyndon B. Johnson of Texas, was well versed in the rougher political arts and could be counted on to make trouble for Nixon's attempt to cultivate the South. Then a series of televised debates between the two Presidential candidates, starting on September 26, left the general impression that the Democrats had taken the lead.

As Eisenhower kept in the background, distress calls for help began to be heard. Tex McCrary, one of the General's original backers, warned that only the President's intervention could provide the dramatic and decisive element that might change the prognosis.[173] Barry Goldwater wired that help from Eisenhower during the campaign's last two weeks would spare the country four years of Kennedy.[174] Suspicions that Eisenhower was, at best, cool toward the Nixon candidacy had already been given considerable nourishment in August. With Nixon advertising himself as the candidate with "experience," the President was asked at the very end of a press conference for an example of a "major idea of his that you had adopted in that role, as the decider and final—"; and Eisenhower, without reflecting, simply replied, "If you give me a week, I might think of one. I don't remember."[175]

Actually, however, between Nixon and Kennedy—or possibly between almost any Republican and the Democrat—Eisenhower had no real choice. His concern for a Nixon victory was very great. After having suggested to the Vice President the possibility of selecting a Catholic as a running mate, perhaps Labor Secretary Jim Mitchell, holding that it would be futile for Nixon to woo the Bible Belt in the South, he later suggested Lodge. It had already been narrowed down to the UN Ambassador and Bob Anderson. But the Texan remained uninterested and Eisenhower's friends, including Aksel Nielsen, thought Lodge would do the most to strengthen the ticket.[176]

Eisenhower's subsequent campaign inactivity had actually been arranged in advance. Both he and Nixon feared that it might make the Vice President look like a mere puppet who could not stand on his own and convince the voters of his readiness for the nation's highest office. "All we want out of Ike," a Nixon aide explained to Theodore H. White, "is for him to handle Khrushchev at the UN and not let things blow up there. That's all."[177] As early as March, Eisenhower told the press he did not wish to appear as Nixon's "patron."[178] On other occasions he hailed the Vice President's "training" to be his successor. Once the campaign started, Eisenhower advanced the dubious concept that he had to limit a personal role because he was still the President and the direction of such problems lay in other hands.[179] Meanwhile, however, the White House staff and Cabinet participated actively. Bryce Harlow, given a leave of absence by the President, worked with Nixon and was sent a continuous flow of memoranda and informational papers by Bob Merriam, the Deputy Assistant to the President for International Affairs. Other items went to Nixon's press aide, Herbert Klein.[180] As the campaign's outlook dimmed and Kennedy accused the Administration of having lowered both American prestige abroad and defenses because of the creation of a "missile gap," Eisenhower waited impatiently to be called into battle.

On October 28 the General delivered a speech for the Vice President in Philadelphia, but his invitation had come from the Nixon for President Committee of Pennsylvania. Three days later, however, after continued appeals by worried Republicans, the two men lunched together at the White House. Writing to Walter Williams, Eisenhower reported, "Today I had a meeting with the Vice President and others to determine what precisely we all should do in the remaining days of the campaign. I prayerfully hope that our efforts will be successful."[181] Then, during the final days of the campaign and until election eve, the President displayed his full vitality and persuasive warmth in a series of vigorous speeches, including four on November 2 in the New York City metropolitan area. Speaking afterward in Cleveland and Pittsburgh, and appealing for Republican votes via television on the final Monday night, he left little doubt about the accuracy of conclusions like Ed Folliard's that "He still has a strong hold on the hearts of most of his countrymen" and could undoubtedly be re-elected if he could run again.[182] The contest narrowed, with Gallup's final poll moving away from talk about a landslide and predicting a narrow Kennedy victory.[183] Out of the sixty-eight and a half million votes cast, the Democratic ticket won by a margin of 118,574 and by 303 to 219 in the electoral college. Asked at his final news conference about what he considered his "heartbreaking failures," Eisenhower explained, "Now if you want, if you want a very particular incident, I'd say November 8th was one of another bad disappointments."[184]

Immediately, for the GOP, one question dominated: "Would the conservatives take over the party? The Kennedy victory had boosted the critics of "me-tooism." Senator Kenneth Keating proposed the formation of a "committee of thirty" to remind the country that the party had alternatives to the conservative doctrines being espoused by Goldwater. The Senator from Arizona, the most popular speaker at GOP rallies, maintained that Nixon would have to be elected to some public office before he could expect recognition as a party leader. By mid-January it was clear that Goldwater's personal following had given him an edge for 1964.[185]

The Democratic victory had also enflamed the radical right. Senator Milton R. Young warned about the growth of the John Birch Society, whose founder had accused Eisenhower of being a Communist. The much older Moral Re-Armament organization ran large newspaper ads with a warning to the American people that "America is at war. A war we are losing. We are under attack by Godless Communism on a world front, and Godless materialism on the home front. Selfishness, perversion and division within our borders are the forces through which Communism takes over."[186] It all sounded familiar, but perhaps even a bit more strident.

In January, President Eisenhower, having already made his plans for returning to Gettysburg and looking forward to spending two months golfing at Palm Springs, California, read the draft of a Farewell Address he planned to deliver to the people. George Washington's, of course, had been notable. Americans had been given a guide for the future. Why not take advantage of the opportunity, of his immense popularity that he was retaining even at the end of eight years in office, to give some advice that was fully within his patriotic obligation? The youthful Democrat about to move into the White House could very likely act on his outrageous contention that the General had destroyed American prestige and neglected military power, all because of concern with something as outmoded as fiscal responsibility and a balanced budget. Looking over the speech that had been drafted by Dr. Malcolm Moos, a political scientist and special assistant to the President, Eisenhower made some changes. Those who knew him said he could never resist editing any paper. He liked it; but first, he thought, perhaps Milton could improve its organization.

CHAPTER 39

Reflections in a Washington Snowstorm

THREE DAYS BEFORE the urbane forty-three-year-old Democrat and his chic wife would move into the White House, Dwight D. Eisenhower, closing fifty years of public service, sat in his office and prepared to speak to the American people. The speech had been further revised by his brother Milton, upon whom Ike had been so dependent throughout the past eight years; and the President was satisfied that he could leave behind no message of greater importance. A few seconds after eight-thirty on the night of January 17, before a battery of television cameras, the President went on the air.

He spoke slowly, earnestly and with no trace of levity. Several words eluded his tongue and, at some points, he departed from the prepared text or corrected his lapses, as though his eyes had been unable to follow the script. One unfamiliar with Eisenhower could have guessed that he was uncertain or nervous. His delivery had often been more vigorous and fluent; but when it was over, liberals and conservatives alike applauded its contents.

About three-quarters of the way through, his theme came into sharper focus. He urged avoidance of "the impulse to live only for today, plundering, for our own ease and convenience, the precious resources of tomorrow." Then, with additional emphasis and deliberation, he said: "We cannot mortgage the material assets of our grandchildren without risking the loss also of their political and spiritual heritage. We want democracy to survive for all generations to come, not to become the insolvent phantom of tomorrow." Noting also, indirectly, the growing political polarization that marked his closing days—despite all his efforts to maintain moderation—he warned that America "must avoid becoming a community of dreadful fear and hate, and be, instead, a proud confederation of mutual trust and respect." Wistfully, addressing himself to international differences that seemed to have undergone few changes, he said, "I wish I could say tonight that lasting peace is in sight."

Most of all, however, he worried about those internal forces that had been propagating themselves so vastly by feeding on the cold war that they were dominating the economic life of the nation. Whole communities had become dependent upon military appropriations. Corporate profits were increasingly tied to government contracts. All kinds of investors and the smallest sub-contractors were leaning on Washington, as were technicians and scientists in need of funds for research. Politicians, expressing their collective desires, solicited additonal "defense" spendng for constituents.. Together, they formed a lobby, an unorganized group of special pleaders, not part of any conspiracy but, nevertheless, one threatening to deflect policy toward particular interests rather than the long-term benefit of the entire nation.[1] It had worried Eisenhower even before his Presidency. On the *Helena* in December of 1952, when discussing the "great equation," he feared that unabated continuation of vast military programs requiring deficit financing would not only destroy the economy and thus weaken the nation but would inevitably lead to a garrison state.[2]

As such, then, it was essentially a fear expressed by conservatives worried about accumulations of power. Back in May of 1952, before Eisenhower's nomination, Lew Douglas warned the General about the consequences to the economy from heavy taxation and inflation and observed that he knew "enough about the terrific power that the Pentagon exercises over the Executive Branch and the Legislature to realize that it can be restrained only by the most courageous and objective controls."[3] Robert Taft, also, speaking in Chicago on February 21, 1953, voiced the same theme. "We could destroy our liberty," he said, "by a military and foreign expenditure in time of peace so great that a free economic system cannot survive." We could even, he added, "be destroyed by expenditures so great as to turn this country into a garrison state in time of peace."[4] Throughout Eisenhower's eight years he weathered continuous criticism that charged him with neglecting the nation's defenses by promoting the New Look program, reducing the number of men in uniform and even risking the political accusation of having created a "missile gap." He had also seen Charlie Wilson succumb to Pentagon insatiability.

What he said then, in the Farewell Address's most widely quoted passage, expressed what he felt all along. "In the councils of government," he read slowly, "we must guard against the acquisition of unwarranted influence, whether sought or unsought, by the military-industrial complex. The potential for the disastrous rise of misplaced power exists and will persist. . . . Only an alert and knowledgeable citizenry can compel the proper meshing on the huge industrial and military machinery of defense with our peaceful methods and goals, so that security and liberty may prosper together." Then, noting the surrender of individual creativity to dependence for subsistence upon the government, he urged that "in holding scientific research and discovery in respect, as we should, we must also be alert to the equal and opposite danger that public policy could itself become the captive of a scientific-technological elite."[5] Nine months later, appearing at the Naval War College in Annapolis, General Eisenhower was asked about the wisdom of utilizing national resources so America could reach the moon. He replied: "I think to make the so-called race to the moon a major element in our struggle to show that we are superior to the Russians is getting our eyes off the right target. I really believe that we don't have that many enemies on the moon."[6] The "right target" for Eisenhower, as he told the nation in his final address, was national solvency and strength that would achieve "the goal of peace with justice." The next morning, at his last news conference, he said that the weaponry and missiles exist only "to protect the great values in which we believe, and they are far deeper even than our own lives and our own property, as I see it."[7]

On Thursday, the nineteenth, he rose early and reached his desk by seven-fifteen. Much correspondence awaited completion, including letters of appreciation to the outgoing team. As a parting gesture, he also signed pardons and parole orders and commuted sentences for more than one hundred persons who had been convicted of breaking federal laws. His most important session of the day was with the Cabinet and President-elect Kennedy's representatives. Photographers were permitted in to take formal pictures of the group, which then turned to the situation in Southeast Asia and heard the President's fears about Laos. More pleasurably, he met for two hours with Kennedy. Newsmen followed along as Eisenhower showed his successor how using the White House helicopters could enable him to get away within five minutes.

By the time the President left his office at 5 P.M. to return to the mansion, where he and Mamie planned to spend their final White House evening alone, Washington was already under a rapidly thickening cover of snow. A large storm moving up the East Coast combined with falling temperatures. At dusk, several inches were on the ground, creating a rush-hour snarl. More alarming was the threat to the next day's elaborate schedule, the noontime swearing-in, the Inaugural parade and the round of balls and parties planned to greet the installation of the forty-three-year-old politician from Harvard and Boston, the youngest man ever elected President of the United States. He was about to replace a man who, at the age of seventy, was the oldest ever to occupy the White House.

Throughout the night snowplows and armies of shovelers worked against the heavy fall; thousands of stranded cars were hauled away from the parade route and Capital Hill. Inside the White House, however, as the snow fell against the windows and piled up on the surrounding lawns, the President and Mamie were detached from the turmoil. For the first time during their forty-four-and-a-half years together, they faced the prospect of living in their own home. Gettysburg seemed like a welcome reward for a long career, one that had moved them from place to place all over the globe. No longer would there be confinement. No longer would he have to hear snide comments and questions about his golfing. The next afternoon, after attending the ceremony and a farewell luncheon hosted by Admiral Strauss, Ike and Mamie would be back at the farm.

He was, in fact, leaving the White House with a remarkable record. After eight years of domestic and international turbulence, accusations and saber-rattling, the man who was universally upheld as a non-politician retained enormous popularity. Few would dare to argue with the observation that, given a chance, the American people would gladly return him for another four years. The final Gallup Poll showed confidence in him at 59 percent, higher—after all the events—than the *average* levels managed by most Presidents. He had averaged 66 percent; only once, during the first quarter of 1958, did it dip below the 50 percent level. Additionally, a study released by Gallup on January 18 showed that 65 percent of the public anticipated that historians would agree that he had been either a "great" or a "good" President. Asked what they considered his greatest single achievement, their reply was simple: "He kept the peace."[8]

Indeed he had. Coming into office at a time of bitter divisions, when the Democratic President—and, to a lesser extent, his party—had lost the confidence of millions of Americans who, rightly or wrongly, were willing to accept the charges calling them responsible for the adversities at home and abroad, Eisenhower had performed a unique service. Fully cognizant of the confidence in his purpose, he became the central link, the conciliator who could stabilize the warriors. Overcoming the popular antipathy to the GOP by winning the election in the first place, it was, fortunately, the General who arranged the Korean peace. Had Stevenson won in 1952, the wild anti-Communist hysteria, ready to denounce every different idea as "treasonous," would have made such a settlement, so close to the original Thirty-eighth Parallel division, virtually impossible. Once effected, the demands for "impeachment" from the Jenners, the McCarthys, the Knowlands, the admirers of General MacArthur would have given massive encouragement to Syngman Rhee to defy the armistice by launching a bold new attack. Refusing to rush to his assistance would have been a "national disgrace." Eisenhower, too, cautious and fully cognizant of the hazards involved in military commitment, held the controls during the Indochinese crisis of 1954 and, together with John Foster Dulles, maneuvered with care and skillfully avoided entice-ments to involvement during the two crises over the islands of Quemoy and Matsu. When the Suez war of 1956 threatened either American intervention or estrangement from the Western allies, Eisenhower avoided either hazard. When he sent the Marines into Lebanon, he did so after choosing a time, place and display of power that minimized the risks and ensured success. Over Berlin, he defied the notion that he offered only "flabby" leadership so successfully that Khrushchev consequently found himself outmaneuvered and in need of an exit. When the Soviet leader exposed the U-2's activities, Eisenhower astonished the world with his admission of responsibility, but it was clear to him that continued "cover" stories would have damaged credibility more than the truth. Over-all, despite the enormous difficulties presented by such varied figures as Eden, Adenauer, De Gaulle and Macmillan, Eisenhower kept NATO alive and maintained relative harmony, his major objectives at the outset. The notion that his policies were mere continuations of the Truman–Acheson containment was, of course, furthered by the Eisenhower–Dulles sponsorship of regional defensive arrangements like SEATO, the Baghdad Pact and its successor, CENTO. It was, of course, containment, but, despite all the talk about "unleashing," "brinkmanship" and "massive retaliation," more efficient and less bloody than under his Democratic predecessors. For Eisenhower's purpose, having Dulles as Secretary of State was perfect. While the shrewd old Puritan employed rhetoric that was music to the right wing and made politic accommodations to avoid Acheson's morass, he followed Eisenhower's lead and steered carefully between sanity and the more fervent desires of the party's holy-war crusaders.

Eisenhower thus lead a double containment policy. William Shannon's characterization of the Administration as the "great postponement" because of the absence of domestic initiative might be more accurately applied to the leashing of the powerful ultraconservative momentum within the Republican party. Originally supported by the liberal and moderate wing, Eisenhower fulfilled most of *their* hopes. By the time 1961 came, Republican isolationism was dead; commitment to inter-nationalism was sufficiently complete to enable his successors, John F. Kennedy and Lyndon B. Johnson, ironically, to find some of the most loyal support and only minimal opposition for their foreign policies within the ranks of the GOP. On domestic matters, by combining with the substantial conservative impulse among the Democrats, particularly in the South, the Republican rightists, adherents of the party's 1950 "Declaration of Principles" and veterans of the conservative Eighty-second Congress, could have made much more of a substantial inroad under a more sympathetic GOP President.

The genesis of the conservatism that erupted after Kennedy's victory and dominated the party during the elections of 1964 and 1968 was, then, certainly present during the 1950s. While he let Joe McCarthy's tyranny continue for perhaps a year after he could have cut him down, with the additional toll upon both individuals and the nation, Eisenhower did keep the right wing from taking over the party. Given the realities, however, he could not effect a permanent change, even though he had managed to moderate the complexion of the national committee. "Modern Republicanism" was not laid aside so much for its vagueness but more for its incompatibility with the heartland of the party. Symbolic of what was unleashed after Eisenhower's departure from Washington was the replacement in 1961 of his final national chairman, Thruston B. Morton, with a vastly more conservative New York State Congressman, William Miller, who became Goldwater's running mate in 1964. While the nomination of Nixon in 1960 did not represent Eisenhower's fondest hope, he was, however, far more acceptable than a Knowland, Bridges or Goldwater.

In his domestic policies, Eisenhower was both less certain and knowledgeable than in relating to the rest of the world. He was conservative in the truest sense, a position akin to nineteenth-century liberalism. He distrusted both the use and accumulation of centers of power and held economics governable mainly by unalterable natural laws. Thus, long after the general acceptance of Keynesian concepts, he proclaimed the virtues of balanced budgets and resisted deficit financing. Long after the New Deal, he railed against overcentralization of government. So he equated fiscal strength with national survival, an indisputable concept, but held that goal obtainable only through the "sound" dollar rather than by substantial investments in the public sector. Careful to preserve the constitutional balance of power beween the federal government and the states, he was loathe to be guilty of violating the strictures of the Tenth Amendment. Therefore, he minimized what could be done about poverty, urban decay, medical care, education and public power; at the same time, however, he utilized existing laws to expand Social Security so that 90 percent of the population was under its coverage by 1960 and undertook the construction of a national interstate highway system which, critics sneered, "paved the countryside from slum to slum." He met the post-Sputnik panic by approving the National Defense Education Act, so that federal outlays for schools by 1960 nearly tripled the 1952 level. Throughout, however, his faith remained in private enterprise and individual initiative with a minimum of government interference. Capital from those encouraged to invest was, to him, immensely preferable to management by the state. Those willing to applaud consistency might consider Eisenhower worthy of their praise. When the great conflict over civil rights coincided with his tenure, he appeared insensitive and ignorant about the plight of the black man in America. Negroes insisted that he did not really understand, and Roy Wilkins has claimed that his attitude served to encourage the racists. Possibly his own essential confidence in the goodness of man kept him convinced that Americans were incapable of such inhumane conduct. While he thought the school-integration decision a serious error, he felt it would have been compounding the situation by forcing social realignment upon those intellectually and emotionally unprepared to make the transition. It was, moreover, a matter best left to the states. Only the pressure of politics and self-evident necessity and the efforts of Herbert Brownell, Jr., and William Rogers brought him to the advocacy of the first civil-rights legislation since Reconstruction. By his closing years, however, the demands that something be done about the internal neglect, about those things that had not been mitigated by either private capital or voluntary behavior, led to stronger demands for action and, by 1960, a massive wave of civil-rights demonstrations, one which could not be repressed any longer. Just as the right wing was becoming impatient, so was the left. Eisenhower's middle-of-the-road moderation was becoming harder to defend. The man whose election had promised a "great crusade" had led not a crusade but a holding action. He was not merely intent on consolidating past gains but in limiting further violence to his conviction that freedom included the toleration of outrage.

While it became fashionable among liberals to blame Eisenhower for the domestic deterioration, to ridicule his conviction that everything was well, there is little evidence that the American people were ready to do much else. Certainly, the Democratic leadership under Lyndon Johnson and Sam Rayburn was moderate, at best. The "loyal opposition" was three parts loyal and only one part opposition. Most Americans were working during the 1950s and, despite the two relatively minor recessions, were enjoying the highest standard of living by any society in history. The children and survivors of the Great Depression had finally come of age; the great new middle class treasured its material well-being and was in no mood to share hard-won gains. Imbued with the American dream and the Protestant ethic, fearing international—and even internal—communism more than the decay of their own society, they were ready to agree that public assistance would kill private initiative. John F. Kennedy, narrowly chosen by them in 1960, had to be pushed by changing times to the advocacy of bolder programs, including civil-rights legislation.

It was not, as some have maintained, a "placid" decade. No years that contained McCarthy and McCarthyism, a war in Korea, constant fear of other conflicts and atomic annihilation, and spreading racial violence, could be so described. Perhaps the placidity of the President promoted that impression. He was a stabilizing force in a time of conflict. He addressed the sinners in terms of high morality. In his own low-keyed way, while critics said he failed to lead, he helped give those years a distinctive tone. "He was popular because he was in tune with the world-wide spirit of the age," wrote James Reston. "He was a good man in a wicked time; a consolidator in a world crying for innovation."[9] John Cogley, in a *Commonweal* eulogy to the outgoing President, observed that it was "hard to imagine any other public figure in either party playing the role Eisenhower performed during the past eight years."[10]

He was not, as some who have tried to shock have suggested, a "political genius," but he knew perhaps better than anyone else around him exactly what the people wanted and how they wanted it. He had, as those who knew him best testify, a remarkable political instinct. Moreover, he knew how to manipulate men, to use them for his purpose and then cut them loose. Those who complained, as did Joe Martin, about his failure to build a solid party organization usually meant that he was not sufficiently partisan and did not give enough jobs to Republicans. In direct contrast to Truman, who had lost all authority by the end, Eisenhower's greatest individual accomplishment was the retention of his own standing with the people. Thus he spared himself from being cited as an example of the destructive effects of the Twenty-second Amendment upon the Presidency. At no time was the quality of his leadership more vigorously praised than after he had suffered key losses among the members of his team—Dulles, Humphrey and Adams. He set up the Presidential office to minimize its dependence upon one man, however much advocates of a "strong" Chief Executive thought he should be in personal command of the myriad details. Much to the consternation of those who bemoaned his frequent vacations, he made it look easy. And, in his insistence upon morality, democracy, decency, distrust of power, and the virtues of Americanism and duty, the man from Abilene preserved a considerable element of the progressivism that had swept his party and country during his youth.

He handled himself with dignity. When he "blew up," it was usually off camera. The moment he became President, few would dare call him "Ike." He was proud of his office and what it represented. When he refused to fight in the "gutter" with McCarthy, he was thinking as much about his position as his pride, although he had plenty of that, too. Fred Morrow believed that the personal defiance inflicted by Governor Faubus prompted Eisenhower to dispatch the troops to Little Rock. His reaction to the reporter who asked about those two helicopters acquired by the

White House was vivid. Most of all, however, perhaps his great asset in both war and peace was his evident warmth and ability to impress people as varied as Khrushchev, capitalists and agitated civil-rights leaders that he was sympathetic and understanding.

His lack of sophistication was a great personal asset with the broad range of the electorate who trusted him despite party labels. Those who complained that the President was a "hayseed" or an innocent equated Ivy League suavity with intelligence and were reluctant to acknowledge that his contribution to history since the early 1940s had been facilitated not only by personal charm but by an astuteness that enabled him to survive the passionate and frequently reckless wiles of lesser men. To label him a great or good or even a weak President misses the point. He was merely necessary.

Notes

Abbreviations
DDEL = Dwight D. Eisenhower Library, Abilene, Kansas
NYHT = New York *Herald Tribune*
NYT = The New York *Times*
PP, 1953–1961 = *Public Papers of the Presidents: Dwight D. Eisenhower.*
8 vols.; Washington: U. S. Government Printing Office, 1960–1961.

PART ONE
Chapter 1

1. NYT, December 29, 1968.
2. Dwight D. Eisenhower, *At Ease: Stories I Tell to Friends* (Garden City, New York: Doubleday and Company, 1967), pp. 388–89.
3. Dwight D. Eisenhower, *Mandate for Change, 1953–1956* (Garden City, New York: Doubleday and Company, 1963), p. 33.
4. NYT, June 5, 1952.
5. Eisenhower, *Mandate*, p. 34.
6. Marquis Childs, *Eisenhower: Captive Hero* (New York: Harcourt, Brace and Company, 1958), p. 139.
7. NYT, June 5, 1952.

Chapter 2

1. Herbert H. Hyman and Paul B. Sheatsley, "The Political Appeal of Eisenhower," *Public Opinion Quarterly* (Winter, 1953–54), p. 460.
2. Eisenhower, *Mandate*, p. 5.
3. Alfred D. Chandler, Jr. (ed.), *The Papers of Dwight David Eisenhower:*

The War Years (5 vols.; Baltimore: The Johns Hopkins Press, 1970), pp. 1518–19.

4. Harry C. Butcher, *My Three Years with Eisenhower* (New York: Simon and Schuster, 1946), p. 434.
5. Eisenhower to Arthur Capper, November 10, 1943, Chandler, *Papers*, p. 1559.
6. Eisenhower to General George Van Horn Mosely, October 7, 1943, *ibid.*, p. 1493.
7. Eisenhower to Hazlett, April 7, 1943, *ibid.*, p. 1082.
8. Dwight D. Eisenhower, *Crusade in Europe* (Garden City, New York: Doubleday and Company, 1948), p. 444.
9. Eisenhower to Edgar Eisenhower, September 26, 1944, Chandler, *Papers*, p. 2192.
10. Butcher, *Three Years*, p. 432.
11. Kenneth S. Davis, *Soldier of Democracy: A Biography of Dwight Eisenhower* (Garden City, New York: Doubleday and Company, 1952), p. 382.
12. *Ibid.*, p. 381; Eisenhower, *Crusade*, pp. 106–14.
13. Eisenhower to John Eisenhower, December 20, 1942, Chandler, *Papers*, p. 855.
14. Cf., Cornelius Ryan, *The Last Battle* (New York: Simon and Schuster, 1966), *passim*; Stephen E. Ambrose, *Eisenhower and Berlin, 1945* (New York: W. W. Norton, 1967), p. 98.
15. Gabriel Kolko, *The Politics of War* (New York: Random House, 1968), p. 6.
16. Eldon Griffin, *Clippers and Consuls* (Ann Arbor, Michigan: University of Michigan Press, 1938), pp. 9–12.

Chapter 3

1. NYHT, January 20, 1952.
2. Hyman and Sheatsley, "Political Appeal," p. 445.
3. Childs, *Eisenhower*, p. 107.
4. John Gunther, *Eisenhower: The Man and the Symbol* (New York: Harper & Bros., 1951), p. 136.
5. Davis, *Soldier*, p. 98.
6. Eisenhower, *At Ease*, p. 336.
7. Confidential information.
8. Confidential information.
9. General Lucius Clay, Eisenhower Oral History Project, Columbia.

Chapter 4

1. Childs, *Eisenhower*, p. 112.
2. Irwin Ross, *The Loneliest Campaign* (New York: New American Library, 1968), pp. 112–13.
3. *Ibid.*, p. 74.
4. Hyman and Sheatsley, "Political Appeal," p. 450.

5. Robert K. Merton, "An Inventory of Communications Addressed to General Eisenhower in the Spring of 1948: A Summary and Digest" (mimeographed), Bureau of Applied Social Research, Columbia University, 1949, p. 5.
6. Robert K. Merton, interview, April 23, 1969.
7. Robert K. Merton to author, May 15, 1969.
8. Merton, "An Inventory . . .," p. 13.
9. *Ibid.*, p. 6.
10. *Ibid.*, p. 9.
11. *Ibid.*, p. 13.
12. *Ibid.*
13. *Ibid.*, p. 24.
14. *Ibid.*, p. 7.
15. Angus Campbell, *et al.*, *The American Voter* (New York: John Wiley, 1960), p. 143.
16. Hyman and Sheatsley, "Political Appeal," p. 448.

Chapter 5

1. NYT, November 4, 1948.
2. Ross, *Loneliest Campaign*, pp. 263, 265.

Chapter 6

1. Lyndon B. Johnson, interview, June 30, 1970.
2. Davis, *Soldier*, p. 207.
3. *Ibid.*, p. 242.
4. NYHT, January 11, 1952.
5. Eisenhower, *At Ease*, p. 105.
6. *Ibid.*, p. 81.
7. *Ibid.*, p. 78.
8. *Ibid.*, p. 76.
9. Eisenhower, *At Ease*, pp. 167, 168.
10. Eisenhower, interview, CBS News Special, September 13, 1966.
11. Eisenhower, *At Ease*, p. 104.

Chapter 7

1. Eisenhower to Ethel Mae Megginson Wyman, December 13, 1942, Chandler, *Papers*, p. 835.
2. General Lucius Clay, Eisenhower Oral History Project, Columbia.
3. General Andrew J. Goodpaster, Eisenhower Oral History Project, Columbia.
4. Sinclair Weeks, interview, April 15, 1969.
5. Gabriel Hauge, interview, November 22, 1968.
6. General Lucius Clay, Eisenhower Oral History Project, Columbia.
7. Sinclair Weeks, interview, April 15, 1969.

8. Eisenhower to Arthur B. Eisenhower, May 18, 1943, Chandler, *Papers*, p. 1149.
9. Eisenhower to Helen E. Eisenhower, October 18, 1943, *ibid.*, p. 1515.
10. Eisenhower to Hazlett, October 20, 1943, *ibid.*, p. 1520.
11. Sir Howard Beale, John Foster Dulles Oral History Project, Princeton.
12. Carter L. Burgess, Eisenhower Oral History Project, Columbia.
13. Confidential source.
14. General Lucius Clay, interview, April 8, 1969.
15. Eisenhower to Milton Eisenhower, June 29, 1943, Chandler, *Papers*, p. 1220.
16. Davis, *Soldier*, p. 512.

Chapter 8

1. Eisenhower, *Mandate*, p. 10.
2. Roy Cohn, interview, May 7, 1969.
3. NYHT, January 16, 1952.
4. *Ibid.*, January 22, 1952.
5. NYT, February 16, 1952.
6. Robert Griffith, *The Politics of Fear: Joseph R. McCarthy and the Senate* (Lexington: University Press of Kentucky, 1970), p. 124.

Chapter 9

1. NYT, November 12, 1950.
2. *Ibid.*, February 13, 1951.
3. Eisenhower, *At Ease*, pp. 371–72.
4. Charles J. V. Murphy, "The Eisenhower Shift," *Fortune* (January, 1956), p. 84.
5. Richard Rovere, *Affairs of State: The Eisenhower Years* (New York: Farrar, Straus and Cudahy, 1956), p. 18.
6. Dwight D. Eisenhower, *Peace With Justice* (New York: Columbia University Press, 1961), p. 15.
7. Eisenhower, *Mandate*, p. 17.
8. Murphy, "Eisenhower Shift," p. 85.
9. George Whitney to Eisenhower, February 23, 1951, Pre-Inaugural Papers, DDEL.
10. Lewis Douglas to Eisenhower, May 26, 1952, *ibid.*
11. Whitney to Eisenhower, August 27, 1951, *ibid.*
12. Cyrus L. Sulzberger, *A Long Row of Candles* (New York: Macmillan, 1969), p. 757.
13. Murphy, "Eisenhower Shift," p. 86.
14. Alvin Wingfield to Hazlett, October 26, 1950, Pre-Inaugural Papers, DDEL.
15. William J. Miller, *Henry Cabot Lodge* (New York: Heineman, 1967), p. 215.
16. Milton S. Eisenhower, interview, June 19, 1969.

17. Gunther, *Eisenhower*, pp. 137–38.
18. Paul T. David, *et al.*, *Presidential Nominating Politics in 1952* (5 vols.; Baltimore: The Johns Hopkins Press, 1954), vol. 2, p. 156.
19. James C. Hagerty, interview, April 9, 1969.
20. Ronald J. Caridi, *The Korean War and American Politics* (Philadelphia: University of Pennsylvania Press, 1968), p. 119.
21. Charles A. Lofgren, *Congress and the Korean Conflict* (unpublished Ph. D. dissertation, Stanford University, 1966), pp. 138–43.
22. NYHT, October 31, 1951.
23. *Ibid.*, October 25, 1951.
24. *Ibid.*, November 2, 1951.
25. Miller, *Lodge*, p. 219.
26. NYHT, October 28 and November 2, 1951.
27. Press release, September 9, 1951, Pre-Inaugural Papers, DDEL.
28. Robert T. Murphy to Matthew J. Connelly, November 20, 1951, OF 408, Harry S Truman Library, Independence, Missouri.
29. Harry A. Bullis to Eisenhower, November 26, 1951, Pre-Inaugural Papers, DDEL.
30. Eugene Meyer to Bullis, December 15, 1951, *ibid.*
31. Sinclair Weeks, interview, April 15, 1969.
32. NYHT, December 22, 1951.
33. Murphy to Connelly, November 20, 1951, OF 408, Truman Library.
34. Bullis to Eisenhower, April 25, 1952, Pre-Inaugural Papers, DDEL.
35. Paul Hoffman to Ralph Flanders, July 25, 1952, Flanders Papers, Syracuse University Library.
36. NYT, October 18, 1951.
37. Dean Acheson, *Present at the Creation* (New York: W. W. Norton, 1969), p. 580.
38. NYT, November 9, 1951.
39. *Ibid.*
40. Flanders to Hoffman, October 18, 1951, Flanders Papers, Syracuse.
41. Hoffman to Flanders, January 30, 1952, and Dulles to Flanders, February 9, 1952, Flanders Papers, Syracuse.
42. Flanders to Dulles, February 5, 1952, *ibid.*
43. NYT, April 12, 1952.

Chapter 10

1. Theodore Achilles, Dulles Oral History, Princeton.
2. Eisenhower to General Clay, December 19, 1951, Pre-Inaugural Papers, DDEL.
3. *Ibid.*, December 27, 1951.
4. Eisenhower to Bullis, December 3, 1951, Pre-Inaugural Papers, DDEL.
5. Eisenhower to Hoffman, February 9, 1952, *ibid.*
6. Eisenhower to Bullis, December 3, 1951, *ibid.*
7. Eisenhower, *Mandate*, p. 18.
8. *Ibid.*, pp. 16, 18.

9. Eisenhower to Bullis, December 3, 1951, Pre-Inaugural Papers, DDEL.
10. Eisenhower to Clay, December 27, 1951, *ibid.*
11. Eisenhower to Lodge, March 18, 1952, *ibid.*
12. Robert Cutler to Eisenhower, March 24, 1952, Hobby Papers, DDEL.
13. General Lucius Clay, interview, April 8, 1969.
14. Winthrop Aldrich to Eisenhower, November 26, 1951, Pre-Inaugural Papers, DDEL.
15. NYHT, January 12, 1952.
16. Bullis to Eisenhower, January 21, 1952, Pre-Inaugural Papers, DDEL.
17. Minneapolis *Morning Tribune*, January 15, 1952.
18. NYHT, January 15, 1952.
19. Eisenhower, *Mandate*, p. 20.
20. Milton S. Eisenhower, interview, June 19, 1969.
21. NYHT, November 2, 1951.
22. Minneapolis *Morning Tribune*, November 7, 1951.
23. General Clay, interview, April 8, 1969.
24. Eisenhower to Clay, December 27, 1951, Pre-Inaugural Papers, DDEL.
25. NYT, November 8, 1951.
26. Arthur Krock, *Memoirs: Sixty Years on the Firing Line* (New York: Funk & Wagnalls, 1968), pp. 268–69.
27. Sulzberger, *Candles*, p. 693.
28. Miller, *Lodge*, p. 218.
29. *Ibid.*, p. 223.
30. NYT, March 12, 1952.
31. NYHT, December 23, 1951.
32. *Ibid.*, January 7, 1952.
33. General Clay, interview, April 8, 1969.
34. Eisenhower to Bullis, April 7, 1952, Pre-Inaugural Papers, DDEL.
35. NYHT, January 7, 1952.
36. *Ibid.*, January 8, 1952.
37. *Ibid.*, February 10, 1952; Sulzberger, *Candles*, p. 702.
38. Sulzberger, *Candles*, p. 731.
39. Eisenhower to Hoffman, January 24, 1952, Pre-Inaugural Papers, DDEL.
40. Aksel Nielsen to Eisenhower, May 20, 1952, *ibid.*
41. Harold Stassen to Eisenhower, December 15, 1951, *ibid.*
42. NYHT, December 23, 1951.
43. *Ibid.*, December 28, 1951.
44. *Ibid.*, December 29, 1951.
45. *Ibid.*, January 4 and 9, 1952.
46. NYT, March 12, 1952.
47. Clifford R. Hope, *et al.*, to Eisenhower, February 22, 1952, Pre-Inaugural Papers, DDEL; NYT, March 18, 1952.
48. Bullis to Eisenhower, March 18, 1952, Pre-Inaugural Papers, DDEL.
49. David, *Nominating Politics*, vol. 2, p. 172.
50. Sulzberger, *Candles*, pp. 737–38.
51. *Time*, February 16, 1953.
52. Harry S Truman, *Memoirs* (2 vols.; Garden City, New York: Doubleday and Company, 1956), vol. 2, 488–89.

53. CBS-TV News Special, "Some Friends of General Eisenhower," March 29, 1969.

54. Sulzberger, *Candles*, p. 755.

55. Roy Roberts to Eisenhower, May 5, 1952, Pre-Inaugural Papers, DDEL.

Chapter 11

1. David Schoenbrun, "Five Weeks That Made a Politician," *The Reporter* (August 5, 1952), p. 7.

2. NYT, June 6, 1952.

3. Eisenhower, *Mandate*, p. 35; NYT, June 6, 1952.

4. NYT, June 6, 1952.

5. Richard Nixon to Eisenhower, January 17, 1952, Pre-Inaugural Papers, DDEL.

6. NYHT, January 19, 1952.

7. Sulzberger, *Candles*, pp. 736, 747–48.

8. NYT, June 1, 1952.

9. David, *Nominating Politics, passim.*

10. NYT, June 8, 1952.

PART TWO

Chapter 12

1. NYT, June 7, 1952.

2. *Ibid.*, June 9, 1952.

3. *Ibid.*, June 14, 1952.

4. Minneapolis *Morning Tribune*, April 24, 1952.

5. David, *Nominating Politics*, vol. 2, p. 273.

6. NYT, June 14, 1952.

7. David, *Nominating Politics*, vol. 1, p. 48.

8. Minneapolis *Morning Tribune*, May 2, 1952.

9. NYT, June 28, 1952.

10. The difficulty was compounded by the variety of primary ground rules. Some, for example, provided for the direct election of unpledged delegates, others for the simultaneous selection of a Presidential candidate and delegates committed to him, and still others where the provision for the direct election of individual delegates made some allowances for indicating Presidential preferences. David, *Nominating Politics*, vol. 1, p. 173.

11. NYT, June 15, 1952.

12. Henry Cabot Lodge, "Eisenhower and the GOP," *Harper's* (May 1952), p. 34.

13. *Ibid.*, p. 35.

14. *Ibid.*, pp. 34–35.

15. *Ibid.*, p. 38.

16. *Ibid.*

17. *Ibid.*, p. 36.

18. Gordon Harrison, "Can Eisenhower Save the GOP?" *Harper's* (January 1952), p. 24.

19. *Congress and the Nation, 1945–1964* (Washington: Congressional Quarterly Service, 1965), p. 56a.
20. *Ibid.*, p. 57a.
21. *Ibid.*
22. NYT, October 17, 1952.
23. *Ibid.*, June 14, 1952.
24. *Ibid.*, June 15, 1952.
25. *Ibid.*, June 17, 1952.
26. *Ibid.*
27. *Ibid.*, June 18, 1952.
28. *Ibid.*, June 19, 1952.
29. *Ibid.*, June 20, 1952.
30. *Ibid.*, June 27, 1952.
31. Sulzberger, *Candles*, p. 764.
32. Schoenbrun, "Five Weeks," p. 7.

Chapter 13

1. NYT, June 11, 1952.
2. *Ibid.*, June 13, 14, 1952.
3. W. H. Francis, Jr., to Orville C. Bullington, May 9, 1952, Hobby Papers, DDEL.
4. David, *Nominating Politics*, vol. 3, p. 319.
5. W. H. Francis, Jr., to Robert L. Johnson, June 26, 1952, Hobby Papers, DDEL.
6. Keith McCanse to Oveta Culp Hobby, May 9, 1952, Hobby Papers, DDEL.
7. David, *Nominating Politics*, vol. 3, p. 321.
8. The Eisenhower for President Club of Texas, "This Is the Story of Texas," n.d., Hobby Papers, DDEL.
9. *Headlines*, March 15, 1952; Francis to William P. Luse, April 30, 1952, Hobby Papers, DDEL.
10. Press Release, May 20, 1952, Citizens for Eisenhower Papers, DDEL.
11. David, *Nominating Politics*, vol. 3, p. 321.
12. Eisenhower, *Mandate*, p. 39.
13. NYT, July 1, 1952.
14. Press Release, June 30, 1952, Citizens for Eisenhower Papers, DDEL.
15. NYT, July 2, 1952.
16. *Ibid.*, July 3, 1952.
17. *Time*, July 14, 1952, p. 18; David, *Nominating Politics*, vol. 3, p. 101.
18. NYT, July 3, 1952.
19. *Ibid.*
20. *Ibid.*, July 4, 1952.
21. *Ibid.*, July 1, 1952.
22. Confidential information.
23. NYT, July 3, 1952.
24. J. Bracken Lee to author, October 8, 1970; Dan Thornton to Sherman

Adams, December 15, 1958, and Walter J. Kohler to Adams, November 21, 1958, Adams Papers, Dartmouth.
25. NYT, July 4, 1952.
26. Confidential information.

Chapter 14

1. *Time*, July 7, 1952, pp. 13–14.
2. NYT, July 5, 1952.
3. *Ibid.*
4. *Ibid.*, July 15, 1952.
5. *Ibid.*
6. *Ibid.*, July 4, 1952.
7. *Ibid.*, July 5, 1952.
8. *Ibid.*
9. *Ibid.*, July 6, 1952.
10. Reprint, *Collier's*, July 27, 1912, Citizens for Eisenhower Papers, DDEL.
11. NYT, July 6, 1952.
12. Eisenhower, *Mandate*, pp. 41–43; NYT, July 7, 1952.
13. Miller, *Lodge*, p. 247.
14. NYT, July 7, 1952.
15. *Ibid.*, July 8, 1952.
16. Miller, *Lodge*, p. 248.
17. *Ibid.*
18. *Time*, July 21, 1952, p. 13; NYT, July 16, 1952.
19. NYT, July 8, 1952.
20. *Ibid.*
21. *Ibid.*
22. *Ibid.*, July 9, 1952.
23. *Ibid.*, July 10, 1952; *Time*, July 21, 1952, p. 15.
24. David, *Nominating Politics*, vol. 1, p. 80.
25. NYT, July 10, 1952.
26. *Ibid.*
27. *Ibid.*, July 9, 1952.
28. *Ibid.*, July 10, 1952.
29. David, *Nominating Politics*, vol. 5, pp. 231–32.
30. Sulzberger, *Candles*, p. 773.
31. *Time*, July 14, 1952, p. 21.
32. NYT, July 10, 1952.
33. *Time*, July 21, 1952, p. 14.
34. NYT, July 10, 1952.
35. *Ibid.*
36. *Ibid.*
37. Marty Snyder, *My Friend Ike* (New York: Frederick Fell, 1956), p. 16.
38. Rovere, *Eisenhower Years*, pp. 27–28; NYT, July 11, 1952.
39. Ralph Flanders to Hoffman, July 30, 1952, Flanders Papers, Syracuse.
40. Eisenhower, *Mandate*, p. 41.

41. *Ibid.*

42. Joseph C. Harsch, interview, August 24, 1970.

43. NYT, July 11, 1952.

44. Sherman Adams, *Firsthand Report* (New York: Harper & Bros., 1961), p. 26.

45. NYT, July 12, 1952; Miller, *Lodge*, p. 251; Eisenhower, *Mandate*, p. 44.

46. NYT, July 12, 1952.

47. NYT, July 15, 1952.

48. Eisenhower, *Mandate*, p. 46.

49. Milton S. Eisenhower, interview, June 19, 1969.

50. NYT, July 12, 1952.

51. *Time*, July 21, 1952, pp. 20–21.

Chapter 15

1. Gabriel Hauge, interview, November 22, 1968.

2. Eisenhower to Thomas Dewey, August 1, 1952, Pre-Inaugural Papers, DDEL.

3. NYT, January 18, 1953.

4. Truman to Eisenhower, August 13, 1952, Truman Papers, OF 1235, Truman Library.

5. Truman, *Memoirs*, vol. 2, p. 513.

6. Eisenhower to Truman, August 14, 1952, OF 1235, Truman Library.

7. Truman, *Memoirs*, vol. 2, p. 513.

8. Eisenhower to Truman, August 14, 1952, OF 1235, Truman Library.

9. Truman, *Memoirs*, vol. 2, p. 513.

10. NYT, July 1–3, 1952.

11. *Ibid.*, July 17, 1952.

12. *Ibid.*, July 12, 1952.

13. *Ibid.*

14. *Ibid.*, July 13, 1952.

15. *Ibid.*, July 14, 1952.

16. *Ibid.*, July 15, 1952.

17. *Ibid.*

18. Eisenhower to Hoffman, July 17, 1952, Pre-Inaugural Papers, DDEL.

19. NYT, July 16, 1952.

20. *Ibid.*, July 21, 1952.

21. *Ibid.*, July 22, 1952.

22. Sherman Adams, interview, July 31, 1969.

23. NYT, August 2, 1952.

24. *Ibid.*, July 27, 1952.

25. Eisenhower, *Mandate*, p. 50.

26. NYT, July 15, 1952.

27. *Ibid.*, August 1, 1952.

28. *Ibid.*, August 14, 1952.

29. *Ibid.*, July 15, August 16, 1952.

30. Neil MacNeil, *Dirksen* (New York: World Publishing Co., 1970), p. 105.

31. *Ibid.*, p. 107.
32. NYT, August 3, 1952.
33. *Ibid.*, July 30, 1952.
34. MacNeil, *Dirksen*, p. 107.
35. NYT, August 5, 1952.
36. *The Reporter*, August 5, 1952, p. 6.
37. Stanley Rumbough, Eisenhower Oral History, Columbia.
38. *Ibid.*
39. Adams, *Report*, p. 19.
40. Charles F. Willis, Jr., Eisenhower Oral History, Columbia.
41. *Ibid.*
42. NYT, August 3, 1952.
43. Flanders to Hoffman, August 5, 1952, Flanders Papers, Syracuse.
44. Eisenhower to J. Lawton Collins, August 5, 1952, Pre-Inaugural Papers, DDEL.
45. NYT, August 5, 6, 1962.
46. *Ibid.*, August 10, 1952.
47. Eisenhower to Frederick C. Downing, August 21, 1952, Pre-Inaugural Papers, DDEL.
48. NYT, August 21, 22, 1952.
49. New York *World Telegram and The Sun*, August 25, 1952.
50. Stephen Benedict, interview, April 9, 1969.
51. *Ibid.*
52. NYT, September 3, 1952.
53. *Ibid.*
54. Rovere, *Eisenhower Years*, p. 41.
55. NYT, October 14, 1952.
56. Stephen Benedict, interview, April 9, 1969.

Chapter 16

1. Adlai E. Stevenson, *Major Campaign Speeches* (New York: Random House, 1953), p. 4.
2. *Ibid.*, p. 9.
3. *Ibid.*, p. 16.
4. *Ibid.*, p. 31.
5. Kenneth S. Davis, *The Politics of Honor* (New York: G. P. Putnam's, 1967), p. 287.
6. *Weekly Report*, Issue No. 25, September 17, 1952, Eisenhower–Nixon Research Service.
7. Nathan B. Blumberg, *One-Party Press?* (Lincoln, Nebraska: University of Nebraska Press, 1954), pp. 31, 45.
8. John Foster Dulles, *War, Peace and Change* (New York: Harper & Bros., 1939), pp. 82–83.
9. *Ibid.*, ix.
10. John Foster Dulles, *War or Peace* (New York: Macmillan, 1950), p. 17.
11. John Foster Dulles, "A Policy of Boldness," *Life* (May 19, 1952), p. 151.

12. John Foster Dulles, Address on Far Eastern Problems, May 15, 1952, Pre-Inaugural Papers, DDEL.
13. Ronald J. Caridi, *The Korean War and American Politics* (Philadelphia: University of Pennsylvania Press, 1968), p. 132.
14. Eisenhower to Dulles, April 15, 1952, Dulles Papers, Princeton.
15. Dulles to Eisenhower, April 25, 1952, Pre-Inaugural Papers, DDEL.
16. Joseph C. Harsch, interview, August 24, 1970.
17. Dwight D. Eisenhower, Dulles Oral History, Princeton.
18. Eleanor Lansing Dulles, interview, January 9, 1970.
19. General Clay, interview, April 4, 1969.
20. Dulles to Eisenhower, May 20, 1952, Dulles Papers, Princeton.
21. Confidential sources.
22. NYT, June 12, 1952.
23. *Ibid.*, July 2, 1952.
24. *Ibid.*, June 25, 1952.
25. Sulzberger, *Candles*, p. 770.
26. Thruston B. Morton, Dulles Oral History, Princeton.
27. NYT, August 26, 1952.
28. *Ibid.*
29. *Ibid.*, August 27, 1952.
30. *Ibid.*, August 28, 1952.
31. Dwight D. Eisenhower, Dulles Oral History, Princeton.
32. *Ibid.*
33. NYT, August 28, 1952.
34. Seymour Martin Lipset and Earl Raab, *The Politics of Unreason* (New York: Harper & Row, 1970), p. 229.
35. Michael Paul Rogin, *The Intellectuals and McCarthy* (Cambridge, Massachusetts: The MIT Press, 1967), p. 96.
36. Richard Rovere, *Senator Joe McCarthy* (New York: Harcourt, Brace and World, 1959), p. 179.
37. Lipset and Raab, *Politics of Unreason*, p. 238.
38. Roy Cohn, interview, May 7, 1969.
39. Earl Latham, *The Communist Controversy in Washington* (Cambridge, Massachusetts: Harvard University Press, 1966), p. 362; Lipset and Raab, *Politics of Unreason*, p. 224.
40. Lipset and Raab, *Politics of Unreason*, p. 235.
41. Ralph E. Flanders, Eisenhower Oral History, Columbia.
42. Lipset and Raab, *Politics of Unreason*, pp. 233, 235.
43. Seymour Martin Lipset, "Sources of the Radical Right," in Daniel Bell (ed.), *The Radical Right* (Garden City, New York: Doubleday Anchor Book, 1964), p. 361.
44. Lipset and Raab, *Politics of Unreason*, pp. 222–23.
45. NYT, October 6, 1952.
46. Stevenson, *Speeches*, p. 20.
47. NYT, November 9, 1952.
48. Confidential source.
49. NYT, September 10, 1952.

50. Robert Cutler, *No Time for Rest* (Boston: Little, Brown, 1965), p. 287.
51. Confidential source.
52. Emmet J. Hughes, *The Ordeal of Power* (New York: Atheneum, 1963), p. 41.
53. NYT, September 11, 1952.
54. *Ibid.*, September 9, 1952.
55. Confidential source.
56. Milton S. Eisenhower, interview, June 19, 1969.
57. NYT, September 13, 1952.
58. *Ibid.*
59. *Ibid.*, September 16, 1952; Davis, *Politics of Honor*, p. 283.
60. NYT, September 14–15, 1952.
61. Adams, *Report*, p. 31.
62. CBS news special, March 29, 1969.
63. Adams, *Report*, p. 32.
64. Gabriel Hauge, interview, November 22, 1968; Cutler, *No Time*, p. 288.
65. NYT, October 4, 1952.
66. Arthur H. Vandenberg, Jr., to Sherman Adams, October 4, 1952, Pre-Inaugural Papers, DDEL.
67. NYT, October 9, 1952.
68. *Ibid.*, October 28, 1952.
69. George A. Sloan to Eisenhower, October 28, 1952, Pre-Inaugural Papers, DDEL.
70. NYT, October 25, 1952.
71. *Ibid.*, September 19, October 3, 14, 18, 19, 25, 1952.
72. *Ibid.*, October 14, 1952.
73. Earl Mazo, *Richard Nixon: A Political and Personal Portrait* (New York: Harper & Bros., 1959), p. 135.

Chapter 17

1. Milton S. Eisenhower, interview, June 19, 1969.
2. Adams, *Report*, p. 37.
3. Richard M. Nixon, *Six Crises* (Garden City, New York: Doubleday and Company, 1962), p. 93.
4. *Ibid.*, p. 83.
5. *Ibid.*, p. 88.
6. Garry Wills, *Nixon Agonistes* (Boston: Houghton Mifflin, 1970), p. 101; Mazo, *Nixon*, p. 121.
7. Nixon, *Six Crises*, p. 100.
8. *Cf.*, *Ibid.*; Mazo, *Nixon*, p. 121; Stewart Alsop, *Nixon and Rockefeller: A Double Portrait* (Garden City, New York: Doubleday and Company, 1960), p. 63; Wills, *Nixon*, p. 104.
9. NYT, September 24, 1952.
10. Nixon, *Six Crises*, p. 110.
11. NYT, September 24, 1952.
12. Alsop, *Nixon and Rockefeller*, p. 65.

13. NYT, October 15, 1952.
14. *Ibid.*, September 24, 1952.
15. Alsop, *Nixon and Rockefeller*, p. 65.
16. Mazo, *Nixon*, p. 132.
17. *Ibid.*; James C. Hagerty, interview, April 11, 1969.
18. Mazo, *Nixon*, p. 133.
19. Adams, *Report*, p. 37.
20. Nixon, *Six Crises*, p. 123.
21. David Rees, *Korea: The Limited War* (New York: St. Martin's Press, 1964), p. 396.
22. Samuel Lubell, *Revolt of the Moderates* (New York: Harper & Bros., 1956), pp. 37–43.
23. Lofgren, *Congress*, pp. 179, 184–85.
24. NYT, June 6, 1952.
25. *Ibid.*, August 22, 1952.
26. *Ibid.*, November 9, 1952.
27. *Ibid.*, October 17, 1952.
28. Davis, *Politics of Honor*, p. 285.
29. NYT, October 25, 1952.
30. Adams, *Report*, pp. 43–44.
31. NYT, November 1, 1952.
32. *The Reporter*, October 28, 1952, p. 5.
33. NYT, November 1, 1952.
34. Irving Berlin to Eisenhower, November 4, 1952, Pre-Inaugural Papers, DDEL.
35. NYT, November 5, 1952.
36. Charles Hook to Eisenhower, November 7, 1952, OF 1–J–4, DDEL.

Chapter 18

1. William Burrow to Sherman Adams, November 10, 1952; Burrow to Wesley Roberts, November 13, 1952; and Adams to Burrow, December 19, 1952, OF 138–C, DDEL.
2. Angus Campbell, *et al.*, *The Voter Decides* (White Plains, New York: Row, Peterson and Company, 1954), pp. 26, 44–46, 58.
3. Lubell, *Moderates*, pp. 37–43.
4. Maston Nixon to Robert Jackson, August 14, 1952, and to Oveta Culp Hobby, August 16, 1952, Hobby Papers, DDEL.
5. George McMillan, "Some Dixiecrats Who Like Ike," *The Reporter* (October 14, 1952), pp. 25, 28.
6. Gallup Poll release, January 12, 1953.
7. Campbell, *Voter Decides*, pp. 48, 61.
8. Cabell Phillips, *The Truman Presidency* (New York: Macmillan, 1966), pp. 427–28.
9. Campbell, *Voter Decides*, p. 65.
10. NYT, November 9, 1952.
11. V. O. Key, Jr., *The Responsible Electorate* (Cambridge, Massachusetts: Harvard University Press, 1966), p. 77.

12. Milton S. Eisenhower to Arthur Vandenberg, Jr., November 17, 1952, OF 138, DDEL.
13. Edward McCabe, Eisenhower Oral History, Columbia.

Chapter 19

1. George M. Humphrey, interview, July 2, 1969.
2. NYT, December 6, 1952; *Time*, December 15, 1952; James C. Hagerty, interview, April 11, 1969.
3. NYT, December 1–2, 1952.
4. George Humphrey, interview, July 2, 1969.
5. NYT, November 4, 1952.
6. *Ibid.*, November 8, 1952.
7. Confidential Korean source.
8. NYT, December 6, 1952.
9. *Ibid.*; Eisenhower, *Mandate*, pp. 93–95.
10. James C. Hagerty, interview, April 11, 1969.
11. NYT, December 6, 1952.
12. Eisenhower, *Mandate*, p. 95.
13. NYT, December 10, 1952.
14. *Ibid.*, December 11, 1952.
15. Eisenhower to General James A. Van Fleet, December 5, 1952, Pre-Inaugural Papers, DDEL.
16. General Clay, interview, April 8, 1969.
17. George M. Humphrey and Herbert Hoover, Jr., Dulles Oral History, Princeton.
18. Eisenhower to Sinclair Weeks, December 9, 1952, Private Papers of Sinclair Weeks, Lancaster, New Hampshire.
19. General Clay, Eisenhower Oral History, Columbia.
20. Eisenhower to David Lawrence, December 15, 1952, Pre-Inaugural Papers, DDEL.
21. Dwight D. Eisenhower, Dulles Oral History, Princeton; Adams, *Report*, p. 48.
22. Robert J. Donovan, *Eisenhower: The Inside Story* (New York: Harper & Bros., 1956), p. 19.
23. Stephen Ambrose, *The Supreme Commander* (Garden City, New York: Doubleday and Company, 1970), p. 105.
24. Agenda, January 12–13, 1953, OF 101-P, DDEL.
25. Sinclair Weeks to Eisenhower, n.d., Weeks Papers.
26. George Humphrey, interview, July 2, 1969.

Chapter 20

1. NYT, January 17, 1953.
2. *The New Republic*, January 26, 1953, p. 7.
3. Eisenhower, *Mandate*, p. 100.
4. NYT, January 21, 1953.

5. Harry S Truman, *Mr. Citizen* (New York: Bernard Geis, 1953), p. 19.
6. Eisenhower, *Mandate*, p. 101.
7. *Ibid.*, p. 20.
8. Milton S. Eisenhower, interview, June 19, 1969.
9. PP, 1953, pp. 1–8.
10. *Ibid.*
11. Washington *Times-Herald*, January 21, 1952.
12. *The Reporter*, February 17, 1953, p. 2; *The Nation*, January 31, 1953, p. 91.
13. NYT, January 21, 1953.
14. *The Reporter*, February 3, 1953, p. 7.

Chapter 21

1. Prescott Bush, Eisenhower Oral History, Columbia.
2. General Clay, Eisenhower Oral History, Columbia; Milton S. Eisenhower, interview, June 19, 1969.
3. Of some interest is Eisenhower's own discussion in his memoirs of the Durkin appointment. Only when referring to the Labor Secretary does Eisenhower cite the need for an exhaustive examination by the FBI, although he does hasten to note that such criteria would have to apply to all other candidates. Eisenhower, *Mandate*, p. 90.
4. William S. White, *The Taft Story* (New York: Harper & Row, 1954), p. 207.
5. NYT, December 31, 1952.
6. George Murphy to Eisenhower, December 30, 1952, Pre-Inaugural Papers, DDEL.
7. NYT, January 18, 1953.
8. *The New Republic*, December 15, 1952, p. 5.
9. *The Nation*, January 24, 1953, p. 61.
10. General Clay, interview, April 8, 1969.
11. NYT, January 17, 22, 1953.
12. Hearings Before the Senate Committee on Armed Services, 83d Congress, 1st Session (Washington: U. S. Government Printing Office, 1953), pp. 25–26.
13. *Time*, February 2, 1953, pp. 16–17.
14. *Ibid.*, February 9, 1953, p. 19.
15. General Clay, Eisenhower Oral History, Columbia; NYT, November 22, 1952.
16. Biographical Summary of Joseph M. Dodge, Dodge Papers, DDEL.
17. NYT, November 25, 1952.
18. Claude Robinson to Sinclair Weeks, March 24, 1953, Weeks Papers.
19. Public Opinion Index for Industry, Opinion Research Corporation, March 1953, Weeks Papers.
20. Robinson to Weeks, March 24, 1953, Weeks Papers.

Chapter 22

1. General Clay, interview, April 8, 1969.
2. James C. Hagerty, interview, April 11, 1969.
3. Quoted in Schoenbrun, "Five Weeks," p. 7.
4. George M. Humphrey, interview, July 2, 1969.
5. Adams, *Report*, p. 72.
6. George M. Humphrey, interview, July 2, 1969.
7. Milton S. Eisenhower, interview, June 19, 1969; E. Frederick Morrow, interview, November 11, 1968; Sherman Adams, interview, August 3, 1969.
8. Confidential source.
9. Ralph Tudor, *Notes Recorded While Under Secretary, Department of Interior, March, 1953—September, 1954* (printed privately by Mrs. M. Lucile Tudor, 1964); p. 9.
10. Benson to Eisenhower, January 28, 1953, OF 101-P, DDEL.
11. Confidential source.
12. Rovere, *Eisenhower Years*, p. 356.
13. E. Frederick Morrow, interview, November 1, 1968.
14. Dwight D. Eisenhower, *Crusade in Europe* (Garden City, New York: Doubleday and Company, 1948), p. 54.
15. Ambrose, *Supreme Commander*, p. 82.
16. W. Bedell Smith to Major General Frank D. Merrill, January 12, 1953, Smith Papers, DDEL.
17. Robert K. Gray, *Eighteen Acres Under Glass* (Garden City, New York: Doubleday and Company, 1961), p. 33.
18. *Ibid.*, pp. 47-48.
19. Sherman Adams, interview, July 31, 1969.
20. George Humphrey, interview, July 2, 1969.
21. Sinclair Weeks, interview, April 15, 1969.
22. *Newsweek*, June 3, 1957, p. 32.
23. Sinclair Weeks to Eisenhower, December 2, 1957, Weeks Papers.
24. Confidential source.
25. Sherman Adams, interview, August 3, 1969.
26. Adams, *Report*, p. 79.
27. Donovan, *Eisenhower*, p. 71.
28. Rovere, *Eisenhower Years*, p. 103.
29. Confidential source.
30. NYT, January 23, 1953.
31. *Ibid.*
32. Confidential source.
33. NYT, March 15, April 3, 10, 1953.
34. Unsigned memorandum, Weeks Papers.
35. George Humphrey, interview, July 2, 1969.
36. *Ibid.*
37. *The Reporter*, February 17, 1953, p. 3.
38. Mrs. Oswald B. Lord, Dulles Oral History, Princeton.
39. Dillon Anderson, Roscoe Drummond, Dulles Oral History, Princeton.

40. Dwight D. Eisenhower, Dulles Oral History, Princeton.
41. General Clay, Eisenhower Oral History, Columbia.
42. Joseph C. Harsch, interview, August 24, 1970, and confidential source.
43. Hughes, *Ordeal*, p. 51.
44. Dwight D. Eisenhower, Dulles Oral History, Princeton.
45. Confidential source.
46. Eleanor Lansing Dulles, interview, January 9, 1970.
47. Adams, *Report*, p. 87.
48. Roscoe Drummond and Gaston Coblentz, *Duel at the Brink* (Garden City, New York: Doubleday and Company, 1960), p. 12.
49. Arthur Larson, *Eisenhower: The President Nobody Knew* (New York: Charles Scribner's, 1968), p. 74.
50. Milton S. Eisenhower, interview, June 19, 1969.
51. Andrew Goodpaster, Dulles Oral History, Princeton.
52. James C. Hagerty, Dulles Oral History, Princeton.
53. John Foster Dulles to Brother Avery Dulles, March 3, 1949, Dulles Additional Papers, Princeton.
54. Richard Harkness, memorandum, n.d., Dulles Additional Papers, Princeton.
55. James Reston, Dulles Oral History, Princeton.
56. Alexander Wiley, Dulles Oral History, Princeton.
57. Confidential source.
58. Clarence B. Randall, Dulles Oral History, Princeton.
59. Eleanor Lansing Dulles, interview, January 9, 1970.
60. Confidential source.
61. Randolph Burgess, Dulles Oral History, Princeton.
62. Confidential source.
63. Adams, *Report*, p. 165.
64. Confidential source.
65. NYT, September 23, 1953.
66. General Clay, Eisenhower Oral History, Columbia.
67. Adams, *Report*, p. 57.
68. Maxwell Rabb, interview, October 1, 1968; Milton S. Eisenhower, interview, June 19, 1969.
69. Tudor, *Notes*, p. 52.
70. PP, 1953, pp. 94–98.
71. *Ibid.*, p. 120.
72. Robert Cutler, "The Development of the National Security Council," *Foreign Affairs* (April 1956), p. 442.
73. Krock, *Memoirs*, p. 281.
74. Confidential source.
75. Dillon Anderson, "The President and National Security," *Atlantic Monthly* (January 1956), p. 45.

Chapter 23

1. NYT, February 2, 14, 1953.
2. *Time*, March 30, 1953, p. 13.

3. Arthur Krock, "Eisenhower Criticized on Score of Leadership," NYT, April 5, 1953, Sect. IV, p. 3.
4. NYT, January 28, 1953.
5. PP, 1953, p. 17.
6. NYT, February 4, 1953.
7. *Ibid.*, February 1, 3, 4, 1953.
8. *Ibid.*, February 1, 1953.
9. *Ibid.*, February 3, 1953.
10. Gallup Poll release, January 30, 1953.
11. C. D. Jackson to Gabriel Hauge, February 23, 1953, OF 101–P, DDEL.
12. *Ibid.*
13. PP, 1953, pp. 13–14.
14. NYT, February 12, 1958.
15. Walter LaFeber, *America, Russia and the Cold War, 1945–1966* (New York: John Wiley and Sons, 1967), p. 106.
16. NYHT, February 17, 1953.
17. NYT, February 21, 1953.
18. Legislative Conference Notes, February 16, 1953, Morgan Papers, DDEL.
19. Donovan, *Eisenhower*, p. 49.
20. NYT, February 22, 1953.
21. *Ibid.*, February 23, 1953.
22. Donovan, *Eisenhower*, p. 49.
23. NYT, February 23–25, 1953.
24. John F. Dulles to Alexander Wiley, March 2, 1953, OF 116–H–4, DDEL.
25. NYT, March 4–5, 1953.
26. PP, 1953, p. 81.
27. Sherman Adams to Robert A. Taft, March 10, 1953, OF 3–A, DDEL.
28. *Congress and the Nation*, p. 357.
29. *Ibid.*
30. NYT, June 6, 1952.
31. Sinclair Weeks, interview, April 15, 1969.
32. Admiral Ben Moreell to Sinclair Weeks, March 9, 1953, Weeks Papers.
33. NYT, November 25, 1952.
34. Edward F. Phelps, Jr., to Tighe E. Woods and Roger L. Putnam, November 25, 1952, OF 13, DDEL.
35. *The New Republic*, March 2, 1953, p. 3.
36. NYT, November 25, 1952.
37. Gabriel Hauge, interview, November 22, 1968.
38. Telephone message, Baruch to Eisenhower, June 25, 1952, Pre-Inaugural Papers, DDEL.
39. NYT, February 3, 1953.
40. Sinclair Weeks, interview, April 15, 1969.
41. Gallup Poll release, January 23, 1953.
42. Joseph Dodge to Gabriel Hauge, January 15, 1953, OF 13, DDEL.
43. Justin Miller to Eisenhower, January 30, 1953, OF 13–A, DDEL.
44. NYT, February 1, 1953.
45. PP, 1953, p. 23.
46. NYT, February 3, 1953.

47. Murphy, "Eisenhower Shift," part 2, p. 113.
48. Weeks to Eisenhower, September 24, 1953, Weeks Papers.
49. Donovan, *Eisenhower*, p. 35.

Chapter 24

1. Sherman Adams to Homer Ferguson, April 22, 1953, OF 101-Y, DDEL.
2. Flanders to Adams, October 20, 1953, Flanders Papers, Syracuse.
3. Donovan, *Eisenhower*, p. 98.
4. Adams, *Report*, p. 79.
5. Hughes, *Ordeal*, pp. 130–31.
6. Eisenhower to Weeks, March 18, 1953, Weeks Papers.
7. David A. Frier, *Conflict of Interest in the Eisenhower Administration* (Ames, Iowa: Iowa State University Press, 1969), pp. 47–51.
8. PP, 1953, pp. 139, 152.
9. Alf Landon to Eisenhower, April 1, 1953, OF 138–C–1, DDEL.
10. Eisenhower to Landon, April 3, 1953, OF 138–C–1, DDEL.
11. NYT, April 11, 1953.
12. Leonard Hall, interview, May 5, 1969.
13. Long Island *Daily Press*, March 30, 1953.
14. Bryce N. Harlow to Eisenhower, April 3, 1953, Harlow Papers, DDEL.
15. Leonard Hall, interview, May 5, 1969; NYT, April 5, 1953.
16. Donovan, *Eisenhower*, p. 96.
17. PP, 1953, p. 205.
18. Benson to Eisenhower, March 16, 1953; Wickard to Eisenhower, March 16, 1953, OF 1–J–3, DDEL.
19. NYT, March 25, 1953.
20. Homer H. Gruenther to Wilton B. Persons, March 25, 1953, OF 1–J–3, DDEL.
21. NYT, April 5, 1953.
22. Wilson Harwood, Eisenhower Oral History, Columbia.
23. *The Reporter*, May 12, 1953, p. 2; NYT, April 26, 1953.
24. Tudor, *Notes*, p. 26.
25. NYT, April 26, 1953.
26. Tudor, *Notes*, pp. 24, 27, 33.
27. *Ibid.*, pp. 66–67.
28. *Time*, July 20, 1953, p. 14.
29. Charles F. Willis, Jr., Eisenhower Oral History, Columbia.
30. Willis to Flanders, June 25, 1954, Flanders Papers, Syracuse.
31. PP, 1954, p. 966.
32. John S. Cooper, Dulles Oral History, Princeton.
33. William R. Biggs, "Memorandum of the Budget," November 28, 1952, Dodge Papers, DDEL.
34. George M. Humphrey, interview, July 2, 1969.
35. PP, 1953, pp. 20–21.
36. NYT, February 9, 1953.
37. *Ibid.*, January 7, 1953.

38. *Ibid.*, February 17, 19, 1953.
39. Bureau of the Budget release, February 3, 1953, OF 72-B, DDEL.
40. NYT, February 10 and March 12, 1953.
41. Adams to Weeks, March 6, 1953, Weeks Papers.
42. PP, 1953, p. 101.
43. Donovan, *Eisenhower*, p. 109.
44. Eisenhower, *Mandate*, p. 130.
45. PP, 1953, pp. 307, 314.
46. NYT, May 24, 1953.
47. Walter Chamblin to Robert W. Welch, Jr., July 22, 1953, Weeks Papers.
48. PP, 1953, p. 546.
49. A. D. Shaver to Humphrey, June 5, 1953, Weeks Papers.
50. Weeks to Peter Hurst, June 29, 1953, Weeks Papers.
51. Chamblin to Welch, July 22, 1953, Weeks Papers.
52. Robert W. Welch, Jr., *The Politician* (Belmont, Massachusetts: Belmont Publishing Company, 1964), p. 279.
53. NYT, March 3, 1953.
54. *Ibid.*, January 17, 1953.
55. *Ibid.*, October 14, 1952.
56. David, *Nominating Politics*, vol. 3, pp. 297, 310, 347.
57. Eisenhower to Clinton P. Anderson, April 24, 1953, PP, 1953, p. 218.
58. NYT, March 3, 4, 1953.
59. Eisenhower to Shivers, May 19, 1958, Rogers Papers, DDEL.
60. Ernest T. Weir to Weeks, July 31, 1953, Weeks Papers.
61. Eisenhower to Weeks, July 30, 1953, Weeks Papers.
62. Hauge to Paul Carroll, July 16, 1953, OF 101-Y, DDEL.

Chapter 25

1. Gallup Poll releases, January 2, February 4, April 17, December 5, 1953.
2. NYT, April 4, February 1, April 26, May 15, May 30, 1953.
3. *Ibid.*, January 12, February 4 ,1954.
4. *Ibid.*, June 19, 1953.
5. A. H. Raskin, "What Communists Can and Can't Do," *ibid.*, April 26, 1953, Sect. IV, p. 12.
6. NYT, January 25, 1953.
7. Griffith, *McCarthy, passim*; Louis Bean, *Influences in the 1954 Mid-Term Elections* (Washington: Public Affairs Institute, 1954), pp. 1-2, 8, 18.
8. NYT, January 31, 1953.
9. *Ibid.*, February 9, 1953.
10. PP, 1953, pp. 24-25.
11. NYT, March 10, 1953.
12. *Ibid.*, March 11, 12, 14, 1953.
13. Gallup Poll release, April 15, 1953.
14. PP, 1953, p. 111.
15. NYT, May 17, 1953.
16. *Ibid.*, March 4, 1953.

17. PP, 1953, p. 350.
18. Ralph Flanders, Eisenhower Oral History, Columbia.
19. Julius C. Holmes, Dulles Oral History, Princeton.
20. Dean Acheson to Walter George, April 18, 1947, Dulles Papers, Princeton.
21. NYT, February 1, 1953.
22. Dean Acheson, *Present at the Creation* (New York: W. W. Norton, 1969), pp. 710–711; Ross Terrill, "When America 'Lost' China," *The Atlantic* (November 1969), p. 79.
23. Alfred Kohlberg to Dulles, January 5, 1953, Dulles Papers, Princeton.
24. Terrill, "When America 'Lost' China," p. 79.
25. NYT, March 5, 1953.
26. Joseph C. Harsch, interview, August 24, 1970.
27. Confidential source.
28. NYT, March 13, 1953.
29. *Ibid.*, May 16, 1953.
30. Philip Crowe, "Recollections of John Foster Dulles," Dulles Additional Papers, Princeton.
31. Edward Corsi, Dulles Oral History, Princeton.
32. Eleanor Bontecou, *The Federal Loyalty-Security Program* (Ithaca, New York: Cornell University Press, 1953), p. 16.
33. Latham, *Communist Controversy*, p. 362.
34. Bontecou, *Loyalty Security Program*, p. 26.
35. Henry Steele Commager, *Documents of American History* (8th ed., New York: Appleton-Century-Crofts, 1968), vol. 2, p. 559.
36. Bontecou, *Loyalty Security Program*, p. 239; for a view that Truman was responsible for helping to create McCarthyism, see Athan Theoharis, "The Escalation of the Loyalty Program," in Barton Bernstein (ed.), *Politics and Policies of the Truman Administration* (Chicago: Quadrangle Books, 1970), pp. 242–68.
37. Confidential source.
38. *Congressional Record*, 83rd Congress, 1st Session, vol. 99, pt. 2, p. 2282.
39. *Time*, March 30, 1953, p. 14.
40. Edward Corsi, Dulles Oral History, Princeton.
41. NYT, November 25, 1953.
42. *Ibid.*
43. Tudor, *Notes*, p. 62.
44. *Congressional Record*, 83rd Congress, 1st Session, pp. 2286–87, 2192, 2293–94, 2297.
45. Robert E. Sherwood, *Roosevelt and Hopkins* (New York: Harper & Bros., 1948), pp. 774, 885–87, 926.
46. Confidential source.
47. NYT, March 3, 1953.
48. Confidential source.
49. NYT, March 22, 1953.
50. *Congressional Record*, 83rd Congress, 1st Session, p. 2282.
51. *Ibid.*, p. 2202.
52. *Ibid.*, p. 2195.

53. NYT, March 15, 1953.
54. *Congressional Record*, 83rd Congress, 1st Session, pp. 2191–92.
55. *Ibid.*, pp. 2192, 2201.
56. *Ibid.*, p. 2189.
57. *Ibid.*, p. 2201.
58. *Ibid.*, p. 2205.
59. *Ibid.*, pp. 2277–81; John Sparkman, Dulles Oral History, Princeton.
60. *Congressional Record*, 83rd Congress, 1st Session, pp. 2282–83, 2285, 2291–92; Theoharis, *Yalta Myths*, p. 174.
61. PP, 1953, p. 130.
62. *Congressional Record*, 83rd Congress, 1st Session, p. 2392.
63. John B. Oakes, "Inquiry into McCarthy's Status," New York *Times Magazine* (April 12, 1953), p. 9.
64. William S. White, *The Taft Story* (New York: Harper & Row, 1954), p. 239.

Chapter 26

1. NYT, June 28, 1953.
2. Roy Cohn, interview, May 7, 1969.
3. Milton Eisenhower to author, December 17, 1969.
4. Bullis to Eisenhower, May 9, 1953, OF 99–R, DDEL.
5. Eisenhower to Bullis, May 18, 1953, OF 99–R, DDEL.
6. Secret ballot, The Links, New York City, June 4, 1953, White House Central Files, Box 723, DDEL.
7. NYT, February 18, 23, March 23, May 17, 22, 25, 1953.
8. *Ibid.*, February 27, March 29, April 15, 1953.
9. Harry A. Bullis to Eisenhower, May 9, 1953, OF 99–R, DDEL.
10. NYT, April 5, 1953.
11. *Ibid.*; Eleanor Lansing Dulles, interview, January 9, 1970; confidential source.
12. Douglas Cater, "The President and the Press," *The Reporter* (April 25, 1953), p. 27.
13. PP, 1953, pp. 149, 153–55.
14. NYT, April 5, 1953.
15. Griffith, *McCarthy*, p. 205.
16. Confidential source.
17. Henry Cabot Lodge to James C. Hagerty, March 24, 1953, OF 101–Y, DDEL.
18. NYT, February 26, 1953.
19. Ralph J. Bunche, interview, January 31, 1970.
20. NYT, May 2, 1953.
21. Ralph J. Bunche, interview, January 31, 1970.
22. NYT, May 26, 1954.
23. Maxwell Rabb, interview, January 12, 1970.
24. Ralph J. Bunche, interview, January 31, 1970; Walter Goodman, *The Committee* (New York: Farrar, Straus & Giroux, 1968), p. 342.

25. Ralph J. Bunche, interview, January 31, 1970.
26. NYT, February 22, 1953.
27. *Ibid.*, March 2, 1953.
28. Martin Merson, Dulles Oral History, Princeton.
29. Martin Merson, *The Private Diary of a Public Servant* (New York: Macmillan, 1955), pp. 68, 158.
30. Martin Merson, Dulles Oral History, Princeton.
31. Merson, *Private Diary*, p. 34.
32. NYT, March 24, 1953.
33. *Ibid.*, May 3, 1953; Anthony Lewis, "What Happens to a Victim of Nameless Accusers," *The Reporter*, March 2, 1954, p. 11.
34. NYT, May 3, 1953.
35. PP, 1953, p. 375.
36. Gabriel Hauge to Bernard C. Duffy, June 22, 1953, and Eisenhower to Hauge and Emmet Hughes, June 20, 1953, OF 101-Y, DDEL; PP, 1953, p. 375.
37. NYT, September 2, 1954.
38. Thomas S. Gates, Jr., to Sherman Adams, August 8, 1956, Morgan Papers, DDEL.
39. Thomas J. Donegan to Herbert Brownell, Jr., September 20, 1956, Morgan Papers, DDEL.
40. Albert Pratt to Frank McCarthy, November 5, 1956, Morgan Papers, DDEL.
41. *Commonweal*, March 8, 1957, p. 591.
42. *America*, February 23, 1957, p. 595.
43. *The New Yorker*, March 23, 1957, p. 103.
44. NYT, March 23, June 13, 15, 17, 18, 20, 1953.
45. Donovan, *Eisenhower*, p. 45.
46. PP, 1954, pp. 446–47.
47. Walter and Miriam Schneir, *Invitation to an Inquest* (Garden City, New York: Doubleday and Company, 1965), p. 168.
48. Theodore Achilles, Dulles Oral History, Princeton.
49. Roy Cohn, *McCarthy* (New York: New American Library, 1968), pp. 75, 88.
50. Martin Merson, Dulles Oral History, Princeton.
51. *Ibid.*
52. Donovan, *Eisenhower*, p. 90.
53. Dwight D. Eisenhower, Dulles Oral History, Princeton.
54. John Foster Dulles to Eisenhower, June 27, 1953, Weeks Papers.
55. *Ibid.*
56. PP, 1953, pp. 300–301.
57. *Ibid.*, pp. 404–405.
58. *Ibid.*, p. 415; NYT, June 15, 16, 1953.
59. NYT, June 17, 1953.
60. *Ibid.*
61. PP, 1953, pp. 426–27, 429, 431–32, 436.
62. *Ibid.*, p. 467.
63. *Cf.*, Donovan, *Eisenhower*, p. 91.

64. PP, 1953, pp. 455, 456.
65. NYT, July 3, 1953.
66. *Ibid.*, July 8–10, 1953; Hughes, *Ordeal,* pp. 94–97; Donovan, *Eisenhower,* p. 95.
67. NYT, July 16, 1953.
68. PP, 1953, p. 506.
69. NYT, July 25, 1953.
70. William S. White, "McCarthy in the Middle of a Widening Storm," NYT, July 12, 1953, Sect. IV, p. 3; NYT, July 26, 1953.
71. *Time,* July 20, 1953, p. 16.
72. Donovan, *Inside,* p. 95.
73. Gallup Poll release, January 15, 1954.
74. Merriman Smith, *Meet Mister Eisenhower* (New York: Harper & Bros., 1955), p. 19.
75. Hughes, *Ordeal,* p. 96.
76. Sulzberger, *Candles,* pp. 921–22.

Chapter 27

1. Gallup Poll reports, November 14, 16, 1952.
2. John Foster Dulles, "European Unity," November 18, 1948, Dulles Additional Papers, Princeton.
3. Department of State, *American Foreign Policy, 1950–1955* (2 vols.; Washington: U. S. Government Printing Office, 1957), vol. 1, pp. 1107–70.
4. NYT, January 7, 1953.
5. Eisenhower, *Mandate,* p. 140.
6. Dulles to Charles E. Wilson, January 16, 1953, Dulles Papers, Princeton.
7. Eisenhower, *Mandate,* p. 142.
8. *American Foreign Policy, 1950–1955,* vol. 1, p. 1444.
9. NYT, February 2, 1953.
10. *Ibid.*, February 5, 1953.
11. Andrew Berding, Dulles Oral History, Princeton; Julius C. Holmes, Eisenhower Oral History, Columbia.
12. Sir Anthony Eden, *Full Circle* (London: Cassell, 1960), p. 64.
13. Dwight D. Eisenhower, Dulles Oral History, Princeton.
14. Flora Lewis, "The Unstable State of Germany," *Foreign Affairs* (July 1960), p. 591.
15. Ronald Steel, *Pax Americana* (New York: The Viking Press, 1967), p. 104.
16. *Ibid.*, pp. 100–102; Barton J. Bernstein, "American Foreign Policy and the Origins of the Cold War," in Bernstein (ed.), *Truman Administration,* p. 49; Gar Alperowitz, "How Did the Cold War Begin?" *New York Review of Books* (March 23, 1967), pp. 11–12; Thomas G. Paterson, "The Abortive American Loan to Russia and the Origins of the Cold War, 1943–1946," The *Journal of American History* (June 1969), pp. 70–92; George C. Herring, Jr., "Lend Lease to Russia and the Origins of the Cold War," *Ibid.*, pp. 93–114.

17. *American Foreign Policy, 1950–1955*, vol. 1, p. 1443.
18. Richard Mayne, *The Recovery of Europe* (New York: Harper & Row, 1970), p. 210.
19. Edward Crankshaw, *Khrushchev: A Career* (New York: The Viking Press, 1966), p. 190.
20. Adam B. Ulam, *Expansion and Coexistence: The History of Soviet Foreign Policy, 1917–67* (New York: Frederick A. Praeger, Inc., 1968), pp. 541–42.
21. NYT, March 29, April 5, April 12, 1953.
22. PP, 1953, p. 104.
23. NYT, April 12, 1953.
24. Ted Bates to C. D. Jackson, May 11, 1953, OF 225–A, DDEL.
25. PP, 1953, pp. 182–84.
26. Tudor, *Notes*, p. 7; Cutler, *No Time*, p. 322.
27. PP, 1953, pp. 187–88.
28. Unsigned and undated memo to Herbert Brownell, Jr., OF 225–A, DDEL.
29. NYT, April 17, 18, 26, 1953.
30. *Ibid.*, April 17, 1953.
31. *Ibid.*, April 18–19, 1953; Text of NATO speech, Paris, April 23, 1953, Dulles Papers, Princeton.
32. Eisenhower, *Mandate*, p. 148.
33. NYT, May 17, 1953.
34. PP, 1953, p. 285.
35. NYT, May 24, 1953.
36. Eisenhower, *Mandate*, p. 242.
37. *Ibid.*
38. PP, 1953, p. 288.
39. NYT, May 24, 1953.
40. PP, 1953, p. 332.
41. NYT, July 5, 1953.
42. Eden, *Full Circle*, p. 53.
43. Richard Harkness, memorandum, August 17, 1953, Dulles Additional Papers, Princeton.
44. *American Foreign Policy, 1950–1955*, vol. 1, pp. 1463–67.
45. Peter V. Curl (ed.), *Documents on American Foreign Relations 1953* (New York: Harper and Bros., 1954), p. 67.
46. Everett Dirksen to Sherman Adams, n.d., OF 116–B, DDEL.
47. Senate and House Committees on Foreign Relations, *The Mutual Security Program for Fiscal Year 1954* (Washington: U. S. Government Printing Office, 1953), p. 28.
48. *Ibid.*, pp. ix, 14–15.
49. Donovan, *Eisenhower*, p. 148.
50. PP, 1953, p. 508.
51. Adams, *Report*, p. 104; Donovan, *Eisenhower*, p. 151.
52. *Congress and the Nation*, p. 185.
53. Eisenhower to Lyndon B. Johnson, August 1, 1958, Harlow Papers, DDEL.

54. Jack Z. Anderson to Bryce Harlow, August 19, 1958, Harlow Papers, DDEL.

55. Eisenhower to Harold Boeschenstein, November 1, 1957, and to George Whitney, November 11, 1957, OF 2, DDEL.

56. Tracy S. Vorhees to Joseph Dodge, May 23, 1960, Dodge Papers, DDEL.

57. O. M. Gale to Robert Gray, June 3, 1960, Harlow Papers.

58. *Congress and the Nation*, p. 185.

59. Christian Herter to Weeks, June 9, 1953, Weeks Papers.

60. Curl (ed.), *Documents 1953*, p. 69.

61. Weeks to Eisenhower, February 25, 1953, Weeks Papers.

62. Marshall M. Smith to Weeks, October 10, 1956, Weeks Papers.

63. 86th Congress, 2d Session, *Special Study Mission to Europe* (Washington: U. S. Government Printing Office, 1960), p. 13.

64. John Foster Dulles, "Memo for the Record," October 1, 1953, Dulles Papers, Princeton.

65. PP, 1957, p. 380.

66. Secret ballot, The Links, New York City, June 4, 1953, White House Central Files, Box 723, DDEL.

67. NYT, February 19, 1953.

68. George Sloan to Eisenhower, February 12, 1953, Weeks Papers.

69. Clarence B. Randall, *A Creed for Free Enterprise* (Boston: Little, Brown, 1952), pp. 147, 156–57.

70. *American Foreign Policy, 1950–1955*, vol. 2, pp. 2898–2930.

71. PP, 1958, pp. 538–39.

72. *Congress and the Nation*, p. 200.

73. Walter S. Robertson to Sinclair Weeks, July 10, 1957, Weeks Papers.

74. Randall to J. Edgar Hoover, May 4, 1960, Morgan Papers, DDEL.

75. Sulzberger, *Candles*, p. 930.

76. Melvin Gurtov, *The First Vietnam Crisis* (New York: Columbia University Press, 1967), pp. 48–49.

77. PP, 1953, pp. 812–13.

78. John Foster Dulles, speech text, December 14, 1953, Dulles Papers, Princeton.

79. C. A. Shoenbrun to Edward R. Murrow, December 15, 1953, Dulles Papers, Princeton.

80. *American Foreign Policy, 1950–1955*, vol. 1, pp. 630, 633.

81. *Ibid.*, p. 641.

82. Eisenhower, *Mandate*, p. 409.

Chapter 28

1. Gallup Poll releases, March 20, April 22, May 20, June 3, 1953.

2. Oliver N. Roberts to Weeks, June 21, 1955; Weeks to Roberts, June 27, 1955, Weeks Papers.

3. White, *Taft*, p. 258.

4. PP, 1953, p. 392.

5. NYT, June 11, 1953.

6. *Ibid.*, May 17, 1963; confidential source.
7. Mark Clark, *From the Danube to the Yalu* (New York: Harper & Bros., 1954), pp. 241–42.
8. Rees, *Korea*, p. 403; Robert Murphy, *Diplomat Among Warriors* (Garden City, New York: Doubleday and Company, 1962), p. 358.
9. Rees, *Korea*, pp. 416–17.
10. Clark, *Danube to the Yalu*, pp. 267, 276.
11. *Ibid.*, p. 258.
12. Hughes, *Ordeal*, p. 105.
13. Larson, *Eisenhower*, p. 74; Gurtov, *Vietnam*, p. 28; PP, 1953, pp. 147–48; NYT, April 14, 1953.
14. General Matthew Ridgway, Dulles Oral History, Princeton; Adams, *Report*, p. 48; James Shepley, "How Dulles Averted War," *Life* (January 16, 1956), p. 71.
15. Confidential source.
16. Murphy, *Diplomat*, p. 350.
17. Clark, *Danube to the Yalu*, p. 262.
18. *Ibid.*, pp. 273–74.
19. NYT, June 6, 1953; Curl (ed.), *Documents 1953*, pp. 303–305.
20. NYT, June 9–10, 1953.
21. Flanders to Hoffman, February 4, 1952, Flanders Papers, Syracuse.
22. Flanders to Hoffman, October 15, 1951, Flanders Papers, Syracuse.
23. Joseph C. Grew to Mrs. Ralph Flanders, February 17, 1954, Flanders Papers, Syracuse.
24. Flanders to Hoffman, August 5, 1952, Flanders Papers, Syracuse; *Congressional Record*, 83rd Congress, 1st Session, July 1, 1953, vol. 99, pt. 6, p. 7765.
25. Flanders to Eisenhower, November 6, 1952, Pre-Inaugural Papers, DDEL; Flanders to Eisenhower, May 7, 1953, Flanders Papers, Syracuse.
26. PP, 1953, p. 922.
27. Flanders to Eisenhower, May 21, 1953, Flanders Papers, Syracuse.
28. Eisenhower to Flanders, May 27, 1953, Flanders Papers, Syracuse.
29. Lofgren, *Congress, passim.*
30. *Ibid.*, pp. 193–94; NYT, May 14, June 2, 1953.
31. Henry Berger, "Senator Robert A. Taft," in Thomas G. Paterson (ed.), *Cold War Critics* (Chicago: Quadrangle Books, 1971), p. 192; Lofgren, *Congress*, p. 142.
32. NYT, April 12, 20, 1953.
33. PP, 1953, p. 327.
34. NYT, May 27, 1953.
35. *Ibid.*, May 31, 1953.
36. *Ibid.*, June 7, 9, 1953.
37. *Ibid.*, May 28, 1953.
38. *Ibid.*, April 21, May 2, 14, 19, 23, 30, 1953.
39. Jacob E. Cooke (ed.), *The Federalist* (Middletown, Connecticut: Wesleyan University Press, 1961), pp. 432–38.
40. NYT, June 14, 1953.
41. John Bricker to Homer Ferguson, January 20, 1954, OF 116-H-4, DDEL.

42. Adams, *Report*, p. 106.
43. John Sparkman, Dulles Oral History, Princeton.
44. *Congress and the Nation*, p. 112.
45. Loyd Wright to Herbert Brownell, Jr., October 28, 1955, and Orie Phillips to Bernard Shanley, March 18, 1956, Morgan Papers, DDEL.
46. NYT, January 26, 1954.
47. Lindsay Rogers, "Senator Bricker Finds a Loophole," *The Reporter* (July 22, 1952), p. 31.
48. *Time*, July 13, 1953.
49. Theoharis, *Yalta*, p. 133.
50. *Economic Council Letter*, April 15, 1953.
51. NYT, February 24, 1954.
52. *Ibid.*, February 3, 16, 1954.
53. *Ibid.*, January 31, 1954; Gallup Poll release, October 7, 1953.
54. Donovan, *Eisenhower*, p. 37.
55. NYT, January 17, 1954.
56. Dwight D. Eisenhower, Dulles Oral History, Princeton.
57. Louis L. Gerson, *John Foster Dulles* (New York: Cooper Square Publishers, 1968), p. 120.
58. Dulles to Adams, January 2, 1953, OF 116-H-4, DDEL.
59. Confidential source.
60. Dwight D. Eisenhower, Dulles Oral History, Princeton.
61. Confidential source.
62. Gerson, *Dulles*, p. 121.
63. Adams, *Report*, p. 106.
64. NYT, June 17, July 4, 1953.
65. PP, 1953, pp. 110, 132.
66. *Ibid.*, 1954, p. 225.
67. Adams, *Report*, p. 108.
68. Eisenhower to Dodge, January 25, 1954, Dodge Papers, DDEL.
69. Eisenhower, *Mandate*, p. 185.
70. NYT, June 26, 1953.
71. Lofgren, *Congress*, p. 201.
72. *Congressional Record*, 83rd Congress, 1st Session, vol. 99, pt. 6, pp. 7764–65.
73. NYT, June 21, 19, 24, July 6, 8, 1953.
74. PP, 1953, pp. 520–22.
75. James C. Hagerty, interview, April 9, 1969.
76. NYT, July 28, 1953.
77. *Time*, August 3, 1953, p. 9.
78. NYT, August 1, 1953; the Washington *Bulletin*, August 4, 1953.
79. White, *Taft*, p. 268.

Chapter 29

1. Bernard Shanley to Weeks, April 18, 1953, Weeks Papers.
2. Minutes of staff meeting, June 25, 1953, Adams Papers, Dartmouth.

3. Barry Goldwater to Eisenhower, November 2, 1955, and supplementary note by Sherman Adams, Adams Papers, Dartmouth.

4. Minutes of staff meeting, March 2, 1953, Adams Papers, Dartmouth.

5. Donovan, *Eisenhower*, p. 14.

6. Roscoe Drummond, Eisenhower Oral History, Columbia.

7. Numan V. Bartley, *From Thurmond to Wallace: Political Tendencies in Georgia, 1948–1968* (Baltimore: Johns Hopkins Press, 1970), pp. 24–27.

8. Sherman Adams, interview, August 3, 1969.

9. Will Herberg, *Protestant, Catholic, Jew* (Garden City, New York: Anchor Books, 1960), p. 84.

10. Donovan, *Eisenhower*, p. 152.

11. PP, 1954, p. 1089; PP, 1955, pp. 267, 270.

12. Eisenhower to Flanders, February 15, 1954, Flanders Papers, Syracuse.

13. Legislative Leaders Conference Minutes, January 8, 1955, Adams Papers, Dartmouth.

14. Cabinet minutes, October 30, 1953, Adams Papers, Dartmouth.

15. *The Reporter*, October 27, 1953, p. 9.

16. NYT, November 2, 4, 1953.

17. New York *Times Magazine*, October 11, 1953, p. 71.

18. NYT, June 6, 1952.

19. *Ibid.*, August 22, September 7, 1952; Edward L. Schapsmeier and Frederick H. Schapsmeier, "Eisenhower and Ezra Taft Benson: Farm Policy in the 1950's," unpublished article in the possession of the authors.

20. Eisenhower to Paul Hoffman, January 24, 1952, Pre-Inaugural Papers, DDEL.

21. Schapsmeier, "Benson," p. 3; Milton Eisenhower, interview, June 19, 1969.

22. Adams, *Report*, p. 203.

23. New York *Times Magazine*, October 11, 1953, p. 17.

24. NYT, February 22, 1953.

25. New York *Times Magazine*, October 11, 1953, pp. 69–70.

26. Schapsmeier, "Benson," p. 4.

27. Arthur V. Watkins to Eisenhower, October 26, 1953, and J. Bracken Lee to Eisenhower, October 27, 1953, OF 1, DDEL.

28. Eisenhower to Benson, July 24, 1953, OF 1, DDEL.

29. PP, 1953, p. 673.

30. Fred A. Seaton to Eisenhower, November 18, 1953, OF 1, DDEL.

31. PP, 1953, p. 712; Gerald Morgan to Louis O. Fish, October 28, 1953, Morgan Papers, DDEL.

32. NYT, October 25, 1953.

33. Lloyd W. Jones to I. Jack Martin, November 2, 1953, OF 101-P, DDEL.

34. Cabinet minutes, February 20 and May 22, 1953, Adams Papers, Dartmouth.

35. Gabriel Hauge, interview, November 22, 1968.

36. Joe McCarthy to Eisenhower, August 24, 1955, and Karl Mundt to Sherman Adams, October 23, 1957, Adams Papers, Dartmouth.

37. Legislative Leaders Conference minutes, February 25, 1958, Adams Papers, Dartmouth.

38. United States Bureau of the Census, *Historical Statistics of the United States, Colonial Times to 1957; Continuation to 1962 and Revisions* (Washington: U. S. Government Printing Office, 1965), pp. 45–46.

39. Martin Durkin, "The Labor Program: Why I Resigned," *Vital Speeches* (October 15, 1953), p. 6.

40. NYT, September 18, 1952; PP, 1953, p. 29.

41. L. Arthur Minnich, memorandum, February 11, 1953, Adams Papers, Dartmouth.

42. Durkin, "The Labor Program," p. 6.

43. Donovan, *Eisenhower*, pp. 33–34.

44. Stephen F. Dunn to Sinclair Weeks, September 28, 1953, Weeks Papers.

45. Dunn to Bernard Shanley, July 31, 1953, Weeks Papers.

46. Weeks to Eisenhower, June 22, 1953, Weeks Papers.

47. Dunn to Weeks, September 28, 1953, Weeks Papers.

48. Stephen F. Dunn, notes of conference, June 18, 1953, Weeks Papers.

49. Dunn to Shanley, July 31, 1953, Weeks Papers.

50. Durkin, "The Labor Program," p. 7.

51. H. W. Prentis, Jr., to H. Alexander Smith, August 22, 1953, and to Weeks, October 15, 1953, Weeks Papers.

52. NYT, August 5, 1953.

53. *Wall Street Journal*, August 3, 1953.

54. NYT, August 6, 1953.

55. Durkin, "The Labor Program," pp. 7–8; Eisenhower, *Mandate*, pp. 197–99.

56. Tudor, *Notes*, p. 52.

57. Eisenhower, *Mandate*, p. 198.

58. James P. Mitchell to Adams, October 4, 1954, Adams Papers, Dartmouth.

59. NYT, September 24, 1953; *Vital Speeches*, October 15, 1953, pp. 8–12; PP, 1953, p. 609.

60. Eisenhower, *Mandate*, p. 197.

61. H. L. Hunt to Eisenhower, September 17, 1953, and Eisenhower to Hunt, September 24, 1953, OF 99, DDEL.

62. Dwight D. Eisenhower, Dulles Oral History, Princeton.

63. James C. Hagerty, interview, April 9, 1969.

64. Adams, *Report*, p. 332.

65. Minnich to Eisenhower, October 13, 1953, OF 99, DDEL.

66. NYT, February 21, 1954.

67. Gerald Morgan to John F. Kennedy, October 28, 1953, Morgan Papers, DDEL.

68. NYT, November 8, 1953.

69. PP, 1953, pp. 738, 747.

70. Eisenhower to Humphrey, *et al.*, November 23, 1953, Adams Papers, Dartmouth.

71. James M. Lambie, Jr., to Sherman Adams, July 11, 1959, Adams Papers, Dartmouth.

72. Weeks to Montgomery, April 8, 1954, Weeks Papers.

73. Cabinet minutes, April 24, 1953, Adams Papers, Dartmouth.
74. NYT, July 26, 1953.
75. *Ibid.*, November 7, 1953.
76. *Ibid.*, November 17, 1953.
77. *Ibid.*, November 11, 16, 1953.
78. PP, 1953, pp. 758–64.
79. Cabinet minutes, November 12, 1953, Adams Papers, Dartmouth.
80. Adams, *Report*, p. 137.
81. NYT, November 16, 1953; PP, 1953, p. 782.
82. NYT, November 22, 1953.
83. PP, 1953, p. 790.
84. NYT, November 19, 1953.
85. *Ibid.*, November 25, 1953.
86. C. D. Jackson to Adams, November 25, 1953, Adams Papers, Dartmouth.
87. Stanley M. Rumbough, Jr., and Charles Masterson to Murray Snyder, December 1, 1953, OF 99–R, DDEL.
88. NYT, December 9, 1953.
89. *U. S. News & World Report*, December 18, 1953, p. 31.
90. Donovan, *Eisenhower*, p. 175.
91. Legislative Leaders Conference agenda, December 19, 1953, OF 99–Q, DDEL.
92. Cohn, *McCarthy*, p. 111; Milton Eisenhower to author, December 17, 1969.
93. Roy Cohn, interview, May 7, 1969.
94. Sherman Adams, "Army McCarthy Chronology," Adams Papers, Dartmouth.
95. Mazo, *Nixon*, pp. 147–48.
96. Gallup Poll release, December 20, 1953.
97. Claude Robinson to Sinclair Weeks, January 5, 1954, Weeks Papers; Donovan, *Eisenhower*, p. 144.
98. *U.S. News & World Report*, December 18, 1953, p. 10.
99. *The Reporter*, January 19, 1954, p. 4.
100. Theoharis, *Yalta*, p. 185; NYT, May 8, 1954.

Chapter 30

1. Gerald Morgan, memorandum for the record, January 13, 1954, Morgan Papers, DDEL.
2. PP, 1954, p. 435.
3. United States Atomic Energy Commission, *In the Matter of J. Robert Oppenheimer, Text of Principal Documents and Letters* (Washington: U. S. Government Printing Office, 1954), pp. 21–23.
4. PP, 1954, p. 573.
5. NYT, February 19, 1967, July 1, 1967.
6. Adams, *Report*, p. 143; NYT, January 23, 1954.
7. NYT, February 26, 1954.
8. *Ibid.*, February 27, 1954.

9. Transcript of telephone conversation between Secretary Stevens and McCarthy, February 20, 1954, quoted in Griffith, *McCarthy*, p. 247.

10. NYT, February 8, 1954.

11. PP, 1954, pp. 254–55.

12. NYT, February 26, 1954.

13. *Ibid.*

14. *Ibid.*

15. *Ibid.*, February 25, 1954.

16. *Ibid.*, February 26, 1954.

17. Adams, *Report*, p. 147.

18. NYT, February 26, 1954.

19. Legislative Leaders Conference minutes, March 1, 1954, Adams Papers, Dartmouth.

20. PP, 1954, pp. 289–91.

21. Tudor, *Notes*, p. 113.

22. John H. Crider to Adams, March 5, 1954, OF 99-R, DDEL; Jack B. Bearwood to Rumbough and Masterson, March 12, 1954, Morgan Papers, DDEL; Gallup Poll release, March 14, 1954; NYT, March 27, 29, 1954.

23. NYT, March 7, 10, 1954.

24. Eisenhower to Flanders, March 9, 1954, Flanders Papers, Syracuse.

25. PP, 1954, p. 301.

26. George Humphrey, interview, July 2, 1969; Ralph Flanders, Eisenhower Oral History, Columbia; Ralph Flanders, *Senator from Vermont* (Boston: Little, Brown, 1961), p. 262.

27. Mazo, *Nixon*, p. 149.

28. NYT, March 14, 1954.

29. *Ibid.*, March 20, 21, 1954.

30. Adams, *Report*, p. 148.

31. NYHT, March 23, 1954.

32. Bernard Fall, *Hell in a Very Small Place* (Philadelphia: J. B. Lippincott, 1967), p. 297; Robert F. Randle, *Geneva 1954: The Settlement of the Indochinese War* (Princeton, New Jersey: Princeton University Press, 1970), pp. 55–56; Joseph Buttinger, *Vietnam: A Dragon Embattled* (2 vols.; New York: Frederick A. Praeger, 1967), vol. 2, pp. 818–19; Drummond and Coblentz, *Duel*, p. 116; Chester L. Cooper, *The Lost Crusade: America in Vietnam* (New York: Dodd, Mead, 1970), pp. 71–72.

33. *Christian Science Monitor*, June 30, 1971.

34. *Ibid.*, July 1, 1971; Acheson, *Creation*, pp. 671–72.

35. *Christian Science Monitor*, July 1, 1971; Gurtov, *Vietnam*, p. 22.

36. Cooper, *Lost Crusade*, p. 62.

37. NYT, July 5, 1971.

38. Dwight D. Eisenhower, Dulles Oral History, Princeton.

39. Eisenhower, *Mandate*, p. 109.

40. Cooper, *Lost Crusade*, p. 64.

41. NYT, May 7, 1953.

42. Eisenhower to Flanders, July 7, 1953, Flanders Papers, Syracuse.

43. Cabinet minutes, May 14, 1954, Adams Papers, Dartmouth.

44. Randle, *Geneva*, p. 11; Fall, *Hell in a Very Small Place*, p. 294.
45. NYT, July 18, 1953.
46. PP, 1953, p. 541.
47. *American Foreign Policy, 1950–1955*, vol. 2, p. 2371.
48. NYT, September 18, 1953.
49. *Ibid.*, November 1, 3, 5, 21, 1953.
50. *Ibid.*, August 19, September 11, 30, 1953; Eisenhower, *Mandate*, p. 341.
51. NYT, November 8, 13, 30, December 1, 1953.
52. Allan B. Cole (ed.), *Conflict in Indo-China and International Repercussions: A Documentary History, 1945–1955* (Ithaca, New York: Cornell University Press, 1956), p. 172.
53. Neil Sheehan, *et al.*, *The Pentagon Papers as Published by The New York Times* (New York: Bantam Books, 1971), pp. 32–35.
54. "Eisenhower at the Naval War College," United States Naval Institute, *Proceedings* (June 1971), pp. 19–20.
55. John Foster Dulles, "Policy for Security and Peace," *Foreign Affairs* (April 1954), p. 357.
56. Peter V. Curl (ed.), *Documents on American Foreign Relations, 1954* (New York: Harper & Bros., 1955), p. 9.
57. Louis J. Halle, *The Cold War as History* (New York: Harper & Bros., 1967), p. 281; Gurtov, *Vietnam*, p. 89.
58. L. Arthur Minnich, memorandum of Legislative Leaders Conference, February 1, 1955, Adams Papers, Dartmouth.
59. Legislative Leaders Conference minutes, March 1, 29, 1955, June 8, 1955, March 28, 1956, and Sherman Adams, memorandum, July 31, 1956, Adams Papers, Dartmouth.
60. Legislative Leaders Conference minutes, February 8, 1954, Adams Papers, Dartmouth.
61. PP, 1954, p. 306.
62. Eisenhower, *Mandate*, p. 343.
63. Randle, *Geneva*, p. 39.
64. Flanders to Warren Austin, March 11, 1954, and to Lodge, April 29, 1954, Lodge to Flanders, April 29, 1954, Flanders Papers, Syracuse.
65. Randle, *Geneva*, p. 48.
66. Fall, *Hell in a Very Small Place*, p. 298; Randle, *Geneva*, pp. 57–58, 62–63; Buttinger, *Vietnam*, vol. 2, p. 819.
67. Cole (ed.), *Indo-China*, p. 173.
68. Cabinet minutes, March 26, 1954, Adams Papers, Dartmouth.
69. *Ibid.*
70. Randle, *Geneva*, pp. 108–110; Eleanor Lansing Dulles, interview, January 9, 1970; Richard Bissell, Dulles Oral History, Princeton.
71. Randle, *Geneva*, pp. 108–110; John Robinson Beal, *John Foster Dulles* (rev. ed.; New York: Harper & Row, 1959), pp. 207–208.
72. Chalmers Roberts, "The Day We Didn't Go to War," *The Reporter*, (September 14, 1954), pp. 31–35; Fletcher Knebel, "We Nearly Went to War Three Times Last Year," *Look* (February 8, 1955), p. 26; Randle, *Geneva*, pp. 63–64.

73. Drummond and Coblentz, *Duel*, p. 117; Gurtov, *Vietnam*, p. 96.
74. *Congressional Record*, 83rd Congress, 2nd Session, vol. 100, pt. 3, pp. 4209–10.
75. *Ibid.*, pt. 4, pp. 4672–81.
76. *Ibid.*, p. 5116.
77. *Ibid.*, pt. 3, p. 4210.
78. PP, 1954, p. 383.
79. Cole (ed.), *Indo-China*, p. 174.
80. James C. Hagerty, interview, April 11, 1969.
81. Eisenhower, *Mandate*, p. 364.
82. Confidential source.
83. Randle, *Geneva*, pp. 72–73.
84. Eden, *Full Circle*, p. 99.
85. Gurtov, *Vietnam*, p. 100; Randle, *Geneva*, pp. 73–74; Legislative Leaders Conference minutes, April 26, 1954, Adams Papers, Dartmouth.
86. Sheehan, *Pentagon Papers*, pp. 38–40.
87. Cabinet minutes, April 9, 1954, Adams Papers, Dartmouth.
88. Washington *Post*, June 18, 1971.
89. Curl (ed.), *Documents . . . 1954*, p. 257.
90. Richard Harkness, memorandum, May 24, 1954, Dulles Additional Papers, Princeton; Eden, *Full Circle*, p. 97; Eleanor Lansing Dulles, interview, January 9, 1970.
91. Eden, *Full Circle*, pp. 102–103, 109.
92. Randle, *Geneva*, pp. 97–99; Cf., Bernard Fall, *The Two Viet-Nams* (New York: Frederick A. Praeger, 1964), p. 230.
93. Dwight D. Eisenhower, Dulles Oral History, Princeton.
94. Legislative Leaders Conference minutes, April 26, 1954, Adams Papers, Dartmouth.
95. Eisenhower, *Mandate*, p. 355.
96. PP, 1954, p. 409.
97. *Congress and the Nation*, p. 1722.
98. Legislative Leaders Conference minutes, May 3, 1954, Adams Papers, Dartmouth.
99. NYT, May 29, 1954.
100. Legislative Leaders Conference minutes, May 17, 1954, Adams Papers, Dartmouth.
101. Bullis to Eisenhower, May 4, 1954, Bullis to Tom Stephens, May 4, 1954, Frank Wood to Eisenhower, May 16, 1954, OF 99–R, DDEL.
102. Griffith, *McCarthy*, p. 262; PP, 1954, pp. 489–90.
103. NYT, June 2, 1954.
104. Gallup Poll release, June 24, 1954.
105. NYT, June 20, August 6, 1954.
106. *Congress and the Nation*, p. 1725.
107. Confidential source.
108. Sheehan, *Pentagon Papers*, pp. 42–43.
109. Curl (ed.), *Documents . . . 1954*, pp. 267–69.
110. Sheehan, *Pentagon Papers*, pp. 35–38.

111. Matthew B. Ridgway, *Soldier* (New York: Harper & Bros., 1956), pp. 276–77.
112. Dwight D. Eisenhower, Dulles Oral History, Princeton.
113. Legislative Leaders Conference minutes, May 3, 1954, Adams Papers, Dartmouth.
114. NYT, May 8, 1954.
115. Sheehan, *Pentagon Papers*, pp. 41–42.
116. Eisenhower, *Mandate*, p. 359.
117. Randle, *Geneva*, pp. 220–21.
118. Sheehan, *Pentagon Papers*, pp. 41–42.
119. *Ibid.*, pp. 12–13.
120. Eisenhower, *Mandate*, pp. 421–26; Richard J. Barnet, *Intervention and Revolution* (New York: World Publishing Company, 1968), pp. 230–34; *American Foreign Policy, 1950–1955*, vol. 1, pp. 1301–02; Richard Bissell, Dulles Oral History, Princeton; Philip Crowe, "Recollections of John Foster Dulles," Dulles Additional Papers, Princeton; Richard Harkness, memorandum, July 1, 1954, Dulles Additional Papers, Princeton.
121. Cabinet minutes, May 14, 1954.
122. Richard Harkness, memorandum of conversations, May 24, 1954, Dulles Additional Papers, Princeton.
123. Gallup Poll release, June 13, 1954.
124. PP, 1954, p. 605.
125. Curl (ed.), *Documents . . . 1954*, pp. 312, 317.
126. NYT, October 30, 1954.
127. *Congress and the Nation*, p. 21.
128. NYT, October 24, 26, 1954.
129. *Congress and the Nation*, p. 21.
130. NYT, December 2, 1954.
131. *Ibid.*, December 3, 1954.
132. *Ibid.*, December 8, 1954.
133. *Ibid.*, December 1, 1954.
134. *Ibid.*, November 24, December 11, 1954.
135. *Ibid.*, February 2, 13, March 28, 1955.
136. *National Review*, November 19, 1955, pp. 6, 12.
137. PP, 1954, pp. 1087–88.

Chapter 31

1. NYT, December 9, 1953.
2. J. Robert Oppenheimer, "Atomic Weapons and American Policy," *Foreign Affairs* (July 1953), pp. 528–31.
3. Lewis L. Strauss, *Men and Decisions* (Garden City, New York: Doubleday and Company, 1962), p. 356.
4. John Lear, "Ike and the Peaceful Atom," *The Reporter* (January 12, 1956), pp. 11–12.
5. Philip Noel-Baker, *The Arms Race.* (New York: Oceana Publications, 1958), p. 5.

6. Flanders to Eisenhower, September 11, and Eisenhower to Flanders, September 22, 1953, Flanders Papers, Syracuse.
7. Andrew Berding, Eisenhower Oral History, Columbia.
8. Strauss, *Men and Decisions*, p. 359.
9. PP, 1953, pp. 813–22.
10. Lear, "Ike and the Peaceful Atom," p. 11.
11. Cabinet minutes, October 23, 1953, Adams Papers, Dartmouth.
12. Robert E. Matteson to Eisenhower, February 8, 1957, Adams Papers, Dartmouth.
13. *Wall Street Journal*, August 16, 1955.
14. Strauss, *Men and Decisions*, p. 363.
15. Noel-Baker, *Arms Race*, pp. 11–14.
16. John Foster Dulles, "Notes for NATO Conference," December 17, 1954, Dulles Papers, Princeton.
17. Legislative Leaders Conference minutes, June 28, 1954, Adams Papers, Dartmouth.
18. Sheehan, *Pentagon Papers*, pp. 14–15; Chicago *Sun-Times*, June 25, 1971.
19. Edward G. Lansdale, "Viet Nam: Do We Understand Revolution?" *Foreign Affairs* (October 1964), p. 77.
20. Sheehan, *Pentagon Papers*, p. 54.
21. *Ibid.*, p. 16.
22. Buttinger, *Vietnam*, vol. 2, pp. 845–47; Robert Scheer and Warren Hinckle, "The 'Vietnam Lobby,'" *Ramparts* (July 1954), pp. 18–19.
23. Cooper, *Lost Crusade*, pp. 124–27.
24. Richard Bissell, Dulles Oral History, Princeton.
25. Confidential source.
26. Cabinet minutes, October 19, 1954, Adams Papers, Dartmouth.
27. Confidential source.
28. Cabinet minutes, October 19, 1954, Adams Papers, Princeton.
29. General J. Lawton Collins, Dulles Oral History, Princeton.
30. Legislative Leaders Conference minutes, April 26, 1955, Adams Papers, Dartmouth.
31. Curl (ed.), *Documents . . . 1954*, pp. 318–23.
32. General Collins, Carlos P. Garcia, Dulles Oral History, Princeton; Cabinet minutes, October 19, 1954, Adams Papers, Dartmouth.
33. Eisenhower, *Mandate*, p. 463.
34. Ridgway, *Soldier*, p. 279.
35. Eisenhower, *Mandate*, pp. 463–64; Richard Harkness, memorandum, February 12, 1955, Dulles Additional Papers, Princeton; Ridgway, *Soldier*, pp. 278–79.
36. Dillon Anderson, Dulles Oral History, Princeton.
37. Confidential source.
38. Chiang Kai-shek, Dulles Oral History, Princeton.
39. PP, 1955, p. 209.
40. *Congress and the Nation*, p. 114.
41. Curl (ed.), *Documents . . . 1955*, p. 299.
42. Confidential source.

43. Richard Harkness, memorandum, February 12, 1955, Dulles Additional Papers, Princeton; Cabinet minutes, February 18, 1955, Adams Papers, Dartmouth.

44. Gallup Poll releases, April 10, May 6, 1955.

45. Noel-Baker, *Arms Race*, pp. 21–22; *National Review*, November 26, 1955, p. 13.

46. PP, 1955, p. 498.

47. *Ibid.*, pp. 676–77.

48. Noel-Baker, *Arms Race*, pp. 23–24.

49. Gerson, *Dulles*, p. 221.

50. Dulles to Eisenhower, June 18, 1955, Dulles Papers, Princeton.

51. John Foster Dulles, "Secret Paper #4: Estimate of Proscript of Soviet Union Achieving Its Goal," n.d., Dulles Papers, Princeton.

52. Harold Macmillan, *Tides of Fortune* (New York: Harper & Row, 1969), pp. 586–87.

53. Eisenhower, *Mandate*, p. 504.

54. Elliott Bell, Dulles Oral History, Princeton.

55. Legislative Leaders Conference minutes, March 22, 1955, Adams Papers, Dartmouth.

56. Macmillan, *Tides*, pp. 586–87.

57. *Ibid.*, pp. 590, 606–607, 613–14.

58. *Ibid.*, p. 591.

59. *American Foreign Policy, 1950–1955*, vol. 2, pp. 1886–87.

60. Rowland Evans and Robert Novak, *Lyndon B. Johnson: The Exercise of Power* (New York: New American Library, 1966), pp. 172–73; NYT, June 23, 1955.

61. Adams, *Report*, p. 176.

62. John Foster Dulles, "Secret Paper #4: Estimate of Proscript of Soviet Union Achieving Its Goals," Dulles Additional Papers, Princeton.

63. Robert B. Anderson, interview, March 11, 1970.

64. Rovere, *Eisenhower Years*, pp. 276–77, 287.

65. Curl (ed.), *Documents . . . 1955*, pp. 215, 216.

66. Robert B. Anderson, interview, March 11, 1970.

67. Confidential source.

68. Eisenhower, *Mandate*, p. 529.

69. Rovere, *Eisenhower Years*, p. 290.

70. Dwight D. Eisenhower, Dulles Oral History, Princeton.

71. NYT, March 20, 1956.

72. Edward Crankshaw (ed.), *Khrushchev Remembers* (Boston: Little, Brown, 1970), p. 398.

73. Curl (ed.), *Documents . . . 1955*, p. 231.

74. Gallup Poll release, August 3, 1955.

75. NYT, August 22, 25, 29, 1955; James Reston, *Sketches in the Sand* (New York: Alfred A. Knopf, 1967), p. 420.

76. Nixon, *Six Crises*, p. 153.

77. NYT, September 25, 1955.

78. PP, 1955, p. 816.

79. Dean Rusk to Gabriel Hauge, September 25, 1955, Hauge Scrapbooks.

PART THREE

Chapter 32

1. Gallup Poll release, September 18, 1955.
2. Dr. Howard Snyder to Wilton Persons, September 29, 1955, Adams Papers, Dartmouth.
3. NYT, September 26, 1955.
4. Gallup Poll release, September 12, 1955.
5. *Ibid.*, September 18, 1955.
6. *Ibid.*, October 8, 1955; C. A. H. Thomson and F. M. Shattuck, *The 1956 Presidential Campaign* (Washington: The Brookings Institution, 1960), p. 19.
7. NYT, September 26, 29, 30, 1955; White House press release, September 26, 1955.
8. Cabinet minutes, September 30, 1955, Adams Papers, Dartmouth.
9. Confidential source.
10. L. Arthur Minnich to Wilton Persons, September 30, 1955, OF 101–P, DDEL; Adams, *Report*, pp. 186–87.
11. Gallup Poll release, October 19, 1955.
12. NYT, September 26, 1955; Rovere, *Eisenhower Years*, p. 325.
13. Nixon, *Crisis*, p. 149.
14. William S. White, "Evolution of Eisenhower as Politician," New York *Times Magazine* (September 23, 1956), p. 60.
15. Drummond and Coblentz, *Duel*, pp. 35–36; Roscoe Drummond, Eisenhower Oral History, Columbia.
16. Hughes, *Ordeal*, p. 173.
17. Confidential source.
18. Confidential source.
19. Ray Scherer, Eisenhower Oral History, Columbia.
20. NYT, February 7, 1953.
21. PP, 1953, p. 108.
22. NYT, April 2, 1953.
23. Donovan, *Eisenhower*, pp. 155–56.
24. *Ibid.*, p. 155.
25. Maxwell Rabb, interview, October 1, 1968.
26. NYT, June 11, 1953.
27. PP, 1953, p. 405.
28. NYT, July 3, 1953.
29. *Ibid.*
30. Robert B. Anderson, interview, March 11, 1970.
31. Dwight D. Eisenhower, *Waging Peace* (Garden City, New York: Doubleday and Company, 1965), p. 7n.
32. NYT, October 18, 1955.
33. Gallup Poll release, November 16, 1955.
34. NYT, November 16, 1955.
35. *National Review*, November 26, 1955, p. 5.
36. Nixon, *Six Crises*, p. 155.
37. NYT, December 18, 1955.

38. *National Review*, December 7, 1955, p. 8.
39. NYT, December 26, 1955.
40. Nixon, *Six Crises*, pp. 158–60.
41. Milton S. Eisenhower, interview, June 19, 1969; James C. Hagerty, interview, April 11, 1969.
42. NYT, December 18, 1955.
43. PP, 1956, pp. 33, 37.

Chapter 33

1. Confidential source.
2. PP, 1956, p. 15.
3. Bryce Harlow to William Rogers, February 6, 1956, Rogers Papers, DDEL.
4. PP, 1956, p. 25.
5. NYT, January 11, 1956.
6. Weeks to Nixon, January 24, 1956, Weeks Papers.
7. PP, 1956, p. 182.
8. *Ibid.*, pp. 175–76.
9. NYT, January 21, 1956.
10. *Business Week*, February 11, 1956, p. 39.
11. PP, 1956, p. 187.
12. Gallup Poll releases, February 11, 12, 15, 1956.
13. NYT, March 2, 1956.
14. *Ibid.*, September 4, 1956.
15. *Ibid.*, February 23, 1956.
16. *Ibid.*, February 12, 1956.
17. E. Frederic Morrow, *Black Man in the White House* (New York: Coward-McCann, 1963), p. 41.
18. General Clay, Eisenhower Oral History, Columbia.
19. PP, 1956, p. 266.
20. *Ibid.*, p. 287.
21. William V. Shannon, "Eisenhower Paradox," *Commonweal* (March 23, 1956), p. 639.
22. Adlai Stevenson, *The New America* (New York: Harper & Bros., 1957), pp. 20–21.
23. NYT, March 1, 1956; Cabinet minutes, March 2, 1956, Adams Papers.
24. *U.S. News & World Report*, March 16, 1956, p. 76; *Newsweek*, March 19, 1956, pp. 31–32.
25. PP, 1956, p. 303.
26. James C. Hagerty, interview, April 11, 1969; Nixon, *Six Crises*, p. 166; Cabinet minutes, April 27, 1956, Adams Papers, Dartmouth.
27. Thomson and Shattuck, *1956 Presidential Campaign*, pp. 55–56.
28. Morrow to Cutler, October 12, 1952, OF 142–A, DDEL.
29. NYT, March 11, 1953; Donovan, *Eisenhower*, p. 160.
30. Ralph A. Rose to Charles F. Honeywell, June 3, 1953, Weeks Papers; Eisenhower to Samuel Spencer, November 30, 1953, Adams Papers, Dartmouth.

31. Benson to Eisenhower, October 22, 1953, OF 1, DDEL.
32. Donovan, *Eisenhower*, p. 160; White House press release, August 13, 1954.
33. Maxwell Rabb to Sherman Adams, December 3, 1953, OF 142–A, DDEL.
34. Marbee William Durhan to Eisenhower, September 5, 1953, and Arthur B. Spingarn, *et al.*, to Eisenhower, September 8, 1953, OF 142–A, DDEL.
35. PP, 1954, p. 293.
36. *Ibid.*, p. 432.
37. Donovan, *Eisenhower*, p. 162.
38. PP, 1954, pp. 491–92.
39. *Ibid.*, p. 700.
40. Richard M. Dalfiume, *Desegregation of the U.S. Armed Forces* (Columbia, Missouri: University of Missouri Press, 1969), p. 167.
41. William C. Berman, "Presidential Politics and Civil Rights: 1952," p. 4. Unpublished article in the possession of the author.
42. Roy Wilkins, interview, August 11, 1970.
43. Cabinet minutes, January 28, 1955, Adams Papers, Dartmouth.
44. Stephen Benedict, interview, April 9, 1969.
45. E. Frederic Morrow, interview, November 1, 1968.
46. Larson, *Eisenhower*, p. 124.
47. George M. Humphrey, interview, July 2, 1969.
48. Sherman Adams, interview, August 3, 1969.
49. James C. Hagerty, interview, April 9, 1969.
50. Numan V. Bartley, *The Rise of Massive Resistance: Race and Politics in the South During the 1950's* (Baton Rouge: Louisiana State University Press, 1969), p. 94.
51. *Ibid.*, pp. 104–48.
52. *Ibid.*, p. 195.
53. Quoted in Valores Washington to Sherman Adams, January 4, 1956, OF 138–A–6, DDEL.
54. Roy Wilkins to Morrow, December 2, 1955, Morrow Papers, DDEL.
55. Morrow to Rabb, November 29, 1955, Morrow Papers, DDEL; Morrow, *Black Man*, pp. 27–29.
56. Morrow to Adams, December 16, 1955, Morrow Papers, DDEL.
57. Rabb to Adams, March 1, 1956, Morgan Papers, DDEL.
58. Morrow, *Black Man*, pp. 29–31.
59. Valores Washington to Adams, January 4, 1956, OF 138–A–6, DDEL.
60. Charles F. Masterson to Howard Pyle, January 19, 1956, Pyle Papers, DDEL.
61. NYT, January 30, 1956.
62. *Ibid.*, January 1, 1956.
63. Bartley, *Massive Resistance*, p. 146.
64. PP, 1956, p. 234.
65. *Ibid.*, p. 269.
66. "A Preview of the Declaration of Segregation," February 10, 1956, Morrow Papers, DDEL.
67. L. Arthur Minnich to Rowland Hughes, January 10, 24, 1956, Harlow Papers, DDEL.

68. Morrow, *Black Man*, pp. 34–35.
69. PP, 1956, p. 187.
70. *Congressional Quarterly* (vol. 12, 1956), p. 83.
71. Gallup Poll release, February 15, 1956.
72. J. W. Anderson, *Eisenhower, Brownell, and the Congress* (University, Alabama: University of Alabama Press, 1964), p. 69.
73. NYT, March 16, 1956.
74. Morrow to Hauge, March 31, 1956, and Rabb to Adams, June 20, 1956, OF 138–A–6, DDEL.
75. PP, 1956, p. 337.
76. Cabinet minutes, December 2, 1955, Adams Papers, Dartmouth.
77. Gerald Morgan to Herbert Brownell, December 8, 1955, Morgan Papers, DDEL.
78. Undated memorandum, "Administration Civil Rights Program," Harlow Papers, DDEL.
79. Marion Folsom to Herbert Brownell, March 19, 1956, Morgan Papers, DDEL.
80. PP, 1956, pp. 304–305.
81. Rabb to Adams, March 30, 1956, Pyle Papers, DDEL.
82. Harlow to Rabb, May 3, 1956, Harlow Papers, DDEL.
83. Anderson, *Congress*, p. 38.
84. L. Arthur Minnich to Rowland Hughes, March 20, 1956, Harlow Papers, DDEL.
85. PP, 1956, p. 567.
86. *Ibid.*, pp. 350–51.
87. S. J. S. to Bryce Harlow, July 17, 1956, Harlow Papers, DDEL; *Congressional Record*, 84th Congress, 2nd Session, vol. 102, pt. 10, p. 13147.
88. Bryce Harlow to General Andrew Goodpaster, July 18, 1956, Harlow Papers, DDEL.
89. NYHT, July 29, 1956.
90. NYT, April 27, 1956.
91. Evans and Novak, *Johnson*, p. 123; Lyndon B. Johnson, interview, June 30, 1970.
92. Morrow, *Black Man*, pp. 85–86.
93. PP, 1956, p. 913.
94. Adams, *Report*, p. 194.
95. *U.S. News & World Report*, August 3, 1956, p. 35.

Chapter 34

1. Harold Stassen to Eisenhower, May 14, 1956, and Eisenhower to Stassen, May 16, 1956, Private Papers of Harold Stassen.
2. Harold E. Stassen, interview, August 23, 1971.
3. Sherman Adams, interview, August 3, 1969; Harold Stassen, "Letter to Republican Delegates," 1956, Weeks Papers.
4. NYT, July 24, 1956.
5. Eisenhower, *Waging Peace*, p. 10.

6. White House press release, July 23, 1956.
7. Adams, *Report*, p. 240.
8. Sinclair Weeks to John E. Dickinson, July 26, 1956, Weeks Papers.
9. *Newsweek*, August 6, 1956, p. 20; Fletcher Knebel, "Did Ike Really Want Nixon?" *Look* (October 30, 1956), pp. 25–27.
10. John D. M. Miller to Weeks, July 27, 1956, Weeks Papers.
11. PP, 1956, pp. 623, 628.
12. *U.S. News & World Report*, August 3, 1956, p. 46.
13. *Ibid.*, August 31, 1956, p. 29.
14. NYT, August 17, 18, 1956; Knebel, "Did Ike Really Want Nixon?" p. 27.
15. Harold Stassen, letter to Republican delegates, 1956, Weeks Papers.
16. Thomson and Shattuck, *1956 Presidential Campaign*, pp. 187–88.
17. *Ibid.*, pp. 188–89.
18. Gallup Poll release, July 25, 1956.
19. For a discussion of the Willkie–Stassen situation in 1944, see Ellsworth Barnard, *Wendell Willkie, Fighter for Freedom* (Marquette, Michigan: Northern Michigan University Press, 1966), pp. 453–54.
20. Eisenhower to Leonard Hall, August 18, 1956, Adams Papers, Dartmouth.
21. *The New Republic*, September 3, 1956, pp. 5–6.
22. Roy Wilkins, interview, August 11, 1970.
23. Thomson and Shattuck, *1956 Presidential Campaign*, p. 202.
24. PP, 1956, p. 669.
25. Thomson and Shattuck, *1956 Presidential Campaign*, pp. 201–204.
26. Arthur Larson, *A Republican Looks at His Party* (New York: Harper & Bros., 1956), p. 39.
27. PP, 1956, p. 722.
28. Howard Pyle to Sherman Adams, October 5, 1956, Pyle Papers, DDEL.
29. NYT, August 23, 1956; Thomson and Shattuck, *1956 Presidential Campaign*, p. 210.
30. PP, 1956, pp. 708–10.
31. *Ibid.*, p. 724.

Chapter 35

1. Gallup Poll release, September 9, 1956.
2. Davis, *Politics of Honor*, p. 339.
3. Bernard C. Duffy to Sherman Adams, September 21, 1956, OF 138-C-4, DDEL.
4. Dewey to Sherman Adams, October 5, 1956, Pyle Papers, DDEL.
5. Bartley, *Massive Resistance*, pp. 163–65; NYT, October 16, 1956.
6. Paul Hoffman, "How Eisenhower Saved the Republican Party," *Collier's* (October 26, 1956), p. 47.
7. *Ibid.*
8. Barry Goldwater to Sherman Adams, October 12, 1956, and Adams to Goldwater, October 16, 1956, OF 123-C-4, DDEL.
9. NYT, October 12, 1956.

10. PP, 1956, p. 891.
11. Eisenhower, *Waging Peace*, p. 11.
12. PP, 1956, pp. 758–59.
13. *Ibid.*, p. 1055.
14. Maxwell Rabb to Sherman Adams, October 24, 1956, OF 138–A–6, DDEL.
15. NYT, September 26, October 12, 30, November 4, 1956.
16. *Ibid.*, September 28, October 11, 1956.
17. NYT, November 2, 1956.
18. Gallup Poll release, October 29, 1956; NYT, November 2, 1956.
19. Thomson and Shattuck, *1956 Presidential Campaign*, p. 351.
20. Tudor, *Notes*, p. 39.
21. Eisenhower to Frank Clement, October 30, 1954, OF 108–E, DDEL.
22. Tudor, *Notes*, p. 9.
23. Eisenhower to John Sherman Cooper, July 26, 1954, OF 108–E, DDEL.
24. Eisenhower to Orie Phillips, November 17, 1954, OF 108–E, DDEL.
25. Frier, *Conflict of Interest*, pp. 57, 66–67.
26. Clapp to Dodge, December 24, 1953, OF 108–E, DDEL.
27. Sherman Adams to Charles Willis, May 13, 1953, OF 51, DDEL.
28. Charles Willis to Sherman Adams, May 14, and Adams to Joseph Dodge, May 20, 1953, OF 31, DDEL.
29. Adams to Sheila Tunney, January 26, 1954, OF 51, DDEL.
30. Joseph Dodge to Sherman Adams, January 26, 1954, OF 51, DDEL.
31. States Rights Finley to Thomas E. Stephens, March 19, 1954, OF 51, DDEL.
32. Rowland Hughes to Sherman Adams, February 9, 1954, OF 51, DDEL.
33. John Sherman Cooper to Sherman Adams, April 3, 1954, OF 51, DDEL.
34. Memoranda to Sherman Adams, July 16, 1954, and Roy Howard to Adams, July 16, 1954, OF 108–E, DDEL.
35. Rowland Hughes to Eisenhower, June 29, 1955, Morgan Papers, DDEL.
36. White House press release, statement by Murray Snyder, July 12, 1955.
37. NYT, October 28, 1956.
38. *Ibid.*, November 4, 6, 1956.
39. *Ibid.*, October 29, 1956.
40. Howard Pyle to Sherman Adams, October 4, 1956, DDEL.
41. NYT, September 23, 1956.
42. I. Jack Martin to Sherman Adams, October 1, 1956, Morgan Papers, DDEL.
43. Henning, J. Prentis to Adams, October 1, 1956, and Robert Cutler to Prentis, October 12, 1956, OF 138–C–4, DDEL.
44. PP, 1956, p. 941.
45. *Ibid.*, pp. 965–66.
46. *Ibid.*, p. 903.
47. Paul E. Zinner (ed.), *Documents on American Foreign Relations 1956* (New York: Harper & Bros., 1957), p. 342.
48. Confidential source.
49. Confidential source; Eisenhower, *Waging Peace*, p. 56; Lyman B. Kirkpatrick, Jr., *The Real CIA* (New York: Macmillan, 1968), pp. 274–75.

50. Andrew Tully, *CIA: The Inside Story* (New York: William Morrow, 1962), pp. 109–10.
51. C. Douglas Dillon, interview, May 26, 1969.
52. PP, 1956, p. 1019.
53. *Ibid.*, pp. 1025–27.
54. Eisenhower, *Waging Peace*, p. 69.
55. Herman Finer, *Dulles Over Suez* (Chicago: Quadrangle Books, 1964), p. 349; Tully, *CIA*, p. 110; Kirkpatrick, *CIA*, pp. 274–75.
56. Eisenhower, *Waging Peace*, p. 70.
57. NYT, October 30, 1956.
58. PP, 1956, p. 1058.
59. Eisenhower, *Waging Peace*, p. 73; Finer, *Dulles*, p. 355.
60. White House press release, October 29, 1956.
61. NYT, October 29, 1956.
62. H. J. Porter to Eisenhower, November 28, 1955, Rogers Papers, DDEL.
63. Richard Goold-Adams, *The Time of Power: A Reappraisal of John Foster Dulles* (London: Weidenfeld & Nicolson, 1962), p. 214.
64. Finer, *Dulles*, p. 495.
65. Tully, *CIA*, p. 107.
66. Eisenhower, *Waging Peace*, pp. 154–55.
67. Sulzberger, *Candles*, p. 850.
68. Eisenhower, *Waging Peace*, p. 23.
69. Ray Carter to Eisenhower, November 18, 1952, Pre-Inaugural Papers, DDEL.
70. Robert Engler, *The Politics of Oil* (Chicago: University of Chicago Press, 1961), pp. 204–205; NYT, July 10, 1953.
71. Beal, *Dulles*, p. 250; confidential source.
72. Confidential source.
73. Finer, *Dulles*, pp. 27–28.
74. George M. Humphrey and Herbert Hoover, Jr., Dulles Oral History, Princeton; Eden, *Full Circle*, p. 420.
75. Robert B. Anderson, interview, March 11, 1970.
76. Kenneth Love, *Suez: The Twice-Fought War* (New York: McGraw-Hill, 1969), p. 309.
77. Eugene Black, Dulles Oral History, Princeton.
78. Eden, *Full Circle*, p. 421.
79. Hugh Thomas, *Suez* (New York: Harper & Row, 1967), p. 22.
80. Thruston Morton, Dulles Oral History, Princeton.
81. Confidential source.
82. Childs, *Eisenhower*, pp. 23–31.
83. Drummond and Coblentz, *Duel*, p. 170.
84. Dillon Anderson, Dulles Oral History, Princeton.
85. Prescott Bush, Eisenhower Oral History, Columbia.
86. Dwight D. Eisenhower, Dulles Oral History, Princeton.
87. Love, *Suez*, p. 315.
88. Department of State press release, July 19, 1956.
89. Finer, *Dulles*, p. 54.
90. NYT, January 16, 1971.

91. Gerard B. Lambert, Dulles Oral History, Princeton.
92. Eugene Black, Dulles Oral History, Princeton.
93. Herman Pleger to Sinclair Weeks, January 7, 1957, Weeks Papers.
94. Dwight D. Eisenhower, Dulles Oral History, Princeton.
95. Thomas, *Suez*, p. 39.
96. Eden, *Full Circle*, pp. 427–28.
97. Eisenhower, *Waging Peace*, p. 664.
98. Winthrop W. Aldrich, "The Suez Crisis: A Footnote to History," *Foreign Affairs* (April 1967), pp. 541–52.
99. Eden, *Full Circle*, pp. 427–28.
100. Loy Henderson, Dulles Oral History, Princeton.
101. Eden, *Full Circle*, p. 435.
102. Zinner (ed.), *Documents . . . 1956*, p. 299.
103. PP, 1956, p. 661.
104. Eden, *Full Circle*, p. 469.
105. Andrew Goodpaster, Dulles Oral History, Princeton.
106. Richard Harkness, memorandum, October 31, 1956, Dulles Additional Papers, Princeton.
107. Richard Bissell, Dulles Oral History, Princeton.
108. PP, 1956, pp. 1064–66.
109. *Ibid.*, p. 1072.
110. NYT, November 2, 1956.
111. PP, 1956, p. 1081.
112. Dr. Leonard D. Heaton, Dulles Oral History, Princeton.
113. Drummond and Coblentz, *Duel*, p. 175.
114. Confidential source.
115. Moses Rischin, *"Our Own Kind": Voting by Race, Creed, or National Origin* (Santa Barbara, California: The Fund for the Republic, 1960), pp. 28–29, 32, 37.
116. Finer, *Dulles*, pp. 446–47; Thomas; *Suez*, p. 149.

Chapter 36

1. *Life*, March 16, 1959, p. 105.
2. PP, 1957, p. 593.
3. *U.S. News & World Report*, October 25, 1957, p. 70.
4. PP, 1957, pp. 214–15.
5. Eisenhower to Charles M. White, April 4, 1957, OF 101-Y, DDEL.
6. NYT, July 31, 1957.
7. Philip K. Crowe, "Recollections of John Foster Dulles," Dulles Papers, Princeton.
8. Philip K. Crowe, Dulles Oral History, Princeton.
9. PP, 1957, pp. 579–80; NYT, August 1, 1957.
10. NYT, August 8, 1957.
11. *Ibid.*, November 7, 1956.
12. PP, 1956, p. 1090.
13. NYT, November 7, 1956.

14. *Ibid.*, July 24, 1957.

15. PP, 1956, pp. 1103–1104.

16. Love, *Suez*, pp. 642–43.

17. PP, 1956, p. 1097.

18. Love, *Suez*, p. 651; Thomas, *Suez*, p. 148.

19. *Life*, March 16, 1959, p. 110.

20. PP, 957, pp. 13, 15.

21. Gallup Poll releases, February 1, 3, 1957.

22. NYT, January 20, 1957.

23. Hughes, *Ordeal*, p. 232.

24. PP, 1957, pp. 63–64.

25. *Ibid.*, pp. 19–21, 23, 26, 27.

26. NYT, November 25, 1956.

27. *Ibid.*, January 18, 1957.

28. *Ibid.*, February 5, 1957.

29. *Ibid.*, February 10, 1957.

30. *Ibid.*, November 25, 1956.

31. Hughes to Eisenhower, March 30, 1956, Pyle Papers, DDEL.

32. Adams, *Report*, p. 365.

33. *Ibid.*, p. 364.

34. Charles J. V. Murphy, "The Budget and Eisenhower," *Fortune* (July 1957), p. 228.

35. *Ibid.*, p. 230.

36. *Ibid.*; Eisenhower, *Waging Peace*, p. 128.

37. Nathaniel R. Howard (ed.), *The Basic Papers of George M. Humphrey as Secretary of the Treasury, 1953–1957* (Cleveland: The Western Reserve Historical Society, 1965), pp. 238, 241–42, 252.

38. PP, 1957, pp. 73–74.

39. Murphy, "The Budget and Eisenhower," p. 230; Eisenhower, *Waging Peace*, p. 130.

40. Sinclair Weeks to Wilton Persons, May 1, 1957, OF 2, DDEL.

41. Adams, *Report*, p. 371.

42. NYT, May 23, 1957.

43. Murphy, "The Budget and Eisenhower," p. 96.

44. NYT, May 3, 1957.

45. *Commonweal*, February 22, 1957, pp. 525–26.

46. Adams, *Report*, p. 380.

47. NYT, November 7, 1957.

Chapter 37

1. NYT, January 1, 1956.

2. *Ibid.*, January 5, 1957.

3. Douglas Cater, "How the Senate Passed the Civil Rights Bill," *The Reporter* (September 5, 1957), pp. 10–13.

4. NYT, January 9 and February 11, 1957.

5. *Amsterdam News*, March 2, 1957; NYT, April 29, 1957.

6. Herbert Brownell to Clarence L. Jordan, February 28, 1957, Morrow Papers, DDEL.
7. Brownell to Marvin Griffin, February 28, 1957, Morrow Papers, DDEL.
8. Morrow, *Black Man*, p. 109.
9. NYT, February 4, 1957.
10. *Ibid.*, January 12, 1957.
11. *Ibid.*, January 13, 1957.
12. *Amsterdam News*, January 19, 1957.
13. NYT, February 7, 1957.
14. Bayard Rustin to author, December 17, 1969; Fred Shuttlesworth, interview, December 10, 1969.
15. *Amsterdam News*, March 9, 1957.
16. New York *Post*, March 22, 1957.
17. Powell to Adams, March 28, 1957, OF 142–A, DDEL.
18. Powell to Eisenhower, March 28, 1957, OF 142–A, DDEL.
19. Warren Olney III to Rabb, April 15, 1957, OF 142–A, DDEL.
20. Rabb to Adams, April 2, 1957, OF 142–A, DDEL.
21. Memorandum to Adams, April 2, 1957, OF 142–A, DDEL.
22. Rabb to Adams, April 3, 1957, OF 142–A, DDEL.
23. *Ibid.*
24. Rabb to Adams, April 17, 1957, OF 142–A, DDEL.
25. *Ibid.*
26. NYT, April 15, 1957.
27. *Ibid.*, May 18, 1957; Coretta Scott King, *My Life with Martin Luther King, Jr.* (New York: Holt, Rinehart and Winston, 1969), p. 159.
28. *Amsterdam News*, May 25, 1957; NYT, May 18, 1957.
29. Roy Wilkins, interview, August 11, 1970.
30. E. Frederic Morrow, interview, November 1, 1968.
31. Morrow to Adams, June 4, 1957, Morrow Papers, DDEL.
32. Maxwell Rabb, memorandum for the record, June 20, 1957, Morrow Papers, DDEL.
33. A. Philip Randolph to Eisenhower, June 10, 1957, Morrow Papers, DDEL.
34. Martin Luther King, Jr., to Nixon, August 30, 1957, Rogers Papers, DDEL.
35. Morrow to Adams, September 12, 1957, Morrow Papers, DDEL.
36. *Ibid.*
37. Orval Faubus to Eisenhower, September 12, 1957, OF 142–A–5–A, DDEL.
38. PP, 1957, p. 546.
39. *Ibid.*, pp. 640, 646.
40. Anthony Lewis, *Portrait of a Decade* (New York: Random House, 1964), p. 49.
41. *Ibid.*, p. 659.
42. Adams, *Report*, pp. 349–52.
43. PP, 1957, p. 689.
44. Woodrow Wilson Mann to Eisenhower, September 24, 1957, OF 142–A–5–A, DDEL.

45. E. Frederic Morrow, interview, November 1, 1968; Adams, *Report*, p. 355.
46. Roy Wilkins, interview, August 11, 1970; Morrow, *Black Man*, p. 234.
47. Gallup Poll release, October 4, 1957.
48. Harold Engstrom to Eisenhower, September 25, 1957, OF 142–A–5–A, DDEL.
49. King to Eisenhower, September 25, 1957, OF 142–A–5–A, DDEL.
50. John Bragdon to Sherman Adams, September 26, 1957, OF 142–A, DDEL.
51. Billy Matthews to Eisenhower, September 27, 1957, OF 142–A, DDEL.
52. Richmond *Times-Dispatch*, October 24, 1957.
53. High Point (North Carolina) *Enterprise*, October 24, 1957.
54. Dulles to Eisenhower, October 31, 1957, Harlow Papers, DDEL.
55. Cabinet minutes, October 18, 1957, Adams Papers, Dartmouth.
56. Governor Joe Foss to Eisenhower, October 20, 1957, OF 1, DDEL.
57. NYT, May 19, 1957.
58. *U.S. News & World Report*, March 29, 1957, p. 74; NYT, April 4, 1957.
59. PP, 1957, p. 354.
60. *Ibid.*, p. 243.
61. NYT, May 25, 1957.
62. *Ibid.*, October 15, 1957.
63. *Ibid.*, November 19, 1957.
64. Gallup Poll release, November 3, 1957.
65. NYT, November 26, 1957.
66. *Ibid.*, December 2, 1957.
67. Nixon, *Six Crises*, pp. 170–74; NYT, November 27, 1957.
68. *Harper's*, February 1958, pp. 10, 18.
69. NYT, December 23, 1957.
70. Sinclair Weeks to George Humphrey, December 3, 1957, Weeks Papers.
71. PP, 1958, p. 4.
72. Eisenhower, *Waging Peace*, pp. 234–35.
73. NYT, March 6, 1958.
74. *Ibid.*, January 21, 1958.
75. *Ibid.*
76. *Ibid.*, January 22, 1958.
77. Bernard Schwartz, *The Professor and the Commissions* (New York: Alfred A. Knopf, 1959), pp. 223–24.
78. Adams, *Report*, p. 440.
79. Frier, *Conflict of Interest*, p. 21.
80. Adams to Oren Harris, June 12, 1958, OF 72–A–2, DDEL.
81. *Ibid.*
82. NYT, June 18, 1958.
83. Frier, *Conflict of Interest*, p. 24.
84. *Congress and the Nation*, p. 1748.
85. Frier, *Conflict of Interest*, pp. 207–10.
86. *Congress and the Nation*, p. 1749.
87. Adams, *Report*, p. 446.

88. Sinclair Weeks to Henry J. Taylor, August 4, 1958, Weeks Papers.
89. *Congress and the Nation*, p. 1749.
90. NYT, July 3, 1958.
91. Ogden Reid to Eisenhower, June 18, 1958, OF 72–A–2, DDEL.
92. Harold Stassen to Eisenhower, June 16, 1958, and Eisenhower to Stassen, June 18, 1958, OF 72–A–2, DDEL.
93. PP, 1958, pp. 479–80.
94. NYT, September 10, 1958.
95. Horace A. Hildreth to Weeks, September 26, 1958, Weeks Papers.
96. John L. Steele, "How the Pros Shot Sherm Adams Down," *Life* (September 29, 1958), p. 28.
97. Eisenhower, *Waging Peace*, p. 316.
98. Morrow, *Black Man*, pp. 223, 257.
99. NYT, October 24, 1958.

Chapter 38

1. PP, 1958, pp. 828–29.
2. William Shannon, "Eisenhower as President," *Commentary* (November 1958), p. 390.
3. *Newsweek*, February 2, 1959, p. 17.
4. NYT, January 18, 1959.
5. *Ibid.*, November 11, 1959.
6. PP, 1958, p. 857.
7. Morrow, *Black Man*, p. 269; E. Frederic Morrow, interview, November 1, 1968.
8. PP, 1959, pp. 503–504.
9. Eisenhower to Owen Cheatham, July 1, 1959, OF 120, DDEL.
10. Robert B. Anderson to W. Allen Wallis, April 1, 1960, Wallis Papers, DDEL.
11. Milton S. Eisenhower, interview, June 19, 1969.
12. NYT, October 28, 1959.
13. Hughes, *Ordeal*, p. 250.
14. Ray Scherer, Eisenhower Oral History, Columbia.
15. NYT, November 13, 1958.
16. *Ibid.*, April 24, 1960.
17. *Ibid.*, January 19, 1959.
18. *Ibid.*, March 12, April 17, 18, 1959.
19. Nixon, *Crises*, pp. 204, 215, 217–18.
20. Douglas Dillon, interview, May 26, 1969.
21. Zinner (ed.), *Documents . . . 1956*, pp. 220–31.
22. PP, 1958, p. 852.
23. Eisenhower, *Waging Peace*, pp. 332, 334.
24. Christian Herter, Dulles Oral History, Princeton.
25. John Foster Dulles, memorandum of conversations, March 24, 1957, Dulles Papers, Princeton.
26. Zinner (ed.), *Documents . . . 1958*, pp. 237–38.

27. Richard P. Stebbins, *The United States in World Affairs 1959* (New York: Vintage Books, 1960), pp. 145–46.

28. President's Report to Congress on the Middle East, July 31, 1957, Harlow Papers, DDEL.

29. Richard Harkness, memorandum, July 21, 1958, Dulles Additional Papers, Princeton.

30. Eisenhower, *Waging Peace*, p. 268.

31. Camille Chamoun, Dulles Oral History, Princeton.

32. Murphy, *Diplomat*, p. 398; Eisenhower, *Waging Peace*, p. 272.

33. James C. Hagerty, interview, April 9, 1969.

34. Zinner (ed.), *Documents . . . 1959*, p. 396.

35. Donald Zagoria, *The Sino-Soviet Conflict 1956–61* (New York: Atheneum, 1967), pp. 206–208.

36. Zinner (ed.), *Documents . . . 1958*, p. 439.

37. Eisenhower, *Waging Peace*, p. 297.

38. Zinner (ed.), *Documents . . . 1958*, pp. 442–52.

39. *Ibid.*, p. 458.

40. Henry A. Kissinger, *Nuclear Weapons and Foreign Policy* (Garden City, New York: Doubleday Anchor Books, 1958), pp. 2, 15.

41. Gallup Poll release, April 6, 1958.

42. Eisenhower, *Waging Peace*, p. 220.

43. Eisenhower to Johnson, January 21, 1958, Harlow Papers, DDEL.

44. Eisenhower, *Waging Peace*, p. 222.

45. Charles J. V. Murphy, "The White House Since Sputnik," *Fortune* (January 1958), p. 100.

46. Stebbins, *U.S. in World Affairs 1959*, p. 9.

47. Stuart Symington, "Where the Missile Gap Went," *The Reporter* (February 15, 1962), p. 22.

48. Roy E. Licklider, "The Missile Gap Controversy," *Political Science Quarterly* (December 1970), pp. 604, 615.

49. Stebbins, *U.S. in World Affairs 1959*, p. 16.

50. Albert Wohlstetter, "The Delicate Balance of Terror," *Foreign Affairs* (January 1959), pp. 211–34.

51. Licklider, "Missile Gap," p. 603.

52. Dwight D. Eisenhower, Dulles Oral History, Princeton.

53. Licklider, "Missile Gap," p. 612.

54. *Ibid.*, p. 601.

55. Eisenhower to Dulles, February 7, 1957, Dulles Papers, Princeton.

56. Eleanor Lansing Dulles, Dulles Oral History, Princeton.

57. Eleanor Lansing Dulles, *John Foster Dulles: The Last Year* (New York: Harcourt, Brace & World, 1963), p. 221.

58. Confidential information.

59. Dr. Leonard Heaton, Dulles Oral History, Princeton.

60. PP, 1959, p. 27.

61. Goold-Adams, *Time of Power*, p. 291.

62. Andrew Berding, *Dulles on Diplomacy* (Princeton, New Jersey: D. Van Nostrand Company), p. 42.

63. Dr. Leonard Heaton, Dulles Oral History, Princeton.
64. David E. Bruce to Dulles, April 2, 1959, Dulles Papers, Princeton.
65. PP, 1959, p. 467.
66. Strauss, *Men and Decisions*, pp. 400–401.
67. Bryce Harlow to Sherman Adams, February 7, 1958, Adams Papers, Dartmouth.
68. Statement by Strauss before the Committee on Interstate and Foreign Commerce, May 6–7, 1959, OF 2, DDEL.
69. Strauss to Wilton Persons, May 28, 1959, OF 2, DDEL.
70. NYT, June 19, 1959; Arthur W. Arundel, "The Most Political Night," privately printed account, OF 2, DDEL.
71. Arundel, "The Most Political Night," OF 2, DDEL.
72. Peter M. Damborg, "Maine Politics," unidentified and undated newspaper clipping, Harlow Papers, DDEL.
73. Eisenhower to Dodge, July 6, 1959, Dodge Papers, DDEL.
74. Leonard Hall, interview, May 5, 1969; Joe Martin, *My First Fifty Years in Politics* (New York: McGraw-Hill, 1960), p. 241; Eisenhower, *Waging Peace*, p. 384; confidential sources.
75. Lyndon B. Johnson, interview, June 30, 1970.
76. Gallup Poll releases, March 29, April 1, June 15, 1959; PP, 1959, p. 573.
77. PP, 1959, p. 581.
78. Dodd to Eisenhower, January 15, 1959, OF 225–A, DDEL.
79. Bridges to Eisenhower, April 2, 1959, OF 116–LL, DDEL.
80. Cardinal O'Hara to Eisenhower, August 3, 1959, OF 225–A, DDEL.
81. Eisenhower, *Waging Peace*, p. 432.
82. NYT, August 13, 1959; Cabell Phillips, "The 'New Look' of the President," New York *Times Magazine*, August 16, 1959, p. 17.
83. Eisenhower, *Waging Peace*, p. 401.
84. G. Bernard Noble, *Christian A. Herter* (New York: Cooper Square Publishers, 1970), p. 40.
85. *Ibid.*, p. 53.
86. Zinner (ed.), *Documents . . . 1959*, pp. 266–68, 277.
87. PP, 1959, pp. 506–507.
88. Murphy, *Diplomat*, p. 438.
89. Eisenhower, *Waging Peace*, p. 407.
90. Wills, *Nixon*, p. 126.
91. Zinner (ed.), *Documents . . . 1959*, pp. 206–208.
92. David Wise and Thomas B. Ross, *The U-2 Affair* (New York: Random House, 1962), p. 179.
93. PP, 1959, pp. 657–58.
94. Keith Funston to Eisenhower, September 17, 1959, OF 225–A, DDEL.
95. NYT, September 19, 1959.
96. Norris Poulson to Eisenhower, September 21, 1959, and John A. Calhoun to General Goodpaster, October 3, 1959, OF 225–A, DDEL.
97. Eisenhower, *Waging Peace*, p. 445.
98. NYT, September 21, 1959.
99. *Ibid.*, January 17, 1959.

100. Eisenhower, *Waging Peace*, p. 447; Zinner (ed.), *Documents . . . 1959*, pp. 192–94.
101. Gallup Poll releases, November 15, 1959, January 17, 1960.
102. Merriman Smith, *A President's Odyssey* (New York: Harper & Bros., 1961), *passim*.
103. NYT, February 3, 1960; Lewis, *Portrait of a Decade*, pp. 85–86.
104. NYT, February 23, 1960.
105. *Ibid.*, March 17, 1960.
106. E. Frederic Morrow, memorandum, March 15, 1960, Morrow Papers, DDEL.
107. Roy Wilkins, interview, August 11, 1970.
108. PP, 1958, pp. 391–94.
109. Robinson to Eisenhower, May 13, 1958, OF 142–A, DDEL.
110. Eisenhower to Robinson, June 4, 1958, OF 142–A, DDEL.
111. Wilkins to Morrow, September 4, 1958, Morrow Papers, DDEL.
112. PP, 1958, p. 647; Morrow to Adams, September 5, 1958, Morrow Papers, DDEL.
113. Francis Moore to Eisenhower, October 7, 1958, Persons Papers, DDEL.
114. Morrow to Gerald Morgan, November 10, 1958, Morgan Papers, DDEL.
115. Foster Rhea Dulles, *The Civil Rights Commission* (East Lansing, Michigan: Michigan State University Press, 1968), p. 69.
116. Gordon M. Tiffany to Gerald Morgan, November 2, 1959, Morgan Papers, DDEL.
117. Rogers to Persons, December 24, 1959, Rogers Papers, DDEL.
118. *Congress and the Nation*, pp. 1630, 81a.
119. PP, 1960–61, p. 398.
120. NYT, June 25, July 10, 1960.
121. Francis Gary Powers and Curt Gentry, *Operation Overflight* (New York: Holt, Rinehart and Winston, 1970), pp. 82–89.
122. Tully, *CIA*, p. 120.
123. Eisenhower, *Waging Peace*, p. 545.
124. *Ibid.*, p. 548n.
125. Wise and Ross, *U–2*, pp. 73–74.
126. Noble, *Herter*, pp. 80–81.
127. NYT, May 8, 1960.
128. *Ibid.*, May 10, 1960.
129. Wise and Ross, *U–2*, pp. 147–48.
130. PP, 1960–61, p. 403.
131. Confidential source.
132. Dwight D. Eisenhower, Dulles Oral History, Princeton.
133. Case to Eisenhower, May 20, 1960, and Eisenhower to Case, June 28, 1960, OF 225–A, DDEL.
134. PP, 1960–61, p. 428.
135. Zagoria, *Sino-Soviet Conflict*, p. 279.
136. LaFeber, *Cold War*, p. 214.
137. Gallup Poll release, June 8, 1960.
138. NYT, June 11, 1960.

139. PP, 1960–61, pp. 562–63.

140. *Ibid.*, p. 567.

141. Philip W. Bonsal, "Cuba, Castro and the United States," *Foreign Affairs* (January 1967), p. 271.

142. Confidential source.

143. Hugh Thomas, *Cuba: The Pursuit of Freedom* (New York: Harper & Row, 1971), p. 1198.

144. Eisenhower, *Waging Peace*, p. 523.

145. Nixon, *Six Crises*, pp. 351–52; Theodore Draper, *Castro's Revolution: Myths and Realities* (New York: Frederick A. Praeger, 1962), p. 62.

146. Eisenhower, *Waging Peace*, p. 533.

147. Confidential source.

148. Arthur M. Schlesinger, Jr., *A Thousand Days* (Boston: Houghton Mifflin 1965), pp. 225–26.

149. Thomas, *Cuba*, p. 1303.

150. Department of Defense, *United States–Vietnam Relations, 1945–1967*, vol. 2, pt. iv. A.5. pp. 25–26.

151. *Ibid.*, p. 61.

152. *Ibid.*, p. 36.

153. *Ibid.*, p. 40.

154. *Ibid.*, p. 57.

155. *Ibid.*, pp. 41, 44, 73.

156. *Ibid.*, p. 63.

157. *Ibid.*, p. 66.

158. Clark Clifford, "A Viet Nam Reappraisal," *Foreign Affairs* (July 1969), p. 604.

159. NYT, July 5, 1959.

160. PP, 1960–61, p. 604.

161. Robert Gray to William Rogers, May 16, 1960, Rogers Papers, DDEL.

162. PP, 1960–61, pp. 615–16.

163. *Congress and the Nation*, p. 36.

164. NYT, June 9, 1960.

165. PP, 1960–61, p. 561.

166. Barry Goldwater, *The Conscience of a Conservative* (Shepherdsville, Kentucky: Victory Publishing Company, 1960), pp. 19, 68, 89, 95, 101.

167. NYT, July 23, 1960.

168. *Ibid.*, July 28, 1960.

169. *Ibid.*, March 8, 1960.

170. *Ibid.*, August 8, 1960.

171. *Ibid.*, March 9, 1961.

172. Gallup Poll release, August 17, 1960.

173. John Reagan "Tex" McCrary to Eisenhower, October 11, 1960, OF 138–C–4.

174. Goldwater to Eisenhower, October 25, 1960, OF 138–C–4, DDEL.

175. PP, 1960–61, p. 658.

176. Sherman Adams, notes of interview with Eisenhower, March 30, 1959, Adams Papers, Dartmouth.

177. Theodore H. White, *The Making of the President 1960* (New York: Atheneum, 1961), p. 309.
178. NYT, March 17, 1960.
179. PP, 1960–61, p. 638.
180. Memoranda in Merriam Papers and Wilton B. Persons to Gerald Morgan, September 7, 1960, Morgan Papers, DDEL.
181. Eisenhower to Williams and Ann Whitman to Barry Leithead, October 31, 1960, OF 138–C–4, DDEL.
182. *Nation's Business*, October 1960, pp. 27–28.
183. Gallup Poll release, November 7, 1960.
184. PP, 1960–61, p. 1044.
185. NYT, November 13, December 2, 1960, and January 10, 11, 15, 1961.
186. *Ibid.*, January 15, March 9, 1961.

Chapter 39

1. United States Naval Institute, *Proceedings*, June 1971, p. 23.
2. Murphy, "The Eisenhower Shift," part 3, *Fortune* (March 1956), p. 112.
3. Douglas to Eisenhower, May 26, 1952, Pre-Inaugural Papers, DDEL.
4. NYT, February 22, 1953.
5. PP, 1960–61, pp. 1038–39.
6. United States Naval Institute, *Proceedings*, June 1971, p. 22.
7. PP, 1960–61, pp. 1045–46.
8. Gallup Poll releases, January 13, 18, 1961.
9. NYT, January 19, 1961.
10. *Commonweal*, January 20, 1961, p. 430.

Bibliography

Interviews

Maxwell M. Rabb, October 1, 1968, and January 12, 1970

E. Frederic Morrow, November 1, 1968

Gabriel Hauge, November 22, 1968

Lucius Clay, April 8, 1969

Stephen Benedict, April 9, 1969

James C. Hagerty, April 9 and 11, 1969

Sinclair Weeks, April 15, 1969

Robert Merton, April 23, 1969

Leonard Hall, May 5, 1969

Roy Cohn, May 7, 1969

C. Douglas Dillon, May 26, 1969

Milton S. Eisenhower, June 19, 1969

George M. Humphrey, July 2, 1969

Sherman Adams, July 31 and August 3, 1969

Rev. Fred L. Shuttlesworth, December 10, 1969

Eleanor Lansing Dulles, January 9, 1970

Clarence Mitchell, January 30, 1970

Ralph J. Bunche, January 31, 1970

Robert B. Anderson, March 11, 1970

Henry Cabot Lodge, May 14, 1970

Lyndon B. Johnson, June 30, 1970

Roy Wilkins, August 11, 1970

Emmet John Hughes, August 14, 1970

Joseph C. Harsch, August 24, 1970

Harold E. Stassen, August 23, 1971

Dwight D. Eisenhower Oral History, Columbia University, Interviews:

Bertha Adkins

George Aiken

Henry Aurand

Ezra Taft Benson

Andrew H. Berding

Samuel Brownell

Percival Brundage

E. La Mar Buckner

Carter L. Burgess

Arthur E. Burns

Prescott Bush

Earl Butz

Lucius Clay

Kenneth Crawford

Wesley A. D'Ewart
Roscoe Drummond
Ralph Flanders
Edward Folliard
Marion B. Folsom
Clarence Francis
Andrew J. Goodpaster
Arthur Gray, Jr.
Charles Halleck
Wilson Harwood
John Hightower
Albert Jacobs
Jacob Javits
Jesse Johnson
Roger Jones
Arthur A. Kimball
James Lambie
J. Bracken Lee
Barry Leithead

Edward A. McCabe
L. Arthur Minnich
William Mitchell
E. Frederic Morrow
Dennis O'Rourke
Richard Pittenger
Ogden Reid
Chalmers Roberts
Richard Rovere
Stanley Rumbough
Leverett Saltonstall
Leonard Scheele
Ray Scherer
Murray Snyder
Elmer Staats
Edward Thye
Anne Wheaton
Charles F. Willis, Jr.
Henry Wriston

JOHN FOSTER DULLES ORAL HISTORY, PRINCETON UNIVERSITY, INTERVIEWS:

Theodore Achilles
Sherman Adams
George Aiken
George V. Allen
Joseph Alsop
Stewart Alsop
Dillon Anderson
Mildred Asbjornson
Sir Howard Beale
Loftus Becker
Elliott V. Bell
Richard Bissell
Eugene Black
Charles Bohlen
Willy Brandt
Herbert Brownell
David K. E. Bruce
Percival Brundage
Wiley T. Buchanan, Jr.
W. Randolph Burgess
Arleigh Burke
W. Walton Butterworth
Charles P. Cabell
John M. Cabot
Isaac W. Carpenter, Jr.

The Right Honorable
   Lord Casey
Camille Chamoun
Dr. Chang Myun
Mme. Chiang Kai-shek
Chiang Kai-shek
Marquis Childs
Chung Il Kwon
Lucius Clay
J. Lawton Collins
John Sherman Cooper
Andrew W. Cordier
Edward Corsi
Maurice Couve de Murville
Philip K. Crowe
Hugh S. Cumming, Jr.
Eugenie Mary Davie
Rafael de la Colina
C. Douglas Dillon
Clarence Dillon
Everett M. Dirksen
Robert J. Donovan
Roscoe Drummond
Eleanor Lansing Dulles
Abba Eban

Dwight D. Eisenhower
Milton S. Eisenhower
Homer Ferguson
Thomas K. Finletter
William C. Foster
George S. Franklin, Jr.
Edward L. Freers
Carlos P. Garcia
Thomas S. Gates
Andrew J. Goodpaster
Gordon Gray
Joseph C. Green
James C. Hagerty
Charles Halleck
John W. Hanes, Jr.
Bryce Harlow
Joseph C. Harsch
Gabriel Hauge
Leonard D. Heaton
Loy Henderson
Christian H. Herter
Yaacov Herzog
Bourke B. Hickenlooper
John Hightower
John B. Hollister
Julius C. Holmes
Emmet John Hughes
George Humphrey and
  Herbert Hoover, Jr.
Jacob J. Javits
U. Alexis Johnson
Walter H. Judd
George F. Kennan
Thanat Khoman
Nobusuke Kishi
Arthur Krock
Gerard Lambert
Arthur Larson
Curtis LeMay
Henry Cabot Lodge
Mary Lord
Donald B. Lourie
Henry R. Luce
Charles Lucet
Douglas MacArthur II

Sir Thomas MacDonald
Phyllis Bernau Macomber
William B. Macomber, Jr.
Charles Malik
Thomas C. Mann
Michael J. Mansfield
Carl W. McCardle
John J. McCloy
John W. McCormack
Neil McElroy
Richard M. Nixon
G. L. Mehta
Martin Merson
James P. Mitchell
Thruston B. Morton
Sir Leslie K. Munro
Frederick E. Nolting, Jr.
Roderic L. O'Connor
Herman Phleger
Christian Pineau
Herbert V. Prochnow
Clarence B. Randall
Ogden Reid
G. Frederick Reinhardt
James Reston
James W. Riddleberger
Matthew Ridgway
William M. Rountree
R. Richard Rubottom, Jr.
John Stewart Service
Bernard M. Shanley
James R. Shepley
Joseph J. Sisco
John Sparkman
Harold E. Stassen
Thomas E. Stephens
Maxwell D. Taylor
Theodore Streibert
Felix Stump
Llewelyn E. Thompson
Nathan F. Twining
James J. Wadsworth
Alexander Wiley
Henry Wriston
Charles W. Yost

MANUSCRIPTS

Dwight D. Eisenhower Library,
  Abilene, Kansas
Pre-Inaugural Papers
White House Central File
Personal Correspondence of President Eisenhower
Citizens for Eisenhower Papers
Bryce Harlow Papers
William P. Rogers Papers
Wilton Persons Papers
W. Allen Wallis Papers
Meyer Kestnbaum Papers
W. Bedell Smith Papers
Gerald Morgan Papers
E. Frederic Morrow Papers
Joseph M. Dodge Papers
Robert Merriam Papers
Oveta Culp Hobby Papers
Don Paarlberg Papers
Howard Pyle Papers
Henry McPhee Papers

Edward A. McCabe Papers
James P. Mitchell Papers
Harry S Truman Library,
  Independence, Missouri
Charles S. Murphy Papers
Sidney Yates Papers
Fred Lawton Papers
New York Public Library
  Schomburg Collection
Syracuse University Library
  Ralph E. Flanders Papers
Library of Congress
  NAACP Papers
Private Papers of Sinclair Weeks,
  Lancaster, New Hampshire
Princeton University Library
  John Foster Dulles Papers
Baker Library, Dartmouth University
  Sherman Adams Papers
Scrapbooks of Gabriel Hauge

GOVERNMENT PUBLICATIONS:

Commission on Foreign Economic Policy, *Report to the President and the Congress, January 1954*. Washington: U. S. Government Printing Office, 1954.

Committee on Banking and Currency, U. S. Senate, 83rd Congress, 1st Session, *Hearings on Standby Economic Controls, March 25–April 1, 1953*. Washington: U. S. Government Printing Office, 1953.

Committee on Foreign Relations, 87th Congress, 1st Session, *United States Foreign Policy: Compilation of Studies*. Washington: U. S. Government Printing Office, 1961.

Committee on Government Operations, U. S. Senate, 84th Congress, 2nd Session, *East-West Trade*. Washington: U. S. Government Printing Office, 1956.

Senate and House Committees on Foreign Relations, *The Mutual Security Program for Fiscal Year 1954*. Washington: U. S. Government Printing Office, 1953.

Congressional Record, 83rd to 87th Congresses.

Department of Defense, *United States–Vietnam Relations, 1945–1967*. 12 vols.; Washington: U. S. Government Printing Office, 1971.

Department of State, *American Foreign Policy, 1950–1960*. 7 vols.; Washington: U. S. Government Printing Office, 1957–1964.

86th Congress, 2nd Session, *Special Study Mission to Europe*. Washington: U. S. Government Printing Office, 1960.

Public Papers of the Presidents: Dwight D. Eisenhower, 1953–1961. 8 vols.; Washington: U. S. Government Printing Office, 1960–1961.

United States Atomic Energy Commission, *In the Matter of J. Robert Oppenheimer*. 2 vols.; Washington: U. S. Government Printing Office, 1954.

United States Bureau of the Census, *Historical Statistics of the United States, Colonial Times to 1957* and *Continuation to 1962 and Revisions*. Washington: U. S. Government Printing Office, 1960, 1965.

PERIODICALS AND NEWSPAPERS (1952–61):

America	*Newsweek*
Atlantic Monthly	*The Reporter*
Business Week	*Time*
Christian Century	*U.S. News & World Report*
Commonweal	*Vital Speeches*
Congressional Quarterly	*Amsterdam News*
Almanac	New York *Herald Tribune*
Fortune	New York *Times*
Harper's	New York *World Telegram and The Sun*
Life	*Wall Street Journal*
The Nation	Washington *Post*
National Review	Washington *Times-Herald*
Nation's Business	American Institute of Public
The New Republic	Opinion Releases (Gallup Poll),
The New Yorker	Princeton, New Jersey

SELECTED ARTICLES:

Aldrich, Winthrop W., "The Suez Crisis: A Footnote to History," *Foreign Affairs* (April 1967), pp. 541–52.

Albjerg, Victor, "Truman and Eisenhower: Their Administrations and Campaigns," *Current History* (October 1964), pp. 221–28.

Alsop, Stewart, "Impact of Eisenhower," *The Saturday Evening Post* (November 9, 1963), p. 14.

———, "Just What Is Modern Republicanism?" *The Saturday Evening Post* (July 27, 1957), pp. 18–19+.*

Anderson, Dillon, "The President and the National Security," *The Atlantic Monthly* (January 1956), pp. 41–46.

Ascoli, Max, "This Spell of Languor," *The Reporter* (March 7, 1957), p. 10.

Berle, Adolph A., Jr., "Businessmen in Government: The New Administration," *The Reporter* (February 3, 1953), pp. 8–12.

Berman, William C., "Presidential Politics and Civil Rights: 1952," unpublished

* + is the symbol employed by the *Readers' Guide to Periodical Literature* to indicate that an article is continued on later pages of the same issue.

typescript in the possession of the author, Dr. William C. Berman, Department of History, University of Toronto, Ontario, Canada.

Bone, Hugh A., "American Party Politics, Elections, and Voting Behavior," *The Annals* (July 1967), pp. 124–37.

Bonsal, Philip W., "Cuba, Castro and the United States," *Foreign Affairs* (January 1967), pp. 260–76.

Burnham, William D., "Eisenhower as a Man, Eisenhower as Mystique," *Commonweal* (December 27, 1963), pp. 408–409.

Byrnes, James F., "The Supreme Court Must be Curbed," *U.S. News & World Report* (May 18, 1956), pp. 50–58.

Cater, Douglas, "Congress and the President," *The Reporter* (May 12, 1953), pp. 15–16.

———, "How the Senate Passed the Civil Rights Bill," *The Reporter* (September 5, 1957), pp. 9–13.

———, "The President and the Press," *The Reporter* (April 28, 1953), pp. 26–28.

———, "Secretary Dulles and the Press," *The Reporter* (November 10, 1953), pp. 22–24.

Collins, Frederic W., "The Education of a Cabinet," *The Reporter* (May 12, 1953), pp. 12–15.

———, "How to Be a President's Brother," New York *Times Magazine* (August 23, 1959), p. 18+.

Commager, Henry Steele, "The Perilous Folly of Senator Bricker," *The Reporter* (October 13, 1953), pp. 12–17.

———, "The Republican Dilemma," *The Reporter* (October 14, 1952), pp. 6–9.

Cutler, Robert, "The Development of the N. S. C.," *Foreign Affairs* (April 1956), pp. 441–58.

Dean, Arthur A., "The Bricker Amendment and Authority Over Foreign Affairs," *Foreign Affairs* (October 1953), pp. 1–19.

Dexter, Lewis Anthony, "Democratic Me-Tooism on Active Opposition," *The Reporter* (October 27, 1953), pp. 16–20.

Dulles, John Foster, "Challenge and Response in United States Policy," *Foreign Affairs* (October 1957), pp. 25–43.

———, "A Policy of Boldness," *Life* (May 19, 1952), pp. 146–60.

———, "Policy for Security and Peace," *Foreign Affairs* (April 1954), pp. 353–64.

Finney, John W., "The Long Trial of John Paton Davies," New York *Times Magazine* (August 31, 1969), pp. 7–9+.

Folliard, Edward T., "Ike Could Win Again, Politicians Agree," *Nation's Business* (October 1960), pp. 27–28.

Gelb, Leslie H., "Vietnam: The System Worked," *Foreign Policy* (Summer 1971), pp. 140–67.

Goodman, William, "Fatal Passion of Harold Stassen," *The New Republic* (August 6, 1956), pp. 7–8.

Graebner, Norman, "Eisenhower's Popular Leadership," *Current History* (October 1960), pp. 230–36.

Hale, William Harlan, "The Double Life in Washington and Bonn," *The Reporter* (January 10, 1957), pp. 8–11.

Hammond, Paul Y., "The NSC as a Device for Interdepartmental Coordination," *American Political Science Review* (December 1960), pp. 899–910.

Hardin, Clifford, "The Republican Department of Agriculture—a Political Interpretation," *Journal of Farm Economics* (May 1954), pp. 210–27.

Harsch, Joseph C., "Eisenhower's First Hundred Days," *The Reporter* (May 12, 1953), pp. 9–12.

———, "What's Happened to Ike?" *The Reporter* (October 28, 1952), pp. 7–10.

Hessler, William H., "George Humphrey: New Name on the Dollar," *The Reporter* (February 17, 1953), pp. 16–17.

Hoffman, Paul G., "How Eisenhower Saved the Republican Party," *Collier's* (October 26, 1956), pp. 44–47.

Horton, Philip, "Voices Within the Voice," *The Reporter* (July 21, 1953), pp. 25–29.

———, "The China Lobby," *The Reporter* (April 29, 1952), pp. 5–18.

Huston, James A., "The Eisenhower Era," *Current History* (July 1969), pp. 24–30+.

Hyman, Sidney, "Absorbing Study of Popularity," New York *Times Magazine* (July 24, 1960), pp. 7, 24–25.

———, "Eisenhower Glow Is Fading Away," *The Reporter* (September 19, 1957), pp. 11–15.

———, "Inner Circles of the White House," New York *Times Magazine* (January 5, 1958), p. 10+.

———, "Portrait of the President as World Leader," New York *Times Magazine* (December 6, 1959), p. 23+.

———, "Problems of a Lame Duck President," New York *Times Magazine* (January 18, 1959), p. 11+.

Hyman, Herbert H., and Sheatsley, Paul B., "The Political Appeal of President Eisenhower," *Public Opinion Quarterly* (Winter 1953–54), pp. 443–60.

Javits, Jacob K., "A Liberal Republican Takes Stock," New York *Times Magazine* (November 15, 1953), p. 12+.

Kempton, Murray, "The Underestimation of Dwight D. Eisenhower," *Esquire* (September 1967), pp. 108–109+.

Kirstein, G. G., "Crusade in America," *The Nation* (November 23, 1963), pp. 349–50.

Knebel, Fletcher, "Did Ike Really Want Nixon?" *Look* (October 30, 1956), pp. 25–27.

———, "We Nearly Went to War Three Times Last Year," *Look* (February 8, 1955), pp. 26–27.

Knowland, William F., "Peace with Honor," *National Review* (November 19, 1955), pp. 9–11.

Koeppen, Sheilah R., "The Republican Radical Right," *The Annals* (March 1969), pp. 73–82.

Krock, Arthur, "Impressions of the President and the Man," New York *Times Magazine* (June 23, 1957), p. 5+.

Lansdale, Edward G., "Viet Nam: Do We Understand Revolution?" *Foreign Affairs* (October 1964), pp. 75–86.

Lear, John, "Ike and the Peaceful Atom," *The Reporter* (January 12, 1956), pp. 11–21.

Lewis, Anthony, "Victim of Nameless Accusers," *The Reporter* (March 2, 1954), pp. 10–17.

Lewis, Flora, "The Unstable States of Germany," *Foreign Affairs* (July 1960), pp. 588–97.

Licklider, Roy E., "The Missile Gap Controversy," *Political Science Quarterly* (December 1970), pp. 600–15.

Lodge, Henry Cabot, "Eisenhower and the GOP," *Harper's* (May 1952), pp. 34–39.

McMillan, George, "Some Dixiecrats Who Like Ike," *The Reporter* (October 14, 1952), pp. 25–28.

Mallon, John P., "Sinclair Weeks: Republican Oligarch," *New Republic* (January 26, 1953), pp. 15–16.

Miller, Helen Hill, "D.P.'s in D. C.: The Riffed and the Miffed," *The Reporter* (August 4, 1953), pp. 27–31.

Mueller, John E., "Presidential Popularity From Truman to Johnson," *American Political Science Review* (March 1970), pp. 18–34.

Murphy, Charles J. V., "Eisenhower's White House," *Fortune* (July 1953), pp. 75–77+.

———, "The Eisenhower Shift," *Fortune* (January, February, March and April 1956), pp. 83–87+, 110–113+, 110–112+, 113–116+.

———, "The Budget and Eisenhower," *Fortune* (July 1957), pp. 96–99.

———, "The White House Since Sputnik," *Fortune* (January 1958), pp. 98–101+.

Oppenheimer, J. Robert, "Atomic Weapons and American Policy," *Foreign Affairs* (July 1953), pp. 525–35.

Palmer, C. B., "Mood of the Farmers of Guthrie Center," New York *Times Magazine* (October 11, 1953), p. 17+.

Phillips, Cabell, "Eisenhower's Inner Circle," New York *Times Magazine* (February 3, 1957), pp. 8–9+.

———, "The 'New Look' of the President," New York *Times Magazine* (August 16, 1959), p. 17+.

Polsby, Nelson W., "Toward an Explanation of McCarthyism," *Political Studies* (October 1960), pp. 250–71.

Randall, Clarence B., "Let's Be Sensible About Foreign Aid," *Saturday Evening Post* (June 22, 1957), p. 30+.

Reston, James, "Dilemma of the White House," New York *Times Magazine* (June 1, 1958), pp. 7–9+.

Rogers, Lindsay, "Senator Bricker Finds a Loophole," *The Reporter* (July 22, 1952), pp. 31–33.

Rovere, Richard, "Eisenhower and the New President," *Harper's* (May 1960), pp. 31–35.

———, "The Presidency on a Part-Time Basis," *The New Yorker* (December 7, 1957), pp. 149–52.

———, "The Civil Rights Bill," *The New Yorker* (August 31, 1957), p. 72+.

———, "The President as His Own Secretary of State," *The New Yorker* (March 14, 1959), pp. 159–63.

Schapsmeier, Edward L., and Schapsmeier, Frederick H., "Eisenhower and Ezra Taft Benson: Farm Policy in the 1950's," unpublished typescript in possession of the authors.

Schattschneider, E. E., "1954: The Ike Party Fights to Live," *The New Republic* (February 23, 1953), pp. 15–17.

Scheer, Robert, and Hinckle, Warren, "The 'Vietnam Lobby,'" *Ramparts* (July 1965), pp. 16–24.

Schilling, Warner R., "The 'New Look' of 1953," in W. R. Schilling, P. Y. Hammond and G. H. Snyder, *Strategy, Politics, and Defense Budgets* (New York: Columbia University Press, 1962), pp. 379–524.

Schlesinger, Arthur, Jr., "Psychological Warfare: Can It Sell Freedom?" *The Reporter* (March 31, 1953), pp. 9–12.

Schoenbrun, David, "Five Weeks That Made a Politician," *The Reporter* (August 5, 1952), pp. 7–10.

Shannon, William V., "Bob Taft, The New Boss," *The New Republic* (February 9, 1953), pp. 9–11.

———, "Eisenhower as President," *Commentary* (November 1958), pp. 390–398.

———, "Eisenhower Paradox," *Commonweal* (March 23, 1956), pp. 639–41.

Shepley, James, "How Dulles Averted War," *Life* (January 16, 1956), pp. 70–72+.

Steele, John L., "How the Pros Shot Sherm Adams Down," *Life* (September 29, 1958), p. 28.

Stone, I. F., "Theatre of Delusion," *New York Review of Books* (April 23, 1970), pp. 15–24.

Symington, Stuart, "Where the Missile Gap Went," *The Reporter* (February 15, 1962), pp. 21–23.

Terrill, Ross, "When America 'Lost' China: The Case of John Carter Vincent," *The Atlantic* (November 1969), pp. 78–86.

Tobin, James, "The Eisenhower Economy and National Security: Defense, Dollars, and Doctrines," in Dean Albertson (ed.), *Eisenhower as President* (New York: Hill and Wang, 1963), pp. 134–46.

White, William S., "Eisenhower Opens the Last Act," *Harper's* (December 1958), pp. 80–83.

———, "Evolution of Eisenhower as a Politician," New York *Times Magazine* (September 23, 1956), p. 11+.

Wohlstetter, Albert, "The Delicate Balance of Terror," *Foreign Affairs* (January 1959), pp. 211–34.

Selected Books:

Acheson, Dean, *Present at the Creation*. New York: W. W. Norton, 1969.
Adams, Sherman, *Firsthand Report*. New York: Harper & Bros., 1961.
Albertson, Dean (ed.), *Eisenhower as President*. New York: Hill and Wang, 1963.

Alsop, Joseph, and Alsop, Stewart, *The Reporter's Trade.* New York: Reynal & Co., 1958.

Alsop, Stewart, *Nixon and Rockefeller: A Double Portrait.* Garden City, New York: Doubleday and Company, 1960.

Ambrose, Stephen, *The Supreme Commander.* Garden City, New York: Doubleday and Company, 1970.

Anderson, Jack, and May, Ronald W., *McCarthy: The Man, the Senator, the "Ism."* Boston: The Beacon Press, 1952.

Anderson, J. W., *Eisenhower, Brownell, and the Congress: The Tangled Origins of the Civil Rights Bill of 1956–1957.* University, Alabama: University of Alabama Press, 1964.

Barber, Hollis W., *The United States in World Affairs 1955.* New York: Harper & Bros., 1957.

Barnet, Richard J., *Intervention and Revolution.* New York: World Publishing Company, 1968.

Bartley, Numan V., *From Thurmond to Wallace: Political Tendencies in Georgia, 1948–1968.* Baltimore: The Johns Hopkins Press, 1970.

———, *The Rise of Massive Resistance: Race and Politics in the South During the 1950's.* Baton Rouge: Louisiana State University Press, 1969.

Beal, John Robinson, *John Foster Dulles.* Rev. ed., New York: Harper & Row, 1959.

Bean, Louis, *Influences in the 1954 Mid-Term Elections.* Washington: Public Affairs Institute, 1954.

Bell, Coral, *Negotiation from Strength.* New York: Alfred A. Knopf, 1963.

Bell, Daniel (ed.), *The Radical Right.* Garden City, New York: Doubleday Anchor Book, 1964.

Benson, Ezra Taft, *Crossfire.* Garden City, New York: Doubleday and Company, 1962.

Berding, Andrew, *Dulles on Diplomacy.* Princeton, New Jersey: D. Van Nostrand Company, 1965.

Berman, Daniel M., *A Bill Becomes a Law.* New York: Macmillan, 1962.

Bernstein, Barton (ed.), *Politics and Policies of the Truman Administration.* Chicago: Quadrangle Books, 1970.

Bickel, Alexander M., *Politics and the Warren Court.* New York: Harper & Row, 1965.

Blumberg, Nathan B., *One Party Press? Coverage of the 1952 Presidential Campaign in 35 Daily Newspapers.* Lincoln, Nebraska: University of Nebraska Press, 1954.

Bolling, Richard, *House Out of Order.* New York: E. P. Dutton, 1965.

Bontecou, Eleanor, *The Federal Loyalty-Security Program.* Ithaca, New York: Cornell University Press, 1953.

Bowles, Chester, *Promises to Keep: My Years in Public Life, 1941–1969.* New York: Harper & Row, 1971.

Brodie, Bernard, *Strategy in the Missile Age.* Princeton, New Jersey: Princeton University Press, 1959.

Buckley, William F., Jr., and Bozell, L. Brent, *McCarthy and His Enemies: The Record and Its Meaning.* Chicago: Henry Regnery Company, 1954.

Burns, James MacGregor, *The Deadlock of Democracy*. Englewood Cliffs, New Jersey: Prentice-Hall, 1963.

———, *John Kennedy: A Political Profile*. New York: Avon Books, 1960.

Buttinger, Joseph, *Vietnam: A Dragon Embattled*. 2 vols., New York: Frederick A. Praeger, 1967.

Campbell, Angus, Gurin, Gerald, and Miller, Warren E., *The Voter Decides*. White Plains, New York: Row, Peterson and Company, 1954.

Caridi, Ronald J., *The Korean War and American Politics*. Philadelphia: University of Pennsylvania Press, 1968.

Chandler, Alfred D., Jr., *The Papers of Dwight David Eisenhower: The War Years*. 5 vols., Baltimore: The Johns Hopkins Press, 1970.

Childs, Marquis, *Eisenhower: Captive Hero*. New York: Harcourt, Brace and Company, 1958.

Clark, Mark, *From the Danube to the Yalu*. New York: Harper & Bros., 1954.

Cleveland, Harlan, *NATO: The Transatlantic Bargain*. New York: Harper & Row, 1970.

Cole, Allan B. (ed.), *Conflict in Indo-China and International Repercussions: A Documentary History, 1945–1955*. Ithaca, New York: Cornell University Press, 1956.

Cook, Fred J., *The Nightmare Decade: The Life and Times of Senator Joe McCarthy*. New York: Random House, 1971.

Cooper, Chester L., *The Lost Crusade: America in Vietnam*. New York: Dodd, Mead & Company, 1970.

Cornwell, Elmer E., Jr., *Presidential Leadership of Public Opinion*. Bloomington, Indiana: Indiana University Press, 1965.

Corwin, Edward S., and Koenig, Louis W., *The Presidency Today*. New York: New York University Press, 1956.

Cox, Archibald, *The Warren Court: Constitutional Decision as an Instrument of Power*. Cambridge, Massachusetts: Harvard University Press, 1968.

Crankshaw, Edward, *Khrushchev: A Career*. New York: The Viking Press, 1966.

———, (ed.), *Khrushchev Remembers*. Boston: Little, Brown, 1970.

Curl, Peter V. (ed.), *Documents on American Foreign Relations, 1953*. New York: Harper & Bros., 1954.

———, *Documents on American Foreign Relations, 1954*. New York: Harper & Bros., 1955.

———, *Documents on American Foreign Relations, 1955*. New York: Harper & Bros., 1956.

Cutler, Robert, *No Time for Rest*. Boston: Little, Brown, 1965.

Dale, Edwin L., *Conservatives in Power: A Study in Frustration*. Garden City, New York: Doubleday and Company, 1960.

David, Paul T. (ed.), *The Presidential Election and Transition, 1960–1961*. Washington: The Brookings Institution, 1961.

———, *et al.*, *Presidential Nominating Politics in 1952*. 5 vols., Baltimore: The Johns Hopkins Press, 1954.

Davis, Kenneth S., *The Politics of Honor: A Biography of Adlai E. Stevenson*. New York: G. P. Putnam's Sons, 1967.

————, *Soldier of Democracy: A Biography of Dwight Eisenhower*. Garden City, New York: Doubleday and Company, 1952.

Donovan, Robert J., *Eisenhower: The Inside Story*. New York: Harper & Bros., 1956.

Dorough, C. Dwight, *Mr. Sam*. New York: Random House, 1962.

Draper, Theodore, *Castro's Revolution: Myths and Realities*. New York: Frederick A. Praeger, 1962.

Drummond, Roscoe, and Coblentz, Gaston, *Duel at the Brink*. Garden City, New York: Doubleday and Company, 1960.

Dulles, Eleanor Lansing, *John Foster Dulles: The Last Year*. New York: Harcourt, Brace & World, 1963.

Dulles, Foster Rhea, *The Civil Rights Commission*. East Lansing: Michigan State University Press, 1968.

Dulles, John Foster, *War or Peace*. New York: Macmillan, 1950.

————, *War, Peace and Change*. New York: Harper & Bros., 1939.

Eden, Sir Anthony, *Full Circle*. London: Cassell, 1960.

Eisenhower, Dwight D., *At Ease: Stories I Tell to Friends*. Garden City, New York: Doubleday and Company, 1967.

————, *Peace with Justice*. New York: Columbia University Press, 1961.

————, *Mandate for Change, 1953–1956*. Garden City, New York: Doubleday and Company, 1963.

————, *Waging Peace*. Garden City, New York: Doubleday and Company, 1965.

Eisenhower, Milton, *The Wine Is Bitter*. Garden City, New York: Doubleday and Company, 1963.

Engler, Robert, *The Politics of Oil*. Chicago: University of Chicago Press, 1961.

Epstein, Benjamin R., and Foster, Arnold, *The Radical Right*. New York: Random House, 1966.

————, *Danger on the Right*. New York: Random House, 1964.

Eulau, Heinz, *Class and Party in the Eisenhower Years*. New York: Free Press, 1962.

Evans, Rowland, and Novak, Robert, *Lyndon B. Johnson: The Exercise of Power*. New York: New American Library, 1966.

Fall, Bernard, *Hell in a Very Small Place*. Philadelphia: J. B. Lippincott, 1967.

————, *The Two Viet-Nams*. New York: Frederick A. Praeger, 1964.

Finer, Herman, *Dulles Over Suez*. Chicago: Quadrangle Books, 1964.

Flanders, Ralph E., *Senator from Vermont*. Boston: Little, Brown, 1961.

Frier, David A., *Conflict of Interest in the Eisenhower Administration*. Ames, Iowa: Iowa State University Press, 1969.

Gerson, Louis L., *John Foster Dulles*. New York: Cooper Square Publishers, 1968.

Goldwater, Barry, *The Conscience of a Conservative*. Shepherdsville, Kentucky: Victor Publishing Company, 1960.

Goodman, Walter, *The Committee*. New York: Farrar, Straus & Giroux, 1968.

Goold-Adams, Richard, *The Time of Power: A Reappraisal of John Foster Dulles*. London: Weidenfeld & Nicolson, 1962.

Gray, Robert K., *Eighteen Acres Under Glass*. Garden City, New York: Doubleday and Company, 1961.

Griffith, Robert, *The Politics of Fear: Joseph R. McCarthy and the Senate*. Lexington: University Press of Kentucky, 1970.

Gunther, John, *Eisenhower: The Man and the Symbol*. New York: Harper & Bros., 1951.

Gurtov, Melvin, *The First Vietnam Crisis*. New York: Columbia University Press, 1967.

Halle, Louis J., *The Cold War as History*. New York: Harper & Row, 1967.

Hammer, Ellen J., *The Struggle for Indo-China, 1940–1955*. Stanford, California: Stanford University Press, 1966.

Henry, Laurin L., *Presidential Transitions*. Washington: The Brookings Institution, 1960.

Hickey, Neil, and Edwin, Ed, *Adam Clayton Powell and the Politics of Race*. New York: Fleet Publishing Company, 1966.

Hofstadter, Richard, *Anti-Intellectualism in American Life*. New York: Alfred A. Knopf, 1963.

——, *The Paranoid Style in American Politics and Other Essays*. New York: Alfred A. Knopf, 1965.

Howard, Nathaniel R. (ed.), *The Basic Papers of George M. Humphrey as Secretary of the Treasury, 1953–1957*. Cleveland: The Western Reserve Historical Society, 1965.

Hughes, Emmet J., *The Ordeal of Power*. New York: Atheneum, 1963.

Huntington, Samuel P., *The Soldier and the State*, Cambridge, Massachusetts: Harvard University Press, 1957.

Hyman, Sidney, *The American Presidency*. New York: Harper & Bros., 1954.

Kalb, Marvin, and Abel, Elie, *Roots of Involvement: The U. S. In Asia, 1784–1971*. New York: W. W. Norton, 1971.

Kaufmann, W. W. (ed.), *Military Policy and National Security*. Princeton, New Jersey: Princeton University Press, 1956.

Kendrick, Alexander, *Prime Time: The Life of Edward R. Murrow*. Boston: Little, Brown, 1969.

Key, V. O., Jr., *The Responsible Electorate*. Cambridge, Massachusetts: Harvard University Press, 1966.

King, Coretta Scott, *My Life with Martin Luther King, Jr*. New York: Holt, Rinehart and Winston, 1969.

King, Martin Luther, Jr., *Stride Toward Freedom*. New York: Perennial Library, 1964.

Kirkpatrick, Lyman B., Jr., *The Real CIA*. New York: Macmillan, 1968.

Kissinger, Henry A., *Nuclear Weapons and Foreign Policy*. Garden City, New York: Doubleday Anchor Books, 1958.

Krock, Arthur, *In the Nation, 1932–1966*. New York: McGraw-Hill, 1966.

——, *Memoirs: Sixty Years on the Firing Line*. New York: Funk & Wagnalls, 1968.

LaFeber, Walter, *America, Russia, and the Cold War, 1945–1966*. New York: John Wiley & Sons, 1967.

Larson, Arthur, *A Republican Looks at His Party*. New York: Harper & Bros., 1956.

———, *Eisenhower: The President Nobody Knew*. New York: Charles Scribner's Sons, 1968.

Latham, Earl, *The Communist Controversy in Washington*. Cambridge, Massachusetts: Harvard University Press, 1966.

Lewis, Anthony, *Portrait of a Decade*. New York: Random House, 1964.

Lewis, David L., *King: A Critical Biography*. New York: Frederick Praeger, 1970.

Lipset, Seymour Martin, and Raab, Earl, *The Politics of Unreason*. New York: Harper & Row, 1970.

Lofgren, Charles Augustin, *Congress and the Korean Conflict*. Unpublished Ph.D. dissertation, Stanford University, 1966.

Lomax, Louis E., *The Negro Revolt*. New York: Signet Books, 1962.

Love, Kenneth, *Suez: The Twice-Fought War*. New York: McGraw-Hill, 1969.

Lubell, Samuel, *The Future of American Politics*. New York: Harper Colophon Books, 1965.

———, *Revolt of the Moderates*. New York: Harper & Bros., 1956.

McCann, Kevin, *The Man from Abilene*. Garden City, New York: Doubleday and Company, 1952.

Macmillan, Harold, *Tides of Fortune*. New York: Harper & Row, 1969.

———, *Riding the Storm, 1956–1959*. New York: Harper & Row, 1971.

MacNeil, Neil, *Dirksen*. New York: World Publishing Company, 1970.

McNeill, William Hardy, *America, Britain, & Russia*. New York and London: Oxford University Press, 1953.

Martin, Joe, *My First Fifty Years in Politics*. New York: McGraw-Hill, 1960.

Mason, Alpheus Thomas, *The Supreme Court from Taft to Warren*. Baton Rouge: Louisiana State University Press, 1958.

Matthews, Herbert L., *Fidel Castro*. New York: Simon and Schuster, 1969.

Mayer, George H., *The Republican Party, 1854–1966*. 2nd ed.; New York: Oxford University Press, 1966.

Mayne, Richard, *The Recovery of Europe: From Devastation to Unity*. New York: Harper & Row, 1970.

Mazo, Earl, *Richard Nixon: A Political and Personal Portrait*. New York: Harper & Bros., 1959.

Merson, Martin, *The Private Diary of a Public Servant*. New York: Macmillan, 1955.

Miller, William J., *Henry Cabot Lodge*. New York: James H. Heineman, 1967.

Miller, William Lee, *Piety Along the Potomac*. Boston: Houghton Mifflin, 1964.

Millis, Walter, *Arms and the State*. New York: The Twentieth Century Fund, 1958.

Morrow, E. Frederic, *Black Man in the White House*. New York: Coward-McCann, 1963.

Murphy, Robert, *Diplomat Among Warriors*. Garden City, New York: Doubleday and Company, 1964.

Neustadt, Richard E., *Presidential Power*. New York: John Wiley, 1960.

Nixon, Richard M., *Six Crises*. Garden City, New York: Doubleday and Company, 1962.

Noble, G. Bernard, *Christian A. Herter*. New York: Cooper Square Publishers, 1970.

Noel-Baker, Philip, *The Arms Race*. New York: Oceana Publications, 1958.

Nutting, Anthony, *No End of a Lesson*. New York: Clarkson N. Potter, 1967.

Osgood, Robert E., *NATO: The Entangling Alliance*. Princeton, New Jersey: Princeton University Press, 1962.

Paterson, Thomas G. (ed.), *Cold War Critics*. Chicago: Quadrangle Books, 1971.

Phillips, Cabell, *The Truman Presidency*. New York: Macmillan, 1966.

Powers, Francis Gary, and Gentry, Curt, *Operation Overflight*. New York: Holt, Rinehart and Winston, 1970.

Pusey, Merlo J., *Eisenhower, the President*. New York: Macmillan, 1956.

Randall, Clarence B., *A Creed for Free Enterprise*. Boston: Little, Brown, 1952.

——, *The Communist Challenge to American Business*. Boston: Little, Brown, 1959.

——, *Over My Shoulder: A Reminiscence*. Boston: Little, Brown, 1956.

Randle, Robert F., *Geneva 1954: The Settlement of the Indochinese War*. Princeton, New Jersey: Princeton University Press, 1970.

Raskin, Marcus G., and Fall, Bernard B., *The Viet-Nam Reader*. Rev. ed.; New York: Vintage Books, 1967.

Reeves, Thomas C., *Freedom and the Foundation: The Fund for the Republic in the Era of McCarthyism*. New York: Alfred A. Knopf, 1969.

Reston, James, *Sketches in the Sand*. New York: Alfred A. Knopf, 1967.

Rees, David, *Korea: The Limited War*. New York: St. Martin's Press, 1964.

Richardson, James, *Germany and the Atlantic Alliance*. Cambridge, Massachusetts: Harvard University Press, 1966.

Ridgway, Matthew B., *Soldier*. New York: Harper & Bros., 1956.

Rischin, Moses, *Our Own Kind: Voting by Race, Creed, or National Origin*. Santa Barbara, California: The Fund for the Republic, 1960.

Roberts, Chalmers, *The Nuclear Year*. New York: Frederick A. Praeger, 1970.

Rogin, Michael Paul, *The Intellectuals and McCarthy*. Cambridge, Massachusetts: The MIT Press, 1967.

Ross, Irwin, *The Loneliest Campaign: The Truman Victory of 1948*. New York: New American Library, 1968.

Rossiter, Clinton, *The American Presidency*. Rev. ed.; New York: Mentor Books, 1962.

——, *Conservatism in America*. New York: Vintage Books, 1962.

Rostow, Walt W., *The United States in the World Arena*. New York: Harper & Brothers, 1960.

Rovere, Richard, *Affairs of State: The Eisenhower Years*. New York: Farrar, Straus and Cudahy, 1956.

——, *Senator Joe McCarthy*. London: Methuen, 1960.

Sawyer, Charles, *Concerns of a Conservative Democrat*. Carbondale: Southern Illinois University Press, 1968.

Scammon, Richard M. (ed.), *America Votes, 1956–57*. New York: Macmillan, 1958.

Schapiro, Leonard, *The Communist Party of the Soviet Union*. Rev. ed.; New York: Vintage Books, 1971.

Schlesinger, Arthur, Jr., *A Thousand Days*. Boston: Houghton Mifflin, 1965.

———, and Israel, Fred L. (eds.), *History of American Presidential Elections, 1789–1968*. 4 vols.; New York: Chelsea House, 1971.

Schneir, Walter, and Schneir, Miriam, *Invitation to an Inquest*. Garden City, New York: Doubleday and Company, 1965.

Schwartz, Bernard, *The Professor and the Commissions*. New York: Alfred A. Knopf, 1959.

Sheehan, Neil, *et al.*, *The Pentagon Papers as Published by The New York Times*. New York: Bantam Books, 1971.

Smith, Earl E. T., *The Fourth Floor: An Account of the Castro Communist Revolution*. New York: Random House, 1962.

Smith, Mark E., III, and Johns, Claude J., Jr. (eds.), *American Defense Policy*. 2nd ed.; Baltimore: The Johns Hopkins Press, 1968.

Smith, Merriman, *Meet Mister Eisenhower*. New York: Harper & Bros., 1955.

Snyder, Marty, *My Friend Ike*. New York: Frederick Fell, 1956.

Stebbins, Richard P., *The United States in World Affairs 1953*. New York: Harper & Bros., 1955.

———, *The United States in World Affairs 1954*. New York: Harper & Bros., 1956.

———, *The United States in World Affairs 1959*. New York: Vintage Books, 1960.

———, *The United States in World Affairs 1960*. New York: Vintage Books, 1961.

Steel, Ronald, *Pax Americana*. New York: The Viking Press, 1967.

Stern, Philip M., *The Oppenheimer Case*. New York: Harper & Row, 1969.

Stevenson, Adlai, *Major Campaign Speeches*. New York: Random House, 1953.

———, *The New America*. New York: Harper & Bros., 1957.

Stone, I. F., *The Haunted Fifties*. New York: Random House, 1963.

———, *The Hidden History of the Korean War*. 2nd ed.; New York: Monthly Review Press, 1969.

Strauss, Lewis L., *Men and Decisions*. Garden City, New York: Doubleday and Company, 1962.

Sulzberger, Cyrus L., *A Long Row of Candles*. New York: Macmillan, 1969.

———, *The Last of the Giants*. New York: Macmillan, 1970.

Thayer, George, *The Farther Shores of Politics*. New York: Simon and Schuster, 1967.

Theoharis, Athan, *The Yalta Myths*. Columbia, Missouri: University of Missouri Press, 1970.

Thomas, Hugh, *Cuba: The Pursuit of Freedom*. New York: Harper & Row, 1971.

————, *Suez*. New York: Harper & Row, 1967.

Thomson, C. A. H., and Shattuck, F. M., *The 1956 Presidential Campaign*. Washington: The Brookings Institution, 1960.

Tudor, Ralph, *Notes Recorded While Under Secretary, Department of Interior, March, 1953–September, 1954*. Printed privately by Mrs. M. Lucile Tudor, 1964.

Tully, Andrew, *CIA: The Inside Story*. New York: William Morrow, 1962.

Ulam, Adam B., *Expansion & Coexistence: The History of Soviet Foreign Policy, 1917–67*. New York: Frederick A. Praeger, 1968.

Welch, Robert W., Jr., *The Politician*. Belmont, Massachusetts: Belmont Publishing Company, 1964.

Westerfield, H. Bradford, *Foreign Policy and Party Politics*. New Haven, Connecticut: Yale University Press, 1955.

White, Theodore H., *The Making of the President 1960*. New York: Atheneum, 1961.

White, William S., *The Professional: Lyndon B. Johnson*. New York: Crest Books, 1964.

————, *The Taft Story*. New York: Harper & Row, 1954.

Wildavsky, Aaron, *Dixon-Yates: A Study in Power Politics*. New Haven and London: Yale University Press, 1962.

Willoughby, William R., *The St. Lawrence Waterway*. Madison: University of Wisconsin Press, 1961.

Wills, Gary, *Nixon Agonistes*. Boston: Houghton Mifflin, 1970.

Wise, David, and Ross, Thomas B., *The Invisible Government*. New York: Bantam Books, 1965.

————, *The U-2 Affair*. New York: Random House, 1962.

Wriston, Henry M., *et al.*, *Goals for Americans*. Englewood Cliffs, New Jersey: Prentice-Hall, 1960.

Yarmolinsky, Adam, *The Military Establishment: Its Impact on American Society*. New York: Harper & Row, 1971.

Zagoria, Donald S., *The Sino-Soviet Conflict 1956–61*. New York: Atheneum, 1967.

Zinner, Paul E. (ed.), *Documents on American Foreign Relations, 1956*. New York: Harper & Bros., 1957.

————, *Documents on American Foreign Relations, 1957*. New York: Harper & Bros., 1958.

————, *Documents on American Foreign Relations, 1958*. New York: Harper & Bros., 1959.

————, *Documents on American Foreign Relations, 1959*. New York, Harper & Bros., 1960.

Index